Women in Canada

A Bibliography, 1965-1982

WOMEN IN CANADA

A Bibliography, 1965-1982

Third Edition

Compiled by

Carol Mazur and Sheila Pepper

OISE Press / The Ontario Institute for Studies in Education

The Ontario Institute for Studies in Education has three prime functions: to conduct program
graduate study in education, to undertake research in education, and to assist in the implemen
tion of the findings of educational studies. The Institute is a college chartered by an Act of t
Ontario Legislature in 1965. It is affiliated with the University of Toronto for graduate stud
purposes.   1984

The publications program of the Institute has been established to make available informatio
and materials arising from studies in education, to foster the spirit of critical inquiry, and t
provide a forum for the exchange of ideas about education. The opinions expressed should be
viewed as those of the contributors.

© The Ontario Institute for Studies in Education 1984
252 Bloor Street West
Toronto, Ontario
M5S 1V6

All rights reserved. No part of this publication may be reproduced in any form without
permission from the publisher, except for brief passages quoted for review purposes.

Canadian Cataloguing in Publication Data

Mazur, Carol
  Women in Canada : a bibliography, 1965-1982

First ed. published: Harrison, Cynthia. Women in Canada, 1965-
1972. Hamilton, Ont. : McMaster University Library Press, 1972.
Includes index.
ISBN 0-7744-0288-1

1.   Women — Canada — Bibliography.
I.   Pepper, Sheila.
II. Harrison, Cynthia. Women in Canada, 1965-1972.
III. Ontario Institute for Studies in Education.
IV. Title.

Z7964.C3M39 1984   016.3054'0971   C84-099526-1

ISBN 0-7744-0288-1   Printed in Canada
1 2 3 4 5 UTP 88 78 68 58 48

CONTENTS

PREFACE

This bibliography was born twelve years ago. That first edition, which covered the years 1965 - 1972, was contained in fifty-one typewritten pages, and was slim and rudimentary in comparison with this third edition, which spans eighteen years of literature by and about Canadian women.

The evolution of the work has been guided and helped by many people, both within and outside McMaster University Library. The brunt of the work has, of course, been borne by the compilers, Sheila Pepper and Carol Mazur, who persevered with the project while carrying full work assignments in the library. The introduction, use and exploitation of word-processing and typesetting technology for the project was a demanding task, that could, as when any technology is used in a certain way for the first time, produce its own unique frustrations and demands. The determination and hard work over many long hours by Marju Kraav, Peggy Budd, Bonnie Quan and Linda Holmes, who were responsible for the automated production are manifest in this volume.

Many other individuals and organizations provided advice and assistance. Members of our staff, too numerous to mention individually, responded willingly to requests for help both big and small. The Interlibrary Loan Department provided extensive assistance in obtaining many publications from other libraries; the staff of the University Printing Department helped us in the production of the copy for publication. Financial assistance was obtained through a grant from the Social Sciences and Humanities Research Council, and Anne-Marie Bélanger gave invaluable assistance to the compilers at the painstaking stage of identifying and locating items for inclusion.

This third edition, so different from the first, represents the coordinated efforts of many hands, and will hopefully be of service to the many who are engaged in research in the field of women's studies.

Graham R. Hill,
University Librarian,
McMaster University,
Hamilton, Ontario.

INTRODUCTION

Up to now, the task of a researcher delving into the ever-broadening field of Canadian women's studies has been formidable, demanding time and fortitude in scanning numerous sources for citations. We hope this bibliography will lessen the burden.

SCOPE

The scope, in terms of subject areas covered, is broad, as the user will find in scanning the subject heading list. The two basic requirements for inclusion were Canadian content and relevance to women's studies. Hence, if a work, even though published in Canada, treated an issue such as abortion philosophically and thus by nature could not be considered Canadian in content, it was excluded. If a similar work included a Canadian survey of public attitude to the morality of abortion, it would be included. General and biographical works on women writers and artists were included, but criticism of their work was excluded unless it dealt with some feminist aspect.

We have limited the bibliography to material published from the year 1965 to 1982, a period important to the Women's Liberation Movement and well represented by a growing mass of writing on women's concerns. Some 1983 publications will also be found, but these are in a minority.

In an effort to make this work comprehensive of all women in Canada, many French-Canadian publications have been included although our aim was not to duplicate existing bibliographies covering women in Quebec.

No restriction has been made on the form of material that has been entered in this bibliography which includes books, articles, pamphlets, theses and government publications. The only type of material that will not be found is audio-visual material which has been excluded. A number of books have been analyzed and their chapters listed individually.

SOURCES

Through the course of this bibliography's editions, from the first printed in 1973, to the present expanded compilation, there has been a growing reliance on both standard and specialized sources in finding citations. Standard tools were searched through systematically. These included *Canadiana*, *Canadian Periodical Index*, *Canadian Education Index*, *Canadian Business Index* and *Index to Canadian Legal Periodical Literature*. Federal and provincial government publications catalogues, indexes to *Profile* and its successor, *Microlog*, were also scanned. Key journals in the field, *Atlantis*, *Branching Out*, *Chatelaine* and *Resources for Feminist Research* were scanned and indexed. Computer searches were conducted mainly for materials after 1975 in *America: History and Life*, *Sociological Abstracts*, *Comprehensive Dissertation Abstracts* and *CODOC (Cooperative Documents Project of the Ontario Universities' Library Cooperative System)*. Finally, requests to some 350 women's organizations across Canada yielded a number of hitherto illusive pamphlets and booklets.

As far as possible, the compilers have attempted to see all the items they have included in order to verify Canadian content, relevance, bibliographic detail and subject. This resulted in heavy use of our own library's resources as well as those of other local libraries and a volume of Interlibrary Loan transactions, particularly of theses. In cases where an item could not be obtained, it was included only if the citation appeared in a reliable source.

USE

The body of the bibliography is arranged by subject, with a list of subject headings and cross references on pages xi—xxi. If a particular work is applicable to several subject areas, it has been listed under each relevant heading and will appear two or possibly three times in the bibliography. The author index at the back lists each entry, whether original or repeated.

The automated sorting of subject headings and entries has resulted in a sequence that does not always follow the conventions of alphabetization. For example, an entry beginning, "The economy ..." will be filed under 't' rather than 'e'.

Abbreviations appearing after certain citations usually refer to the number of a microform collection of which the item is part.

(Can. theses, no.53404)   Canadian thesis on microform order number. National Library of Canada

(Canedex 76-4126)   *Candex: Canadian education monographs on microfiche.* Toronto: Micromedia, 1974-76.

(Microlog 79-0393)   *Microlog.* [Canadian federal, provincial and local government publications]. Toronto: Micromedia, 1979-   .

(Profile 74-4126)   *Profile.* [Canadian provincial and municipal publications]. Toronto: Micromedia, 1973-78.

(UM, 81-10998)   University Microfilms International order number. See *Dissertation Abstracts International.*

(Urban Canada 78-4120)   *Urban Canada, a current index to Canadian publications in the field of urban and regional planning and development.* Toronto: Micromedia, 1977-78.

LIST OF SUBJECT HEADINGS

Note to users: In most cases, women employed in professional occupations are entered under the field rather than the name of profession, as in the case of *Physicians*, entered under *Medicine*.

ABORTION

1. "Abortion setback," *Broadside*, 3:7, Oct. 1981.
2. "Abortion: two views," *Chatelaine*, 46:38, 105-7, Nov. 1973.
3. Allen, Patrick. "20 fois plus d'avortements thérapeutiques dans les hôpitaux anglophones," *L'Action nationale*, 67:157-8, oct. 1977.
4. _____. "43,201 avortements au Canada en 1973," *L'Action national*, 65:402,fév. 1976.
5. Amiel, Barbara. "All freedoms are not free: the tab for abortions should be picked up by those who want them," *Maclean's*, 94:11, July 27, 1981.
6. "An age-old issue simmers," *Globe & Mail*, Nov.20, 1982, p.10.
7. Balakrishnan, T. R. and others. "Attitudes toward abortion of married women in Toronto," *Social Biology*, 19(1):35-42, 1972.
8. Barrett, Michael and Malcolm Fitz-Earle. "Student opinion on legalized abortion at the University of Toronto," *Canadian Journal of Public Health*, 64:294-9, May-June 1973.
9. Batten, Jack. "Abortion: the issue hots up," *Chatelaine*, 47:42-3, 98-102, Oct. 1974.
10. "BC women slam hospital approach to abortion," *Health Care in Canada*, 20:8, June 1978.
11. Berger, Charlene. "Psychological characteristics of anglophone and francophone initial and repeat aborters and contraceptors." PhD diss., ConcordiaUniversity, 1978. 205p. (Can. theses, no.38528)
12. "Bishops of Canada propose alternatives," *National Catholic Reporter*, 4:5, Feb. 14, 1968.
13. Bourne, Paula. "Abortion," in her, *Women in Canadian society*. Toronto: Ontario Institute for Studies in Education, 1976, pp.44-62.
14. Boyce, R. M. and R. W. Osborn. "Therapeutic abortion in a Canadian city," *Canadian Medical Association. Journal*, 103:461-6 Sept. 12, 1970.
15. _____. "Therapeutic abortion in a Canadian city," in Carl F. Grindstaff and others, eds.,*Population issues in Canada*. Toronto: Holt, Rinehart & Winston, 1971, pp.39-48.
16. Boyd, Monica and Deirdre Gillieson. "Canadian attitudes on abortion: results of the gallup polls," *Canadian Studies in Population*, 2:53-64, 1975.
17. Canada. Statistics Canada. *Basic facts on therapeutic abortions, Canada, 1980-* . Ottawa, 1982- . Annual. (Cat. no.82-215) Continues *Therapeutic abortions, Canada*, (Cat. no.82-211P).
18. _____. *Therapeutic abortions, 1972-* . [Avortements thérapeutiques]. Ottawa, 1973- . Annual. (Cat. no.82-211)
19. Canadian Abortion Rights Action League. *Childbirth by choice*. [Choisir de donner naissance]. Toronto: Canadian Abortion Rights Action League, 1980. 11, 13p.
20. _____. "Brief to the Special Joint Committee of the Senate and of the House of Commons on the Constitution of Canada," in the committee's, *Minutes of proceedings and evidence*, no.24, Dec. 11, 1980, pp.98-117.
21. Clarke, Allan B. "Abortion: an analysis and survey of empirical data concerning the abortion issue," *Crime and/et Justice*, 6(1):16-21, 1978.
22. Comité de lutte pour l'avortement libre et gratuit. *C'est à nous de décider: l'avortement: la situation actuelle, les méthodes médicales d'avortement, comment obtenir un avortement au Québec*. Montréal: Éditions du remue-ménage, 1978. 56p.
23. Constantineau, Gilles. "Une séance chez l'avorteur numéro l de Montréal," *Le Magazine Maclean*, 6:18-9, 50-2, nov. 1966.
24. Damude, Earl. "Attitudes after abortion," *Chatelaine*, 50:18, May 1977.
25. Dingman, Jocelyn. "Abortion Lib," *Chatelaine*, 43:4, July 1970.
26. _____. "Jet-service abortion," *Chatelaine*, 43:4, June 1970.
27. Dunlop, John. "That controversial anti-abortion ad - Grey nuns were behind it," *Marketing*, 82:2, Jan. 10, 1977.
28. Emanuel, Elliott. "I was always against it, but... ," *Canadian Medical Association Journal*, 113:723-4, Oct. 18, 1975.
29. "L'épiscopat canadien et l'avortement," *Relations*, no. 334:3-4 janv.1969.
30. "En attendant," *Relations*, 42:101, avr. 1982.

31. Evans, Ruth. "Voting against motherhood," *Canadian Forum*, 51:9-11, June 1971.

32. Farkas, Edie. "How many trials will Morgentaler face?" *Last Post*, 5:13-14, Dec. 1976.

33. Freeman, Beverly A. "A descriptive study of women approved for abortions in a general hospital." MSW thesis, University of Windsor, 1976. 153p. (Can. theses, no.29149)

34. Gentles, Ian. "Gentles' reply," *Canadian Forum*, 59:29, June-July 1979.

35. _____. "Measuring tragedy [book review]," *Canadian Forum*, 58:34-7, Apr. 1978. For commentary see Lillian Robinson below.

36. Gillen, Mollie. "Why women are still angry over abortion," *Chatelaine*, 43:34-5, 80, Oct. 1970.

37. Gillen, Mollie. "Your replies to the abortion quiz," *Chatelaine*, 44:23, 62-3, Mar. 1971.

38. Grescoe, Audrey. "Rebirth of the abortion furore," *Maclean's*, 93:46-7, June 2, 1980.

39. Hepworth, H. Philip. *Personal social services in Canada: a review.* Vol. 5: *Family planning and abortion services and family life education programs.* Ottawa: Canadian Council on Social Development, 1975. 146p.

40. Hunter, Marlene E. "Application for abortion at a community hospital," *Canadian Medical Association Journal*, 111:1088-9, 1092, Nov. 16, 1974.

41. "Hypocrisy shows in Canada's abortion policy," *Globe & Mail*, June 25, 1981, p.T5.

42. Isbiter, Sarah R. "Abortion," *Queen's Quarterly*, 86:127-33, Spring 1979.

43. Johnson, Eva. "The lost cause," *Weekend Magazine*, 29:18-20, June 23, 1979.

44. Keate, Kathryn. "Out from under, women unite," *Saturday Night*, 85:15-20 July 1970.

45. Kettle, J. "Numbers racket," *Canada Month*, 9:11, Jan. 1969.

46. Kettle, John. "Population, abortion, birth rates," *Executive*, 17:47-8, Nov. 1975.

47. Kimber, Stephen. "Getting a second opinion," *Maclean's*, 92:25, Sept. 3, 1979.

48. Kostash, Myrna. "The rising of the women," *Broadside*, 2:12-13, 15, Mar. 1981.

49. Kremer, E. J. and E. A. Synan, eds. *Death before birth: Canada and the abortion question*. Toronto: Griffin House, 1974. 196p.

50. Krishnamoni, Devaki. "An investigation into the motives of women seeking therapeutic abortion in Newfoundland." MSW thesis, Memorial University of Newfoundland, 1979. 90p. (Can. theses, no.40846)

51. Krotko, K. J. and S. A. McDaniel. *Three estimates of illegal abortion in Alberta, Canada: survey, mail-back questionnaire and randomized response technique.* Population reprints, no. 24. Edmonton: University of Alberta. Population Research Laboratory, 1977. [5]p.

52. Leblond, Georges. "Phénomènes perçus à travers le discours québécois sur l'avortement." MA thèse, Université du Québec à Rimouski, 1980. 143p. (Can. theses, no.50750)

53. Ligue des droits de l'homme. *La société québécoise face à l'avortement* Montréal: Leméac, 1974. 180p.

54. Lipper, Irene and others. "Abortion and the pregnant teenager," *Canadian Medical Association Journal*, 109:852-6, Nov. 3, 1973.

55. *L'Avortement: la résistance tranquille du pouvoir hospitalier: une enquête de la coordination nationale pour l'avortement libre et gratuit* [Montréal]: Editions du Remue-Ménage, 1980. 94p.

56. Maeots, Krista. "Abortion Caravan," *Canadian Forum*, 50:157, July-Aug. 1970.

57. Marchand, Philip. "Men and abortion," *Chatelaine*, 51:63, 168+ , Nov. 1978.

58. Marcotte, Marcel. "L'avortement est un meurtre," *Relations*, no. 304:106-7, avr. 1966.

59. _____. "L'avortement, la morale et la loi," *Relations*, no. 324:30-6, fév.1968.

60. _____. "En marge du Rapport Bird: la femme devant l'avortement," *Relations*, no. 358:81-5, mars 1971.

61. _____. "Hôpitaux et médecins catholiques face à l'avortement légal," *Relations*, no. 342:273-6, oct. 1969.

62. _____. "Respect de la vie et moralité de l'avortement," *Relations*, no. 360:132-7, mai 1971.

63. Marcus, Robert J. "Evaluating abortion counselling," *Dimensions in Health Service*, 56:16-18, Aug. 1979.

64. Martin, Louis. "On préfère tuer la mère et l'enfant," *Le Magazine Maclean*, 7:84, mai 1967.

65. McArthur, Laura. "Protect the innocents," *Canada & the World*, 46:19, Jan. 1981.

66. McDaniel, Susan A. and Karol J. Krotki. "Estimates of the rate of illegal abortion and the effects of eliminating therapeutic abortion, Alberta 1973-74," *Canadian Journal of Public Health*, 70:393-8, Nov.-Dec. 1979.

67. McGill University. Medical Students' Society. *Brief no. 344 to the Royal Commission on the Status of Women in Canada*. Montreal, 1968. 13p.

68. McLaren, Angus. "Birth control and abortion in Canada, 1870-1920," *Canadian Historical Review*, 59(3):319-40, 1978.

69. Melançon, Louise. "Mouvement de libération des femmes et avortement: pour une réflexion éthico-théologique," dans Rodrigue Bélanger et autres, eds., *Devenirs de femmes*. Cahiers de recherche éthique, no. 8. Montréal: Éditions Fides, 1981, pp.89-101.

70. Nett, Emily M. "An ecological analysis of urban therapeutic abortion rates," *Social Biology*, 25:235-42, Fall 1978.

71. Nowlan, Alden. "Legalized abortion is not 'progress'," *Atlantic Advocate*, 61:64-5, Mar. 1971.

72. Ogino, Prudence. *L'avortement, les évêques et les femmes*. Montréal: Editions du Remue-ménage, [1979?] 32p.

73. Pape, G. "Women are turning on the heat," *Monetary Times*, 138:46, June 1970.

74. Pelrine, Eleanor. *Abortion in Canada*. Toronto: New Press, 1971. 133p.

75. _____. *Morgentaler: the doctor who couldn't turn away*. Toronto: Gage, 1975. 210p.

76. Perreault, Michel. "La planification et l'avortement dans les CLSC," *Canadian Women's Studies / Les cahiers de la femme*, 1:16-17, Summer 1979.

77. Québec. Counseil des affaires sociales et de la famille. *Dossier sur l'avortement: contribution du CASF à une information et une réflexion collective sur un problème d'actualité*. [Québec, 1974]. 48p.

78. _____. *La question de l'avortement*. [Sillery, Québec], 1977. 52p.

79. _____. *Le Conseil du statut de la femme et sa position face à l'interruption volontaire de grossesse* Québec, 1975. 3p.

80. "Report conclusions opposed," *Dimensions in Health Service*, 54:23, Dec. 1977.

81. Robertson, Lloyd W. *Abortion: what the provinces can do*. [Edmonton]: Alberta. Legislative Assembly, 1980. 30p. (Microlog 80-3113)

82. Robinson, Lillian. "Abortion and the 'right to life': a rejoinder," *Canadian Forum*, 59:20-2, Apr. 1979.
    For reply see Gentles above.

83. Ross, Alexander. "Meet your friendly local abortionist," *Maclean's*, 81:30, 65-7, May 1968.

84. Ross, Shirley Ann. "Abortion: attitudes of married women." MA thesis, University of Western Ontario, 1968. 175p. (Can. theses, no.2994)

85. Rosta, Helen "Conscience came first [book review]," *Branching Out*, 3:38, Feb.-Mar. 1976.
    Book review of *Morgentaler - the doctor who couldn't turn away*, by Eleanor Wright Pelrine.

86. Rosta, Helen J. "Cruel and unusual punishment: Pelrine reports on Morgentaler," *Branching Out*, 3:36-7, Feb.-Mar. 1976.

87. Rozovsky, Lorne E. "A husband's consent to his wife's abortion," *Dimensions in Health Service*, 57:34, 36, Jan. 1980.

88. Sachdev, Paul, ed. *Abortion: readings and research*. Toronto: Butterworths, 1981. 237p.

89. Schwenger, Cope W. "Abortion in Canada as a public health problem and as a community health measure," *Canadian Journal of Public Health*, 64:223-9, May-June 1973.

90. Stein, David Lewis and Erna Paris. "Abortion: is it a right or is it murder?" *Chatelaine*, 51:22, Aug. 1978.

91. Sullivan, Gail and Susan Watt. "Legalized abortion: myths and misconceptions," *Social Worker*, 43:78-86, Summer 1975.

92. Tarrab, Gilbert, ed. *La polémique québécoise autour de la question del'avortement et l'affaire Morgentaler*. Montréal: Éditions Aquila, 1975. 194p.

93. Toronto Abortion Committee. "Abortion - it's not free and easy," *Broadside*, 2:12-13, 21, Feb. 1981.

94. _____. "Our abortions, our selves," *Broadside*, 2:6-7, Mar. 1981.

95. "TTC finds the better way," *Broadside*, 3:2, Dec. 1981-Jan. 1982.

96. Vézina, Marie-Odile. *Journal d'une avortée*. Montréal: Éditions de la Presse, 1974. 134p.

97. Watters, Wendell W. *Compulsory parenthood: the truth about abortion*. Toronto: McClelland and Stewart, 1976. 304p.

98. "*Weekend* poll: abortion," *Weekend Magazine*, 29:3, June 23, 1979.

ABORTION - BIBLIOGRAPHY

99. Adams, David W. *Therapeutic abortion: an annotated bibliography*. [Hamilton, Ont.]: McMaster University Medical Centre, 1973. 69, xip.

ABORTION - LAW

100. Adams, Scott. *Abortion and our Canadian Laws*. 3rd. ed. [Toronto, Ont.: S.C.M. Book Room, 1976]. 108p. 1st ed. published 1971; 2nd ed., 1973.

101. Anderson, D. "Change the abortion law now," *Chatelaine*, 43:1, Sept. 1970.

102. Anderson, Doris. "Abortion: let the silent majority prevail," *Chatelaine*, 50:2, January 1977.

103. Baglow, John and Louise Dulude. "Henry who?" *Branching Out*, 5(1):5-6, 1978.

104. Béliveau, Pierre. "La réforme de l'avortement et l'avortement d'une réforme," *Revue du Barreau*, 35:563-92, 1975.

105. Campbell, Tom. "Abortion law in Canada: a need for reform," *Saskatchewan Law Review*, 42:221-50, 1978.

106. Canada. Advisory Council on the Status of Women. *Abortion in Canada; background notes on the proposed amendments to the Criminal Code*, by Louise Dulude. Ottawa, 1975. 26p.

107. Canada. Dept. of Justice. Committee on the Operation of the Abortion Law. *Report*. Ottawa, 1977. 474p.

108. Cheung, K. W. *Essays on abortion*. [n.p.]: University of Windsor Printshop, 1977. 116p.

109. Collison, Robert. "Abortion in the '80's: confrontation and crisis, *Chatelaine*, 56:47, 118+ July 1983.

110. Damude, Earl. "Legal abortion: but not abortion on demand," *Maclean's*, 80:79, May 1967.

111. De Valk, Alphonse. "Worst law ever: ten years of legalized abortion," *Chelsea Journal*, 5:111-19, May-June 1979.

112. Dickens, Bernard M. "The Morgentaler case: criminal process and abortion law," *Osgoode Hall Law Journal*, 14:229-74, Oct. 1976.

113. Dulude, Louise. "Medical rights: beyond the written law," *Branching Out*, 4:5-6, Nov.-Dec. 1977.

     For commentary and reply see John Baglow and Louise Dulude above.

114. Dumont, Hélène. "L'abolition du crime d'avortement dans la perspective de la réforme du droit criminel," *La Revue juridique Thémis*, 15:149-92, 1981.

115. Eisler, Dale. "Legal clout without a trial," *Maclean's*, 95:17, June 28, 1982.

116. Fleck, J. C. "Canada debates abortion, homosexuality," *Christian Century*, 86:354-8, Mar. 12 1969.

117. Friedenberg, E. Z. "Evolution of Canadian justice: the Morgentaler case," *Canadian Forum*, 55:28-30, June 1975.

118. Gillen, Mollie. "Our new abortion law: already outdated?" *Chatelaine*, 42:29, 102, Nov. 1969.

119. Glenn, H. Patrick. "The constitutional validity of abortion legislation: a comparative note," *McGill Law Journal*, 21:672-84, Winter 1975.

5

120. Gordon, Margie and Shelly Gavignan. "The prosecution of Dr. Morgentaler," *Canadian Dimension*, 10:9-11, June 1975.
121. Haliburton, Jane. *"Report of the Committee on Operation of the Abortion Law, 1977* [book review]," *Atlantis*, 4:205-10, Spring 1979.
122. Hawkes, Cheryl. "Attention may have shifted from it, but abortion remains a major issue," *Maclean's*, 90:80, Nov. 14, 1977.
123. Le Bourdais, E. "Badgley committee: abortion law retained," *Dimensions in Health Service*, 54:34-5, Apr. 1977.
124. Monopoli, William. "Judicial doors open a little more: law and life," *Financial Post*, 75:9, Dec. 12, 1981.
125. Oliver, Carole. "Abortion under attack," *Canadian Forum*, 62:37, 42, Mar.1983.
126. Pearson, Mary. *Certain aspects of therapeutic abortion in Canada.* Ottawa: Canada. Advisory Council on the Status of Women, Ottawa: Canada. 1975. 21p.
127. Playfair, Patrick. "Parliament faces up," *Canadian Welfare*, 44:4-7, Jan.-Feb. 1968.
128. *Pregnancy termination: an overview of Canadian law and practice.* Childbearing families and the law: a law review series. Winnipeg, Man.: Community Task Force on Maternal and Child Health, 1981. 20p. and app.
    Bound with Pregnancy termination: rights of the fetus and the father.
129. Robb, W. "Abortion reform," *Canadian Business*, 40:13-14, Dec. 1967.
130. Rozovsky, Lorne E. "Legal consequences of 'right' to abortion," *Dimensions in Health Service*, 53:14-15, Apr. 1976.
131. Ryan, H. R. S. "Abortion and criminal law," *Queen's Law Journal*, 6:362-71, 1981.
132. Tierney, Ben. "Abortion: where it's at, where it's going?" *Canadian Bar Journal*, 3:26-8, Apr. 1972.
133. Veevers, J. E. "The liberalization of Canadian abortion laws," in C. Boydell and others, eds., *Critical issues in Canadian society.* Toronto: Holt, Rinehart & Winston of Canada, 1971, pp.33-9.
134. Wilson, Edward. "The organization and function of therapeutic abortion committees," *Canadian Hospital*, 48:38-40, Dec. 1971.
135. Wouk, Judith. "Halifax right-to-lifers appointed guardian to foetus," *Branching Out*, 7(1):7, 1980.

ABORTION - PSYCHOLOGICAL ASPECTS

136. Bacon, Hugh M. "Psychiatric aspects of therapeutic abortion," *Canada's Mental Health*, 17:18-21, Jan.-Feb. 1969.
137. Damude, Earle. "After abortion," *Chatelaine*, 51:20, July 1978.
138. Giroux, Claire. *Impact psycho-social de l'avortement clandestin: perceptions de 101 femmes qui ont vécu cette expérience.* Montréal: Centre de planning familial du Quebec, 1971. 600p.
139. Greenglass, Esther R. *After abortion.* Don Mills, Ont.: Longman Canada, 1976. 149p.
140. _____. "Therapeutic abortion and its psychological implications: the Canadian experience," *Canadian Medical Association Journal*, 113:754-7, Oct. 18, 1975.
141. Guyatt, Doris Elsie. "Adolescent pregnancy: a study of pregnant teenagers in a suburban community in Ontario." DSW diss., University of Toronto, 1976. 304p. (Can. theses, no.35036)
142. Heath, David S. "Psychiatry and abortion," *Canadian Psychiatric Association. Journal*, 16: 55-63, Feb. 1971.
143. Lawrence, William J. "Anxiety and other personality factors in teenagers before and after abortion." MA thesis, Sir George Williams University, 1972. 80p.
144. McKay, Reta Lynn. "Expressed needs of women having abortions." MSN thesis, University of British Columbia, 1974. 88p. (Can. theses, no.19585)
145. Rinfret, Michèle et autres. *100 femmes devant l'avortement.* Montréal: Éditions du Centre de planning familial du Québec, 1972. 30p.
146. Skinner-Gardner, Jo-Anne. "Induced abortion: a psychological perspective." PhD diss., York University, 1975. 287p. (Can. theses, no.25751)

147.   Taylor, Amy. "Heartbreak pregnancy," *Chatelaine*, 50:36,110-16, March 1977.

ACCOUNTING

148.   "Break with the past," *Executive*, 23:44, Feb. 1981.
149.   Fairclough, Ellen L. "Women as chartered accountants," *Canadian Chartered Accountant*, 88:469-71, June 1966.
150.   Farlinger, Shirley. "Women in chartered accountancy," *Chatelaine*, 54:42, Apr. 1981.
151.   "Female CPA's equal" *Canadian Chartered Accountant*, 98:378, June 1971.
152.   Harel-Giasson, Francine et Marie-Françoise Marchis-Mouren. *La femme comptable agrée vue à travers la litterature specialisée.* Working paper series, no. 81-19. Montreal: Ecole des hautes études commerciales, 1981. 53p.
153.   Luscombe, Nelson. "The women are coming, the women are coming! [La comptabilité au féminin]," *CA Magazine*, 113:3-4, Jan. 1980.
154.   Muse, A. "Ladies first," *CA Magazine*, 110:24-5, Jan. 1977.
155.   Russell, Bettina. "Women in accountancy," *Canadian Women's Studies / Les cahiers de la femme*, 1:48-9, Winter 1978-1979.
156.   "Woman on the move," *Cost and Management*, 49:53, July-Aug. 1975.

ACHIEVEMENT MOTIVATION

157.   Berens, Anne Elizabeth. "Sex-role stereotypes and the development of achievement motivation," *Ontario Psychologist*, 5(2):30-5, 1973.
158.   Berens, Anne Elizabeth. "The socialization of achievement motives in boys and girls." PhD diss., York University, 1972. 224p. (Can. theses, no.15681)
159.   Bird, Barbara Jean. "Differences in achievement motivation in women: the sex-role orientation of the situation." MA thesis, University of Western Ontario, 1972. 113p. (Can. theses, no.12,518)
160.   Lazar, Frances E. "Sex role identity and achievement motivation in women." MA thesis, University of Ottawa, 1979. 142p. (Can. theses, no.44061)
161.   Press, Marjorie Jean P. "Achievement motivation in women: some consequences for familial and professional careers." MA thesis, Memorial University of Newfoundland, 1970. 133p. (Can. theses, no.15,665)
162.   Short, Judith-Ann Catherine. "The effect of the sex-role orientation of the situation on the arousal of the motive to avoid success in women." MA thesis, University of Western Ontario, 1973. 134p. (Can. theses, no.14975)
163.   Silverman, Bernice. "The role of social desirability in the achievement behaviour of female undergraduates." MA thesis, University of Guelph, 1976. 65p.
164.   Stacy, Stanley. "Perceptions of male and female success in sex-linked occupations in relation to the sex of subject and the stance of spouse: impressions of conflicts, consequences, and attributions." MA thesis, Concordia University, 1976. 65p. (Can. theses, no.28470)

ADVERTISING

165.   Aaron, Dorothy. *About face: towards a positive image of women in advertising.* Toronto: Ontario Status of Women Council, 1975. 30p.
166.   "Advertising: has it really come a long way?" *Globe & Mail*, July 19, 1979, p.T1.
167.   "Adwomen told of serious threat," *Marketing*, 85:1, 21, Jan. 28, 1980.
168.   Anderson, Patricia. "Greater push against sex role stereotyping," *Financial Post*, 75:12, May 16, 1981.
169.   "CAAB Peterborough test: in women and advertising study, liberated way wins," *Marketing*, 82:53, 55, Nov. 21, 1977.
170.   Canada. Dept. of National Health and Welfare. Office of the Minister of National Health and Welfare and Minister Responsible for the Status of Women. *The media mirage.* An address by the Honourable Marc Lalonde, to the Ottawa Women's Canadian Club. Ottawa, 1975. 17p.

171. Canadian Advertising Advisory Board. Task Force on Women and Advertising. *Women and advertising: today's messages - yesterday's images?* Toronto, 1977. 30p.

  French edition: *La femme et la publicité: des messages contemporains projetant une image désuète?*

172. Canadian Radio-Television and Telecommunications Commission. *Images of women; report of the Task Force on Sex-Role Stereotyping in the Broadcast Media.* [Ottawa], 1982. 189p.

173. Chiasson, Gail. "Grey wins doubtful honors from Quebec women's group," *Marketing*, 87:4, 14, June 14, 1982.

174. Courtney, Alice. "Count the open shirt buttons on each Belvedere model," *Financial Post*, 68:A23, Oct. 5, 1974.

175. Courtney, Alice and Thomas Whipple. "Women in TV commercials," *Journal of Communication*, 24:110-8, Spring 1974.

176. _____. *Canadian perspectives on sex stereotyping in advertising.* Ottawa: Canada. Advisory Council on the Status of Women, 1978. 117p.

177. _____. *Reaction to traditional versus liberated portrayals of women in TV advertising: a pilot study.* Toronto: York University. Faculty of Administrative Studies, 1976. 63p.

178. Craig, Sheri. "What women say on sex bias in advertising," *Marketing*, 79:3, Feb. 11, 1974.

179. "CRTC task force gets behind ad industry guidelines on sex-role stereotyping issue," *Marketing*, 85:31, Dec. 1, 1980.

180. Curley, Bill. "Fight for the 'right' to stereotype," *Marketing*, 85:8, Aug. 4, 1980.

181. Davis, Curt. "Women bring an extra dimension to sales competition," *Marketing*, 81:8-9, 12-13, July 12, 1976.

182. _____. "Women in sales: a different response," *Marketing*, 81:7-8, May 31, 1976.

183. Edmonds, Elizabeth. "Ad image of women: advertisers way behind in portrayal of women and may get worse," *Marketing*, 79:8, Feb. 18, 1974.

184. "Feminine hygiene commercials will require approval of standards council," *Globe & Mail*, May 16, 1979, p.B4.

185. "Film combats sex-role stereotyping," *Marketing*, 86:2, May 11, 1981.

186. First National Farm Women's Conference. *"The invisible pitch fork" or the portrayal of farm women in the Canadian media.* Status of Rural Women Project. [Ottawa], 1980. 39, [10]p.

  French edition: *"L'outil invisible" ou le portrait de la femme en agriculture dans les média canadiens.*

187. Fisher, John. "Despite what the CAAB says about women in advertising, those rotten sex-stereotyped ads sell, dammit! *Marketing*, 83:17-18, 20, Mar. 6, 1978.

188. _____. "From here to reality: advertising's improved since the sexist '60s, but still ignores the reality of that 50%," *Marketing*, 84:19-20, Oct. 22, 1979.

189. _____. "Sexual stereotyping: opponents have been cast as 'vociferous minority' but it looks like their ranks are swelling," *Marketing*, 81:46-9, Oct. 4, 1976.

190. Godbout, Jacques. "Faut-il censurer la publicité sexiste?" *L'Actualité*, 5:17, juill., 1980.

191. Grass, Jennifer. "TV ads slow to change view of women," *Financial Times*, 66:16-17, Nov. 21, 1977.

192. Harris, Marjorie. "Women in advertising," *Chatelaine*, 55:58-9, 93+ , June 1982.

193. Heath, Brian. "Another probe into 'sexist' advertising," *Marketing*, 83:2, Aug. 28, 1978.

194. "Housewife seen as butt of TV commercials," *Globe & Mail*, Sept. 22, 1976, p.B5.

195. "How should an advertiser proposition a woman? [CAAB pilot study]," *Marketing*, 82:14-15, Feb. 21, 1977.

196. Hughes, Jane. "You've got it all wrong, says a sex task force member," *Marketing*, 85:10, 12, 14, Mar. 10, 1980.

197. "Industry takes fresh look at women's buying power," *Globe & Mail*, Aug. 29, 1979, p.B4.

198. Istona, Mildred. "Redefining the 'women's market'," *Chatelaine*, 52:2, Oct. 1979.

199. "It's no time to be a gentleman [CRTC task force]," *Marketing*, 85:4, Feb. 11, 1980.

8

200. "It's time to really look at women's ads," *Marketing*, 80:12, Dec. 22/29, 1975.
201. "Jean ads gets them into a jam," *Marketing*, 84:51, June 25, 1979.
202. Kaite, Berkeley. "The intimacy of commodities: social control, subjectivity and feminine hygiene." MA thesis, McMaster University, 1981. 182p.
203. Klassen, Rita. "A content analysis of women's roles in TV ads in Ontario." Undergraduate thesis, Dept. of Consumer Studies, University of Guelph, 1977. 43p.
204. Lalonde, Michele. "Images: la femme active," *Le Maclean*, 14:11-12, 31, mars 1974.
205. Lanken, Dane. "Interest, hard work and a bit of good timing," *Broadcaster*, 37:6-7, June 1978.
206. McCoubrey, James. "Opportunities for women opening up in advertising," *Marketing*, 82:16, Mar. 14, 1977.
207. Mehr, Martin. "Progress on role stereotype issue [CRTC task force on sex role stereotyping in the broadcast media]," *Financial Post*, 74:12, Apr. 5, 1980.
208. Messer, Tom. "Sex-symbol ad inquiry?" *Marketing*, 84:1, Mar. 26, 1979.
209. _____. "Survey of women to probe 'sexist' advertising," *Marketing*, 84:8, July 9, 1979.
210. Morrison, Suzanne. "Women and advertising: task force report presents 11-point program," *Journal (The Board of Trade of Metropolitan Toronto)*, Jan. 1978, pp.35-8.
211. Morrissey, Mary and others. *Women and advertising; a study of the opinions of Nova Scotian women regarding the portrayal of women in Canadian media advertising*. [Halifax]: Nova Scotia Human Rights Commission, 1979. 70p. and app. (Microlog 80-0885)
212. "Now CAAB looks at women's role in advertising," *Marketing*, 80:2, Nov. 17/24, 1975.
213. "Ottawa to probe 'sexist' broadcast ads," *Marketing*, 84:2, May 7, 1979.
214. Patrick, Ed. "Milk girl causes a 'sexist' ad row," *Marketing*, 85:1, 4, Aug. 11, 1980.
215. Phillips, Frances. "Industry can continue to act on sex-stereotyping. [CRTC Task Force report]," *Financial Post*, 76:11, Sept. 11, 1982.
216. _____. "Women have firm grip on top advertising rungs," *Financial Post*, 76:20, July 31, 1982.
217. Proulx, Serge. "L'image de la femme dans la publicité: une analyse du contenu des annonces publicitaires de certaines publications québécoises et canadiennes (1954 et 1967)." MA thèse, Université de Montréal, 1969. 397p.
218. "Quebec acts on stereotype ad issue," *Marketing*, 84:1, 45, Dec. 10, 1979.
219. Québec. Conseil du statut de la femme. *L'image des femmes dans la publicité*, préparée par Catherine Lord. Québec, 1979. 103p.
220. "Quebec council acts to fight sexism in ads," *Marketing*, 85:2, Jan. 7, 1980.
221. "Quebec govt. campaigns against sexist ads," *Marketing*, 84:42, Oct. 15, 1979.
222. Rae, Jane. "Today's woman: a description," *Stimulus*, May-June 1978, pp.20-1.
223. "Recognition - as time goes by [Women's Advertising and Sales Club of Winnipeg]," *Marketing*, 83:24, Apr. 24, 1978.
224. "Research group pans women's ad study," *Marketing*, 81:3, Jan. 26, 1976.
225. Reynolds, O. J. "One woman's view of how ads see women," *Stimulus*, May-June 1978, pp.18-19.
226. Ross, Mary Lowrey. "Television," *Saturday Night*, 80:41-2, May 1965.
227. "'Sexist' milk spot pulled in Ontario, edited for final run in Maritimes," *Marketing*, 85:16, Aug. 25, 1980.
228. "Sex role [CRTC task force] study dispute," *Financial Post*, 74:14, Feb. 16, 1980.
229. "Sex role stereotyping admitted," *Globe & Mail*, May 7, 1980, p.B4.
230. "Sexual stereotypes are target of CRTC talks," *Globe & Mail*, May 15, 1979, p.5.
231. Singbeil, Beverly. "Sex in advertising," *Business Life in Western Canada*, 9:27-30, 33-4, Dec. 1981.
232. Snowden, Annette. "You've come an even longer way, baby," *Maclean's*, 91:53, Sept. 4, 1978.
233. "Study finds women like liberated slant in ads," *Globe & Mail*, Jan. 25, 1977, p.5.
234. "Talking about talking about women," *Stimulus*, May-June 1978, pp.14-16.
235. "Task force is not headed for censorship: president," *Marketing*, 85:1, Feb. 18, 1980.
236. Thompson, Tony. "Don't fall into the gender trap," *Marketing*, 83:24-5, Oct. 30, 1978.

237. "TV ranked as 'most persuasive' and also 'most annoying' ad medium by Canadian women," *Marketing*, 84:53, Oct. 15, 1979.
238. "Use education and persuasion to end sex stereotyping in ads, report recommends," *Marketing*, 83:4, 19, July 3, 1978.
239. Vancouver Status of Women. *Sexist ads kit*. Vancouver, 1975. 12p.
240. "Watch advertising tactics, women warn," *Marketing*, 80:25, Sept. 8, 1975.
241. Watson, Elizabeth. "ACA and CRTC Task Force take softer line [sex stereotype]," *Marketing*, 85:2, Mar. 24, 1980.
242. _____. "ACA prepares to fight against 'sexism' censors: CRTC task force finds 32 out of 35 commercials are 'objectionable'," *Marketing*, 85:1, 21, Jan. 28, 1980.
243. _____. "Ad industry seeks united front in 'sexism' battle [task force]," *Marketing*, 85:2, 21, Feb. 4, 1980.
244. _____. "CRTC brings out plan to end sex stereotyping," *Marketing*, 84:1, 31, Oct. 8, 1979.
245. _____. "ICA tells CRTC: 'we quit': 'pointless' to stay on sex stereotype task force," *Marketing*, 85:1, 21, Feb. 18, 1980.
246. _____. "Minister who began 'sex-role' task force defeated," *Marketing*, 85:1, 21, Feb. 25, 1980.
247. _____. "New 'study group' on sexist stereotyping," *Marketing*, 84:27, Aug. 13, 1979.
248. _____. "Sex-role stereotyping: 'last-ditch' action plan pushes for self-regulation," *Marketing*, 85:1, 17, Aug. 18, 1980.
249. "With Women, magazines have edge over TV, study shows," *Marketing*, 86:35, Feb. 16, 1981.
250. "Women and advertising: CAAB's report revisited," *Stimulus*, May-June 1978, pp.11-13.
251. "Women urged to change advertising attitudes," *Marketing*, 80:3, Apr. 28, 1975.
252. "Women's ad club wants to take stand on sex stereotyping," *Marketing*, 85:2, June 23, 1980.
253. "Women's role in advertising: editorial," *Marketing*, 79:4, Feb. 11, 1974.
254. Wood, Ted. "CAAB women's report - it's real!" *Marketing*, 82:12-13, Dec. 5, 1977.
255. _____. "Hey ladies! How'd you like this bacon fat to add to the fire?" *Marketing*, 85:8, 10, Apr. 14, 1980.
256. _____. "I don't believe what's in vogue these days," *Marketing*, 86:28, Apr. 20, 1981.
257. _____. "Must advertisers poke around in ladies' nooks and crannies on TV?" *Marketing*, 82:18, 45, Nov. 7, 1977.
258. _____. "Zesty moment in the girls' locker room," *Marketing*, 85:17-18, Mar. 17, 1980.
259. Young Women's Christian Association. Sexism in Advertising Committee. *Sexism in advertising: report of the Montreal YWCA "Sexism in Advertising" Committee*. Montreal, 1978. 39p.
       French edition: *Publicité et sexisme*.

ADVERTISING — BIBLIOGRAPHY
260. "Stereotyping of women in advertising: a selected bibliography," *Labour Topics (Ontario Ministry of Labour Library)*, 2:1-4, July 1979.

AFFIRMATIVE ACTION
261. "A helping hand up the ladder: [promoting women]," *Financial Times*, 67:19, Oct. 16, 1978.
262. Anderson, Doris. "'Push now by companies will pay'," *Financial Post*, 75:8, Oct. 10, 1981.
263. Avard, Phyllis. "Equal opportunity at Canada Life," *Canadian Personnel and Industrial Relations Journal*, 24:32-3, Mar. 1977.
264. Axworthy, Lloyd. "Status of women: affirmative action in Canada; address," *Canadian Personnel and Industrial Relations Journal*, 27:13-15, Sept. 1980.
265. Bagnall, James. "Ma Bell reverses sex discrimination," *Financial Post*, 71:24, Oct. 15, 1977.

266. Bennett, James. "Equal opportunities for women: why and how companies should take action," *Business Quarterly*, 40:22-9, Winter 1975.

267. Bennett, James and Pierre Loewe. "Stop hemming and hawing - act on equal opportunity," *Financial Post*, 69:11-12, June 21, 1975.

268. British Columbia. Task Force on Women's Issues. *A future for women: a proposal for an equal employment opportunity program for women in the Attorney General's department*. Victoria: British Columbia. Dept. of the Attorney-General, 1976. 43p.

269. Canada. Advisory Council on the Status of Women. *What's been done?* Ottawa, 1974. 40p.
    Assessment of the federal government's implementation of the recommendations of the Royal Commission on the Status of Women.

270. Canada. Co-ordinator, Status of Women. *Status of women in Canada, 1972*. [Ottawa: Information Canada, 1972]. 35, 39p.

271. Canada. Dept. of Employment and Immigration. *Affirmative action study*, prepared by Complan Research Associates Ltd. Ottawa, 1979. 25p.

272. Canada. Dept. of Labour. *Equal opportunities for women program: report and action plan.* [*Programme d'égalité d'accès aux chances pour les femmes: rapport et plan d'action*]. Ottawa, 1981. [103, 105]p.

273. _____. *Status of women in Canada, 1973*. [*La situation de la femme au Canada, 1973.*] By the Honourable John C. Munro, Minister of Labour, Minister Responsible for the Status of Women. Ottawa, 1972. 43, 45p.

274. Canada. Dept. of National Health and Welfare. *Equal opportunities for women: program report, 1976-77*. Ottawa, 1977. 130p.

275. Canada. Dept. of National Health and Welfare. Equal Opportunities for Women Program. *Annual report, 1977-78, including Objectives and action plans, 1978-79*. [*Rapport annuel, 1977-78, comprenant les Objectifs et plans d'action, 1978-79*]. Ottawa, 1978. v.p.

276. Canada. Employment and Immigration Commission. Affirmative Action Program. *Some thoughts about affirmative action in Canada in the 1980's*, prepared by Peter C. Robertson. [Ottawa]: Canada. Dept. of Employment and Immigration, 1980. 43p.

277. Canada. Office of the Co-ordinator, Status of Women. *Status of women in Canada*. [*La situation de la femme au Canada*]. Ottawa, 1975. 56, 54p.

278. Canada. Public Service Commission. Office of Equal Opportunities for Women. *Proceedings of information day on the Public Service. Equal Opportunities Program and the affirmative action strategy*. [Ottawa], 1981. 72, 100p.

279. _____. *Program guidelines: equal opportunities for women*. Ottawa, 1973. 5p.

280. _____. *Response of the Public Service Commission to departmental action plans on equal opportunities for women, 1978-1979*. [Ottawa], 1979. 74, 74p.
    Includes French edition.

281. _____. *Women in the Public Service of Canada, Report 1976*. [*La femme dans la fonction publique du Canada*]. Ottawa, 1976. 28, 28p.

282. Canada. Public Service Commission. Staffing Branch. *Policy: equal opportunities for women in the Public Service of Canada*. [Ottawa, 1975]. 10p.

283. Canada. Treasury Board Secretariat. Human Resources Program Group. *Equal opportunities for women in the Public Service of Canada; a summary of departmental plans-1977*. Ottawa, 1978. 135p. (Microlog 79-1363)

284. Canada. Treasury Board. Personnel Policy Branch. *Equal opportunities for women in the Public Service of Canada, 1978*. [*L'égalité d'accès à l'emploi pour la femme dans la Fonction publique du Canada*]. [Ottawa, 1979]. 252, 275p.

285. Canadian Union of Public Employees. Education Dept. *Affirmative action: putting a stop to sex discrimination: an outline for locals*. Ottawa, n.d. 6p.

286. Canadian Union of Public Employees. *Equal opportunity at work: a CUPE affirmative action manual*. Ottawa: CUPE, 1976. 218p.

287. Clark, John. "Ottawa push for women's job rights," *Financial Post*, 74:1-2, Aug. 2, 1980.

288. Dingman, Jocelyn. "Affirmative action: putting some muscle into equal opportunity," *Chatelaine*, 48:20, July 1975.

289. Dowling, Deborah. "Ontario wants action on women," *Financial Post*, 75:6, Oct. 3, 1981.

290. Duncan, Linda. "Human rights: what the law can - and can't - do," *Branching Out*, 4:6-11, May-June 1977.

291. Eady, Mary. "Affirmative action; Action positive," *Canadian Labour | Travailleur canadien*, 21:14-15, [English]; 15-16, 26, [French], Sept. 1976.

292. Eastham, Kay. "How affirmative should affirmative action be?" *Canadian Personnel and Industrial Relations Journal*, 23:23-6, Nov. 1976.

293. _____. "Women on move: affirmative action for women crown employees in Ontario," *Canadian Business Review*, 3:34-5, Spring 1976.

294. English, Robert. "'Natural forces will make jobs for women'" *Financial Post*, 75:12, Oct. 24, 1981.

295. "Ford has better idea: pay equality for women," *Globe & Mail*, July 20, 1977, p.4.

296. Francis, Anne. "Action from the blueprint: the Royal Commission on the Status of Women," *Canadian Business Review*, 2:2-5, Summer 1975.

297. Gillmeister, Dorothy. "The equal opportunity fantasy: a hard look at voluntary affirmative action," *Status of Women News*, 6:17-19, Spring 1980.

298. Gordon, Sheldon E. "Banking on equal opportunity," *Financial Post*, 72:16, Jan. 21, 1978.

299. Grass, Jennifer. "Affirmative action programs," *Chatelaine*, 54:28, Jan. 1981.

300. _____. "For them, a slow climb up the corporate ladder," *Financial Times*, 68:1, 16-17, July 9, 1979.

301. Harris, Marjorie. "Redressing the balance," *Canadian Business*, 54:52-6, 59-61, June 1981.

302. "International Women's Year 1975 [editorial]," *Canadian Personnel and Industrial Relations Journal*, 21:9, Nov. 1974.

303. Jain, Harish C. and Diane Carroll, eds. *Race and sex equality in the workplace: a challenge and an opportunity*. Proceedings of a conference sponsored by Industrial Relations Research Association, Hamilton and District Chapter and Canadian Industrial Relations Association, McMaster University, Hamilton, Ont., Sept. 28-9, 1979. Ottawa: Canada. Dept. of Labour. Women's Bureau, 1980. 236p.
    Panels on equal pay, affirmative action and seniority, promotion and layoffs.

304. Johnson, Pat. "Women start a blue-collar revolution; but myths, stories must be overcome," *Financial Times*, 70:35, 37 Oct. 19, 1981.

305. Kowalski, Edita. "Women as peers in the organization," *Canadian Banker & ICB Review*, 86:40-3, Feb. 1979.

306. Lee, Betty. "Affirming women's place: it's still inside the corral," *The Canadian*, Nov. 12, 1977, p.19.

307. Liberal Party of Canada. *Woman in Canada*. Ottawa, [1975?] Brochure.

308. Livingston, Martin. "Company's responsibility to change negative attitudes towards women," *Bus & Truck Transport*, 55:43-5, Apr. 1979.

309. "McMaster University seminar: some views on affirmative-action programs," *Labour Gazette*, 78:253-5, June 1978.

310. Mitchell, Nancy. "Equal opportunities," *Civil Service Review*, 53:3-5, June 1980.

311. Monopoli, William. "Court boosts affirmative action policy," *Financial Post*, 75:6, July 25, 1981.

312. Moore, Joy and Frank Laverty. "Affirmative action: a sadly passive event," *Business Quarterly*, 41:22-6, Autumn 1976.

313. _____. "Positive action for integrating women into management," *Canadian Personnel and Industrial Relations Journal*, 22:15-21, Mar. 1975.

314. New Brunswick. Advisory Council on the Status of Women. *Improving opportunities for groups with special employment needs: a response to the Dodge Task Force*, prepared by Susan Shalala. Moncton, 1981. 15p.

315. New Brunswick. Executive Council. *Government of New Brunswick plan of action on the status of women*. [Fredericton], 1980. 11p.

316. North York Board of Education. Ad Hoc Committee Respecting the Status of Women in the North York System. *Interim report no. 2*. [Willowdale, Ont.], May 29, 1975. [16]p.
　　　Published as Appendix C in Minutes of North York Board of Education, [1975?].

317. North York Board of Education. Affirmative Action/Women's Studies Office; Toronto. Board of Education. Affirmative Action/Equal Opportunity Office; Ontario Ministry of Labour. Women's Bureau. *Understanding affirmative action; a glossary of terms*. [Toronto], 1982. Brochure.

318. North York Board of Education. Office of the Director of Education. *Affirmative action and women's studies report*. [Willowdale, Ont.], 1982. [14]p. and app. A & B.

319. _____. *Affirmative Action*. [Willowdale, Ont.], 1981. [8]p. Appendix A, Positive action plan; Appendix B, Affirmative action program in North York.

320. Ontario Status of Women Council. *Brief on contract compliance*. [Toronto], 1978. 12p.

321. Ontario. Advisory Council on Equal Opportunity for Women. *Three-year report on Affirmative Action*. [Toronto], 1982. 28, [53]p. (Microlog 82-3928)
　　　Includes Ontario Minister of Labour's response.

322. Ontario. Ministry of Culture and Recreation. Office of the Women's Advisor. *Affirmative action program*. [Toronto, 1979]. 9p.

323. Ontario. Ministry of Labour. Office of the Executive Coordinator, Women's Programs. *Report of the Executive Coordinator of Women's Programs on the status of women Crown employees in Ontario*. Toronto, 1974/75- . Annual.
　　　Issued also in abridged edition.

324. Ontario. Ministry of Labour. Women Crown Employees Office. *Guidelines for ministries and crown agencies of the Ontario government on affirmative action for women crown employees*. Toronto, 1974. 8p.

325. _____. *Status of women crown employees. Report*. 8th, 1981/82. [Toronto, 1982]. 136p. and app. (Microlog 83-3000)

326. Ontario. Ministry of Labour. Women's Bureau. *Affirmative action consulting service: an interim report*. Toronto, 1979. 14, [4]p.

327. _____. *Affirmative action; a consulting service for your organization*. Toronto, [1979]. Leaflet.

328. Ontario. Ministry of Labour. Women's Bureau. Research Branch. *Affirmative action for women in Ontario; survey of the incidence and scope of affirmative action activities for women in Ontario - a summary*. [Toronto], 1980. 22p.

329. Ontario. Office of the Provincial Secretary for Social Development. *Equal opportunity for women in Ontario: a plan for action*. Toronto, 1973. 73 p. (Profile 73-0373)

330. Phillips, Rhys D. *Affirmative action as an effective labour market planning tool of the 1980s*. Technical study, no. 29. Ottawa: Canada. Task Force on Labour Market Development, 1981. 69p.

331. Pié, Bette. "Affirmative Action: can the voluntary approach work?" *Business Quarterly*, 41:14-19, Spring 1976.

332. "Pipeline employing Natives [Northern Pipeline Agency]," *Native People*, 14:14-15, Oct. 30, 1981.

333. Pratt, Heather. "Women in CN," *Canadian Personnel and Industrial Relations Journal*, 25:47-8, Mar. 1978.

334. Purdy, Kris. "Affirmative action: are we fer it or agin it?," *Branching Out*, 4:33-6, July-Aug. 1977.

335. Québec. Conseil du statut de la femme. *Programme d'égalité de chances à la fonction publique du Québec*. Québec, 1974. 29, 8p.

336. Québec. Ministère de la Fonction publique. *Égalité en emploi pour les femmes dans la fonction publique*. Québec, 1980. 12p. (Microlog 81-0270)

337. Québec. Ministère des affairs sociales. Direction du personnel. *Égalité des chances pour les femmes au Ministère des affairs sociales: plan d'action, 1980/81-* . [Québec], 1980- . Annual.

338. "Recruiting in a changing environment," *Canadian Business Review*, 8:37-40, Spring 1981.

339. Saskatchewan Advisory Council on the Status of Women. *Social progress for the 80's: affirmative action brief*. Saskatoon, Sask., 1980. 25p.

340. Seneca College of Applied Arts and Technology. *Report on equality of opportunity: (Part 1: employees)*. [Willowdale, Ont.: Seneca College, 1978]. 178p.

341. Service de la condition féminine CSN. *Un vieux problème, la discrimination; un nouveau moyen, l'action positive*. Montréal: CSN, 1982. 15p.

342. "Still near the bottom of the totem pole," *Financial Post*, 71:24-5, Oct. 15, 1977.

343. "We've got the finest EEO program in the country," *Office Equipment & Methods*, 24:44, 50, May 1978.

344. Wiebe, Heather Rachael. "Women in traditionally male jobs at Sask Tel: a baseline for affirmative action." MSW thesis, University of Regina, 1981. 121, [42]p. (Can. theses, no.50668)

345. "Women in business: policies of three Canadian corporations," *Canadian Business Review*, 2:8-11, Summer 1975.

346. "Women's cause hits barriers: corporations switching priority to bottom line," *Financial Times*, 69:21, 24, Dec. 15, 1980.

347. Young, Leslie. "Behind the noble slogan," in Canadian Federation of Business and Professional Women's Clubs, *A collection of papers delivered at the National Conference: Women & Work in the 80's: a Decade of Change*. Ottawa: The Federation, 1981, pp.113-119.

AFFIRMATIVE ACTION - BIBLIOGRAPHY

348. Mathews, Catherine and Marnie Shea. *Affirmative action: a selected bibliography*. Toronto: Ontario. Ministry of Labour. Research Library, 1975. 17p.

349. Ontario. Ministry of Labour. Women's Bureau. *Selected bibliography: affirmative action for women in employment and academia*. Toronto, 1974. 4p. Addendum, Apr. 1974. 1p.

AGING

350. Abu-Laban, Sharon McIrvin and Baha Abu-Laban. "Women and the aged as minority groups: a critique," in Victor W. Marshall, ed., *Aging in Canada: social perspectives*. Toronto: Fitzhenry & Whiteside, 1980, pp.63-79.

351. Arel, Louise. "Être pauvre parce que femme et âgée," *Perception*, 4:36-7, Jan.-Feb. 1981.

352. Begin, Monique. "The unladylike business of growing old in Canada," in *Canadian Conference on Social Development, 1978. Proceedings*. Ottawa: Canadian Council on Social Development, 1979, pp.3-18.

353. Cameron, Carmen. *Women and aging: towards tomorrow*. St. John's, Nfld.: Newfoundland Status of Women Council, 1981. 16p.

354. Canadian Advisory Council on the Status of Women. *Women and aging*. [*Vieillir au féminin*]. Ottawa, [1977?] 6p.

355. Cape, Elizabeth. "Aging women in rural society: out of sight, out of mind," *Resources for Feminist Research*, 11:214-15, July 1982.

356. Chappell, Neena L. and Betty Havens. "Old and female: testing the double jeopardy hypothesis," *Sociological Quarterly*, 21:157-71, Spring 1980.

357. Chappell, Neenah. "Elderly women discriminated against," *Perception*, 3:17, Jan.-Feb. 1980.

358. Conrad, Margaret. "'No discharge in this war': a note on the history of women and aging," *Resources for Feminist Research*, 11:216-18, July 1982.

359. Dulude, Louise. *Women and aging: a report on the rest of our lives*. Ottawa: Canadian Advisory Council on the Status of Women, 1978. 123p.

360. Elliott, Jean Leonard. "Retirement without tears: the report of the Special Senate Committee on Retirement Age Policies [review]," *Atlantis*, 5:216-18, Spring 1980.

361. Fernet-Martel, Florence. "Trois ou quatre fois vingt ans," *Canadian Women's Studies / Les cahiers de la femme*, 3(1):32-3, 1981.

14

362. Fletcher, Susan and Leroy O. Stone. *The living arrangements of Canada's older women.* [*Les modes d'habitation des femmes âgées au Canada*]. Ottawa: Statistics Canada, 1982. 77p. (Microlog 83-1124)

363. _____. "The living arrangements of older women," *Essence*, 4(3):115-33, 1980.

364. Frenette, Lyse et Suzanne Messier. "Notes et documents: approche féministe du vieillissement," *Cahiers québécois de demographie*, 9:143-6, avr. 1980.

365. Grenier, Pierre. "Les projets éducatifs de femmes agées: objets d'apprentissage et moyens privilegies." Mémoire de maîtrise inédit, Université de Montréal, 1980. 167p.

366. Hill, Mary W. "Old women: the invisible majority." MA thesis, Simon Fraser University, 1981. (Can. theses, no.53444)

367. Istona, Mildred. "Is there life after 30?" *Chatelaine*, 51:2, June 1978.

368. Kozak, John Francis. "Attitudes toward the elderly: the relationship between self-ratings and ratings assigned to an elderly woman." MA thesis, University of British Columbia, 1975. 152p. (Can. theses, no.49975)

369. National Council of Women of Canada. *The financial situation of older women: a study guide.* Ottawa: The Council, 1978. 23p.

370. _____. *The financial situation of older women: report on a survey of opinion.* Ottawa, 1979. 14p.

371. New Brunswick. Advisory Council on the Status of Women. *Older women: numerous and needy*, prepared by Susan LeBlanc. Presentation to the Advisory Committee for the Development of Programs and Services for Senior Citizens in New Brunswick. Fredericton, 1982. 12, [24]p.

372. Neysmith, Sheila M. "Parental care: another female family function?" *Canadian Journal of Social Work Education*, 7(2):55-63, 1981.

373. Norris, Joan E. "The social adjustment of single and widowed older women," *Essence*, 4(3):135-44, 1980.

374. Ontario. Status of Women Council. *Brief to the Ontario government on women and aging.* [Toronto], 1982. 35p. (Microlog 82-4715)

375. Posner, Judith. "Old and female: the double whammy," *Essence*, 2(1):41-8, 1977.

376. _____. "Old and female: the double whammy," in Victor W. Marshall, ed., *Aging in Canada: social perspectives.* Toronto: Fitzhenry & Whiteside, 1980,pp.80-7.

377. Senior Citizens' Forum of Montreal. *Brief no. 316 to the Royal Commission on the Status of Women in Canada.* Montreal, 1968. 8p.

378. Stone, Leroy O. and Susan Fletcher. "The growing predominance of females," in their, *A profile of Canada's older population.* Montreal: Institute for Research on Public Policy, 1980, pp.14-16.

379. Webster, Loyola Cathleen. "Effects of a programme of regular exercise on institutionalized elderly women." MA thesis, University of Western Ontario, 1978. 87p. (Can. theses, no. 36335)

AGING - BIBLIOGRAPHY

380. Jaffee, Georgina and Emily M. Nett. "Annotated bibliography on women as elders," *Resources for Feminist Research*, 11:253-88, July 1982.

ALCOHOLISM

381. Alcoholism and Drug Dependency Commission of New Brunswick. Research and Evaluation Division. *Profile of female admissions to treatment.* [Fredericton], 1982. 19p. (Microlog 83-2261)

382. Ashley, Mary Jane and others. "Morbidity in alcoholics: evidence for accelerated development of physical disease in women," *Archives of Internal Medicine*, 137:883-7, July 1977.

383. Badiet, Patricia. "Women and legal drugs: a review," in Anne MacLennan, ed., *Women: their use of alcohol and other legal drugs: a provincial consultation - 1976.* Toronto: Addiction Research Foundation of Ontario, 1976, pp.57-81.

384. Birchmore, Doreen, Rodeen Walderman and Karen McNama. *A retrospective study of female and male addiction*. Toronto: Donwood Institute, 1978. 17, [12]p.

385. Bryant, Lee. *The magic bottle*. Toronto: G.R. Welch, 1978. 253p.

386. Burton, Constance Kadota. *Women and alcohol: problems and services, Vancouver*. Vancouver: Water Street Research Group, 1976. 53p.

387. Burton, Constance. *Female alcoholism*. Vancouver: Alcoholism Foundation of British Columbia, 1973. 16p.

388. Carver, Virginia. "The female alcoholic in treatment," *Canadian Psychological Review*, 18:96-103, Jan. 1977.

389. "Female alcoholics," *Chatelaine*, 50:18, Nov. 1977.

390. Ferrence, Roberta G. "Sex differences in the prevalence of problem drinking," in Oriana Josseau Kalant, ed., *Alcohol and drug problems in women*. Research advances in alcohol and drug problems, vol. 5. New York: Plenum Press, 1980, pp.69-124.

391. Fraser, Judy. *The female alcoholic*. Toronto: Addiction Research Foundation of Ontario, 1974. 16p.
　　　　Reprinted from *Addictions*, 20:64-80, Fall 1973.

392. Fraser, Winnie. "The alcoholic woman: attitudes and perspectives," in Anne MacLennan, ed., *Women: their use of alcohol and other legal drugs: a provincial consultation - 1976*. Toronto: Addiction Research Foundation of Ontario, 1976, pp.45-56.

393. Gabriel, Lynn. "The special problems of women alcoholics," *Reader's Digest (Canada)*, 116:57-60, Feb. 1980.

394. Gilmore, Alan and Gustave Oki. *The female chronic drunkenness offender*. The chronic drunkenness offender. Chapter xix. Toronto: Addiction Research Foundation, 1972. 135p.

395. Govier, Katherine. "Ladies on the rocks: the anonymous alcoholics," *Weekend Magazine*, 26:4-6, 8, Apr. 3, 1976.

396. MacLennan, Anne, ed. *Women: their use of alcohol and other legal drugs: a provincial consultation - 1976*. Toronto: Addiction Research Foundation, 1976. 144p.

397. _____. *Women: their use of alcohol and other legal drugs: a provincial consultation, 1976*. Toronto: Addiction Research Foundation of Ontario, 1976. 144p.

398. McCarron, Mary L. "Personality characteristics as affected by variable stress situations in wives of alcoholics." MA thesis, University of Regina, 1977. 89p. (Can. theses, no.33451)

399. McLachlan, John and others. *The woman alcoholic*. Toronto: Donwood Institute, 1975. 32p.

400. Orr, Jody, Mary Downey and Mike DeVillaer. *Report on the need for women's detoxication facilities in Hamilton-Wentworth*. Hamilton, Ont.: Social Planning and Research Council of Hamilton and District, 1981. [35]p. and app.

401. Poole, Nancy. "Self-help groups for alcoholic women - an interview with Nancy Poole," *Canadian Women's Studies / Les cahiers de la femme*, 1:44-6, Summer 1979.

402. Sanders, Willie James. "Thirty female addicts: a descriptive study of thirty females who are addicted to alcohol." MSW thesis, University of Toronto, 1965.

403. Schmidt, Wolfgang and Jan de Lint. "Mortality experiences of male and female alcoholic patients," *Quarterly Journal of Studies on Alcohol*, 30:112-18, Mar. 1969.

404. Schmidt, Wolfgang and Robert E. Popham. "Sex differences in mortality: a comparison of male and female alcoholics," in Oriana Josseau Kalant, ed., *Alcohol and drug problems in women*. Research advances in alcohol and drug problems, vol. 5. New York: Plenum Press, 1980, pp.365-84.

405. "Treatment lacking for female alcoholics [New Brunswick]," *Canada's Mental Health*, 26:22, Sept. 1978.

406. Tuohimaa, Anne. "Sex role adjustment and alcoholism in women." MA thesis, University of Windsor, 1980. 142p. (Can. theses, no.49254)

407. Wilson, Rod. "Sex differences in teenage drinking." MA thesis, York University, 1976. 109p. (Can. theses, no.30958)

408. "Women working, women drinking," *Canada's Mental Health*, 26:24, Mar. 1978.

ARCHIVES

409. Alberta. Provincial Archives. *Some sources for women's history at the Provincial Archives of Alberta*, by Jean E. Dryden. Provincial Archives of Alberta. Occasional paper, no. 2. n.p.: Alberta Culture. Historical Resources Division, 1980. 189p.

410. _____. *Women in Alberta*. Information leaflet, no. 5. Edmonton, 1977. [9]p. (Profile 78-0037)

411. Anderson, Ann Leger and Patricia Marie Chuchryk. "Archival holdings in Saskatchewan women's history: preliminary survey," *Resources for Feminist Research*, 8:44-55, July 1979.

412. Bellingham, Susan. "Special collections: University of Waterloo library special collection related to women," *Canadian Women's Studies / Les cahiers de la femme*, 2(2): 18-20, 1980.

413. Brown, Catherine. *Sources on women in the Toronto City Hall Archives*. Women in Canadian History Project. Informal publication, no. 6. Toronto: Ontario Institute for Studies in Education, [1977].

414. Conrad, Margaret. "Report on the archival resources of the Atlantic provinces on the subject of women's history," *Canadian Newletter of Research on Women*, 7:103-12, July 1978.

415. Hale, Linda Louise. *Selected bibliography of manuscripts and pamphlets pertaining to women held by archives, libraries, museums and associations in British Columbia*. Canadian women's history series, no. 9. [Toronto: Ontario Institute for Studies in Education. Women in Canadian History Project], 1978. 185p.

416. Light, Beth. *Sources in women's history at the Public Archives of Ontario. 1976*. Canadian women's history series. Toronto: Ontario Institute for Studies in Education. Dept. of History and Philosophy of Education, 1977. 37p.

417. _____. "An inventory of sources on women in the personal papers, family papers and manuscript collection in the Archives of Ontario," *Canadian Newsletter of Research on Women*, 6:171-95, Feb. 1977, suppl.

418. Nesmith, Tom. "Sources for the history of women at the Public Archives of Canada," *Canadian Women's Studies / Les cahiers de la femme*, 3(1):113, 1981.

419. Nesmith, Tom, comp. *Post-Confederation sources in manuscripts for the history of women: thematic guide*. 2v. Finding aid, no.1069. Ottawa: Canada. Public Archives, 1979. Rev. 1980. Looseleaf.

420. Rielly, Heather and Marilyn Hindmarch. *Some sources for women's history in the Public Archives of Canada*. Canada. National Museum of Man. History Division. Paper no. 5. Ottawa: Canada. National Museum of Man, 1974. 93p.

421. Royce, Marion. "An inventory of manuscript holdings in the Baldwin Room of the Metropolitan Toronto Public Library," *Canadian Newsletter of Research on Women*, 6:[197]-214, Feb. 1977, suppl.

422. Silverman, Eliane Leslau and Rodney Anne Muir. "Archival holdings in Canadian Women's history: Alberta, Manitoba and Saskatchewan," *Canadian Newsletter of Research on Women*, 6:127-30, Feb. 1977.

423. "Sources on women at the York University Archives," *Canadian Newsletter of Research on Women*, 7:112-6, July 1978.

424. *Sources on women in religious archives in Toronto*. Women in Canadian History Project. Informal publication, no. 8. Toronto: Ontario Institute for Studies in Education. Women in Canadian History Project, [1978?].

425. Women's Movement Archives [Canadian Herstory Project]. *Holdings on group and subject titles as of May 1981*. Toronto, 1981. 14p.

ARMED FORCES

426. Ayling, Vera. "Girls hit all-male bastion [air force reserves]," *Atlantic Advocate*, 64:32-3, Sept. 1973.

427. Bowman, Phylis. *We skirted the war*! Prince Rupert, B.C.: P. Bowman, 1975. 133p.

428. Danson, Barney. *The role of women in the Canadian forces*. Remarks to the Young Women's Christian Association and the Provincial Council of Women of Manitoba. [Ottawa]: Canada. Dept. of National Defence, 1979. 30p.

429. Frewer, Barry. "Chippawa's girls," *Sentinel*, 9(5):23-5, 1973.

430. Griffiths, Alison. "Women on the march," *Today*, Apr. 5, 1980, pp.9-12.

431. Haswell, Geof. "Women in the Canadian Forces," *Sentinel*, 10(5):16-19, 1974.

432. Jacobsen, Carl G. "Women in the Canadian Forces: past, present and future: a critique," *Atlantis*, 4:284-86, Spring 1979, Part II.

433. Labreche, Julianne and Catherine Fox. "Women in arms: they'll stand on guard for thee," *Maclean's*, 91:40, Dec. 18, 1978.

434. Laws, Margaret. "Women are equal in everything except combat," *Financial Post*, 73:1, 6, Mar. 24, suppl. 1979.

435. Louttit, Neil. "This woman's army [Royal Military College]," *Today*, May 23, 1981, pp.8-10.

436. "Military colleges to accept women?" *University Affairs*, 19:22, May 1978.

437. Pierson, Ruth Roach. "Ladies or loose women: the Canadian Women's Army Corps in World War II," *Atlantis*, 4:245-66, Spring 1979, Part II.

438. ---------. "The double bind of the double standard: VD control and the CWAC in World War II," *Canadian Historical Review*, 62:31-58, Mar. 1981.

439. ---------. "The double bind of the double standard: VD control and the CWAC in World War II," *Canadian Historical Review*, 62:31-58, Mar. 1981.

440. ---------. "'Jill Canuck': CWAC of of all trades, but no 'pistol packing momma'," *Canadian Historical Association. Historical Papers*, 1978, pp.106-33.

441. "Professions and personhood," in Canadian Research Institute for the Advancement of Women, *Women as persons. [La femme en tant que personne]*. Toronto: Resources for Feminist Research, 1980, pp.61-9.
     Proceedings of the 3rd annual meeting.

442. Roe, Kathleen Robson. *War letters from the C.W.A.C. (Canadian Women's Army Corp)*. Toronto: Kakabeka Pub. Co., 1975. 169p.

443. Scanlan, Larry. "Royal Military College cadets," *Chatelaine*, 54:32, June 1981.

444. Simpson, Suzanne, Doris Toole and Cindy Player. "Women in the Canadian forces: past, present and future," *Atlantis*, 4:266-83, Spring 1979, Part II.

445. Sloan, Harriet J. T. "Nursing in the Canadian Armed Forces," *Canadian Nurse*, 62:23-5, Nov. 1966.

ART AND ARTISTS

446. Allain, Marie-Hélène. "Marie-Hélène Allain, sculpteure [interview]," *Canadian Woman Studies / Les cahiers de la femme*, 3:27-9, Spring 1982.

447. Allodi, Mary. "Two gentlewomen of Upper Canada," *Rotunda*, 10:2-3, Summer 1977.

448. Arbour, Rose-Marie et Suzanne Lemerise. "Le rôle des Québécoises dans les arts plastiques depuis trente ans; The role of Quebec women in the plastic arts of the last thirty years," *Vie des Arts*, 20:16-23, [French]; 65-7, [English], printemps 1975.

449. Baker, Marilyn. "Women in exhibition: a review," *Branching Out*, 5(2):10-11, 1978.

450. Bawden, Anne. "Woman as viewer," *Canadian Dimension*, 11:41-2, Mar. 1976.

451. Blackridge, Persimmon. "Persimmon Blackridge [interview]," *Fireweed*, 13:135-40, July 1982.

452. Bobak, Molly Lamb. "What is it like to be a woman in art?" Art *Magazine*, 5:10-15, Fall 1973.

453. Boggs, Jean S. "In Canada, a place for women," *Art News*, 7:30-2, Sept. 1974.

454. Boughton, Noelle. "Sharron Corne: from solitary artist to radical feminist," *Canadian Woman Studies / Les cahiers de la femme*, 3:61-3, Spring 1982.

455. Boyce, Eleanor. "Carrying on a North American tradition: Eleanor Boyce, quilt-maker [interview]," *Canadian Women's Studies / Les cahiers de la femme*, 1:8-10, Spring 1979.

456. Brickman, Julie. "Women and the erotic art," *Canadian Dimension*, 11:42-5, Mar. 1976.

457. Brunet-Weinmann, Monique. "La gravure: Angèle, Carmen, Claude, et les autres," *Canadian Woman Studies / Les cahiers de la femme*, 3:40-3, Spring 1982.

458. _____. "Suzanne Olivier," *Canadian Women's Studies / Les cahiers de la femme*, 2(2):80-1, 1980.

459. _____. "Voir et se voir - chronique sur les arts - Lorraine Bénic," *Canadian Women's Studies / Les cahiers de la femme*, 1:80-1, Spring 1979.

460. _____. "Voir et se voir - les femmes artistes d'un océan à l'autre," *Canadian Women's Studies / Les cahiers de la femme*, 1:106-8, Summer 1979.

461. Burgess, Catherine. "Women artists: bright young newcomers on Canada's art scene," *Chatelaine*, 54:84-7, Oct. 1981.

462. "Canada's 'First Lady' of culture: Jean Sutherland Boggs," *Communiqué*, no. 8:18-20, May 1975.

463. Corne, Sharon. "Women in exhibition: the politics of pioneering art feminism on the Prairies," *Branching Out*, 5(2):7-10, 1978.

464. Crean, Susan. "Guess who wasn't invited to 'The dinner party'," *This Magazine*, 16:18-25, Nov. 1982.

465. Davis, Gayle R. "Visibility: the slide registry of Nova Scotia artists," *Canadian Woman Studies / Les cahiers de la femme*, 3:52-3, Spring 1982.

466. Edinborough, Arnold. "Judy Chicago throws awe-inspiring party [at Art Gallery of Ontario]," *Financial Post*, 76:26, June 5, 1982.

467. Elliott, Marnie. "Inviting the eye inside: Maryon Kantaroff," *Canadian Woman Studies / Les cahiers de la femme*, 3:23-4, Spring 1982.

468. Elwood, Marie. "The State Dinner Service of Canada, 1898," *Material History Bulletin*, 3:41-9, Spring 1977.

469. Evans, Eileen. "Jean Kamins: cabbages and crushed taffeta," *Canadian Woman Studies / Les cahiers de la femme*, 3:7-3, Spring 1982.

470. Farr, Dorothy and Natalie Luckyj. *From women's eyes: women painters in Canada*. Kingston, Ont: Agnes Etherington Art Centre, 1975. 81p.

471. Fleisher, Pat. "Love or art? A historical survey," *Art Magazine*, 5:18-21, Fall 1973.

472. Ford, Judy and Ellen McDonald. "The crafts of Labrador women," *Canadian Women's Studies / Les cahiers de la femme*, 1:96, Spring 1979.

473. Graham, Mayo. *Some Canadian women artists. [Quelques artistes canadiennes]*. Ottawa: National Gallery of Canada, 1975. 112p.

474. Gwyn, Sandra. *Women in the arts in Canada*. Royal Commission on the Status of Women in Canada. Study no. 7. Ottawa, 1971. 98p.

475. _____. "Women in the arts in Canada," *Communiqué*, no.8:3-5, 43-4, May 1975.

476. Harris, Marjorie. "Woman's work," *Chatelaine*, 51:34,37,79+ , July 1978.

477. Hayman, Sasha and Joan Barfoot. "Reclaiming an art: the tapestries of Sasha Hayman," *Fireweed*, 3/4:164-9, Summer 1979.

478. Hayman, Sasha. "Sasha Hayman - spinster hag," *Canadian Women's Studies / Les cahiers de la femme*, 1:38-9, Spring 1979.

479. Heiman, Trudie. "Strange happenings [Festival of life and learning, University of Manitoba]," *Canadian Dimension*, 13(1):21-2, [1978].

480. Hobart, Cathy. "Art for the audience [Maureen Paxton]," *Branching Out*, 6(1):22-5, 1979.

481. _____. "Art transformed," *Branching Out*, 7(1):12-13, 1980.

482. _____. "Does art have a sex?" *Branching Out*, 5(2):4-6, 1978.

483. Hunt, J. Doris. "Annora Brown of Fort Macleod," *Canadian Women's Studies / Les cahiers de la femme*, 1:91-3, Spring 1979.

484. Joyce-Jones, Susannah. "Sasha McInnis-Hayman," *Canadian Woman Studies / Les cahiers de la femme*, 3:70-1, Spring 1982.

485. Julien, Pauline. "Suzanne Guité n'est plus," *Canadian Woman Studies / Les cahiers de la femme*, 3:16-18, Spring 1982.

486. Kantaroff, Maryon. "Breaking out of the female mould," in Gwen Matheson, *Women in the Canadian mosaic*. Toronto: Peter Martin, 1976, pp.274-87.

487.   Kelly, Susan A. "A sister-in-law writes: Susan E. Kelly [Weaver]," *Canadian Woman Studies / Les cahiers de la femme*, 3:76-8, Spring 1982.

488.   Kirkwood, Hilda. "Space and sculpture: an interview with Almuth Lutkenhaus," *Canadian Forum*, 60:5-9, Dec. 1980-Jan. 1981.

489.   Landsberg, Michèle. "Joyce Wieland: artist in movieland," *Chatelaine*, 49:57-9, 110-11, Oct. 1976.

490.   Larson, Doris. "New perspectives: Saskatchewan women artists, 1981," *Canadian Woman Studies / Les cahiers de la femme*, 3:11-14, Spring 1982.

491.   Lemoine, Christine. "Quand l'art est social: une lutte à mener...," *Canadian Woman Studies / Les cahiers de la femme*, 3(2):30-1, 1981.

492.   Lindsay-Szilasi, Doreen. "Notes from Spiracle: 5 young women in Montreal with a co-operative approach," *Art Magazine*, 5:28-30, Fall 1973.

493.   Long, Inga. "Art as my link with history," *Canadian Women's Studies / Les cahiers de la femme*, 1:41, Spring 1979.

494.   "Lynne Munro - apprentice weaver," *Canadian Women's Studies / Les cahiers de la femme*, 1:40, Spring 1979.

495.   MacKay, Susanne. "Women artists in Canada: an 'Atlantis' gallery of women's art," *Atlantis*, 5:Fall 1979.

496.   Maranda, Jeanne. "Louisette Gauthier-Mitchell, une artiste québécoise," *Canadian Woman Studies / Les cahiers de la femme*, 3:48-50, Spring 1982.

497.   ----------. "Pnina Granirer: une artiste de l'ouest canadien," *Canadian Woman Studies / Les cahiers de la femme*, 3:4-6, Spring 1982.

498.   Martin, Jane. "Who judges whom: a study of some male/female percentages in the art world," *Atlantis*, 5:127-9, Fall 1979.

499.   McDougall, Anne. *Anne Savage: the story of a Canadian painter*. Montreal: Harvest House, 1977. 215p.

500.   McGrath, Judy. "Craftswomen of the North West Territories," *Canadian Women's Studies / Les cahiers de la femme*, 1:97-8, Spring 1979.

501.   McInnes-Hayman, Sasha. *Contemporary Canadian women artists: a survey*. London, Ont.: Womanspirit Art Research and Resource Centre, [1981] 16p. and app.

502.   Micillo-Villata, Sylvana. "Découragement: encouragement," *Canadian Women's Studies / Les cahiers de la femme*, 1:11-12, Spring 1979.

503.   Montagnes, Anne. "Joyce Wieland: myth in many media," *Communiqué*. no. 8:36-9, May 1975.

504.   Morgan, Joanna. "Sarah Jackson, Halifax 'xerographer'," *Chatelaine*, 50:18, April 1977.

505.   Mount Saint Vincent University. Art Gallery. *Some Nova Scotia women artists*. Halifax, N.S., 1975. 45p.

506.   Munro, Mary. "Pangnirtung women carvers," *North*, 22:46-9, Oct. 1975.

507.   Murray, Joan. "Some contemporary women artists in Canada: an introduction," *Fireweed*, 3/4:86-101, Summer 1979.

508.   Narayana, Hélène. "Cécile Szaszkiewicz," *Canadian Woman Studies / Les cahiers de la femme*, 3:59-60, Spring 1982.

509.   Neering, Rosemary. *Emily Carr*. Don Mills, Ont.: Fitzhenry & Whiteside, 1975. 62p.

510.   Nemiroff, Diana. "Suzy Lake and Sorel Cohen," *Artscanada*, 34:59-60, Oct./Nov. 1977.

511.   Nix, Kalene. "A tree rooted in a stark pure land: Suzanne Guité, 1927-1981," *Canadian Woman Studies / Les cahiers de la femme*, 3:47, Spring 1982.

512.   Norris, J. A., comp. *The book of giving: a history of the Ontario Handweavers and Spinners, 1956-1979*. Toronto: Ontario Handweavers and Spinners, 1979. 129p.

513.   O'Brien, Paddy. "Mary Pratt," *Canadian Woman Studies / Les cahiers de la femme*, 3:36-9, Spring 1982.

514.   Parsons, Alison. "Alison Parsons - textile designer and printer [interview]," *Canadian Women's Studies / Les cahiers de la femme*, 1:83-6, Spring 1979.

515.   Pazdro, Roberta J. "Mildred Valley Thornton (1890-1967): painter of the native people," *Canadian Women's Studies / Les cahiers de la femme*, 1:103-4, Spring 1979.

516. Pazdro, Roberta. "The importance of minutiae: Valerie Pugh," *Canadian Woman Studies / Les cahiers de la femme*, 3:56-8, Spring 1982.

517. Poteet, Susan K. "Who is the new Eve?: the feminist art of Freda Guttman Bain," *Branching Out*, 2:11-13, 37, Mar.-Apr. 1975.

518. Provincial Council of Women of Manitoba. Arts and Letters Committee. *Women artists in Manitoba*. [Winnipeg], 1981 36p.

519. Robertson, Heather. "Those wonderful high-powered volunteers," *Chatelaine*, 56:59, 140+ , Apr. 1983.

520. Rosenberg, Avis Lang. *Mirrorings: women artists of the Atlantic Provinces*. Halifax, N.S.: At Gallery, Mount Saint Vincent University, 1982. 45p.

521. _____. "Women artists and the Canadian art world: a survey," *Atlantis*, 5:107-26, Fall 1979.

522. Roy, Monique. "Nicole Gagné," *Canadian Woman Studies / Les cahiers de la femme*, 3:67-8, Spring 1982.

523. Sabat, Christina. "The delectable art of Mary Pratt," *Atlantic Advocate*, 73:12-15, Nov. 1982.

524. Sands, Gwen. "From pioneer to professional: women in crafts," *Communiqué*, no. 8:24-6, 47, May 1975.

525. Sisler, Rebecca. *The girls: a biography of Frances Loring and Florence Wyle*. Toronto: Clarke Irwin, 1972. 120p.

526. Sparling, Mary. "'The lighter auxiliaries': women artists in Nova Scotia in the early nineteenth century," *Atlantis*, 5:83-106, Fall 1979.

527. "Stitches in time," *Canadian Women's Studies / Les cahiers de la femme*, 3(1):28-9, 1981.

528. Stoffman, Judy. "The rediscovery of Paraskeva Clark," *Chatelaine*, 56:40, 102+ , Aug. 1983.

529. Tippett, Maria. *Emily Carr: a biography*. Toronto: Oxford University Press, 1979. 314p.

530. Van Raalte, Sharon. "Inuit women and their art," *Communiqué*, no. 8:21-3, May 1975.

531. Waisman, Chaika. "Old woman at play - an interview with Chaika Waisman," *Canadian Women's Studies / Les cahiers de la femme*, 1:53-5, Spring 1979.

532. Watterson, Georgia. "Aferdita Shehu," *Canadian Women's Studies / Les cahiers de la femme*, 1:13-15, Spring 1979.

533. _____. "When my vision is cohesive, I draw: Banakonda Kennedy-Kish (Bambi)," *Canadian Woman Studies / Les cahiers de la femme*, 3:20-2, Spring 1982.

534. Whitehead, Ruth Holmes. "Christina Morris: Micmac artist and artist's model," *Material History Bulletin*, 3:1-14, Spring 1977.

535. Wieland, Joyce. "Joyce Wieland: she speaks in colours [interview]," *Broadside*, 2:13, 17, May 1981.

536. Zwarun, Suzanne. "The lady is a champ [Lynn Johnston]," *Quest*, 11:25-34, June-Aug. 1982.

ART GALLERIES

537. Brunet-Weinmann, Monique. "La galerie Powerhouse," *Canadian Women's Studies / Les cahiers de la femme*, 2(1):84-9, 1980.

538. Kask, Janet. "Women artists: radical and unique [Powerhouse Art Gallery, Montreal]," *Chatelaine*, 48:40, Nov. 1975.

539. Morrison, Suzanne. "McGibbon Culture Centre planned as showcase for Canadian women," *Journal (The Board of Trade of Metropolitan Toronto)*, Fall 1978, pp.5-6, 9-10.

540. Nash, Joanna. "Montreal's Powerhouse gallery: the evolution of a women's art space," *Fireweed*, 3/4:22-7, Summer 1979.

541. Poteet, Susan K. "Powerhouse: Montreal women's gallery," *Branching Out*, 2:19-21, Sept.-Oct. 1975.

542. Prost, Viviane. "D'une coopérative artistique: Powerhouse," *Possibles*, 4:163-6, automne 1979.

543. Rogers, Janet. "Where the spirit of women is gathered," *Broadside*, 3:4-5, Apr. 1982.

ASSERTIVENESS

544. Cammaert, Lorna. "A cross-cultural comparison of assertiveness in women," in Cannie Stark-Adamec, ed., *Sex roles: origins, influences and implications for women*. Montreal: Eden Press, 1980, pp.100-10.

545. Emmott, Shelagh. "Assertiveness training for improved conflict resolution style," in Cannie Stark-Adamec, ed., *Sex roles: origins, influences and implications for women*. Montreal: Eden Press, 1980, pp.111-26.

546. Kahn, Sharon E. and Leslie S. Greenberg. "Beyond a cognitive/behavioural approach: congruent assertion training," in Cannie Stark-Adamec, ed., *Sex roles: origins, influences and implications for women*. Montreal: Eden Press, 1980, pp.127-38.

547. McVicar, Pauline A. "A study of assertiveness, self-actualization, and locus of control in women." MSc thesis, University of Calgary, 1979. 92p. (Can. theses, no.42054)

548. Plenge, Viviann C. "The effects of assertive training and group counseling on assertiveness and self esteem in middle class women." MSc thesis, University of Calgary, 1976. 88p. (Can. theses, no.28554)

549. Reed, Carol. "Assertiveness as a key to success," *Canadian Banker & ICB Review*, 84:42-7, May-June 1977.

550. Smye, Marti Diane and Jeri Dawn Wine. *A comparison of female and male adolescents' social behaviors and cognitions: a challenge to the assertiveness literature*. GROW paper, no. 11. Toronto: Ontario Institute for Studies in Education. Group for Research on Women, [1977?]. 31p.

551. Smye, Marti Diane, Jeri Dawn Wine and Barbara Moses. "Sex differences in assertiveness: implications for research and treatment," in Cannie Stark-Adamec, ed., *Sex roles: origins, influences and implications for women*. Montreal: Eden Press, 1980, pp.164-75.

552. Wine, Jeri Dawn and others. "Assertiveness: sex differences in relationships between self-report and behavioural measures," in Cannie Stark-Adamec, ed., *Sex roles: origins, influences and implications for women*. Montreal: Eden Press, 1980, pp.176-86.

ATHLETICS AND SPORTS

553. "A woman's place is in the gym [body building]," *Financial Post Magazine*, [75]:5, Mar. 1981.

554. Agger, Ellen. "Out of the kitchen and into the streets," *Canadian Women's Studies / Les cahiers de la femme*, 2(2):90-1, 1980.

555. Aitken, John. "She shoots, she scores!" *Weekend Magazine*, 27:10, Feb. 12, 1977.

556. Barrett, Cindy. "Female jab at the rules [boxing]," *Maclean's*, 95:60b Nov. 15, 1982.

557. Batt, Sharon. "Editorial," *Branching Out*, 5(4):2, 1978.

558. Batten, Jack. "The ecstasy of long drives," *Macleans*, 86:34-5,44,46,48,50, July 1973.

559. Bird, Evelyn I. "Personality structure of Canadian intercollegiate women ice hockey players," in G. S. Kenyon, ed., *Contemporary psychology of sport: proceedings of the Second International Congress of Sport Psychology*. Chicago: Athletic Institute, 1970, pp.149-56.

560. Bow, Jane. "The great recreation rip-off," *Chatelaine*, 50:20, July 1977.

561. Bratton, Robert D. "Participation in school and community sports by adolescents from a Calgary junior high school," *CAHPER Journal*, 44:6-12, 14, Nov.-Dec. 19

562. Breen, Mary Catherine. "The self-concepts of female athletes: an explanatory study of role strain in intercollegiate athletics." MA thesis, University of Windsor, 1977. 103p. (Can. theses, no.33185)

563. Buhrmann, Hans G. and Robert D. Bratton. "Athletic participation and status of Alberta high school girls," *International Review of Sport Sociology*, 12(1):57-69, 1977.

564. Butcher, Janice. *Physical activity participation of adolescent girls*. Edmonton: Alberta. Dept. of Education. Planning and Research Branch, 1979. 17p. and app.

565. _____. "A study of the differences between high school girls who elect physical education and high school girls who do not." MSc thesis, Dalhousie University, 1976. 159p. (Can. theses, no.31476)

566. _____. "Physical activity participation of adolescent girls." PhD diss., University of Alberta, 1980. 315p. (Can. theses, no.44707)

567. Butler, Elaine. "Shop talk, interviews by Elaine Butler," *Branching Out*, 5(4):29-31, 1978.

568. Butt, Dorcas Susan. "Perspectives from women on sport and leisure," in Cannie Stark-Adamec, ed., *Sex roles: origins, influences and implications for women*. Montreal: Eden Press, 1980, pp.70-88.

569. Canada. Dept. of National Health and Welfare. Fitness and Amateur Sport. *Survey [of] women in sport in Canada: leaders and participants from a national perspective. [Enquête sur la participation des femmes aux sports au Canada]*. [Ottawa, 1980?] 9, 10p.

570. Canada. Fitness and Amateur Sport. Women's Program. *Canadian directory of women in sport leadership*. Ottawa, 1982- .

571. _____. *Women in sport leadership; summary of national survey. [Les femmes dans le leadership sportif; résumé de l'enquête nationale]*. Ottawa, 1982. 11, 11p.

572. Cochrane, Jean, Abby Hoffman, and Pat Kincaid. *Women in Canadian sports*. Toronto: Fitzhenry & Whiteside, 1977. 96p.

573. Day, Helen and Josephine Budgell. "A look at female involvement in sports," *Newfoundland Teachers' Association. Bulletin*, 25:5+ , Nov. 16, 1981.

574. Di Manno, Rosie. "Zip! There goes Angella Taylor," *Chatelaine*, 56:54, 258, 260, Oct. 1983.

575. Dranoff, Linda Silver. "Ask a lawyer," *Chatelaine*, 53:25-6, Sept. 1980.

576. Fisher, Margaret Ada. "Sex-role socialization and female sport participation." MEd thesis, University of New Brunswick, 1976. 122p. (Can. theses, no.30399)

577. Fournier, Jean-Pierre. "Le sport: la fin du sexe faible," *Le Maclean*, 14:15, oct. 1974.

578. Gilverson, Pamela G. "The female in physical recreation: a study of participation and its relationship to lifestyle." MA thesis, University of Alberta, 1980. 118p. (Can. theses, no.48952)

579. Gould, Allan M. "Susan Nattrass: Canada's shooting star," *Chatelaine*, 56:52, 110, 112, Dec. 1983.

580. Greaves, Helen. "Law: the view from the bench," *Branching Out*, 5(4):34-5, 1978.

581. Greene, Nancy. *Nancy Greene: an autobiography*. Toronto: Pagurian Press, 1968. 189p.

582. Griffiths, Alison. "They who risked their delicate organs," *Branching Out*, 5(4):10-13, 1978.

583. Gzowski, Peter. "Sports," *Saturday Night*, 81:50-1, Mar. 1966.

584. Hall, Ann. "On track: interview with Ann Hall," *Branching Out*, 5(4):20-3, 1978.

585. Hall, Ann, Jane Cameron and Debbie Shogan. *Women in athletic administration at Canadian universities*. Report of a National Conference sponsored by the Faculty of Physical Education and Recreation, University of Alberta, May 15-17, 1981. 60p.

586. Hall, M. Ann and Dorothy A. Richardson. *Fair ball: towards sex equality in Canadian sport*. Ottawa: Canadian Advisory Council on the Status of Women, 1982. 124p.

587. Hall, M. Ann and Patricia A. Lawson. "Womansport: implications of the changing roles of women," in Frank J. Hayden, ed., *Body and mind in the 90's*. [n.p.]: Canadian Council of University Physical Education Administrators, 1980, pp.341-64.

588. Hall, M. Ann. *Sport and gender: a feminist perspective on the sociology of sport*. Ottawa: Canadian Association for Health, Physical Education and Recreation, 1978. 83p.

589. _____. *Sport, sex roles and sex identity*. CRIAW papers, no. 1. Ottawa: Canadian Research Institute for the Advancement of Women, 1981. 41p.

590. _____. "Rarely have we asked why: reflections on Canadian women's experience in sport," *Atlantis*, 6:51-60, Fall 1980.

591. _____. "Sport and physical activity in the lives of Canadian women," in Richard S. Gruneau and John G. Albinson, eds., *Canadian sport: sociological perspectives*. Don Mills, Ont.: Addison-Wesley, 1976, pp.170-99.

592. Harrison, Donna J. "The perceived image of the female athlete in relation to other female social roles." MA thesis, University of Alberta, 1978. 116p. (Can. theses, no.40172)

593. Hoffman, Abby. "Running for gold," *Macleans*, 86:31-3, Feb. 1975.

594. _____. "Super-jock in decline: liberating sport from sexist stereotypes," *Canadian Dimension*, 8:41-2, Aug. 1971.

595. _____. "The champions!" *Chatelaine*, 49:26-8, Jan. 1976.

596. Holman, Roy Paul. "The perceived status of female athletes by male and female athletes and non-athletes in Canada and the United States." EdD diss., University of North Carolina at Greensboro, 1978. 207p.

597. Huot, François. "Loisirs: de la cuisine au stade," *L'Actualité*, 2:12, juill. 1977.

598. Hynes, Maureen. "Athletic council gives in: U. of T. women win soccer ruling," *Branching Out*, 5(3):6, 1978.

599. Kennedy, Linda Marie. "Mother-daughter relationships and their influence on female sport socialization." MA thesis, University of Alberta, 1975. 217p. (Can. theses, no.26797)

600. Kennedy, Linda. "Mother-daughter relationships and female sport socialization," *CAHPER Journal*, 43:22-6, Jan.-Feb. 1977.

601. Keyes, Mary. "Administration of the Canadian Women's Intercollegiate Athletic Union," *CAHPER Journal*, 40:21-3, 32-3, July-Aug. 1974.

602. Koziol, Carol Ann. "Role conflict in female athletes." MPEd thesis, University of New Brunswick, 1980. 111p. (Can. theses, no.47757)

603. Layton, Nancy. "The current status of girls' secondary school physical education programs in selected Canadian independent schools." MPE thesis, University of New Brunswick, 1979. (Can. theses, no.43908)

604. Leslie, Susan. "Coming on strong," *Weekend Magazine*, 29:14-16, Aug. 11, 1979.

605. Lewis, Pamela J. "Fitness and amateur sport branch policies as they pertain to women in sport in Canada from 1974 to 1979." MA thesis, University of Western Ontario, 1980. 123p.

606. Lord, Catherine. "Une charte des droits de la golfeuse," *L'Actualité*, 3:14, fév. 1978.

607. Loverock, Patty. "Pink bows and sweat," *Branching Out*, 5 (4):32-3, 1978.

608. MacDuff, Nicole. "Womansport: implications of the changing roles of women. A response to Hall and Lawson," in Frank J. Hayden, ed., *Body and mind in the 90's*. [n.p.]: Canadian Council of University Physical Education Administrators, 1980, pp.365-8.

609. Mann, Brenda and Peat O'Neil. "Corsets unlaced: the beginning of women in sport," *Branching Out*, 3:32-5, July-Aug. 1976.

610. McCart, Joyce. "Goodbye to the Powder Puffs: women stake their claim in stock car racing," *Branching Out*, 3:11-13, Apr.-June 1976.

611. McDonald, David and Lauren Drewery. *For the record: Canada's greatest women athletes*. Toronto: Mesa Associates, 1981. 270p.

612. McFadden, Fred. *Abby Hoffman*. Don Mills, Ont.: Fitzhenry & Whiteside, 1977. 47p.

613. Miscisco, Daniel Robert. "The influence of distinct coaching styles on personality and sportsmanship attitudes of elementary age girls playing competitive basketball." MPE thesis, University of British Columbia, 1976. 165p. (Can. theses, no.29907)

614. Myers, Anita M. and Hilary M. Lips. "Participation in competitive amateur sports as a function of psychological androgyny," *Sex Roles*, 4(4):571-8, 1978.

615. National Conference on Women and Sport. *Report*. 1st. May 1974. Ottawa: Information Canada, 1975. 80p.
     Published by authority of the Minister of National Health and Welfare.

616. New Brunswick. Advisory Council on the Status of Women. *Amateur sport in New Brunswick*, prepared by Pamela Easterbrook. [Moncton], 1980. 7p.

617. Ontario Status of Women Council. *About face: towards a positive image of women in sport*, by Abby Hoffman. Toronto, 1976. 30p.

618. Ontario. Task Force on Equal Opportunity in Athletics. *Can I play?* [Toronto], 1983. 113, [37]p.

619. O'Malley, Martin. "She shoots, she scores. Now what, one may ask, is so remarkable about that?" *Maclean's*, 90:64, Nov. 28, 1977.

24

620. Popma, Anne, ed. *The female athlete: proceedings of a national conference about women in sports and recreation, March 21-23, 1980, Institute for Human Performance, Simon Fraser University, Burnaby, British Columbia*. Burnaby, B.C.: Simon Fraser University. Institute for Human Performance, 1980. 205p.
621. Purdy, Kris. "Fair coverage," *Branching Out*, 5(4):6-9, 1978.
622. Rockett, Eve. "Karen Magnussen, the girl who won't lose," *Chatelaine*, 47:30-1, 69-71, Jan. 1974.
623. Ross, Val. "Chatelaine's first woman of the year: who said it was easy being a champ? [Diane Jones Konihowski]," *Chatelaine*, 52:32-35, 103+ , Jan. 1979.
624. Rubenstein, Lorne. "A swing and three misses [golfers]," *Today*, pp.6-8, July 4, 1981.
625. Samler, Jolanta and Frankie Ford. "Can this sport be liberated?" *Branching Out*, 5(4):37-8, 1978.
626. Shore, Valerie. "Women's university athletics: equality still far off," *University Affairs*, 20:11-12, Feb. 1979.
627. Sport and Recreation As It Affects Women Conference. *Sport and recreation as it affects women: Conference report, proceedings*. Regina: Saskatchewan. Dept. of Culture and Youth, 1975. 23p.
628. "Sport: fit for women," *Urban Reader*, 3:18-20, May 1975.
629. Steed, Judy. "New Amazons," *The Canadian*, Oct. 28, 1978, pp.5-6, 8+ .
630. Stein, David Lewis and Erna Paris. "Should girls play hockey with boys?" *Chatelaine*, 51:17, Dec. 1978.
631. Swan, Susan. "Barbara Ann, are you still happy, Happy?" *Chatelaine*, 48:51, 74+ , Nov. 1975.
632. Syrotuik, Janice Letitia. "Fear of success in sport among adolescent girls." MA thesis, University of Alberta, 1975. 117p.
633. Thomas, Gregory Charles. "The relationship between personality and performance of Canadian women intercollegiate basketball players." MPE thesis, University of British Columbia, 1977. 85p. (Can. theses, no.34965)
634. Tyrwhitt, Janice. "Women in sport: winners or losers?" *Reader's Digest. Can. ed.*, 107:60-4, Oct. 1975.
635. Vail, Susan E. "The effect of female athletic involvement on femininity and self-esteem." MA thesis, University of Western Ontario, 1975. 77p. (Can. theses, no.28368)

636. Vertinsky, Patricia. "Female activism through sport from a cross-national perspective," *ARENA Review*, 3:3-12, May 1979.
637. Vickers, Joan and others. *A comparative study: relative opportunities for women in the C.I.A.U. 1978 to 1981, athletes, coaches, administrators*. n.p., [1981?] 26p.
        Study funded by Fitness and Amateur Sport Canada.
638. Walton, Yvette M. "The life and professional contributions of Ethel Mary Cartwright, 1880-1955." MA thesis, University of Western Ontario, 1976. 199p. (Can. theses, no.28372)
639. Wayne, Jamie. "Women race into sports market," *Financial Post*, 73:37, Nov. 10, 1979.
640. Whitson, David. "Jock and Jill in Toronto," *Community Schools*, Oct. 1972, pp.8-10.
641. Wolfe, Jennifer. "Coed physed," *Orbit*, 8:6-7, Dec. 1977.
642. "Women and sport: a position paper prepared by CAHPER," *HPEC Runner*, 18:14-15, Spring 1980.
643. "Women and sport: report on the 1974 national conference, May 24-26," *HPEC Runner*, 13:20-5, Summer 1975.
644. Women's Hockey Workshop. *Proceedings*. Ottawa: Canadian Amateur Hockey Association / Canada. Dept. of National Health and Welfare. Fitness and Amateur Sport Branch, 1977. 14p. and app.

ATHLETICS AND SPORTS - BIBLIOGRAPHY

645. "Sex discrimination in sports: a selected bibliography," *Labour Topics (Ontario Ministry of Labour Library)*, 5(11):1-4, Nov. 1982.

ATHLETICS AND SPORTS - HISTORY

646. Gurney, Helen. *A century of progress: girls' sports in Ontario high schools*. Don Mills, Ont.: Ontario Federation of School Athletic Associations, [1979]. 102p.
647. Hall, Margaret Ann. "History of women's sport in Canada prior to World War I." MA thesis, University of Alberta, 1968. 198p.
648. Hall, M. Ann. "Women's sport in Canada prior to 1914," in Canadian Symposium on the History of Sport and Physical Education. *Proceedings. 1st, 1970*. Ottawa: Canada. Dept. of National Health and Welfare. Fitness and Amateur Sport Directorate, [1970?], pp.71-89.
    Based on the author's thesis, "History of women's sport in Canada prior to World War I."
649. Hoffman, Abby. "1923-1935: the golden age of women's sport," *Branching Out*, 7(1):23-5, 52, 1980.
650. Keyes, Mary Eleanor. "The history of the Women's Athletics Committee of the Canadian Association for Health, Physical Education and Recreation, 1940-1973." PhD diss., Ohio State University, 1980. 188p.
651. Korchinsky, Nestor Nick. "The equality of men and women in sport as portrayed through the history, development and the analysis of performance in age class competition of selected Canadian sports." PhD diss., University of Oregon, 1978. 416p.
652. Lindsay, Peter L. "Woman's place in nineteenth century Canadian sport," *CAHPER Journal*, 37:25-8, Sept.-Oct. 1970.
653. _____. "Woman's place in nineteenth century Canadian sport," *Canadian Women's Studies / Les cahiers de la femme*, 1:22-4, Summer 1979.
654. Mitchell, Sheila Louise. "The organizational development of women's competitive sport in Canada in the 1920's." MHK thesis, University of Windsor, 1977. 171p. (Can. theses, no.33212)
655. Pitters-Caswell, Marian Irene. "Woman's participation in sporting activities as an indicator of femininity and cultural evolution in Toronto, 1910 to 1920." MHK thesis, University of Windsor, 1975. 194p. (Can. theses, no.29223)
656. Pitters-Caswell, Marian. "Women's participation in sporting activities as an indicator of a feminist movement in Canada between 1867 and 1914," in Canadian Symposium on the History of Sport and Education. *Proceedings. 3rd, 1974*, Dalhousie University, Halifax, Nova Scotia. [1974?] 21p.
657. Randall, Nora Delahunt. "Ladies of the court; the Edmonton grads 1915-1940," *Makara*, 1:12-17, Aug.-Sept. 1976.
658. Schrodt, Barbara. "Canadian women at the Commonwealth Games: 1930-1974," *CAHPER Journal*, 44:30-7, Mar.-Apr. 1978.
659. _____. "Canadian women at the Olympics: 1924-1972," *CAHPER Journal*, 42:34-42, Mar.-Apr. 1976.
660. Swain, Sue. "History of the Ontario Women's Intercollegiate Athletic Association (OWIAA)," *CAHPER Journal*, 49:26-8, Nov.-Dec. 1982.
661. Van Trigt, Maria. "Girls and boys on the same team," *Canadian Women's Studies / Les cahiers de la femme*, 1:111-12, Summer 1979.
662. Wasylynchuk, Mary Ann. "The development of women's field hockey in Alberta: 1962-1973." MA thesis, University of Alberta, 1975. 163p. (Can. theses, no.26948)

ATTITUDES

663. Balderstone, Helen and others. *Women in the community*. Winnipeg: Manitoba. Dept. of Labour. Women's Bureau, 1975. 98p. (Profile 77-0097)
664. Boyd, Monica. "English-Canadian and French-Canadian attitudes toward women: results of the Canadian gallup polls," *Journal of Comparative Family Studies*, 6:153-169, Autumn 1975.
665. Brown, Caree Rozen and Marilyn Levitt Hellinger. "Therapists' attitudes toward women," *Social Work*, 20:266-70, July 1975.

7884

666. Canada. Privy Council Office. International Women's Year Secretariat. *Women in Canada*. 2nd ed. Prepared by Decision Marketing Research Ltd. Ottawa: Canada. Office of the Co-ordinator, Status of Women, [1976]. 256p.

667. Canadian Broadcasting Corporation. Research Dept. *Attitudes of Canadians to certain aspects of population growth*. Ottawa, 1971.

668. De Sincay, Beatrice. "Modernité des attitudes féminines et planification des naissances." MA thèse, Université de Montréal, 1967.

669. Employers Council of British Columbia. *Female employment in non-traditional areas: some attitudes of managers and working women*. Vancouver, 1975. 33p. and tables.

670. Geoffroy, Renée and Paule Sainte-Marie. *Attitude of union workers to women in industry*. Royal Commission on the Status of Women in Canada. Study no.9. Ottawa, 1971. 137p.

671. Ghan, Sherman L. "Women's attitudes toward oral contraceptives." MA thesis, University of Regina, 1974. 114p. (Can. theses, no.20031)

672. Gibbins, Roger, J. Rick Ponting and Gladys Symons. "Attitudes and ideology: correlates of liberal attitudes towards the role of women," *Journal of Comparative Family Studies*, 9:19-40, Spring 1978.

673. Gray, Charlotte. "Baby boom women: high hopes, uncertain prospects," *Chatelaine*, 56:50-1, 68-70, Aug. 1983.

674. Kimball, Meredith M. and Vicky A. Gray. "Feedback and performance expectancies in an academic setting," *Sex Roles*, 8(9):999-1007, 1982.

675. Morrissey, Mary and others. *Women and advertising: a study of the opinions of Nova Scotian women regarding the portrayal of women in Canadian media advertising*. [Halifax]: Nova Scotia Human Rights Commission, 1979. 70p. and app. (Microlog 80-0885)

676. Proulx, Monique Cecile. "Personal, family, and institutional factors associated with attitudes toward women's roles among French-Canadian college students," PhD diss., Michigan State University, 1976. 143p. (UM, 77-5871)

677. Van der Merwe, Sandra. "Women as managers - the current attitudes and programs of Canadian businessmen," *Business Quarterly*, 44:35-9, Spring 1979.

678. Vickers, Joan. "Sex and age differences in attitude toward the concepts. 'male', 'female', 'male athlete', 'female athlete'." MSc thesis, University of Calgary, 1976. 91p. (Can. theses, no.30590)

AUDIOVISUAL MATERIALS

679. Moore, Catherine. "A checklist of some audio visual materials in Canadian women's history," *Resources for Feminist Research*, 8:39-41, July 1979.

680. Newton, Jennifer L. "Audio-visual guide: resources for teaching women and ethnicity," *Resources for Feminist Research*, 8:74-85, Nov. 1979.

681. Ontario Educational Communications Authority. *Women's studies: a multimedia approach*. Toronto, 1977. 122p.
    Joint project of Centennial College of Applied Arts and Technology and the Ontario Educational Communications Authority.

682. Roberts, Barbara. "Seeing is believing: audio-visual aids in Canadian women's history," *Resources for Feminist Research*, 8:37-8, July 1979.

AUDIOVISUAL MATERIALS - BIBLIOGRAPHY

683. Deane, Marie and others. "Women and film: a filmography," *Ontario Library Review*. 59:44-51, Mar. 1975.

684. Laplante, Michelle. *Répertoire des productions audio-visuelles sur la condition féminine*. Québec: Conseil du statut de la femme, 1983. 206p.

685. National Film Board of Canada. *A catalogue of films projecting women*. [Ottawa], 1975. 57p.

686. Ontario Educational Communications Authority. *Women's studies: video resource catalogue*. Toronto, 1979. 116p.

687. Québec. Conseil du statut de la femme. *Les Québécoises: guide bibliographique suivi d'une filmographie*. Québec: Editeur officiel du Québec, 1976. 160p.
688. Toronto. Metropolitan Toronto Library Board. Audio-Visual Services. *Women: a filmography*. Toronto, 1975. 19p.

AUTHORS

689. Atwood, Margaret. "Face to face: Margaret Laurence, as seen by Margaret Atwood," *Macleans*, 87:38-9, 43-4, May 1974.
690. _____. "Paradoxes and dilemmas: the woman as writer," in Gwen Matheson, *Women in the Canadian mosaic*. Toronto: Peter Martin, 1976, pp.256-72.
691. _____. "The curse of Eve - or, what I learned in school," in Ann B. Shteir, ed., *Women on women*. Toronto: York University, 1978, pp.13-26.
692. Bauchman, Rosemary. "A profile of Helen Creighton," *Atlantic Advocate*, 72:26-7, 29-30, Dec. 1981.
693. Beattie, Jessie L. *A walk through yesterday*. Toronto: McClelland and Stewart, 1976. 320p.
694. Berd, Francoise. "Marthe Blackburn," in *Mon héroine: les lundis de l'histoire des femmes: an 1: Conférences du Théâtre expérimental des femmes 1980-81*. Montréal: Editions du Remue-Ménage, 1981, pp.97-115.
695. Bersianik, Louky and others. *Au fond des yeux: 25 Québècoises qui écrivent*. Montréal: Nouvelle optique, 1981. 110p.
    Collection of photographs.
696. Brossard, Nicole. "Nicole Brossard: fantasies and realities [interview]," *Broadside*, 2:11, 18, June 1981.
697. Bursey, Maureen. "Maria Campbell: putting the pieces together," *Branching Out*, 7(1):6-7, 1980.
698. Creighton, Helen. *A life in folklore*. Toronto: McGraw-Hill Ryerson, 1975. 244p.
699. Engel, Marian. "Marian Engel: beyond kitchen sink realism [interview]," *Branching Out*, 5(2):12-13, 40, 1978.
700. _____. "Woman as storyteller," *Communiqué*, no. 8:6-7, 44-5, May 1975.
701. Frankel, Vivian. "Margaret Atwood," *Branching Out*, 2:24-6, Jan.-Feb. 1975.
702. French, William. "The women in our literary life," *Canadian Author and Bookman*, 51:1-3, 5-6, Spring 1976.
703. _____. "The women in our literary life," *Imperial Oil Review*, 59(1):3-7,1975.
704. Geirsson, Freya. "Does sex make a difference? Some propositions on Canadian novelists," *Emergency Librarian*, 2:5-8, Oct. 1974.
705. Gillen, Mollie. *Lucy Maud Montgomery*. Don Mills, Ont.: Fitzhenry & Whiteside, 1978. 62p.
706. _____. *The wheel of things: a biography of L. M. Montgomery, author of "Anne of Green Gables"*. Don Mills, Ont.: Fitzhenry & Whiteside, 1975. 200p.
707. Harvor, Beth. "Special world of the WW's...," *Saturday Night*, 84:33-5, Aug. 1969.
708. James, Donna. *Emily Murphy*. Toronto: Fitzhenry & Whiteside, 1977. 63p.
709. Johnson, Valerie Miner. "The matriarch of Manawaka," *Saturday Night*, 89:17-20, May 1974.
710. Knelman, Martin. "The past, the present, and Alice Munro," *Saturday Night*, 94:16-18, 19+ , Nov. 1979.
711. Kostash, Myrna. "Rating the chauvinists on the Richler scale," *Macleans*, 87:75, Jan. 1974.
712. Lamy, Suzanne. *D'elles*. Montréal: L'hexagone, 1979. 110p.
713. Laurence, Margaret. "Revolution and resolution: an interview with Margaret Laurence," *Canadian Forum*, 59:15-18, Mar. 1980.
714. Lawrence, Karen. "From the other Paris: interview with Mavis Gallant," *Branching Out*, 3:18-19, Feb.-Mar. 1976.
715. _____. "Word from the authors," *Branching Out*, 6(3):9, 1979.

716.   Lequin, Lucie. "Les femmes québécoises ont inventé leurs paroles," *American Review of Canadian Studies*, 9:113-24, Autumn 1979.

717.   Lever, Bernice. "An interview with Dorothy Livesay," *Canadian Forum*, 55:45-52, Sept. 1975.

718.   Lischke-McNab, Ute and David McNab. "Petition from the backwoods [Catharine Parr Traill]," *Beaver*, 308:52-7, Summer 1977.

719.   Lister, Rota. "An interview with Carol Bolt," *World Literature Written in English*, 17:144-53, Apr. 1978.

720.   Makward, Christiane. "Quebec women writers," *Women and Literature*, 7:3-11, Winter 1979.

721.   March, Kem. "Alice Munro. Occupation: writer," *Chatelaine*, 48:43, 69-72, Aug. 1975.

722.   Martel, Suzanne. "La famille dans le mur," *Canadian Women's Studies | Les cahiers de la femme*, 2(1):78-80, 1980.

723.   McClung, M. G. *Women in Canadian literature*. Toronto: Fitzhenry & Whiteside, 1977. 96p.

724.   McClung, Nellie. *The stream runs fast: my own story*. Toronto: Thomas Allen, 1965. 316p. First published in 1945.

725.   McCord, Joanne. "Alberta first Native appointment: Maria Campbell new writer-in-residence at university," *Native People*, 12:1-2, Sept. 28, 1979.

726.   Miner, Valerie. "The many faces of Margaret Atwood," *Chatelaine*, 48:33, 66, 68, 70, June 1975.

727.   Montgomery, Lucy Maud. *My dear Mr. M.: letters to G. B. MacMillan from L. M. Montgomery*, edited by Francis W. P. Bolger and Elizabeth R. Epperly. Toronto: McGraw-Hill Ryerson, 1980. 212p.

728.   _____. *The alpine path: the story of my career*. Don Mills, Ont.: Fitzhenry & Whiteside, 1974. 96p.

729.   Morin, Lisette. "Madeleine Gleason-Huguenin: un demi-siècle d'écriture au féminin," *Revue d'histoire du Bas Saint-Laurent*, 5:28-31, déc. 1978.

730.   Nelson, Sharon H. "Bemused, branded, and belittled: women and writing in Canada," *Fireweed*, 15:64-102, Winter 1982.

731.   Poitras, Huguêtte. "Toutes les femmes en cachent un," *Le Maclean*, 15:24f-24h, sept. 1975.

732.   Reid, Gayla. "Alive and well in B.C.," *Emergency Librarian*, 2:10-13, Dec. 1974.
            Brief selective report on B.C. writers.

733.   Rhodes, Ann. "The perfectionist on the third floor," *Chatelaine*, 55:59, 165-6, 168, Dec. 1982.

734.   Roden, Lethem Sutcliffe. "Laure Conan: the first French-Canadian woman novelist." PhD diss., University of Toronto, 1956 (c1974). 167p. (Can. theses, no.19732)

735.   Ross, Val. "Merle Shain and the business of loving," *Chatelaine*, 51:68, 96+, Oct. 1978.

736.   Rule, Jane. "Seventh waves," *Branching Out*, 6(1):16-17, 1979.

737.   Saumart, Ingrid. *La vie extraordinaire de Jean Despréz*. Montréal: Éditions du jour, 1965. 115p.

738.   Simon, Sherry. "Feminist writing in Québec," *Canadian Forum*, 60:5-8, Aug. 1980.

739.   Smart, Patricia. "Voices of commitment and discovery: women writers in Quebec," *Room of One's Own*, 4(1/2):7-18, 1978.

740.   Smyth, Donna E. "Interview with Myrna Kostash—'a western, Ukrainian, regionalist, feminist, socialist writer'," *Atlantis*, 6:178-85, Spring 1981.

741.   Swan, Susan. "Why women write the most interesting books: the astonishing matriarchy in Canadian letters," *Saturday Night*, 93:21-3, Nov. 1978.

742.   Thomas, Clara. "Happily ever after: Canadian women in fiction and fact," *Canadian Literature*, 34:43-53, Autumn 1967.

743.   Timson, Judith. "The magnificent Margaret Atwood," *Chatelaine*, 54:42-3, 56+, Jan. 1981.

744.   Turner, Marion Diane. "Manawaka woman: a study of the personal and literary development of Margaret Laurence." MA thesis, McMaster University, 1970. 112p.

745. Van Herk, Aritha. "Aritha van Herk: her time and place [interview]," *Branching Out*, 55(2):26-9, 1978.
746. Webster, Jackie. "Antonine Maillet prize winning writer," *Chatelaine*, 54:32, Mar. 1981.
747. Young, Mildred. "For a long time in the Maritimes," *Emergency Librarian*, 2:14-15, Dec. 1974.

BANKING

748. "Bank policy, practice for women differed," *Globe & Mail*, July 12, 1978, p.B12.
749. "Bank unions: when they come, expect changes," *Financial Times*, 65:1, 4, Mar. 21, 1977.
750. "Banks & women," *Financial Times*, 65:26, Jan. 3, 1977.
751. Bossen, Marianne. *Employment in chartered banks, 1969-1975*. [Ottawa]: Advisory Council on the Status of Women / Canadian Bankers' Association, 1976. 71p.
752. _____. *Manpower utilization in Canadian chartered banks*. Royal Commission on the Status of Women in Canada. Study no. 4. Ottawa, 1971. 60p.
753. _____. "Utilizing womanpower," *Canadian Banker and ICB Review*, 82:27-9, July-Aug. 1975.
754. Bureau, Yvon. "Woman's work...if she could find it," *Canada Commerce*, 138:15, suppl., Anniversary Issue, 1974.
755. "Critical look at women in Canadian banking," *Burroughs Clearing House*, 59:46, June 1975.
756. Day, Sonia. "Seminars for women only," *Canadian Banker and ICB Review*, 82:44-7, July-Aug. 1975.
757. "First Women's Bank chief emphasizes professionalism," *Globe & Mail*, Mar. 2, 1977, p.B4.
758. Frazee, Rowland. "A president's perspective," *Executive Bulletin (Conference Board in Canada)*, no. 4:1-4, Mar. 1978.
759. Gordon, Sheldon E. "Banking on equal opportunity," *Financial Post*, 72:16, Jan. 21, 1978.
760. Hansen, Barbara. "A historical study of women in Canadian banking, 1900-1975," *Canadian Women's Studies / Les cahiers de la femme*, 1:17-22, Winter 1978-1979.
761. Hartwick, Paul. "What's your MCQ (male chauvinism quotient)?" *Canadian Banker & ICB Review*, 83:40-2, May-June 1976.
762. Ivens, W. G. "A telling blow for bank women," *Canadian Banker & ICB Review*, 83:4-5, May-June 1976.
763. Krossel, Martin. "Pages from the past [1929]," *Canadian Banker & ICB Review*, 86:59, Dec. 1979.
764. Lowe, Graham S. "Problems and issues in the unionization of female workers: some reflections on the case of Canadian bank employees," in Naomi Hersom and Dorothy E. Smith, [eds.], *Women and the Canadian labour force*. Working document. Ottawa: Social Sciences and Humanities Research Council of Canada, 1982, pp.307-42.
765. Mann, Brenda. "The woman bank employee," *Branching Out*, 3:7, July-Aug. 1976.
766. "Metro Toronto Women's C.U. a first in Canada," *Ontario Credit Union News*, 38:9, Dec.-Jan. 1976.
767. Pitt, Cathie. "FICB: what's in it for the female banker?" *ICB Review*, 5:11-12, Summer, 1972.
768. "Proposed trust company for women may settle for male chief exec," *Globe & Mail*, July 17, 1976, p.B11.
769. "Royal Bank task force studied status of women," *Journal (The Board of Trade of Metropolitan Toronto)*, July-Aug. 1978, p.39.
770. "Royal, Scotia bank tussle with women directors issue," Financial Times, 65:10, Sept. 27, 1976.
771. "Staid banks may start chasing after women," *Marketing*, 79:6, Mar. 25, 1974.

772. Steklasa, Robert. "Women make some telling gains in banks," *Financial Post*, 70:15, May 22, 1976.

773. "The big five's ladies-in-waiting," *Maclean's*, 92:38, Mar. 12, 1979.

BATTERED WOMEN

774. Backhouse, Constance and others. *London battered women's legal handbook*. [London: University of Western Ontario. Faculty of Law, 1980?] 28p. (Microlog 80-3462)
    Research funded by Canada. Dept. of Justice.

775. Beirne, Anne. "Marital rape," *Chatelaine*, 55:61, 176+ , Nov. 1982.

776. Bell, Garry L. "Inter-spousal violence: discovery and reporting," in John M. Eekelaar and Sanford N. Katz, eds., *Family violence: an international and interdisciplinary study*. Toronto: Butterworths, 1978, pp.208-15.

777. Burris, Carole Anne and Peter Jaffe. "Wife abuse as a crime: the impact of police laying charges," *Canadian Journal of Criminology*, 25:309-18, July 1983.

778. Byles, John A. "Family violence in Hamilton," *Canada's Mental Health*, 28:4-6, Mar. 1980.

779. _____. "Family violence in Hamilton - revisited," *Canada's Mental Health*, 30:10-11, Dec. 1982.

780. Canada. Parliament. House of Commons. Standing Committee on Health, Welfare and Social Affairs. *Report on violence in the family; wife battering*. Ottawa, 1982. [35, 39p.]

781. Canada. Secrétariat d'État. Programme de promotion de la femme. *La violence faite aux femmes en milieu conjugal: le produit d'une société sexiste: une étude québécoise*, par Micheline Carrier et Monique Michaud. Ottawa, 1982. 106p.

782. Canadian Advisory Council on the Status of Women. *A brief on wife battering with proposals for federal action*, prepared by Debra J. Lewis. Ottawa, 1982. 24p. (Microlog 83-2127)

783. Canadian Association of Social Workers. *Policy statement on social work practice with assaulted women and their families*. Ottawa, 1983. Leaflet.

784. Chadourne, Michèle. "Mon vécu," *Canadian Women's Studies / Les cahiers de la femme*, 2(1):49-51, 1980.

785. Chan, Kwok Bun. "Husband-wife violence in Toronto." PhD diss., York University, 1978. 350p. (Can. theses, no.36980)

786. Cole, Susan G. "Adding insult to injury: injury… ," *Broadside*, 3:10-11, Apr. 1982.

787. Costigliola, Bozica. "Wife battering report: law policies perpetuate violence," *Perception*, 3:8, Mar.-Apr. 1980.

788. De Koninck, Maria. *Réflexion sur la condition des femmes violentées*. Québec: Conseil du statut de la femme, 1977. 23p.

789. Dixon, Jean. *Domestic violence; the tip of the iceberg*. Charlottetown: Prince Edward Island. Dept. of Justice, 1980. 39p. and app.

790. Downey, Joanne and Jane Howell. *Wife battering: a review and preliminary enquiry into local incidence, needs and resources*. Vancouver: United Way of Greater Vancouver, 1976. 93, xxviip.

791. D'Oyley, Vincent., ed. *Domestic violence: issues and dynamics*. Informal series, no. 7. Toronto: Ontario Institute for Studies in Education, 1978. 268p.

792. Dranoff, Linda Silver. "Ask a lawyer," *Chatelaine*, 54:26, 28, June 1981.

793. Epstein, Rachel, Roxana Ng and Maggi Trebble. *Social organization of family violence: an ethnography of immigrant experience in Vancouver*. [Vancouver]: Women's Research Centre, 1978. 52p.
    Report to the Non-Medical Use of Drugs Directorate, Health and Welfare, Canada.

794. Fleming, Thomas S. "Violent domestic assault." MA thesis, University of Toronto, 1975. [76]p. and app.

795. Freedman, Lisa and Susan Ursel. "Adding insult to injury: insult… ," *Broadside*, 3:10-11, Apr. 1982.

796. Gabor, Agota. "I am Joe's punching bag!" *Homemaker's Magazine*, 11:136-8, 140+ , May 1976.
797. Gelles, Richard J. "Abused wives: why do they stay?" in Mary A. B. Gammon, ed., *Violence in Canada*. Toronto: Methuen, 1978, pp.77-89.
798. Goldman, Pearl. "Violence against women in the family." LLM thesis, McGill University, 1978. 187p. (Can. theses, no.39677)
799. Gordon, Marie. "Battered wives: the gagged victims," *Branching Out*, 6(2):26-9, 1979.
800. Gropper, Arlene and Janet Currie. *A study of battered women*. [Ottawa, Ont.: Vanier Institute of the Family], 1976. 100p. and app.
801. Gropper, Arlene and Joyce Marvin. "Violence begins at home," *The Canadian*, Nov. 20, 1976, pp.4-7, 9.
802. Hannell, Lesley. "Perceptions of conjugal violence." MA thesis, University of Guelph, 1980. 104p. (Can. theses, no.52498)
803. Hauser, Anne M. and June N. Wilton. "An approach to the etiology of wife abuse." MSW thesis, University of Windsor, 1977. 167p. (Can. theses, no.34544)
804. Horlick, Sharon Debra. "Personality correlates of battered women." MA thesis, University of Windsor, 1980. 82p. (Can. theses, no.51197)
805. Istona, Mildred. "Wife assault: no joke," *Chatelaine*, 55:2, July 1982.
806. Jaffe, Peter and Carole Anne Burris. "No place to turn," *Canadian Lawyer*, 5:13-15, Oct. 1981.
807. Killoran, Margaret Maureen. "The sound of silence breaking: toward a metatheory of wife abuse." MA thesis, McMaster University, 1981. 253p.(Can. theses, no.57037)
808. Larouche, Ginette. "Une étude sur la violence conjugal." MSc thesis, Université de ntréal, 1980. 178, [33]p.
809. LeFeuvre, Joan. *Fresh start ... is this book for you?* Peterborough, Ont.: YWCA, 1982. 72p.
810. "Les femmes battues au Québec," *Ligue des femmes du Québec. Bulletin*, 1:14-18, janv. 1981.
811. Lord, Catherine. "L'auberge des femmes battues," *Le Maclean*, 16:8, juill. 1976.
812. MacDonald, Deborah and others. *The P.E.I. legal handbook for battered women*. Charlottetown: National Association of Women and the Law, P.E.I. Caucus, 1981. 28p. (Microlog 82-2455)
813. MacKay, Harry. "Law and poverty and access to social services," *Perception*, 5:28, June 1982.
814. MacLeod, Flora, ed. *Family violence: report of the Task Force on Family Violence*. Vancouver: United Way of the Lower Mainland, 1979. 25p. and app.
815. MacLeod, Linda and Andrée Cadieux. *Wife battering in Canada: the vicious circle*. Ottawa: Canadian Advisory Council on the Status of Women, 1980. 72p.
816. McGregor, Julie. "Wife battering in Canada," *Perception*, 6:14-15, Jan.-Feb. 1983.
817. Meade-Ramrattan, Joanne, Mary L. Cerré and Mary Lynn Porto. "Physically abused women: satisfaction with sources of help," *Social Worker*, 48:162-6, Winter 1980.
818. Miller, Donna Jean. "Battered women: perceptions of their problems and their perception of community response." MSW thesis, University of Windsor, 1980. 236p. (Can. theses, no.49233)
819. "Not a family affair: report on wife battering; Surtout pas une affaire de famille," *Liaison*, 8:23-5, July-Aug. 1982.
820. Ontario Status of Women Council. *Brief on behalf of battered women*. Toronto, 1980. 38p. "Report and recommendations arising from the Symposium on Family Violence."
821. Ontario. Legislative Assembly. Standing Committee on Social Development. *First report on family violence: wife battering*. [Toronto], 1982. 63, 70p.
822. Orr, Jody. *The support services network for battered women in the Hamilton area*. Hamilton, Ont.: Social Planning and Research Council of Hamilton and District, 1980. 37p.
823. Ostrowski, Margaret V. *Legal process for battered women*. Vancouver: United Way of the Lower Mainland, 1979. 50p.

32

824. _____. *Legal process for battered women*. Rev. and expanded by Leslie Baker. Vancouver: United Way of the Lower Mainland, 1982. 34p.

825. Page, Barbara. "Silence, la femme battue parle," *Canadian Women's Studies / Les cahiers de la femme*, 1:76-7, Summer 1979.

826. Québec. Conseil du statut de la femme. *Réflexion sur la condition des femmes violentées*. [Québec, 1977]. 23p.

827. Québec. Ministère de la justice. Comité d'orientation. *Rapport: colloques régionaux sur la violence envers les femmes et les enfants et dans la pornographie*. Québec: Québec. Ministère de la justice. Direction des communications, 1980. 83p.

828. Rasminsky, Judy. "How battered women can get help," *Reader's Digest (Canada)*, 113:183-4, 186+ , Dec. 1978.

829. Rinehart, Dianne. "Violence in the home: crime without punishment," *Canada & the World*, 48:18-19, Sept. 1982.

830. Roberts, Barbara. "No safe place: the war against women," *Our Generation*, 15:7-26, Spring 1983.

831. Rose, Marie-Georgette. "Le problème du masochisme: une plainte cachée: les femmes battues." MA mémoire, Université du Québec à Montréal, 1979. 189p. (Can. theses, no.47669)

832. Routledge, Janet. "How many bruises make a battered wife?; Le problème des femmes maltraitrées," *Civil Service Review / Revue du Service Civil*, 53:12-15, [English]; 12-15, [French], Dec. 1980.

833. Schendlinger, Mary. *Makara*, 3(2):34-8, [1978].

834. Schlesinger, Benjamin. "Abused wives: Canada's silent screamers," *Canada's Mental Health*, 28:17-20, June 1980.

835. Schneider, Elizabeth M. and others. "Representation of women who defend themselves in response to physical or sexual assault," *Family Law Review*, 1:118-32, 1978.

836. Secord, R. C. "Competence and compellability of wives at common law," *Alberta Law Review*, 17(2):313-17, 1979.

837. Small, Shirley Endicott. *Wife assault; an overview of the problem in Canada*. Toronto: Education, Wife Assault, [1980?] 32p.

838. _____. "Wife assault: an overview of the problem in Canada," *Fireweed*, 14:9-24, Fall 1982.

839. Social Planning Council of Peel. Interim Place Steering Committee. *Feasibility study and programme proposal: interim place*. [Draft]. Mississauga, Ont., 1979. 14p.

840. Thompson, Judy and Rhonda Gilby. "Correlates of domestic violence and the role of police agencies," in Robert A. Silverman and James J. Teevan, eds., *Crime in Canadian society*. 2d ed. Toronto: Butterworths, 1980, pp.298-306.

841. University of Saskatchewan. Women and the Law Committee. *Help for battered women*, by Anne Wirth, Bob Patton, and Cindy Biddell. Saskatoon: The Public Legal Education Association of Saskatchewan, Inc., 1981. 53p.

842. Vancouver Transition House and the Women's Research Centre. *'Battered and blamed' - a report on wife assault from the perspective of battered women*, by Jan Barnsley and others. Vancouver, B.C.: Women's Research Centre, 1980. 131, [29]p.

843. Women in Transition Research Project. *One step at a time; alternatives to domestic assault (wife-battering); a 1978 Canada Works Project*. Thunder Bay, Ont.: Northwestern Ontario Women's Centre, 1978. 19p.

844. Women's Research Centre. *A study of protection for battered women*. Vancouver, B.C., 1982. 237, [11]p.

845. Young Women's Christian Association of Canada. *Brief to the Standing Committee on Health, Welfare and Social Affairs for its study on intra-family violence*. [Toronto: YWCA], 1982. 13, [8]p.

846. _____. *Violence against women: a project of the YWCA of Metropolitan Toronto*. Coordinated by Barbara Waisberg. Toronto: YWCA of Canada, [1980]. [31]p.

BATTERED WOMEN - BIBLIOGRAPHY

847. *Battered wives in Canada: a list of references, 1973-1978*. [Ottawa]: Canada. Dept. of National Health and Welfare. Departmental Library Services, [1979?] 5p.
848. Pethick, Jane. *Battered wives: a select bibliography*. Toronto: University of Toronto. Centre of Criminology, 1979. 114p. Includes some Canadian material.

BIOGRAPHY

849. Allaire, Émilia (Boivin). *Profils féminins: trente figures de proue canadiennes*. Québec: Éditions Garneau, 1967. 283p.
850. _____. *Têtes de femmes: essais biographiques*. 4 éd. rev. Québec: Éditions de l'Equinoxe, 1971. 242p.
851. Allen, Charlotte Vale. *Daddy's girl*. Toronto: McClelland and Stewart, 1980. 255p.
852. Allison, Susan. *A pioneer gentlewomen in British Columbia: the recollections of Susan Allison*, edited and introduced by Margaret A. Ormsby. Vancouver: University of British Columbia Press, 1976. 210p.
853. Association féminine d'éducation et d'action sociale. *Dans l'histoire...des femmes aussi...au Saguenay-Lac-St-Jean*. 2 vols. Chicoutimi, Qué.: Éditions Science Moderne, 1978-1980.
854. _____. *Pendant que les hommes travaillaient, les femmes elles...: 266 fiches biographiques de femmes qui ont marqués le Québec entre 1820 et 1950*. Montréal: Guérin, [1978?]. 405p.
855. Bannerman, Jean (MacKay). *Leading ladies, Canada, 1639-1967*. Dundas, Ont.: Carrswood, 1967. 332p.
856. Bassett, Isabel. *The parlour rebellion: profiles in the struggle for women's rights*. Toronto: McClelland and Stewart, 1975. 223p.
857. Bassett, John M. *Elizabeth Simcoe: first lady of Upper Canada*. Don Mills, Ont.: Fitzhenry & Whiteside, 1974. 61p.
    French edition: *Elisabeth Simcoe: la première dame du Haut-Canada*.
858. Beamish, Rahno M. *Fifty years a Canadian nurse: devotion, opportunities and duty*. New York: Vantage Press, 1970. 344p.
859. Beattie, Jessie L. *A walk through yesterday*. Toronto: McClelland and Stewart, 1976. 320p.
860. Bell, Lily M. and Kathleen E. Bray. *Women of action: St. Catharines and area, 1876-1976* St. Catharines: Published for the Local Council of Women for International Women's Year 1975 and St. Catharines Centennial 1976, 1976. 134p.
861. Benham, Mary Lile. *Nellie McClung*. Don Mills, Ont.: Fitzhenry & Whiteside, 1975. 61p.
862. Bertrand, Réal. *Emile Nelligan*. Montréal: Lidec, 1980. 62p.
863. _____. *Thérèse Casgrain*. Montréal: Lidec, 1981. 63p.
864. Best, Carrie M. *That lonesome road: the autobiography of Carrie M. Best*. New Glasgow, N.S.: Clarion Pub. Co., 1977. 258p.
865. Bird, Florence. *Ann Francis: an autobiography*. Toronto: Clarke Irwin, 1974. 324p.
866. Black, Martha Louise. *My ninety years*. Anchorage, Alaska: Alaska Northwest Pub., 1976. 166p.
867. Boechler, M. A. *Dawn to dusk*. [Spiritwood, Sask.: n.p., 1979]. 53p.
868. Bouchard, Laurette. *Courtepointe d'une grand-mère*. Hull, Québec: Editions Asticou, 1981. 89p.
869. Brotman, Ruth C. *Pauline Donalda: the life and career of a Canadian prima donna* n.p., 1975. 125p.
870. Burnford, Sheila. *One woman's Arctic*. Toronto: McClelland and Stewart, 1973. 222p.
871. Burtin. *Bienheureuse Kateri Tekakwitha vierge iroquoise: 1656-1680*. St.-Jovite, Québec: Editions Magnificat, 1980. 111p.
872. Campbell, Helen Richards. *From chalk dust to hayseed*. Belleville, Ont.: Mika Pub. Co., 1975. 116p.

873. Carter, Charles Ambrose and Thomas Melville Bailey, eds. *The diary of Sophia MacNab*. 2nd ed. rev. Hamilton, Ont.: W. L. Griffin, 1974. 88p.

874. Casgrain, Thérèse F. *Woman in a man's world*. Translated by Joyce Marshall. Toronto: McClelland and Stewart, 1972. 192p.
    French edition: *Une femme chez les hommes*.

875. *Cercle des femmes journalistes. Vingt-cinq à la une: biographies*. Montréal: La Presse, 1976. 189p.

876. Chalmers, J. W. "Marguerite Bourgeoys, preceptress of New France," in Robert S. Paterson, and others, eds., *Profiles of Canadian educators*. n.p.: D. C. Heath Canada, 1974, pp.4-20.

877. Chartrand, Simonne Monet. *Ma vie comme rivière: récit autobiographique*. Vol. 1 :*1919-1942* Vol. 2 :*1939-1949*. Montréal: Éditions du Remue-ménage, 1981-82.

878. Cimichella, André-M. *Marguerite Bourgeoys, lumière sur notre ville*. Montréal: Éditions Jésus Marie et notre temps, 1974. 71p.

879. Cochrane, Felicity. *Margaret Trudeau: the prime minister's runaway wife*. Scarborough, Ont.: New American Library of Canada, 1978. 173p.

880. Cochrane, Jean. *Kate Aitken*. Don Mills, Ont.: Fitzhenry & Whiteside, 1979. 63p.

881. Cook, Janet McLaren. *Through cloud and sunshine*. Lethbridge, Alta.: Southern Print Co., 1975. 96p.

882. Cook, Ramsay. "Francis Marion Beynon and the crisis of Christian reformism," in Carl Berger and Ramsay Cook, eds., *The west and the nation: essays in honour of W. L. Morton*. Toronto: McClelland and Stewart, 1976, pp.187-208.

883. Corbett, Gail. *Portraits: Peterborough area women past and present*. Peterborough: Portraits' Group, 1975. 206p.

884. Cormack, Barbara. *Perennials and politics: the life story of the Hon. Irene Parlby*. Sherwood Park, Alta.: Printed by Professional Print, [1968]. 160p.

885. Courchesne, Ginette. "Laure Hurteau, journaliste: étude bio-bibliographique." MA mémoire, Université de Montréal, 1975. 222p.

886. Cox, Barbara J. *Summer of childhood*. n.p.: B. J. Cox, 1978. 96p.

887. Creighton, Helen. *A life in folklore*. Toronto: McGraw-Hill Ryerson, 1975. 244p.

888. Cunningham, John. *She has done what she could: Mark 14:8 N A S V: biography of Mother Cunningham, who was Dean of Bible School Women at Prairie Bible Institute from 1955 to 1962*. Three Hills, Alta: Prairie Press, 1976. 56p.

889. *C.W.O.N., Canadian women of note*. [Downsview, Ont.]: York University, [1981]. Microfiche.

890. Davidson, Margaret Rutherford, ed. *I came from Pictou County: the recollections of a Prairie Bluenose, Jane MacKay Rutherford*. Ottawa: n.p., 1975. 67p.

891. Davidson, True. "The life force: Vida Peene," in her, *Golden strings*. Toronto: Griffin House, 1973, pp.48-54.

892. _____. "The mother: Pauline Vanier," in her, *Golden strings*. Toronto: Griffin House, 1973, pp.127-33.

893. Davison, James Doyle. *Alice of Grand Pre: Alice T. Shaw and her GrandPre seminary, female education in Nova Scotia and New Brunswick*. Wolfville, N.S.: Acadia University, 1981.

894. Davison, James D. "Alice Shaw and her Grand Pre seminary: a story of female education," in Barry M. Moody, ed., *Repent and believe: the Baptist experience in maritime Canada*. Hantsport, N.S.: Acadia Divinity College, 1980, pp.124-37.

895. Dempsey, Lotta. *No life for a lady*. Don Mills, Ont.: Musson Book, 1976. 207p.

896. Desjardins, Paul. *La vie toute de grâce de Jeanne Mance: fondatrice de l'Hôtel-Dieu de Montréal et première infirmière laique*. Montréal: Les Èditions Bellarmin, 1979. 188p.

897. Douville, Raymond. *Nos premières mères de famille: les "filles du roi" aux origines de Sainte-Anne*. Trois Rivières, Qué.: Éditions du Bien public, 1976. 46p.

898. Doyle, James. *Annie Howells and Achille Fréchette*. Toronto: University of Toronto Press, 1979. 131p.

899. Duguay, Marie-Anne. *Lettres d'une paysanne à son fils*, compilé par Jeanne L'Archevêque-Duguay. Montréal: Leméac, 1977. 214p.

900. Dupont, Théodora. *Mes mémoires*. Québec: La Pocatière, 1980. 712p.

901. Durham, Louise Elizabeth Grey, Countess. *Letters and diaries of Lady Durham*, edited by Patricia Godsell. [n.p.]: Oberon Press, 1979. 203p.

902. Duval, Germaine. *Par le chemin du roi, une femme est venue: Marie-Rose Durocher, 1811-1849*. Montréal: Ed. Bellarmin, 1982. 398p.

903. Eaton, Sara. *Lady of the backwoods: a biography of Catharine Parr Traill*. Toronto: McClelland & Stewart, 1969. 175p.

904. Fadette. *Journal d'Henriette Dessaulles, 1874-1880*. Montréal: Editions Hurtubise, 1971. 325p.

905. *Fast, Vera. Missionary on wheels: Eva Hasell and the Sunday School caravan missions.* Toronto: Anglican Book Centre, 1979. 158p.

906. Ferguson, Ted. *Kit Coleman: queen of hearts*. Toronto: Doubleday Canada, 1978. 182p.

907. Fergusson, C. Bruce. *Alderman Abbie Lane of Halifax*. Windsor, N.S.: Lancelot Press, 1976. 40p.

908. *Figures du temps de nos grand'mères*. Sainte-Anne-de-la-Pérade, Qué.: Éditions du Bien public, 1976. 39p.

909. Firth, Sophia. *The urbanization of Sophia Firth*. Toronto: Peter Martin, 1974. 271p.

910. Fitts, Mary Pauline. *Hands to the needy: Blessed Marguerite d'Youville, apostle to the poor*. Garden City, N.Y.: Doubleday, 1971. 332p.

911. Fortier-Langlois, Suzanne et autres. *Personnalités féminines: Sita Riddez, Marguerite Paquet, Gertrude Néron, Edouardina Dupont, Jeanne L'Archevêque-Duguay*. Chicoutimi; Qué. Editions Science moderne, 1975. 176p.

912. Fowler, Marian. *The embroidered tent: five gentlewomen in early Canada, Elizabeth Simcoe, Catharine Parr Traill, Susanna Moodie, Anna Jameson, Lady Dufferin*. Toronto: Anansi, 1982. 239p.

913. Francis, Alice Katharine. *From Ty Mawr to Two Bar*. Brandon, Man.: A. K. Francis, 1975. 136p.

914. Francis, Anne. *Anne Francis: an autobiography*. Toronto: Clarke, Irwin & Co., 1974. 324p.

915. Fredrickson, Olive A. *The silence of the north*. Leicester, Eng.: Ulverscroft, 1978. 357p. French edition: *Une femme dans le Grand Nord*.

916. French, Alice. *My name is Masak*. Winnipeg: Peguis Publishers, 1976. 110p.

917. Gillen, Mollie. *Lucy Maud Montgomery*. Don Mills, Ont.: Fitzhenry & Whiteside, 1978. 62p.

918. Gillen, Mollie. *The wheel of things: a biography of L. M. Montgomery, author of "Anne of Green Gables"*. Don Mills, Ont.: Fitzhenry & Whiteside, 1975. 200p.

919. Gorham, Deborah. "Flora MacDonald Denison: Canadian feminist," in Linda Kealey, ed., *A not unreasonable claim: women and reform in Canada, 1880s-1920s*. Toronto: Women's Press, 1979, pp.47-70.

920. Goudie, Elizabeth. *Woman of Labrador*. Toronto: Peter Martin Associates, 1973. 166p.

921. Greenland, Cyril. "Mary Edwards Merrill, 1858-1880: 'the psychic'", *Ontario History*, 68:81-92, June 1976.

922. Hacker, Carlotta. *E. Cora-Hind*. Don Mills, Ont.: Fitzhenry & Whiteside, 1979. 63p.

923. Hamel, Réginald. *Gaëtane de Montreuil, journaliste québécoise (1867-1951)*. Montréal: L'Aurore, 1976. 205p.

924. Head, Gertrude. *Saga of a homesteader*. n.p., 1977. 72p.

925. Henry, Ann. *Laugh, baby, laugh*. Toronto: McClelland and Stewart, 1970. 187p.

926. Holmes, Peggy. *It could have been worse*. Toronto: Collins, 1980. 190p.

927. Holt, Simma. *The other Mrs. Diefenbaker*. Toronto: Doubleday Canada, 1982. 378p.

928. Hopkins, Monica. *Letters from a lady rancher*. Calgary: Glenbow Museum, 1981. 172p.

929. Innis, Mary (Quayle). *The clear spirit: twenty Canadian women and their times*. Toronto: University of Toronto: Press, 1966. 304p.

36

930. Jackson, Florence E. *North wind blowing backwards*. Cobalt, Ont.: Highway Book Shop, 1977. 91p.

931. James, Donna. *Emily Murphy*. Toronto: Fitzhenry & Whiteside, 1977. 63p.

932. Johnson, Arthur. *Margaret Trudeau*. Markham, Ont.: PaperJacks, 1977. 210p.

933. Johnson, Georgiana May. *Life in the parsonage: memoirs of Georgiana May Johnson (née Harrison)*. n.p., [1976]. 202p.

934. Johnston, Jean. *Wilderness women: Canada's forgotten history*. Toronto: Peter Martin, 1973. 242p.

935. Jordan, Mary. *De ta soeur, Sara Riel*. Sainte-Boniface, Man.: Editions des Plaines, [1980?] 180p.

936. Keller, Betty. *Pauline, a biography of Pauline Johnson*. Vancouver: Douglas & McIntyre, 1981. 317p.

937. Klassen, Annie. *Mountains removed*. n.p., 1976. 143p.

938. Knight, Rolf. *A very ordinary life*. Vancouver: New Star Books, 1974. 317p.

939. Konantz, Gail. *Edith Rogers*. Winnipeg: Peguis Publishers, 1981. 52p.

940. Kostash, Myrna and others. *Her own woman: profiles of ten Canadian women*. Toronto: Macmillan, 1975. 213p.

941. Laframboise, Philippe. *La poune*. Montréal: Éditions Héritage, 1978. 139p.
   Biography of Rose Ouellet.

942. Lafrenière, Suzanne. *Moisette Olier: femme de lettres de la Mauricie*. Hull, Québec: Éditions Asticou, 1980. 224p.

943. LaMarsh, Judy. *Memoirs of a bird in a guilded cage*. Toronto: McClelland and Stewart, 1969. 367p.

944. Lambert, Thérèse. *Marguerite Bourgeoys, éducatrice, 1620-1700: mère d'un pays et d'une église*. Montréal: Les Éditions Bellarmin, 1978. 137p.

945. Laplante, Germaine. *Une journaliste intemporelle: Germaine Bernier*. Montréal: Éditions Bellarmin, 1978. 446p.

946. Lemieux, Thérèse et Gemma Caron. *Silhouettes acadiennes*. n.p.: [Fédération des dames d'Acadie], 1981. 374p.

947. Linder, Norma West and Hope Morritt. *Pauline: a warm look at Ontario Lt.-Gov. Pauline McGibbon*. Sarnia, Ont.: River City Press, 1979. 125p.

948. Lipsitz, Edmond Y., ed. *Canadian Jewish women of today: who's who of Canadian Jewish women, 1983*. Downsview, Ont.: J.E.S.L. Educational Products, 1983. 142p.

949. Livesay, Dorothy. *Right hand, left hand*. Erin, Ont.: Press Porcepic, 1977. 280p.

950. MacEwan, Grant. *...And mighty women too: stories of notable western Canadian women*. Saskatoon, Sask.: Western Producer Prairie Books, 1975. 275p.

951. MacGill, Elsie Gregory. *My mother the judge: a biography of Helen Gregory MacGill*. Toronto: Peter Martin Associates, 1981. 248p.

952. McKenzie, Ruth. *Laura Secord: the legend and the lady*. Toronto: McClelland and Stewart, 1971. 142p.

953. Maher, Florentine Morvan. *Florentine raconte....* Montreal: Domino, 1980. 238p.

954. Martin, Claire. *In an iron glove: an autobiography*. Translated by Philip Stratford. Montreal: Harvest House, 1975. 161p.
   Translation of *Dans un gant de fer, v. 1, La joue gauche*.

955. _____. *The right cheek: an autobiography*. Translated by Philip Stratford. Montreal: Harvest House, 1975. 161p.
   Translation of *Dans un gant de fer, v. 2, La joue droite*.

956. McCallan, N. J. and Katherine Roback. *An ordinary life: life histories of women in the urban core of Vancouver*. CRIAW working papers. Sponsored by the Canadian Research Institute for the Advancement of Women. n.p., n.d. 36p. and app.

957. McClung, M. G. *Women in Canadian literature*. Toronto: Fitzhenry & Whiteside, 1977. 96p.

958. McClung, Nellie. *The stream runs fast: my own story*. Toronto: Thomas Allen, 1965. 316p.
   First published in 1945.

959. McDonald, David and Lauren Drewery. *For the record: Canada's greatest women athletes*. Toronto: Mesa Associates, 1981. 270p.

960. McDougall, Anne. *Anne Savage: the story of a Canadian painter*. Montreal: Harvest House, 1977. 215p.

961. McDowell, Linda. "Harriet Dick. A lady ahead of her time?" *Manitoba Pageant*, 20:11-13, Summer 1975.

962. McFadden, Fred. *Abby Hoffman*. Don Mills, Ont.: Fitzhenry & Whiteside, 1977. 47p.

963. McGuire, Rita. *Marguerite d'Youville: a pioneer for our times: a biography based on the life and times of Marguerite d'Youville, Foundress of the Sisters of Charity (Grey Nuns) of Montreal*. Ottawa: Novalis, 1982. 309p.

964. Metcalf, Vicky. *Catherine Schubert*. Don Mills, Ont.: Fitzhenry & Whiteside, 1978. 62p.

965. Mitchell, Dorothea. *Lady lumberjack*. Vancouver: Mitchell Press, 1967. 135p.

966. Monté, Denyse. *On l'appelle toujours...Lise*. Montréal: La Presse, 1975. 214p.

967. Montgomery, Lucy Maud. *My dear Mr. M.: letters to G. B. MacMillan from L. M. Montgomery*, edited by Francis W. P. Bolger and Elizabeth R. Epperly. Toronto: McGraw-Hill Ryerson, 1980. 212p.

968. _____. *The alpine path: the story of my career*. Don Mills, Ont.: Fitzhenry & Whiteside, 1974. 96p.

969. Murphy, Emily F. *Janey Canuck in the West*. Heritage books, no. 2. Toronto: McClelland and Stewart, 1975. 223p.

970. Murray, Florence J. *At the foot of Dragon Hill*. New York: E. P. Dutton, 1975. 240p.

971. Norcross, Elizabeth Blanche. *Pioneers every one: Canadian women of achievement*. Toronto: Burns & MacEachern, 1979. 159p.

972. O'Brien, Mary Sophia. *Journals of Mary O'Brien: 1828-1838*. Edited by Audrey S. Miller. Toronto: MacMillan of Canada, 1968. 314p.

973. Payette, Lise. *Le pouvoir? Connais pas!* Montréal: Québec/Amérique, 1982. 212p.

974. Peterkin, Audrey and Margaret Shaw. *Mrs. Doctor: reminiscences of Manitoba doctors' wives*. Winnipeg: Prairie Publishing Co., 1976. 168p.

975. Plamondon, Lilianne. "Une femme d'affaires en Nouvelle-France, Marie-Anne Barbel." MA thèse, Université Laval, 1976.

976. Proulx, Marcienne. "L'action sociale de Marie Gérin-Lajoie, 1910-1925." MA mémoire, Université de Sherbrooke, 1976. 127p. (Can. theses, no.27019)

977. Ray, Janet. *Emily Stowe*. Don Mills, Ont.: Fitzhenry and Whiteside, 1978. 63p.

978. Reynolds, Louise. *Agnes: the biography of Lady Macdonald*. Toronto: Samuel Stevens, 1979. 229p.

979. Robertson, Heather. "The prime of Ms. Judy LaMarsh," *Maclean's*, 88:73-7, Mar. 1975.

980. Roger, Gertrude Minor. *Lady rancher*. Saanichton, B.C.: Hancock House Publishers, 1979. 182p.

981. Rooke, Patricia T. and R. L. Schnell. "'An idiot's flowerbed' - a study of Charlotte Whitton's feminist thought, 1941-50," *International Journal of Women's Studies*, 5:29-46, Jan.-Feb. 1982.

982. Rosenberg, Leah. *The errand runner: reflections of a rabbi's daughter*. Toronto: John Wiley and Sons Canada, 1981. 149p.

983. Salverson, Laura Goodman. *Confessions of an immigrant's daughter*. Toronto: University of Toronto Press, 1981.
    First published in 1939.

984. Saumart, Ingrid. *La vie extraordinaire de Jean Despréz*. Montréal: Éditions du jour, 1965. 115p.

985. Siggins, Maggie. "One woman's search for herself," *Chatelaine* 47:35, 70-2, Dec. 1974.

986. Smith, Elizabeth. *'A woman with a purpose': the diaries of Elizabeth Smith, 1872-1884*, edited and introduced by Veronica Strong-Boag. Toronto: University of Toronto Press, 1980. 298p.

38

987. Stamp, R. M. "Adelaide Hoodless, champion of women's rights," in Robert S. Patterson and others, eds., *Profiles of Canadian educators*. n.p.: D.C. Heath Canada, 1974, pp.213-32.

988. Stephenson, Patricia. *Hidden voices: the life experiences of women who have worked and studied at Queen's University*. Kingston, Ont.: Queen's University. Office of the Dean of Women, 1980. 60p.
     Catalogue of abstracts of oral history recordings; a student group project extending over four years (1976-1980).

989. Stirling, Lilla. *In the vanguard: Nova Scotia women, mid-twentieth century*. Windsor, N.S.: Lancelot Press, 1976. 72p.

990. Storrs, Monica. *God's galloping girl: the Peace River diaries of Monica Storrs, 1929-1931*, edited and introduced by W. L. Morton. Vancouver: University of British Columbia Press, 1979. 307p.

991. Street, Margaret M. *Watch-fires on the mountains: the life and writings of Ethel Johns*. Toronto: University of Toronto Press, 1973. 336p.

992. Strong-Boag, Veronica. "Canada's women doctors: feminism constrained," in Linda Kealey, ed., *A not unreasonable claim: women and reform in Canada, 1880s-1920s*. Toronto: Women's Press, 1979, pp.109-29.

993. Tausky, Thomas E. *Sara Jeannette Duncan: novelist of empire*. Port Credit: P. D. Meany, 1980. 300p.

994. Thomas, Clara. *Love and work enough: the life of Anna Jameson*. Toronto: University of Toronto Press, 1967. 252p.

995. Tippett, Maria. *Emily Carr: a biography*. Toronto: Oxford University Press, 1979. 314p.

996. Tivy, Louis. *Your loving Anna: letters from the Ontario frontier*. Toronto: University of Toronto Press, 1972. 120p.

997. Trudeau, Margaret. *Beyond reason*. New York: Paddington Press, 1979. 256p.
     French edition: *A coeur ouvert*.

998. _____. *Consequences*. Toronto: McClelland Stewart, 1982. 192p.

999. Turcotte, Bobbie and Mary Hemlow. "Searching for the real Margaret Trudeau," *Chatelaine*, 48:65, 127-132, Oct. 1975.

1000. Vance, Catharine. *Not by gods but by people: the story of Bella Hall Gauld*. Toronto: Progress Books, 1968. 65p.

1001. Van Steen, Marcus. *Pauline Johnson, her life and work*. Toronto: Hodder and Stoughton, 1965, 1973 printing. 279p.

1002. Vincens, Simone. *Madame Montour et son temps*. Montréal: Québec/Amérique, 1979. 331p.

1003. Walton, Yvette M. "The life and professional contributions of Ethel Mary Cartwright, 1880-1955." MA thesis, University of Western Ontario, 1976. 199p. (Can. theses, no.28372)

1004. Ward-Harris, E. D. *A nun goes to the dogs: a biography of Mother Cecilia Mary, O.S.B.* Rev. ed. Victoria, B.C.: Sono Nis Press, 1977. 136p.

1005. Watson, Louise. *She was never afraid: the biography of Annie Buller*. Toronto: Progress Books, 1976. 129p.

1006. Whissel-Tregonning, Marguerite. *Kitty, le gai pinson: résumé de la vie d'une pionnière du nord de l'Ontario écrit en français-canadien*. Sudbury, Ont.: Prise de parole, 1978. 218p.

1007. *Who's who of American women: a biographical dictionary of notable living American women*. Chicago: Marquis Who's Who, 1958/59- . Annual.

1008. *Who's who of Canadian women*. Toronto: Trans-Canada Press, 1984- .

1009. Willis, Jane. *Geniesh: an Indian girlhood*. Toronto: New Press, 1973. 199p.

1010. Wilson, Mary Carol. *Marion Hilliard*. Don Mills, Ont.: Fitzhenry & Whiteside, 1977. 63p.

1011. Wright, Helen K. *Nellie McClung and women's rights*. Agincourt, Ont.: Book Society of Canada Ltd., 1980. 75p.

1012. Wright, James Frederick Church. *The Louise Lucas story. This time tomorrow*. Montreal: Harvest House, 1965. 137p.
1013. Zonta Club, Charlottetown, P.E.I. *A century of women*. Charlottetown, 1967. 107p.

BIRTH CONTROL AND FAMILY PLANNING

1014. Addy, Cenovia. "Planification familiale au Canada: une vision d'ensemble des progrès réalisés," dans J. H. Gourges, G. Leclerc et J. Tremblay, *Sexualité, fertilité, planification des naissances*. Sherbrooke, Québec: Éditions Prince, 1978, pp.157-62.
1015. Angers, Maurice. *Pouvoir dans la famille et planification des naissances en milieu défavorisé urbain québécois*. Laboratoire de recherches sociologiques. Rapports de recherches. Cahier 4. Québec: Université Laval. Dept. de sociologie, Faculté des sciences sociales, 1973. 509p.
1016. Arnold, Robert, Cyril Greenland and Marylen Wharf. *Family planning in Hamilton*. Ottawa: Canada. Dept. of National Health and Welfare, 1974. 188p.
1017. Balakrishnan, T. R., J. F. Kantner and J. D. Allingham. *Fertility and family planning in a Canadian metropolis*. Montreal: McGill-Queen's University Press, 1975. 217p.
1018. Beaujot, Roderic Paul. "Ethnic fertility differentials in Edmonton." PhD diss., University of Alberta, 1975. 271p. (Can. theses, no.26707)
1019. Boivin, Micheline. *Communication conjugale et planification des naissances en milieu défavorisé urbain québécois*. Laboratoire de recherches sociologiques. Rapports de recherches. Cahier 1. Québec: Université Laval. Dept. de sociologie, Faculté des sciences sociales, 1973. 372p.
1020. Bouma, Gary D. and Wilma J. Bouma. *Fertility control: Canada's lively social problem*. Don Mills, Ont.: Longman Canada, 1975. 144p.
1021. Bracher, Michael David. "A stochastic model of family planning." MA thesis, University of Alberta, 1976. 67p. (Can. theses, no.27620)
1022. Canada. Advisory Council on the Status of Women. *A statement on birth planning: ACSW recommendations*. Ottawa, 1976. 4p.
1023. _____. *Birth planning; the right to know. [Planification des naissances]*. The person papers. 2nd. ed. Ottawa, 1976. 16, 16p.
1024. Canadian Advisory Council on the Status of Women. *CACSW recommendations on birth planning*. Ottawa, 1979. 4p.
1025. Carrara, Angelo. "Attitudes et comportements d'un groupe de femmes québécoises face au problème de la régulation des naissances." MScSoc thèse, Université Laval, 1971. 89p. (Can. theses, no.18930)
1026. Cloutier-Cournoyer, Renée. *Interaction conjugale et planification des naissances en milieu défavorisé urbain québécois*. Laboratoire de recherches sociologiques. Rapports de recherches. Cahier 7. Québec: Université Laval. Dept. de sociologie, Faculté des sciences sociales, 1974. xxxx, 725p.
1027. _____. "Théorie du développement: aspirations féminines et comportements contraceptifs." MA thèse, Université de Montréal, 1970.
1028. Cole, Peter. "The sterilization trap," *Canadian Women's Studies / Les cahiers de la femme*, 2(1):42-3, 1980.
1029. Comité pour la planification des naissances de Gaspé. *Regards sur la sexualité des Gaspésiens: étude des connaissances, attitudes et comportements des Gaspésiens et des Madelinots en matière de sexualité*. Gaspé, Que., 1976. 226p.
1030. Cook, Judith K. "An investigation of the family planning of post-partum mothers." MSc thesis, University of Guelph, 1974. 75p. (Can. theses, no.17977)
1031. Cowell, Carol A. "Wilful exposure to unwanted pregnancy," *Canadian Medical Association. Journal*, 111:1045, 1047, Nov. 16, 1974.
1032. De Sincay, Beatrice. "Modernité des attitudes féminines et planification des naissances. MA thèse, Université de Montréal, 1967.
1033. Elahi, Virginia. "Family planning survey in Halifax, Nova Scotia," *Canadian Journal of Public Health*, 64:515-20, Nov.-Dec. 1973.

1034.   _____. *A family planning survey of Halifax*. Halifax: Dalhousie University. Dept. of Preventive Medicine, 1973. 218p.

1035.   Family Planning Federation of Canada. *Brief no. 15 to the Royal Commission on the Status of Women in Canada*. Montreal, n.d. 4p.

1036.   Fortin, J. N. and others. "Side effects of oral contraceptive medication: a psychosomatic problem," *Canadian Psychiatric Association. Journal*, 17:3-10, Feb. 1972.

1037.   Ghan, Sherman L. "Women's attitudes toward oral contraceptives." MA thesis, University of Regina, 1974. 114p. (Can. theses, no.20031)

1038.   Gourgues, Jules-Henri. *Sexualité et planification des naissances en milieu défavorisé urbain québécois*. Laboratoire de recherches sociologiques. Rapports de recherches. Cahier 6. Québec: Université Laval. Dept. de sociologie, Faculté des sciences sociales,1974. 631p.

1039.   Grauer, H. "A study of contraception as related to multiple unwanted pregnancies," *Canadian Medical Association. Journal*, 111:1083-4, 1087, Nov. 16, 1974.

1040.   _____. "A study of contraception as related to unwanted pregnancy," *Canadian Medical Association. Journal*, 107:739-41, Oct. 21, 1972.

1041.   Hepworth, H. Philip. *Personal social services in Canada: a review*. Vol. 5: *Family planning and abortion services and family life education programs*. Ottawa: Canadian Council on Social Development, 1975. 146p.

1042.   Herold, Edward S. "Contraceptive embarrassment and contraceptive behavior among young single women," *Journal of Youth and Adolescence*, 10:233-42, June 1981.

1043.   Herold, Edward S. and Lynne M. Samson. "Differences between women who begin pill use before and after first intercourse Ontario, Canada," *Family Planning Perspectives*, 12:304-5, Nov.-Dec. 1980.

1044.   Herold, Edward S. and Marilyn R. Goodwin. "The adoption of oral contraceptives among adolescent females: reference group influence," in K. Ishwaran, ed., *Childhood and adolescence in Canada*. Toronto: McGraw-Hill Ryerson, 1979, pp.232-48.

1045.   Herold, Edward S. and Marilyn Shirley Goodwin. "Premarital sexual guilt and contraceptive attitudes and behavior," *Family Relations*, 30:247-53, Apr. 1981.

1046.   _____. "Why adolescents go to birth-control clinics rather than to their family physicians," *Canadian Journal of Public Health*, 70:317-20, Sept.-Oct. 1979.

1047.   Herold, Edward S. and Roger E. Thomas. "Sexual and contraceptive attitudes and behavior of high school and college females," *Canadian Journal of Public Health*, 69:311-14, July-Aug. 1978.

1048.   Holmberg, R. "Prognosis for family planning," *Canadian Welfare*, 53:21, Mar.-Apr. 1977.

1049.   Lalonde, Marc. "Major initiatives in family planning," *Chelsea Journal*, 3:102, 104, May-June 1977.

1050.   Lapierre-Adamcyk, Evelyne et Nicole Marcil-Gratton. "La contraception au Québec," *Canadian Studies in Population*, 2:23-51, 1975.

1051.   Le Centre de planification familiale. "Les implications de la planification des naissances." Royal Commission on the Status of Women in Canada. Brief no. 368. Montréal, 1968. 35p.

1052.   Le Riche, N. and J. Howard. *A survey of teenage attitudes to sex and contraception in Kingston*. Queen's University. Dept. of Community Medicine, 1974. 62p.

1053.   Love, E. J., ed. *Non-medical issues in contraception*. n.p.: Canadian Committee for Fertility Research, 1980. 168p.
         Proceedings of a seminar sponsored by the Canadian Committee for Fertility Research with the support of a grant-in-aide from the Family Planning Division of Health & Welfare, Canada.

1054.   Mackenzie, C. J. G. "The Vancouver family planning clinic: a comparison of two years' experience," *Canadian Journal of Public Health*, 59:257-65, July 1968.

1055.   Major, Henri. *Notes on the law of birth planning in Canada*. Ottawa: Canada. Advisory Council on the Status of Women, 1975. 10p.

1056.   Marcil-Gratton, Nicole. "La pratique de la contraception au Québec." MSc thèse, Université de Montréal, 1975. 159p.

1057. McGill University. Medical Students' Society. *Brief no. 344 to the Royal Commission on the Status of Women in Canada*. Montreal, 1968. 13p.

1058. McKilligan, Helen R. "Deliveries in teenagers at a Newfoundland general hospital," *Canadian Medical Association Journal*, 118:1252-4, May 20, 1978.

1059. McLaren, Angus. "Birth control and abortion in Canada, 1870-1920," *Canadian Historical Review*, 59(3):319-40, 1978.

1060. _____. "'What has this to do with working class women?': birth control and the Canadian Left, 1900-1939," *Histoire sociale / Social History*, 14:435-54, Nov. 1981.

1061. Munz, Diane and others. "Contraceptive knowledge and practice among undergraduates at a Canadian university," *American Journal of Obstetrics and Gynecology*, 124:499-505, Mar. 1, 1976.

1062. Myers, Anita M. "Psychological androgyny and its relationship to contraceptive use." MA thesis, York University, 1977. 90p. (Can. theses, no.33647)

1063. Orton, Maureen Jessop and Ellen Rosenblatt. *Adolescent birth planning needs: Ontario in the eighties*. n.p.: Planned Parenthood Ontario, 1981. 84p.

1064. Paquette, Lucie. *Rôles familiaux et planification des naissances en milieu défavorisé urbain québécois*. Laboratoire de recherches sociologiques. Rapports de recherches. Cahier 5. Québec: Université Laval. Dept de sociologie, Faculté des sciences sociales, 1974. xxii, 313p.

1065. Parakulam, George G. "Wives who have unwanted children: an examination of some of the determinants of the control over reproductive behaviour among metropolitan wives in Canada." MA thesis, University of Western Ontario, 1970. 69p. (Can. theses, no.6680)

1066. Pearson, Mary. *Background notes on family planning, conception and birth control*. Ottawa: Canada. Advisory Council on the Status of Women, 1975. 50p.

1067. _____. *Background notes on birth planning and conception control*. Ottawa: Canadian Advisory Council on the Status of Women, 1979. 44p.

1068. Playfair, Patrick. "Parliament faces up," *Canadian Welfare*, 44:4-7, Jan.-Feb. 1968.

1069. Pool, Janet Sceats and D. Ian Pool. *Contraception and health care among young Canadian women*. Ottawa: Carleton University. Dept. of Sociology and Anthropology, 1978. 218p.

1070. Richard, Yvan. "Planification des naissances au Québec," in J. H. Gourges, G. Leclerc et J. Tremblay, *Sexualité, fertilité, planification des naissances*. Sherbrooke, Qué.: Éditions Prince, 1978, pp.165-7.

1071. Roberts, Liz. "Female teenagers and contraception," in Benjamin Schlesinger, ed., *Sexual behaviour in Canada: patterns and problems*. Toronto: University of Toronto Press, 1977, pp.35-44.

1072. Ross, Anne. *Teenage mothers / teenage fathers*. Toronto: Personal Library, 1982. 128p.

1073. Samson, Linda M. "A study of oral contraceptor and pregnancy groups." MSc thesis, University of Guelph, 1979. 164p. (Can. theses, no.43839)

1074. Sawyer, Alison. "Women's bodies, men's decisions," *Canadian Women's Studies / Les cahiers de la femme*, 3(2):92-3, 1981.

1075. Schlesinger, Benjamin. *Family planning in Canada: a source book*. Toronto: University of Toronto Press, 1974. 291p.
    Contents: Family planning and women's rights in Canada, by L. Marsden; The pregnant schoolgirl, by M. Powell; Family planning and the adolescent girl, by D. Guyatt.

1076. _____. "Use and misuse of contraception among teenagers in Canada," *School Guidance Worker*, 32:38-42, Nov./Dec. 1976.

1077. "Sexuality and personhood," in Canadian Research Institute for the Advancement of Women, *Women as persons*. [*La femme en tant que personne*]. Toronto: Resources for Feminist Research, 1980, pp.70-5.
    Proceedings of the 3rd annual meeting.

1078. Shirley, Marilyn R. "A study of the oral contraceptive adoption process among sexually active adolescent females." MSc thesis, University of Guelph, 1977. 205p. (Can. theses, no.33974)

1079. Stoffman, Judy. "The first lady of birth control [Dr. Elizabeth Bagshaw]," *Weekend Magazine*, 27:8-9, Oct. 1, 1977.

1080. United Community Services of the Greater Vancouver Area. Social Policy and Research Dept. *Babies by choice, not by chance: a demonstration project in outreach family planning services*. Vol. 1: *Contraceptive practices*. Vol. 2: *Outreach services*. Vancouver: United Community Services of the Greater Vancouver Area, 1972-73.

1081. Weyer, John. "Alberta Sterilization Act," *University of Toronto Law Journal*, 19:424-29, Sept. 1969.

1082. Wright, Pat and Doris Wilson. "Sterilization: what's the law when there is none?" *Branching Out*, 4:3-5, Sept.-Oct. 1977.

BUSINESS

1083. Annesley, Pat. "Myra Richman [stockbroker] is not in the market for a lark," *Impetus*, June 1973, p.7-9, 41-2.

1084. "Barbara Rae of Office Assistance: equal opportunity in a competitive business," *B.C. Business Magazine*, 9:28-31, Feb. 1981.

1085. Becker, Mary. "The outdoors is her business," *Status of Women News*, 6:14-15, Spring 1980.
      Re: Sheila Kaighin, editor of *Outdoor Canada*.

1086. Bennett, James. "Equal opportunities for women: why and how companies should take action," *Business Quarterly*, 40:22-9, Winter, 1975.

1087. Bennett, James and Pierre Loewe. "Despite our equal-pay laws, lower salaries and benefits persist for female workers," *Financial Post*, 69:E6-8, June 7, 1975.

1088. _____. "'Females need not apply': sex segregation might not be that obvious, but it exists," *Financial Post*, 69:C2-4, May 31, 1975.

1089. _____. "Stop hemming and hawing - act on equal opportunity," *Financial Post*, 69:11-12, June 21, 1975.

1090. _____. *Women in business: a shocking waste of human resources*. Toronto: Maclean-Hunter Ltd., 1975. 150p.

1091. _____. "Women in business: Canadian business isn't really committed to extending equal opportunities to women," *Financial Post*, 69:C1-3 May 24, 1975.

1092. Brien, Pat. "Role of women in business is outlined," *Office Administration*, 11:67, Feb. 1965.

1093. Briggs, Margaret. "Women in business: a unique, feminine contribution," *Western Business and Industry*, 39:47, Feb. 1965.

1094. Brown, Ian. "Isabel's folly?" *Chatelaine*, 56:94, 262+ , Oct. 1983.

1095. Canada. Dept. of Industry, Trade and Commerce. Small Business Secretariat. *Canadian women owner/managers*. Small Business Secretariat working paper. [Ottawa], 1982. 16p.

1096. Cook, Jane T. and Jane Widerman. "Women: the best entrepreneurs," *Canadian Business*, 55:68-73, June 1982.

1097. Davidson, Jane. "Will companies become baby-sitters, too?" *Financial Post*, 66:1, 8, July 15, 1972.

1098. Drake, Robin. "Can you identify your 'type two' women?" *Canadian Personnel and Industrial Relations Journal*, 20:38, 41-2, Jan. 1973.

1099. Eastman, Barbara C. "Women entrepreneurs: the role has ready models," *Canadian Woman Studies / Les cahiers de la femme*, 3:93-6, Summer 1982.

1100. "Emily Post revisited," *Business Journal of the Board of Trade of Metropolitan Toronto*, 67(8):33-6, Sept. 1977.

1101. "Ex-Chimo president says women in travel should stick together," *Canadian Travel Courier*, 10:23,25, Sept. 11, 1975.

1102. Fraser, Karen, comp. *The women's business directory*. Toronto: Personal Library, 1981. 103p.

1103. "Girls woo gas customers," *Service Station and Garage Management*, 8:20, Sept. 1978.

1104. Gooding, Wayne. "Women business owners organize," *Financial Post*, 75:4, May 23, 1981.

1105. Govier, Katherine. "Does success spoil love?" *Chatelaine*, 51:58-9, 105+ , Mar. 1978.
1106. Grass, J. "Taking their place in Business Hall of Fame," *Financial Post*, 75:21, Apr. 11, 1981.
1107. Greenglass, Esther. "New perspectives on women in management," *Chatelaine*, 52:32, 36, Nov. 1979.
1108. "Group offers encouragement, advice to women entrepreneurs," *Globe & Mail*, May 16, 1981, p.B5.
1109. Gwyn, Sandra. "She thinks like a man," *Saturday Night*, 92:21-6, July-Aug. 1977.
1110. Harris, Marjorie. "Helen Moffett: suite success," *Financial Post Magazine*, [76]:12-14, 16+ , June 1982.
1111. "Hotels adapting to needs of women on business travel," *Globe & Mail*, Feb. 22, 1982, p.B30.
1112. "Husband, wife enter Business Hall of Fame," *Financial Post*, 75:4, Feb. 28, 1981.
1113. Hustvedt, Eric. "Ruth Hernden: 'a symbol of hope for single parents'," *Atlantic Advocate*, 72:60-2, Nov. 1981.
1114. "Jobs gap narrowing in market research," *Marketing*, 79:16, March 25, 1974.
1115. Johnson, Brian D. "Pat Johnston: economist and rebel," *Chatelaine*, 56:68, 110, 114, Oct. 1983.
1116. Kee, Y. T. "Don't raise your daughter to behave 'like a lady'," *Business Quarterly*, 40:4-5, 7-8, Spring 1975.
1117. Kirk, Patti and Marie Prins. "The Toronto Women's Bookstore - an interview with Patti Kirk and Marie Prins," *Canadian Women's Studies / Les cahiers de la femme*, 1:113-14, Spring 1979.
1118. Lerch, Renate. "No special treatment please," *Financial Post*, 76:51, Mar. 13, 1982.
1119. Levine, Sybil and Christine Magraken. "Trending towards equality," *Financial Post*, 72:20, Feb. 11, 1978.
1120. MacBeth, Mike. "Fast-track women MBAs," *Chatelaine*, 53:22, Feb. 1980.
1121. "Male-female behavior on the job. A round table discussion," *ICB Review*, 5:6-8, Summer 1972.
1122. "[Marion Van Dyke]," *Canadian Business*, 44:43, Sept. 1971.
1123. McGibbon, Pauline. "Women's Year: a hopeful milestone," *Canadian Business Review*, 2:1, Spring 1975.
1124. Moore, Joy and Frank Laverty. "Women in the front window," *Optimum*, 5(3):28-35, 1974.
1125. Morgan, Joanna. "Meet five Montreal women who wanted to be their own boss," *Chatelaine*, 51:22, 80-1, Jan. 1978.
1126. Mungall, Constance. "10 most powerful women in Canada," *Chatelaine*, 50:54-5, 102+ , Dec. 1977.
1127. O'Neil, Peat. "From Atwood to Zaremba: founding a feminist bookstore," *Branching Out*, 3:11-12, Feb.-Mar. 1976.
1128. "Opinions of experts on women in business," *Canadian Business*, 44:46, Sept. 1971.
1129. Paris, Erna. "How are nice girls doing in places like the banks...The Bell...Air Canada?" *Chatelaine*, 46:48-9, 101-6, Sept. 1973.
1130. _____. "Women and business: some conclusions," *Chatelaine*, 47:38, 42, 119, Nov. 1974.
1131. Peal, Emma. "Corporate chic: success in the skirted suit," *Journal (The Board of Trade of Metropolitan Toronto)*, Spring 1979, pp.5-6, 8, 10, 12.
1132. Pfeifer, Pat and Stanley J. Shapiro. "Male and female MBA candidates: are there personality differences?" *Business Quarterly*, 43:77-80, Spring 1978.
1133. Plowman, Shirley. "Are women (managers) treated differently?" *Canada Commerce*, [146]:18-20, May 1982.
1134. Praskey, Sally. "Working women: limitless potential for success [in hardware & building supply industries]," *Hardware Merchandising*, Aug. 1982, pp.8-11.
1135. Rae, Barbara J. "Woman as manager 1979: choices, choices, choices," *Canadian Manager*, 4:9,20, Nov.-Dec. 1979.

44

1136. Roberts, Imla. "Networks are not for men only," *Canadian Training Methods*, 13:25-6, Aug. 1980.
1137. Ross, Aileen D. "Some comments on the home roles of businesswomen in India, Australia and Canada," *Journal of Comparative Family Studies*, 8:327-40, Autumn 1977.
1138. Ross, A. D. "Businesswomen and business cliques in three cities: Delhi, Sydney, and Montreal," *Canadian Review of Sociology and Anthropology*, 16(4):425-35, 1979.
1139. Ross, Eleanor C. "Nurse to entrepreneur," *Canadian Woman Studies / Les cahiers de la femme*, 3:98-9, Summer 1982.
1140. Ross, Henry. "You've come a long way baby: but not quite far enough," *Marketing*, 80:4, 25, Sept. 22, 1975.
1141. Rumball, Donald. "Managing now means you can't act like a 'boss'," *Financial Post*, 67:7, June 16, 1973.
1142. Shack, Sybil. *Saturday's stepchildren: Canadian women in business.* [Toronto]: University of Toronto. Faculty of Education. Guidance Centre. 1977. 184p.
1143. Simard-Pilote, Vivianne. "Quand les femmes deviennent chefs d'entreprises," *Actualité*, 15:22-5, juill. 1975.
1144. Sinclair, Sonja. "Women: growing force in business," *Canadian Business*, 44:42,44+, Sept. 1971.
1145. Sorensen, J. "West: support for businesswomen," *Financial Post*, 75:7, Sept. 26, 1981.
1146. Timson, Judith. "5 dazzling examples of women as entrepreneurs," *Chatelaine*, 53:42-3, 66+, Mar. 1980.
1147. Townson, Monica. "Breaking down the barriers," *Financial Times of Canada*, 61:5ff, Feb. 12, 1973.
1148. _____. "Business shuns the women," *Synoptic*, 14:12-14, Summer 1974.
1149. "Wendy McDonald: not your average grandmother," *B.C. Business Magazine*, 7:21-4, Nov. 1979.
1150. "Women are still 'half-persons' in the whole corporate spectrum," *Financial Post*, 69:1-2, May 31, 1975.
1151. Winter, Maridee Allen. "Risk takers: women are different," *Financial Post*, 75:23, Mar. 14, 1981.
1152. "Women in business: policies of three Canadian corporations," *Canadian Business Review*, 2:8-11, Summer 1975.
1153. *Women like me: the women's business directory.* Southern Ontario [ed.]. Maple, Ont.: Belsten Pub., [1982]. Annual.
    Continues Women's business directory.
1154. "Working paper profiles women as owner/managers," *Canada Commerce*, [146]:26, Apr. 1982.

BUSINESS - BIBLIOGRAPHY

1155. Bégin, Diane, Francine Harel-Giasson, Marie-Françoise Marchis-Mouren. *Portraits de Québécoises gestionnaires: une bibliographie annotée.* Rapport de recherche, no. 82-07. Montréal: Université de Montréal. École des hautes études commerciales, 1982. 64p.

CANADIAN ADVISORY COUNCIL ON THE STATUS OF WOMEN

1156. Campbell, Bonnie. "Under fire: Advisory Council on the Status of Women," *Labour Gazette*, 73:663-7, Oct. 1973.
1157. Canada. Advisory Council on the Status of Women. *Annual Report.* 2nd, 1974/75- . Ottawa, 1975- .
    First Annual report entitled, *What's been done?*
1158. Canadian Advisory Council on the Status of Women. *As things stand: ten years of recommendations.* Ottawa, 1983. 175p.
1159. _____. *Equality and equalization.* Brief to the Parliamentary Task Force on Federal Provincial Fiscal Arrangements. Ottawa, 1981. 27p.
1160. _____. *It's your turn: a handbook for Canadian women.* Ottawa, 1983. 44p.

1161. _____. *Recommendations of the Canadian Advisory Council on the Status of Women*, by subject. Ottawa, 1981. 104p.

1162. "CLC proposes revised women's council; 'Restructurez le Conseil de la femme' (le CTC)," *Canadian Labour / Travailleur canadien*, 26:7, [English]; 7, [French], Feb. 1981.

1163. Cole, Susan G. and others. "What price status?" *Broadside*, 2:1, 3, Feb. 1981.

1164. De Villiers, Marq. "The unsinkable Katie Cooke: a powerful swimmer against a tide of discrimination," *Weekend Magazine*, Apr. 13, 1974, pp.2-4

1165. Gray, Elizabeth. "The exit of an iron will: 'he's a bully and I don't see why women should be bullied'," *Maclean's*, 94:28-9, Feb. 2, 1981.

1166. Laws, Margaret. "Deciding housewives' worth requires an attitude change [Advisory Council on the Status of Women study]," *Financial Post*, 72:7, July 1, 1978.

1167. Rousseau, Yvette. "The status of women in the labour market," *Civil Service Review*, 51:13-16, June 1978.

1168. "Women's status [Advisory Council on the Status of Women Report]," *Labour Gazette*, 74:457, July 1974.

CAREERS AND OCCUPATIONS

1169. Alberta. Women's Bureau. *Jobs without gender*. [Edmonton], 1977. 87p. (Profile 77-0723)
    Interviews with women in different careers.

1170. Barnes, Angela. "The voice of women [interviews]," *Journal (The Board of Trade of Metropolitan Toronto)*, Easter 1977, pp.34-44.

1171. Boyd, Monica. "Occupational segregation: a review," in *Sexual equality in the workplace*. Ottawa: Canada. Dept. of Labour. Women's Bureau, 1982, pp.66-92.

1172. _____. "Sex differences in the Canadian occupational attainment process," *Canadian Review of Sociology and Anthropology*, 19:1-28, Feb. 1982.

1173. Boyd, M. *Occupational attainment of native born Canadian women: results from the 1973 Canadian National Mobility Study*. Working paper, no. 77-26. Madison: University of Wisconsin. Center for Demography and Ecology, 1977. 42p.

1174. Canada. Dept. of Employment and Immigration. *Manual of sex free occupational titles*. Ottawa, 1977. 87p.

1175. Canada. Dept. of Labour. Women's Bureau. *If I go to university*. Ottawa, 1966. 36p.

1176. Canada. Dept. of Transport. Canadian Marine Transportation Administration. *National consolidation: Equal Opportunities For Women Availability Research Study*. [*Aperçu national: promotion de la femme étude disponibilité*]. [Ottawa, 1980]. 96, 99p. (Microlog 81-0773)

1177. Canadian Teachers' Federation. *Challenge '77: strategies for action*. Ottawa: The Federation, 1977. [4]p.
    French edition: *Défi '77 tratégies pour action*.

1178. Charlesworth, Maxine A. "Sexual attitudes and career choice." MA thesis, Queen's University, 1972. 109 p. (Can. theses, no.12983)

1179. Cohen, Leah. *Review of women's participation in the non-traditional occupations*. Technical study, no. 8. Ottawa: Canada. Task Force on Labour Market Development, 1981. 27p.

1180. Cohen, Shaughnessy Murray. "Patterns of occupational segregation by sex in the Canadian labour force." MA thesis, University of Windsor, 1973. 174p. (Can. theses, no.19877)

1181. Corner Brook Status of Women Council. *No need to just pretend: new work choices for women*. [Ottawa]: Employment and Immigration Canada, [1981?] 24p.

1182. Echenberg, Havi. "Canada's women: victims of job ghettos and unequal pay," *Canadian Business Review*, 7:30-2, Spring 1980.

1183. Glaze, Avis. "Factors which influence career choice and future orientations of females: implications for career education." EdD diss., University of Toronto, 1979. 215p. (Can. theses, no.50267)

1184. Goodings, Sidlofsky, Goodings and Associates. *Female engineering technicians and technologists*. [Toronto]: Ontario. Ministry of Colleges and Universitites, 1975. 78, [9]p.

1185. Greve, Rose Marie. "Careers in modelling: a study in occupational socialization." MA thesis, University of Windsor, 1973. 132p. (Can. theses, no.19896)

1186. Guppy, L. N. and J. L. Siltanen. "A comparison of the allocation of male and female occupational prestige," *Canadian Review of Sociology and Anthropology*, 14(3):320-30, 1977.

1187. Kalin, Rudolf, and others. "Sex-role ideology and sex bias in judgements of occupational suitability," in Cannie Stark-Adamic, ed., *Sex roles: origins, influences and implications for women*. Montreal: Eden Press, 1980, pp.89-99.

1188. Kimball, Meredith M. "Returning to work or school: women's career decisions," *Atlantis*, 4:212-21, Spring 1979, Part II.

1189. Lautard, Emile Hugh. "Occupational segregation by sex and industrialization in Canada: 1891-1971." PhD diss., University of British Columbia, 1978. 128p. (Can. theses, no.40678)

1190. Lee, Betty. "Job prospects for women in the '80's," *Chatelaine*, 53:44-5, 176+ , Apr. 1980.

1191. Leith, Nancy Louise. "The effect of exposure to film-mediated career information of traditionally defined male occupations on the vocational interest level of girls." MEd thesis, University of Alberta, 1977. 67p. (Can. theses, no.34407)

1192. Livingston, Marilyn. "Nova Scotia's lady auctioneer," *Atlantic Advocate*, 71:85-6, Nov. 1980.

1193. Long, Bonita Clarice. "An evaluation of lifeplanning interventions: comparing a career development course with a personal development course and lifeplanning interviews for women." MA thesis, University of British Columbia, 1978. 147p. (Can. theses, no.40686)

1194. MacLennan, Barbara. "Careers in museology," *Chatelaine*, 52:32, 36, Oct. 1979.

1195. McCreary, Gillian, Beverly Lambert and Jeff Jones. *Saskatchewan women in the labour force; some Saskatchewan women and their careers*. [Regina]: Saskatchewan. Dept. of Labour. Women's Division, [1978?]. 32p. (Microlog 79-0684)

1196. Mungall, Constance. "Eighty-eight best jobs for women today," *Chatelaine*, 47:insert 1-12, Oct. 1974.

1197. Nadeau, Elaine. "Careers for women: tinker, tailor, teacher, nurse," *Canada and the World*, 40:18-19, Dec. 1974.

1198. Newfoundland Status of Women Council. Education Group. *This is our work: some Newfoundland women talk about their careers*. St. John's, Nfld., 1975. 40p.

1199. Ontario. Dept. of Labour. Women's Bureau. *You're a what?* Toronto, n.d. 32p.

1200. Ontario. Ministry of Labour. Women's Bureau. *Career selector*. Rev. ed. Toronto, 1978. v.p.
   Series of booklets on careers: Business, finance and office; Communication and creative arts; Community service and education; Health and paramedical; Science and technical; Service and retailing; Trades and industry.

1201. Paris, Erna. "Which professions pay off for women - if any?" *Chatelaine*, 47:37, 86, 88-90, Sept. 1974.

1202. Pepperdene, Barbara J. "The occupation of nursing and careers: a study of the careers of diploma and degree nurses." PhD diss., University of Toronto, 1974. 401p. (Can. theses, no.27944)

1203. "Pipeline inspector getting high from job," *Native People*, 15:10, May 14, 1982.

1204. Press, Marjorie Jean. "Achievement motivation in women: some consequences for familial and professional careers." MA thesis, Memorial University of Newfoundland, 1970. 133p. (Can. theses, no.15665)

1205. "Recruiting in a changing environment," *Canadian Business Review*, 8:37-40, Spring 1981.

1206. Reeves, John. "Celebration of women," *Chatelaine*, 48:68-72, Oct. 1975.

1207. Ryten, Eve. "Our best educated women," *Canadian Business Review*, 2:12-16, Summer 1975.

1208. Schreck, David Donald. "Occupational segregation by sex." PhD diss., University of British Columbia, 1978. 196p. (Can. theses, no.37717)
1209. Sheinin, Rose. "The rearing of women for science, engineering and technology," *International Journal of Women's Studies*, 4:339-47, Sept.-Oct. 1981.
1210. University of British Columbia. Student Counselling and Resources Centre. *Tinker, tailor, soldier, sailor....* [Vancouver], 1979. 48p.
1211. Walton, Jo Anne. "Organizing lobbies for tradeswomen," *Perception*, 4:9-10, Jan.-Feb. 1981.

CAREERS AND OCCUPATIONS, NON-TRADITIONAL

1212. Andresen, Susan A. *Introduction to Non-traditional Occupations Program (INTO) evaluation: expanding women's career options*. [London, Ont.: Women's Workshop, Continuous Learning Project, 1981]. 175p. (Microlog 82-3760)
        Study funded by Ontario Ministry of Colleges and Universities.
1213. Atkins, J. Louise. "Female environmental planners," *Status of Women News*, 6:5-6, Winter 1979-80.
1214. Barriault, Rachel and Shirley Hawes. "Women at Inco: speakout [interview]," *Canadian Women's Studies / Les cahiers de la femme*, 1:72-8, Winter 1978-1979.
1215. Braid, Kate. "Invisible women: women in non-traditional occupations in British Columbia." MA thesis, Simon Fraser University, 1979. 213p. (Can. theses, no.44862)
1216. _____. *Resumé of research: women in non-traditional occupations in British Columbia*. Prepared for the B.C. Human Rights Commission Conference, Dec. 7-9, 1979. n.p., 1979. 7p. (Microlog 80-0851)
1217. _____. "Woman in man's territory: the sexuality of the non-traditional workplace," *Canadian Women's Studies / Les cahiers de la femme*, 3(2):65-71, 1981.
1218. _____. *Women in non-traditional occupations in British Columbia*. CRIAW working papers. Ottawa: Canadian Research Institute for the Advancement of Women, n.d. 19p.
        "A preliminary study prep'd for C.S.A.A. Annual Meeting, June 1, 1979."
1219. Braid, Kathleen. "Zen construction: wherein a woman learns harmony, balance and how to lay 'im down," *Branching Out*, 6(4):18-19, 1979.
        For replies see Kathy Poff and Naomi Wakan below.
1220. British Columbia. Apprenticeship Training Programs Branch. *Women's exploratory apprenticeship training course outline*. Victoria, B.C., 1978.
1221. Burrows, Jean. "Operation skywatch: women pilots fly pollution patrols to protect Ontario lakes," *Civic*, 31:14-15, Aug. 1979.
1222. Butler, Diana. "Women in planning career development," *Plan Canada*, 15:62-7, Sept. 1975.
1223. Canada. Dept. of Transport. Canadian Marine Transportation Administration. *National consolidation: Equal Opportunities For Women Availability Research Study*. [*Aperçu national: promotion de la femme étude disponibilité*]. [Ottawa, 1980]. 96, 99p. (Microlog 81-0773)
1224. Canadian Advisory Council on the Status of Women. *Critical skill shortages: new opportunities for women*. Brief to the Parliamentary Task Force on Employment Opportunities for the 80's. Ottawa, 1981. 29p.
1225. Cohen, Leah. *A review of women's participation in the non-traditional occupations*. Technical study, no. 8. Ottawa: Canada. Task Force on Labour Market Development, 1981. 27p.
1226. _____. "The barriers to women seeking non-traditional jobs," *Canadian Women's Studies / Les cahiers de la femme*, 3(1):40-3, 1982.
1227. de Blicquy, Lorna. "Move over fellas," *Canadian Aviation*, (50th anniversary issue), June 1978, pp.106-11, 133.
1228. De Pauw, Karen. "Training women for non-traditional occupations." MA thesis, Concordia University, 1980. 144p. (Can. theses, no.49598)
1229. Employers' Council of British Columbia. *Female employment in non-traditional areas: some attitudes of managers and working women*. Vancouver, 1975. 33p. and app.

1230. "Female welders to the rescue!" *Labour Gazette*, 66:93, Mar. 1966.

1231. "First 4 women start jobs at Stelco," *Globe & Mail*, Mar. 27, 1980, p.11.

1232. "Gerri Bissonnette, construction executive," *Engineering and Contract Record*, 88:38, Nov. 1975.

1233. Good, D. B. "Women in planning: a citizen's view," *Plan Canada*, 15:68-71, Sept. 1975.

1234. Grescoe, Audrey. "The new 'woman's' work," *Homemaker's Magazine*, 15:54-6, 58+ , June 1980.

1235. "Hard hats hard to fill, women find," *Globe & Mail*, Feb. 7, 1978, p.1.

1236. Henderson, Karen. "Women in trades," *Broadside*, 1(9):8, 1980.

1237. Holmes, Barry. "Human Rights Act: Ottawa strikes again [truck drivers]," *Motor Truck*, 48:15-17, Jan. 1979.

1238. Irvine, D. M. "Food technology: a new career for women," *Labour Gazette*, 67:638-9, Oct. 1967.

1239. Johnson, Pat. "Women start a blue-collar revolution; but myths, stories must be overcome," *Financial Times*, 70:35, 37 Oct. 19, 1981.

1240. Lester, Tanya. "Women shift to non-traditional jobs," *Perception*, 4:9-10, Mar.-Apr. 1981.

1241. List, Wilfred. "A new blue-collar vanguard," *Industrial Management*, 4:17-19, 22, 28, Apr. 1980.

1242. Livingston, Martin. "Company's responsibility to change negative attitudes towards women," *Bus & Truck Transport*, 55:43-5, Apr. 1979.

1243. MacLean, Margaret. "Western development may speed entry of women into skilled labour ranks," *Canadian Vocational Journal*, 17:4-5, 49, May 1981.

1244. Maxwell, Denise. "Fear & loathing in the machine shop [interview]," *Fireweed*, 9:21 , Winter 1981.

1245. National Conference of Women in Trades. 1st, Sept. 26-8, 1980. *Proceedings*. n.p., [1980?] 92p.

1246. "News briefs [steel workers]," *Labour Gazette*, 70:550, Aug. 1970.

1247. Newton, Jennifer L. "Boa constrictor in the back seat only: women driving taxis," *Canadian Women's Studies / Les cahiers de la femme*, 1:50-1, Winter 1978-1979.

1248. Ontario. Ministry of Colleges and Universities. *Women and the skilled trades*. [Toronto, 1976?] Brochure.

1249. _____. *Women into trades and technology: a training profile*. [Toronto], 1982. 156, 9p. (Microlog 82-4713)

1250. Ontario. Ministry of Labour. Women's Bureau. *New skills for women: technology and the skilled trades*. Toronto, 1980. [13]p.

1251. _____. *"But...what else can a girl be?"* [Toronto, 1975]. n.p. Collection of newspaper articles of women in non-traditional occupations.

1252. Poff, Kathy and Naomi Wakan. "Readers respond," *Branching Out*, 7(1):3-5, 1980.

1253. "Prefab plant finds women good workers," *Plant Management and Engineering*, 35:80, June 1976.

1254. "Quota for women workers rejected [steel workers]," *Globe & Mail*, Mar. 14, 1980, pp.1-2.

1255. Rothberg, Diane. "Womanly advice: an experienced pilot offers guidelines for the woman thinking of a flying career," *Canadian Aviation*, 55:52-4, Apr. 1982.

1256. Rovan, Rhonda. "Women in environmental design," *Chatelaine*, 53:26, Aug. 1980.

1257. Schom-Moffatt, Patti and Cynthia Dale Telfer. *Women and work: introduction to non-traditional work*. CRIAW working papers. Ottawa: Canadian Research Institute for the Advancement of Women, [1979?]. 28p. and app.

1258. "Shortage of skilled manpower in Canadian planer mills opens up more jobs for women," *Canadian Forest Industries*, 99:25, June 1979.

1259. Skolnick, H. "Women in industrial sales: from their perspective and that of management," *Marketing*, 85:24, Mar. 24, 1980.

1260. "Special report on women in construction," *Engineering and Contract Record*, 88:35+, Nov. 1975.
1261. Stunell, Linda. *The non-traditional woman*. Vancouver: Amazon Women's Employment Society, 1976. 157p.
1262. "There's room in trucking for these determined gals," *Motor Truck*, 50:40, Oct. 1981.
1263. Thompson, Patricia. "Working in a man's world is not difficult for female navigator," *Seaports and the Shipping World*, Apr. 1980, pp.30-1, 69.
1264. Travers, Lincolne. "Women find opportunity as construction foremen," *Native People*, 9:8, Aug. 6, 1976.
1265. Whittington, Hugh. "Unwitting pioneer," *Canadian Aviation*, 51:6, Sept. 1979.
1266. Wisniewski, Lawrence. "Choosing a man's job: the effect of socialization on female occupational entry." PhD diss., McMaster University, 1977. 339p. (Can. theses, no.36572)
1267. "Woman's place is in the home," *Financial Times*, 65:11, Feb. 7, 1977.
1268. "Women breaking into sweaty, tough world of fire fighting in Northern Ontario," *Globe & Mail*, May 26, 1977, p. 4.
1269. "Women in the woods," *Pulp and Paper Canada*, 76:21-4, Aug. 1975.
1270. "Women in trucking: a man's world no longer," *Motor Truck*, 47:21-2, Apr. 1978.
1271. "Women open building chapter," *Globe & Mail*, Jan. 15, 1982, p.B4.
1272. "You've come a long way baby: [women in the petroleum industry]," *Oilweek*, 31:30, 32, Nov. 24, 1980.
1273. Working Women's Association [Vancouver]. *Women's work: a selection of articles by working women*. Vancouver: Press Gang, 1972. 24p.

CHILD CUSTODY

1274. Edmonds, Alan. "Child custody: don't fathers have rights too?" *Chatelaine*, 50:36, 69-71, Jan. 1977.
1275. Freeland, Halyna. "Custody rights for the nonconformist," *Branching Out*, 5(1):4-5, 1978.
1276. Gerus, Claire. "Motherhood without children: some women walk out on their families. Others have them torn away," *Today*, Nov. 22, 1980, pp.7-9.
1277. Hobbs, Lisa. "The parent-kidnappers," *Chatelaine*, 50:43, 76-84, May 1977.
1278. Middleton, Kate. "Custody battles - not child's play," *Broadside* 1(6):8, 1980.
1279. Wyland, Francie. *Motherhood, lesbianism and child custody*. Toronto: Wages Due Lesbians Toronto / Falling Wall Press, 1977. 36p.

CHILDBIRTH

1280. Bradley, Christine Felecia. "The effects of hospital experience on postpartum feelings and attitudes of women." PhD diss., University of British Columbia, 1978. 171p. (Can. theses, no.34766)
1281. Buckley, Suzann. "Efforts to reduce infant maternity mortality in Canada between the two world wars," *Atlantis*, 2:76-84, Spring 1977, Part II.
1282. _____. "Ladies or midwives? Efforts to reduce infant and maternal mortality," in Linda Kealey, ed., *A not unreasonable claim: women and reform in Canada, 1880s-1920s*. Toronto: Women's Press, 1979, pp.131-49.
1283. Coquatrix, Nicole. "Donner sa vie, garder son corps," *Perception*, 4:40-1, Mar.-Apr. 1981.
1284. Dean, Joanna and Jannie Edwards. "Home birth revival," *Branching Out*, 4:14-16, Sept.-Oct. 1977.
1285. Jackson, Marni. "All in the family: the quiet revolution in the Canadian way of birth," *The Canadian*, Aug. 12, 1978, pp.5-8.
1286. Keywan, Zonia. "Hospitals: are they any place to have a baby?" *Branching Out*, 4:10-12, Sept.-Oct. 1977.
1287. Lord, Catherine. "Accouchements et chaînes de montage," *L'Actualité*, 3:24, nov. 1978.

1288. McDonnell, Kathleen. "From here to maternity," *Broadside*, 1(3):1, 17, 1979.

1289. McQuaig, Linda. "Doctor's choice, mother's trauma," *Maclean's*, 93:46-7, July 28, 1980.

1290. "Midwifery re-examined," *Branching Out*, 3:5, Apr.-June 1976.

1291. Mitchinson, Wendy. "Historical attitudes toward women and childbirth," *Atlantis*, 4:13-34, Spring 1979, Part II.

1292. Naissance-Renaissance. *Depuis que le monde est monde: l'accouchement au Québec en 1980*. Montréal, 1982. 41p.

1293. Pannell, Beverly Walters. "Midwives? What midwives!?" *Canadian Women's Studies / Les cahiers de la femme*, 1:42-4, Winter 1978-1979.

1294. Robertson, Joann. "Sharing the post-partum blues," *Makara*, 2:46-7, Feb.-Mar. 1977.

1295. _____. "A treatment model for post-partum depression," *Canada's Mental Health*, 28:16-17, June 1980.

1296. Rogers, June. "Back to maternity wards," *Maclean's*, 94:20d, June 1, 1981.

1297. Rosenberg, Harriet. "The woman I am is not what you see," *Canadian Dimension*, 15:43-5, Apr. 1981.

1298. Swedlo, Mavis D. "Childbirth at home," *Canadian Journal of Public Health*, 70:307-9, Sept.-Oct. 1979.

CHURCH

1299. Anglican Church of Canada. General Synod Task Force on the Ordination of Women to the Priesthood. *Report*. Toronto, 1972. 11p.

1300. Archevêché de Montréal. *La femme, un agent de changement dans l'église: dossier de travail*. Montreal, 1976. 103p.

1301. Association féminine d'éducation et d'action sociale. *Participation de la femme dans la société et dans l'église*. Montréal: Secrétariat général de l'A.F.E.A.S., 1974.

1302. Boucher, Marie Gratton. "Les droits des femmes dans l'église," dans Rodrigue Bélanger et autres, eds., *Devenirs de femmes*. Cahiers de recherche éthique, no. 8. Montréal: Éditions Fides, 1981, pp. 131-46.

1303. Boyer, Ginette. "Pour s'épanouir, l'Église a besoin des femmes," *Relations*, 40:136, mai 1980.

1304. _____. "Reconnaître le travail des femmes dans l'Église," *Relations*, 42:245-6, Oct. 1982.

1305. Daigeler, Hanow, comp. *Survey on the participation of women in the official pastoral work of the Catholic Church in Canada*. Ottawa: Canadian Conference of Catholic Bishops, 1979. 52p.
    French edition: Sondage sur la participation des femmes dans le travail pastoral officiel de l'Église catholique au Canada.

1306. Dingman, J. "Why not clergywomen?" *Saturday Night*, 80:32-4, Nov. 1965.

1307. Dumais, Monique. "Féminisme et religion au Québec," in Peter Slater, ed., *Religion and culture in Canada*. [*Religion et culture au Canada*]. [Toronto]: Canadian Corporation for Studies in Religion, 1977, pp.149-86.

1308. _____. "La femme dans l'Église du Québec," *Relations*, 37:244-50, Sept. 1977.

1309. _____. "Les femmes et la religion dans les écrits de langue française au Québec," *Atlantis*, 4:152-62, Spring 1979.

1310. _____. "Perspectives pour les femmes telles que proposées par un évêque entre 1928-1950," *Revue d'histoire du Bas Saint-Laurent*, 5:33-6, déc. 1978.

1311. Duncan, Muriel. "You haven't made it...until we've all made it," *United Church Observer*, new ser., 38:12-15, Mar. 1975.

1312. Egginton, Joyce. "Women priests: the Anglicans tell the Episcopals to butt out," *Macleans*, 88:62, Oct. 20, 1975.

1313. Fitzpatrick, Helen. "Catholic women speak out," *Branch Out*, 2:30-1,47, July-Aug. 1975.

1314. Freitag, Walter. *The ordination of women: challenge for Canadian Lutheran unity*. Saskatoon: n.p., 1978. 134p.

1315.   Garr, Allen. "Female rites: for the Anglican Church of Canada this was no ordinary ordination," *Weekend Magazine*, 27:10-12, Mar. 5, 1977.

1316.   Hallet, Mary E. "Nellie McClung and the fight for the ordination of women in the United Church of Canada," *Atlantis*, 4:2-16, Spring 1979.

1317.   Harvey, Julien. "La femme dans l'église: une commission," *Relations*, no. 386:262, oct. 1973.

1318.   Headon, Christopher. "Women and organized religion in mid and late nineteenth century Canada," *Canadian Church Historical Society. Journal*, 20:3-18, Mar.-June 1978.

1319.   Kieran, Sheila. "Are women more equal in the church?" *Chatelaine*, 48:40-1, 74-8, Mar. 1975.

1320.   Krotz, Larry. "Mr. and Mrs. Minister," *United Church Observer*, new ser., 39:22-4, Sept. 1975.

1321.   Lacelle, Élisabeth J. *La femme et la religion au Canada français: un fait socio-culturel, perspectives....* Montréal: Éditions Bellarmin, 1979. 232p.

1322.   Lane, Grace. "Mary Haggart: at home on the range," *United Church Observer*, new ser., 38:26-8, Feb. 1975.

1323.   Lazar, Morty M. "The role of women in synagogue ritual in Canadian Conservative congregations," *Jewish Journal of Sociology*, 20:165-71, Dec. 1978.

1324.   Legendre, Anne Carmelle. "The Baptist contribution to nineteenth century education for women: an examination of Moulton College and McMaster University." MA thesis, McMaster University, 1981. 221p. (Can. theses, no.54178)

1325.   Lord, Catherine. "Au nom du père et de la fille," *L'Actualité*, 3:12, jan. 1978.

1326.   Marchand, Philip. "Priests," *The Canadian*, Apr. 2, 1977, pp.10-12, 14.

1327.   _____. "Women as clergy: what's the verdict?" *Chatelaine*, 53:158-9, 176+ , May 1980.

1328.   Mitchinson, Wendy. "Canadian women and church missionary societies in the nineteenth century: a step towards independence," *Atlantis*, 2:57-75, Spring 1977, Part II.

1329.   O'Rourke, J. J. "Women and the reception of orders," *Revue de l'Université d'Ottawa*, 38:290-8, avr.-juin, 1968.

1330.   Pelletier-Baillargeon, Hélène. "La Québécoise et l'église," *Communauté Chrétienne*, no. 95:450-62, sept.-oct. 1977.

1331.   Presbyterian Church in Canada. Board of Evangelism and Social Action. *Brief no. 73 to the Royal Commission on the Status of Women in Canada*. Toronto, 1968. 6, [19]p.
        Includes pamphlet: "Putting woman in her place." 1964.

1332.   Presbyterian Church in Canada. Committee of the Order of Deaconesses. *A history of the deaconess in the Presbyterian Church in Canada*. Toronto: n.p., 1975. [24]p.

1333.   Rhodes, Kathleen. "Equality for Anglican women? Well...," *United Church Observer*, 28:26-7, Sept. 15, 1966.

1334.   Saint-Martin, Fernande. *La femme et la société cléricale*. Montréal: Mouvement laique de langue française, 1967. 16p.

1335.   "Theology and personhood," in Canadian Research Institute for the Advancement of Women, *Women as persons.[La femme en tant que personne]*. Toronto: Resources for Feminist Research, 1980, pp.34-45.
        Proceedings of the 3rd annual meeting.

1336.   Toupin, R. "Un dossier sur la femme dans l'Église." *Relations* 39:136-7, mai 1979.

1337.   Tyrwhitt, Janice. "Women in the clergy," *Reader's Digest (Canada)*, 112:84-8, Mar. 1978.

1338.   Wallace, Cecelia. "Changes in the churches," in Gwen Matheson, *Women in the Canadian mosaic*. Toronto: Peter Martin, 1976, pp.92-128.

1339.   "Why not? [Anglican church]," *Time. Can. ed.*, 106:10, Oct. 13, 1975.

1340.   "A woman's place," *United Church Observer*, new ser., 38:32-4, Jan. 1975.

1341.   "...Women ministers: are they really worth stalling church union for?" *United Church Observer*, 30:12-15, 40, Mar. 1, 1968.

CIVIL SERVICE

1342. Anderson, Doris. "Now is the time for all good women to come to the aid of themselves [editorial]," *Chatelaine*, 47:1, Feb. 1974.

1343. _____. "Women: never mind the world, start with Ottawa," *Chatelaine*, 45:3, Mar. 1972.

1344. Archibald, Kathleen. "Men, women and persons," *Canadian Public Administration*, 16:14-24, Spring 1973.

1345. _____. *Sex and the public service*. Report to Public Service Commission. Ottawa: Queens Printer, 1970. 218p.

1346. "Asexuons les SM," *Optimum*, 12(2):17-26, 1981.

1347. Bain, George. "A woman of substance [Sylvia Ostry]," *Saturday Night*, 96:21-4, 26+ , Nov. 1981.

1348. Cadwell, Dorothy. "The development of maternity leave in the Civil Service of Canada," in *Report of a Consultation on the employment of women with family responsibilities*. Ottawa: Canada. Dept. of Labour. Women's Bureau, 1965, pp.19-22.

1349. Canada. Dept. of Labour. *Equal opportunities for women program: report and action plan*. [*Programme d'égalité d'accès aux chances pour les femmes: rapport et plan d'action*]. Ottawa, 1981. [103, 105]p.

1350. Canada. Dept. of National Health and Welfare. *Equal opportunities for women: program report, 1976-77*. Ottawa, 1977. 130p.

1351. Canada. Dept. of National Health and Welfare. Equal Opportunities for Women Program. *Annual report, 1977-78, including Objectives and action plans, 1978-79*. [*Rapport annuel, 1977-78, comprenant les Objectifs et plans d'action, 1978-79*]. Ottawa, 1978. v.p.

1352. Canada. Public Service Commission. *A study of the existing sex restrictions in the correctional group CX(COF-LUF-STI): an emotional and controversial issue*. [Ottawa], 1977. 67, 75p. Report of a committee. Includes French text under title: Étude sur les restrictions d'ordre sexuel dans le groupe des services correctionnels CX(COF-LUF-STI): une question fort controversée.

1353. _____. *Representation of women in the public service. Data sampler, 1975*. Ottawa, 1976. 46p.

1354. Canada. Public Service Commission. Office of Equal Opportunities for Women. *A chance to be yourself*. Ottawa, 1971. Folder.

1355. _____. *Career path study of a selected sample in the program administration group*. Ottawa, 1972. 32p.

1356. _____. *Employment of women in the Public Service of Canada: mandate for change*. 2nd ed. Ottawa, 1974. 16p.

1357. _____. *Facts and figures: administrative and foreign service category*. Ottawa, 1972. 41p.

1358. _____. *Facts and figures: administrative support*. Ottawa, 1972.

1359. _____. *Group and level profile - scientific and professional category*. Ottawa, 1973. 90p.

1360. _____. *Group and level profile - technical category*. Ottawa, 1975. xviii, 65p.

1361. _____. *Implementation report on status of women: report recommendations by the Public Service Commission*. Ottawa, 1973. 6p.

1362. _____. *Its up to you*. Ottawa, 1974. Folder.

1363. _____. *Proceedings of information day on the Public Service Equal Opportunities Program and the affirmative action strategy*. [Ottawa], 1981. 72, 100p.

1364. _____. *Program guidelines: equal opportunities for women*. Ottawa, 1973. 5p.

1365. _____. *Response of the Public Service Commission to departmental action plans on equal opportunities for women*, 1978-1979. [Ottawa], 1979. 74, 74p. Includes French edition.

1366. Canada. Public Service Commission. Human Resource Planning Division. Staffing Branch. *A study of the separation of women from the Public Service of Canada, 1976-1979*. [*Étude sur les cessations d'emploi des femmes à la Fonction publique du Canada, 1976-1979*]. Ottawa, 1979. 46, 48p. (Microlog 80-2118)

1367.   Canada. Public Service Commission. Office of Equal Opportunities for Women. *Women in the Public Service of Canada: report 1976. [Le femme dans la fonction publique du Canada]*. Ottawa, 1976. 29, 28p.

1368.   Canada. Public Service Commission. Staffing Branch. *Policy: equal opportunities for women in the Public Service of Canada*. [Ottawa, 1975]. 10p.

1369.   Canada. Treasury Board Secretariat. Human Resources Program Group. *Equal opportunities for women in the Public Service of Canada; a summary of departmental plans - 1977*. Ottawa, 1978. 135p. (Microlog 79-1363)

1370.   Canada. Treasury Board Secretariat. Personnel Policy Branch. *Secretaries in the public service. [Les secrétaires dans la fonction publique]*. Ottawa, 1976. 37, 38p. and app.

1371.   Canada. Treasury Board. Personnel Policy Branch. *Equal opportunities for women in the Public Service of Canada, 1978. [L'égalité d'accès à l'emploi pour la femme dans la Fonction publique du Canada]*. [Ottawa, 1979]. 252, 275p.

1372.   Canadian Advisory Council on the Status of Women. *Women in the public service: barriers to equal opportunity*, by Linda MacLean and others. Ottawa,1979. 80p.

1373.   _____. *Women in the public service: overlooked and undervalued*. Ottawa, 1980. 62p. and app.

1374.   _____. *Women in the public service; what progress has been made? An analysis of employment statistics for 1975*. Ottawa, 1977. 25p.

1375.   Carson, J. J. "Sex and the public service," *Canadian Personnel and Industrial Relations Journal*, 17:13-17, Mar. 1970.

1376.   Carson, Susan. "Getting there is the battle," *Weekend Magazine*, 22:18, 20, 23, Nov. 4, 1972.

1377.   Clark, John. "Ottawa push for women's job rights," *Financial Post*, 74:1-2, Aug. 2, 1980.

1378.   Collins, Winston. "Rebel with a cause [Abby Hoffman]," *Saturday Night*, 96:57-8, July 1981.

1379.   Cornell, Bonnie. "June Menzies, new woman at AIB," *Chatelaine*, 50:24, 28, Apr. 1977.

1380.   _____. "What has Beryl Plumptre done for you lately?" *Chatelaine*, 48:43, 82, 84, 87-90, May 1975.

1381.   DeVilliers, Marq. "The unsinkable Katie Cooke: a powerful swimmer against a tide of discrimination," *Weekend Magazine*, Apr. 13, 1974, pp.2-4.

1382.   "Equal opportunities for women in the federal public service [advertisement]," *Branching Out*, 6(1):26, 1979.

1383.   "Federal equal pay settlement; Égalisation de salaires à la Fonction publique du Canada," *Canadian Labour / Travailleur canadien*, 27:7, [English]; 7, [French], Mar. 1982.

1384.   "Feminism among the mandarins," *Saturday Night*, 93:6, Sept. 1978.

1385.   Judek, Stanislaw. *Women in the public service: their utilization and employment*. Ottawa: Canada. Dept. of Labour. Economics and Research Branch,1968. 142p.

1386.   Kates, Joanne. "Report from Canada: they stopped typing - and stopped the country: Trudeau's new constitution," *Ms.*, 10:77-80, Aug. 1981.

1387.   Lauzon, Sylvie. "La promotion de la femme dans la fonction publique du Canada; Equal opportunities for women in the Public Service of Canada," *Civil Service Review / Revue du Service Civil*, 47:51-3, [French]; 53-5, [English], Sept. 1974.

1388.   Laws, Margaret. "Ottawa slipping on equal opportunity goals," *Financial Post*, 73:13, Jan. 27, 1979.

1389.   Lutes, Carol. "Room at the top: a view of women in management," *Optimum*, 2(1):49-52, 1971.

1390.   Mitchell, Nancy. "Equal opportunities; La promotion des membres," *Civil Service Review / Revue du Service Civil*, 53:3-5, [English]; 3-5, [French], June 1980.

1391.   National Action Committee on the Status of Women. *Women in the public service*. A brief presented to the Special Committee to Review Personnel Management and the Merit Principle in the Public Service. Toronto, 1978. 10p.

1392.   "One step forward, two back," *Labour Gazette*, 75:4, Jan. 1975.

54

1393. Ottawa Conference on the Role of Women in the Public Service, Jan. 24-25, 1974. *Conference report*. Ottawa: Canada. Public Service Commission. Office of Equal Opportunities for Women, 1975. 57p.

1394. "Public service opportunities for university women," *Labour Gazette*, 67:685, Nov. 1967.

1395. Rickenbacker, Louise. "Women in the PSAC; Les femmes de l'AFPC," *Civil Service Review / Revue du Service Civil*, 48:3-14, Dec. 1975.

1396. "Sex and the public service," *Canadian Labour*, 16:17, 19, Feb. 1971.

1397. Smith, Donald J. "Federal employees: differential perceptions of the work role of women." MA thesis, Carleton University, 1977. 183p.

1398. Smith, Janet. "Equal opportunity in the public service," *Canadian Labour*, 20:13-15, 24, June 1975.

1399. _____. "We are women - in numbers too big to ignore," in McGill University. Industrial Relations Centre. *Women and work*. Montreal, 1974. v.p. Annual conference proceedings, 23rd, Apr. 1974.

1400. Swan, H. F. "Housewives - an overlooked source of senior executives for government?" *Optimum*, 3(4):19-25, 1974.

1401. "The civil service: to the top [Sylvia Ostry]," *Time. Can. ed.*, 105:13, Feb. 10, 1975.

1402. "The public and private Sylva Gelber," *Branching Out*, 2:14-17, Sept.-Oct. 1975.

1403. Townson, Monica. "Equality of opportunity for women in the federal public service," *Labour Gazette*, 77:309-12, July 1977.

1404. _____. *Women in the public service: an analysis of employment statistics 1972-1974*. Ottawa: Canada. Advisory Council on the Status of Women, Sept. 1975. 34p.

1405. Vallely-Fischer, Lois. "'Dear Mr. Minister: Equal opportunities—why not?' IWY revisited," *Atlantis*, 4:190-200, Spring 1979.

1406. "Women at the top; Postes supérieurs confiés à des femmes," *Interaction*, 3:1-4, [English]; 1-4, [French], Jan. 1974.

1407. "Women in Canada's federal undertakings and public service," *Labour Gazette*, 67:492, Autumn 1967.

1408. "Women in the federal service," *Labour Gazette*, 68:630-4, Nov. 1968.

1409. "Women must change attitudes to get equal breaks," *University Affairs*, 13:12-13, Apr. 1972.

CIVIL SERVICE - ALBERTA

1410. Reich, Carol. *Occupational segregation and its effects: a study of women in the Alberta Public Service*. [Edmonton]: Alberta. Human Rights Commission, 1979. 203p. and app.

CIVIL SERVICE - BRITISH COLUMBIA

1411. British Columbia. Task Force on Women's Issues. *A future for women: a proposal for an equal employment opportunity program for women in the Attorney General's department*. Victoria: British Columbia. Dept. of the Attorney-General, 1976. 43p.

CIVIL SERVICE - MANITOBA

1412. Cooper, Joy and others. *Women in the Manitoba civil service*. Winnipeg: Manitoba. Planning and Priorities Committee of the Cabinet Secretariat, 1975. 124p. (Profile 76-0053)

1413. Manitoba. Task Force on Equal Opportunities in the Civil Service of Manitoba. *Report*. Submitted to the Hon. A. R. Paulley, Minister of Labour. Winnipeg: Manitoba. Civil Service Commission, 1974. 82p. (Profile 74-0088)

CIVIL SERVICE - ONTARIO

1414. Fraser, Sylvia. "Laura Sabia: not exactly mom and apple pie," *Chatelaine*, 48:54-5, 98, 100, 102-4, 106, Nov. 1975.

1415. Ontario. Civil Service Commission and Ontario. Women Crown Employees Office. *Selection process in the Ontario Civil Service: equality of opportunity for employment.* Toronto, [1979]. 5p.

1416. Ontario. Ministry of Culture and Recreation. Office of the Women's Advisor. *Affirmative action program.* Toronto, 1979. [10]p.

1417. Ontario. Ministry of Labour. Office of the Executive Coordinator, Women's Programs. *Report of the Executive Coordinator of Women's Programs on the status of women Crown employees in Ontario.* Toronto, 1974/75- . Annual.
　　　　Issued also in abridged edition.

1418. Ontario. Ministry of Labour. Women Crown Employees Office. *Comparative survey of pregnancy and maternity policies in the provincial governments of Canada and Ontario crown agencies.* [Toronto], 1974. 54p. (Profile 76-0245)

1419. _____. *Guideline for ministries and crown agencies of the Ontario government on affirmative action for women crown employees.* Toronto, 1974. 8p.

1420. _____. *Status of women crown employees. Report.* 8th, 1981/82. [*Toronto, 1982*]. 136p. and app. (Microlog 83-3006)

1421. _____. *Summary report of maternity leave in the Ontario Public Service: survey results for 1976-77*, prepared by Dawna Burt and Sharon Peregrine. Toronto, 1978. 39p.

1422. _____. *Report on two-month survey of competition statistics.* Toronto, 1975. 21p. (Profile 76-0244)

1423. _____. *Women Crown Employees Office: a place for action and a plan for action.* 1974. Folder.

CIVIL SERVICE - QUEBEC

1424. De Sève, Michel et Marlen Carter. "Les inégalités salariales entre les travailleurs féminins et masculins: effet de qualification ou effet de statut?" *Recherches sociographiques*, 21:253-82, sept.-déc. 1980.

1425. Gagnon, Lysiane. *Les femmes, c'est pas pareil.* Montréal: Éditions de la Presse, 1976. 36p.

1426. Québec. Conseil du statut de la femme. *Programme d'égalité de chances à la fonction publique du Québec.* Québec, 1974. 29p. and app.

1427. Garneau, Hélène. "Le statut de la femme dans la fonction publique québécoise." MA thèse, Université Laval, 1977. 142p. (Can. theses, no.39137)

1428. Gosselin, Hélène. "Signification des activités de travail (professionnelles) et hors travail (extra-professionnelles) pour des femmes occupant certains postes de professionnelles à la Fonction Publique du Québec." MScSoc thèse, Université Laval, 1978. 155, [50]p. (Can. theses, no.39141)

1429. Québec. Conseil du statut de la femme. *Programme d'égalité de chances à la fonction publique du Québec.* Québec, 1974. 29, 8p.

1430. Québec. Ministère de la Fonction publique. Programmes égalité des chances. *Égalité en emploi pour les femmes dans la fonction publique.* Québec, 1980. 12p. (Microlog 81-0270)

1431. _____. Programmes égalité des chances. *Présence des femmes et des hommes dans la fonction publique du Québec. Vol. 1.* [Québec], 1980. 313p.

1432. Québec. Ministère des affairs sociales. Direction du personnel. *Égalité des chances pour les femmes au Ministère des affairs sociales: plan d'action, 1980/81- .* [Québec], 1980- . Annual.

CLOTHING WORKERS

1433. Baril, Michèle. "Women in the textile industry: an interview with Yvette Rousseau," *Branching Out*, 4:10-11, Mar.-Apr. 1977.

1434. Berlin, Simon, Paul Jones and Janet Jorge. "Decline of a union," *Canadian Dimension*, 12(7):40-7, [1978].

1435. Brandt, Gail Cuthbert. "Industry's handmaidens: women in the Quebec cotton industry," *Canadian Women's Studies / Les cahiers de la femme*, 3(1):79-82, 1981.

56

1436. Gauthier, Gilles. "Les midinettes de Montréal: entrevue accordée par Gilles Gauthier," *Canadian Women's Studies / Les cahiers de la femme*, 1:58-63, Winter 1978-79.
1437. "ILGU Women's Year seminar," *Canadian Labour*, 20:26-7, 36, June 1975.
1438. Ligue des femmes du Québec. *De fil en aiguille*. Montréal, [1980]. 12p.
1439. Murphy, Pat. "A Portuguese garment worker talks about her work and her union," *Rikka*, 7:42-4, Spring 1980.
1440. Oikawa, Dulce. "Speaking 'garmentese'," *Branching Out*, 4:14, Mar.-Apr. 1977.
1441. Rouilland, Jacques. *Les travailleurs du coton au Québec 1900-1915*. Montréal: Presses de l'Université du Québec, 1974. 152p.
1442. Spink, Marilyn. "Factory women go to class," *Canadian Women's Studies / Les cahiers de la femme*, 1:31, Fall 1978.
1443. Szlamp, Terry. "Garment workers: a bleak future?" *Branching Out*, 4:12-14, Mar.-Apr. 1977.

CLUBS

1444. Desrosiers, Lise. "Touch of class at [Elmwood] women's club," *Financial Post*, 76:12, Feb. 20, 1982.
1445. "Feminism and fitness at 21 McGill," *Saturday Night*, 94:5-6, July-Aug. 1979.
1446. Harris Marjorie. "New clubbiness of women," *Chatelaine*, 55:66-7, 152+ , Apr. 1982.
1447. Hilts, Daniel. "Club where women come in by front door [Twenty-one McGill street]," *Financial Post*, 70:32, June 12, 1976.
1448. "Networking moves to classy quarters," *Globe & Mail*, Dec. 30, 1982, p.T1.
1449. "No women allowed [University Club of Vancouver]," *Time Canada*, 106:10, July, 1975.
1450. "Women's club strikes right mix," *Financial Times*, 65:12, Mar. 28, 1977.
1451. Zwarun, Suzan. "Turning the tables: a separate reality," *Maclean's*, 93:38b, Mar. 31, 1980.

COMMUNITY DEVELOPMENT AND ORGANIZATION

1452. Balderstone, Helen and others. *Women in the community*. Winnipeg: Manitoba. Dept. of Labour. Women's Bureau, 1975. 98p. (Profile 77-0097)
1453. Bilgin, Bahir. *The roles of women and community development*. Hicksville, N.Y.: Exposition Press, 1978. 43p.
1454. Ellis, Diane. "Women and economic development; Les femmes et le développement économique," *Status of Women News / Statut: Bulletin de la femme*, 5:14-16, [English]; 15-17, [French], Sept. 1978.
1455. Jacobson, Helga E. *How to study your own community: research from the perspective of woman*. Vancouver: Women's Research Centre, 1977. 20p.
1456. _____. Women in community studies and research: the practice of exclusion. Vancouver: Women's Research Centre, 1978. 11p.
     Address given to the Canadian Research Institute for the Advancement of Women,November 1978.
1457. Lawrence, Wendy. "Transportation: an innovative approach in Whitehorse," *Status of Women News*, 6:8, Winter 1979-80.
1458. National Workshop on the Concerns of Women in Shaping the Urban Environment. *Proceedings*, by Nan Griffiths and N.C.C. Women's Task Force. Ottawa: National Capital Commission, 1975. 42p.
     Cover title: Women in the urban environment. [La femme en milieu urban].
1459. Twidale, Peter. "Women-run bus line cures Whitehorse blues; Ligne d'autobus gérée par des femmes," *Transport Canada*, July/Aug., 1976, pp.4, 6+ , [English]; 5, 7+ , [French].
1460. Women's Research Centre. *Energy development and social institutions: community research from the perspective of women in northern communities impacted by the Alaska Highway Gas Pipeline*. Papers presented at The Human Side of Energy: 2nd International Forum, University of Alberta, August 16-19, 1981. 35p.

CONSTITUTION

1461. Canadian Abortion Rights Action League. "Brief to the Special Joint Committee of the Senate and of the House of Commons on the Constitution of Canada," in the committee's, *Minutes of proceedings and evidence*, no. 24, Dec. 11, 1980, pp.98-117.

1462. Canadian Advisory Council on the Status of Women. "Brief to the Special Joint Committee of the Senate and of the House of Commons on the Constitution of Canada," in the committee's, *Minutes of proceedings and evidence*, no. 9,Nov. 20, 1980, pp.123-52.

1463. _____. *Women and the constitution*, edited by Audrey Doerr and Micheline Carrier. Ottawa: Minister of Supply and Services, Canada. 1981. 223p.
  Papers prepared for the conference, 'Women and the constitution.' Contents: I. Women and constitutional renewal II. Entrenchment of rights for women III. Family law IV. Overlapping jurisdictions and women's issues V. Economic and social issues facing women.

1464. _____. *Women, human rights the constitution*, by Beverley Baines. Ottawa, 1980. 58p.

1465. Canadian Committee on Learning Opportunities for Women. "Brief to the Special Joint Committee of the Senate and of the House of Commons on the Constitution of Canada," in the committee's, *Minutes of proceedings and evidence*, no. 24, Dec. 11, 1980, pp.60-82.

1466. Canadian Congress for Learning Opportunities for Women. *Freedom to learn: comments on the proposed Canadian Charter of Rights and Freedoms*. Presented to The Special Joint Committee on the Constitution of Canada, Dec. 11, 1980. 12p.

1467. Chartrand, Larry. "Women against patriation," *Native People*, 14:1-2, Mar. 20, 1981.

1468. Eberts, Mary. "Women fight for place in debate," *Perception*, 4:27, Nov.-Dec. 1980.

1469. Hastings, Jane and Judith Lawrence. "Constitutional conference: Valentine's Day revenge," *Broadside*, 2:4, Mar. 1981.

1470. Hosek, Chaviva. "How women fought for equality," *Canadian Forum*, 63:6-14, May 1983.

1471. Indian Rights for Women Group. "Brief to the Special Joint Committee of the Senate and of the House of Commons on the Constitution of Canada," in the committee's, *Minutes of proceedings and evidence*, no. 17, Dec. 2, 1980, pp.83-103.

1472. Kates, Joanne. "Trudeau's new constitution," *Ms.*, 10:79-80, Aug. 1981.

1473. Kome, Penney. *The taking of 28: women challenge the Constitution*. Toronto: Women's Press, 1983.

1474. _____. "Anatomy of a lobby," *Saturday Night*, 98:9-11, Jan. 1983.

1475. _____. "Women and the Constitution conference," *Homemaker's Magazine*, 16:92, 92B+ , May 1981.

1476. _____. "Women and the constitutional renewal," *Homemaker's Magazine*, 16:152, 154+ , Apr. 1981.

1477. Lawrence, Judith and Jane Hastings. "Bill of Rights: one preposition for all," *Broadside*, 2:7, Dec. 1980/Jan. 1981.

1478. Macpherson, Kay. "Constitutional conference: women make it happen," *Broadside*, 2:5, Mar. 1981.

1479. McDonald, Lynn. "Charter of rights and the subjection of women," *Canadian Forum*, 61:17-18, June-July 1981.

1480. National Action Committee on the Status of Women. "Brief to the Special Joint Committee of the Senate and of the House of Commons on the Constitution of Canada," in the committee's, *Minutes of proceedings and evidence*, no. 9, Nov. 20, 1980, pp.57-75.

1481. National Association of Women and the Law. "Brief to the Special Joint Committee of the Senate and of the House of Commons on the Constitution of Canada," in the committee's, *Minutes of proceedings and evidence*, no. 22, Dec. 9, 1980, pp.50-73.

1482. Native Women's Association of Canada. "Brief to the Special Joint Committee of the Senate and of the House of Commons on the Constitution of Canada," in the committee's, *Minutes of proceedings and evidence*, no. 17, Dec. 2, 1980, pp.63-81.

1483. Ontario Native Women's Association. *What does the future hold for native women - aboriginal entitlement?* by Priscilla A. Simard. Thunder Bay, Ont.: Guide Printing & Publishing, 1982. Report of a conference, 1982.

1484. Richardson, Karen. "No Indian women...no Indian nation," *Ontario Indian*, 4:10-12, May 1981.

1485. Riley, Susan. "Up from the Cow Café," *Maclean's*, 94:32-3, Apr. 20, 1981.

1486. Simard, Priscilla. *Nations within a nation; an aboriginal right?* Report on the [Ontario Native Women's Association] Conference Proceedings, Nov. 12-14, 1982. Thunder Bay: Ontario Native Women's Association, 1983. 67p.

1487. "Women and the Constitution," *Atlantis*, 6:147-66, Spring 1981.

1488. "Women fearful of provincial override," *Globe & Mail*, Nov. 19, 1981, p.8.

1489. "Women mount campaign against charter," *Globe & Mail*, Nov. 21, 1981, p.14.

CONSUMERS

1490. "Advertisers who mass market to today's woman are 'doomed to failure'" *Marketing*, 86:17-18, June 8, 1981.

1491. Althoff, Roly. "Population dynamics and the 'old age' myth," *Marketing*, 86:15-16, June 8, 1981.

1492. Clements, George. "Marketers: why pay lip service to the 'ideal' or 'normal' family and ignore what's real?" *Marketing*, 83:14, 16, Jan. 30, 1978.

1493. "Clout of working women," *Marketing*, 84:3, Apr. 23, 1979.

1494. Craig, Sheri. "TV day: just one thing missing," *Marketing*, 85:3, 57, Nov. 10, 1980.

1495. Fisher, J. "Such are not the dreams of the everyday housewife," *Marketing*, 80:8, 10, Oct. 6, 1975.

1496. Foley, Christine. "Consumerism, consumption and Canadian feminism: 1900-1930." MA thesis, University of Toronto, 1979. 107p.

1497. Kaite, Berkeley. "The intimacy of commodities: social control, subjectivity and feminine hygiene." MA thesis, McMaster University, 1981. 182p. (Can. theses, no. 57036).

1498. Katz, Bill. "Hitting the target: the influence of lifestyle on women's media habits," *Marketing*, 85:20-2, 24+, Apr. 21, 1980.

1499. _____. "Time to tune in to changing 'mediastyle' of today's women," *Marketing*, 85:24-7, Mar. 10, 1980.

1500. "Lifestyle is where it's at, says researcher," *Marketing*, 87:8, Feb. 15, 1982.

1501. Marney, Jo. "Advertising research: reaching the new woman of today," *Marketing*, 87:9,Mar. 1, 1982.

1502. "New ways needed to woo working women," *Marketing*, 84:8, May 28, 1979.

1503. Payette, Lise. *Consommation et condition féminine: conférence prononcée devant les membres du Cercle des fermières de Ahuntsic,* [le] 21 nov. 1977. Québec: Québec. Cabinet du ministre, 1977. 29p.

1504. "Quebec women have different outlook, says study," *Marketing*, 81:5, 7, Oct. 25, 1976.

1505. "Working women are 'best-educated' buyers," *Marketing*, 84:12, Jan. 8, 1979.

1506. "Working women boost economy," *Marketing*, 84:14, Sept. 3, 1979.

1507. "Working women govern retailers' future," *Marketing*, 86:24, Mar. 9, 1981.

1508. "Working women, a force to be reckoned with," *Marketing*, 84:9, Nov. 26, 1979.

COUNSELLING

1509. British Columbia. Ministry of Education. Post-Secondary Dept. *Finding my own way; a guide for British Columbia users*. Victoria, 1981. 138p. (Microlog 82-2111)
    Manual for a telecourse based on a counselling course for women, "Contemporary woman: options and opportunities," produced by Carolyn Larsen and Lorna Cammaert.

1510. Canadian Committee on Learning Opportunities for Women. *Programme packages*. 1977.
    Descriptive essays of sample programs for women across Canada.

1511. Canadian Psychological Association. "Guidelines for therapy and counselling with women," *Ontario Psychologist*, 13:20-5, Apr. 1981.

1512.   Clarke, Marnie A. "Transitional women: implications for adult educators," *Adult Leadership*, 24:123-7, Dec. 1975.

1513.   "Counselling and personhood," in Canadian Research Institute for the Advancement of Women, *Women as persons. [La femme en tant que personne]*. Toronto: Resources for Feminist Research, 1980, pp.110-18.
        Proceedings of the 3rd annual meeting.

1514.   David, Sarah Joy. "A decade of personal change," *Canadian Women's Studies / Les cahiers de la femme*, 2(2):74-5, 1980.

1515.   Doyon, Helen and Pat Hacker. "Feminist career counselling - an account of one successful experience," *Canadian Women's Studies / Les cahiers de la femme*, 1:12-14, Winter 1978-1979.

1516.   Egger, Larry Robert. "The effects of a training program designed for the contemporary woman, on attitudes toward self, children and child-bearing." MSc thesis, University of Calgary, 1978. 123p. (Can. theses, no.42000)

1517.   Griffith, Alison. "Feminist counselling," *School Guidance Worker*, 31:21-4, Sept.-Oct. 1975.

1518.   Jacobs, Bryna. "Sex differences in psychiatric diagnosis and treatment." MA thesis, McMaster University, 1980. 234p.

1519.   James, Alice. "The Women's Resources Centre - 1974." MA thesis, University of British Columbia, 1975. 85p. (Can. theses, no.25886)

1520.   Kennedy, M. Sandra L. "The effect on persuasibility of the client's self-esteem, his or her sex and the sex of the counseller." DEd diss., McGill University, 1975. 140p. (Can. theses, no.24350)

1521.   Kinzel, Mary Kathleen. "A study of the influence of sex-role stereotypes on marriage counsellors' personal and clinical evaluations of their clients." MA thesis, University of Regina, 1974. 272p. (Can. theses, no.23642)

1522.   Krakauer, Renate. *Career development workshop for women: outline*. Toronto: Ontario. Ministry of Labour. Women's Bureau, 1978. 20p. and app.

1523.   Larsen, Carolyn and Lorna Cammaert. *A follow-up study on contemporary women: a group counselling program for women on assistance*. Calgary: University of Calgary. Student Counselling Services, 1975. 27p. and app.

1524.   Levine, Helen. "Feminist counselling," *Canadian Dimension*, 13:32-6, May 1979.

1525.   Lord, Catherine. "Femmes: sois folle et tais-toi," *Le Maclean*, 16:42, janv. 1976.

1526.   Loughner-Gillin, Cheryl. "Sex of the therapist: an exploration of competence attributions as a function of therapists's gender." PhD diss., University of Windsor, 1981. 92p. (Can. theses, no.51202)

1527.   Mitchell, Samuel. *Report on the survey of Calgary women for the Alberta Human Research Council*. [Calgary?], 1972. 131p.

1528.   Myhr, Ronald Peder. "Sex-role and counsellor evaluation." PhD diss., University of Toronto, 1976. 151p. (Can. theses, no.30350)

1529.   Nadeau, Denise. "Women and self-help in resource-based communities," *Resources for Feminist Research*, 11:65-7, Mar. 1982.

1530.   Pendergast, Barbara. "Specialized counseling for women." MA thesis, University of Victoria, 1975. 89p. (Can. theses, no.27323)

1531.   Robertson, Joann. "A treatment model for post-partum depression," *Canada's Mental Health*, 28:16-17, June 1980.

1532.   Roney, Bronwen. "Self-actualization and marital adjustment scores of adult women as affected by a group counselling program." MSc thesis, University of Calgary, 1975. 74p. (Can. theses, no.23775)

1533.   Simpkins, Joan. *Counselling services: profile and follow-up*. Winnipeg: Manitoba. Dept. of Labour. Women's Bureau, 1976. 15p.

1534.   Thom, Patricia, Anne Ironside and Eileen Hendry. "The Women's Resources Centre: an educational model for counselling women," *Adult Leadership*, 24:129-32, Dec. 1975.

1535.   Women's Counselling Collective. *Report of a research project, sponsored by the Women's Faculty and Staff Group of the Maritime School of Social Work*. [Halifax, N.S.], 1981. 58p. and app.A-D.

CREDIT

1536. Berkeley, Ann. "Women: the great credit-ability gap," *Chatelaine*, 48:24, 63-5, Aug. 1975.

1537. Daley, Pat. "The Ottawa Women's Credit Union: a banking alternative," *Perception*, 4:32-4, Nov.-Dec. 1980.

1538. "Equal credit opportunity guidelines," *Ontario Credit Union News*, 38:12, Dec.-Jan. 1976.

1539. First National Farm Women's Conference. *"Credit where credit is due": women and farm credit in Canada*. Status of Rural Women Project. [Ottawa], 1980. 21,[7]p.

    French edition: *"Le crédit à qui en a besoin." Les femmes et le crédit agricole au Canada*.

1540. Glenister, Betty. *Women and credit*. [Halifax]: Nova Scotia. Human Rights Commission, [1976]. [72]p. (Profile 76-0951)

1541. Goldenberg, S. "Credit: a major problem for women," *Financial Post*, 68:E8, Apr. 13, 1974.

1542. Hipwell, Anne. "Women must know credit rights to beat discrimination," *Financial Post*, 73:33, Apr. 28, 1979.

1543. Kryzanowski, Lawrence and Elizabeth Bertin-Boussu. "Equal access to credit: lenders' attitudes toward an applicant's sex and marital status," *International Journal of Women's Studies*, 4:213-33, May-June 1981.

1544. Lipkin, Mary Jane. "Brawn not brain: women & farm credit in Canada," *Canadian Woman Studies / Les cahiers de la femme*, 3:53-6, Summer 1982.

1545. "Lock, stock and filing cabinet," *Broadside*, 3:2, Apr. 1982.

1546. Masters, Philinda. "Toronto Women's Credit Union: merging ahead?" *Broadside*, 2:5, June 1981.

1547. "Metro Toronto Women's C.U. a first in Canada," *Ontario Credit Union News*, 38:9, Dec.-Jan. 1976.

1548. Noonan, P. "Women and credit," *Chitty's Law Journal*, 21:220-2, 1973.

1549. Ontario. Ministry of Consumer and Commercial Relations. *Credit and you: women's access to credit in Ontario*. Toronto, 1976. 15p.

1550. O'Leary, Patricia. "Giving women credit where it's due," *Branching Out*, 3:15-16, Apr.-June 1976.

1551. "Separate credit files recommended for wives," *Globe & Mail*, Oct. 22, 1977, p.B1.

1552. Stoffman, Judith. "Men must begin to give credit to women," *Financial Post*, 70:C6, Jan. 31, 1976.

1553. Townson, Monica. "Family laws make lenders cautious," *Financial Post*, 76:16, Jan. 16, 1982.

1554. Whittingham, Anthony. "Ontario pushes equal credit for women," *Financial Post*, 69:1, 4, Nov. 15, 1975.

1555. "Women & credit," *Ontario Credit Union News*, 37:9, Nov. 1975.

1556. Zaremba, Eve. "Caught in the squeeze: Women's Credit Union," *Broadside*, 2:4, Feb. 1981.

CRIME AND CRIMINALS

1557. Bell, Lorna E. "Effects of sex of juror, sex of defendant, and sex of victim on the decisions of simulated jurors." MA thesis, University of Windsor, 1979. 94p. (Can. theses, no.41930)

1558. Benson, Margaret. *Admission to the Provincial Correctional Centre for Women in Ontario*. Adult female offenders. Working paper, no. 5. Toronto: Elizabeth Fry Society, 1971. 111p.

1559. _____. *Adult female offenders: an examination of the nature of their offences: the criminal process and service patterns: [summary of findings of seven independent but related research studies]*. [Ottawa: Solicitor General of Canada, 1974?] 35, 46p.

1560. _____. *Fines imposed on women in the provincial courts, Toronto*. Adult female offenders. Working paper, no. 7. Toronto: Elizabeth Fry Society, 1973. 44p.

1561. _____. *From arrest to trial for female offenders appearing in the former magistrates' courts in Toronto from September 1961 to February 1962*. Adult female offenders. Working paper, no. 2. Toronto: Elizabeth Fry Society, [1969?]. 47p.

1562. _____. "Special problems related to the adult female offender," *Canadian Journal of Corrections*, 10:206-16, Jan. 1968.

1553. _____. *Statistics of criminal and other offences as related to adult women convicted in Canada with special reference to Ontario and York County*. Adult female offenders. Working paper no. 1. Toronto: Elizabeth Fry Society, 1968. 58p.

1564. _____. *The Elizabeth Fry Society, Toronto: clients, contact patterns and agency services*. Adult female offenders. Working paper, no. 6. Toronto: Elizabeth Fry Society, 1973. 115p.

1565. _____. *Women on probation in Metropolitan Toronto*. Adult female offenders. Working paper, no. 3. Toronto: Elizabeth Fry Society, [1975?]. 82p.

1566. Bertrand, Marie-Andrée. *La femme & le crime*. Montréal: L'Aurore, 1979. 224p.

1567. _____. "*L'augmentation accelérée de la criminalité des femmes*," *Atlantis*, 3:63-71, Spring 1978, Part II.

1568. Bienvenue, Rita and A. H. Latif. "Arrests, disposition and recidivism: a comparison of Indians and Whites," *Canadian Journal of Corrections*, 16(2):105-16, 1974.

1569. Biron, Louise, Rosette Gagnon et Marc LeBlanc. *La délinquance des filles*. Inadaptation juvénile cahier 3. Montréal: Université de Montréal. Groupe de recherche sur l'inadaptation juvénile, 1980. 208p.

1570. Canada. National Advisory Committee on the Female Offender. *The female offender - selected statistics*. [Ottawa]: Canada. Solicitor General, 1977. 34p.
Preliminary report prepared as a statistical appendix to the report of the committee.

1571. Canadian Corrections Association. *Brief on the woman offender*. Royal Commission on the Status of Women in Canada. Brief no. 398. Ottawa, 1968. 56p. and app.

1572. Chimbos, Peter D. "Marital violence: a study of husband-wife homicide," in K. Ishwaran, *The Canadian family*. Rev. ed. Toronto: Holt, Rinehart and Winston of Canada, 1976, pp.580-99.

1573. _____. "Marital violence: a study of interspouse homicide." PhD diss., York University, 1976. 233p. (Can. theses, no.26616)

1574. Denys, Rudi G. "Lady paperhangers," in W. E. Mann, ed., *Social deviance in Canada*. Vancouver: Copp Clark, 1971, pp.110-27.

1575. _____. "'Lady paperhangers': a study of the relationships of 'lady paperhangers' to five social institutions." MA thesis, University of Toronto, 1968. 138p.

1576. Dubec, Bernice. *Native women and the criminal justice system: an increasing minority*. [Thunder Bay, Ont.]: Ontario Native Women's Association, 1982. 50p. and app.

1577. Fox, John and Timothy F. Hartnagel. "Changing social roles and female crime in Canada," in Robert A. Silverman and James J. Teevan, eds., *Crime in Canadian society*. 2d ed. Toronto: Butterworths, 1980, pp.369-78.

1578. _____. "Changing social roles and female crime in Canada: a crime series analysis," *Canadian Review of Sociology and Anthropology*, 16(1):96-104, 1979.

1579. Gillan, Mary Ellen and Brenda J. Thomas. "Law: the forgotten offenders," *Branching Out*, 5(3):30-3, 1978.

1580. Gilmore, Alan and Gustave Oki. *The female chronic drunkenness offender*. The chronic drunkenness offender. Chapter XIX. Toronto: Addiction Research Foundation, 1972. 135p.

1581. Gray, Charlotte. "Raging female hormones in the courts: several cases boost legal recognition for premenstrual syndrome as a factor in female crime," *Maclean's*, 94:46-7, 49, June 15, 1981.

1582. Greenland, Cyril and Ellen Rosenblatt. "Female crimes of violence," *Canadian Journal of Corrections*, 16(2):173-80, 1974.

1583. Griffiths, Curt Taylor and Margit Nance, eds. *The female offender: selected papers from an international symposium*. Burnaby, B.C.: Simon Fraser University. Criminology Research Centre, 1980. 331p.

1584. Hagan, John and Nancy O'Donnel. "Sexual stereotyping and judicial sentencing: a legal test of the sociological wisdom," *Canadian Journal of Sociology*, 3:309-19, Summer 1978.

1585. Hartnagel, Timothy F. "The effect of age and sex compositions of provincial populations on provincial crime rates," *Canadian Journal of Criminology*, 20:28-33, Jan. 1978.

1586. Haslam, P. "The woman offender." Address delivered at the annual meeting of the John Howard Society of Ontario, Apr. 30, 1970.

1587. Haslam, Phyllis G. "The woman offender," in W. T. McGrath, ed., *Crime and its treatment in Canada*. 2nd ed. Toronto: Macmillan of Canada, 1976, pp.470-82.

1588. Henriksen, Sheila P. "Personality and deviance: a study of female prisoners and welfare recipients." MA thesis, Queen's University, 1972. 120p. and app. (Can. theses, no.15012)

1589. Lambert, Leah R. and Patrick G. Madden. *The adult female offender before-during-after incarceration*. Vanier Centre research report, no. 3. Toronto: Ontario. Ministry of Correctional Services, 1975. 114p. (Profile 76-0416)

1590. _____. "The adult female offender: the road from institution to community life," *Canadian Journal of Criminology and Corrections*, 18:319-31, 1976.

1591. Landau, Barbara. "Adolescent female offender: our dilemma," *Canadian Journal of Criminology and Corrections*, 17:146-53, April 1975.

1592. Lawson, Darlene. "Women shut up," *Broadside*, 1(6):11, 1980.

1593. Layton, Monique. "Street women and their verbal transactions: some aspects of the oral culture of female prostitute drug addicts." PhD diss., University of British Columbia, 1978. 264p. (Can. theses, no.37662)

1594. Lindsay, Peter H. and Peggy Ann Walpole. "Crimes of violence and the female offender," in Mary A. B. Gammon, ed., *Violence in Canada*. Toronto: Methuen, 1978, pp.40-50.

1595. Lord, Catherine. "Le crime au féminin," *Le Maclean*, 16:15, avr. 1976.

1596. McCaldon, R. J. "Lady paperhangers," *Canadian Journal of Corrections*, 9:243-56, [July] 1967.

1597. Nova Scotia. Dept. of Attorney General. *The female offender, Nova Scotia and New Brunswick*. [Halifax]: Nova Scotia. Dept. of Attorney General. Correctional Services / New Brunswick. Dept. of Justice. Correctional Services, 1977. 90p. and tables.

1598. Reid, Linda. *The self concept of the adult female offender*. Adult female offenders. Working paper, no. 4. Toronto: Elizabeth Fry Society, 1971. 86p.

1599. Russell, Mary. "Groups for women who shoplift," *Canadian Journal of Criminology*, 20:73-4, Jan. 1978.

1600. Taylor, K. Wayne, Neena L. Chappell, and Stephen Brickey. "A critical comment on Hagan and O'Donnell's 'Sexual stereotyping and judicial sentencing: a legal test of the sociological wisdom'," *Canadian Journal of Sociology*, 5:55-61, Winter 1980.

1601. "The female offender," *Liaison*, 5, no. 2, 1979 (Special issue).

1602. Townesend, Michael. *Study of rehabilitative halfway house program for women of previously inadequate social performance*. Vancouver: Elizabeth Fry Society of British Columbia, 1972. 19p.

1603. Travis, Gail Lesley. "The courtroom experience as perceived by the female appearing on a first charge of shoplifting." MA thesis, University of Toronto, 1975. 101p.

1604. Walshaw, Anne. "Women and crime as a social problem," in W. E. Mann, ed., *Social deviance in Canada*. Vancouver: Copp Clark, 1971, pp.98-109.

DANCERS, BURLESQUE

1605. Daly, Janis. "Canadian Association of Burlesque Entertainers," *Broadside*, 1(2):9, 1979.
1606. Withdrawn.

1607. McLean, Anne. "Taking it off: a strip act with a difference," *Branching Out*, 4:18-19, Sept.-Oct. 1977.
1608. Michaels, Diane. "'Pulling our own strings': Diane Michaels in conversation with Constance Brissenden [interview]," *Fireweed*, 7:77-82, Summer 1980.
1609. Paquin, Carole. *Une esclave bien payée*. Montréal: Les Editions Quinze, 1978. 165p.
1610. Withdrawn.
1611. Salutin, Marilyn. "Stripper morality," in C. L. Boydell, C. F. Grindstaff and P. C. Whitehead, eds., *Deviant behaviour and societal reaction*. Toronto: Holt, Rinehart & Winston, 1972, pp.532-45.

DAY CARE

1612. Adams, David. "Among society's neglected - the working mother," *Canadian Welfare*, 46:18-19, July-Aug. 1970.
1613. Anderson, Doris. "Three good ideas we can't afford to cut," *Chatelaine*, 49:2, May 1976.
1614. Baar, E. "Provincial regulation of day care: child protection or child growth?" *Canadian Welfare*, 49:12-17, Mar.-Apr. 1973.
1615. Bella, Leslie. "Day care: view from the top," *Branching Out*, 4:11-14, May-June 1977.
1616. Cameron, Barb and others. *Day care book*. Toronto: Canadian Women's Educational Press, [1972]. 48p.
1617. Canada. Dept. of Labour. Women's Bureau. *Working mothers and their child-care arrangements*. Ottawa, 1970. 58p.
1618. Canada. Dept. of National Health and Welfare. *Canadian day care survey*. Ottawa, 1972. 24p.
1619. _____. *Day care: a resource for the contemporary family*. Papers and proceedings of a seminar, Ottawa, Sept. 1969. Ottawa, 1974. 70p.
1620. _____. *Policy guidelines relating to the provision of day care services for children under the Canada Assistance Plan*. Ottawa, 1974. 10p.
1621. Canadian Council on Social Development. "National guidelines for developing day care services," *Canadian Welfare*, 49:21-3, Sept.-Oct. 1973.
1622. "Chatelaine day-care survey results," *Chatelaine*, 50:14, Aug. 1977.
1623. Citizen's Committee on Children. Committee of the Day Care Section. *Brief no. 324 to the Royal Commission on the Status of Women in Canada*. Ottawa, 1968. 8p.
1624. "CLC urges local day-care centres," *Canadian Library Journal*, 13:40, Oct. 1968.
1625. Davidson, Jane. "Will companies become baby-sitters, too?" *Financial Post*, 66:1, 8, July 15, 1972.
1626. "Day care centres," *World Affairs*, 34:12-13, Nov. 1968.
1627. "Day care debate," *Canadian Consumer*, 12:34, June 1982.
1628. "Day care: 1980 update," *Perception*, 5:11, Feb. 1982.
1629. Family Planning Federation of Canada. Brief no.15 to the Royal Commission on the Status of Women in Canada. Montreal, n.d. 4p.
1630. Gentleman, Ainslee Gail. "Decision factors in parents' choice of a child care arrangement." MSc thesis, University of Guelph, 1979. 162p. (Can. theses, no.43795)
1631. Hepworth, Philip. *600,000 children: report of a survey of day care needs in Canada*. n.p., [1975?] 12p.
1632. Hepworth, P. "600,000 children: report of a survey of day care needs in Canada," *Canadian Welfare*, 50:10-13, Nov.-Dec. 1974.
1633. Herzog, Carol. "Company daycare can pay dividends," *Financial Post*, 75:20, July 25, 1981.
1634. _____. "Day-care issues fast becoming management's," *Financial Post*, 75:4, Jan. 31, 1981.
1635. Johnson, Laura Climenko and Janice Dineen. *The kin trade: the day care crisis in Canada*. Toronto: McGraw-Hill Ryerson, 1981. 147p.
1636. Johnson, Laura Climenko. *The search for child care*. Project child care working paper, no. 3. Toronto: Project Child Care, 1978. 22p.

64

1637.	_____. *Who cares? A report of the project child care survey of parents and their child care arrangements*. Toronto: Project Child Care, 1977. 287p.

1638.	_____. "A decade of day care in Canada: women & children last," *Canadian Women's Studies / Les cahiers de la femme*, 2(2):51-2, 1980.

1639.	Kerwin, P. "Canadian day care survey [and] the day care book," *Canadian Labour*, 18:33, March, 1973.

1640.	Kidd, Joanna. "Caring for the little children: as the demand for day care heightens, canny entrepreneurs flood in to fill the void," *Maclean's*, 94:66, 69-70, Dec. 7, 1981.

1641.	Lange, Linda. "Daycare and the union movement [conference]," *Canadian Dimension*, 14:16-17, Aug. 1980.

1642.	MacKeracher, Dorothy. *Roadblocks to women's learning: issues for advocacy*. [Toronto: Canadian Committee on Learning Opportunities for Women, 1978]. [172]p.
		Consists of the following units: Unit 1, Introduction; Unit II, Day Care Services; Unit III, Employment (Manpower) and Immigration.

1643.	McGowan, Shirley and others. *Childreach; an exploratory, descriptive study of day care needs in the city of London*. Presented to the Day Care Services Committee of United Community Services of Greater London. [London, Ont.], 1974. 62p.

1644.	McGowan, Shirley. "New extended family: an orientation towards the care and education of young children," *Canada's Mental Health*, 23:3-6, Sept. 1975, suppl.

1645.	McLeod, E. M. *A study of child care services at Canadian universities*. Ottawa: Association of Universities and Colleges of Canada, 1975. 44p. (Canedex 76-0007)
		French edition: Une étude sur les services de garderie dans les universités canadiennes.

1646.	Nursery Education Association of Ontario. *Brief no. 436 to the Royal Commission on the Status of Women in Canada*. Ottawa, n.d. 14p.

1647.	Pappert, Ann. "In search of quality child care," *Homemakers' Magazine*, 17:96H, 96J, Oct. 1982.

1648.	Pioneer Women's Organization of Canada. *Brief no. 65 to the Royal Commission on the Status of Women in Canada*. Montreal, 1968. 12p.

1649.	Pringle, Brenda. "Minding the children," *Canadian Dimension*, 12(7):39-40, [1978].

1650.	"Reductions in day care standards may be poor economy," *Canadian Welfare*, 50:23-4, Sept.-Oct. 1974.

1651.	Ross, Kathleen Gallagher, ed. *Good day care: fighting for it, getting it, keeping it*. Toronto: Women's Press, 1978. 223p.

1652.	Sales, Judith. "Cooperative preschool associations: apprenticeship for what?" *Canadian Women's Studies / Les cahiers de la femme*, 2(1):35-6, 1980.

1653.	Saskatchewan. Dept. of Labour. Women's Division. *Childcare needs of working women*. Regina, 1978. 11p.

1654.	Shumiatcher, M. C. "Movement for L.I.F.E. - a revolution in embryo," *Canada Month*, 12(5):13-14, 1972.

1655.	"The poor mother and child - day-care centres," in Canada. Senate. Special Senate Committee on Poverty, *Poverty in Canada*. Ottawa: Information Canada, 1971, pp.155-65.

1656.	"Working mothers and their child care arrangements in Canada, 1973," *Labour Force* [*Statistics Canada*], 31:83-91, Sept. 1975.

1657.	"Working mothers' child care study released," *Canadian Welfare*, 46:23, July-Aug. 1970.

DAY CARE - ALBERTA

1658.	Brunelle, Heather. "'Down here with us parents'," *Branching Out*, 4:11-14, May-June 1977.

1659.	Calgary Social Planning Council. *A study of day care needs in Calgary*. Calgary, Alta., n.d.

1660. Edmonton Social Services. *Policy guidelines regarding the expansion of day care services in Edmonton.* Edmonton, 1975. 27p. and app. A & B
    Appendix A, Analysis of the need for expanded day care services in the city of Edmonton; Appendix B, Position paper on after school care.

1661. Edmonton Welfare Council. *Brief to the city of Edmonton on the establishment of day care services.* Edmonton, Alta., 1966. 13p.

1662. Family Service Association of Edmonton. *Day care brief.* Edmonton, Alta., 1966. 2p.

DAY CARE - BIBLIOGRAPHY

1663. Canada. Dept. of National Health and Welfare. National Day Care Information Centre. *Day care: guide to reading. [Garde de jour: guide du lecteur].* Ottawa, 1975. 168p.

1664. Canadian Welfare Council. Research Branch. *The day care of children: an annotated bibliography.* Ottawa, 1969. 68p.

1665. "Employer-sponsored day care: a selected bibliography," *Labour Topics (Ontario Ministry of Labour Library)*, 5:1-4, May 1982.

DAY CARE - BRITISH COLUMBIA

1666. Alperovitz, Cath and Women's Research Centre. *Overview of child care in B. C., 1971-1977.* [Vancouver]: Women's Research Centre, [1978?] 9p.

1667. Cohen, Marcy and others. *Cuz there ain't no daycare (or almost none she said): a book about daycare in B.C.* [Vancouver: Press Gang Publishers], 1973. 128p.

1668. United Community Services of the Greater Vancouver Area. *Day care services for working mothers.* Royal Commission on the Status of Women in Canada. Brief no. 105. Vancouver, 1968. 11p.

1669. Vancouver Welfare and Recreation Council. *Report on day care needs.* Vancouver, 1965. 22p.

DAY CARE - MANITOBA

1670. Epstein, Joyce. *Day care: a research report to the Community Day Care Study Commission.* [Winnipeg]: University of Winnipeg. Institute of Urban Studies, 1979. 103p.

1671. Family Bureau of Greater Winnipeg. *Brief no. 298 to the Royal Commission on the Status of Women in Canada.* Winnipeg, 1968. 22p. and app.

1672. Manitoba. Dept. of Labour. Women's Bureau. *Mothers in the labour force: their child care arrangements.* Winnipeg, 1974. [39p.] and app. (Profile 75-0198)

1673. Simpkins, Joan and others. *Employment in day care.* Winnipeg: Manitoba. Dept. of Labour. Women's Bureau, 1976. 23p. (Profile 77-0277)

DAY CARE - NEW BRUNSWICK

1674. New Brunswick. Advisory Council on the Status of Women. *Day care: a support service to the contemporary family.* Brief to the Hon. Leslie I. Hull, Minister of Social Services. [Moncton, N.B.], 1981. [23]p.

1675. University of New Brunswick. Faculty of Law. Women and the Law Project. *Day care in New Brunswick.* Moncton, N. B.: New Brunswick Advisory Council on the Status of Women, 1979. 19p. (Microlog 80-1619)

DAY CARE - NOVA SCOTIA

1676. Marra, Glenna. "When mothers work: their need for child care services." MA thesis, Dalhousie University, 1977. 147p. (Can. theses, no.36137)

1677. Community Information Centre of Metropolitan Toronto. *Survey of inquiries relating to full-day care of children August 17 to September 12, 1981.* Toronto, 1981. 34p.

66

DAY CARE - ONTARIO

1678. Dineen, Jacqueline. *A study of the problems of the working mother and the need for adequate day care*. Royal Commission on the Status of Women in Canada. Brief no. 341. Toronto, 1967. 15p.

1679. Fancy, Gail P. "Working mothers and private day nurseries: with special emphasis on day care as a service for pre-school children." MSW thesis, University of Toronto, 1965. 133p.

1680. Herzog, Carol. "Daycare funding increased [Toronto]," *Financial Post*, 74:4, Aug. 30, 1980.

1681. Krashinsky, Michael. *Day care and public policy in Ontario*. Ontario Economic Council research studies, no. 11. Toronto: University of Toronto Press for Ontario Economic Council, 1977. 139p.

1682. Leah, Ronnie. "Women's labour force participation and day care cutbacks in Ontario," *Atlantis*, 7:36-44, Fall 1981.

1683. Li, Selina. *Between neighbours, between kin: a study of private child care arrangements in Metropolitan Toronto*. Toronto: Project Child Care, 1978. 106p.

1684. Lightman, Ernie S. and Laura C. Johnson. *Child care patterns in Metropolitan Toronto*. Project Child Care working paper, no. 2. Toronto: Social Planning Council of Metropolitan Toronto. Project Child Care, 1977. 48p. (Urban Canada 78-4126)

1685. Li, Selina. *Options for single mothers*. Project Child Care working paper, no. 4. Toronto: Project Child Care, 1978. 44p.

1686. Manson, Freda. "Day care facilities and services for children of employed mothers," in *Report of a consultation on the employment of women with family responsibilities*. Ottawa: Canada. Dept. of Labour. Women's Bureau, 1965, pp.13-19.

1687. McIntyre, Eilene Lifsha Goldberg. "The provision of day care in Ontario: responsiveness of provincial policy to children at risk because their mothers work." PhD diss., University of Toronto, 1979. 349p.

1688. Ontario Coalition for Better Daycare. *Daycare, deadline 1990: brief to the government of the province of Ontario on the future of daycare service in Ontario*. Don Mills, Ont.: Ontario Federation of Labour, 1981. 19p.

1689. Ontario. Ministry of Community and Social Services. *Day care policy: background paper*. Toronto, 1981. 65, [40]p.

1690. Ontario. Ministry of Community and Social Services. Advisory Council on Day Care. *Final Report*. Toronto, 1976. 46p. (Profile 76-0582)

1691. Ontario. Ministry of Labour. Women's Bureau. *Women in the labour force. "Child care"*. Factsheet, no. 4. Toronto, [1976]. [3]p.

1692. Ontario. Status of Women Council. Child Care Committee. *Towards expanding quality child care in Ontario: a plan for action*. [Toronto], 1978. 23p.

1693. Orr, Jody. *Planning for child care; a brief to the Ontario Federation of Labour Panel 'Sharing the caring.'* Hamilton, Ont.: Social Planning and Research Council of Hamilton and District, 1981. 12p.

1694. Pennock, Mike and Mark Goldenberg. *The utilization of day care services in Hamilton-Wentworth*. Hamilton, Ont.: Social Planning and Research Council of Hamilton and District, 1977. 13p. and app.

1695. Social Planning and Research Council of Hamilton and District. *Day care: some reactions to the policy changes, a statement adopted by the Board of Directors*. Hamilton, Ont.: The Council, 1974. 6p.

1696. Social Planning Council of Hamilton and District. *Nursery and day care centres*. Hamilton, Ont., 1965.

1697. Social Planning Council of Metropolitan Toronto. *Brief on day care services*. Toronto, 1967.

1698. _____. *The need for nursery and day care centres in the western section of the city*. Toronto, 1966. 9p.

1699. _____. *Report on family day care of children*. Toronto, 1966. 58p. and app.

1700. Social Planning Council of Ottawa and District. Committee on Day Care for Children. *Report 1965-1967*. Ottawa, [1967]. 76p.
1701. Toronto. Dept. of Social Services. Day Care Planning Task Force. *Future directions for day care services in Metro Toronto: Final report*. Presented to the Metropolitan Toronto Social Services and Housing Committee. Toronto, 1981. 141p.
1702. Toronto. Planning Council. Governing Committee. *Meeting day care needs in North York*. Toronto, 1966. 15p.
1703. Victoria Day Care Services. *Brief no. 168 to the Royal Commission on the Status of Women in Canada*. Toronto, 1968. 21p.
1704. Windsor Social Planning (A division of United Community Services). *A study of day care in the greater Windsor area*. Windsor, Ont., 1968.

DAY CARE - QUEBEC

1705. Conféderation des syndicats nationaux et le Syndicat canadien de la fonction publique. *Dossier garderies pour un réseau universel gratuit*. n.p., [1980?].
1706. Corporation des enseignants du Québec et Centrale de l'enseignement du Québec. *Condition féminine: XXIVième congrès de la Corporation des enseignants du Québec: 1er congrès de la Centrale de l'enseignement du Québec*.Québec: CEQ, 1974. 52p.
1707. Dumont-Johnson, Micheline. "Des garderies au XIXe siècle: les salles d'asile des Soeurs Grises à Montréal," *Revue d'histoire de l'Amérique française*, 34:27-55, juin 1980.
1708. Hétu, Renée. "Les mères en emploi et la garde de leurs enfants: une étude des dispositions prises par un groupe de mères au travail (paroisses St-Henri et St-Irénée) pour assurer la garde de leurs enfants pendant leurs heures ouvrées." MA thèse, Université de Montréal, 1966. 95p.
1709. Québec. Conseil du statut de la femme. *Position du Conseil du statut de la femme sur la question des garderies*. Québec, 1975. 4p.

DAY CARE - SASKATCHEWAN

1710. Burton Zenny. *Brief no. 211 to the Royal Commission on the Status of Women in Canada*. Regina, 1968. 10p. and app.
1711. Saskatchewan. Advisory Council on the Status of Women. *Brief on day care*. Saskatoon, 1980. 5p.
1712. Saskatchewan. Dept. of Labour. Women's Division.*Industry and day care*. Regina, 1978. 5p.
1713. Saskatchewan Federation of Labour, C.L.C. Women's Ad Hoc Committee. *Brief no. 296 to the Royal Commission on the Status of Women in Canada*. Regina, 1968. 11p. and app.
1714. Turner, Janice Shirlene. "Day care and women's labour force participation: an historical study." MA thesis, University of Regina, 1981. 231p. (Can. theses, no. 50667)
1715. University Women's Club of Regina. *Working mothers in Regina and their child care arrangements: a study*. n.p., 1975. 57p.

DESERTION AND NON-SUPPORT

1716. Canada. Dept. of National Health and Welfare. Planning and Evaluation Branch. Welfare Research Division. *Deserted wives and childrens' maintenance legislation in Canada*. Ottawa, 1973. 107p.
1717. Canadian Welfare Council. *A study of family desertion in Canada*. Report to the Royal Commission on the Status of Women in Canada. Ottawa, 1968. 93p. and app.
1718. Dranoff, Linda Silver. "Ask a lawyer," *Chatelaine*, 54:18, 20, Jan. 1981.
1719. Fodden, Simon. "Dependent wives and the requirement to sue," *Bulletin of Canadian Welfare Law*, 3:22-30, Spring 1974.
1720. Kieran, Sheila. "Women in the Crunch no. 1. The crunch: he left her with four kids and not enough money," *Chatelaine*, 48:41-3, 64-7, Feb. 1975.
1721. Silverman, H. W. "Deserted wife's dilemma," *Reports of Family Law*, 3:235-53, 1971.

68

DIRECTORIES

1722. *Annuaire des femmes de Montréal*. [Montréal]: Centre d'information et de référence pour femmes, [1982]- .
   Continues Montreal women's yellow pages.
1723. Bode, Carolyn. "How I spent my summer [Toronto Women's Yellow Pages]," *Branching Out*, 2:33-4, 43, Mar.-Apr. 1975.
1724. Bode, Carolyn, Larraine Brown and Mary Ann Kelly, eds. *Toronto women's yellow pages*. [Toronto]: Amazon Press, 1974. 48p.
1725. Canadian Federation of Business and Professional Women's Clubs. *List of women in public life in Canada*. Ottawa, 1975. v.p.
1726. *Federal services for women: a guide to federal programs, services and grants of interest to women, including special responsibility centres*. Ottawa: Information Canada, 1975. 63p.
1727. *Guide to the B.C. women's movement*. Vancouver: Western Canadian Women's News, 1975. 27p.
1728. *Montreal women's yellow pages*. [Montreal, Que.: Feminist Communication Collection, 1973-].
   French edition: *Les pages jaunes des femmes de Montréal*.
1729. Ottawa Women's Network. *Directory of women's groups within Ottawa-Carleton*. [*Répertoire des groupes de femmes d'Ottawa-Carleton*]. Ottawa, 1982. [88, 87]p.

DISCRIMINATION

1730. Aitchison, Douglas Wayne. "Sexism and sexual discrimination." PhD diss., University of Waterloo, 1978. 150p. (Can. theses, no.36196)
1731. Bayefsky, Anne. "The Jamaican women case and the Canadian Human Rights Act: is government subject to the principle of equal opportunity?" *University of Western Ontario Law Review*, 18:461-92, 1980.
1732. Canada. Employment and Immigration Commission. Affirmative Action Division. *Provincial human rights legislation*, prepared by Noel A. Kinsella. Ottawa: Canada. Dept. of Employment and Immigration, 1980. 132p.
1733. *Convention on the elimination of all forms of discrimination against women. [Convention sur l'élimination de toutes les formes de discrimination à l'égard des femmes]*. A United Nations publication reprinted by the Human Rights Program, Dept. of Secretary of State, Ottawa, 1982. 12, 12p.
1734. Delta Kappa Gamma Society. Delta Chapter. *Brief no. 232 to the Royal Commission on the Status of Women in Canada*. Toronto, 1968. 11p. and app.
1735. Dranoff, Linda Silver. "Ask a lawyer," *Chatelaine*, 53:25-6, Sept. 1980.
1736. Dulude, Louise. "Sweet reason," *Branching Out*, 7(1):38, 1980.
1737. Dumont-Henry, Suzanne. "Les femmes ont-elles les mêmes chances?" *Prospectives*, 17:67-70, Apr. 1981.
1738. "Federal human rights bill introduces anti-discrimination provisions," *Information - Status of Women*, 1(2):1-2, 1977.
1739. Gelber, Sylva M. "Injustice to one - injustice to all," in, *Women's Bureau '72*. Ottawa: Canada. Dept. of Labour. Women's Bureau, 1973, pp.29-36.
1740. Gladstone, Bill and Joanne Kates. "Car repairs: his story / her story," *Chatelaine*, 52:44-5, 118+ , June 1979.
1741. Goldberg, Joel O. "Defensive styles and women's reactions to discrimination." MA thesis, University of Waterloo, 1981. 86p. (Can. theses, no.49780)
1742. Jacobson, Helga E. *Women in community studies and research: the practice of exclusion*. Vancouver: Women's Research Centre, 1978. 11p.
   Address given to the Canadian Research Institute for the Advancement of Women, November 1978.
1743. Jain, Harish C. and Peter J. Sloane. *Race, sex and minority group discrimination legislation in North America and Britain*. Working paper series, no. 144. Hamilton, Ont.: McMaster University. Faculty of Business, 1978. 37p.

1744. Kelgard, Daphne Sylvia. "Bureaucracy and racism: their interrelationship: a case study of the cooperative home for Indian women." MA thesis, University of British Columbia, 1974. 180p. (Can. theses, no.22133)
1745. Menzies, S. June. "The uncounted hours: the perception of women in policy formulation," *McGill Law Journal*, 21:615-30, Winter 1975.
1746. Perkins, Craig. "Sex discrimination and the Canadian constitution," *New Feminist*, 4:3-14, Mar. 1973.
1747. Rowan, Renée. "La femme et la culture," *Canadian Women's Studies / Les cahiers de la femme*, 1:82, Spring 1979.
1748. Ruff, Kathleen. "Good news, and bad," *Branching Out*, 5(4):5, 1978.
1749. Strouch, Kathleen and Joan McFarland. *Equality for women?* Fredericton: New Brunswick. Human Rights Commission, 1974. 53p.
1750. Wachtel, Eleanor. "5 clear cases of sex discrimination," *Chatelaine*, 53:44-5, 156+ , Mar. 1980.
1751. "Women panelists charge sex bias in real estate industry," *CREA Reporter*, 5:3, Dec. 1975.

DISCRIMINATION IN EDUCATION

1752. Andersen, Margaret. "Economics and sex roles in academe," *CAUT/ACPU Bulletin*, 24:6-8, Sept. 1975.
1753. Archer, Maureen. "Women - a minority group in the academic professions," *Branching Out*, 1:21,24, Mar.-Apr. 1974.
1754. Asper, Linda. "Bibliographical essay on women in education," *Manitoba Journal of Education*, 9:29-33, Nov. 1973.
1755. Boyd, Monica. *Rank and salary differentials in the 1970's: a comparison of male and female full-time teachers in Canadian universities and colleges*. Ottawa: Association of Universities and Colleges of Canada, 1979. 59p.
    French edition: *Écarts dans les traitements et les rangs au cours des années 1970: comparaison entre les professeurs du sexe féminin en emploi à plein temps dans les universités et collèges du Canada.*
1756. B. C. Teachers' Federation. *Indicators of equality*. Vancouver, 1977. 28p.
1757. Canadian Teachers' Federation. *Socialization and life skills: report of the proceedings of the Canadian Teachers' Federation workshop on the Status of Women in Education held in Winnipeg, Manitoba, November 6-8, 1977*. Ottawa: Canadian Teachers' Federation, 1978. 59p.
    French edition: *La socialisation et les aptitudes à la vie.*
1758. Christiansen-Ruffman, Linda. "Positions for women in Canadian sociology and anthropology," *Society*, 3:9-12, Sept. 1979.
1759. "Discrimination against women still common in universities," *CAUT/ACPU Bulletin*, 23:4, Feb. 1975.
1760. Galloway, Priscilla. *What's wrong with high school English?...It's sexist...un-Canadian...out-dated*. Curriculum series, no. 43. Toronto: OISE Press, 1980. 150p.
1761. Gelber, Sylva M. "Discriminatory practices in the universities and a proposed role for the Canadian Federation of University Women," in, *Women's Bureau '70*. Ottawa: Canada. Dept. of Labour. Women's Bureau, 1971, pp.15-19.
1762. Gillett, Margaret. "Seahorse society." *McGill Journal of Education*, 10:40-8, Spring 1975.
1763. _____. "Sexism in higher education," *Atlantis*, 1:68,81, Fall 1975.
1764. Henderson, Jule and John Briere. "Sexism and sex roles in letters of recommendation to graduate training in psychology," *Canadian Psychological Review*, 21:75-80, Apr. 1980.
1765. "Interview with the minister of education", *ATA Magazine*, 55:40-1, Jan.-Feb. 1975.
1766. Julian, Marilyn. "You've come a long way, baby," *OSSTF Bulletin*, 52:245-54, Dec. 1972.
1767. Nelson, Fiona. "Sex stereotyping in Canadian schools," in Gwen Matheson, *Women in the Canadian mosaic*. Toronto: Peter Martin, 1976, pp.166-80.

1768. Nemiroff, Greta. "Women and education," *McGill Journal of Education*, 10:3-19, Spring 1975.

1769. Nixon, Mary. "Equal opportunity: still empty words," *ATA Magazine*, 55:18-20, Jan.-Feb. 1975.

1770. Pyke, Sandra W. "Sex-role socialization in the school system," in Richard A. Carlton, and others, eds., *Education, change and society: a sociology of Canadian education*. Toronto: Gage, 1977, pp.426-38.

1771. Reich, Carol M. *Effect of a teacher's sex on career development*. Research service report, no. 131. [Toronto]: Board of Education, 1975. 77p.

1772. _____. *The effects of sex on careers within education: implications for a plan of action*. [Toronto: Ontario Institute for Studies in Education. Group for Research on Women, 1976]. 37p. and app.

1773. Reich, Carol and Helen La Fountaine. "The effects of sex on careers within education: implications for a plan of action," *Canadian Journal of Education*, 7(2):64-84, 1982.

1774. Ricks, Frances and Sandra Pyke. "Teacher perceptions and attitudes that foster or maintain sex role differences," *Interchange*, 4(1):26-33, 1973.

1775. Robson, R. A. H. *A comparison of men's and women's salaries and employment fringe benefits in the academic profession*. Royal Commission on the Status of Women in Canada. Study no. 1. Ottawa, 1971. 39p.

1776. Schafer, Juliet. "Where discrimination flowers: a walk through the backyards of the teaching profession," *Manitoba Teacher*, 52:5, Feb. 1974.

1777. Schrank, William E. "Sex discrimination in faculty salaries: a case study," *Canadian Journal of Economics*, 10:411-33, Aug. 1977.

1778. Shack, Sybil. "No females need apply," *Education Canada*, 15:28-31, Winter 1975.

1779. Smith, Dorothy E. "On the implications of declining enrolments for women public school teachers: the Ontario case." *Resources for Feminist Research*, 8:6-9, Mar. 1979.

1780. Smith, Dorothy E. and others. *Working paper on the implications of declining enrolment for women teachers in public elementary and secondary schools in Ontario*. Working paper, no. 24. Toronto: Ontario. Commission on Declining School Enrolments in Ontario, 1978. 81p.

1781. Stuckey, Johanna H. "Status of women in education, the importance of attitudinal change," *School Guidance Worker*, 31:29-33, Sept.-Oct. 1975.

1782. Symons, Gladys L. "Equality of opportunity in American and Canadian graduate education: a comparison of gender differences," *Alberta Journal of Educational Research*, 26:96-112, June 1980.

1783. Synge, Jane. "The sex factor in social selection processes in Canadian education," in Richard A. Carlton, and others, eds., *Education, change and society: a sociology of Canadian education*. Toronto: Gage, 1977, pp.298-310.

1784. Tremblett, Josephine. "We haven't really come a long way!" *Newfoundland Teachers' Association. Bulletin*, 24:18, Apr. 15, 1981.

1785. Trew, Marsha. "Women and education: road to poverty," in *Empowering adults: education policies in a crisis*. Vancouver: Educational Resource Group, 1982, pp.77-85.

1786. Whittingham, Ken. "Sex bias at universities in Canada: no change in 20 years, study finds," *Chronicle of Higher Education*, 20:15, July 7, 1980.

1787. Willis, Janet. "Where we stand," *Learning*, 1:3-5, Fall 1977.

1788. Wolfe, Jennifer. "Coed physed," *Orbit*, 8:6-7, Dec. 1977.

1789. "Women academics in Canadian universities: little change in status over past decade," *CAUT Bulletin*, 26:9, Dec. 1979.

1790. Wright, Susan, Andrew Griffith and others. *About face: is anybody out there listening? A study of sexism in a secondary school*. Toronto: Ontario Status of Women Council, [1977]. 41p.

DISCRIMINATION IN EMPLOYMENT

1791. Apostle, Richard and Don Clairmont. "Income dynamics in the marginal work world," *Atlantis*, 6:47-61, Spring 1981.

1792. Armstrong, Pat and Hugh Armstrong. *The double ghetto: Canadian women and their segregated work*. Toronto: McClelland and Stewart, 1978. 199p.

1793. "Asexuons les SM," *Optimum*, 12(2):17-26, 1981.

1794. "Bank policy, practice for women differed," *Globe & Mail*, July 12, 1978, p.B12.

1795. Bannon, Sharleen. "International Women's Year: women in the workplace," *Labour Gazette*, 76:69-74, Feb. 1976.

1796. Bennett, James and Pierre Loewe. "'Females need not apply': sex segregation might not be that obvious, but it exists," *Financial Post*, 69:C2-4, May 31, 1975.

1797. _____. "Two barriers that stymie females in the work force," *Financial Post*, 69:E2-4, June 14, 1975.

1798. _____. *Women in business: a shocking waste of human resources*. Toronto: Maclean-Hunter Ltd., 1975. 150p.

1799. _____. "Women in business: Canadian business isn't really committed to extending equal opportunities to women," *Financial Post*, 69:C1-3, May 24, 1975.

1800. Bhérer, Jacinthe et Monique des Rivières. *Lois québécoises discriminatoires à l'égard des femmes*. Québec: Conseil du statut de la femme, 1974. v.p.

1801. Bhérer, Jacinthe. *Étude sur les distinctions fondées sur le sexe dans les conventions collectives et décrets*. Québec: Conseil du statut de la femme, 1974. v.p.

1802. Biles, Penny. "Sex differences and work patterns: a case study of a community college." MA thesis, McMaster University, 1978. 301p. (Can. theses, no.36570)

1803. "Breaking the job barrier," *Canadian Labour*, 16:11, 18, Mar. 1971.

1804. Canada. Public Service Commission. *A study of the existing sex restrictions in the correctional group CX(COF-LUF-STI): an emotional and controversial issue*. [Ottawa], 1977. 67, 75p.
  Report of a committee. Includes French text under title: Étude sur les restrictions d'ordre sexuel dans le groupe des services correctionnels CX(COF-LUF-STI):une question fort controversée.

1805. Carson, Susan. "The female unit," *Weekend Magazine*, 27:18-19, Feb. 19, 1977.

1806. "Causes of sex bias," *Labour Gazette*, 75:787-8, Nov. 1975.

1807. "CLC brief: 'Women suffer job discrimination'," *Canadian Labour*, 13:7, 40, Oct. 1968.

1808. Coffey, Mary Anne. *Inequality at work*. [Toronto]: Social Planning Council of Metropolitan Toronto / Toronto. Board of Education. Women's Studies and Affirmative Action Dept., [1982?] 32p. (Microlog 83-2362)

1809. Colwill, Nina. "Women in business: discrimination, why does it work?" *Business Quarterly*, 47:20-2, Oct. 1982.

1810. Confédération des syndicats nationaux. *La lutte des femmes: pour le droit au travail social: deuxième rapport du comité de la condition féminine, 49e congrès de la CSN, Montréal, juin 1978*. Montréal, 1978. 67p.

1811. _____. *La lutte des femmes: une lutte permanente, une lutte collective: rapport du comité de la condition féminine de la CSN au 50e congrès de la CSN, mai 1980, reçu et amendé par le conseil confédéral du mars 1981*. n.p., 1981. 64p.

1812. Confédération des syndicats nationaux. Comité de condition féminine. *On n'a pas les moyens de reculer! Les conséquences de la crise sur les femmes*. n.p., [1981]. 55p.

1813. Constantineau, G. "L'Expo: cherchez la femme!" *Le Magazine Maclean*, 6:44, janv. 1966.

1814. Canadian Union of Public Employees. Education Dept. *Affirmative action: putting a stop to sex discrimination: an outline for locals*. [Ottawa], n.d. 6p.

1815. Cook, Gail. "Working women's role not rated high priority," *Journal (The Board of Trade of Metropolitan Toronto)*, July-Aug. 1978, pp.37-9.

1816. Cummings, Joan E. "Sexism in social work: the experience of Atlantic social work women," *Atlantis*, 6:62-79, Spring 1981.

1817. David, Hélène. *La lutte des femmes, combat de tous les travailleurs: rapport du comité de la condition féminine, 47e congrès, Québec, juin 1976 (document 4) tel qu'amendé par le congrès et le conseil confédéral*. 3e ed. n.p.: Confédération des syndicats nationaux, 1979. 72p.

1818. Dunphy, Jill. "Tradition, men, and other women no help to woman who tries to scale exec wall," *Office Equipment & Methods*, 23:32-3, Feb. 1977.

1819. Echenberg, Havi. "Canada's women: victims of job ghettos and unequal pay," *Canadian Business Review*, 7:30-2, Spring 1980.

1820. Eichler, Margrit. "The double standard as an indicator of sex-status differentials," *Atlantis*, 3:1-21, Autumn 1977.

1821. Erickson, L. Diane Lindgren. "Organizational determinants of the use of sex in hiring decisions: a case study." MA thesis, University of British Columbia, 1974. 86p. (Can. theses, no.19527)

1822. "Federal plan aims at improved attitudes to working women," *Globe & Mail*, Oct. 16, 1976, p.B3.

1823. "Female employee discrimination thought possible despite laws," *Globe & Mail*, Jan. 14, 1977, p.B10.

1824. "Feminist union leader feels improved women's job role 'hoax, mirage'," *Globe & Mail*, Oct. 29, 1979, p.B10.

1825. Fraser, Joan. "Profit, not charity rationale for more women workers," *Financial Times*, 64:10, May 10, 1976.

1826. Frazee, Rowland. "A president's perspective," *Executive Bulletin (Conference Board in Canada)*, no. 4:1-4, Mar. 1978.

1827. Gauthier, Kathleen. "The task ahead: for business, industry and government," in Canadian Federation of Business and Professional Women's Clubs, *A collection of papers delivered at the National Conference: Women & Work in the 80's: a Decade of Change*. Ottawa: The Federation, 1981, pp.97-111.

1828. Gelber, Sylva. "Communicating with the press - education for business: women in management," in, *Women's Bureau '72*. Ottawa: Canada. Dept. of Labour. Women's Bureau, 1973, pp.37-41.

1829. _____. "Highly qualified manpower policies and the Canadian woman graduate: what price discrimination," in, *Women's Bureau '69*. Ottawa: Canada. Dept. of Labour. Women's Bureau, 1970, pp.27-31.

1830. _____. "The importance of perseverance," in, *Women's Bureau '71*. Ottawa: Canada. Dept. of Labour. Women's Bureau, 1972, pp.13-19.

1831. _____. "The importance of perseverance," in, *Women's Bureau '71*. Ottawa: Canada. Dept. of Labour. Women's Bureau, 1972, pp.13-19.

1832. _____. "Unequal pay, opportunity persist," *Canadian Labour*, 16:21, Dec. 1971.

1833. _____. "Which side are you on?" in, *Women's Bureau '72*. Ottawa: Canada. Dept. of Labour. Women's Bureau, 1973, pp.7-12.

1834. Gillett, Margaret. "...Faintly the inimitable rose," *Canadian Library Journal*, 32:277-9, Aug. 1975.

1835. Godard, Lorraine. "La femme et le droit au travail," *Atlantis*, 3:21-39, Spring 1978, Part II.

1836. Goodman, Eileen. "Still a long way to go," *Canadian Business*, 50:70, 72+, July 1977.

1837. Gripton, James. "Sexism in social work: male takeover of a female profession," *Social Worker*, 42:78-89, Summer 1974.

1838. Gunderson, Morley and Frank Reid. *Sex discrimination in the Canadian labour market: theories, data and evidence*. Discussion paper series. Series A, equality in the workplace, no. 3. Ottawa: Canada. Dept. of Labour. Women's Bureau, 1983. 77p.

1839. Hall, O. "Gender and the division of labour," *Office Administration*, 11:74, Sept. 1965.

1840. Hartman, Grace. "Women in the labour movement; Les femmes dans le mouvement syndical," *Civil Service Review / Revue du service civil*, *46:38+*, [English]; 39+, [French], Dec. 1973.

1841. "IAM fights sexist hiring policy; L'AIM combat le sexisme dans l'embauche," *Canadian Labour / Travailleur canadien*, 25:8, [English]; 8, [French], Sept. 5, 1980.

1842. Jain, Harish C. "Race and sex discrimination in employment in Canada: theories, evidence and policies," *Industrial Relations*, 37(2):344-66, 1982.

73

1843. "Job barriers to women's employment," *Canada Manpower and Immigration Review*, 8(1):9-13, 1975.
1844. "Labour minister sides with female underdog," *Industrial Management*, May 1982, p.20.
1845. Landau, Barbara. "Women pushing for job equality - but old attitudes won't die; digest of address," *Financial Post*, 71:18, Feb. 26, 1977.
1846. Laws, Margaret. "Equality when necessary but not necessarily equality," *Financial Post*, 72:29-30, 32, Oct. 7, suppl. 1978.
1847. Lennon, Elizabeth Shilton. "Sex discrimination in employment: the Nova Scotia Human Rights Act," *Dalhousie Law Journal*, 2:593-632, July 1976.
1848. Lord, Catherine. "La révolte des vieilles dames pas indignes," *L'Actualité*, 1:90, déc. 1976.
1849. _____. "On demande barman topless," *Le Maclean*, 16:8, juin 1976.
1850. MacCormack, Terrance. "Women in industry - a staggering waste of skills," *Plant Administration and Engineering*, 29:27, Aug. 1970.
1851. McKenzie, Grace. "Crack in the liberation bell. [McGill industrial relations conference]," *Labour Gazette*, 74:497-9, July, 1974.
1852. Moore, Joy and Frank Laverty. "Women in the front window," *Optimum*, 5(3):28-35, 1974.
1853. Morrison, Suzanne. "Corporate women: the slow climb to the top," *Journal (The Board of Trade of Metropolitan Toronto)*, July-Aug. 1978, pp.33-7.
1854. _____. "The career woman: the progress and problems," *Journal (The Board of Trade of Metropolitan Toronto)*, Apr. 1979, pp.23-8, 31-3.
1855. Myette, J. M. "The equal opportunity syndrome," *Canadian Underwriter*, 46:48-52, May 1979.
1856. New Brunswick. Advisory Council on the Status of Women. *Improving opportunities for groups with special employment needs: a response to the Dodge Task Force*, prepared by Susan Shalala. Moncton, 1981. 15p.
1857. Ontario Human Rights Commission. *A study of employment policies in downtown hotel dining rooms and coffee shops*, submitted by Janet McMurtry and Pam McGibbon. Toronto: Ontario Status of Women Council, 1978. 5p.
1858. Ontario. Ministry of Labour. Women's Bureau. *Sex discrimination in employment; how to file a complaint under the Human Rights Code*. Rev. ed. [Toronto], 1978. Leaflet.
1859. Paris, Erna. "How are nice girls doing in places like the banks...the Bell...Air Canada?" *Chatelaine*, 46:48-9, 101-6, Sept. 1973.
1860. _____. "Looking for a dead-end job? For a start, try department stores and supermarkets," *Chatelaine*, 46:41, 113-5, 118-9, Nov. 1973.
1861. _____. "Women and business: some conclusions," *Chatelaine*, 47:38, 42, 119, Nov. 1974.
1862. Patterson, R. Allan. "The effects of sex and marital status on personnel decisions," in Patricia Marchak, ed., *The working sexes: symposium papers on the effects of sex on women at work*. Vancouver: University of British Columbia. Institute of Industrial Relations, 1977, pp.72-87.
1863. Peal, Emma. "Companies slow to acknowledge women's role in business," *Canadian Business*, 49:51-2, Nov. 1976.
1864. _____. "[Howe] report outlines goals for women," *Journal (The Board of Trade of Metropolitan Toronto)*, Easter 1977, pp.22, 24-5.
1865. Pyke, Sandra W. "Selected characteristics of the female psychologist in the labour force," *Canadian Psychological Review*, 18:23-33, Jan. 1977.
1866. Quebec. Conseil du statut de la femme. *Parce que vous êtes une femme: la discrimination au travail et la Charte des droits de la personne*. Québec: Éditeur officiel du Québec, 1975. 17p.
1867. Rose-Lizée and Ginette Dussault. "Discrimination against women and labour market segregation: the case of office workers in Montreal," in *Reflections on Canadian incomes: selected papers presented at the Conference on Canadian Incomes, May 10-12, 1979*. Ottawa: Economic Council of Canada, 1980, pp.421-50.

1868. "Royal chief clarifies remarks about women," *Globe & Mail*, Sept. 11,1976, p.B2.

1869. Sallot, Lynne. "Is industry making full use of female labor resources?" *Plant Management & Engineering*, 34:7-9, Dec. 1975.

1870. Schreck, David Donald. "Occupational segregation by sex." PhD diss., University of British Columbia, 1978. 196p. (Can. theses, no.37717)

1871. "Sex discrimination and the division of labour," *Canadian Banker and ICB Review*, 83:59-61, Feb. 1975.

1872. Strumpfer, D. J. W. "Harnessing impatience to organization goals I," *Canadian Personnel and Industrial Relations Journal*, 24:11-18, May 1977.

1873. _____. "Harnessing impatience to organizational goals II," *Canadian Industrial Relations and Personnel Journal*, 24:13-18, Sept. 1977.

1874. _____. "You and the impatient people," *Canadian Personnel and Industrial Relations Journal*, 24:12-18, Mar. 1977.

1875. Swan, Carole. *Women in the Canadian labour market*. Technical study, no. 36. Ottawa: Canada. Task Force on Labour Market Development, 1981. [89]p.

1876. _____. "Broken promises: fresh assaults on the working woman," *Branching Out*, 6(2):8-10, 1979.

1877. Tellier, Marie. "Les femmes dans les entreprises: où est leur place?" *Canadian Woman Studies / Les cahiers de la femme*, 3:90-2, Summer 1982.

1878 "Testing job bias," *Labour Gazette*, 75:488, Aug. 1975.

1879 "The short-changed sex," *Urban Reader*, 3:12-14, May 1975.

1880. Townson, Monica. "Business shuns the women," *Synoptic*, 14:12-14, Summer 1974.

1881. _____. "The status of women," *Executive*, 19:37-8, 40, Sept. 1977.

1882. _____. "Women and the economic crisis," *Branching Out*, 7(1):9-11, 1980.

1883. _____. "Women in the executive suite: you're an engineer? How's your shorthand?" *Financial Times of Canada*, 62:9, July 8, 1973.

1884. "Traditional trends seen hindering women," *Globe & Mail*, Sept. 11, 1976, p.B2.

1885. Van der Merwe, Sandra. "Using career planning to buffer sex discrimination," *Canadian Women's Studies / Les cahiers de la femme*, 1:109-11, Winter 1978-1979.

1886. Wallace, Catherine. "Four-fifths minority: continuing education for library personnel," *Canadian Library Journal*, 33:75-9, Apr. 1976.

1887. Wallace, Joan. "The case of the pregnant stewardesses," *Status of Women News*, 2:5-6, Nov. 1975.

1876. Wendell, Susan. "Discrimination, sex prejudice and affirmative action," *Atlantis*, 6:39-50, Fall 1980.

1889. "Women are still 'half-persons' in the whole corporate spectrum," *Financial Post*, 69:1-2, May 31, 1975.

1890. "Women panelists charge sex bias in real estate industry," *CREA Reporter*, 5:3, Dec. 1975.

1891. "Women still lose top jobs to males," *Globe & Mail*, Jan. 22, 1982, pp.1-2.

1892. Wyckham, Robert. "What would you do? Testing equal opportunity," *ICB Review*, 5:15-17, Summer 1972. Replies: IBC Review, 5:14, Fall/Winter 1972.

DIVORCE

1893. Abernathy, Thomas J. and Margaret E. Arcus. "The law and divorce in Canada," *Family Coordinator*, 26:409-13, Oct. 1977.

1894. Alberta. Women's Bureau. *Ending a marriage: the legal aspects of separation, annulment and divorce*. Edmonton, 1979. 33p.

1895. Ambert, Anne-Marie. *Divorce in Canada*. Don Mills, Ont.: Academic Press Canada, 1980. 235p.

1896. Anderson, Doris. "Let's plug the loopholes before this law goes through," *Chatelaine*, 50:2, May 1977.

1897. Appel, David. "On divorcing yourself," *Weekend Magazine*, 26:22, June 5, 1976.

1898. Beaulieu, Michel. "Le couple en morceaux," *Le Maclean*, 16:25-8, fév. 1976.

1899. Boyd, Monica. "The forgotten minority: the socioeconomic status of divorced and separated women," in Patricia Marchak, ed., *The working sexes: symposium papers on the effects of sex on women at work*. Vancouver: University of British Columbia. Institute of Industrial Relations, 1977, pp.46-71.

1900. Brière, Germain. "Famille et divorce: chroniques régulières," *Revue du Barreau*, 76:247-52, 410-13, 565-68, 1976.

1901. Buchanan, Roberta. "Divorce: Newfoundland style," *Canadian Dimension*, 10:16-18, June 1975.

1902. Canada. Advisory Council on the Status of Women. *Divorce law reform; ACSW recommendations*. Ottawa, 1976. 4p.

1903. Canada. Law Reform Commission. *Divorce*. Working paper, no. 13. Ottawa: Information Canada, 1975. 70p.

1904. _____. *Studies on divorce*. Ottawa: Information Canada, 1975. 203p.
     Also includes: Maintenance on divorce, Working paper no. 12; Divorce, Working paper no. 13.

1905. Chapman, F. A. R. *Everything you should know about law and marriage*. Toronto: Pagurian Press, 1971. 163p.

1906. Clark, Wayne. "Divorce by fire: getting burned in the courts," *Weekend Magazine*, 26:10-11, 14-15, June 5, 1976.

1907. Cook, David and others. "Separation and divorce in Canada: can we get closer to accurate data?" *Canadian Journal of Public Health*, 70:271-4, July/Aug. 1979.

1908. de Mestier du Bourg, Hubert J. M. "Étude comparative des causes et les effets du divorce en droit canadien." DCL thèse, McGill University, 1974. 515p. (Can. theses, no.20773)

1909. Diamond, Robyn Moglore. "Divorce jurisdiction," *Canadian Forum*, 61:34-5, May 1981.

1910. "Do-it-yourself divorce for only $167?" *Atlantic Advocate*, 62:69, Mar. 1972.

1911. Dranoff, Linda Silver. "Ask a lawyer," *Chatelaine*, 55:32, Aug. 1982.

1912. Duff, Diane Marie. "The problems of post-divorce adjustment." MA thesis, McMaster University, 1968. 73p.

1913. Fleishman, Neil. *Counsel for the damned*. Vancouver: J. J. Douglas, 1973. 206p.

1914. Frosst, Sandra and Wendy Thomson. "A study of the concerns of divorcing women," *Canadian Journal of Social Work Education*, 6(2/3):25-44, 1980.

1915. Gillen, M. "Lawyer: divorce isn't fair to women," *Chatelaine*, 44:19, 52-4, July, 1971.

1916. Hahlo, H. R. *Nullity of marriage in Canada: with a sideways glance at concubinage and its legal consequences*. Toronto: Butterworths, 1979. 67p.

1917. Hanif, Muhammad. "Separation trends: a functional analysis of changing dynamics in relationships." MA thesis, University of Windsor, 1977. 85p. (Can. theses, no.33195)

1918. Harris, S. "Do-it-yourself divorce," *Chatelaine*, 43:44, 92-5, Sept. 1970.

1919. Hawkes, Cheryl. "The bills of divorcement: how to ease the pain," *Canadian Business*, 55:153, Oct. 1982.

1920. Irving, Howard H. *Family law: an interdisciplinary perspective*. Toronto: Carswell, 1981. 215p.

1921. Jahn, Penelope and Charles Campbell. *The self-help guide to divorce, children, welfare: an up-to-date handbook on Canadian family law*. Toronto: Anansi, 1976. 108p.

1922. Jamieson, Laura. "Divorce: women have it tougher," *Canadian Secretary*, 6:6-7, Nov. 1981.

1923. King, Lynn. *What every woman should know about marriage, separation and divorce*. Toronto: James Lorimer, 1980. 165p.

1924. La Chambre des Notaires de la Province de Québec. *Brief no. 307 to the Royal Commission on the Status of Women in Canada*. Montreal, 1968. 41p.

1925. *Les régimes matrimoniaux et le partage dans la séparation et le divorce*. Montréal: Barreau du Québec, 1976. 122p.

1926. Little, W. T. "The domestic illness profile seen in a family court setting," in W. E. Mann, ed., *Deviant behaviour in Canada*. Toronto: Social Science Publishers, 1968, pp.310-18.

76

1927. MacDonald, James C. and Lee K. Ferrier. *Canadian divorce law and practice*. Toronto: Carswell, 1969- . Loose-leaf.

1928. MacKay, Harry. "Law and poverty and access to social services," *Perception*, 5:28, June 1982.

1929. Makabe, Tomoko. "Provincial variations in divorce rates: a Canadian case," *Journal of Marriage and the Family*, 42:171-6, Feb. 1980.

1930. Marcotte, M. "Vers une nouvelle loi du divorce," *Relations*, no. 323:2-3, janv. 1968.

1931. McDonnell, Kathleen. "To smooth the waters of stormy divorces [mediation]," *Maclean's*, 95:50-1, Mar. 8, 1982.

1932. Nowack, Paul. "Till divorce do us part," *Maclean's*, 89:26-8, 30+ , Apr. 19, 1976.

1933. Palmer, Sally E. "Divorcing families: a case study in southwestern Ontario," in K. Ishwaran, ed., *The Canadian family*. Rev. ed. Toronto: Holt, Rinehart and Winston of Canada, 1976, pp.614-30.

1934. _____. "Reasons for marriage breakdown: a case study in southwestern Ontario (Canada)," in George Kurian, ed., *Cross-cultural perspectives of mate selection and marriage*. Contributions in family studies, no. 3. Westport, Conn.: Greenwood Press, 1979, pp.364-75.

1935. Peters, John F. *Divorce*. Social problems in Canada, no. 8. Toronto, Ont.: University of Toronto. Faculty of Education. Guidance Centre, 1979. 47p.

1936. _____. "Divorce in Canada: a demographic profile," in George Kurian, ed., *Cross-cultural perspectives of mate selection and marriage*. Contributions in family studies, no. 3. Westport, Conn.: Greenwood Press, 1979, pp.376-90.

1937. Peters, J. F. "Divorce in Canada: a demographic profile," *Journal of Comparative Family Studies*, 7:335-49, Summer 1976.

1938. Pike, Robert. "Legal access and the incidence of divorce in Canada: a sociohistorical analysis," *Canadian Review of Sociology and Anthropology*, 12(2):115-33, 1975.

1939. Pineau, Jean. *Mariage, séparation, divorce: l'état du droit au Québec*. Montréal: Presses de l'Université de Montréal, 1976. 289p.

1940. Playfair, Patrick. "Parliament faces up," *Canadian Welfare*, 44:4-7, Jan.-Feb. 1968.

1941. "Proposing a move to no-fault divorce," *Time Canada*, 106:8-9, Aug. 11, 1975.

1942. Québec. Conseil du statut de la femme. *Mieux divorcer: conseils pratiques aux femmes du Québec*. [2e éd. rév. et corr.]. Québec: Conseil du statut de la femme, 1978. 38p.

1943. Québec. Ministère de la justice. Service d'information. *Séparation et divorce*. 2e éd., [Québec], 1974. 30p.
      English edition: Separation and divorce.

1944. Rioux, Marcia H. *Study paper on divorce*. Ottawa: Canadian Advisory Council on the Status of Women, 1976. 42p.

1945. Roberts, Lance and P. Krishnan. *Age specific incidence and social correlates of divorce in Canada*. Edmonton: University of Alberta. Dept. of Sociology. Population Research Laboratory, 1973. 9p. and tables.
      Paper presented at the 14th Annual Meetings of the Western Association of Sociology and Anthropology, Calgary, Alberta, Dec. 30, 1982.

1946. Roy, Laurent. *Le divorce au Québec: évolution récente*. [Préparé pour la] Division des études démographiques, Registre de la population. [Québec]: Québec. Ministère des affaires sociales. Direction des communications, 1978. 41 [6]p.

1947. Schlesinger, Benjamin, ed. *The Chatelaine guide to marriage*. Toronto: MacMillan, 1975. 218p.

1948. Shorter, Edward. "The dark side of the sexual revolution: left-behind women," *Chatelaine*, 50:56-7, 101-3, Mar. 1977.

1949. Stein, David Lewis and Erna Paris. "Divorce: do men get all the sympathy?" *Chatelaine*, 52:22, Feb. 1979.

1950. Temins, Irving D. *Law of divorce in Canada*. Toronto: Primrose Publishing Co., 1969. 120p.

1951. "The marriage contract," *Financial Times*, 66:41-2, Mar. 13-19, 1978.

1952. Vancouver People's Law School. *Matrimony and divorce*. 2nd. ed. Vancouver, 1976. 32p.

1953. Wanadi-Mboyo, Ea Booto. "Mariage et rupture institutionnelle et non institutionnelle du lien conjugal chez les couples dont l'âge de la femme se situe entre 30 et 45 ans." MSS thèse, Université de Sherbrooke, 1977. 165p. (Can. theses, no.37045)

1954. Wires, David. "Comment on working paper no. 13 of the Law Reform Commission of Canada: Divorce," *Ottawa Law Review*, 8:358-64, 1976.

1955. Woodsworth, K. C., ed. *Family law: proceedings of a conference held May 17-19, 1978 at the Bayshore Inn, Vancouver, B.C.* Vancouver: University of British Columbia. Continuing Legal Education Society of British Columbia, 1979. 160p.

1956. "You asked us: splitting up: in a divorce, you'll share your pension, too," *Today*, Dec. 12, 1981, p.4b.

1957. Zinck, Cynthia Hasting. "Divorce Canadian style," *Broadside*, 2:6, Dec. 1980/Jan. 1981.

DIVORCE - BIBLIOGRAPHY

1958. Canada. Dept. of National Health and Welfare. Departmental Library Services. *Divorce: a bibliographical look at the world. [Le divorce: bibliographie internationale]*. [Ottawa], 1977. 183p.

DOMESTIC WORK

1959. Armstrong, Pat. "Domestic labour and wage labour," *Atlantis*, 7:1-2, Fall 1981.

1960. Barber, Marilyn. "The women Ontario welcomed: immigrant domestics for Ontario homes, 1870-1930," *Ontario History*, 72:148-72, Sept. 1980.

1961. Black, Karen. "Interceding for domestics," *Broadside*, 2:10, Feb. 1981.

1962. Bouchard, Danielle. "Association du personnel domestique," *Canadian Women's Studies / Les cahiers de la femme*, 1:38-40, Winter 1978-1979.

1963. Dimano, Rosie. "To serve and protest," *The Canadian*, Sept. 15-16, 1979, pp.2-4, 6.

1964. Epstein, Rachel. "I thought there was no more slavery in Canada!" *Canadian Dimension*, 14:29-35, May 1980.

1965. _____. "West Indian domestic workers on employment visas: I thought there was no more slavery in Canada!" *Canadian Women's Studies / Les cahiers de la femme*, 2(1):22-9, 1980.

1966. Farkas, Edie. "It's a field day for the household tyrants: victimizing domestic workers," *Last Post*, 6:17-19, Jan. 1978.

1967. Gregory, Frances. "Domestic workers and the International Coalition to End Domestics' Exploitation," *Rikka*, 7:59-60, Spring 1980.

1968. "Improving the position of household workers," *Labour Gazette*, 67:123, Feb. 1967.

1969. Lacelle, Claudette. "Les domestiques dans les villes canadiennes au XIXe siècle: effectifs et conditions de vie," *Histoire sociale / Social History*, 15:181-207, mai 1982.

1970. Poulton, Terry. "When nanny is an outlaw," *Maclean's*, 92:50, Dec. 17, 1979.

1971. Silvera, Makeda. "Immigrant domestic workers: whose dirty laundry?" *Fireweed*, 9:53-9, Winter 1981.

DRESS

1972. Abrahamson, U. "Women's clothes: what's wrong," *Chatelaine*, 43:84-6, Sept. 1970.

1973. Amiel, Barbara. "Pursuing the working woman," *Maclean's*, 92:37-40, June 25, 1979.

1974. Audet, Bernard. "Le costume féminin," in his, *Le costume paysan dans la région de Québec au XVIIe siècle*. Ottawa: Leméac, 1980, pp.61-80.

1975. Brett, Kathrine Beatrice. *Women's costume in Ontario (1867-1907)*. [Toronto: Royal Ontario Museum, 1966]. 16p.

1976. Collard, Eileen. *Decade of change, circa 1909-1919: women's clothing in Canada just prior to, during and after the First World War*. Burlington, Ont.: E. Collard, 1981. 92p.

1977. _____. *Women's dress in the 1920's: an outline of women's clothing in Canada during the roaring twenties*. Burlington, Ont.: E. Collard, 1981. 48p.

1978. Harris, M. "Brief to the Royal Commission on the Status of Women," *Maclean's*, 81:30-3, Aug. 1968.

1979. Lambert, Anne. "Images for sale: how Eaton's saw us," *Branching Out*, 4:30-3, Mar.-Apr. 1977.

1980. MacDonald, Ann Clarice. "Selected motivational aspects of clothing conformity and compartmentalization among female university students." MSc thesis, University of Guelph, 1977. 127p.

1981. Miall, Charlene Elizabeth. "Mass media and adolescent female fashion decisions." MA thesis, University of Calgary, 1972. 158p.

1982. Peal, Emma. "Corporate chic: success in the skirted suit," *Journal (The Board of Trade of Metropolitan Toronto)*, Spring 1979, pp.5-6, 8, 10, 12.

1983. Schlesinger, B. "Miniskirted girls," *Chatelaine*, 43:12, Jan. 1970.

1984. Shaheen, Ghazala and Cecilia A. Gonzales. "Clothing practices of Pakistani women residing in Canada," *Canadian Ethnic Studies*, 13(3):120-6, 1981.

1985. Tyrchniewicz, Mabel Eleanor. "Clothing attitudes, body - and self-cathexis among females from early adulthood to old age." MSc thesis, University of Manitoba, 1972. 101p.

DRUGS AND DRUG ADDICTION

1986. Alcoholism and Drug Dependency Commission of New Brunswick. Research and Evaluation Division. *Profile of female admissions to treatment*. [Fredericton], 1982. 19p. (Microlog 83-2261)

1987. Alexander, Gay, Betty Campbell and Gilda Jubas. *Self acceptance, substance use and sole support mothers in Toronto: an examination of the relationship*. n.p., [1978?] 57p. and app.
Funded by Non-Medical Use of Drugs Directorate, Health and Welfare Canada.

1988. Dudiet, Patricia. "Women and legal drugs: a review," in Anne MacLennan, ed., *Women: their use of alcohol and other legal drugs: a provincial consultation - 1976*. Toronto: Addiction Research Foundation of Ontario, 1976, pp.57-81.

1989. Birchmore, Doreen, Rodeen Walderman and Karen McNama. *A retrospective study of female and male addiction*. Toronto: Donwood Institute, 1978. 17, [12]p.

1990. Cooperstock, Ruth. "A review of women's psychotropic drug use," *Canadian Journal of Psychiatry*, 24:29-34, Feb. 1979.

1991. _____. "Psychotropic drug use among women," *Canadian Medical Association. Journal*, 115:760-3, Oct. 23, 1976.

1992. _____. "Sex differences in the use of mood-modifying drugs: an explanatory model," *Journal of Health and Social Behavior*, 12:238-44, Sept. 1971.

1993. _____. "Special problems of psychotropic drug use among women," *Canada's Mental Health*, 28:3-5, June 1980.

1994. _____. "Understanding women's psychotropric drug use," *Fireweed*, 2:57-62, Spring 1979.

1995. Dowsling, Janet and Anne MacLennan. *The chemically dependent woman: Rx recognition, referral, rehabilitation*. Toronto: Addiction Research Foundation, 1978. 115p.
Proceedings of a conference sponsored by the Donwood Institute, Toronto, June 4, 1977.

1996. Eveson, Mark. "The female addict," *Canadian Journal of Corrections*, 9(3):227-33, 1967.

1997. Ferrence, Roberta G. and Paul C. Whitehead. "Sex differences in psychoactive drug use: recent epidemiology," in Oriana Josseau Kalant, ed., *Alcohol and drug problems in women*. Research advances in alcohol and drug problems, v.5. New York: Plenum Press, 1980, pp.125-201.

1998. MacLennan, Anne, ed. *Women: their use of alcohol and other legal drugs: a provincial consultation - 1976*. Toronto: Addiction Research Foundation of Ontario, 1976. 144p.

1999. Thomas, Eleanor. "Maternity and narcotic addiction," *Canada's Mental Health*, 23:13-16, Sept. 1975, Suppl.

EDUCATION

2000. Aubert, Lucienne. "L'éducation des filles: un processus aux objectifs ambigus," *Statut: Bulletin de la femme*, 5:5-6, automne 1979.

2001. Brien, Jasmine. "L'éducation chez les femmes," *Canadian Women's Studies / Les cahiers de la femme*, 1:124-6, Winter 1978-1979.

2002. British Columbia. Apprenticeship Training Programs Branch. *Women's exploratory apprenticeship training course outline*. Victoria, B.C., 1978.

2003. Campbell, S. F. "Further education facilities recommended after study," *Labour Gazette*, 66:164, Apr. 1966.

2004. Canadian Committee on Learning Opportunities for Women. "Brief to the Special Joint Committee of the Senate and of the House of Commons on the Constitution of Canada," in the committee's, *Minutes of proceedings and evidence*, no. 24, Dec. 11, 1980, pp.60-82.

2005. *Conference '80. Women and the economy*. n.p., 1980. 48p. Conference sponsored by New Brunswick Advisory Council on the Status of Women, New Brunswick. Dept. of Youth, Recreation and Cultural Resources, and others.

2006. Cook, Gail C., ed. *Opportunity for choice: a goal for women in Canada. [L'objectif pour les canadiennes: pouvoir choisir]*. Ottawa: Statistics Canada / C. D. Howe Research Institute, 1976. 217p.

2007. Coulter, J. M. "Dangers in educating women," *Continuous Learning*, 4:110-14, May-June 1965.

2008. "C.E.A. [Canadian Education Association] resolution on sex discrimination," *Education Nova Scotia*, 7:1, Feb. 9, 1977.

2009. "Education and personhood," in Canadian Research Institute for the Advancement of Women, *Women as persons. [La femme en tant que personne]*. Toronto: Resources for Feminist Research, 1980, pp.103-9.
    Proceedings of the 3rd annual meeting.

2010. Erickson, Gaalen, Lynda Erickson and Sharon Haggerty. *Gender and mathematics / science education in elementary and secondary schools*. Victoria: British Columbia. Ministry of Education. Information Services, 1980.

2011. Feldhammer, Louis. "The liberation of women and the educational system," *McGill Journal of Education*, 5:13-28, Spring 1970.

2012. Fischer, Linda. "See Jane change. Change Jane change," *Status of Women News*, 5:11-12, Fall 1979.

2013. Gaskell, Jane S. "Equal educational opportunity for women," in J. Donald Wilson, ed., *Canadian education in the 1980's*. Calgary: Detselig Enterprises, 1981, pp.173-93.

2014. Gaskell, Jane S. and Marvin Lazerson. "Between school and work: perspectives of working class youth," in J. Donald Wilson, ed., *Canadian education in the 1980's*. Calgary: Detselig Enterprises, 1981, pp.197-211.

2015. Gaskell, Jane. "Education and job opportunities for women: patterns of enrolment and economic returns," in Naomi Hersom and Dorothy E. Smith, [eds.], *Women and the Canadian labour force*. Working document. Ottawa: Social Sciences and Humanities Research Council of Canada, 1982, pp.257-306.

2016. _____. "Sex inequalities in education for work: the case of business education," *Canadian Journal of Education*, 6(2):54-72, 1981.

2017. _____. "Training, education and socialization," in *Sexual equality in the workplace*. Ottawa: Canada. Dept. of Labour. Women's Bureau, 1982, pp.93-122.

2018. Glasspool, Janet. "A sexy topic," *Orbit*, 11:9-10, Feb. 1980.

2019. Grenier, Pierre. "Les projets éducatifs de femmes agées: objets d'apprentissage et moyens privilegies." Mémoire de maîtrise inédit, Université de Montréal, 1980. 167p.

2020. Handelman, Esther. "Differential socialization by female elementary school teachers." MA thesis, Concordia University, 1977. 94p. (Can. theses, no.34694)

2021. Handfield, M. "Éducation familiale versus femmes universitaires," *Action nationale*, 54:671-81, mars 1965.

80

2022. Hiscock, Pamela Ruth. "A report on the development of two instructional units on women of Newfoundland and Labrador entitled Mary Southcott and Georgina Stirling." MEd thesis, University of Newfoundland, 1982. (Can. theses, no.53330)

2023. Humber College of Applied Arts and Technology. *Education-training opportunities for women - a summer at Humber survey - June 21-Aug. 27, 1971*. [Rexdale, Ont., 1971?] 89p.

2024. Ironside, Anne. *Women's access centres: a proposal*. Discussion paper 03/79. [Victoria]: British Columbia. Ministry of Education, Science and Technology, 1979. 40p.

2025. Kettle, John. "From school to work," *Executive*, 23:22, Aug.-Sept. 1981.

2026. _____. "More school - more work," *Executive*, 23:14, Feb. 1981.

2027. Kincaid, Pat J. "Response to 'A sexy topic': sex stereotyping imprisons boys and girls," *Orbit*, 11:10, Feb. 1980.

2028. Knoepfli, Heather E. "Origin of women's autonomous learning groups." PhD diss., University of Toronto, 1971. 284p.

2029. MacKeracher, Dorothy. *Roadblocks to women's learning: issues for advocacy*. [Toronto: Canadian Committee on Learning Opportunities for Women, 1978]. [172]p.
    Consists of the following units: Unit I, Introduction; Unit II, Day Care Services; Unit III, Employment (Manpower) and Immigration.

2030. _____. *Adult basic education for women; a model for policy development*. [Toronto: Canadian Congress for Learning Opportunities for Women, 1980]. 144p.

2031. Mahon, Barbara M. "Educational alternatives for the pregnant schoolgirl." MA thesis, University of Calgary, 1976. 113p. (Can. theses, no.30554)

2032. McKenzie, Francine. *Interventions dans le domaine de l'éducation et actions éducatives proposées (plan d'orientation)*. Québec: Conseil du statut de la femme, 1974. 14p.

2033. "Ministries renew efforts to improve status of women in every sector of education," *Education Ontario*, Spring 1980, p.3.

2034. Nemiroff, Greta. "Éduquer les femmes en vue de la maturité," *Critère*, no. 9:52-67, juin 1973.

2035. Newfoundland. Dept. of Education. Division of School Services. *Statistical presentation for the Minister's Advisory Committee on Women's Issues in Education*. [St. John's], 1980. 53p. (Microlog 80-3460)

2036. Ontario. Ministry of Education. *Changing roles in a changing world: a resource guide focusing on the female student*. [Toronto, 1976?] 24p.

2037. Ontario. Ministry of Labour. Research Branch. *Ontario women: selected occupational and educational data*. [Toronto], 1975. 7p.

2038. Pattillo, Margaret. "Education and vocational training of rural women," in *The family in the evolution of agriculture*. Ottawa: Vanier Institute of the Family, 1968, pp.32-46.

2039. Prentice, Alison and Susan Houston. "Places for girls and women," in their, *Family, school and society in nineteenth-century Canada*. Toronto: Oxford University Press, 1975, pp.244-69.

2040. Québec. Conseil du statut de la femme. *L'accès à l'éducation pour les femmes du Québec: mémoire*. Québec, 1977. 43, [22]p.

2041. Québec. Ministère de l'éducation. *Les actions du ministère de l'éducation dans le dossier de la condition féminine: dossier synthèse*. [Québec], 1980. 26p.

2042. Québec. Ministère de l'éducation. Direction générale de l'éducation des adultes. *La condition féminine et l'éducation populaire dans les commissions scolaires: répertoire d'activités et outils*. [Québec], 1979, [1981]. 60p.

2043. Storey, John W. "Ministry of education policy," in Sex-Role Stereotyping and Women's Studies Conference, Sept.28-30, 1978. *Report*. [Toronto]: Ontario. Ministry of Education, [1978], pp.23-8.

2044. Synge, Jane. "The sex factor in social selection processes in Canadian education," in Richard A. Carlton, *Education, change and society*. Toronto: Gage, 1977, pp.298-310.

2045. Therien, C. "Évolution du travail féminin et préparation scolaire au Québec," *Canadian Vocational Journal*, 10:42-5, mai 15, 1974.

2046. Turrittin, Anton H., Paul Anisef and Neil J. MacKinnon. "Gender differences in educational achievement: a study of social inequality," *Canadian Journal of Sociology*, 8:395-419, Fall 1983.

2047. University of British Columbia. Committee of Mature Women Students. *Brief no. 217 to the Royal Commission on the Status of Women in Canada*. Vancouver, 1968. 19p. and app.

2048. Vancouver Women's Caucus. *Women teachers and the education process, or "It's something you can always fall back on."* Victoria, B.C.: Social Science Research, [1969?] 3p.

2049. Welch, Joan Sally Shewchuk. "Factors relating to female enrollment in high school physics." MEd thesis, University of Manitoba, 1974. 110p. (Can. theses, no.20468)

2050. Wigney, L. *The education of women and girls*. Toronto: University of Toronto Press, 1965. 89p.

2051. Williams, Trevor. "Educational ambition: teachers and students," *Sociology of Education*, 48:432-56, Fall 1975.

2052. Willis, Janet. "Women's continuing education: back to frills?" *Branching Out*, 5(1):12-15; correction 5(2):3, 1978.

EDUCATION - HISTORY

2053. Chalmers, J. W. "Marguerite Bourgeoys, preceptress of New France," in Robert S. Patterson and others, eds., *Profiles of Canadian educators*. n.p.: D. C. Heath Canada, 1974, pp.4-20.

2054. Davey, Ian E. "Trends in female school attendance in mid-nineteenth century Ontario," *Histoire Sociale / Social History*, 8:238-54, Nov. 1975.

2055. Davison, James Doyle. *Alice of Grand Pre: Alice T. Shaw and her Grand Pre Seminary, female education in Nova Scotia and New Brunswick*. Wolfville, N.S.: Acadia University, 1981. 197p.

2056. Davison, James D. "Alice Shaw and her Grand Pré seminary: a story of female education," in Barry M. Moody, ed., *Repent and believe: the Baptist experience in maritime Canada*. Hantsport, N.S.: Acadia Divinity College, 1980, pp.124-37.

2057. Delisle, Gertrude. *Une expérience d'éducation-vie: respectueusement dédié aux dames universitaires, Montréal, et aux anciennes élèves de la "Ruche"*. Québec: Editions Le Renouveau, 1976. 109p.

2058. Fair, Myrtle. *I remember the one-room school*. Cheltenham, Ont.: Boston Mills Press, 1979. 184p.

2059. Feltmate, Peggy. "Mount Allison: in the forefront of women's education," *Atlantic Advocate*, 71:32-4, Dec. 1980.

2060. Gillett, Margaret. *We walked very warily: a history of women at McGill*. Montreal: Eden Press Women's Publications, 1981. 476p.

2061. Legendre, Anne Carmelle. "The Baptist contribution to nineteenth century education for women: an examination of Moulton College and McMaster University." MA thesis, McMaster University, 1981. 221p.

2062. Lemieux, Lucien. "La fondation de l'École ménagère St.-Pascal, 1905-1909," *Revue d'histoire d'Amérique française*, 25:552-7, mars 1972.

2063. L'Espérance, Jeanne. *The widening sphere: women in Canada 1870-1940. [Vers des horizons nouveaux: la femme canadienne de 1870 à 1940]*. [Ottawa]: Public Archives Canada, 1982. 63p.

2064. Milner, Elizabeth Hearn. *The history of King's Hall, Compton, 1874-1972*. Lennoxville, Que.: Secretary of the B.C.S. Alumni Association, 1979. 251p. Originally presented as the author's thesis, Bishop's University.

2065. Ontario Ladies' College. *Vox collegii: centennial ed., 1874-1974*. [Whitby, Ont.], 1974. 173p. Includes a history of the Ontario Ladies' College, by Brian Winter, pp.6-80.

2066. Plante, Lucienne. "La fondation de l'enseignement classique féminin au Québec, 1908-1926." MA thèse, Université Laval, 1967. 187p.

2067. _____. "L'enseignement classique chez les soeurs de la Congrégation de Notre-Dame, 1908-1971." DesL thèse, Université Laval, 1971. 367p. (Can. theses, no.19024)

2068. Royce, Marion V. *Education for girls in Quaker schools in Ontario*. Canadian women's history series, no. 3. Toronto: Ontario Institute for Studies in Education. Dept. of History and Philosophy of Education. The Women in Canadian History Project, 1977. 22p.

2069. _____. *Landmarks in the Victorian education of 'young ladies' under Methodist Church auspices*. n.p., 1977. [60]p.

2070. _____. *Notes on schooling for girls in Upper Canada from the pre-conquest period until the mid-nineteenth century*. Canadian women's history series, no. 10. Toronto: Ontario Institute for Studies in Education. Dept. of History and Philosophy of Education. The Women in Canadian History Project, 1978. 32p.

2071. Royce, Marion. "A landmark in Victorian education for young ladies," *Improving College and University Teaching*, 23:9-11, Winter 1975.

2072. Royce, Marion V. "Arguments on the education of girls - their admission to grammar schools in the province," *Ontario History*, 67:1-13, Mar. 1975.

2073. Stamp, R. M. "Adelaide Hoodless, champion of women's rights," in Robert S. Patterson and others, eds., *Profiles of Canadian educators*. n.p.: D. C.Heath Canada, 1974, pp.213-32.

2074. Temple, Anna. "The development of higher education for women in Ontario, 1867-1914." PhD diss., Wayne State University, 1981. 251p.

2075. Thivierge, Nicole. *Histoire de l'enseignement ménager-familial au Québec 1882-1920*. Québec: Institut québécois de recherche sur la culture, 1982. 475p.

2076. Women in Canadian History Project. (Ontario Institute for Studies in Education). "An inventory of articles on the education of women in the Journal of Education (for Upper Canada and Ontario), 1848-1877," *Canadian Newsletter of Research on Women*, 7:60-1, Mar. 1978.

EDUCATION,CONTINUING

2077. Bowen, Sally and others. "Women practitioners comment," *Learning*, 1:6-8, Fall 1977.

2078. "Brief to the Royal Commission on the Status of Women in Canada," *Continuous Learning*, 8:27-30, Jan.-Feb. 1969.

2079. British Columbia. Ministry of Education. Post-Secondary Dept. *Finding my own way: a guide for British Columbia users*. Victoria, 1981. 138p. (Microlog 82-2111)
    Manual for a telecourse based on a counselling course for women, "Contemporary woman: options and opportunities," produced by Carolyn Larsen and Lorna Cammaert.

2080. Campbell, Sylvia F. *A study prepared for Atkinson College, York University, on continuing education for women in Metropolitan Toronto*. Toronto: S. F. Campbell, 1965. 28p.

2081. Canadian Association for Adult Education. *The next step: a CAAE workshop on continuing education for women*. Saskatoon, Oct. 25-27, 1973.

2082. Canadian Congress for Learning Opportunities for Women. *Freedom to learn: comments on the proposed Canadian Charter of Rights and Freedoms*. Presented to The Special Joint Committee on the Constitution of Canada, Dec. 11, 1980. 12p.

2083. Canadian Federation of University Women. *An exploratory survey of women university graduates: their views on, their plans for continuing education and employment*. With the co-operation of the Women's Bureau, Canada Dept. of Labour. Toronto, 1967. 6p.

2084. "Continuing education of women," *Labour Gazette*, 65:716, Aug. 1965.

2085. Dansereau, J. "Les mamans a l'école," *Le Magazine Maclean*, 8:20-1, fév. 1968.

2086. Dumont-Henry, Suzanne et Michèle Jean. "L'expérience 'Repartir' du CEGEP Bois-de-Boulogne de Montréal: 'Quand maman reprend son sac d'école'," *Canadian Women's Studies / Les cahiers de la femme*, 1:152-6, Fall 1978.

2087. "Further educational facilities recommended after study," *Labour Gazette*, 66:164, Apr. 1966.

2088. Gagné, Christiane Bérubé. "L'Aféas, précurseur en éducation des adultes," *Canadian Women's Studies / Les cahiers de la femme*, 1:25-8, Fall 1978.

2089. Hoek, Margaretha. "A descriptive study of women enrolled in the office careers programmes at selected community colleges." MA thesis, University of Victoria, 1978. 126p. (Can. theses, no.39399)

2090. Humber College of Applied Arts and Technology. *Education-training opportunities for women - a summer at Humber survey, June 21-Aug. 27, 1971*. [Rexdale, Ont., 1971?] 89p.

2091. Justus, Marian. "A descriptive study of the female nonpersisters enrolled in the office careers programs at Douglas College between 1976-1979." MA thesis, Simon Fraser University, 1981. 127p. (Can. theses, no.51028)

2092. Kassirer, Eve. *Female participation in the Canada NewStart Program*. [Ottawa]: Canada. Dept. of Regional and Economic Expansion. Social and Human Analysis Branch, 1970. 26p.

2093. Kiely, Margaret. "Programme of college education for mothers with small children: an evaluation of its effects on mental health," *Canadian Counsellor*, 8:240-9, Oct. 1974.

2094. Krakauer, Renate. *Back to school; a study on access to continuing education and employment for women*. Rexdale, Ont.: Humber College of Applied Arts and Technology. Centre for Women / Centre for Continuous Learning, 1976. 57p. and app.

2095. Ladan, C. J. and Maxine M. Crooks. "Some factors influencing the decision of mature women to enroll for continuing education," *Canadian Counsellor*, 10:29-36, Oct. 1975.

2096. La Fédération des femmes du Québec. *L'éducation des femmes au Québec*. Royal Commission on the Status of Women in Canada. Brief no. 155. Montreal, 1968. 92p. and app.

2097. L'Association des Femmes Diplômées des Universités. *La femme mariée face aux études et au travail*. Royal Commission on the Status of Women in Canada. Brief no. 349. Montreal, 1968. 108p.

2098. Long, Bonita Clarice. "An evaluation of lifeplanning interventions: comparing a career development course with a personal development course and lifeplanning interviews for women." MA thesis, University of British Columbia, 1978. 147p. (Can. theses, no.40686)

2099. Michaels, J. Dale. "A study of the reasons women give for participation in adult career education courses and a comparative analysis of some demographic characteristics." MA thesis, University of British Columbia, 1979. 118p. (Can. theses, no.46211)

2100. Moorcroft, Robert. "The origins of women's learning projects." MA thesis, University of Toronto, 1975. 199p. (Can. theses, no.27926)

2101. Newman, Joel and Mary Jane McLachlan. "Adult education: self-exploration for women," *Canadian Counsellor*, 13:215-18, July 1979.

2102. Ontario Institute for Studies in Education. Dept. of Adult Education. *Continuing education of women: an informal discussion*. Toronto, 1968. Proceedings of a conference held May 9, 1968 at OISE.

2103. Royce, Marion V. *Continuing education for women in Canada: trends and opportunities*. Monographs in adult education, no. 4. Toronto: Ontario Institute for Studies in Education, 1970. 167p.

2104. _____. "The continuing education of women," *International Review of Education*, 19:81-7, Special Number 1973.

2105. _____. "Geared to change," *Continuous Learning*, 4:23-7, Jan.-Feb. 1965.

2106. Selman, G. R. "Two important reports on continuing education for women," *Continuous Learning*, 6:183-7, July-Aug. 1967.

2107. Skelhorne, J. M. *Adult learner in the university: does anybody care?* Toronto: Ontario Institute for Studies in Education. Dept. of Adult Education, 1975. 53 p.

2108. Thom, Pat. "Tokenism," *Learning*, 1:8-10, Fall 1977.

2109. Thring, Beverley R. "Homemaking responsibilities as a factor influencing a mother's educational plans." MA thesis, University of Toronto, 1966. 127p.

2110. University of Alberta. Dept. of Extension. *Women and advanced education*. Royal Commission on the Status of Women in Canada. Brief no. 90. Edmonton, 1968. 7p. and app.

2111. University Women's Club of Edmonton. *Brief no. 82 to the Royal Commission on the Status of Women in Canada*. Edmonton, n.d. 19p.

2112. Waniewicz, Ignacy. *Demand for part-time learning in Ontario*. Toronto: Ontario Institute for Studies in Education, 1976. 216p.

2113. Webster, Daisy. "The need for adult education of married women in the lower socio-economic levels in Vancouver." MA thesis, University of British Columbia, 1978. 91p.

2114. Western Conference on Opportunities for Women. *Report*. Vancouver: University of British Columbia. Centre for Continuing Education / Vancouver Status of Women, 1973. 96p.

2115. Willis, Janet. *Learning opportunities for women in Canada: perceptions of educators; a working paper*. [Toronto]: Canadian Committee on Learning Opportunities for Women, [1977?] 55p.

2116. _____. *Learning opportunities for women: an impressionistic overview*. [Toronto]: Canadian Committee on Learning Opportunities for Women, 1977. 10p.

2117. _____. "Where we stand," *Learning*, 1:3-5, Fall 1977.

2118. Wilson, I. "Seminar on continuing education for women university graduates, York University," *Continuous Learning*, 4:221-2, Sept.-Oct. 1965.

EDUCATION,HIGHER

2119. Bacave, Christiane et Michèle Jean. "Faut-il interdire l'université aux femmes?" *Chatêlaine*, 9:36-7, 59-60, 62, déc. 1968.

2120. Black, Naomi. *Women and post-secondary education in Ontario*. Toronto: Ontario Status of Women Council, 1974. 16p.

2121. Brown, M. Jennifer. *"A disposition to bear the ills...": rejection of a separate college by University of Toronto women*. Canadian Women's History Series, no. 7. Toronto: Ontario Institute for Studies in Education, n.d. 20p.

2122. Coffin, Susan Dianne. "Sex differences in educational aspirations of Newfoundland youth: the effects of family, school and community variables." MEd thesis, Memorial University of Newfoundland, 1976. 111p. (Can. theses, no.31391)

2123. Favreau, Marianne. "Les étudiantes au CEGEP: y prépare-t-on un nouveau type de femmes?" *Châtelaine*, 13:22-3, 64-7, avr. 1972.

2124. Fisher, Esther. "Economics A, marriage F," *Quest*, 9:38L-38N, 38P+ , Oct. 1980.

2125. Frederickson, Margaret C. "Mature women students: a survey." MA thesis, University of British Columbia, 1975. 99p. (Can. theses, no.25863)

2126. Gelber, Sylva M. "Economic and academic status of women in relation to their male colleagues," in, *Women's Bureau '74*. Ottawa: Canada. Dept. of Labour. Women's Bureau, 1975, pp.39-44.

2127. Hitchman, Gladys Symons. "The professional socialization of women and men in two Canadian graduate schools." PhD diss., York University, 1976. 346p. (Can. theses, no.26639)

2128. Kiely, Margaret. "Programme of college education for mothers with small children: an evaluation of its effects on mental health," *Canadian Counsellor*, 8:240-9, Oct. 1974.

2129. Krakauer, Renate. "Make colleges responsive to women's needs, educator urges," *College Canada*, 1:16, Nov. 1976.

2130. Lussier, Thelma G. "The task ahead: in education and training," in Canadian Federation of Business and Professional Women's Clubs, *A collection of papers delivered at the National Conference: Women & Work in the 80's: a Decade of Change*. Ottawa: The Federation, 1981, pp.65-72.

2131. Mackay, Isobel. *A report on women taking part-time degree courses at the University of Waterloo*. Waterloo, Ont.: University of Waterloo, 1973. 85p.

2132. Marsden, Lorna and Edward Harvey. "Equality of educational access reconsidered: the postsecondary case in Ontario," *Interchange*, 2(4):11-26, 1971.

2133. McDonald, Lynn. *Women in post-secondary education: an approach to improved participation*. Ontario. Commission on Post-Secondary Education in Ontario. Brief no. 330. n.p., 1971. 5p.

2134. Nuechterlein, Dorothea I. Allwardt. "The self and the mid-course correction: the mature woman's return to school." MA thesis, Queen's University, 1977. 182p. (Can. theses, no.37533)

2135. Ontario. Ministry of Labour. Women's Bureau. *Women in the labour force. "Education".* Rev. ed. Factsheet, no. 5. Toronto, 1980. [5]p.

2136. Ronish, Donna Ann. "The development of higher education for women at McGill University from 1857 to 1899 with special reference to the role of Sir John William Dawson." MA thesis, McGill University, 1972. 126p. (Can. theses, no.14546)

2137. Ronish, Donna Ann. "The Montreal Ladies' Educational Association, 1871-1885," *McGill Journal of Education*, 6:78-83, Spring 1971.

2138. Skelhorne, J. M. *Adult learner in the university: does anybody care?* Toronto: Ontario Institute for Studies in Education. Dept. of Adult Education, 1975. 53p.

2139. *The education of women.* Submission no. 73 to the Commission on Post-Secondary Education in Ontario, by a group of individuals, June 1971. 10p.

2140. Thompson, Nancy Ramsay. "The controversy over the admission of women to University College, University of Toronto." MA thesis, University of Toronto, 1974. 144p.

2141. Tremblay, Andrée. "L'enseignement supérieur féminin au Québec: l'action concertée des femmes." MA thèse, Université d'Ottawa, 1981. (Can. theses, no.53298)

2142. Vickers, Jill McCalla and June Adam. *But can you type? Canadian universities and the status of women.* CAUT monograph series. Toronto: Clarke, Irwin & Co. / Canadian Association of University Teachers, 1977. 142p.

2143. Wintermute, Dianne. *'Breaking away': women's issues in the student movement.* Toronto: Canadian Federation of Students-Ontario / Ontario Federation of Students, 1980. Reprinted 1983. [18]p.

2144. Zimmerman, Lillian and Marsha Trew. *A report on non-traditional learning programs for women at B. C. post-secondary institutions.* Discussion paper 02/79. Victoria: British Columbia. Ministry of Education, Science and Technology. Information Services, 1979. 57p. (Microlog 79-0393)

ELECTRONIC DATA PROCESSING

2145. Thompson, Jennifer. "DP management doors open for committed women," *CIPS Review*, 6:8-9, July-Aug. 1982.

2146. "Why more women should be DP managers," *Canadian Datasystems*, 10:49-51, June 1978.

2147. "Women in computing: part 1," *ComputerData*, 5:40-4, Nov. 1980.

2148. "Women in computing: part 2," *ComputerData*, 5:72, 74, 76, 78, 80, Dec. 1980.

2149. "Women in computing: part 3," *ComputerData*, 6:41-5, Jan. 1981.

2150. "Absenteeism and women workers," *Labour Gazette*, 65:41, Jan. 1965.

EMPLOYMENT

2151. Allingham, John D. *Demographic background to change in the number and composition of female wage-earners in Canada, 1951-1961.* Canada. Dominion Bureau of Statistics. Special labour force studies, Ser. B, no. 1. Ottawa: Queens Printer, 1967. 26p.

2152. _____. *Women who work: pt. 1: relative importance of age, education and marital status for participation in the labour force.* Canada. Dominion Bureau of Statistics. Special labour force studies, no. 5. Ottawa: Queens Printer, 1967. 26p.

2153. Anderson, Doris. "'Gains made by women in job rights may be in jeopardy'," *Financial Post*, 76:8, Aug. 7, 1982.

2154. Anschutz, Martha. "Something to think about - sex and the business world," *Canada Commerce*, 138:21-2, May 1974.

2155. Armstrong, Hugh and Pat Armstrong. "The segregated participation of women in the Canadian labour force, 1941-71," *Canadian Review of Sociology and Anthropology*, 12:370-84, Nov. 1975.

2156. Armstrong, Pat and Hugh Armstrong. *A working majority: what women must do for pay*. Ottawa: Canadian Advisory Council on the Status of Women, 1983. 280p.

2157. _____. *Job creation and unemployment for Canadian women*. CRIAW working papers. Funded in part by the Canadian Research Institute for the Advancement of Women. Vanier College, Montreal, Quebec, 1980. 46p.
   Prepared for the NATO Symposium "Women and the World of Work" Portugal, Aug. 4-8, 1980.

2158. _____. "Job creation and unemployment for Canadian women," in Naomi Hersom and Dorothy E. Smith, [eds.], *Women and the Canadian labour force*. Working document. Ottawa: Social Sciences and Humanities Research Council of Canada, 1982, pp.209-55.

2159. _____. *Women and jobs: the Canadian case*. Ottawa: Canadian Centre for Policy Alternatives, 1981. 22p.

2160. Armstrong, Patsy Lauraine. "Women and their work: the Canadian experience." MA thesis, Carleton University, 1976. 184p.

2161. Armstrong, Pat. "Unemployed & underemployed: not to mention underpaid & overworked," *Canadian Woman Studies / Les cahiers de la femme*, 3:41-3, Summer 1982.

2162. Arnopoulos, Sheila McLeod. *Problems of immigrant women in the Canadian labour force*. Ottawa: Canadian Advisory Council on the Status of Women, 1979. 79p.

2163. Attenborough, Susan. *Bargaining for equality*. Ottawa: National Union of Provincial Government Employees, 1982. 70p.

2164. Axworthy, Lloyd. "Women and work in the 80's" in Canadian Federation of Business and Professional Women's Clubs, *A collection of papers delivered at the National Conference: Women & Work in the 80's: a Decade of Change*. Ottawa: The Federation, 1981, pp.121-38.

2165. Bank of Montreal. "Women in the labour force," *Bank of Montreal. Business Review*, June 27, 1973, pp.1-4.

2166. Bannon, Sharleen. "International Women's Year. Part 2: Women in the workplace," *Labour Gazette*, 76:69-74. Feb. 1976.

2167. Bell Telephone Co. of Canada. *Brief no. 116 to the Royal Commission on the Status of Women in Canada*. Montreal, n.d. 4p.

2168. Boulet, Jac-André and Laval Lavallée. *Women and the labour market: an analytical framework*. Discussion paper, no. 207. Ottawa: Economic Council of Canada, 1981. 204p.

2169. Boyd, Monica and Elizabeth Humphreys. *Labour markets and sex differences in Canadian incomes*. Discussion paper, no. 143. Ottawa: Economic Council of Canada, 1979. 81p.

2170. _____. "Sex differences in Canada: incomes and labour markets," in *Reflections on Canadian incomes; selected papers presented at the Conference on Canadian Incomes, May 10-12, 1979*. Ottawa: Economic Council of Canada, 1980, pp.401-20.

2171. "Breaking the job barrier," *Canadian Labour*, 16:11, 18, Mar. 1971.

2172. Canada. Advisory Council on the Status of Women. *Women and work*. [*Les femmes et le travail*]. Fact sheet, no. 1. Ottawa, [1979]. 6p.

2173. Canada. Dept. of Labour. *Women at work in Canada: a fact book on the female labour force*. Rev. ed. [Ottawa: Queen's Printer, 1965]. 108p.

2174. Canada. Dept. of Labour. Women's Bureau. *Administrative arrangements for handling questions relating to women workers*. Bulletin no. 20. Ottawa, 1966. 17p.

2175. _____. *Changing patterns in women's employment: report of a consultation held March 18, 1966, Sir Wilfred Laurier Building*. Ottawa, 1966. 71p.

2176. _____. *Domaines de travail accessibles aux femmes: sciences physiques, géosciences, mathématiques*. Ottawa, 1966. 47p.

2177. _____. *Women in the labour force: facts and figures*. Ottawa, 1965- .
   Annual. Beginning with 1976 published in three sections: Pt.1, Labour force survey; Pt.2, Earnings of women and men; Pt.3, Miscellaneous.

2178. Canada. Dept. of National Health and Welfare. Policy Research and Long Range Planning Branch. *The changing dependence of women: roles, beliefs and inequality*. [*La dépendance changeante de la femme: rôles, croyances et inégalité*]. Social security research report, no. 5. Ottawa, 1978. 45, 49p.

2179. Canada. Statistics Canada. *Canada's female labour force*. One of a series from the 1976 Census of Canada. Ottawa, 1980. [32]p. (Cat. no. 98-804E)

2180. Canadian Air Line Flight Attendants Association. *Brief no. 441 to the Royal Commission on the Status of Women in Canada*. Vancouver, 1968. 7p.

2181. Canadian Federation of Business and Professional Women's Clubs. *A collection of papers delivered at the National Conference: Women and Work in the 80's: a Decade of Change. Chateau Lake Louise, Lake Louise, Alberta, October 9 - 12, 1981*. Ottawa: The Canadian Federation of Business and Professional Women's Clubs, 1981. 163p.

2182. Canadian Labour Congress. Women's Bureau. *Equal partners for change: women and unions*. Ottawa, 1981. Folder, 11 pieces.

2183. Canadian Union of Public Employees. *The new status of women in CUPE: a report on past progress and the challenges ahead*. Ottawa: CUPE, 1975. 16p.
    French edition: La nouvelle situation de la femme dans le SCFP.

2184. _____. *The status of women in CUPE; a special report approved by the CUPE national convention, September 1971*. [Ottawa, 1971]. 35p.

2185. "Canadian women in labor force," *World Affairs*, 30:15-16, Jan. 1955.

2186. "Career choice, advancement and personhood," in Canadian Research Institute for the Advancement of Women, *Women as persons. [La femme en tant que personne]*. Toronto: Resources for Feminist Research, 1980, pp.25-33.
    Proceedings of the 3rd annual meeting.

2187. Carmel, Alan. "Femmes et nouveaux horaires," *Labour Gazette*, 74:21-3, Jan. 1974.

2188. _____. "Implications of the new workweek patterns for women in the workforce," *Labour Gazette*, 73:803-6, Dec. 1973.

2189. Cavanagh, Judy. "The plight of women farmworkers," *Resources for Feminist Research*, 11:6-7, Mar. 1982.

2190. Chalkley, Hugh. "Changes in the work environment and implications for employees," in Canadian Federation of Business and Professional Women's Clubs, *A collection of papers delivered at the National Conference: Women & Work in the 80's: a Decade of Change*. Ottawa: The Federation, 1981, pp.29-33.

2191. "Changing patterns in women's employment," *Labour Gazette*, 66:229, May 1966.

2192. Chappell, Neena Lane. "Work, commitment to work and self-identity among women." PhD diss., McMaster University, 1978. 399p.

2193. "Characteristics of women in the labour force—1965," *Labour Gazette*, 66:452, Aug. 1966.

2194. "Chart story: women in the Canadian labour force," *Canadian Business Review*, 2:6-7, Summer 1975.

2195. Charte des droits de la femme au travail," *Canadian Labour*, 10:37, Oct. 1965.

2196. "Charter of rights of working women, eighth World Congress of ICFTU...Resolution," *Labour Gazette*, 65:912-14, Oct. 1965.

2197. Cockburn, Patricia and Yvonne R. Raymond. *Women university graduates in continuing education and employment: an exploratory study initiated by the Canadian Federation of University Women, 1966*. [Toronto, 1967]. 196p. Text in English and French.

2198. Cohen, J. "Women workers," *Canadian Business*, 38:134, May 1965.

2199. Cohen, Marjorie. "Damned if they do: double jeopardy for working women," *Ontario Report*, 3:18-19, Sept. 1978.

2200. Cohen, Shaughnessy M. "Patterns of occupational segregation by sex in the Canadian labour force." MA thesis, University of Windsor, 1973. 174p. (Can. theses, no.19877)

2201. *Conference '80. Women and the economy*. n.p., 1980. 48p.
    Conference sponsored by New Brunswick Advisory Council on the Status of Women, New Brunswick. Dept. of Youth Recreation and Cultural Resources, and others.

2202. Congrès des relations industrielles de l'Université Laval. *Le travail féminin*. Québec: Presses de l'Université Laval, 1967. 177p.

2203. Connelly, M. Patricia. "Canadian women as a reserve army of labour." PhD diss., University of Toronto, 1976. 169p. (Can. theses, no.30337)

2204. _____. "The economic context of women's labour force participation in Canada," in Patricia Marchak, ed., *The working sexes: symposium papers on the effects of sex on women at work*. Vancouver: University of British Columbia. Institute of Industrial Relations, 1977, pp.10-27.

2205. _____. "Women workers and the family wage in Canada," in Anne Hoiberg, ed., *Women and the world of work*. New York: Plenum Press, 1982, pp.223-37.

2206. Connelly, Patricia. *Last hired, first fired: women and the Canadian work force*. Toronto: Women's Press, 1978. 122p.

2207. Cook, Gail C., ed. *Opportunity for choice: a goal for women in Canada. [L'objectif pour les Canadiennes: pouvoir choisir]*. Ottawa: Statistics Canada / C. D. Howe Research Institute, 1976. 217p.

2208. Cook, Gail. "Working women's role not rated high priority," *Journal (The Board of Trade of Metropolitan Toronto)*, July-Aug. 1978, pp.37-9.

2209. Cooper, Jack Edward. "An analysis and evaluation of a multi-agency rehabilitation program for disadvantaged women." MA thesis, Simon Fraser University, 1972. 173p. (Can. theses, no.12564.)

2210. Dale, Patricia. *Women and jobs: the impact of federal government employment strategies on women*. Ottawa: Canadian Advisory Council on the Status of Women, 1980. 119p. and app.

2211. Darling, Martha. *Role of women in the economy: a summary based on ten national reports*. Paris: Organization for Economic and Cultural Development,1975. 127p.

2212. Davies, Sarah. "What women could tell men about work," *Chatelaine*, 47:44, 80, 82, Mar. 1974.

2213. Decore, Anne Marie. "Women and work in Canada, 1961 and 1971." PhD diss., University of Alberta, 1976. 180p. (Can. theses, no.30657)

2214. Devereaux, M. S. and Edith Rechnitzer. *Higher education - hired? Sex differences in employment characteristics of 1976 postsecondary graduates*. Ottawa: Statistics Canada. Projections Section. Education, Science and Culture Division, 1980. 212p.

2215. Dingman, J. "Women's jobs," *Chatelaine*, 42:3-4, Sept. 1969.

2216. Dupont, Claire. *The brain versus the womb*. Royal Commission on the Status of Women in Canada. Brief no. 64. Montreal, 1968. 20p.

2217. Duval, Thérèse. *99.9% des femmes au travail finissent toujours par dire "O.K. boss"*. Montréal: Éditions Libre Expression, 1978. 294p.

EMPLOYMENT

2218. Employers' Council of British Columbia. *Female employment in non-traditional areas: some attitudes of managers and working women*. Vancouver, 1975. 33p. and app.

2219. English, Robert. "'Natural forces will make jobs for women'," *Financial Post*, 75:12, Oct. 24, 1981.

2220. "Establish the rules," *Monetary Times*, 137:50, Oct. 1969.

2221. Fairclough, E. L. "Women's liberation to enter boardrooms: excerpts from address," *Canadian Chartered Accountant*, 97:218, Oct. 1970.

2222. _____. "Women's liberation to enter boardrooms: excerpts from address," *Canadian Chartered Accountant*, 97:218, Oct. 1970.

2223. "Female labour-force participation: putting modern trends in perspective," *Canadian Business Review*, 8:30-2, Summer 1981.

2224. Fox, Bonnie J. and John Fox. "Effects of women's employment on wages," *Canadian Journal of Sociology*, 8:319-28, Summer 1983.

2225. Gagnon, Mona-Josée. "Women and paid work - a difficult equation," *Canada's Mental Health*, 23:12-13, Sept. 1975, suppl.

2226. Gallagher, Diane May. "Factors affecting fertility and female labor force participation in Canada and the United States." MA thesis, University of Alberta, 1973. 141p. (Can. theses, no.17516)

2227. Gaskell, Jane S. and Marvin Lazerson. "Between school and work: perspectives of working class youth," in J. Donald Wilson, ed., *Canadian education in the 1980's*. Calgary: Detselig Enterprises, 1981, pp.197-211.

2228. _____. "Education and job opportunities for women: patterns of enrolment and economic returns," in Naomi Hersom and Dorothy E. Smith, [eds.], *Women and the Canadian labour force*. Working document. Ottawa: Social Sciences and Humanities Research Council of Canada, 1982, pp.257-306.

2229. _____. "Training, education and socialization," in *Sexual equality in the workplace*. Ottawa: Canada. Dept. of Labour. Women's Bureau, 1982, pp.93-122.

2230. Gelber, Sylva M. "Highly qualified manpower policies and the Canadian woman graduate. What price discrimination?" in *Women's Bureau '69*. Ottawa: Canada. Dept. of Labour. Women's Bureau, 1970, pp.27-31.

2231. _____. "The underemployed, underpaid third of the labour force," in *Women's Bureau '71*. Ottawa: Canada. Dept. of Labour. Women's Bureau, 1972, pp.7-12.

2232. Geoffroy, Renée and Paule Sainte-Marie. *Attitude of union workers to women in industry*. Royal Commission on the Status of Women in Canada. Study no. 9. Ottawa, 1971. 137p.

2233. Gillen, M. "Women at work," *Chatelaine*, 42:38, 58-9, Feb. 1969.

2234. Goldenberg, Shirley B. "Female labour and the law in Canada," *Bulletin of Comparative Labour Relations*, 9:55-95, 1978.

2235. Goodman, E. "How management can give women a better break," *Industrial Canada*, 66:28-33, Sept. 1965.

2236. Gunderson, Morley. *Logit estimates of labour force participation based on census cross tabulations*. Working Paper, no. 77-11. Toronto: University of Toronto. Faculty of Management Studies, 1977. 13p.

2237. Hall, O. "Gender and the division of labour; excerpts," *Office Administration*, 11:74, Sept. 1965.

2238. Hersom, Naomi and Dorothy E. Smith. "Brief report and summary of workshop papers and discussion," in their *Women and the Canadian labour force*. Working document. Ottawa: Social Sciences and Humanities Research Council of Canada, 1982, pp.1-27.

2239. _____. *Women and the Canadian labour force*. Working document: not copy edited. Ottawa: Social Sciences and Humanities Research Council of Canada, 1982. 588p.
    Proceedings and papers from a workshop held at the University of British Columbia, Jan. 1981 to evaluate strategic research needs in Women and the Canadian Labour Force.

2240. Hersom, Naomi and Lucy Scott. "Women and the Canadian labour force: report of a Delphi study," in Naomi Hersom and Dorothy E. Smith, [eds.], *Women and the Canadian labour force*. Working document. Ottawa: Social Sciences and Humanities Research Council of Canada, 1982, pp.545-88.

2241. Hersom, Naomi et Dorothy E. Smith. *Les femmes et la population active canadienne: bref exposé et résumé des débats de l'atelier et des rapports présentés*. Ottawa: Conseil de recherche en sciences humaines du Canada, 1982. 24p.

2242. Hickling-Johnston, Ltd. *The status of women in employment in Canada, 1968*. 2v. Report for the Royal Commission on the Status of Women in Canada. Toronto, 1969.

2243. Hill, Christina Maria. "Women in the Canadian economy," in Robert Laxer, ed., *(Canada) Ltd: the political economy of dependency*. Toronto: McClelland & Stewart, 1973, pp.84-106.

2244. Hollobon, J. "Are women people?" *Continuous Learning*, 4:245-50, Nov.-Dec. 1965.

2245. Hossie, Helen. "Women in the work force," *Manitoba Business Review*, 1(4):8-10, May 1976.

2246. Howell, Shelley and Margaret Malone. "Immigrant women and work," *Rikka, 7:35-41, Spring 1980*.

2247. Jain, Harish C. and Diane Carroll, eds. *Race and sex equality in the workplace: a challenge and an opportunity*. Proceedings of a conference sponsored by Industrial Relations Research Association, Hamilton and District Chapter and Canadian Industrial Relations Association, McMaster University, Hamilton, Ont., Sept. 28-29, 1979. Ottawa: Canada. Dept. of Labour. Women's Bureau, 1980. 236p.
    Panels and workshops on equal pay, affirmative action and seniority, promotion and layoffs.

2248. Jewett, P. "Working woman," *Continuous Learning*, 4:216-20, Sept.-Oct. 1965.

2249. Kassirer, Eve. *Female participation in the Canada NewStart Program*. [Ottawa]: Canada. Dept. of Regional and Economic Expansion. Social and Human Analysis Branch, 1970. 26p.

2250. _____. *Female participation in the Canada NewStart Program*. [Ottawa]: Canada. Dept. of Regional and Economic Expansion. Social and Human Analysis Branch, 1970. 26p.

2251. Kehoe, Mary. "CLC conference on equal opportunity; Conférence du CTC sur l'égalité des chances," *Canadian Labour / Travailleur canadien*, 23:30-3, [English]; 31-5, [French], Mar. 1978.

2252. Kettle, John. "From school to work," *Executive*, 23:22, Aug.-Sept. 1981.

2253. _____. "More school - more work," *Executive*, 23:14, Feb. 1981.

2254. _____. "More work = fewer kids," *Executive*, 23:14, Mar. 1981.

2255. Kowalski, Edita. "Women as peers in the organization," *Canadian Banker & ICB Review*, 86:40-3, Feb. 1979.

2256. "L'accroissement de l'effectif ouvrier féminin," *Canadian Labour*, 10:2-3, June 1965.

2257. Leaper, Richard John. "Female labor force attachment: an analysis of unemployment rates in the United States and Canada." PhD diss., Duke University, 1976. 183p. (UM,76-8757)

2258. "L'égalité dans l'emploi est la clé—SCFP," *Canadian Labour*, 13:9, Oct. 1968.

2259. Levine, G. "All male clerical force may result from automation," *Labour Gazette*, 66:430, Aug. 1966.

2260. "Look-out, she's coming: long the victim of discrimination: the female worker...is on the brink of revolution," *Monetary Times*, 137:47-52, Oct. 1969.

2261. MacCormack, Terrance. "Women in industry - a staggering waste of skills," *Plant Administration and Engineering*, 29:27, Aug. 1970.

2262. "Laval's 22nd Industrial Relations Conference: women in the labour force," *Labour Gazette*, 67:486, 488, Aug. 1967.

2263. MacKay, Harry and David Ross. "Fewer jobs, less training for women and youth," *Perception*, 4:30-1, Mar.-Apr. 1981.

2264. MacKenzie, Ruth. "What are women doing with all those rights?" *Citizen*, 14:21-9, Feb. 1968.

2265. MacMillan, S. E. "Women in the labor pool," *Executive*, 7:53-4, Mar. 1965.

2266. "Male-female behaviour on the job: a round table discussion," *ICB Review*, 5:6-8, Summer 1972.

2267. Marchak, M. Patricia. "The Canadian labour force: jobs for women," in Marylee Stephenson, *Women in Canada*. Toronto: New Press, 1973, pp.202-12.

2268. Marsden, Lorna and others. "Female graduates: their occupational mobility and attainments," *Canadian Review of Sociology and Anthropology*, 12:385-405, Nov. 1975.

2269. Marsden, Lorna R. "The relationship between the labor force employment of women and the changing social organization in Canada," in Anne Hoiberg, ed., *Women and the world of work*. New York: Plenum Press, 1982, pp.65-76.

2270. _____. "Unemployment among Canadian women: some sociological problems raised by its increase," in Patricia Marchak, ed., *The working sexes: symposium papers on the effects of sex on women at work*. Vancouver: University of British Columbia. Institute of Industrial Relations, 1977, pp.28-45.

2271. McGill University. Industrial Relations Centre. *Women and work*. Montreal: [n.p.], 1974. 115p.
    Unedited collection of papers presented at its 23rd annual conference, 1974.

2272. McGillivray, Don. "More jobs being created for women than men," *Financial Times*, 65:7, Nov. 15, 1976.

2273. _____. "More new jobs go to women," *Financial Times*, 66:6, May 15, 1978.

2274. _____. "Women becoming major economic force," *Financial Times*, 67:6, Feb. 5 1979.

2275. Menzies, Heather. *Women and the chip: case studies of the effects of informatics on employment in Canada*. Montreal: Institute for Research on Public Policy, 1981. 98p.

2276. "Montreal co-eds get break as 'summer girls' at Bell," *Financial Post*, 60:10, Apr. 23, 1966.

2277. "More women sought," *Labour Gazette*, 75:487, Aug. 1975.

2278. Morissette, Y. R. *Brief no. 322 to the Royal Commission on the Status of Women in Canada*. [Expo]. Montreal, 1968. 22p.

2279. "Myths about women in the labour force," *IR Research Reports*, 3:16, July-Aug. 1979.

2280. Nadeau, J. R. "Sex parity: the real obstacles," *Canadian Personnel and Industrial Relations Journal*, 22:11-12, Mar. 1975.

2281. National Action Committee on the Status of Women. *The economic outlook*. Presentation to the Cabinet of the Government of Canada. Ottawa, 1978. 17p.

2282. New Brunswick. Advisory Council on the Status of Women. *Employment opportunities for the 80's*, prepared by Pamela Easterbrook. [Moncton], 1980. 15p.
    Brief to the Special Committee on Employment Opportunities for the 80's.

2283. Nickson, May. "Current patterns in the female labor force: Canada, 1972," *Notes on Labour Statistics, (Statistics Canada)*, 1972, pp.14-31.

2284. "Night work for women," *Labour Gazette*, 69:740, Dec. 1969.

2285. Northcott, Herbert C. *Women, work, health and happiness*. Edmonton, Alta.: University of Alberta, 1981. (Microlog 81-2175)

2286. _____. "Women, work, health and happiness," *International Journal of Women's Studies*, 4:268-76, May-June 1981.

2287. Nova Scotia Home Economics Association. *Brief no. 31 to the Royal Commission on the Status of Women in Canada*. Wolfville, Nova Scotia, n.d. 17p.

2288. Ontario. Ministry of Labour. Women's Bureau. *Job search*. Rev. ed. Toronto, 1980. 48p.

2289. "OECD study of working women," *Canadian Labour*, 10:44, Nov. 1965.

2290. "Older women valued," *Labour Gazette*, 75:487, Aug. 1975.

2291. Ontario Dept. of Labour. Women's Bureau. *What women think about working!* Toronto, 1970. 20p.

2292. "Opportunity for choice," *Canadian Welfare*, 52:23, July-Aug. 1976.

2293. Ostry, Sylvia. *The female worker in Canada*. 1961 Census monograph. Ottawa: Dominion Bureau of Statistics, 1968. 63p.

2294. Paltiel, Freda L. "International perspective on equal opportunity," *Canadian Labour*, 20:19-22, June 1975.

2295. Parizeau, Alice. "La femme: pupille ou paria?" *Maintenant*, 41:158-60, mai 1965.

2296. Paul, Patricia. "Women derive special benefits from government 'make-work' programs," *Labour Gazette*, 75:723-4, Oct. 1975.

2297. Peal, Emma. "[Howe] report outlines goals for women," *Journal (The Board of Trade of Metropolitan Toronto)*, Easter 1977, pp.22, 24-5.

2298. Penney, Jennifer. *Hard earned wages: women fighting for better work*. Toronto: Women's Press, 1984. 250p.

2299. Perly, C. *Women in the work force: a class analysis*. Ottawa: Canadian Union of Students. Secretariat, 1969. 13p.

2300. Plowman, Shirley. "From 'why not?' to 'when?'" *Labour Gazette*, Anniversary Issue, 1975, pp.663-5.

2301. _____. "Woman's place in the home?" *Labour Gazette*, 75:245-6, Apr. 1975.

2302. "Problems of women workers studied by ILO meeting of consultants," *Labour Gazette*, 66:300, June 1966.

2303. Ram, Bali. *Women's labour-force participation, life cycle stage, and current fertility in Canada: some causal inferences*. [Ottawa: Statistics Canada, 1976?] 15,[7]p.

2304. Randall, S. J. "'Weaker sex' third of work force," *Financial Post*, 60:52, May 14, 1966.

2305.   Rasky, Deena. "For whom the bell toils," *Broadside*, 1(6):1, 1980.

2306.   Recherches opérationnelles technique économiques. *Projected market conditions for female labour in 1980: final report*. Rotec-contract no. 141. Report for the Royal Commission on the Status of Women in Canada. Montreal, 1968. 78p.

2307.   Rioux, Marcia. "Position of women in the Canadian labour force: a sociological analysis." MA thesis, Carleton University, 1973.

2308.   Roberts, Imla. "Making sense out of some new findings," *Canadian Training Methods*, 9:43, Aug. 1976.

2309.   Rosenfeld, Rachael A. "Sex difference in socioeconomic achievement: an overview of findings and explanations," in *Reflections on Canadian incomes; selected papers presented at the Conference on Canadian Incomes, May 10-22, 1979*. Ottawa: Economic Council of Canada, 1980, pp.383-99.

2310.   Ross, Henry. "You've come a long way baby: but not quite far enough," *Marketing*, 80:4, 25, Sept. 22, 1975.

2311.   Rousseau, Yvette. "The status of women in the labour market," *Civil Service Review*, 51:13-16, June 1978.

2312.   Royce, M. V. "Employment of women," *Labour Gazette*, 65:723-4, Aug. 1965.

2313.   Ryten, Eva. "Our best educated women," *Canadian Business Review*, 2:12-16, Summer 1975.

2314.   Saskatchewan. Dept. of Labour. Women's Division. *Trends in women's employment*. [Regina], 1978. 13p. (Microlog 79-1181)

2315.   _____. *Women - employed and unemployed*. Regina, [1979?] 9p.

2316.   Schlesinger, B. "Women workers," *Chatelaine*, 44:12, Sept. 1971.

2317.   Schreiner, J. "Rising female 'participation' shouldn't have been a surprise," *Financial Post*, 65:36, Dec. 4, 1971.

2318.   _____. "Women workers," *Financial Post*, 61:28, Feb. 18, 1967.

2319.   *Sexual equality in the workplace*. Proceedings of a conference sponsored by the Women's Bureau, Labour Canada, Mar. 17-19, 1982, Toronto. Ottawa: Canada. Dept. of Labour. Women's Bureau, 1982. 152p.

2320.   Skolnik, Michael L. "Toward some new emphases in empirical research on women and the Canadian labour force," in Naomi Hersom and Dorothy E. Smith,[eds.], *Women and the Canadian labour force*. Working document. Ottawa: Social Sciences and Humanities Research Council of Canada, 1982, pp.105-32.

2321.   Smith, Elizabeth. "Women, an untapped human resource," *ICB Review*, 5:2-5, Summer 1972.

2322.   Spencer, Byron G. "The increase in female labour force participation in Canada: a survey of some causes and consequences," in Harish C. Jain, *Contemporary issues in Canadian personnel administration*. Scarborough, Ont.: Prentice-Hall, 1974, pp.86-95.

2323.   "Status of women today and tomorrow," *Bank Canadian National*, 7:1-4, Jan. 1976.

2324.   Swan, Carole. *Women in the Canadian labour market*. Technical study, no.36. Ottawa: Canada. Task Force on Labour Market Development, 1981. [89]p.

2325.   _____. "Women in the Canadian labour force: the present reality," in Naomi Hersom and Dorothy E. Smith, [eds.], *Women and the Canadian labour force*. Working document. Ottawa: Social Sciences and Humanities Research Council of Canada, 1982, pp.29-103.

2326.   Tandan, Nand. "Decline in the female-male unemployment rate differential in Canada, 1961-72," *Notes on Labour Statistics (Statistics Canada)*, 1973, pp.5-12.

2327.   Thibault, André. *Étude sur l'absentéisme et le roulement de la main d'oeuvre féminine*. Report for the Royal Commission on the Status of Women in Canada. n.p., 1968. 39p.

2328.   "Third of women in 25-44 group at work," *Financial Post*, 64:18, Apr. 4, 1970.

2329.   "'Third shift' for women sought," *Financial Post*, 59:39, July 24, 1965.

2330.   Turcotte, E. "Dear Ottawa: about jobs for women, put up or shut up," *Maclean's*, 83:21, Feb. 1970.

2331.   "Useful facts for countering popular myths about working women," in Lynda Turner, comp., *Woman in Canadian society*. n.p., 197?, pp.99-103.

2332. Walker-Leigh, Vanya. "Our man stands up for working women," *Financial Post*, 74:9, May 10, 1980.

2333. Walsh, William D. "A time series analysis of female labour force participation rates disaggregated by marital status," *Relations industrielles / Industrial Relations*, 37(2):367-84, 1982; correction, 37(3):703, 1982.

2334. Warskett, George. "The choice of technology and women in the paid work force," in Naomi Hersom and Dorothy E. Smith, [eds.], *Women and the Canadian labour force*. Working document. Ottawa: Social Sciences and Humanities Research Council of Canada, 1982, pp.133-64.

2335. "Weekend poll: are working women still being exploited?" *Weekend Magazine*, 28:3, Mar. 4, 1978.

2336. Western Conference on Opportunities for Women. *Manpower/womanpower: proposals concerning manpower policies and practices*. Brief to the Minister of Manpower and Immigration, the Honourable Robert Andras, 1973. 11p.

2337. White, Terrence H. "Autonomy in work: are women any different?" in Marylee Stephenson, *Women in Canada*. Toronto: New Press, 1973, pp.213-26.

2338. Wilson, S. J. *Women, the family and the economy*. Toronto: McGraw-Hill Ryerson, 1982. 176p.

2339. "Women and the labour force," in M. Burstein and others, *Canadian work values: findings of a work ethic survey and a job satisfaction survey*. Ottawa: Canada. Dept. of Manpower and Immigration, Strategic Planning and Research, 1975, pp.50-9.

2340. "Women at work in Canada," *Labour Gazette*, 65:801, Sept. 1965.

2341. "Women at work," *Financial Post*, 59:6, May 8, 1965.

2342. "Women get majority of new jobs but are hardest hit by unemployment," *Labour Gazette*, 78:487, Nov.-Dec. 1978.

2343. "Women in business: policies of three Canadian corporations," *Canadian Business Review*, 2:8-11, Summer 1975.

2344. "Women in the labour force," *Canadian Labour*, 10:11-12, June 1965.

2345. "Women in the labour force, 1966," *Labour Gazette*, 67:305, May 1967.

2346. "Women in the labour force, 1967," *Labour Gazette*, 68:272, May 1968.

2347. "Women in the labour force: recent trends," *Canada Manpower and Immigration Review*, 8(1):15-24, 1975.

2348. "Women in the labour market," *Labour Research Bulletin* (British Columbia. Dept. of Labour), 10:12-8, Sept. 1982.

2349. "Women in the workforce," *Labour Gazette*, 74:457, July 1974.

2350. "Women of the world," *Financial Post*, 61:6, Mar. 4, 1967.

2351. "Women organizing for big breaks in job training, access to capital," *Globe & Mail*, Feb. 26, 1977, p.B1.

2352. "Woman represents CUPE at international conference," *Labour Gazette*, 69:75, Feb. 1969

2353. "Women told they outnumber men at most agencies," *Globe & Mail*, Feb. 23, 1977, p.B3.

2354. "Women workers," *Canadian Labour*, 17:2-3, May 1972.

2355. "Women's work," in Irving Abella and David Millar, eds., *The Canadian worker in the twentieth century*. Toronto: Oxford University Press, 1978, pp.151-215.

2356. "Working women," *Canadian Business*, 39:49, July 1966.

EMPLOYMENT - ALBERTA

2357. Alberta. Dept. of Manpower and Labour. Research Divison. *Women in the labour force - Alberta*. 1972. 20p.

2358. Bilgin, Bahir. *The roles of women and community development*. Hicksville, N.Y.: Exposition Press, 1978. 43p.

2359. Edmonton Social Planning Council. Task Force on Women in the Albertan Labour Force. *Report*. Edmonton, 1974. 20p.

EMPLOYMENT - BIBLIOGRAPHY

2360. Bayefsky, Evelyn. "Women and work: a selection of books and articles," *Ontario Library Review*, 56:79-90, June 1972.
2361. Boulet, Jac-André and Laval Lavallée. *Women and the labour market: an analytical framework*. Discussion paper, no. 207. Ottawa: Economic Council of Canada, 1981. 204p.
2362. Connelly, M. Patricia, comp. *Women in the Canadian economy: an annotated selected bibliography*. Compiled with support from the Humanities and Social Science Committee, University of Toronto, 1974. 24p.
2363. Diamond, Sara. *Women's labour history in British Columbia: a bibliography, 1930-1948*. Vancouver: Press Gang Publishers, 1980. 80p.
2364. McKay, Margaret. *Women in the labour force, with an emphasis on the clerical and service occupations: a selected bibliography*. [Ottawa: Social Sciences and Humanities Research Council of Canada, 1982]. 59p. (Microlog 83-0920)
2365. Metropolitan Toronto Library Board. Business Library. *Working women in Canada*. Toronto, 1973. 11p. Suppl. no. 1 (Dec. 1973); suppl. no. 2 (Sept. 1974).

EMPLOYMENT - BRITISH COLUMBIA

2366. Braid, Kate. "Invisible women: women in non-traditional occupations in British Columbia." MA thesis, Simon Fraser University, 1979. 213p. (Can. theses, no.44862)
2367. Diamond, Sara. *Women's labour history in British Columbia: a bibliography, 1930-1948*. Vancouver: Press Gang Publishers, 1980. 80p.
2368. Leonard, Anne Hewitt. "Employment trends for women in British Columbia." MA thesis, University of British Columbia, 1966. 116p.
2369. Mitchell, M. "Recent trends in women's labour force activity in British Columbia," *BC Labour Research Bulletin*, 7:23-31, July 1979.
2370. Stanton, Patrick. "Women in the labour market - industries, occupations and earnings," *BC Labour Research Bulletin*, 7:15-23, Aug. 1979.
2371. Working Women's Association, [Vancouver]. *Women's work: a selection of articles by working women*. Vancouver: Press Gang, 1972. 24p.

EMPLOYMENT - HISTORY

2372. "Chart story: women in the Canadian labour force," *Canadian Business Review*, 2:6-7, Summer 1975.
2373. The Corrective Collective. *Never done: three centuries of women's work in Canada*. Toronto: Canadian Women's Educational Press, 1974. 150p.
2374. Denis, Ann B. "Femmes: ethnie et occupation au Québec et en Ontario, 1931-1971," *Canadian Ethnic Studies*, 13(1):75-90, 1981.
2375. Kearney, Kathryn. "Canadian women and the First World War," *Canadian Women's Studies / Les cahiers de la femme*, 3(1):95-6, 1981.
2376. Klein, Sheila. "Biscuitmakers, dressmakers, ironers and pressers," *Branching Out*, 7(1):11, 1980.
2377. Lacelle, Claudette. "Les domestiques dans les villes canadiennes au XIXe siècle: effectifs et conditions de vie," *Histoire sociale / Social History*, 15:181-207, mai 1982.
2378. Le Rougetel, Katy. "Cats, mothers, nut trappers," *Branching Out*, 4:38-41, July-Aug. 1977.
2379. Lenskyj, Helen. "Social change affecting women in urban Canada, 1890-1930, and its impact upon immigrant women in the labour force." MA thesis, University of Toronto, 1980. 152p.
2380. Lowe, Graham S. "Women, work and the office: the feminization of clerical occupations in Canada, 1901-1931," *Canadian Journal of Sociology*, 5:361-81, Fall 1980.
2381. Pierson, Ruth. "Women's emancipation and the recruitment of women into the Canadian labour force in World War II," *Canadian Historical Association. Historical Papers*, 1976, pp.141-73.

2382. .... "Women's emancipation and the recruitment of women into the labour force in World War II," in Susan Mann Trofimenkoff and Alison Prentice, eds., *The neglected majority: essays in Canadian women's history*. Toronto: McClelland and Stewart, 1977, pp.125-45.

2383. Strong-Boag, Veronica. "The girl of the new day: Canadian working women in the 1920's," *Labour / Le Travailleur*, 4:131-64, 1979.

2384. .... "Working women and the state: the case of Canada 1889-1945," in Naomi Hersom and Dorothy E. Smith, [eds.], *Women and the Canadian labour force*. Working document. Ottawa: Social Sciences and Humanities Research Council of Canada, 1982, pp.439-61.

2385. Trofimenkoff, Susan Mann. *One hundred and two muffled voices: Canada's industrial women in the 1880's*. GROW paper, no. 10. Toronto: Ontario Institute for Studies in Education. Group for Research on Women, [197?]. 20, [4]p.

2386. "Women's employment in Canada: a look at the past," *Canada Manpower and Immigration Review*, 8(1):1-8, 1975.

EMPLOYMENT - MANITOBA

2387. Clatworthy, Stewart J. *Issues concerning the role of native women in the Winnipeg labour market*. Technical study, no. 5. Ottawa: Canada. Task Force on Labour Market Development, 1981. 14p. and app.

2388. Phillips, Paul. "Women in the Manitoba labour market: a study of the changing economic role," in Henry C. Klassen, ed., *The Canadian West: social change and economic development*. Calgary: University of Calgary / Comprint Pub., 1977, pp.79-92.

2389. Simpkins, Joan and others. *Employment in day care*. Winnipeg: Manitoba. Dept. of Labour. Women's Bureau, 1976. 23p. (Profile 77-0277)

EMPLOYMENT - NEW BRUNSWICK

2390. New Brunswick. Interdepartmental Committee on the Role of Women in the New Brunswick Economy and Society. *Report*. [Fredericton], 1975. 169p. (Profile 76-0068)

EMPLOYMENT - NEWFOUNDLAND

2391. Adams, Janet, "Role of women in the labour force of Newfoundland." BA thesis, Memorial University at Newfoundland, 1967. 64p.

2392. Basha, Rosemary. "St. John's women in the labour force (1900-1920)". Paper presented in fulfillment of the requirements for History 4230, Memorial University of Newfoundland, 1973. 24p.

2393. Batten, Elizabeth and others. *Working women in Newfoundland*. St. John's: Women's Place, 1975. 46p.

2394. Newfoundland Status of Women Council. Education Group. *This is our work: some Newfoundland women talk about their careers*. St. John's, Nfld., 1975. 40p.

2395. Women's Employment Counselling. *No need to just pretend: new work choices for women*. Corner Brook, Nfld.: Canada. Dept. of Employment and Immigration / Corner Brook Status of Women Council, [1982]. 24p.

EMPLOYMENT - NOVA SCOTIA

2396. Bianchi, Maria Teresa and Joyce Sterling Brodie. "Decision to work among Halifax women," in C. Beattie and S. Crysdale, eds., *Sociology Canada: readings*. Toronto: Butterworth and Co., 1974, pp.179-89.

2397. Conrad, Joyce D. "Women as reserve labour: the Nova Scotia case." MA thesis, Dalhousie University, 1978. 53p. (Can. theses, no.38377)

2398. Halifax Women's Bureau. *Women at work in Nova Scotia*. Halifax, 1973. 47p.

2399. .... "Women's work in Nova Scotia," *This Magazine*, 9:24-8. Mar.-Apr. 1975. Excerpts from Halifax Women's Bureau, *Women at work in Nova Scotia*, 1973.

96

2400. Nova Scotia. Dept. of Labour. Economics and Research Division. *Working women in Nova Scotia*. Information bulletin. [Halifax], 1976. 13p.

2401. _____. *Women workers in Nova Scotia*. Halifax, 1967. 48p.

2402. Voice of Women [Halifax]. *Brief no.429 to the Royal Commission on the Status of Women in Canada*. n.d. 6p.

EMPLOYMENT - ONTARIO

2403. Acton, Janice, Penny Goldsmith and Bonnie Shepard, eds. *Women at work: Ontario, 1850-1930*. Toronto: Canadian Women's Educational Press, 1974. 405p.

2404. Bird, Patricia. "Hamilton working women in the Great Depression," *Canadian Woman Studies / Les cahiers de la femme*, 3:101-2, Summer 1982.

2405. Bohnen, Linda. "Women workers in Ontario: a socio-legal history," *University of Toronto. Faculty of Law Review*, 31:45-74, 1973.

2406. Davis, N. H. W. *Some methods of analysing cross-classified census data: the case of labour force participation rates*. Canada. Dominion Bureau of Statistics. Special labour force studies, series B, no. 3. Ottawa, 1969. 37p.

2407. Eastham, Katherine. *Working women in Ontario*. Toronto: Ontario. Dept. of Labour, Women's Bureau, [1971]. 62p.

2408. Kealey, Greg. *Working class Toronto at the turn of the century*. Toronto: New Hogtown Press, 1973. 23p.

2409. London, Ont. City Council. *Status of equal employment opportunities for male and female employees*. London, Ont., 1975. [48]p.

2410. Matthew, Barbara A. "Women's work: the Northwestern Ontario case [review]," *Resources for Feminist Research*, 11:185-6, Mar. 1982.

2411. McLellan, Ethel. "Counselling and training for women entering or re-entering the labour force - findings of a survey [précis]," in *Report of a consultation on the employment of women with family responsibilities*. Ottawa: Canada. Dept. of Labour. Women's Bureau, 1965, pp.4-12.

2412. Ontario. Dept. of Labour. Women's Bureau. *Who are Ontario's working women?* Toronto, 1967. 4p.

2413. _____. *Women in Ontario's economy*. Toronto, 1966. 26p.

2414. Ontario. Ministry of Labour. Research Branch. *Ontario women: selected occupational and educational data*. [Toronto], 1975. 7p.

2415. Ontario Status of Women Council. *Comments on the work incentives program for family benefits recipients announced by Ministry of Community and Social Services*. [Toronto], 1979. 12p.

2416. _____. *Employment strategies for women in the 1980's: recommendations for action: a brief to the Government of Ontario*. [Toronto], 1980. 18p.

2417. Ontario. Ministry of Labour. Women's Bureau. *Options: a sourcebook on employment and education for women*. Toronto, 1977. 63p.

2418. _____. *Two out of five women in Ontario are employed, and other interesting statistics....* Toronto, 1976. [4]p.

2419. _____. *Women in the labour force. "Basic facts"*. Rev. ed. Factsheet, no. 2. Toronto, 1981. [6]p.

2420. _____. *Women in the labour force. "Fact & fiction"*. Factsheet, no. 1. [Toronto, 1975] [4]p.

2421. _____. *Women in the workplace: blueprint for employers*. Rev. ed. Toronto, [1982]. 32p.

2422. _____. *Report of the Premier's meeting on equal employment opportunity for women*. [Toronto, 1975]. 17p.

2423. Roberts, Wayne. *Honest womanhood: feminism, femininity and class consciousness among Toronto working women, 1893 to 1914*. Toronto: New Hogtown Press, 1976. 60p.

2424. Spears, Kasia and Jan Barnsley. *Working relationship. A report on the status of women employees in the Addiction Research Foundation*. Toronto: Alcoholism and Drug Addiction Research Foundation, 1977. 170p.

EMPLOYMENT - PRINCE EDWARD ISLAND

2425. Prince Edward Island. Dept. of Labour. Research and Planning Branch. *Women in the Prince Edward Island labour force*. [Charlottetown], 1983. 17p. and app. (Microlog 83-3371)

EMPLOYMENT - QUEBEC

2426. Association des femmes diplômées des universités (Montréal). *Analyse de politiques d'égalité en emploi*. Montréal, 1979. [166]p.

2427. Barry, Francine. *Le travail de la femme au Québec: l'évolution de 1940 à 1970*. Montréal: Les Presses de l'Université du Québec, 1977. 80p.

2428. Beattie, Margaret. "La politique d'ensemble. 'Pour les Québécoises: éqalité et indépendance' du Conseil du Statut de la Femme du Québec..." *Resources for Feminist Research*, 9:32-4, Nov. 1980.

2429. Bhérer, Jacinthe. *Étude sur les distinctions fondées sur le sexe dans les conventions collectives et décrets*. Québec: Conseil du statut de la femme, 1974. v.p.

2430. Centrale de l'enseignement du Québec et Confédération des syndicats nationaux. *Etats généraux des travailleuses salariées québécoises: 3 mars 1979: la lutte des femmes: une lutte permanente, une lutte collective: manifeste (deuxième) version*. n.p., C.E.Q., 1979. 11p.

2431. Centrale de l'enseignement du Québec. *Le droit au travail pour toutes les femmes: défis d'aujourd'hui, réalités de demain: rapport du XXVIIe congrès général, Québec*. n.p., 1980. 43p.

2432. _____. *Lutte des femmes: un présent à organiser, un futur à défier: forum sur la condition des femmes 10-11-12 avril 1981*. n.p., 1981. 31p.

2433. Confédération des syndicats nationaux. *Les travailleuses et l'accès à la syndicalisation: états généraux II des travailleuses salariées québécoises*. Produit par le comité d'action "accès à la syndicalisation et normes minimales d'emploi". n.p., [1979?] 60p.

2434. Copp, Terry. "Women and children in the labour force," in his *The anatomy of poverty: the condition of the working class in Montreal, 1897-1929*. Toronto: McClelland and Stewart, 1974, pp.44-56.

2435. Daigle, Johanne. "L'évolution des revendications des travailleuses salariées québécoises depuis la crise," *Relations*, 41:200-4, juill.-août 1981.

2436. Descarries-Bélanger, Francine. *L'école rose...et les cols roses: la reproduction de la division sociale des sexes*. [Laval, Québec]: Editions coopératives Albert Saint-Martin, 1980. 128p.

2437. Després, J. P. and others. *Le travail féminin*. Québec: Les Presses de l'Université Laval, 1967. 177p.

2438. Fédération des travailleurs du Québec. *Travailleuses et syndiquées: rapport du comité FTQ sur la situation de la femme*. Montréal, 1973. 87p. Rapport du 13e congrès du 3 décembre au 7 décembre 1973 à Montréal.

2439. Fortin, Carrier. "Egalité ou privilège pour la femme au travail," in Jacques Boucher et André Morel, eds., *Livre du centenaire du Code civil*. Vol. 1: *Le droit dans la vie familiale*. Montréal: Presses de l'Université de Montréal, 1970, pp.287-96.

2440. Fournier, Francine. "Les femmes et le travail au Québec," dans Rodrigue Bélanger et autres, eds., *Devenirs de femmes*. Cahiers de recherche éthique, no. 8. Montréal: Éditions Fides, 1981, pp.111-21.

2441. Fournier, Gaétane et Sylvia Morin. *Des femmes au pouvoir*. Sherbrooke, Québec: Éditions Sherbrooke, 1978. 119p.

2442. Freeman, Jody. "Au bas de l'échelle" - la condition des travailleuses non syndiquées [entrevue]," *Relations*, 41:205-7, juill-août 1981.

2443. Gendron, Diane et Kim Chi Tran Van. *Les travailleuses au Québec*. Québec: Québec. Ministère du travail et de la main-d'oeuvre. Service des communications, 1975. 11p.

2444. Gosselin, Hélène. "Signification des activités de travail (professionnelles) et hors travail (extra-professionnelles) pour des femmes occupant certains postes de professionnelles à la Fonction Publique du Québec." MScSoc thèse, Université Laval, 1978. 155, [50]p. (Can. theses, no. 39141)

2445. "La condition économique des femmes au Québec. Collection études et dossiers, la documentation Québécoise, Ministère des communications, éditeur officiel du Québec; Québec 1978, recense par Monique B. Boulanger," *Orientation professionnelle*, 14:181-2, été 1978.

2446. "La femme canadienne au travail," *Canadian Labour*, 10:35, nov. 1965.

2447. Lavigne, Marie et Jennifer Stoddart. "Analyse du travail féminin à Montréal entre les deux guerres." MA thèse, Université du Québec à Montréal, 1973. 268p. (Can. theses, no.32321)

2448. _____. "Les travailleuses Montréalaises entre les deux guerres," *Labour / Le Travailleur*, 2:170-83, 1977.

2449. _____. "Ouvrières et travailleuses Montréalaises 1900-1940," dans Marie Lavigne et Yolande Pinard, *Les femmes dans la société québécoise: aspects historiques*. Montréal: Éditions du Boréal Express, 1977, pp.125-43.

2450. _____. "Women's work in Montreal at the beginning of the century," in Marylee Stephenson, *Women in Canada*. Rev. ed. Toronto: General Publishing Co., 1977, pp.129-47.

2451. Lavigne, Marie et autres. *Travailleuses et féministes: les femmes dans la société québécoise*. Études d'histoire du Québec, no. 13. Montréal: Boréal Express, 1983. 430p.

2452. Lepage, Francine et autres. *Syndicalisation: droit à acquérir, outil à conquérir: étude sur les travailleuses non syndiquées au Québec*. [Québec]. Conseil du statut de la femme, [1901?] 275p.

2453. Quebec. Comité chargé d'étudier le problème du travail de nuit de la main-d'oeuvre féminine dans les établissements industriels. *Rapport du Comité chargé d'étudier le problème de travail de nuit de la main-d'oeuvre féminine dans les établissements industriels*. Québec: Le Comité, 1966. 44p.

2454. Roch, Marcelle Hardy. *Travail féminin*. Québec: Québec. Ministère de l'éducation. Direction générale de l'éducation permanente, 1968. 245p.

2455. Simard, Monique et Carmen Bazzy, eds. *Les femmes à la CSN n'ont pas les moyens de reculer*. 4e Rapport du Comité de la condition feminine CSN. Montréal: Comité de la condition féminine CSN, [1982]. 108p.

2456. Therien, C. "Évolution du travail féminin et préparation scolaire au Québec," *Canadian Vocational Journal*, 10:42-5, mai 15, 1974.

2457. Université du Québec à Montréal. Laboratoire sur la répartition et la securité du revenu / Québec. Conseil du statut de la femme. *La condition économique des femmes au Québec*. Vol.1: *L'exposé de la question. Vol.2: L'évaluation de la réponse apportée par l'État*. Québec: Éditeur officiel du Québec, 1978.

2458. Vinet, Alain, Francine Dufresne et Lucie Vézina. *La condition féminine en milieu ouvrier: une enquête auprès des travailleuses de cinq usines de la région du Québec*. Identité et changements culturels, no. 3. Québec: Institut québécois de recherche sur la culture, 1982. 222p.

2459. "Women in Quebec industry, graveyard shift," *Labour Gazette*, 67:359, June 1967.

EMPLOYMENT - SASKATCHEWAN

2460. Saskatchewan. Dept. of Labour. Women's Bureau. *Women at work in Saskatchewan*. Regina, n.d. 2p.

2461. Saskatchewan. Dept. of Labour. Women's Division. *Women in the Saskatchewan labour force*. Regina, 1978. 32p.

EMPLOYMENT - YUKON

2462. Scrivener, Leslie. "The unstoppable women of the Yukon," *Canadian Women's Studies / Les cahiers de la femme*, 3(1):26-7, 1981.

EMPLOYMENT, RE-ENTRY INTO LABOUR FORCE

2463. Axford, R. W. "Stage of the empty nest!" *Continuous Learning*, 6:233-7, Sept.-Oct. 1967.

2464. Bell, Linda. *Women returning to the labour force*. Toronto: Ontario. Dept. of Labour. Women's Bureau, 1969. 26p.

2465. Benmouyal-Acoca, Viviane. *Le retour des femmes sur le marché du travail: rapport d'étude*. Études et recherches, no. 2. Québec: Québec. Ministère du travail et de la main-l'oeuvre. Direction générale de la recherche, 1978. 195p.

2466. Canada. Commission of Employment and Immigration. *Creative job search technique: appendix. Women returning to work*. [Ottawa], 1979. 8p.

2467. Clarke, Marnie A. "Transitional women: implications for adult educators," *Adult Leadership*, 24:123-7, Dec. 1975.

2468. Delisle, Lucie. "La femme et sa seconde carrière," *Orientation professionnelle*, 14:118-27, été 1978.

2469. Gillen, M. "Back to work...guide to re-employment," *Chatelaine*, 42:24-5, 36-8, Aug. 1969.

2470. Harris, Marjorie. "Going back to work," *Chatelaine*, 47:52, 103, Oct. 1974.

2471. _____. "How Sally Ballantine went back to work," *Chatelaine*, 47:53, 105, Oct. 1974.

2472. Hoek, Margaretha. "A descriptive study of women enrolled in the office careers programmes at selected community colleges." MA thesis, University of Victoria, 1978. 126p. (Can. theses, no.39399)

2473. "Housewives don't go back to first career: report," *Globe & Mail*, Nov. 13, 1978, p.11.

2474. Kostash, Myrna. "Coming back from motherhood," *Maclean's*, 88:8, Aug. 1975.

2475. L'Association des femmes diplômées des universités. *La femme mariée face aux études et au travail*. Royal Commission on the Status of Women in Canada. Brief no. 349. Montreal, 1968. 108p.

2476. McLellan, Ethel. "Counselling and training for women entering or re-entering the labour force - findings of a survey [précis]," in *Report of a consultation on the employment of women with family responsibilities*. Ottawa: Canada. Dept. of Labour. Women's Bureau, 1965, pp.4-12.

2477. Pearson, Mary. *The second time around: a study of women returning to the work force*. Women and work, [no. 2]. Ottawa. Canadian Advisory Council on the Status of Women, 1979. 69p.

2478. Simard, Lucie. "La situation de la femme qui retourne au marche du travail," *Orientation professionnelle*, 14:145-9, été 1978.

2479. Simpkins, Joan. *Counselling services: profile and follow-up*. Winnipeg: Manitoba. Dept. of Labour. Women's Bureau, 1976. 15p.

2480. Sinclair, Sonja. *I presume you can type: the mature woman's guide to second careers*. [Toronto]: Canadian Broadcasting Corp., [1969]. 161p.

2481. Toscani, Ave. "Le retour au travail et l'estime de soi chez la femme au passage des quarante ans." MA mémoire, Université du Québec à Montréal, 1980. 109p. (Can. theses, no.47683)

2482. Wilcox, V. and E. Dollery. "3 who went back," *Chatelaine*, 42:26-31, Aug. 1969.

ENGINEERING

2483. Bouchard, Micheline. "What it's like to be a woman, an engineer, a wife, a mother & a president," *CIM Bulletin*, 72:46, 48-9, June 1979.

2484. Canada. Dept. of Transport. Canadian Marine Transportation Administration. *National consolidation: Equal Opportunities For Women Availability Research Study. [Aperçu national: promotion de la femme étude disponibilité]*. [Ottawa, 1980]. 96, 99p. (Microlog 81-0773)

2485. Ellis, Dormer. *These women are engineers. [Ces femmes sont des ingénieures]*. Ottawa: Canadian Council of Professional Engineers, 1983. 27, 28p. Summary report of a questionnire survey for the 2nd Convention of Women Engineers of Canada.

2486. Hawley, Brendan, ed. "Women and engineering," *Engineering Manpower News*, no. 34, May-June 1982. [4]p.

2487. Ordre des ingénieurs du Québec. *Sondage sur le rôle de la femme ingénieur au Québec: rapport final*. n.p., 1980. (Microlog 81-2148)

2488. Sidlofsky, Samuel and Gloria Goodings. "The Canadian female engineer: role confusion - oh, no!" *Sociological Focus*, 6:14-29, Winter 1973.

2489. _____. "Female professional engineers in Canada," *Engineering Digest*, 18(2):31-3, 1972.

2490. "Survey shows Quebec's women engineers find gaining acceptance hard," *Globe & Mail*, Jan. 24, 1981, p.B6.

2491. "This issue is dedicated Elsie Gregory McGill, 1905-1980," *Canadian Women's Studies / Les cahiers de la femme*, 3(1):119, 1981.

2492. Whitton, Bob. "Meet Marjory Loveys in her final year in Waterloo's systems design program," *Canadian Personnel and Industrial Relations Journal*, 22:26-7, Mar. 1975.

ENVIRONMENT

2493. Liefschultz, Judy. "Nuclear power: child of the patriarchy," *Broadside*, 1(9):5, 1980.

2494. Mayo, Susan and Susan Holtz. "Ecological decision making: where politics, morality and technology meet, who makes the rules? [interview]," *Branching Out*, 5(3):8-11, 1978.

2495. Peterson, Rebecca, Gerda R. Wekerle and David Morley. "Women and environments: an overview of an emerging field," *Environment and Behavior*, 10:511-34, Dec. 1978.

2496. Porter, Sylvia. "One woman's journey," *Branching Out*, 5(3):15, 48, 1978.

EQUAL PAY FOR EQUAL WORK

2497. "A day to remember," *Canadian Nurse*, 77:4, May 1981.

2498. "A helping hand up the ladder: [promoting women]," *Financial Times*, 67:19, Oct. 16, 1978.

2499. Acheson, Shelley. "Equal pay: a myth - equal value: a joke," *Labour Review [Ontario Federation of Labour]*, Nov.-Dec. 1976, p.9.

2500. Agarwal, Naresh C. and Harish C. Jain. *Pay discrimination against women in Canada: issues and policies*. Working paper series, no. 143. Hamilton, Ont.: McMaster University. Faculty of Business, 1978. 9p.

2501. _____. "Pay discrimination against women in Canada: issues and policies," *International Labour Review*, 117:169-177, Mar.-Apr. 1978.

2502. Agarwal, N. C. "Male-female pay inequity and public policy in Canada and the United States," *Industrial Relations*, 37(4):780-804, 1982.

2503. Albert, Richard G. "Be sure your pay scales don't discriminate," *Benefits Canada*, 5:38-9, July-Aug. 1981.

2504. Bell, Sandra. "Librarians and historical researchers: equal value?" *Status of Women News*, 5:21-2, Summer 1979.

2505. Bennett, James and Pierre Loewe. "Despite our equal-pay laws, lower salaries and benefits persist for female workers," *Financial Post*, 69:E6-8, June 7, 1975.

2506. Blaker, Gloria. "Some of us are more equal than others," *Canadian Nurse*, 76:6, May 1980.

2507. Bourne, Paula. "The case of Lois Beckett," in her, *Women in Canadian Society*. Toronto: Ontario Institute for Studies in Education, 1976, pp.63-86.

2508. _____. "The Greenacres case," in her, *Women in Canadian society*. Toronto: Ontario Institute for Studies in Education, 1976, pp.86-103.

2509. Canada. Dept. of Labour. International Labour Affairs Branch. *Equal remuneration for work of equal value*. Ottawa: Queen's Printer, 1970. 55p. and app.

2510. Canadian Association of Administrators of Labour Legislation. Women's Policy Committee. *Equal pay in Canada*. Report prepared for the 36th Annual Conference of the Canadian Association of Administrators of Labour Legislation. Saskatoon, Sask., Sept. 13-15, 1977. n.p., 1977. 56p.

2511. Canadian Human Rights Commission. *Equal pay for male and female employees who are performing work of equal value; interpretation guide for section 11 of the Canadian Human Rights Act*. Ottawa, 1981. 8, 8p.

2512. Canadian Human Rights Commission. Task Force on Equal Pay. *Equal pay for work of equal value*. [*Rémunération égale entre les hommes et les femmes qui éxecutent des fonctions équivalentes*]. [Ottawa]: The Commission, 1978. 35, 46p.

2513. Canadian Labour Congress. *Equal pay for work of equal value / equal opportunity: background paper to report of Committee on Equality of Opportunity and Treatment for Women Workers*. Ottawa, 1980. 12p.
     Report and recommendations of the CLC Working Group on Equal Pay for Work of Equal Value.

2514. Chruscinski, Theresa. "Equal pay front pushes forward," *Financial Post*, 75:7, Jan. 3, 1981.

2515. Clark, John. "Local 31 award sets uneasy precedent on women's wages," *Financial Post*, 72:5, May 13, 1978.

2516. Daley, Pat. "Ontario: Tories call on equal pay amendment," *Perception*, 3:41-2, May-June 1980.

2517. Davidson, Jane. "Women start to win the 'equal work, equal pay' argument," *Financial Post*, 67:C1, Feb. 17, 1973.

2518. "'Don't quit equal pay fight' TUC warns women unionists," *Canadian Labour*, 15:64, June 1970.

2519. Dowling, Deborah. "Equal pay progress hampered by lack of comparison system," *Financial Post*, 74:23, May 3, 1980.

2520. Dranoff, Linda Silver. "Ask a lawyer," *Chatelaine*, 54:26, Feb. 1981.

2521. Duncan, Linda. "Legal notes: equal wage guidelines," *Branching Out*, 6(1):36, 44, 1979.

2522. Eady, Mary I. "What about equal pay?" *Canadian Labour*, 20:11-12, Sept. 1975.

2523. "Economics and personhood," in Canadian Research Institute for the Advancement of Women, *Women as persons*. [*La femme en tant que personne*]. Toronto: Resources for Feminist Research, 1980, pp.94-102. Proceedings of the 3rd annual meeting.

2524. Employers' Council of British Columbia. *A review of equal pay for work of equal value*. [Vancouver]:The Council, 1981. 10p.

2525. "Equal pay," *Labour Gazette*, 69:743, Dec. 1969.

2526. Equal Pay Coalition. "Bill 3: false rumours of equal pay's death," *Broadside*, 1(6):19, 1980.

2527. "Equal pay for work of equal value [Ontario]," *Canadian Welfare*, 53:25-6, Mar.-Apr. 1977.

2528. Equal Pay / Equal Opportunity Conference. *Issues and options: equal pay / equal opportunity*. Papers presented at the conference, Toronto, Jan. 16-17, 1978. Toronto: Ontario. Ministry of Labour, 1978. 76p. (Microlog 79-1156)

2529. Equal Remuneration Convention, 1951. *Convention concerning equal remuneration for men and women workers for work of equal value (No.100)*. Canada. Treaty series, no. 37, 1973. Ottawa: Queen's Printer for Canada, 1975. 10p.

2530. "Equal value standard needs army of autocrats," *Globe & Mail*, Mar. 4, 1980, p.B2.

2531. "Federal equal pay settlement; Égalisation de salaires à la Fonction publique du Canada," *Canadian Labour / Travailleur canadien*, 27:7, [English]; 7, [French], Mar. 1982.

2532. "Federal government librarians win equal pay," *APLA Bulletin*, 44:61, Mar. 1981.

2533. Finn, Ed. "Equal rights: fact or fantasy?" *Labour Gazette*, 78:189-194, May 1978.

2534. Fisher, Christine. "Ontario Ministry of Labour Conference: equal pay and equal opportunity - part 1," *Labour Gazette*, 78:256-62, June 1978.

2535.   _____. "Ontario Ministry of Labour Conference: equal pay and equal opportunity - part 2," *Labour Gazette*, 78:289-95, July 1978.

2536.   "Ford has better idea: pay equality for women," *Globe & Mail*, July 20, 1977, p.4.

2537.   Gelber, Sylva M. "Equal pay programs in Canada and the United States of America," *Women's Bureau '74*, Ottawa: Canada. Dept. of Labour. Women's Bureau, 1975, pp.45-77.

2538.   Gostick, Kim. "Equal pay: fifty percenters," *Canada & the World*, 46:16-17, Nov. 1980.

2539.   Grass, Jennifer. "No agreement in scrap to close pay gap for women [Ontario]," *Financial Post*, 74:15, Feb. 2, 1980.

2540.   Gray, Elizabeth. "Underpaid women, undervalued jobs," *Maclean's*, 93:48, 50, Apr. 7, 1980.

2541.   Gunderson, Morley. "Equal pay in Canada: history, progress and problems," in Barrie O. Pettman, ed., *Equal pay for women: progress and problems in seven countries*. Washington: Hemisphere, 1977, pp.129-46.

2542.   _____. "Male-female wage differentials and the impact of equal pay legislation," *Review of Economics and Statistics*, 57:462-9, Nov. 1975.

2543.   _____. "Sex discrimination in wage payments," in S. M. A. Hameed, ed., *Canadian Industrial Relations*. Toronto: Butterworth, 1975, pp.309-19.

2544.   _____. *The male-female earnings gap in Ontario: a summary*. [Toronto]: Ontario. Ministry of Labour. Research Branch, 1982. 23p. (Microlog 82-2600)

2545.   _____. *Time pattern of male-female wage differentials: Ontario 1946-71*. Working Paper, no. 75-09. Toronto: University of Toronto. Faculty of Management Studies, 1975. 18p.

2546.   Holmes, Barry. "Human Rights Act: Ottawa strikes again," *Motor Truck*, 48:15-17, Jan. 1979.

2547.   Innes, Eva. "Equal pay basis of [Human Rights Commission] ruling," *Financial Post*, 76:7, Mar. 13, 1982.

2548.   Jain, Harish C. "Canadian legal approaches to sex equality in the workplace," *Monthly Labor Review*, 105:38-43, Oct. 1982.

2549.   _____. "Discrimination in employment: legal approaches are limited," *Labour Gazette, 78:284-8, July 1978*.

2550.   Jain, Harish C. and Diane Carroll, eds. *Race and sex equality in the workplace: a challenge and an opportunity*. Proceedings of a conference sponsored by Industrial Relations Research Association, Hamilton and District Chapter and Canadian Industrial Relations Association, McMaster University, Hamilton, Ont., Sept. 28-9, 1979. Ottawa: Canada. Dept. of Labour. Women's Bureau, 1980. 236p.
         Panels and workshops on equal pay, affirmative action and seniority, promotion and layoffs.

2551.   Johnston, Robert F. "Equal pay for work of equal value," *Canadian Personnel and Industrial Relations Journal*, 28:59-65, Mar. 1981.

2552.   Kaye, Lynn. "Equal pay for work of equal value - enforcement and setbacks; A travail d'égale valeur, salaire égal: application de la loi et reculs," *Status of Women News / Statut: Bulletin de la femme*, 5:7, [English]; 8-9, [French], Dec. 1978.

2553.   Kehoe, Mary. "Equal rights in 1975," *Canadian Labour*, 20:1, June 1975.

2554.   "Law and personhood," in Canadian Research Institute for the Advancement of Women, *Women as persons*. [La femme en tant que personne]. Toronto:Resources for Feminist Research, 1980, pp.76-81.
         Proceedings of the 3rd annual meeting.

2555.   Laws, Margaret. "Ready for 'equal value' pay law? [Canadian Human Rights Act]," *Financial Post*, 72:1, 4, May 13, 1978.

2556.   "Librarians awarded landmark settlement," *Quill & Quire*, 47:38, Feb. 1981.

2557.   "Male-female gap widens," *Labour Gazette*, 78:486-7, Nov.-Dec. 1978.

2558.   Manitoba. Dept. of Labour. Women's Bureau. *Working paper on equal pay for work of equal value*. [Winnipeg, 1976]. 18p. (Profile 77-0097)

2559.   Man, Angela. "Women must stand up, speak out," *Native People*, 15:5, Apr. 9, 1982.

2560. Marsden, Lorna R. "The role of the National Action Committee on the Status of Women in facilitating equal pay policy in Canada," in Ronnie Steinberg Ratner, ed., *Equal employment policy for women: strategies for implementation in the United States, Canada, and Western Europe*. Philadelphia: Temple University Press, 1980, pp.242-60.

2561. McDonald, Lynn. "Equal pay - how far off?" *Canadian Dimension*, 14:21-4, May 1980.

2562. _____. "Wages of work: a widening gap between women and men," *Canadian Forum*, 55:4-7, Apr.-May 1975.

2563. Mitchell, Nancy. "Equal opportunities," *Civil Service Review*, 53:3-5, June 1980.

2564. Moon, Peter. "A note on the equal pay issue (Position Analysis Questionnaire)," *Canadian Training Methods*, 13:26-7, Oct. 1980.

2565. Morrison, Suzanne. "Toronto Conference: business women put focus on equal pay/-equal opportunity," *Journal (The Board of Trade of Metropolitan Toronto)*, Spring 1978, pp.47-50.

2566. "News briefs," *Labour Gazette*, 70:395, June 1970.

2567. "News briefs," *Labour Gazette*, 71:222, Apr. 1971.

2568. Niemann, Lindsay. "Equality and compensation: the secondary economic status of women in the paid workforce," in *Sexual equality in the workplace*. Ottawa: Canada. Dept. of Labour. Women's Bureau, 1982, pp.45-65.

2569. "Ontario Court of Appeal [nurses' aides and orderlies]," *Labour Gazette*, 70:651-2, Sept. 1970.

2570. "Ontario enforces equal pay laws," *Canadian Labour*, 14:36, Oct. 1969.

2571. Ontario. Ministry of Labour. *Equal pay for work of equal value; a discussion paper*. [Toronto], 1976. 106p.

2572. Osler, Richard. "Equality is only skin deep," *Financial Post*, 71:16, Feb. 26, 1977.

2573. _____. "Myths that impede equality for working women," *Financial Post*, 72:39, Feb. 4, 1978.

2574. Pilkington, Harry. "Complying with the legislation: some areas of concern," *Executive Bulletin (Conference Board in Canada)*, no. 4:15-16, Mar. 1978.

2575. Ramkhalawansingh, Ceta, ed. *(Un) equal pay: Canadian and international perspectives*. Toronto: Ontario Institute for Studies in Education, 1979. 145p.

2576. Ritchie, Laurell. "This A.I.B.: a setback for women," *This Magazine*, 11:7-11, Oct. 1977.

2577. Shapiro, Daniel M. and Morton Stelcner. *Earnings determination: the role of language and sex: Quebec 1970*. Working Paper, no. 1981-1. Montreal: Concordia University. Dept. of Economics, 1981. 223p.

2578. "Sizeable pay gaps between men and women," *Canadian Labour*, 13:7, 40, Oct. 1968.

2579. Sonnemann, Sabine and Jean L'Espérance. "A case of discrimination," *Canadian Library Journal*, 40:9-12, Feb. 1983.

2580. "Tax burden on working wives: outdated and unfair," *Maclean's*, 79:4, Dec. 3, 1966.

2581. Thompson, David. "Equality: deal with what, precisely?" *Executive*, 20:17, 19-20, May 1978.

2582. "Too many loopholes on human rights bill, women and the law assoc. tell Basford," *Globe & Mail*, Jan. 29, 1977, p.19.

2583. "TUC equal pay campaign," *Canadian Labour*, 10:24, June 1965.

2584. "TUC launches new equal-pay study," *Canadian Labour*, 13:32, Nov. 1968.

2585. "TUC seeks earlier enactment of legislation for equal pay," *Canadian Labour*, 15:66, Apr. 1970.

2586. University of Saskatchewan. Saskatoon Women and Law Committee. *Equal pay*. Saskatoon, [197?] 4p.

2587. Vohanka, Sue. "Labour notes...the fifty-seven per cent solution," *This Magazine*, 16:25, July 1982.

2588. "Volley number 3," *Broadside*, 1(3):2, 1979.

2589. "Wage quality," *Labour Gazette*, 74:458, July, 1974.

2590. "Women still earning less, study shows," *Globe & Mail*, Apr. 28, 1982, pp.1-2.

2591. "Women's cause hits barriers: corporations switching priority to bottom line," *Financial Times*, 69:21, 24, Dec. 15, 1980.
2592. "Women's Commission," *Canadian Labour*, 16:17, Jan. 1971.
2593. "Women's Committee urges equal pay," *Canadian Labour*, 12:37, Jan. 1967.
2594. "Women's groups see too many loopholes in [Rights] bill" *Globe & Mail*, Mar. 30, 1977, p.10.
2595. "Year after lodging equal-pay complaint, woman wonders if she really won," *Globe & Mail*, June 11, 1977, p.15.
2596. Zachon, Vivian. "Negotiating equal pay; Négociation de l'égalité en rémunération," *Canadian Labour / Travailleur canadien*, 21:19-21, [English]; 20-2, [French], Sept. 1976.

EQUAL PAY FOR EQUAL WORK - BIBLIOGRAPHY

2597. Haist, Dianne. *Equal pay for work of equal value: a selected bibliography.* Bibliography series, no. 3. Toronto: Ontario. Ministry of Labour. Research Library, 1976. 15p.

EQUAL RIGHTS

2598. Alberta. Women's Bureau. *Women are persons! A tribute to the women of Alberta and the 'person case'.* [Edmonton], 1979. Booklet.
2599. Anderson, D. "Rights: U.S. women have more," *Chatelaine*, 42:1, Sept. 1969.
2600. Anderson, Doris. "The Supreme Court and women's rights," *The Supreme Court Law Review*, 1(1980), pp.457-60.
2601. _____. "Women's rights: long road to equality," *Canada & the World*, 46:14-15, Nov. 1980.
2602. _____. "51-per-cent minority," *Maclean's*, 93:5, Jan. 28, 1980.
2603. Ayim, Maryann. "A comparison of women's rights and minority group rights within the framework of the Confederation debate," in Stanley G. French, ed., *Philosophers look at Canadian Confederation. [La Confédération canadienne: qu'en pensent les philosophes?]*. Montreal: Canadian Philosophical Association, 1979, pp.343-48.
2604. Bassett, Isabel. *The parlour rebellion: profiles in the struggle for women's rights.* Toronto: McClelland and Stewart, 1975. 223p.
2605. Bird, Florence. "Solidarity for women," *Policy Options*, 2:29-34, Sept.-Oct. 1981.
2606. Canada. Dept. of National Health and Welfare. *Equality: a principle in practice.* Notes for an address by the Honourable Marc Lalonde, Minister Responsible for the Status of Women, to Action '75+ . Ottawa, 1975. 14p.
2607. _____. Office of the Minister of National Health and Welfare and Minister Responsible for the Status of Women. *Equal rights - a new era.* Statement by the Honourable Marc Lalonde to the National Women's Organizations' Consultation, Department of the Secretary of State. Ottawa, 1977. 11p.
2608. Canada. Minister Responsible for the Status of Women. *Towards equality for women. [Femme en voie d'égalité]*. Ottawa: Minister of Supply and Services Canada, 1979. 42, 42p.
2609. Canadian Advisory Council on the Status of Women. "Brief to the Special Joint Committee of the Senate and of the House of Commons on the Constitution of Canada," in the committee's, *Minutes of proceedings and evidence*, no. 9, Nov. 20, 1980, pp.123-52.
2610. _____. *Women, human rights and the constitution.* Submission to the Special Joint Committee on the Constitution. Ottawa, 1980. 34p.
2611. _____. *Women, human rights and the constitution*, by Beverley Baines. Ottawa, 1980. 58p.
2612. Casgrain, T. F. "Les droits de la femme au Québec," *Québec*, 5(14):46-55, oct. 1968.
2613. "Charte des droits de la femme au travail," *Canadian Labour*, 10:37, Oct. 1965.
2614. "Charter of rights of working women, Eighth World Congress of ICFTU...resolution," *Labour Gazette*, 65:912-4, Oct. 1965.
2615. Cohen, Marjorie. "Economic barriers to liberation," *Canadian Woman Studies / Les cahiers de la femme*, 3:4-8, Summer 1982.

2616. Connelly, M. Patricia and Linda Christiansen-Ruffman. "Women's problems: private troubles or public issues?" *Canadian Journal of Sociology*, 2:167-78, Spring 1977.

2617. "C.E.A. [Canadian Education Association] resolution on sex discrimination," *Education Nova Scotia*, 7:1, Feb. 9, 1977.

2618. Dubuc, C. "Ce que femme veut," *Commerce*, 72:73-4, déc. 1970.

2619. Engel, Joan J. *The 'persons case', 50th anniversary Oct. 18, 1929-Oct. 18, 1979*. Edmonton: Alberta. Women's Bureau, 1979. 28p. (Microlog 80-1592)
    Learning kit prepared for application to Grades 8B and 10A Social Studies programs.

2620. "Equality of opportunity and treatment for women workers; L'égalité de chances et de traitement pour les travailleuses," *Canadian Labour / Travailleur canadien*, 21:2-9, [English]; 2-9, [French], Sept. 1976.

2621. Federation of Women Teachers' Associations of Ontario. *The visible woman: a history of women and of women's rights in Canada*, by Beryl Fox with Annette Cohen and Jean Cochrane. [Toronto]: The Federation, n.d. [22]p.

2622. Fish, Karen. "Native women fight unique battle," *Native People*, 10:6, 12, July 8, 1977.

2623. Fox, Beryl and Annette Cohen. *Visible woman: a history of women and of women's rights in Canada*. n.p.: Federation of Women Teachers' Associations of Ontario, [1975?] [21]p.

2624. Gagnon, Jacques. "Femmes: on veut l'égalité," *Sentinelle*, 10(9):5-9, 1974.

2625. Gelber, Sylva M. "Rights of man and the status of women," *Women's Bureau '73*. Ottawa: Canada. Dept. of Labour. Women's Bureau, 1974, pp.25-38.

2626. _____. "Women's responsibility in the search for equality of rights," *Women's Bureau '72*. Ottawa: Canada. Dept. of Labour. Women's Bureau, 1973, pp.21-8.

2627. Gellatly, C. and N. K. Thompson. "Women's rights: two perspectives," *Canada and the World*, 37:10-11, Nov. 1971.

2628. Harel, Louise. "L'affirmation des Québécoises," *Canadian Women's Studies / Les cahiers de la femme*, 3(1):44, 1981.

2629. Hosek, Chaviva. "How women fought for equality," *Canadian Forum*, 63:6-14, May 1983.

2630. "ICFTU and women's rights; La CISL et les droits de la femme," *Canadian Labour*, 10:14[English]; 15[French], June 1965.

2631. Kome, Penney. *The taking of 28: women challenge the Constitution*. Toronto: Women's Press, 1983.

2632. Major, Henri. *Background notes on the proposed Canadian Human Rights Act (Bill C-72)*. Ottawa: Canada. Advisory Council on the Status of Women, 1975. 38p.

2633. *Manifeste de femmes québécoises*, [par] un groupe de femmes de Montréal. Montréal: L'Étincelle, [1971]. 58p.

2634. McDonough, Peggy. "1929: round one," *Body Politic*, no. 57: 18-19, Oct. 1979.

2635. Morton, F. L. "Sexual equality and the law: a comparative review and analysis of judicial policy-making in the American and Canadian Supreme Courts." Paper presented at The 49th Annual meeting of the Canadian Political Science Association at the University of New Brunswick, Fredericton, N.B., June 9-11, 1977. 47p.

2636. National Action Committee on the Status of Women. "Brief to the Special Joint Committee of the Senate and of the House of Commons on the Constitution of Canada," in the committee's, *Minutes of proceedings and evidence*, no. 9, Nov. 20, 1980, pp.57-75.

2637. National Council of Women of Canada. "Brief submitted to the Special Joint Committee of the Senate and House of Commons on the Constitution of Canada," in the committee's, *Minutes of proceedings and evidence*, no. 74, May 4, 1971, pp.83-7.

2638. "Obstacles contre l'égalité de femmes," *Canadian Labour*, 14:53, Apr. 1969.

2639. O'Connor, Karen and Nancy E. McGlen. "The effects of government organization on women's rights: an analysis of the status of women in Canada, Great Britain and the United States," *International Journal of Women's Studies*, 1:588-601, Nov.-Dec. 1978.

2640. Ontario Status of Women Council. *Brief to the Government of Ontario respecting suggested revisions to Bill 7, proposed Ontario Human Rights Code*. [Toronto], 1981. 15p.

2641. Plowman, Shirley. "Fighting cheesecake and chauvinism [UN Seminar in Ottawa]," *Labour Gazette*, 75:10-22, Jan. 1975.

106

2642. Québec. Conseil du statut de la femme. *Commentaires du Conseil du statut de la femme sur la Charte des droits et libertés de la personne*. Québec, 1975. 3p.

2643. _____. *Recommandations du Conseil du statut de la femme concernant le projet de Loi 50, loi sur les droits et libertés de la personne*. Québec, 1975. 7p.

2644. Ray, Janet. *Towards women's rights*. Focus on Canadian history series. Toronto: Grolier, 1981. 96p.

        Secondary school level.

2645. Réaume, Denise. "Women and the law: equality claims before courts and tribunals," *Queen's Law Journal*, 5:3-45, 1980.

2646. Repo, S. "Are women necessary?" *Saturday Night*, 84:28-31, Aug. 1969.

2647. Réseau d'action et d'information pour les femmes. *Le livre rouge de la condition féminine et critique de la politique d'ensemble du Conseil du statut de la femme contenue dans "Pour les Québécoises: égalité et indépendance"*. Sillery, Qué., 1979. 67, 263p.

2648. Robillard, Laurette Champigny. "Pour les Québécoises: égalité et indépendance," *Commerce*, 81:88-90, 92+ , mai 1979.

2649. Siggins, Maggie. "Affirmative actions," *Toronto Life*, June 1982, pp.15-16, 19-20+ .

2650. Sluzhbovets, N. "Rights of women in Canada," *Ukrainian Canadian*, Mar. 1972, pp.25-32.

2651. "Speech by the Honourable Marc Lalonde on the second reading of the omnibus bill on the status of women (Bill C-16)," in Canada. Parliament. House of Commons. *Debates*, 1st sess., 30th parl., v.6, 1975, pp.6238-42.

2652. Stanton-Jean, M. "Liberté, égalité - féminité: allocution," *Relations*, no. 297:262-3, sept. 1965.

2653. Stone, Olive M. "Canadian women as legal persons: the jubilee of Edwards v. the Attorney-General for Canada," *Alberta Law Review*, 17(3):331-71, 1979.

2654. Strouch, Kathleen and Joan McFarland. *Equality for women!* Fredericton. New Brunswick. Human Rights Commission, 1974. 53p.

2655. Townson, Monica. "What it doesn't [Canadian Human Rights Act]," *Perception*, 1:11,13, Jan.-Feb. 1978.

2656. Vancouver Status of Women Council. *Status anyone?* Vancouver, 1972. 42p.

2657. Wasylyzia-Leis, Judy. "Economic prospects & policies for women," *Canadian Woman Studies / Les cahiers de la femme*, 3:115-6, Summer 1982.

2658. "Women: equality? Not yet," *Canada & the World*, 42:4-5, Nov. 1976.

EXECUTIVES

2659. "Banks & women," *Financial Times*, 65:26, Jan. 3, 1977.

2660. "Barbara Rae of Office Assistance: equal opportunity in a competitive business," *B.C. Business Magazine*, 9:28-31, Feb. 1981.

2661. Becker, Jane. "Board directors: a push for women," *Executive*, 22:55, Aug. 1980.

2662. "Bias, own attitudes limit women's promotions," *Globe & Mail*, Nov. 4, 1978, p.B1.

2663. Boileau, Jacqueline. "Female manager - contradiction?," *Optimum*, 3(1):36-45, 1972.

2664. _____. "The female manager in Canada-contradiction?" in Harish C. Jain, *Contemporary issues in Canadian personnel administration*. Scarborough, Ont.: Prentice-Hall, 1974, pp.123-8.

2665. Bower, Anne. "Women directors: where they are - and aren't," *Financial Post*, 70:42, Oct. 9, 1976.

2666. Brown, Dick. "Take a letter, Ralph," *Canadian Magazine*, 23:2, 4, 7, Mar. 17, 1973.

2667. Carson, Susan. "How women get to the top," *Weekend Magazine*, 22:16-7, Sept. 2, 1972.

2668. Davidson-Palmer, Judith. "They're ready and able but few make executive suite," *Financial Post*, 75:43, Mar. 21, 1981.

2669. "Directorship for woman 'inevitable' appointee says," *Globe & Mail*, Oct. 16, 1976, p.17.

2670. Douglas, Marcia. "Woman traveller doesn't want special treatment," *Financial Post*, 76:S4, Mar. 27, 1982.

2671. Dunphy, Jill. "Tradition, men, and other women no help to woman who tries to scale exec wall," *Office Equipment & Methods*, 23:32-3, Feb. 1977.

2672. Fairclough, E. L. "Women's liberation to enter boardrooms," *Canadian Chartered Accountant*, 97:218, Oct. 1970.

2673. "First Women's Bank chief emphasizes professionalism," *Globe & Mail*, Mar. 2, 1977, p.B4.

2674. "Follow the code and get ahead, women executive hopefuls told," *Globe & Mail*, Feb. 12, 1977, p.B2.

2675. Forbes, Rosalind. "Stress and the executive woman," *Journal (The Board of Trade of Metropolitan Toronto)*, June 1980, pp.31-3.

2676. Fournier, Gaetane et Sylvia Morin. *Des femmes au pouvoir*. Collection Dossiers. Sherbrooke, Qué.: Éditions Sherbrooke, 1978. 119p.

2677. Gauthier, Linda. "For a woman, landing a job is the hard part," *Marketing*, 80:15-16, Aug. 18, 1975.

2678. "Gerri Bissonnette, construction executive," *Engineering and Contract Record*, 88:38, Nov. 1975.

2679. Goneau, Marilyn. "'Pressures greater on executive women'," *Financial Post*, 75:29, Oct. 31, 1981.

2680. Goodman, E. "How management can give women a better break," *Industrial Canada*, 66:28-33, Sept. 1965.

2681. Goodman, Eileen. "Still a long way to go," *Canadian Business*, 50: 70, 72+ , July 1977.

2682. Gould, Allan M. "Women in TV: new power behind the scenes," *Chatelaine*, 56:86-7, 182+ , Nov. 1983.

2683. Gray, Charlotte. "Do women have a place in the boardrooms of the nation?" *Chatelaine*, 54:56-7, 89+ , Apr. 1981.

2684. Harris, Marjorie. "The soft cell: why more women are going into PR - and excelling at it," *Financial Post Magazine*, [76]:20-1, 24+ , Nov. 1982.

2685. Hart, L. B. "What women on way up should know; interview by Alan Pearson," *Financial Post*, 74:19, Apr. 26, 1980.

2686. Hoeschen, Susan. "Service with a smirk," *Business Life in Western Canada*, 10:50-2, Apr. 1982.

2687. Jabes, Jak. "Causal attributions and sex-role stereotypes in the perceptions of women managers," *Canadian Journal of Behavioural Science*, 12(1):52-63, 1980.

2688. _____. *Sex-role stereotypes and success attributions of women and men managers as perceived by women managers*. Working paper, no. 78-12. Ottawa: University of Ottawa. Faculty of Management Science, 1978. 33p.

2689. Johnson, Pat. "Liberating the boardroom: virtues of women managers finally being recognized," *Financial Times* 69:14, Aug. 18, 1980.

2690. Kome, Penney. "Reading between the lines [Anna Porter, publisher]" *Quest*, 12:38a-h, Mar. 1983.

2691. Kowalski, Edita. "Why women are not going into in-house management training programs," *Canadian Industrial Relations and Personnel Journal*, 26:17-24, Nov. 1979.

2692. _____. "Women managers learn professional development," *Life Insurance in Canada*, 5:16,18, Mar.-Apr. 1978.

2693. Laws, Margaret. "Avant-garde of career women needs army following behind," *Financial Post*, 73:7, Feb. 3, 1979.

2694. Lee, Betty. "Women at the top," *The Canadian*, June 11, 1977, p.9.

2695. Lerch, Renate. "Programs help women clear office hurdles," *Financial Post*, 76:19, Feb. 6, 1982.

2696. Lutes, Carol. "Room at the top: a view of women in management," *Optimum*, 2(1):49-52, 1971.

2697. McArthur, John. "Why aren't there more women managers?" *Canadian Business*, 47:34, 36, Dec. 1974.

2698. "Meet our career woman," *Monetary Times*, 135:51-3, Apr. 1967.

108

2699. Moore, Joy and Frank Laverty. "Positive action for integrating women into management," *Canadian Personnel and Industrial Relations Journal*, 22:15-21, Mar. 1975.

2700. Morneau, François. "La femme et les affaires au Québec," *L'Action nationale*, 72:325-36, déc. 1982.

2701. Morrison, Suzanne. "Corporate women: the slow climb to the top," *Journal (The Board of Trade of Metropolitan Toronto)*, July-Aug. 1978, pp.33-7.

2702. _____. "Margaret Hamilton: pacesetter," *Journal (The Board of Trade of Metropolitan Toronto)*, 67:33-4, July-Aug. 1977.

2703. _____. "The career woman: the progress and problems," *Journal (The Board of Trade of Metropolitan Toronto)*, Apr. 1979, pp.23-8, 31-3.

2704. _____. "Women: career route rough," *Journal (The Board of Trade of Metropolitan Toronto)*, Christmas 1977, pp.43-5.

2705. Myrtle, Jeanne-Marie. "Past attitudes must change: digest of address," *Financial Post*, 67:26, May 5, 1973.

2706. Ontario. Ministry of Labour. Women's Bureau. *Women in management*. Toronto, Oct. 1972. 7p.

2707. Peal, Emma. "Women MBAs: the new elite?" *Journal (The Board of Trade of Metropolitan Toronto)*, Spring 1978, pp.38-9.

2708. Pettigrew, Eileen. "Women must establish old girls' network," *Financial Post*, 72:15, July 8, 1978.

2709. "Popular belief of successful woman executive," *Atlantic Advocate*, 63:60-1, Sept. 1972.

2710. "Post's who's who of women directors; table," *Financial Post*, 70:43, Oct. 9, 1976.

2711. "Proposed trust company for women may settle for mail chief exec," *Globe & Mail*, July 17, 1976, p.B11.

2712. Rae, Barbara J. "Woman as manager 1979: choices, choices, choices," *Canadian Manager*, 4:9-20, Nov.-Dec. 1979.

2713. Rankin, Linda. "Women at work - a threat?" *Canadian Personnel and Industrial Relations Journal*, 25:13-15, Sept. 1978.

2714. Reed, Carol. "Assertiveness as a key to success," *Canadian Banker & ICB Review*, 84:42-7, May-June 1977.

2715. Robert, Véronique. "Quand les femmes sont d'affaires," *L'Actualité*, 7:45-6, juin 1982.

2716. Roberts, Imla. "For and about women in management. (4) Work stresses," *Canadian Training Methods*, 7:15, Aug. 1974.

2717. _____. "Women in management: revolution or evolution?" *Canadian Training Methods*, 6:22-3, Oct. 1973.

2718. "Royal chief clarifies remarks about women," *Globe & Mail*, Sept. 11, 1976, p.B2.

2719. "Royal, Scotia bank tussle with women directors issue," *Financial Times*, 65:10, Sept. 27, 1976.

2720. Sanders, Doreen. "Here come the women MBAs - and it's about time," *Financial Post*, 67:C4, July 14, 1973.

2721. Sinclair, Sonja. "Acting out the way to promotion: no room at the top if you're too nice," *Financial Post*, 71:13, Jan. 15, 1977.

2722. _____. "Women learning rules of the road," *Financial Post*, 74:23, May 10, 1980.

2723. _____. "Women working hard to achieve top positions," *Financial Post*, 71:28-30, Oct. 1, 1977, suppl.

2724. Squires, Nicole-marie. "Women have made it - more to follow," *Health Care*, 22:17-21, May 1980.

2725. Steward, Gillian. "Women in the oil industry," *Business Life in Western Canada*, 9:64-6, 69, Dec. 1980-Jan. 1981.

2726. Taylor, Linda. "Women in leadership: the achievers," *Canada & the World*, 46:20-1, Nov. 1980.

2727. "The real world of a woman MBA," *Journal (The Board of Trade of Metropolitan Toronto)*, Spring 1978, pp.40-2.

2728. "The upward-mobile WP secretary: unlearning the 'go-fer' route," *Office Equipment & Methods*, 21:33-4, 36, July 1975.

2729. Tindal, Doug. "These women mean business," *Today*, Mar. 7, 1981, pp.16-18.

2730. Townson, Monica. "Women in the executive suite: you're an engineer? How's your shorthand?" *Financial Times of Canada*, 62:9, July 8, 1973.

2731. "Training women for management: some defend it, others call it sexist: only results will tell," *Financial Times*, 66:17, Apr. 10, 1978.

2732. Vaillancourt, Louise B. "Une femme au Conseil d'administration," *Commerce*, 80:144-6, 148, Oct. 1978.

2733. Van Der Merwe, Sandra. "A portrait of the Canadian woman manager," *Business Quarterly*, 43:45-52, Autumn 1978.

2734. _____. "What personal attributes it takes to make it in management," *Business Quarterly*, 43:28-35, Winter 1978.

2735. _____. "Women as managers - the current attitudes and programs of Canadian businessmen," *Business Quarterly*, 44:35-9, Spring 1979.

2736. Ward, Eleanor. "Not the sort of women, it seems, Earle McLaughlin was looking for," *Maclean's*, 89:67, Oct. 4, 1976.

2737. "Why are so few women in management?" *Labour Gazette*, 68:405, July 1968.

2738. "Woman executive is a rare species," *Monetary Times*, 137:48-9, Oct. 1969.

2739. "Women executives organize," *Journal (The Board of Trade of Metropolitan Toronto)*, Easter 1977, pp.25-6, 28-9.

2740. "Women in management, or who want to be, speak out. (Part 2)," *Canadian Training Methods*, 6:17-8, Dec. 1973.

2741. "Women managers help a company's image...but few firms have many around," *Financial Times of Canada*, 61:11, Oct. 2, 1972.

2742. "Women travellers - a special growing market in the hospitality industry," *Foodservice and Hospitality*, 12:20-1,24, Aug. 1979.

2743. Wood, Jean. "The games organizations play and what women don't know about them," *Municipal World*, 90: 297-9, Nov. 1980.

2744. Worzel, Richard. "Grooming for change: the women are coming," *Financial Post*, 69:E3, Oct. 18, 1975.

2745. Zwarun, Suzanne. "Women in oil," *Chatelaine*, 55:52, 119+ , Nov. 1982.

EXECUTIVES - BIBLIOGRAPHY

2746. Cheda, Sherrill. "Women and management: a selective bibliography, 1970-73," *Canadian Library Journal*, 31:18-27, Jan.-Feb. 1974.

2747. Haist, Dianne. *Women in management: a selected bibliography, 1970-1975*. Bibliography series, no. 4. Toronto: Ontario. Ministry of Labour. Research Library, 1976. 18p.

FAMILY

2748. Arès, Richard. "Recensement 1976: la famille au Québec," *Relations*, 38:270-2, oct. 1978.

2749. Beaulieu, Lucien A. "Media, violence and the family: a Canadian view," in John M. Eekelaar and Sanford N. Katz, eds., *Family violence: an international and interdisciplinary study*. Toronto: Butterworths, 1978, pp.58-68.

2750. Bosher, John F. "The family in New France," in Barry M. Gough, *In Search Of the visible past*. Waterloo, Ont.: Wilfrid Laurier University Press, 1975, pp.1-13.

2751. Boyd, Monica. "Family size ideals of Canadians: a methodological note," *Canadian Review of Sociology and Anthropology*, 11:360-70, Nov. 1974.

2752. B.-Dandurand, Renée. "Famille du capitalisme et production des êtres humains," *Sociologie et sociétés*, 13:95-111, Oct. 1981.

2753. Canada. Dept. of Manpower and Immigration. *Family life through women's eyes: final report*. n.p., [1978]. 84, [21]p.
    Report of a government sponsored project; a survey of Sudbury miners' wives.

2754. Canada. Statistics Canada. *Characteristics of wives in husband-wife families*. Canada. 1976 Census. Supplementary bulletins: housing and families. Ottawa, 1978. [42]p. (Cat. no.93-834)

110

2755. "Canada's families," *Canada & the World*, 46:19, Nov. 1980.

2756. Carisse, Colette. "Family values of innovative women," in C. Beattie and S. Crysdale, eds., *Sociology Canada: readings*. Toronto: Butterworth, 1974, pp.190-202.

2757. Carisse, Colette and Joffre Dumazedier. "Valeurs familiales de sujets féminins novateurs: perspectives d'avenir," *Sociologie et sociétés*, 2:265-82, nov. 1970.

2758. Children's Aid Society of Vancouver, B.C. *Brief no. 188 to the Royal Commission on the Status of Women in Canada*. Vancouver, 1968. 21p.

2759. Clements, George. "Marketers: why pay lip service to the 'ideal' or 'normal' family and ignore what's real?" *Marketing*, 83:14, 16, Jan. 30, 1978.

2760. Cook, Gail C., ed. *Opportunity for choice: a goal for women in Canada. [L'objectif pour les Canadiennes: pouvoir choisir]*. Ottawa: Statistics Canada / C. D. Howe Research Institute, 1976. 217p.

2761. Cunningham, Charnie and Laurel Limpus. "The myth of motherhood," in Bryan Finnigan, *Making it: the Canadian dream*. Toronto: McClelland & Stewart, 1972, pp.61-70.

2762. Davids, Leo. "Family change in Canada: 1971-1976," *Journal of Marriage and the Family*, 42:177-83, Feb. 1980.

2763. D'Oyley, Vincent, ed. *Domestic violence: issues and dynamics*. Toronto: Ontario Institute for Studies in Education, 1978. 268p.

2764. Elkin, Frederick. *Family in Canada*. Ottawa: Vanier Institute of the Family, 1969. 197p.

2765. Family Service Association of Edmonton. *Brief no. 70 to the Royal Commission on the Status of Women in Canada*. Edmonton, 1968. 17p.

2766. Garigue, Philippe. *La vie familiale des canadiens français*. Montréal: Presses de l'Université de Montréal, 1970. 143p.

2767. Gaulin, Hélène Caron. "La famille [étendue] nouvelle unité de prestation de services," *Perception*, 3:6-9, nov.-déc. 1979.

2768. Gee, Ellen Margaret Thomas. "Fertility and marriage patterns in Canada: 1851-1971." PhD diss., University of British Columbia, 1978. 344p. (Can. theses, no.37608)

2769. Gingras, J. B. "Le masculinisme et la famille," *L'Action nationale*, 59:559-65, fév. 1970.

2770. Harris, Marjorie and Benjamin Schlesinger. "Men and women: where we're at: coming out of the stone age: the myths and the facts separated," *Quest*, 6:24-6, 28, 30, Sept.-Oct. 1977.

2771. Henripin, Jacques et Evelyne Lapierre-Adamcyk. *La fin de la revanche des berceaux: qu'en pensent les Québécoises?* Montréal: Presses de l'Université de Montréal, 1974. 164p.

2772. Ishwaran, K., ed. *Canadian families: ethnic variations*. Toronto: McGraw-Hill, Ryerson, 1980. 291p.

2773. _____. *The Canadian family: a book of readings*. Toronto: Holt, Rinehart and Winston of Canada, 1971. 557p.

2774. Jaffe, Peter and Judy Thompson. "The family consultant service with the London (Ontario) police force," in John M. Eekelaar and Sanford N. Katz, eds., *Family violence: an international and interdisciplinary study*. Toronto: Butterworths, 1978, pp.216-23.

2775. Kirk, H. David. "Differential sex preference in family formation: a serendipitous datum followed up," in James E. Gallagher and Ronald D. Lambert, eds., *Social process and institution: the Canadian case*. Toronto: Holt, Rinehart and Winston, 1971, pp.415-32.

2776. Kleiber, Nancy. "Family size and family organization in selected subcultural groups in Vancouver, British Columbia." PhD diss., University of California, Davis, 1972. 165p. (UM73-19088)

2777. Krahn, Harvey, John Gartrell and Lyle Larson. "The quality of family life in a resource community," *Canadian Journal of Sociology*, 6:307-24, Summer 1981.

2778. Lachance, Micheline. "La famille de l'an 2000," *L'Actualité*, 6:55-7, août 1981.

2779. Larson, Lyle E. *The family in Alberta*. Edmonton: Human Resources Research Council of Alberta, 1971. 101p.

2780. McConnell, Wanda. "Family facing transition," *Free Press Report on Farming*, 97:15, Nov. 2, 1977.

2781. Moreux, Colette. "The French-Canadian family," in Marylee Stephenson, *Women in Canada*. Toronto: New Press, 1973, pp.157-82.

2782. Morrison, T. R. "'Their proper sphere' feminism, the family, and child-centered social reform in Ontario, 1875-1900," *Ontario History*, 68:45-64 Mar.; 65-74, June 1976.

2783. Nett, Emily M. "Canadian families in socio-historical perspective," *Canadian Journal of Sociology*, 6:239-60, Summer 1981.

2784. _____. "The family," in Robert Hagedorn, ed., *Sociology*. 2d ed. Toronto: Holt, Rinehart & Winston, 1983, pp.331-67.

2785. Neysmith, Sheila M. "Parental care: another female family function?" *Canadian Journal of Social Work Education*, 7(2):55-63, 1981.

2786. Parr, Joy, ed. *Childhood and family in Canadian history*. Toronto: McClelland and Stewart, 1982. 221p.

2787. Paquette, Lucie. *Rôles familiaux et planification des naissances en milieu défavorisé urbain québécois*. Laboratoire de recherches sociologiques. Rapports de recherches. Cahier 5. Québec: Université Laval. Dept. de sociologie, 1974. xxii, 313p.

2788. Posner, Michael. "Marriage on the rocks," *Maclean's*, 90: 28-30, 35-6+ , May 16, 1977.

2789. Québec. Conseil des affaires sociales et de la famille. *La situation des familles québécoises*. [Sillery, Québec, 1978]. 108p.

2790. Ramu, G. N., ed. *Courtship, marriage and the family in Canada*. Toronto: Macmillan of Canada, 1979. 219p.

2791. Ramu, G. N. "The family and marriage in Canada," in G. N. Ramu and Stuart D. Johnson, eds., *Introduction to Canadian society: sociological analysis*. Toronto: Macmillan of Canada, 1976, pp.295-348.

2792. Rowley, J. C. R. and D. W. Henderson. "The relative economic position of female-headed families in Canada, 1965-1975: some basic information," in *Reflections on Canadian incomes; selected papers presented at the Conference on Canadian Incomes, May 10-12, 1979*. Ottawa: Economic Council of Canada, 1980, pp.451-61.

2793. Schlesinger, Benjamin. *Families: Canada*. Toronto: McGraw-Hill Ryerson, 1979. 193p.

2794. _____. "Family patterns are changing with the times," *Canadian Banker & ICB Review*, 82:40-4, May-June 1975.

2795. Smith, Dorothy E. "Women, class and family," in Naomi Hersom and Dorothy E. Smith, [eds], *Women and the Canadian labour force*. Working document. Ottawa: Social Sciences and Humanities Research Council of Canada, 1982, pp.367-437.

2796. Smith, Dorothy. "Women, the family and corporate capitalism," in Marylee Stephenson, *Women in Canada*. Toronto: New Press, 1973, pp.2-35.

2797. Stirling, Robert M. *Effects of wife's employment on family relations*. Report for the Royal Commission on the Status of Women in Canada. Calgary, 1968. 56p.

2798. Tomeh, Aida K. "Sex roles in a cross-cultural perspective - Canada," in her, *Family and sex roles*. Toronto: Holt, Rinehart and Winston of Canada, 1975, pp.75-83.

2799. Veevers, J. E. *The family in Canada*. Canada. 1971 Census. Profile studies. Ottawa: Statistics Canada, 1977. 72p. (Cat. no.99-725)

FAMILY - BIBLIOGRAPHY

2800. Bracher, Michael D. and P. Krishnan. "Family and demography: a selected Canadian bibliography," *Journal of Comparative Family Studies*, 7:367-72, Summer 1976.

2801. Nowosielski, Maryna. *Marriage and the family: preliminary check list of National Library holdings*. [*Mariage et famille: inventaire préliminaire des fonds de la Bibliothèque nationale*]. Ottawa: National Library of Canada / Vanier Institute of the Family, 1980. 130p.

FAMILY BUSINESS

2802. First National Farm Women's Conference. *AFEAS report: the wife contributing with her husband to an enterprise for profit*. Montreal: L'Association féminine d'éducation et d'action sociale, [1980]. [43]p.

2803. Marchessault-Lussier, Lucie. "Une femme pas comme les autres, ou la femme col-laboratrice - une travailleuse non-reconnue," *Canadian Women's Studies / Les cahiers de la femme*, 1:7-11, Winter 1978.

2804. Marmer, Jack. "Divorce can threaten a company's survival," *Financial Post*, 75:16, July 18, 1981.

2805. _____. "Marriage and business often go hand in hand," *Financial Post*, 75:18, July 25, 1981.

2806. Marmer, Jack. "When divorce may cost a business," *Financial Post*, 75:1-2, July 11, 1981.

FAMILY LAW

2807. Abella, Rosalie Silberman. "Family law in Ontario: changing assumptions," *Ottawa Law Review*, 13:1-22, 1981.

2808. _____. "Family law perspectives," *The Law Society Gazette*, 16:204-19, 1982.

2809. Andrews, H. T. G., ed. *Family law in the family courts*. Toronto: Carswell, 1973. 232p.

2810. Attorney General of Manitoba. "Manitoba's position paper on family law for the First Ministers Conference, September 1980," *Reports of Family Law*, 2d ser., 16:42-57, 1980.

2811. Bailey, Stella. "Intrafamily tort immunity: Alberta's position," *Alberta Law Review*, 16(3):417-45, 1978.

2812. Bala, Nicholas. "Consequences of separation for unmarried couples: Canadian developments," *Queen's Law Journal*, 6:72-149, 1980.

2813. Basford, Ron. "Notes for a speech delivered to the Family Law Section, Ontario Bar Association, Toronto, 26 January 1977," *Reports of Family Law*, 26:61-7, 1977.

2814. Baxter, Ian F. G. "Family law reform in Ontario," *University of Toronto Law Journal*, 25:236-80, Summer 1975.

2815. Beamish, James and Arthur Gans. *Family and juvenile law (Ontario)*. Vancouver: Coast Legal Publication Ltd., 1971. 81p.

2816. Beaupré, Gerard. "L'évolution du droit familial au Québec," *Canadian Bar Journal*, new ser., 2:1-3, Oct. 1971.

2817. Bisson, Alain-F. et François Héleine. "Chronique de droit familial," *Revue générale de droit*, 5(2):333-82, 1974.

2818. Bohémier, A. "Le droit de la famille au Québec," *Relations*, no. 305:132-6, mai 1966.

2819. Boucher, Jacques et André Morel, eds. *Livre du centenaire du Code civil*. Vol. 1: *Le droit dans la vie familiale*. Montréal: Presses de l'Université de Montréal, 1970. 302p.

2820. Brière, Germain. "Famille et divorce: chroniques régulières," *Revue du Barreau*, 76:247-52, 410-413, 565-68, 1976.

2821. Canada. Law Reform Commission. *Report on family law*. [*Rapport, Le droit de la famille*]. Ottawa, 1976. 73, 79p.

2822. *Canadian family law guide*. 2v. Don Mills, Ont.: Commerce Clearing House Canadian Ltd., 1976- . Loose-leaf service.

2823. Carr, Robert. *Report on the state of family law in Manitoba: recommendations for change*. [Winnipeg, Man.]: Taylor, Brazzell, McCaffrey, 1982. 176p. (Microlog 82-3834)
        Report prepared for the Honourable Roland Penner, Attorney-General of Manitoba.

2824. Castelli, Mireille D. "La notion de famille et son impact en droit social," *Cahiers de droit*, 22:5-54, 1981.

2825. Cullity, Maurice C. "Family law reform - a legislative response!" *Estates and Trusts Quarterly*, 3:129-50, 1976.

2826. Deleury, Edith et M. Rivet. "Droit civil: chroniques régulières," *Revue du Barreau*, 40:330-6, 483-90, 1980.

2827. Dussault, Hélène. *Synthèse et critique du rapport de l'Office de révision du Code civil*. Québec: Conseil du statut de la femme, 1974. 18p.

2828. Gargrave, Tony. "The Family Relations Act of British Columbia," *Advocate*, 38:225-7, 1980.

2829. Gaudet, Bérengère. *Étude sur certains aspects du droit familial au Canada*. Royal Commission on the Status of Women in Canada. Study no. 11. Ottawa: Information Canada, 1971. 380p.

2830. Greenberg, S. "Ontario's Family Law Reform Act: how it works, what it means," *Perception*, 2:26-9, Jan.-Feb. 1979.

2831. Guay-Archambault, Denyse. "Regards sur le nouveau droit de la famille au Canada anglais et au Québec," *Cahiers de droit*, 22:723-84, 1981.

2832. Harvey, Cameron. "Manitoba family law reform legislation and succession," *Manitoba Law Journal*, 9(3):247-53, 1979.

2833. Hewett, Adlyn M. *Family laws for Albertans*. Revised. Edmonton: Women of Unifarm, 1974. 44p.

2834. Hovius, Berend. *Family law: cases, notes, materials*. Toronto: Carswell, 1982. 885p.

2835. Irving, Howard H., ed. *Family law: an interdisciplinary perspective*. Toronto: Carswell, 1981. 215p.

2836. Jahn, Penelope and Charles Campbell. *The self-help guide to divorce, children, welfare: an up-to-date handbook on Canadian family law*. Toronto: Anansi, 1976. 108p.

2837. Khetarpal, S. P. "Family law: annual survey of Canadian law," *Ottawa Law Review*, 10:384-447, 1978.

2838. Kieran, Sheila. *"Kramer vs. Kramer* vs. reality: all about what really goes on in family law in Canada today," *Homemaker's Magazine*, 16:26-8, 30+ , Jan.-Feb. 1981.

2839. Kronby, Malcolm C. *Canadian family law*. Rev. and updated ed. Don Mills, Ont.: General Publishing, 1981. 214p.

2840. Kronby, Malcolm. *The guide to family law*. Toronto: New Press, 1972. 168p.

2841. MacDonald, James C. and others. *Law and practice under the Family Law Reform Act of Ontario*. 2v. Toronto: Carswell, 1980- . Loose-leaf service.

2842. Manitoba. Dept. of the Attorney-General. *Family law in Manitoba*. [Winnipeg], 1978. 27p.

2843. _____. *Family law in Manitoba*. [Rev. ed.] Winnipeg, 1981. 55p. (Microlog 82-0347)

2844. McBean, Jean. *Marriage and family law in Alberta: the rights of husbands, wives, children and common law spouses*. 2nd ed. Vancouver: International Self-Counsel Press, 1980. 203p.

2845. Mendes da Costa, Derek, ed. *Studies in Canadian family law*. Toronto: Butterworths, 1972. 2v.

2846. National Action Committee on the Status of Women. "Annual meeting and conference, March 18-21, 1977, Ottawa: proposals arising from workshops: women and family law," *Status of Women News*, 3:9-12, [English]; 13-16, [French]; May 1977.

2847. Newfoundland. Family Law Study. *Family law in Newfoundland*. St. John's, 1973. 675p.

2848. Ontario. Law Reform Commission. *Report on family law. Part I, torts*. Toronto: Ontario. Dept. of Justice, 1969. 114p.

2849. Ontario. Ministry of the Attorney General. *Family law reform: your new rights*. [Toronto, 1978]. [6]p.

2850. Ouellette, Monique. "Droit civil: chroniques régulières," *Revue du Barreau*, 41:279-82, 483-5, 1981.

2851. P.E.I. Civil Liberties Association, P.E.I. Federation of Agriculture and Island Information Service. *Family laws in P.E.I.: a simple guide for you*. n.p., 1975? v.p.
    Contents: 1. The family court of P.E.I. 2. Marriage law 3. Family property law 4. Ending the marriage 5. Children and family laws

2852. Prince Edward Island. Dept. of Justice. *Family law*. [Charlottetown, 1978]. 14p.

2853. Québec. Conseil du statut de la femme. *Droit de la famille, droit des femmes?: dossier d'information à l'intention des femmes*. [Québec], 1979. 69p.
    English edition: Rights of the family, rights of women?: an information tool prepared for women.

2854. _____. *Mémoire présenté à la Commission parlementaire sur la réforme du droit de la famille*. Québec, 1979. 38, [16]p.

114

2855. Québec. Office de revision du code civil. Comité du droit des personnes et de la famille. *Rapport sur la famille. Partie 2*. [Québec]:Éditeur officiel du Québec, 1975. 326p.

2856. _____. *Rapport sur la famille*. 2v. Montréal: Le Comité, 1974-1975.

2857. Rivet, Michèle et E. Deleury. "Personne, famille, divorce: chroniques régulières," *Revue du Barreau*, 40:111-18, 1980.

2858. Saskatchewan. Advisory Council on the Status of Women. *Position paper on the constitutional proposal to transfer family law to the provincial jurisdiction*. Saskatoon, 1980. 19p.

2859. Vancouver Status of Women. *Submission to the Royal Commission on Family and Children's Law*. 1974. 6p.

2860. Webb, Peter. "The Family Law Reform Act, 1978," *Advocates' Quarterly*, 1:367-73, 1978.

2861. Woloski, R. "Manitoba: sexual politics," *Maclean's*, 90:14, Dec. 26, 1977.

2862. Wouk, Judith. "Halifax right-to-lifers appointed guardian to foetus," *Branching Out*, 7(1):7, 1980.

FARMERS' WIVES

2863. Bacchi, Carol. "Divided allegiances: the response of farm and labour women to suffrage," in Linda Kealey, ed., *A not unreasonable claim: women and reform in Canada, 1880s-1920s*. Toronto: Women's Press, 1979, pp.89-107.

2864. Bains, Amar. "Conditions of farm work [interview]," *Resources for Feminist Research*, 11:5-6, Mar. 1982.

2865. "Breakthrough in Quebec - wages for farm wives," *Report on Farming*, 100:31, Apr. 1980.

2866. Carey, Patricia. "Farm wives: the forgotten women," *Canadian Women's Studies / Les cahiers de la femme*, 1:4-5, Winter 1978-1979.

2867. Dion, Suzanne. *Les femmes dans l'agriculture au Québec*. Longueuil, Québec: Éditions la Terre de chez nous, 1983. 165p.

2868. First National Farm Women's Conference. *"Credit where credit is due": women and farm credit in Canada*. Status of Rural Women Project. [Ottawa], 1980. 21,[7]p.
    French edition: *"Le crédit à qui en a besoin." Les femmes et le crédit agricole au Canada*.

2869. _____. *Equal partner or "just a wife": farm wives and property law in Canada*. Status of Rural Women Project. [Ottawa], 1980. 27, [19]p.
    French edition: *Partenaire à part égale ou "rien qu'une femme"*.

2870. _____. *"The invisible pitch fork" or the portrayal of farm women in the Canadian media*. Status of Rural Women Project. [Ottawa], 1980. 39, [10]p.
    French edition: *"L'outil invisible" ou le portrait de la femme en agriculture dans les média canadiens*.

2871. _____. *The socio-economic status of farm women - an overview*. Status of Rural Women Project. [Ottawa], 1980. 13p.
    French edition: *Un apercu de la situation socio-économique de la femme en agriculture*.

2872. Fortin, Gerald. "Woman's role in the evolution of agriculture in Quebec," in *The family in the evolution of agriculture*. Ottawa: Vanier Institute of the Family, 1968, pp.25-31.

2873. Gervais, Solange Fernet. "Regroupement des femmes au Québec," *Resources for Feminist Research*, 11:64-5, Mar. 1982.

2874. Graff, Linda L. "Industrialization of agriculture: implications for the position of farm women," *Resources for Feminist Research*, 11:10-11, Mar. 1982.

2875. _____. "The changing nature of farm women's work roles under the industrialization of agricultural production." MA thesis, McMaster University, 1979. 333p. (Can. theses, no.46869)

2876. Hedley, Max J. "Relations of production of the 'family farm': Canadian prairies," *Journal of Peasant Studies*, 9:71-85, Oct. 1981.

2877. "Keeping women down on the farm," *Canadian Dimension*, 15:33-6, Apr. 1981.

2878. Kohl, Seena B. "Women's participation in the North American family farm," *Women's Studies International Quarterly*, 1(1):47-54, 1978.

2879. Koutecky, Teri. "Manitoba's marital law—being against Bill 61 like opposing mother-hood," *Free Press Report on Farming*, 97:22, Oct. 5, 1977.
2880. New Brunswick. Dept. of Agriculture and Rural Development. Planning and Development Branch. *Agriculture training for farm wives*. [Fredericton], 1972. 11p.
2881. "New ruling allows split in husband-wife [farm] income," *Farm and Country*, 42:M4, June 20, 1978.
2882. Research, Action and Education Centre. "Keeping women down on the farm," *Resources for Feminist Research*, 11:12-14, Mar. 1982.
    Slightly revised version of article in *Canadian Dimension*, 15:33-6, Apr. 1981.
2883. Saskatchewan. Dept. of Labour. Women's Division. *Farm women*. Regina, [1977]. 31p. (Profile 77-0912)
2884. Sawer, Barbara. "Predictors of the wife's involvement in farm decision-making." PhD diss., University of British Columbia, 1972. 121p. (Can. theses, no.11255)
2885. _____. *The role of the wife in farm decisions*. Rural sociology monograph, no.5. Vancouver: University of British Columbia. Adult Education Research Center, 1974. 96p.
2886. Sawer, Barbara J. "Predictors of farm wife's involvement in general management and adoption decisions," *Rural Sociology*, 38:412-26, Winter 1973.
2887. Schulz, Linda Z. "Feminism, down on the farm," *Branching Out*, 6(1):37-8, 1979.
2888. Taylor, Norma. "All this for three and a half a day: the farm wife," in Gwen Matheson, *Women in the Canadian mosaic*. Toronto: Peter Martin, 1976, pp.150-64.
2889. Williamson, Lenny. "Farm women," *Canada Agriculture*, 26(3):21-2, 1981.

FARMING

2890. "Farm women expanding into agricultural industry," *Free Press Report on Farming*, 98:19, Jan. 11, 1978.
2891. Lipkin, Mary Jane. "Brawn not brain: women & farm credit in Canada," *Canadian Woman Studies / Les cahiers de la femme*, 3:53-6, Summer 1982.
2892. Piéri, Monique. "Seule sur ses arpents verts," *Châtelaine*, 20:50+ , fév. 1979.
2893. Watson, Julie. "Women get involved in sheep farming," *Atlantic Advocate*, 72:29-31, June 1982.
2894. "When 2 city women went farming," *Farm and Country*, 42:24-5, June 20, 1978.
2895. "Women head back to the land," *Farm and Country*, 41:28, Jan. 18, 1977.

FEMINISM

2896. Anderson, D. "How to get along with (or raise the hackles of) a feminist," *Chatelaine*, 43:1, Oct. 1970.
2897. _____. "Women's Lib — a short (forgotten) history," *Chatelaine*, 43:1, Nov. 1970.
2898. Batten, J. "After black power, woman power," *Chatelaine*, 42:36-7, 105-7, Sept. 1969.
2899. Bertrand, Marie-Andrée. "La Québecoise entre hier et demain," *Forces*, no. 45:3-15, 1978.
2900. Borgman, A. E. and A. Ansara. *A woman who took a rifle to Moncade had to be a liberated woman: interview with Haydee Santamaria*. Ottawa: Canadian Union of Students. Secretariat, n.d. 6p.
2901. Callwood, J. and others. "Do we need Women's Lib? We asked a cross section of prominent Canadian women," *Chatelaine*, 43:26-7, 82+ , Nov. 1970.
2902. Charney, Ann. "Quebec: no more 'happiness' schools," *Ms*, 42:27-30, Mar. 1976.
2903. Cheda, Sherrill, Johanna Stuckey, and Maryon Kantaroff. "New feminists now," *Canadian Women's Studies / Les cahiers de la femme*, 2(2):27-30, 1980.
2904. Cheda, Sherrill. "On the way to liberation," *Chatelaine*, 47:57, 97-9, Nov. 1974.
2905. Chuchryk, Patricia Marie. "Ideological perspectives in contemporary North American feminism: a critical assessment." MA thesis, University of Regina, 1979. 204p. (Can. theses, no. 39062)

2906. Cloutier, Renée et autres. *Femmes et culture au Québec: un avant-projet de chantier*. Documents préliminaires, no. 3. Québec: Institut québécois de recherche sur la culture, 1982. 105p.

2907. Cohen, Marjorie. "The need for independent feminism," *Canadian Forum*, 60:4, Mar. 1981.

2908. Corbeil, Christine et autres. *L'intervention féministe: l'alternative des femmes au sexisme en thérapie*. Montréal: Éditions coopératives Albert Saint-Martin, 1983. 188p.

2909. Dubin, Gloria Louise Joachim. "Nursing, leadership and the women's liberation movement." MScN thesis, University of British Columbia, 1976. 70p. (Can. theses, no.29824)

2910. *Education and women's liberation*. Toronto: Young Socialists, 1968. 11p.

2911. Eichler, Margrit. *The double standard: a feminist critique of feminist social science*. New York: St. Martin's Press, 1980. 151p.

2912. _____. "Women as personal dependents," in Marylee Stephenson, *Women in Canada*. Toronto: New Press, 1973, pp.36-55.

2913. Fine, Judylaine. "Can single men find happiness with the new woman?" *Chatelaine*, 48:49, 80-2, 84-5, Feb. 1975.

2914. Fitzgerald, Maureen, Connie Guberman and Margie Wolfe, eds. *Still ain't satisfied! Canadian feminism today*. Toronto: Women's Educational Press, 1982. 318p.

2915. Frum, B. "What women have to lose: instant support, instant identity — and some chains," *Chatelaine*, 43:28, 56 +, Nov. 1970.

2916. Germain, Nicole, pseud. et Liette Desjardins. *La femme émancipée*. Montréal: Éditions de l'homme, 1971. 119p.

2917. Gingras, J. B. "Féminisme ou masculinisme: égalité vs. similarité," *L'Action nationale*, 59:111-16, oct. 1969.

2918. Goldfield, Evelyn, Sue Munaker, and Naomi Weisstein. *A woman is a sometime thing: or, cornering capitalism by removing 51% of its commodities*. [Toronto]: Toronto Women's Liberation and Hogtown Press, [1971?] 30p.

2919. G.R.A.F.S. *Nous, notre santé, nos pouvoirs*. Montréal: Éditions coopératives Albert Saint-Martin, 1983. 204p.

2920. Griffiths, N. E. S. *Penelope's web: some perceptions of women in European and Canadian society*. Toronto: Oxford University Press, 1976. 249p.

2921. Hawley, A. *Men's and women's liberation*. Ottawa: Canadian Union of Students. Secretariat, n.d. 5p.

2922. Jean, Michele. "Les Québecoises, ont-elles une histoire?" *Forces*, no. 27:4-14, 1974.

2923. Johnson, Ronald W. and others. "Perceived attractiveness as a function of support for the feminist movement," *Canadian Journal of Behavioural Science*, 10(3):214-21, 1978.

2924. Johnson, Valerie Miner. "Suburban housewife as feminist organizer," *Saturday Night*, 88:15-18, July 1973.

2925. Kieran, Sheila H. "Who's downgrading women? Women," *Maclean's*, 81:18-19, 40-2, Aug. 1968.

2926. Kostash, Myrna. "How to get into consciousness raising," *Chatelaine*, 46:41, 106, 108-9, 111-2, Oct. 1973.

2927. Kreps, Bonnie. *Brief no. 373 to the Royal Commission on the Status of Women in Canada*. Toronto, 1968. 16p.

2928. Landsberg, Michele. *Women and children first: a provocative look at modern Canadian women at work and at home*. Toronto: MacMillan of Canada, 1982. 239p.

2929. Leblanc, Claudette. "Féminisme et sciences sociales: emergence du discours féministe dans la sociologie. MA thèse, Université d'Ottawa, 1981. (Can. theses, no.53249)

2930. LeBourdais, E. "What men have to gain: sex object? It's a lot worse being a 'work' object," *Chatelaine*, 43:26, 61-2, Nov. 1970.

2931. Lubka, N. "Ins and outs of women's liberation," *Canadian Dimension*, 7:24-9, June-July 1970.

2932. Lumsden, Barbara L. "Women's dependency: the interrelationship of structure and ideology." MA thesis, University of Guelph, 1981. 118p. (Can. theses, no.52521)

2933. MacDonald, D. "Women's liberation: year 2," *Chatelaine*, 43:25, 52+, Nov. 1970.

2934. MacLeod, Donna Jean. "A study of nursing students from a feminist perspective." MA thesis, University of Calgary, 1976. 113p. (Can. theses, no.30551)

2935. Malmo-Levine, Cheryl Lynne. "Behaviour of women in consciousness-raising groups." MEd thesis, University of Alberta, 1972. 126p. (Can. theses, no.13475)

2936. Maroney, Heather Jon. "Sexual politics in Quebec: the structure and dynamics of class, national and sex oppression." MA thesis, McMaster University, 1978. 308p. (Can. theses, no.46913)

2937. McDonald, Marci. "Carole Taylor doesn't want to be perfect," *Maclean's*, 88:50-6, Oct. 6, 1975.

2938. McLean, Julia. "Militantly impotent: has the women's movement come to this?" *Branching Out*, 3:8-10, 48, Apr.-June 1976.

2939. McVeigh, Gregory E. "Women's liberation and psychopathology: an examination of the relationship between attitudes towards women's liberation and personality traits." MA thesis, York University, 1974. 75p. and app. (Can. theses, no.20017)

2940. Michalski, Andrzej B. "Essex County social workers: their attitudes toward women." MSW thesis, University of Windsor, 1976. 187p. (Can. theses, no.29198)

2941. Miles, Angela. "Le féminisme, parole authentique et autonome des femmes," in Yolande Cohen, *Femmes et politique*. Montréal: Le Jour, 1981, pp.67-78.

2942. Miles, Angela R. and Geraldine Finn, eds. *Feminism in Canada: from pressure to politics*. Montreal: Black Rose Books, 1982. 315p.

2943. Morgan, Joanna. "20 women questions to test you," *Chatelaine*, 48:56, 127, Nov. 1975.

2944. "New feminists," *Canada and the World*, 36:8-10, Dec. 1970.

2945. Nicholson, Barbara. "Feminism in the Prairie provinces to 1916." MA thesis, University of Calgary, 1974. 203p. (Can. theses, no.21331)

2946. Nunes, Maxine and Deanna White. *The lace ghetto*. Toronto: New Press, 1972. 152p.

2947. "Out from under, women unite!" *Saturday Night*, 85:15-20, July 1970.

2948. Preston, Patricia. "Confrontations: most of us avoid conflict and the women's movement suffers," *Branching Out*, 6(1):32-4, 1979.

2949. Rich, J. "Watching all the liberated girls go by," *Chatelaine*, 44:34, 85-6+ , Apr. 1971.

2950. Sabia, Laura. "Women and politics," in Margaret Atwood and others, *Women on women*. Toronto: York University, 1978, pp.29-42.

2951. Saint-Arnaud-Beauchamp, Jocelyne. "Nature féminine et égalité," dans Rodrigue Bélanger et autres, eds., *Devenirs de femmes*. Cahiers de recherche éthique, no. 8. Montréal: Éditions Fides, 1981, pp.39-49.

2952. "Towards a Canadian feminist party," *Atlantis*, 5:142-5, Fall 1979.

2953. Usher, Sarah. "Self-esteem in the mature married woman as a function of working status and feminist attitudes." PhD diss., York University, 1977. 141, [42]p. (Can. theses, no.33665)

FEMINISM - HISTORY

2954. Brigden, Beatrice. "One woman's campaign for social purity and social reform," in Richard Allen, ed., *Social gospel in Canada*. Ottawa: Canada. National Museums of Man, 1975, pp.36-62.

2955. Danylewycz, Marta. "Changing relationships: nuns and feminists in Montreal, 1890-1925," *Histoire sociale / Social History*, 14:413-34, Nov. 1981.

2956. Foley, Christine. "Consumerism, consumption and Canadian feminism: 1900-1930." MA thesis, University of Toronto, 1979. 107p.

2957. Gorham, Deborah. "Singing up the hill," *Canadian Dimension* 10:26-38, June 1975.

2958. Hynes, Maureen. *History of the rise of women's consciousness in Canada and Quebec...with some conclusions drawn concerning the struggle of women today*. Toronto: Hogtown Press, 1971.

2959. Jean, Michèle. "Histoire des luttes féministes au Québec," *Possibles*, 4:17-32, automne 1979.

2960. Lavigne, Marie, Yolande Pinard et Jennifer Stoddart. "La Fédération nationale Saint-Jean-Baptiste et les revendications féministes au début du 20e siècle," dans Marie Lavigne et Yolande Pinard, *Les femmes dans la société québécoise: aspects historiques*. Montréal: Éditions du boréal express, 1977, pp.89-108.

2961. Laws, Margaret. "Women: for 50 years 'persons'," *Financial Post*, 73:2, May 5, 1979.

2962. MacKenzie, Suzanne. *Women and the reproduction of labour power in the industrial city: a case study*. Brighton, Eng.: University of Sussex. Urban and Regional Studies, 1980. 172p.

2963. MacLellan, Margaret. "History of women's rights in Canada," *Status of Women News*, 1(2):16-20, 1974.

2964. MacPherson, Kay. "The seeds of the seventies," *Canadian Dimension*, 10:39-41, June 1975.

2965. Morrison, T. R. "'Their proper sphere' feminism, the family, and child-centered social reform in Ontario, 1875-1900," *Ontario History*, 68:45-64 Mar.; 65-74, June 1976.

2966. Pinard, Yolande. "Les débuts du mouvement des femmes," dans Marie Lavigne et Yolande Pinard, *Les femmes dans la société québécoise: aspects historiques*. Montréal: Éditions du boréal express, 1977, pp.61-87.

2967. Pitters-Caswell, Marian. "Women's participation in sporting activities as an indicator of a feminist movement in Canada between 1867 and 1914," in Canadian Symposium on History of Sport and Education. *Proceedings. 3rd, 1974*, Dalhousie University, Halifax, N.S. 21p.

2968. Pyke, S. W. and C. Stark-Adamec. "Canadian feminism and psychology: the first decade," *Canadian Psychological Review*, 22:38-54, Jan. 1981.

2969. Roberts, Wayne. "'Rocking the cradle for the world': the new woman and maternal feminism, 1877-1914," in Linda Kealey, ed., *A not unreasonable claim: women and reform in Canada, 1880s-1920s*. Toronto: Women's Press, 1979, pp.15-45.

2970. Siu, Bobby. "Comparative women's movements: a study of the organizational pre-requisites of the women's movements in the United States, Canada and China." Prepared for the Annual New York State Conference of the Association of Asian Studies. State University of New York, Buffalo, N.Y., Oct. 14-16, 1977. 20p.

2971. Stoddart, Jennifer and Veronica Strong-Boag. "...and things were going wrong at home," *Atlantis*, 1:38-44, Fall 1975.

2972. Strong-Boag, Veronica. "Cousin Cinderella: a guide to historical literature pertaining to Canadian women," in Marylee Stephenson, *Women in Canada*. Toronto: New Press, 1973, pp.262-90.

2973. _____. "'Setting the stage': national organization and the women's movement in the late 19th century," in Susan Mann Trofimenkoff and Alison Prentice, eds., *The neglected majority: essays in Canadian women's history*. Toronto: McClelland and Stewart, 1977, pp.87-103.

2974. _____. *The parliament of women: The National Council of Women of Canada 1893-1929*. Canada. National Museum of Man. Mercury series / History Division paper, no.18. Ottawa: National Museums of Canada, 1976. 492p.

2975. Strong-Boag, Veronica. "The roots of modern Canadian feminism: the National Council of Women, 1893-1929," *Canada: an Historical Magazine*, 3:22-33, Dec. 1975.

2976. Trofimenkoff, Susan Mann. "Nationalism, feminism and Canadian intellectual history," *Canadian Literature*, 83:7-20, Winter 1979.

FEMINISM, SOCIALIST

2977. Adamson, Nancy and Kathy Arnup. "A committee for all seasons [International Women's Day Committee]," *Broadside*, 3:4, Mar. 1982.

2978. Brand, Johanna and Ester Koulack. "Liberation: more than equality," *Canadian Dimension*, 13(1):18-21, [1978].

2979. Connelly, Patricia. *Last hired, first fired: women and the Canadian work force*. Toronto: Women's Press, 1978. 122p.

2980. Connelly, Patricia. "The economic context of women's labour force participation in Canada," in John Allan Fry, ed., *Economy, class and social reality: issues in contemporary Canadian society*. Toronto: Butterworths, 1979, pp.206-23.

2981. Denis, Roch. *Les marxistes et l'émancipation de la femme*. Documents du groupe socialiste des travailleurs du Québec, no. 2. Montréal: Presses socialistes internationales, 1976. 47p.

2982. Fox, Bonnie, ed. *Hidden in the household: women's domestic labour under capitalism*. Toronto: Women's Educational Press, 1980. 325p.

2983. Jamieson, Kathleen. "Sisters under the skin: an exploration of the implications of feminist-materialistic perspective research," *Canadian Ethnic Studies*, 13(1):130-43, 1981.

2984. Maroney, Heather Jon. "Sexual politics in Quebec: the structure and dynamics of class, national and sex oppression." MA thesis, McMaster University, 1978. 308p. (Can. theses, no.46913)

2985. McDonald, L. "Women and the left," *Canadian Forum*, 59:13-14, May 1979.

2986. Revolutionary Workers' League. *Women's liberation and socialism*. Revolutionary workers league papers, no. 1. Toronto: Vanguard Publications, 1978. 119p.

2987. Smith, Dorothy E. *Feminism and Marxism: a place to begin, a way to go*. Vancouver: New Star Books, 1977. 54p.

FEMINIST PARTY OF CANADA

2988. Brown, Heather. "New times/new tactics," *Broadside*, 1(1):5, 18, [1979].

2989. _____. "The press vs. the Feminist Party," *Broadside*, 1(1):5, [1979].

2990. Carey, Patricia. "Feminist Party of Canada," *Canadian Women's Studies / Les cahiers de la femme*, 1:119-20, Summer 1979.

2991. Evans, Marg. "Feminist Party of Canada," *Broadside*, 1(1):8, [1979].

2992. "Feminist Party of Canada: first principles," *Broadside*, 1(7):6, 1980.

2993. Hynes, Maureen. "Feminist Party of Canada: entering the electoral mainstream," *Branching Out*, 7(1):8, 1980.

2994. McIntyre, Sheila. "FPC: growing pains," *Broadside*, 1(9):7, 17, 1980.

FEMINISTS

2995. Alberta. Women's Bureau. *The famous five*. Alberta facts. Edmonton, n.d. 2p.

2996. Bassett, Isabel. *The parlour rebellion: profiles in the struggle for women's rights*. Toronto: McClelland and Stewart, 1975. 223p.

2997. Benham, Mary Lile. *Nellie McClung*. Don Mills, Ont.: Fitzhenry & Whiteside, 1975. 61p.

2998. Burton, Betty. "Nellie McClung," *Manitoba Pageant*, 20:1-10, Summer 1975.

2999. "Dorise Nielsen, 1902-1980: a tribute," *Atlantis*, 6:138-46, Spring 1981.

3000. Ferguson, Ted. "Emily Murphy, the forgotten feminist," *Chatelaine*, 50:20, May 1977.

3001. Francis, Anne. "Nellie McClung: her soul goes marching on," *Readers Digest. Can. ed.*, 105:111-14, 116, 118, Aug. 1974.

3002. Gane, Margaret Drury. "Dr. Margaret Fulton: feminist in academe," *Chatelaine*, 53:25, 28-9, Feb. 1980.

3003. Jean, Michèle. "Idola Saint-Jean, féministe (1880-1945)," in *Mon héroine: les lundis de l'histoire des femmes: an 1: conférences du Théâtre expérimental des femmes 1980-81*. Montréal: Editions du Remue-ménage, 1981, pp.117-47.

3004. Lishman, Judith. "Her Honor, Sir, was not a person [Emily Murphy]," *The Canadian*, Oct. 13-14, 1979, pp.14, 16.

3005. MacKenzie, Jean. "Nellie was a lady," *United Church Observer*, new ser., 37:18-19, Oct. 1973.

3006. Matheson, Gwen. "Nellie McClung," *Canadian Dimension*, 10:42-8, June 1975.

3007. Matheson, Gwen and V. E. Lang. "Nellie McClung: not a nice woman," in Gwen Matheson, *Women in the Canadian mosaic*. Toronto: Peter Martin, 1976, pp.1-20.

3008.   _____. "No 'Nice Nelly' was Nellie," *Chatelaine*, 47:55, 102-5, Nov. 1974.

3009.   McClung, Nellie. *In times like these*. Edited by Veronica Strong-Boag. Toronto: University of Toronto Press, 1972. 129p.

3010.   Ray, Janet. *Emily Stowe*. Don Mills, Ont.: Fitzhenry and Whiteside, 1978. 63p.

3011.   Roberts, Wayne. "Six new women: a guide to the mental map of women reformers in Toronto," *Atlantis*, 3:145-64, Autumn 1977.

3012.   Savage, Candace. *Our Nell: a scrapbook biography of Nellie L. McClung*. Saskatoon: Western Producer Prairie Books, 1979. 253p.

3013.   Skarsgard, Anne. "Violet McNaughton: Saskatchewan's forgotten crusader," *Chatelaine*, 52:148, 150, Dec. 1979.

3014.   Strong-Boag, Veronica. "Canadian feminism in the 1920s: the case of Nellie L. McClung," *Journal of Canadian Studies*, 12:58-68, Summer 1977.

3015.   Wade, Susan. "Her work for wages earned the vote [Helena Gutteridge]," *Canadian Women's Studies / Les cahiers de la femme*, 3(1):60-1, 1981.

3016.   Wright, Helen K. *Nellie McClung and women's rights*. Agincourt, Ont.: Book Society of Canada , 1980. 75p.

3017.   Zaremba, Eve. "Can't fight the right without feminism: a political profile of Angela Miles, activist and theorist," *Broadside*, 3:4-5, 17, Dec. 1981-Jan. 1982.

FERTILITY

3018.   Arès, Richard. "La dénatalité: des recommandations à connaître et à appliquer," *L'Action nationale*, 64:617-21, avr. 1975.

3019.   _____. "La question sociale au Québec," *L'Action nationale*, 65:93-104, oct. 1975.

3020.   Balakrishnan, T. R., G. E. Ebanks and C. F. Grindstaff. *Patterns of fertility in Canada, 1971. 1971 Census of Canada. Census analytical study.* Ottawa: Statistics Canada, 1979. 269p. (Cat. no.99-759E)

3021.   Balakrishnan, T. R., J. F. Kantner and J. D. Allingham. *Fertility and family planning in a Canadian metropolis*. Montreal: McGill-Queen's University Press, 1975. 217p.

3022.   Bisson, Antonio F. et Victor Piché. "L'Accord conjugal en matière de fécondité et de planification familiale: une enquête au Québec," *Population*, 32:184-93, janv.-fév. 1977.

3023.   Carliner, Geoffrey, Christopher Robinson and Nigel Tomes. "Female labour supply and fertility in Canada," *Canadian Journal of Economics*, 13:46-64, Feb. 1980.

3024.   Collishaw, Neil. *Fertility in Canada. [La fécondité au Canada]*. 1971 Census of Canada. Vol. V, pt.1:Profile studies. Ottawa. Statistics Canada, 1976. 69p. (Cat. no.99-706)

3025.   Condon, Richard G. "Inuit natality rhythms in the central Canadian Arctic," *Journal of Biosocial Science*, 14:167-77, Apr. 1982.

3026.   Duchesne, Louis. *Tendances passées et perspectives d'évolution de la fécondité au Québec*. Série analyse et prévision démographiques, v. 4. [Québec]: Bureau de la statistique du Québec. Direction de l'analyse et de l'information statistiques / Service de la démographie et du recensement, 1976. 83p.

3027.   Festy, M. Patrick. "La fécondité des mariages au Québec, d'après l'enquête famille de 1971," *Population*, 31:875-900, juill.-oct. 1976.

3028.   Frenette, Lyse. "Étude des femmes mariées du Quebec qui desirent peu d'enfants." MA thèse, Université de Montreal, 1974. 266p.

3029.   Gallagher, Diane May. "Factors affecting fertility and female labor force participation in Canada and the United States." MA thesis, University of Alberta, 1973. 141p. (Can. theses, no.17516)

3030.   Gee, Ellen M. Thomas. "Early Canadian fertility transition: a components analysis of census data," *Canadian Studies in Population*, 6:23-32, 1979.

3031.   Grindstaff, Carl F. "The baby bust: changes in fertility patterns in Canada," *Canadian Studies in Population*, 2:15-22, 1975.

3032.   _____ ,T. R. Balakrishnan and G. Edwards Ebanks. "Socio-demographic correlates of childlessness: an analysis of the 1971 Canadian census," *Canadian Journal of Sociology*, 6:337-51, Summer 1981.

3033. Henripin, Jacques. *Trends and factors of fertility in Canada*. 1961 Census monograph. Ottawa: Statistics Canada, 1972. 421p.

3034. _____. "Justice sociale et politiques familiales [entrevue]," *Relations*, 39:81-6, mars 1979.

3035. _____. "La natalité au Québec: y a-t-il un problème? [entrevue]," *Relations*, 39:44-8, fév. 1979.

3036. _____. and Jacques Légaré. "Recent trends in Canadian fertility," *Canadian Review of Sociology and Anthropology*, 8(2):106-18, 1971.

3037. Kelly, John J. "Timing of the birth of the first child within marriage for women of Metropolitan Toronto." MA thesis, University of Western Ontario, 1970. 97p. (Can. theses, no.6677)

3038. Kettle, John. "Delay or decline?" *Executive*, 23:20, Aug.-Sept. 1981.

3039. _____. "Small families for 25 years," *Executive*, 23:20, Nov. 1981.

3040. Kyriazis, Natalie. "Parity-specific analysis of completed fertility in Canada," *Canadian Review of Sociology and Anthropology*, 19:29-43, Feb. 1982.

3041. _____. "Sequential fertility decision making: Catholics and Protestants in Canada," *Canadian Review of Sociology and Anthropology*, 16(3):275-86, 1979.

3042. _____. and J. Henripin. "Women's employment and fertility in Quebec," *Population Studies*, 36:431-40, Nov. 1982.

3043. "La revanche des berceaux avortée," *Commerce*, 82:147-8, Sept. 1980.

3044. Lachapelle, Réjean. "La fécondité au Québec et en Ontario: quelques éléments de comparaison," *Canadian Studies in Population*, 1:13-28, 1974.

3045. Lapierre-Adamcyk, Evelyne. "Activité féminine et fécondité: une enquête au Québec (1971)," *Population*, 33:609-32, mai-juin 1978.

3046. Légaré, Jacques. "Demographic highlights on fertility decline in Canadian marriage cohorts," *Canadian Review of Sociology and Anthropology*, 11:287-307, Nov. 1974.

3047. Lapierre-Adamcyk, Evelyne. *Socio-economic correlates of fertility in Canadian metropolitan areas, 1961 and 1971*. 1971 Census of Canada. Census analytical study. Ottawa: Statistics Canada, 1979. 101p. (Cat. no.99-757E)

3048. Macleod, Betty. "Regional fertility differentials in Ontario," in Betty Macleod, ed., *Demography and educational planning*. Monograph series, no. 7. Toronto: Ontario Institute for Studies in Education, 1970, pp.157-81.

3049. McAlpine, Phyllis J. and Nancy E. Simpson. "Fertility and other demographic aspects of the Canadian Eskimo communities of Igloolik and Hall Beach," *Human Biology*, 48:113-38, Feb. 1976.

3050. Morah, Benson Chukwuma. "Timing of births in Edmonton: patterns and consequences." PhD diss., University of Alberta, 1977. 208p. (Can. theses, no.32034)

3051. Oatman, Marlene A. "Social structural and social psychological predictors of fertility expectations." MA thesis, University of Guelph, 1977. 112p. (Can. theses, no.37447)

3052. Page, H. G. "Changes in the fertility pattern in Quebec," *Canadian Journal of Public Health*, 58:197-203, May 1967.

3053. Pool, D. Ian and M. D. Bracher. "Aspects of family formation in Canada," *Canadian Review of Sociology and Anthropology*, 11:308-23, Nov. 1974.

3054. Pool, Janet Sceats. "Family-building in a Canadian city: an analysis of the timing and spacing of pregnancies," *Population Studies*, 32:583-92, Nov.1978.

3055. Québec. Bureau de la statistique. Service de la démographie et du recensement. *Tendances passées et perspectives d'évolution de la fécondité au Québec*. Analyse et prévision démographiques, v. 4. Québec, 1976. 83p.

3056. Ram, Bali. *Women's labour-force participation, life cycle stage, and current fertility in Canada: some causal inferences*. [Ottawa: Statistics Canada, 1976?] 15, [7]p.

3057. Rao, N. Baskara. "An overview of the fertility trends in Ontario and Quebec," *Canadian Studies in Population*, 1:37-42, 1974.

3058. _____. "Fertility and income in Canada: a time series and cross section analysis," PhD diss., University of Alberta, 1973. 167p. (Can. theses, no.15323)

3059. *Report on multidisciplinary extension programme in human sexuality and fertility, offered by School of Adult Education, School of Social Work and Faculty of Health Sciences at McMaster University, Hamilton, Ont. 1975*. [Ottawa]: Canada. Dept. of National Health and Welfare. Family Planning Division. 1976. v.p.

3060. Robinson, Chris and Nigel Tomes. "Family labour supply and fertility: a two-regime model," *Canadian Journal of Economics*, 15:706-34, Nov. 1982.

3061. Romaniuk, A. "Increase in natural fertility during the early stages of modernization: Canadian Indians case study," *Demography*, 18:157-72, May 1981.

3062. Romaniuk, Anatole. "Modernization and fertility: the case of the James Bay Indians," *Canadian Review of Sociology and Anthropology*, 11(4):344-59, 1974.

3063. _____. and Victor Piché, "Natality estimates for the Canadian Indians by stable population models, 1900-1969," *Canadian Review of Sociology and Anthropology*, 9(1):1-20, 1972.

3064. "Solution, for some, is no kids," *Maclean's*, 90:32, May 16, 1977.

3065. Trovato, Frank and Carl F. Grindstaff. "Decomposing the urban-rural fertility differential: Canada, 1971," *Rural Sociology*, 45:448-68, Aug. 1980.

3066. Trovato, Frank. "Canadian ethnic fertility," *Sociological Focus*, 14:57-74, Jan. 1981.

3067. _____. and T. K. Burch. "Minority group status and fertility in Canada," *Canadian Ethnic Studies*, 12(3):1-18, 1980.

3068. Turner, Jean and Alan B. Simmons. "Sex roles and fertility: which influences which?" *Canadian Studies in Population*, 4:43-60, 1977.

3069. Veevers, J. E. "Childlessness and age at first marriage," *Social Biology*, 18(3):292-5, 1971.

3070. _____. "Declining childlessness and age at marriage: a test of an hypothesis," *Social Biology*, 19(3):285-8, 1972.

3071. _____. "Factors in the incidence of childlessness in Canada: an analysis of census data," *Social Biology*, 19(3):266-74, 1972.

3072. _____. "Rural-urban variation in the incidence of childlessness," *Rural Sociology*, 36:547-53, Dec. 1971.

3073. _____. "The violation of fertility mores: voluntary childlessness as deviant behaviour," in C. L. Boydell, C. F. Grindstaff and P. C. Whitehead, eds., *Deviant behaviour and societal reaction*. Toronto: Holt, Rinehart & Winston, 1972, pp.571-92.

3074. _____. "Voluntarily childless wives: an exploratory study," *Sociology and Social Research*, 57:356-66, Apr. 1973.

3075. Verma, Ravi, B. P. "Variations in family size among Canadian women by generation and ethnic group," *International Journal of Comparative Sociology*, 20:293-303, Sept.-Dec. 1979.

3076. Vlassoff, Carol and J. W. Gartrell. *Frontier fertility: a study of Fort McMurray families*. Discussion paper, no. 21. [Edmonton, Alta.: University of Alberta. Population Research Laboratory], 1980. 27p. (Microlog 80-4536)

3077. Wolowyna, Jean E. "Income and childlessness in Canada: a further examination," *Social Biology*, 24:326-31, Winter 1977.

FILMS AND FILMING

3078. Anderson, D. M. "How real are reel-life women?" *Chatelaine*, 42:1, July, 1969.

3079. _____. "Why we need women making films about women [editorial]," *Chatelaine*, 46:1, Aug. 1973.

3080. Antonelli, Marylu. "Impossible situations [NFB series on working mothers]," *Branching Out*, 1:8-11, Nov.-Dec. 1974.

3081. Armatage, Kay. "Canadian women's cinema," *Canadian Forum*, 61:24-5, Feb. 1982.

3082. _____. "Exploring the status of woman as spectacle [interview]," *Fireweed*, 7:71-6, Summer 1980.

3083. _____. "Feminist film-making: theory and practice," *Canadian Women's Studies / Les cahiers de la femme*, 1:49-50, Spring 1979.

3084. Barling, Marion. "Film as an ideological process; Karen: women in sport." MA thesis, University of British Columbia, 1977. 37p. (Can. theses, no.34758)
> Consists of a paper, "Film as an ideological process" and a film, "Karen: women in sport."

3085. Batt, Sharon. "Ruth, Harriet and Barbara; [two women of the Peace and one who filmed them]," *Branching Out*, 1:31-2, Mar.-Apr. 1974.

3086. Berd, Francoise. "Marthe Blackburn," in *Mon héroïne: les lundis de l'histoire des femmes: an 1: Conférences du Théâtre expérimental des femmes 1980-81*. Montréal: Éditions du Remue-Ménage, 1981, pp.97-115.

3087. Berger, Sara. "Women in focus," *Branching Out*, 6(1):45-8, 1979.

3088. Chisholm, Elspeth and Patricia Thorvaldson. "Women in documentary: the early years," *Motion*, 4:14-19, Nov. 1975.

3089. Cooper, Margaret. "The Central Character: an interview with Patricia Gruben," *Branching Out*, 6(2):36-9, 1979.

3090. Deane, Marie and others. "Women and film: a filmography," *Ontario Library Review*, 59:44-51, Mar. 1975.

3091. Delaney, M. "Jean-Luc Godard's woman of parts: a film director's view," *Saturday Night*, 80:38-40, 45, Nov. 1965.

3092. "En tant que femme: quatre films de société nouvelle," *Relations*, 34:126, avr. 1974.

3093. Gay, Richard. "En tant que femmes: des films avec les femmes, par les femmes, pour les femmes...et les hommes," *Maintenant*, 140:28-30, nov. 1974.

3094. Geering, Jacqueline. "Funnel vision," *Broadside*, 1(7):14, 1980.

3095. Joyce-Jones, Susannah. "Marian Barling: from long shot to close-up...womansize," *Canadian Woman Studies / Les cahiers de la femme*, 3:72-4, Spring 1982.

3096. "Kay Armitage interviews Joyce Wieland," *Take One*, 3(2):23-5, 1970.

3097. Kreps, Bonnie. "Towards a women's film aesthetic," *Makara*, 1:7-9, Aug.-Sept. 1976.

3098. Landsberg, Michèle. "Joyce Wieland: artist in movieland," *Chatelaine*, 49:57-9, 110-11, Oct. 1976.

3099. Longfellow, Brenda. "Women in gear," *Cinema Canada*, no. 85:20-1, June 1982.

3100. Martineau, Barbara. "Innovators in animation," *Branching Out*, 5(2):21-5, 1978.

3101. _____. "Leading ladies behind the camera," *Cinema Canada*, no. 71:17-32, Jan.-Feb. 1981.

3102. _____. "Thought about the objectification of women," *Take One*, 3:15-18, Nov.-Dec. 1970.

3103. _____. "Women in film: many women film makers: few films," *Communiqué*, no. 8:32-5, May 1975.

3104. Mathews-Klein, Yvonne. "How they saw us: images of women in National Film Board films of the 1940's and 1950's," *Atlantis*, 4:20-33, Spring 1979.

3105. Morissette, Brigitte. "Treize femmes à la recherche des femmes," *Le Maclean*, 12:18-19, 46-8, oct. 1972.

3106. Poirier, Anne-Claire. "Être femme et cinéaste, être femme et artiste, pourquoi pas?" *Canadian Women's Studies / Les cahiers de la femme*, 1:45, Spring 1979.

3107. Poitras, Huguette. "Le cinéma: par des femmes, sur des femmes, pour les femmes," *Le Maclean*, 13:66,68, nov. 1973.

3108. Prost, Vivian and Nell Tenhaaf. "Powerhouse," *Branching Out*, 6(1):49-51, 1979.

3109. Pyros, J. "Notes on women directors," *Take One*, 3:709, Nov.-Dec. 1970.

3110. Reid, Alison. *Canadian women film-makers: an interim filmography*. Canadian filmography series, no. 8. Ottawa: Canadian Film Institute, 1972. 11p.

3111. Sky, Laura. "I am not objective: filmmaker Laura Sky talks with Fireweed about her work [interview]," *Fireweed*, 8:26-30, Fall 1980.

3112. Smith, Sharon. "Women who make movies," *Women in Film*, July 1973, pp.77-90.

3113. Spring, S. "Women on women in films," *Take One*, 3:10-14, Nov.-Dec. 1970.

3114. Wollheim, Peter. "*Not a love story*: a dissenting opinion," *Canadian Forum*, 62:26-7, Sept. 1982.

FINANCE

3115.   Ash, Stephen B. *Consumer satisfaction with financial services and insurance: the case of the working woman*. Submitted to and distributed by Consumer and Corporate Affairs Canada. 1980. 40p. (Microlog 83-1316)

3116.   *Conference '80. Women and the economy*. n.p., 1980. 48p.
         Conference sponsored by New Brunswick Advisory Council on the Status of Women, New Brunswick. Dept. of Youth, Recreation and Cultural Resources, and others.

3117.   National Association of Women and the Law. Victoria Caucus. *Legal and financial management for women*. [Victoria]: British Columbia. Ministry of Consumer and Corporate Affairs, 1981. 126p. (Microlog 82-3109)

FOOD SERVICE INDUSTRY

3118.   Agger, Ellen. "Tipping: the waitress pays," *Branching Out*, 4:26-8, July-Aug. 1977.

3119.   Bazilli, Susan. "We also serve who only stand and wait," *Fireweed*, 9:7-19, Winter 1981.

3120.   Martens, Debra. "Hot tip," *Broadside*, 1(6):12, 1980.

3121.   Novack, Ellen. "Women in our industry," *Canadian Hotel & Restaurant*, 55:13-16, Dec. 1977.

3122.   Ontario Human Rights Commission. *A study of employment policies in downtown hotel dining rooms and coffee shops*, submitted by Janet McMurtery and Pam McGibbon. Toronto: Ontario Status of Women Council, 1978. 5p.

3123.   "Women in foodservice: Rose can never look back since her first pizza," *Canadian Hotel & Restaurant*, 57:28, 38, Dec. 1979.

FRINGE BENEFITS

3124.   Bossen, M. and Associates. *Sex discrimination in fringe benefits*. Ottawa: Canada. Advisory Council on the Status of Women, 1975. 60p.

3125.   Canada. Advisory Council on the Status of Women. *Fringe benefits*. [*Les avantages sociaux*]. 2nd ed. The person papers. Ottawa, 1976. 16, 16p.

3126.   Dulude, Louise. "Legal notes: the fringe takes centre stage," *Branching Out*, 6(2):29-30, 1979.

3127.   Gelber, Sylvia M. "Discrimination in fringe benefits," *Labour Gazette*, 78:81-3, Feb.-Mar. 1978.

3128.   Juneja, Diljit. "Impact of the Ontario Human Rights Code on employee benefit plans," *Canadian Personnel and Industrial Relations Journal*, 22:22-5, Mar. 1975.

3129.   Landsberg, Michele. "Fringe benefits," *Chatelaine*, 47:35, 94-5, May 1974.

3130.   New Brunswick. Human Rights Commission. *Guidelines for ensuring compliance with the New Brunswick Human Rights Code in the matter of discrimination on the grounds of sex, age or marital status under employee benefit programs*. Fredericton, 1975. 16p. and app.

3131.   Ontario. Task Force on Employee Benefits Under Part X of the Employment Standards Act. *Report*. Toronto: Ontario. Ministry of Labour, 1975. 169p.

3132.   Ray, Ratna. "Problems of employees with family responsibilities and implications for employers," in Canadian Federation of Business and Professional Women's Clubs, *A collection of papers delivered at the National Conference: Women & Work in the 80's: a Decade of Change*. Ottawa: The Federation, 1981, pp.35-49.

GOVERNMENT OFFICIALS

3133.   Canada. Advisory Council on the Status of Women. *A preliminary review of the appointments within the power of the federal government to boards, commissions, councils, committees and corporations; a draft paper*, by Marcia Rioux for Mary Pearson. Ottawa, 1975. 16p.

3134.   Carlyle-Gordge, Peter. "The crowning achievement of Pearl McGonigal," *Chatelaine*, 55:38, 166+ , Sept. 1982.

3135.   Champagne, Lyse. *Not how many but how few: women appointed to boards, commissions, councils, committees and crown corporations within the power of the federal government*. Ottawa: Canadian Advisory Council on the Status of Women, 1980. 27p.

3136.   Engel, Marian. "Pauline McGibbon: the woman behind all those 'first women' jobs," *Chatelaine*, 47:46-7, 88-91, Oct. 1974.

3137.   Guggi, Anita. "Steady increase of women in [local] government," *Civic*, 33:6, 47, Sept. 1981.

3138.   Hardy, Allison Taylor. "Women: always diplomatic and more recently diplomats," *International Perspectives*, [5]:26-32, July-Aug. 1976.

3139.   Heald, Tim. "Jean Wadds and the politics of patriation," *Saturday Night*, 97:13-20, Jan. 1982.

3140.   Kohn, Walter S. G. "The Canadian House of Commons," in his *Women in national legislatures: a comparative study of six countries*. New York: Praeger, 1980, pp.113-34.

3141.   Labreche, Julianne. "The unsinkable Jeanne Sauvé," *Chatelaine*, 53:48-9, 100+ , Oct. 1980.

3142.   Saskatchewan. Advisory Council on the Status of Women. *Report on female participation on boards, commissions, committees and crown corporations in Saskatchewan*. Saskatoon, 1981. 15p. and app. (Microlog 82-1583)

GOVERNMENT PROGRAMS

3143.   Bannon, Sharleen. "International Women's Year: the government's program," *Labour Gazette*, 76:18-24, Jan. 1976.

3144.   Belfry, Ron. "Boost in the arm for Native women," *Native People*, 15:12, May 14, 1982.

3145.   Canada. Dept. of National Health and Welfare. *Equality: a principle in practice*. Notes for an address by the Honourable Marc Lalonde, Minister Responsible for the Status of Women, to Action '75+. Ottawa, 1975. 14p.

3146.   Canada. Dept. of the Secretary of State. *Native Women's Program: discussion paper*. [*Programme des femmes autochtones: document de travail*]. [Ottawa], 1980. 11p.

3147.   Canada. Minister Responsible for the Status of Women. *Towards equality for women*. [*Femme en voie d'égalité*]. Ottawa: Minister of Supply and Services Canada, 1979. 42, 42p.

3148.   Canada. Office of the Co-ordinator, Status of Women. *Federal services for women*. [*Ressources fédérales pour la femme*]. Rev. ed. [Ottawa]: Minister of Supply and Services Canada, 1977. 64, 63p.

3149.   _____. *We are... . Ottawa, 1978. Leaflet*.

3150.   Canada. Secretary of State. *Women's program: discussion paper*. [*Programme de promotion de la femme: document de travail*]. [Ottawa], 1980. 15p.

3151.   Canadian Committee on Learning Opportunities for Women. *Cutbacks to training allowances and outreach programs: their impact on women*. n.p., 1979. 35p.
         Brief presented to representatives of the Liberal Party, New Democratic Party and the Progressive Conservative Party.

3152.   "Equal opportunities for women in the federal public service [advertisement]," *Branching Out*, 6(1):26, 1979.

3153.   *Federal services for women: a guide to federal programs, services and grants of interest to women, including special responsibility centres*. Ottawa: Information Canada, 1975. 63p.

3154.   *Feminist Services Training Programme: a Youth Job Corps project*, sponsored by the Women's Programme Department of the Secretary of State. n.d. [5]p.

3155.   Lester, Tanya. "Women shift to non-traditional jobs," *Perception*, 4:9-10, Mar.-Apr. 1981.

3156.   "Minister announces plan of action [address by Marc Lalonde]," *Information - Status of Women*, 2(2):1-2, 4, 6, [English]; 1, 3, 5 [French],1978

3157.   Ontario. Ministry of Labour. Women's Bureau. *Evaluation research of the Introduction to Non-Traditional Occupations Program*, by Lynn Dzeoba. [Toronto], 1979. 24p.

126

3158. Ontario Status of Women Council. *Comments on the work incentives program for family benefits recipients announced by Ministry of Community and Social Services*. [Toronto], 1979. 12p.

3159. Status of Women Canada. *Towards equality for women. [Femme en voie d'égalité]*. Ottawa: Supply and Services Canada, 1979. 42, 42p.

HANDICAPPED

3160. Canadian Advisory Council on the Status of Women. *Women with handicaps*. Brief to the Special Committee on the Disabled and the Handicapped. Ottawa, 1980. 38p. and app.

3161. Luce, Sally R. and Barbara Wand. "Sex differences in referrals to a rehabilitation facility for the physically disabled: a research note," *Canadian Psychological Review*, 18:92-5, Jan. 1977.

3162. Vargo, J. W. "The disabled wife and mother: suggested goals for family counselling," *Canadian Counsellor*, 13:108-111, Jan. 1979.

3163. Weintraub, Laura S. "Invisible disabilities: women with handicap," *Fireweed*, 9:89-124, Winter 1981.

HEALTH

3164. Campeau, Nicole. "Une invitation à prendre en charge nôtre santé," *Canadian Women's Studies / Les cahiers de la femme*, 1:11-12, Summer 1979.

3165. Canadian Advisory Council on the Status of Women. *Women, caring and curing: submission of the CACSW to Health Services Review '79*. Ottawa, 1980. 22p. and app.
   Appendix A, Detailed recommendations on birth planning and occupational health

3166. Cassels, Derek. "More women dying from lung cancer," *Canadian Secretary* (Supplement to *Office Equipment & Methods*), Sept. 1976, pp.17, 21.

3167. Chappell, Neena L. and Betty Havens. "Old and female: testing the double jeopardy hypothesis," *Sociological Quarterly*, 21:157-71, Spring 1980.

3168. Cochrane, Jean. "Menopause: its onset and effects vary," *Drug Merchandising*, 59:22-4, June 1978.

3169. Community Task Force on Maternal and Child Health. *Manitoba native Indian mother and child: a discussion paper on a high risk population*. Winnipeg, Man., 1981. 45p.

3170. Dean, Loral. "The 12 main causes of death among Canadian women," *Chatelaine*, 56:80, 82, 84, 86, Apr. 1983.

3171. DeKoninck, Maria, Francine Saillant et Lise Dunningan. *Essai sur la santé des femmes*. Québec: Conseil du statut de la femme. Service de la recherche, 1981. 342p. Contents: Partie 1: Pouvoir, dépendance et santé des femmes. Partie 2: Réflexion sur la sexualité.

3172. DeLuca, Rayleen V. and Manly N. Spigelman. "Effects of models on food intake of obese and non-obese female college students," *Canadian Journal of Behavioural Science*, 11(2):124-9, 1979.

3173. Duvall, Donna and Alan Booth. "The housing environment and women's health," *Journal of Health and Social Behavior*, 19:410-17, Dec. 1978.

3174. Dyck, F. J. and others. "Are hysterectomies necessary?" *Canadian Family Physician*, 22:75-7, Oct. 1976.

3175. Filion, Jean-Paul. "Les causes de l'invalidité chez les femmes. [The causes of disability among women]," *Bulletin statistique; Régime de rentes du Québec*, 10:vii-xiii, [French]; xxi-xxvii [English], sept. 1976.

3176. Griffiths, G. Audrey. "Health and the working woman in the 80's," in Canadian Federation of Business and Professional Women's Clubs, *A collection of papers delivered at the National Conference: Women & Work in the 80's: a Decade of Change*. Ottawa: The Federation, 1981, pp.51-5.

3177. Herman, Sheryl Frances. "A social engineering approach to the treatment of obese women." MA thesis, University of Western Ontario, 1978. 182p. (Can. theses, no.36275)

3178. Levine, Helen. "On women and on one woman," in Anne MacLennan, ed., *Women: their use of alcohol and other legal drugs: a provincial consultation - 1975*. Toronto: Addiction Research Foundation of Ontario, 1976, pp.21-43.

3179. Luce, Sally R. and Barbara Wand. "Sex differences in health and illness," *Canadian Psychological Review*, 18:79-95, Jan. 1977.

3180. "Ma santé: je m'en occupe," *Canadian Women's Studies / Les cahiers de la femme*, 1:47-8, Summer 1979.

3181. Magidson, Debbie and Judy Wright. "Poster politics," *Broadside*, 1(1):9, [1979].

3182. McDonnell, Kathleen. "The women's health movement in Canada: new directions," *Canadian Dimension*, 13:30-2, May 1979.

3183. Meikle, Stewart. "The psychological effects of hysterectomy," *Canadian Psychological Review*, 18:128-41, Apr. 1977.

3184. Mitchinson, Wendy. "Gynecological operations on insane women: London, Ontario, 1895-1901," *Journal of Social History*, 15:467-84, Spring 1982.

3185. _____. "Gynecological operations on the insane," *Archivaria*, 10:125-44, Summer 1980.

3186. New Brunswick. Advisory Council on the Status of Women. *An ounce of prevention or a pound of cure: women, emergency and outpatient services*, prepared by Paula Wilson. [Moncton, N.B.], 1981. 33p.

3187. Northcott, Herbert C. *Women, work and health*. Edmonton area series, no. 12. Edmonton: University of Alberta. Dept. of Sociology. Population Research Laboratory, 1979. 13p. (Microlog 80-1490)

3188. _____. *Women, work, health and happiness*. Edmonton, Alta.: University of Alberta, 1981. (Microlog 81-2175)

3189. _____. "Women, work, and health," *Pacific Sociological Review*, 23:393-404, Oct. 1980.

3190. _____. "Women, work, health and happiness," *International Journal of Women's Studies*, 4:268-76, May-June 1981.

3191. Olmsted, Marion. "Anorexic-normal differences and predictors of concern with dieting in college women." MA thesis, University of Guelph, 1981. 110p. (Can. theses, no.52544)

3191.1 Ontario. Ministry of Health. Health Education, Promotion Unit and Ontario Interagency Council on Smoking and Health. *Workshop on women and smoking. Queen's Park, Toronto, Ont., Jan. 28, 1980*. Toronto, 1980. 21p.

3192. Ontario Status of Women Council. *About face: towards a positive image of women and health*, by Naomi Mallovy. Toronto, 1978. 26p.

3193. Ontario Status of Women Council. Health Committee. *Brief to Joint Advisory Committee of the Government of Ontario and the Ontario Medical Association on methods to control health care costs*. [Toronto], 1977. [13]p.

3194. Pettit, Laura. "Regina healthsharing: Healthsharing Inc.," *Broadside*, 2:8, June 1981.

3195. Phillips, A. J. and M. E. Brennan. "Reactions of Canadian women to Pap tests and breast self-examination," *Canadian Family Physician*, 22:71-4, Oct. 1976.

3196. Rahn, M. Julie-Anne. "Nutrition knowledge of a sample of urban women." MSc thesis, University of Guelph, 1980. 135p. (Can. theses, no.43832)

3197. Ross, Hazel Miriam. "Women and wellness: defining, attaining and maintaining health in Eastern Canada." PhD diss., University of Washington, 1982. 393p.

3198. Rozovsky, Lorne E. "Can a married woman give valid consent?" *Dimensions in Health Service*, 53:8-9, Oct. 1976.

3199. Saskatchewan. Task Force on Women's Health. *Report of the Task Force on Women's Health*. Regina, 1980. 124, [10]p.

3200. Sherrard, Debbie and Camille Fouillard, comps. *Women's Health Education Project - Newfoundland and Labrador survey analysis - 1981*. [St. John's, Nfld.: Women's Health Education Project], 1982. [53]p.

3200.1 Thompson, Edward. "Women and smoking," *Canadian Newsletter of Research on Women*, 7:94-6, July 1978.

3201. Van der Merwe, Marina Suzanne. "The relationship between physical fitness and the health status of selected Canadian college women." PhD diss., Ohio State University, 1981. 180p. (UM, no.81-21866)

3202. Weintraub, Laura S. "Invisible disabilities: women with handicap," *Fireweed*, 9:89-124, Winter 1981.

HEALTH - BIBLIOGRAPHY

3203. Pederson, Diana. *Women and health: an annotated bibliography of articles in selected Canadian medical periodicals 1970-1979*. CRIAW working papers. Ottawa: Canadian Research Institute for the Advancement of Women, 1979. 104p.

HEALTH CENTRES

3204. Atcheson, Beth. "Our own 'Catch 22': [Toronto] women's health clinic proposal rejected; Rejet d'un projet de clinique pour la santé de la femme," *Status of Women News / Statut: Bulletin de la femme*, 5:12-13, [English]; 12-13, [French], Dec. 1978.

3205. Campbell, Janet. "Nova Scotia Well Woman clinics; Les cliniques 'Well Woman' de la Nouvelle-Écosse. Elles dénoncent le contrôle de notre corps par la société," *Status of Women News / Statut: Bulletin de la femme*, 5:26-7, [English]; 30-1, [French], Dec. 1978.

3206. Haliburton, Jane C. "Establishing a Well Woman Clinic in Yarmouth, Nova Scotia," *Atlantis*, 4:141-45, Spring 1979, Part II.

3207. Hall, Audrey. "A self-help clinic for women," *Canadian Nurse*, 70:33-6, May 1974.

3208. Lockey, Ottie. "Feminist services and research mental health collectives: cooperation for survival," *Atlantis*, 4:128-32, Spring 1979, Part II.

HEALTH, OCCUPATIONAL

3209. Canada. Advisory Council on the Status of Women. *Health hazards at work*. [Le travail et les risques à la santé]. The person papers. Ottawa, 1977. 16, 16p.

3210. Canada. Advisory Council on the Status of Women. *Position paper: reproductive health hazards in the workplace*. Ottawa, 1980. 15p.

3211. Chenier, Nancy Miller. *Reproductive hazards at work; men, women and the fertility gamble*. Ottawa: Canadian Advisory Council on the Status of Women, 1982. 105p.

3212. George, Anne. *Occupational health hazards to women, a synoptic view*. Ottawa: Canada. Advisory Council on the Status of Women, 1976. 128p.

3213. George, Anne. "Occupational health hazards," *Canadian Women's Studies / Les cahiers de la femme*, 1:82-4, Summer 1979.

3214. "High miscarriage rates linked to VDT's?" *Ontario Labour*, May-June 1982, p.12.

3215. New Brunswick. Advisory Council on the Status of Women. *Women and occupational health: a submission to the New Brunswick Occupational Health and Safety Commission*, prepared by Susan Shalala. Moncton, N.B., 1981. 23p.

3216. "Pregnancy difficulties [among women operators of VDT's] a concern for government employees," *Ontario Labour*, May-June 1982, p.Ins.4.

3217. "VDT pregnancy fear grounds for transfer; Les écrans cathodiques peuvent motiver une mutation," *Canadian Labour / Travailleur canadien*, 27:6, [English]; 6, [French], Mar. 1982.

3218. "Women's health workplace issue," *Ontario Labour*, July-Aug. 1981, p.8.

3219. Wynn, Sheila. "The task ahead: in health," in Canadian Federation of Business and Professional Women's Clubs, *A collection of papers delivered at the National Conference: Women & Work in the 80's: a Decade of Change*. Ottawa: The Federation, 1981, pp. 83-8.

HOME LABOUR

3220. Home Economics International Development Workshop, Halifax, N.S., 1979. *Women's participation in economic growth*. Sponsored by Canadian Home Economics Association and the Canadian International Development Agency. [Ottawa: Canadian Home Economics Association, 1979]. 36p. (Microlog 80-4571)

3221. Johnson, Laura Climenko. "The homeworkers," *Perception*, 3:32-4, Sept.-Oct. 1979.

3222. Johnson, Laura C. and Robert E. Johnson. *The seam allowance: industrial sewing in Canada*. Toronto: Women's Press, 1982. 128p.

3223. McQuaig, Linda. "The ever-so-humble and low pay at home," *Maclean's*, 93:54-5, Nov. 10, 1980.

HOME LABOUR - BIBLIOGRAPHY

3224. McPherson, Kathryn. *A 'round the clock job': a selected bibliography on women's work at home in Canada*. Ottawa: Social Sciences and Humanities Research Council of Canada, 1983. 45p.

HOUSEWORK

3225. Adler, Hans J. and Oli Hawrylyshyn. "Estimates of the value of household work Canada, 1961 and 1971," *Review of Income and Wealth*, 24:333-55, Dec. 1978.

3226. Armstrong, Pat and Hugh Armstrong. *The double ghetto: Canadian women and their segregated work*. Toronto: McClelland and Stewart, 1978. 199p.

3227. Canada Pension Plan Advisory Committee. *More effective participation of homemakers in the Canada Pension Plan: majority and minority reports*. [Submitted] to Minister of National Health and Welfare. [Ottawa], 1983. 41, 7p. (Microlog 83-3264)
    Includes French edition.

3228. Centre de recherche sur la femme. *Analyse socio-économique de la ménagère québécoise*, par Carmell Benoit et autres. Montréal, 1972. 287p.

3229. Chisholm, Marjorie. "Businessmen look around," *Canadian Business Magazine*, 46:62, June 1973.

3230. Clark, Susan and Andrew S. Harvey. "The sexual division of labour: the use of time," *Atlantis*, 2:46-66, Autumn 1976.

3231. Derow, Ellan Odiorne. "Married women's employment and domestic labour." PhD diss., University of Toronto, 1977. 474p. (Can. theses, no.36631)

3232. Edds, J. A. "Businessman, learn thy lesson!" *Canadian Business Magazine*, 46:28, Feb. 1973.

3233. Eichler, Margrit. "The prestige of the occupation housewife," in Patricia Marchak, ed., *The working sexes: symposium papers on the effects of sex on women at work*. Vancouver: University of British Columbia. Institute of Industrial Relations, 1977, pp.152-75.

3234. Fox, Bonnie, ed. *Hidden in the household: women's domestic labour under capitalism*. Toronto: Women's Educational Press, 1980. 325p.

3235. Gelber, Sylva M. "Housework services: the orphan in economic reckoning," in *Women's Bureau '69*. Ottawa: Canada. Dept. of Labour. Women's Bureau, 1970, pp.22-6.

3236. _____. "The labour force, the G.N.P.: and unpaid housekeeping services," in *Women's Bureau '70*. Ottawa: Canada. Dept. of Labour. Women's Bureau, 1971, pp.20-6.

3237. Geraci, Francine. "That immutable housework," *Maclean's*, 95:44h, Apr. 5, 1982.

3238. Gillen, Mollie. "Housewives: what's your work worth? Would you believe $8,600?" *Chatelaine*, 46:20, 63, Dec. 1973.

3239. Hawrylyshyn, Oli. *Estimating the value of household work in Canada*. [*L'estimation de la valeur du travail ménager au Canada*]. Ottawa: Statistics Canada, 1978. 57p.

3240. Istona, Mildred. "Housework: for love or money?" *Chatelaine*, 50:4, Oct. 1977.

3241. Kome, Penney. *About face: towards a positive image of housewives*. Toronto: Ontario Status of Women Council, 1977. 40p.

3242.   _____. *Somebody has to do it: whose work is housework?* Toronto: McClelland & Stewart, 1982. 223p.

3243.   _____. "How Canadian women really feel about housework," *Homemaker's Magazine*, 13:26-8, 30+ , Oct. 1978.

3244.   Lacasse, François D. *Women at home: the cost to the Canadian economy*. Commission on the Status of Women in Canada. Study no. 2. Ottawa, 1970. 28p.

3245.   "La mère de famille, devrait-elle recevoir un salaire?" *Châtelaine*, 13:14, 74, 76-7, mai 1972.

3246.   Laws, Margaret. "Deciding housewives' worth requires an attitude change [Advisory Council on the Status of Women study]," *Financial Post*, 72:7, July 1, 1978.

3247.   Luxton, Margaret. "Why women's work is never done: a case study from Flin Flon, Manitoba of domestic labour in industrial capitalist society." PhD diss., University of Toronto, 1978. 364p. (Can. theses, no.38766)

3248.   Luxton, Meg. *More than a labour of love: three generations of women's work in the home*. Toronto: Women's Educational Press, 1980. 260p.

3249.   Meissner, Martin. "No exit for wives: sexual division of labour and the cumulation of household demands," *Canadian Review of Sociology and Anthroplogy*, 12:424-39, Nov. 1975.

3250.   _____. "The domestic economy: now you see it, now you don't," in Naomi Hersom and Dorothy E. Smith, [eds.], *Women and the Canadian labour force*. Working document. Ottawa: Social Sciences and Humanities Research Council of Canada, 1982, pp.343-66.

3251.   Muir, Margaret. "The paid housekeeper: socialization and sex roles in two fishing villages," in Richard J. Preston, ed., *Canadian Ethnology Society: papers from the fourth annual congress, 1977*. National Museum of Man. Mercury Series. Ottawa: National Museums of Canada, 1978, pp.85-98.

3252.   Proulx, Monique. *Five million women: a study of the Canadian housewife*. Women and work, [no. 1]. Ottawa: Canada. Advisory Council on the Status of Women, 1978. 92p.

3253.   Siggins, Maggie. "Should this woman get a salary?" *Chatelaine*, 45:25, 57-9, 61, July 1972.

3254.   Stein, David Lewis and Erna Paris. "Who should pay the housewife?" *Chatelaine*, 51:26, Oct. 1978.

3255.   Ursel, Jane. "Women's work, women's consciousness," *Canadian Dimension*, 13(3):24-5, 1978.

3256.   "What price housework? $80b," *Globe & Mail*, June 27, 1978, p.l.

3257.   White, Charles A. "Housewife mother vs. working father: whose job is tougher? You decide," *Canada and the World*, 39:16-17, Oct. 1973.

HOUSEWORK - BIBLIOGRAPHY

3258.   McPherson, Kathryn. *A 'round the clock job': a selected bibliography on women's work at home in Canada*. Ottawa: Social Sciences and Humanities Research Council of Canada, 1983. 45p.

HOUSING

3259.   Dranoff, Linda Silver. "Ask a lawyer," *Chatelaine*, 52:16, Nov. 1979.

3260.   Duvall, Donna and Alan Booth. "The housing environment and women's health," *Journal of Health and Social Behavior*, 19:410-17, Dec. 1978.

3261.   Fletcher, Susan and Leroy O. Stone. *The living arrangements of Canada's older women*. [*Les modes d'habitation des femmes âgées au Canada*]. Ottawa: Statistics Canada, 1982. 77p. (Microlog 83-1124)

3262.   _____. "The living arrangements of older women," *Essence*, 4(3):115-33, 1980.

3263.   Goliger, Gabriella. "Constance Hamilton Co-op: housing by women for women," *Habitat*, 26(1):22-6, 1983.

3264.   Hannley, Lynn and Marsha Mitchell. "The castle revisited," *Branching Out*, 5(3):16-17, 1978.

3265. Harrison, Brian R. "Fertility differentials and living arrangements of older widows," in his *Living alone in Canada: demographic and economic perspectives, 1951-1976*. Ottawa: Statistics Canada, 1981, pp.41-50. (Cat. no. 98-811)

3266. _____. "Increases in living alone by age and sex characteristics," in his *Living alone in Canada: demographic and economic perspectives, 1951-1976*. Ottawa: Statistics Canada, 1981, pp.24-6. (Cat. no. 98-811)

3267. McClain, Janet and Cassie Doyle. *Women and housing*. Toronto: James Lorimer, for the Canadian Council on Social Development, 1983.

3268. McClain, Janet. "Access, security and power...; Accession à la propriété, sécurité et pouvoir... ," *Status of Women News / Statut: Bulletin de la femme*, 6:15-16, [English]; 9-10, [French], Winter 1979-80.

3269. Padgham, Terry. "Canadian precedent set in N.W.T. Supreme Court," *Status of Women News*, 2:5, Feb. 1976.

HUSBAND AND WIFE

3270. Abrioux, Marie-Louise. "Marital perceptions and life satisfactions of middle-aged husbands and wives." MEd thesis, University of Alberta, 1977. 193p. (Can. theses, no.34276)

3271. Angers, Maurice. *Pouvoir dans la famille et planification des naissances en milieu défavorisé urbain québécois*. Laboratoire de recherches sociologiques. Rapports de recherches. Cahier 4. Québec: Université Laval. Dept. de sociologie, Faculté des sciences sociales, 1973. 509p.

3272. Boivin, Micheline. *Communication conjugale et planification des naissances en milieu défavorisé urbain québécois*. Laboratoire de recherches sociologiques. Rapports de recherches. Cahier 1. Québec: Université Laval. Dept. de sociologie, Faculté des sciences sociales, 1973. 372p.

3273. Brinkerhoff, Merlin and Eugen Lupri. "Theoretical and methodological issues in the use of decision-making as an indicator of conjugal power: some Canadian observations," *Canadian Journal of Sociology*, 3:1-20, Winter 1978.

3274. Burke, Ronald and Tamara Weir. "The husband-wife relationship: how significant in career and life success?" *Business Quarterly*, 40:62-7, Autumn 1975.

3275. Chimbos, Peter D. "Marital violence: a study of husband-wife homicide," in K. Ishwaran, *The Canadian family*. Rev. ed. Toronto: Holt, Rinehart and Winston of Canada, 1976, pp.580-99.

3276. Cloutier-Cournoyer, Renée. *Interaction conjugale et planification des naissances en milieu défavorisé urbain québécois*. Laboratoire de recherches sociologiques. Rapports de recherches. Cahier 7. Québec: Université Laval. Dept. de sociologie, Faculté des sciences sociales, 1974. xxxx, 725p.

3277. Colby, Marion. "Juggling the roles," *Canadian Women's Studies / Les cahiers de la femme*, 2(2):41-3, 1980.

3278. "Corporate couples: when it's good it's very good and when it's bad it's horrid," *Financial Times*, 66:21, Apr. 17, 1978.

3279. Delisle, Mary Ann. "Bonding behaviour in newly married couples." MSW thesis, University of British Columbia, 1979. 123p. (Can. theses, no.46112)

3280. Dunnigan, Barbara. "Survival suggestions for the executive wife," *Canadian Personnel and Industrial Relations Journal*, 20:27-8, Oct. 1973.

3281. Edinborough, Arnold. "A new kind of liberated woman," *Financial Post*, 68:10, Sept. 7, 1974.

3282. Edmonds, Alan. "War brides, 30 years later," *The Canadian*, May 15, 1976, pp.16-20.

3283. Eichler, Margrit. "The equalitarian family in Canada?" in S. Parvez Wakil, ed., *Marriage, family and society: Canadian perspectives*. Toronto: Butterworth and Company, 1975, pp.223-35.

3284. Finlayson, Judith. "Loving and working together," *Homemaker's Magazine*, 13:9-10, 12+ , May 1978.

3285. Garigue, Philippe. *La vie familiale des canadiens français*. Montréal: Presses de l'Université de Montréal, 1970. 143p.

3286. Grescoe, Paul and Audrey Grescoe. "24-hours-a-day marriage," *Financial Post Magazine*, [70]:42-4, Nov. 20, 1976.

3287. Guay, Chantal. "Comment le changement de rôle chez la femme peut entraîner un reajustement des rôles dans la relation conjugale," *Orientation professionnelle*, 14:138-44, été 1978.

3288. Hedlund, David. "An investigation of the marriage encounter program." MEd thesis, University of Alberta, 1980. 209p. (Can. theses, no.48965)

3289. Herman, Sheryl Frances. "A social engineering approach to the treatment of obese women." MA thesis, University of Western Ontario, 1978. 182p. (Can. theses, no.36275)

3290. Howard, Paul. "Mothering is a legitimate male occupation," *Canadian Women's Studies / Les cahiers de la femme*, 2(1):14-16, 1980.

3291. Landsberg, Michele. "How liberated are Canadian husbands," *Chatelaine*, 48:32, 55-8, Jan. 1975.

3292. Leclerc, Marie. *Mieux vivre à deux*. 2e éd. Québec: Conseil du statut de la femme, 1979. 38p.

3293. Leginsky, Patricia Anne. "Problem solving resources for dual career couples." MSc thesis, University of Alberta, 1980. 163p. (Can. theses, no.44768)

3294. Lumsden, Barbara L. "Women's dependency: the interrelationship of structure and ideology." MA thesis, University of Guelph, 1981. 118p. (Can. theses, no.52521)

3295. Lurie, Christine. "Association between marital adjustment and the wife's employment in her profession." MSc thesis, University of Calgary, 1974. 49p. (Can. theses, no.21306)

3296. Martin-Matthews, Anne E. "Wives' experiences of relocation: status passage and the moving career." PhD diss., McMaster University, 1980. 337p. (Can. theses, no.46914)

3297. Maynard, Fredelle. "New norm: the two-income couple: double the pleasure or double the stress?" *Chatelaine*, 54:39-41, 64+ , June 1981.

3298. Meissner, Martin. "Sur la division du travail et l'inégalité des sexes," *Sociologie du travail*, 17:329-50, oct.-déc. 1975.

3299. _____. "Women and inequality: at work - at home," *Our Generation*, 11:59-71, Winter 1976.

3300. Paquette, Lucie. *Rôles familiaux et planification des naissances en milieu défavorisé urbain québécois*. Laboratoire de recherches sociologiques. Rapports de recherches. Cahier 5. Québec: Université Laval. Dept. de sociologie, Faculté des sciences sociales, 1974. xxii, 313p.

3301. Pierzchalski, Paul. "Marital resources: some variables examined." MA thesis, University of Calgary, 1974. 95p. (Can. theses, no.21338)

3302. Ribeyron, Marie-Thérèse. "Les amoureux du travail conjugal," *L'Actualité*, 5:46-9, août 1980.

3303. Ross, Valerie. "She stoops-grovels!-to conquer," *Maclean's*, 88:67, Dec. 15, 1975.

3304. Sexton, Christine S. "Career orientation, sex role orientation, and perceived equity as factors affecting marital power." PhD diss., University of Manitoba, 1979. 165p. (Can. theses, no.40048)

3305. Sheppard, Deborah L. "Awareness and decision-making in dual-career couples." PhD diss., York University, 1981. 235p. (Can. theses, no.47861)

3306. Sheppard, Mary. "Profiting from equal partnership: demand for skilled professionals and career-minded women is promoting corporate couples," *Maclean's*, 94:50, May 11, 1981.

3307. Simpson, Judith Deanne. "A study of mothers' perception of parental dominance in the family as related to socio-economic status." MSW thesis, University of Toronto, 1968. 91p. (Can. theses, no.17808)

3308. Stacy, Stanley. "Perceptions of male and female success in sex-linked occupations in relation to the sex of subject and the stance of spouse: impressions of conflicts, consequences, and attributions." MA thesis, Concordia University, 1976. 65p. (Can. theses, no.28470)

3309. Thompson, Judy and Rhonda Gilby. "Correlates of domestic violence and the role of police agencies," in Robert A. Silverman and James J. Teevan, eds., *Crime in Canadian society*. 2d ed. Toronto: Butterworths, 1980, pp.298-306.

3310. Wachowich, Elizabeth Louise. "Role competence and marital satisfaction of dual-career couples: a replication study." MSc thesis, University of Alberta, 1979. 151p. (Can. theses, no.40523)

3311. Weir, Tamara and Ronald J. Burke. "Two people, two careers, and one relationship! Making it work," *Business Quarterly*, 44:47-53, Spring 1979.

IMMIGRANTS

3312. Alberro, Ana and Gloria Montero. "The immigrant woman," in Gwen Matheson, *Women in the Canadian mosaic*. Toronto: Peter Martin, 1976, pp.131-48.

3313. _____. "The land of beginning again," *Canadian Forum*, 55:23-8, Sept. 1975.

3314. Arnopoulos, Sheila McLeod. *Problems of immigrant women in the Canadian labour force*. Ottawa: Canadian Advisory Council on the Status of Women, 1979. 79p.

3315. Baril, Joan. *The fringes of society: immigrant women in Thunder Bay, "catch 22, catch 22, catch 22...".* n.p.: Lakehead Social Planning Council, 1981. 9p.

3316. Barndt, Deborah, Ferne Cristall and Dian Marino. *Getting there: producing photostories with immigrant women*. Toronto: Between the Lines, 1982. 110p.

3317. Bernardin-Haldemann, Verena. "Femmes haitiennes à Montréal." MA thesis, Université Laval, 1972. 283p. (Can. theses, no.18907)

3318. Bodnar, Ana and Marilee Reimer. "The organization of social services and its implications for the mental health of immigrant women," *Resources for Feminist Research*, 8:63-5, Nov. 1979.

3319. Boyd, Monica. "Occupations of female immigrants and North American immigration statistics," *International Migration Review*, 10:73-80, Spring 1976.

3320. _____. "Status of immigrant women in Canada," *Canadian Review of Sociology and Anthropology*, 12:406-16, Nov. 1975.

3321. Canada. Dept. of the Secretary of State. Multiculturalism Directorate. *The immigrant woman in Canada; a right to recognition. Part 1, Report of the proceedings of the conference, Toronto, Ont., Mar. 20-22, 1981*. Ottawa: Minister of Supply and Services Canada, 1981. 31, 31p.
   French edition: Les immigrantes au Canada; le droit à la reconnaissance. Partie 1, Actes de la conférence, Toronto (Ontario), les 20, 21 et 22 mars 1981.

3322. _____. *The immigrant woman in Canada; a right to recognition. Part 2, Recommendations from the conference, Toronto, Ont., Mar. 20-22, 1981*. Ottawa: Minister of Supply and Services Canada, 1981. 27, 29p.
   French edition: Les immigrantes au Canada; le droit à la reconnaissance. Partie 2, Recommandations de la conférence, Toronto (Ontario), les 20, 21 et 22 mars 1981.

3323. Danziger, Kurt. "The acculturation of Italian immigrant girls," in K. Ishwaran, ed., *The Canadian family*. Rev. ed. Toronto: Holt, Rinehart and Winston of Canada, 1976, pp.200-12.

3324. De Schepper, Gladys. "Immigrant and female," *Homemaker's Magazine*, 11:102-3, 106-8, May 1976.

3325. Diane. "Femmes chiliennes," *Canadian Women's Studies / Les cahiers de la femme*, 1:114-15, Winter 1978-1979.

3326. Diebel, Linda. "Black women in white Canada: the lonely life [West Indians]," *Chatelaine*, 46:38, 84, 86-8, Mar. 1973.

3327. Edmonds, Alan. "War brides, 30 years later," *The Canadian*, May 15, 1976, pp.16-20.

3328. Epstein, Rachel. "I thought there was no more slavery in Canada!" *Canadian Dimension*, 14:29-35, May 1980.

3329. _____. "West Indian domestic workers on employment visas: I thought there was no more slavery in Canada!" *Canadian Women's Studies / Les cahiers de la femme*, 2(1):22-9, 1980.

3330. Epstein, Rachel, Roxana Ng and Maggi Trebble. *Social organization of family violence: an ethnography of immigrant experience in Vancouver*. [Vancouver]: Women's Research Centre, 1978. 52p. Report to the Non-Medical Use of Drugs Directorate, Health and Welfare, Canada.

3331. Ferguson, Edith. *Immigrant women in Canada*. Report for the Royal Commission on the Status of Women in Canada. n.p., n.d. 23p.

3332. Greenglass, Esther R. "A comparison of maternal communication style between immigrant Italian and second-generation Italian women living in Canada," *Journal of Cross-Cultural Psychology*, 3:185-92, June 1972.

3333. Horna, Jarmila L. A. "The entrance status of Czech and Slovak immigrant women," in Jean Leonard Elliott, ed., *Two nations, many cultures: ethnic groups in Canada*. Scarborough, Ont.: Prentice-Hall, 1979, pp.270-9.

3334. Howell, Shelley and Margaret Malone. "Immigrant women and work," Rikka, 7:35-41, Spring 1980.

3335. "Immigrant women," *Multiculturalism*, 2, no. 4, 1979, Special issue.

3336. Kainola, May Ann and Margie Bruun-Meyer. *Making changes: employment orientation for immigrant women*. Toronto: Cross Cultural Communication Centre, 1982. 136p. and app.

3337. Khosla, Renu Chopra. "A Canadian perspective on the Hindu woman: a study in identity transformation." MA thesis, McMaster University, 1980. 154, 4p. (Can. theses, no.20313)

3338. Knight, Rolf. *A very ordinary life*. Vancouver: New Star Books, 1974. 317p.

3339. Krehm, Gladys. "The illegals," *Canadian Forum*, 56:5-7, Oct. 1976.

3340. Lash, Ronnie and Gwen Morgan. "Immigrant women fight back: the case of the seven Jamaican women," *Resources for Feminist Research*, 8:23-4, Nov. 1979.

3341. MacKeracher, Dorothy. *Roadblocks to women's learning: issues for advocacy*. [Toronto: Canadian Committee on Learning Opportunities for Women, 1978].
    Consists of the following units: Unit I, Introduction; Unit II, Day Care Services; Unit III, Employment (Manpower) and Immigration.

3342. Magloire Chancy, Adeline. *L'analphabétisme chez les femmes immigrants haitiennes*. [Montréal]: Librairie de l'Université de Montréal, [1981?] 168p.

3343. Menozzi, Anna. "Employment services for immigrants," *Rikka*, 7:10-12, Spring 1980.

3344. Mickelson, Edward. *Language needs of immigrant women*. MEd thesis, University of Alberta, 1978. 147p. (Can. theses, no.40245)

3345. Montero, Gloria. "Carmen Lopez' tough fight to make it as a Canadian," *Chatelaine*, 49:34, 38-40, 113-15, May 1976.

3346. _____. "Immigrant women," *Emergency Librarian*, 3:21-4, Sept.-Oct. 1975.

3347. Morgan, Gwen and Michael David. "Caribbean women and immigration," *Rikka*, 7:20-2, Spring 1980.

3348. Moudgil, Ranvir. "Changes in sex-role identity among Ugandan Asians in Canada," *State University of New York, Buffalo. Occasional Papers in Anthropology*, no. 1:123-31, Apr. 1979.

3349. Murphy, Pat. "A Portuguese garment worker talks about her work and her union," *Rikka*, 7:42-4, Spring 1980.

3350. Naidoo, Josephine C. *The (East) Indian woman*. Toronto: Indian Immigration Aid Services, [1977?] 18p.

3351. Naidoo, Josephine C. "Women of South Asian and Anglo-Saxon origins in the Canadian context," in Cannie Stark-Adamec, ed., *Sex roles: origins, influences and implications for women*. Montreal: Eden Press, 1980, pp.50-69.

3352. Ng, Roxana and Judith Ramirez. *Immigrant housewives in Canada: a report*. Toronto: Immigrant Women's Centre, 1981. 76p.

3353. Ng, Roxana and Tania Das Gupta. "Nation builders? The captive labour force of non-English-speaking immigrant women," *Canadian Women's Studies / Les cahiers de la femme*, 3(1):83-5, 1981.

135

3354. Ng, Roxana. "Constituting ethnic phenomenon: an account from the perspective of immigrant women," *Canadian Ethnic Studies*, 13(1): 97-108, 1981.

3355. _____. "Moving around in the everyday world," *Rikka*, 7:14-16, Spring 1980.

3356. Oikawa, Dulce. "Speaking 'garmentese'," *Branching Out*, 4:14, Mar.-Apr. 1977.

3357. Ontario. Joint Task Force on Immigrant Women, September 1979. *Report*. Toronto, 1980. 42p.
  Sponsored by the Ontario Advisory Council on Multiculturalism, with the Ontario Advisory Council on Senior Citizens and the Ontario Status of Women Council.

3358. Poulton, Terry. "When nanny is an outlaw," *Maclean's*, 92:50, Dec. 17, 1979.

3359. Ramkhalawansingh, Ceta. "Language and employment training for immigrant women," *Canadian Ethnic Studies*, 13(1):91-6, 1981.

3360. _____. "Sexual and cultural politics among immigrants in Toronto [interview]," *Resources for Feminist Research*, 8:28-30, Nov. 1979.

3361. Rayfield, J. R. "Maria in Markham Street: Italian immigrants and language-learning in Toronto," *Ethnic Groups*, 1(2):133-50, 1976.

3362. Rosenberg, Leah. *The errand runner: reflections of a rabbi's daughter*. Toronto: John Wiley and Sons Canada, 1981. 149p.

3363. Scrutton, R. Edgar. "Intergenerational value conflicts in the Italian families, Amherstburg, Ontario: a study of mother-daughter responses." MA thesis, University of Windsor, 1978. 100p. (Can. theses, no.37164)

3364. Siddique, Muhammad. "Changing family patterns: a comparative analysis of immigrant Indian and Pakistani families of Saskatoon, Canada," *Journal of Comparative Family Studies*, 8:179-200, Summer 1977.

3365. Silvera, Makeda. "Broken dreams: West Indian women in Toronto," *Rikka*, 7:17-19, Spring 1980.

3366. _____. "Immigrant domestic workers: whose dirty laundry?" *Fireweed*, 9:53-9, Winter 1981.

3367. Smith, Bruna. "Centro femminile: a source of help to immigrant women," *Multiculturalism*, 1(1):18-21, 1977.

3368. Srivastava, Ram P. "Family organization and change among the overseas Indians with special reference to Indian immigrant families of British Columbia, Canada," in George Kurian, ed., *The family in India: a regional view*. The Hague: Mouton, 1974, pp.369-91.

3369. Turritin, Jane Sawyer. "Networks and mobility: the case of West Indian domestics from Montserrat," *Canadian Review of Sociology and Anthropology*, 13(3):305-20, 1976.

3370. Turrittin, Jane S. "Networks to jobs: case studies of West Indian women from Montserrat." MA thesis, University of Toronto, 1975. 176p.

3371. Turrittin, Jane Sawyer. "'We don't look for prejudice': migrant mobility culture among lower status West Indian women from Montserrat," in Jean Leonard Elliott, ed., *Two nations, many cultures: ethnic groups in Canada*. Scarborough, Ont.: Prentice-Hall, 1979, pp.311-24.

3372. Uwaegbute, Adaoha C. "Infant feeding practices of Nigerians and Ghanian women living in the Guelph-Kitchener-Waterloo area." MSc thesis, University of Guelph, 1978. 202p. (Can. theses, no.39013)

IMMIGRANTS - BIBLIOGRAPHY

3373. Gulbinowicz, Eva. *Problems of immigrant women: past and present: a bibliography*. Bibliography, no. 16. [Toronto]: Ontario. Ministry of Labour, Library, 1979. 45p.

3374. "Resource guide [on immigrant women]," *Multiculturalism*, 2(4):29-32, 1979.

3375. Working Women (Formerly Women's Community Employment Centre). *A report on the research and development phase*. Submitted to Secretary of State. [Toronto], 1975. 39p. and app.

IMMIGRANTS - HISTORY

3376. Barber, Marilyn. "The women Ontario welcomed: immigrant domestics for Ontario homes, 1870-1930," *Ontario History*, 72:148-72, Sept. 1980.

3377. Buckley, Suzann. "British female emigration and imperial development: experiments in Canada, 1885-1931," *Hecate*, 3(2):26-40, 1977.

3378. Emblem, Edith Lawrence. "In her own words," in E. Blanche Norcross, ed., *Nanaimo retrospective: the first century*. Nanaimo, B.C.: Nanaimo Historical Society, 1979, pp.147-51.

3379. Hibbert, Joyce, ed. *The war brides*. Toronto: PMA Books, 1978. 160p.

3380. Jackel, Susan, ed. *A flannel shirt and liberty: British emigrant gentlewomen in the Canadian west, 1880-1914*. Vancouver: University of British Columbia Press, 1982. 229p.

3381. Lenskyj, Helen. "Social change affecting women in urban Canada, 1890-1930, and its impact upon immigrant women in the labour force." MA thesis, University of Toronto, 1980. 152p.

3382. Parr, Joy. "'Transplanting from dens of iniquity': theology and child emigration," in Linda Kealey, ed., *A not unreasonable claim: women and reform in Canada, 1880s-1920s*. Toronto: Women's Press, 1979, pp.169-83.

3383. Petroff, Lillian. *The Macedonian community in Toronto to 1930: women and emigration*. Canadian Women's History series, no. 5. Toronto: Ontario Institute for Studies in Education, 1977. 23p.
    A paper presented to the 1977 meeting of the Canadian Historical Association.

3384. _____. "'A work of empire': Canadian reformers and British female immigration," in Linda Kealey, ed., *A not unreasonable claim: women and reform in Canada, 1880s-1920s*. Toronto: Women's Press, 1979, pp.185-201.

3385. Roberts, Barbara. "Sex, politics and religion: controversies in female immigration reform work in Montreal, 1881-1919." *Atlantis*, 6:25-38, Fall 1980.

3386. Salverson, Laura Goodman. *Confessions of an immigrant's daughter*. Toronto: University of Toronto Press, 1981. 415p. First published in 1939.

INHERITANCE AND SUCCESSION

3387. Charron, Camille. "Le conjoint survivant et la succession légitime en droit québécois," *Revue de droit*, 8(2):197-336, 1977.

3388. Dranoff, Linda Silver. "Ask a lawyer," *Chatelaine*, 52:12, 18, Sept. 1979.

3389. _____. "Ask a lawyer," *Chatelaine*, 53:22, 25, Apr. 1980.

3390. Rocchi, Rosanne. *Understanding family law reform in Ontario*. Toronto: Coles, 1979. 141p.

INSURANCE

3391. Alberta. Women's Bureau. *Life insurance and disability insurance; the woman's point of view*. Rev. ed. Edmonton, 1979. 16p.

3392. "An all-female agency: is it really that much different?" *Canadian Insurance*, 82:22, 24, Dec. 1977.

3393. Anderson, Helen. "Consumers apprehensive about 'Unisex' rating," *Canadian Insurance*, 84:61-2, Nov. 1979.

3394. Ash, Stephen B. *Consumer satisfaction with financial services and insurance: the case of the working woman*. Submitted to and distributed by Consumer and Corporate Affairs Canada. 1980. 40p. (Microlog 83-1316)

3395. Belton, Ted. "Unisex rating perversion of human rights," *Canadian Insurance*, 84:68-78, Nov. 1979.

3396. "Decision on [annuity] payments to women spotlights key insurers' problems," *Globe & Mail*, May 30, 1979, p.B1.

3397. Dumont, Monique. "L'assurance-vie et les femmes: commentaires sur une documentation récente," *Assurances*, 47:274-8, oct. 1979.

3398. Eustace, David F. "Three widows," *Life Insurance in Canada*, 4:6, 8, 48-9, 54, May-June 1977.

3399. Gelber, Sylva M. "Time to reform traditional insurance practices to eliminate sex discrimination," in, *Women's Bureau '74*. Ottawa: Canada. Dept. of Labour. Women's Bureau, 1975, pp.99-106.

3400. Laws, Margaret. "Women courted by insurance industry as sales increase," *Financial Post*, 72:23, May 6, 1978.

3401. Lee, Betty. "Women & insurance," *Chatelaine*, 50:16, 20, Sept. 1977.

3402. McBride, Russ. "Age, sex, marital status are valid rating criteria," *Canadian Insurance*, 84:64, 66, Nov. 1979.

3403. "More women trying life insurance sales," *Financial Times*, 66:26, Oct. 17-23, 1977.

3404. Osler, Richard. "Facts of life on insurance disturb some women," *Financial Post*, 70:14, Jan. 17, 1976.

3405. "Women can combine career and family," *Life Insurance in Canada*, 5:5, 9, Jan.-Feb. 1978.

3406. "Women need financial planning, rather than emotional blackmail," *Canadian Underwriter*, 46:54, Nov. 1979.

INTERNATIONAL WOMEN'S YEAR

3407. Anderson, Doris. "International Women's Year: will Canadian women get their $5 millions worth? [editorial]," *Chatelaine*, 48:4, Feb. 1975.

3408. _____. "Women's Year should try to meet women's real needs [editorial]," *Chatelaine*, 48:4, July 1975.

3409. Bannon, Sharleen. "International Women's Year: the government's program," *Labour Gazette*, 76:18-24, Jan. 1976.

3410. _____. "International Women's Year: women in the workplace," *Labour Gazette*, 76:69-74, Feb. 1976.

3411. Bird, Florence. "Update on International Women's Year: national and international experience with women's rights," *International Perspectives*, [7]:20-6, Jan.-Feb. 1978.

3412. Brown, Sharon. "International Women's Year," *Canada Commerce*, 139:2-5, Jan. 1975.

3413. Canada. Dept. of the Secretary of State. *International Women's Year*. [*Année internationale de la femme*]. [Ottawa], 1975. 13, 14p.

3414. Cooke, Katie. "International Women's Year: what it means to all of us," *Chatelaine*, 48:20, Jan. 1975.

3415. "CUPE programme for women's year," *Canadian Labour*, 20:16-18, June 1975.

3416. De Villiers, Marq. "The year of the she: but now what?" *Weekend Magazine*, 26:2-4, 7, Jan. 3, 1976.

3417. Dick, Jane. "Why not? Because..." *Branching Out*, 2:6-7, Nov.-Dec. 1975.

3418. Hillmer, Sandra. "Prelude to IWY," *Branching Out*, 1:26-8, Nov.-Dec. 1974.

3419. "International Women's Year," *Canadian Welfare*, 50:23, Nov.-Dec. 1974.

3420. Kostash, Myrna. "Women: this, ladies, is your very own year: two cheers," *Maclean's*, 88:9, Feb. 1975.

3421. Krehm, Gladys. "Straws in the wind," *Canadian Forum*, 55:9-11, Sept. 1975.

3422. Landsberg, Michele. "Has Women's Year laid an egg?" *Chatelaine*, 48:53, 113-14, 116, 118, Nov. 1975.

3423. Lee, Betty. "The aftermath of IWY: some of us moved in the right direction, almost as many went wrong," *The Canadian*, Aug. 21, 1976, p.3.

3424. MacPherson, Kay. "Doing it ourselves," *Canadian Forum*, 55:39-41, Sept. 1975.

3425. Marsden, Lorna. "Why now? The mirage of equality: IWY in Canada," *Canadian Forum*, 55:12-17, Sept. 1975.

3426. Ollsen, Andree. "IWY is not going to turn Canada into Amazonia," *Broadsheet: New Zealand's Feminist Magazine*, no. 31:13-14, July 1975.

3427. Ontario. Ministry of Labour. Women's Programs Division. *Women on the move, equal opportunity, 1975, International Women's Year*. [1975]. Folder.

3428. Pelrine, Eleanor Wright. "IWY postscript with Dr. Katie Cooke," Chatelaine, 50:26, 60-2, Feb. 1977.

3429. Québec. Ministère des communications. Direction générale de l'édition. Centre de documentation. *L'Année internationale de la femme: rétrospectives 1975*. [Québec], 1976. 233p.

3430. Robillard, Laurette. *Impact actuel de l'Année internationale de la femme*. Causerie prononcée, le 23 sept. 1975 devant La Societé des comptables en administration industrielle du Québec. Québec: Conseil du Statut de la Femme, 1975. 10p.

3431. _____. "Impact actuel de l'Année internationale de la femme," *Cost and Management*, 49:58-9, Nov.-Dec. 1975.

3432. "What did you think of IWY?" *Branching Out*, 2:8-11, Nov.-Dec. 1975.

3433. White, Charles A. "International Women's Year: a new deal for women?" *Canada and the World*, 40:6-7, May 1975.

INVESTMENT

3434. Best, Patricia. "Brokers take aim at women investors," *Financial Post*, 76:5, June 19, 1982.

3435. Codère, Clarisse. "Les clubs d'Épargne-femmes," *Canadian Woman Studies / Les cahiers de la femme*, 3:108-9, Summer 1982.

3436. Collins, Catherine. "Women's stock is on the rise in the investment business," *Canadian Business*, 53:28, 32, Oct. 1980.

3437. Jamieson, Laura. "Fifteen ways to invest," *Canadian Secretary*, 5:10-11, May 1980.

3438. Noble, Winifred. "A wily guide for the novice investor," *Canadian Secretary* (Supplement to *Office Equipment & Methods*), Sept. 1976, pp.10-11.

3439. Pappert, Ann. "Lone bull meets little lady: wooing women investors," *Canadian Business*, 54:138, Feb. 1981.

3440. Reid, Laura. "Women flock to investment courses," *Canadian Secretary*, 6:8, Nov. 1981.

3441. Ward, Eleanor. "Not the sort of women, it seems, Earle McLaughlin was looking for," *Maclean's*, 89:67, Oct. 4, l976.

JOURNALISM

3442. Best, Carrie M. *That lonesome road: the autobiography of Carrie M. Best*. New Glasgow, N.S.: Clarion Pub. Co., 1977. 258p.

3443. Boivin, Aurélien et Kenneth Landry. "Françoise et Madeleine: pionnières du journalism féminin au Québec," *Atlantis*, 4:63-74, Autumn 1978.

3444. Cash, Gwen. *Off the record: the personal reminiscences of Canada's first woman reporter*. Langley, B.C.: Stagecoach Pub. Co., 1977. 170p.

3445. Cercle des femmes journalistes. *Vingt-cinq à la une: biographies*. Montréal: La Presse, 1976. 189p.

3446. Cochrane, Jean. *Kate Aitken*. Don Mills, Ont.: Fitzhenry & Whiteside, 1979. 63p.

3447. Cook, Ramsay. "Francis Marion Beynon and the crisis of Christian reformism," in Carl Berger and Ramsay Cook, eds., *The west and the nation: essays in honour of W. L. Morton*. Toronto: McClelland and Stewart, 1976, pp.187-208.

3448. Courchesne, Ginette. "Laure Hurteau, journaliste: étude bio-bibliographique." MA mémoire, Université de Montréal, 1975. 222p.

3449. Dempsey, Lotta. *No life for a lady*. Don Mills, Ont.: Musson Book, 1976. 207p.

3450. Drobot, Eva. "Half begun, half done," *Content*, no. 85: 3, 5-7, 26-31, May 1978.

3451. Ferguson, Ted. *Kit Coleman: queen of hearts*. Toronto: Doubleday Canada, 1978. 182p.

3452. Francis, Daniel. "Sara Jeannette Duncan: the Victorian rebel reporter who breached the Globe's men's club'," *Chatelaine*, 49:30, May 1976.

3453. Gorham, Deborah. "Pen and buckskin: women journalists in the west who knew wheat and justice," *Content*, 85:22-3, May 1978.

3454. Gould, Allan M. "CTV's Pam Wallin: a skyrocket from Saskatchewan," *Chatelaine*, 56:60-1, 102+ , Apr. 1983.

3455. Govier, Katherine. "...Women's Press - staying small and thriving," *Quill & Quire*, 45:15-16, July 1979.
3456. Hacker, Carlotta *E. Cora-Hind*. Don Mills, Ont.: Fitzhenry & Whiteside, 1979. 63p.
3457. Hamel, Reginald. *Gaëtane de Montreuil. Journaliste québécoise (1867-1951)*. Montréal: L'Aurore, 1976. 205p.
3458. Harvey, Dona. "June Sheppard, woman in the media," *Branching Out*, 1:23-4, 29, June-July 1974.
3459. Henry, Ann. *Laugh, baby, laugh*. Toronto: McClelland and Stewart, 1970. 187p.
3460. Laplante, Germaine. *Une journaliste intemporelle: Germaine Bernier*. Montréal: Éditions Bellarmin, 1978. 446p.
3461. "Operation visiting press women," *Citizen*, 13:23-6, Oct. 1967.
3462. "Presswomen: their status in Canada," *Labour Gazette*, 66:518, Sept. 1966.
3463. Robinson, Gertrude Joch. *Female print journalists in Canada and the United States: a professional profile and comparison*. n.p., [1975]. 27p.
3464. Rowland, Robin. "Kit Watkins: the journalist who opened the way for Canadian newspaper women," *Content*, no. 85:13-19, May 1978.
3465. Rowland, Robin. "Kit: '... an adornment to any paper'," *Content*, no. 85:19-20, May 1978.
3466. "Spy in the house of men [Joanne Kates]," *Saturday Night*, 93:5-6, Sept. 1978.
3467. "Women's rights and the newspaper guild," *Labour Gazette*, 71:245, Apr. 1971.

JUSTICE

3468. Alberta. Women's Bureau. *Women on juries*. Alberta facts. Edmonton, n.d. 3p.
3469. Morrow, W. G. "Women on juries," *Alberta Law Review*, 12:321-6, 1974.
3470. Nelson, Susan Hess. "An experimental study concerning jury decisions in rape trials," *Criminal Reports*, 3rd ser., 1:265-83, 1978.
3471. Nelson, Susan Hess. "Jurors' verdicts in a mock rape trial experiment: a social learning approach." PhD diss., Carleton University, 1979. 178p. (Can. theses, no.49524)
3472. McKie, Craig and Paul Reed. "Women in Canadian civil courts," *Canadian Journal of Sociology*, 6:485-504, Fall 1981.
3473. McKie, C. and P. Reed. *Women in the civil courts*. Research study, no. 9. Ottawa: Statistics Canada. Justice Statistics Division, 1979. 73p.

JUVENILE DELINQUENCY

3474. Barnhorst, Sherrie. "Female delinquency and the role of women," *Canadian Journal of Family Law*, 1:254-73, Apr. 1978.
3475. Bertrand, Marie-Andrée. "Le caractère discriminatoire et unique de la justice pour mineurs: les filles dites 'delinquantes' au Canada," *Deviance et societé*, 1(2):187-202, 1977.
3476. Butt, Dorcas Susan. "Psychological styles of delinquency in girls," *Canadian Journal of Behavioural Science*, 4(4):298-306, 1972.
3477. Coupland, Michael W. "Antecedents of juvenile prostitution: a test of social control theory." MA thesis, Simon Fraser University, 1979. 122p. (Can. theses, no.44880)
3478. DeJordy, Micheline. "La délinquance cachée," *Canadian Woman Studies / Les cahiers de la femme*, 4:53-4, Fall 1982.
3479. Deschênes, Diane. "Délinquance féminine et traits descriptifs de la personnalité," Mémoire de maîtrise, Université de Montréal, 1980.
3480. Fillmore, Cathy. "Sex and juvenile delinquency." MA thesis, University of Manitoba, 1977. 184p.
3481. Gagnon, Rosette, Louise Biron et Marie-Andrée Bertrand. *Aspirations et délinquance révélée chez les adolescentes. Rapport no. 3*. Montréal: Université de Montréal. Groupe de Recherche sur l'inadaptation juvénile, 1980. 198p.
3482. Geller, Gloria Rhea. "Streaming of males and females in the juvenile justice system." PhD diss., University of Toronto, 1981. 383p. (Can. theses, no.50264)

3483. Geller, Gloria. "Sexism in the juvenile justice system," *Canadian Woman Studies | Les cahiers de la femme*, 4:56-8, Fall 1982.

3484. Landau, Barbara. "The adolescent female offender," *Ontario Psychologist*, 5(2):56-62, 1973.

3485. Lando, Bella. "Male and female delinquents under the law." MA thesis, University of Toronto, 1979. 93p.

3486. Linden, Rick and Cathy Fillmore. "A comparative study of delinquency involvement," *Canadian Review of Sociology and Anthropology*, 18:343-61, Aug. 1981.

3487. Neilson, Kathryn Elizabeth. "The delinquency of Indian girls in British Columbia: a study in socialization." MA thesis, University of British Columbia,1969. 85p.

3488. Offord, David R. and others. "Broken homes, parental psychiatric illness, and female delinquency," *American Journal of Orthopsychiatry*, 49:252-64, Apr. 1979.

3489. Oostveen-Romaschin, Maria Albertine. "The family as an affected agent in female delinquent behavior." MA thesis, University of Windsor, 1978. 102p. (Can. theses, no.39586)

3490. Ross, R. R. *Rewards for offenders: behavior modification in an institution for female adolescents*. n.p.: Ontario Ministry of Correctional Services / University of Waterloo, 1974. 5p.

3491. Ross, R. R. and others. "Self-mutilation in adolescent female offenders," *Canadian Journal of Criminology*, 20:375-92, Oct. 1978.

3492. Stankiewicz-Bleszynski, Teresa I. "Juvenile offences, personality, sociometric status and behaviour in training schools as predictors of adult criminality: a follow-up study of training girls." MA thesis, University of Ottawa, 1975. 132p.

3493. Trottier, Michel Jacques. "'Délinquance' et 'protection' dans une institution pour jeunes filles," *Canadian Journal of Criminology and Corrections*, 15:239-47, Apr. 1973.

3494. _____. "'Delinquance' et 'protection' dans une institution pour jeunes filles." MA thèse, Université de Montréal, 1972. 108p.

LABOUR LAWS AND LEGISLATION

3495. Canada. Dept. of Labour. Women's Bureau. *Canadian women and job related laws, 1981*. [*Les Canadiennes et la législation relative au travail, 1981*]. Ottawa, 1982. 61, 67p. Previous edition: *Legislation relating to working women, 1979*.

3496. _____. *Legislation relating to working women*. [*La législation touchant la femme en emploi*]. 4th ed. [Ottawa]: Minister of Supply and Services, 1979. 43, 43p.

3497. _____. *The law relating to working women*. 3rd ed. [Ottawa] 1975. 26p.

3498. Canada. Employment and Immigration Commission. Affirmative Action Division. *Provincial human rights legislation*, prepared by Noel A. Kinsella. Ottawa: Canada. Dept. of Employment and Immigration, 1980. 132p.

3499. Collectif. "Comment lutter au bas de l'échelle," *Possibles*, 4:167-73, automne 1979.

3500. Des Rivières, Monique. *Législations canadiennes sur l'emploi féminin dans les mines*. Québec: Conseil du statut de la femme, 1975. [12]p.

3501. _____. *Législations fédérales et provinciales concernant plus particulièrement les travailleuses au Canada*. Québec: Conseil du statut de la femme, 1973. 21p.

3502. Fairweather, Gordon. "The need for human rights legislation," *Executive Bulletin (Conference Board in Canada)*, no. 4, 11-13, Mar. 1978.

3503. Gelber, Sylva M. "A year after the report: where are we now?" in *Women's Bureau '71*. Ottawa: Canada. Dept. of Labour. Women's Bureau, 1972, pp.20-8.

3504. _____. "Women and work in Canada: a study of legislation," in *Women's Bureau '74*. Ottawa: Canada. Dept. of Labour. Women's Bureau, 1975, pp.17-20.

3505. _____. "Women and work - the legislative base," *Canadian Labour*, 20:7-10, June 1975.

3506. Godard, Lorraine. "La femme et le droit au travail," *Atlantis*, 3:21-39, Spring 1978, Part II.

3507. Goldenberg, Shirley B. "Female labour and the law in Canada," *Bulletin of Comparative Labour Relations*, 9:55-95, 1978.

3508. Hunt, Keith. "The impact of legislation on collective bargaining," *Executive Bulletin (Conference Board in Canada)*, no. 4:13-15, Mar. 1978.

3509. Jain, Harish C. "Canadian legal approaches to sex equality in the workplace," *Monthly Labor Review*, 105:38-43, Oct. 1982.

3510. _____. "Discrimination in employment: legal approaches are limited," *Labour Gazette*, 78:284-8, July 1978.

3511. "Legislation for women," *Labour Gazette*, 74:318, May 1974.

3512. MacGuigan, Mark. "A legislator's perspective," *Executive Bulletin (Conference Board in Canada)*, no. 4, 6-8, Mar. 1978.

3513. "Meeting the problems of female workers," *Labour Gazette*, 70:567, Aug. 1970.

3514. Morgan, Joanna. "Fired while pregnant," *Chatelaine*, 50:14, May 1977.

3515. "Night work for women," *Labour Gazette*, 69:740, Dec. 1969.

3516. Pilkington, Harry. "Complying with the legislation: some areas of concern," *Executive Bulletin (Conference Board in Canada)*, no. 4:15-16, Mar. 1978.

3517. Plowman, Shirley. "From 'why not?' to 'when?'" *Labour Gazette*, Anniversary Issue, 1975, pp.633-5.

3518. Ramkhalawansingh, Ceta, ed. *(Un) equal pay: Canadian and international perspectives*. Toronto: Ontario Institute for Studies in Education, 1979. 145p.

3519. Ruff, Kathleen. "A view from the provincial level," *Executive Bulletin (Conference Board in Canada)*, no. 4:8-11, Mar. 1978.

3520. "Sex and age are important factors for employers," *Financial Post*, 71:6, Dec. 3, 1977.

3521. Stewart, Andrew. "A union president's perspective," *Executive Bulletin (Conference Board in Canada)*, no. 4:16-18, Mar. 1978.

3522. Strong-Boag, Veronica. "Working women and the state: the case of Canada, 1889-1945," *Atlantis*, 6:1-9, Spring 1981.

3523. Townson, Monica. "Working women: business to face tough laws," *Financial Times of Canada*, 62:15, Mar.4, 1974.

3524. Tremblay, Henri. "The impact of the legislation on human resources management," *Executive Bulletin (Conference Board in Canada)*, no. 4:18-20, Mar. 1978.

3525. Woods, Sandra. "Equality of opportunity: the emerging challenge," *Labour Gazette*, 78:195-8, May 1978.

LABOUR LAWS AND LEGISLATION - ALBERTA

3526. Alberta. Women's Bureau. *Alberta labour legislation of interest to women in the paid work force*. Rev. ed. Edmonton, 1981. 12p.

LABOUR LAWS AND LEGISLATION - BRITISH COLUMBIA

3527. Vancouver Status of Women. *Brief proposing legislative changes to equalize the position of men and women workers in the province of British Columbia*. Submitted to the Special Advisors to the Minister of Labour. [Vancouver], 1973. 18p.

LABOUR LAWS AND LEGISLATION - NEW BRUNSWICK

3528. New Brunswick. Human Rights Commission. *Women workers and the law*. Fredericton, [1972]. 10p.

LABOUR LAWS AND LEGISLATION - NOVA SCOTIA

3529. Lennon, Elizabeth Shilton. "Sex discrimination in employment: the Nova Scotia Human Rights Act," *Dalhousie Law Journal*, 2:593-632, July 1976.

142

LABOUR LAWS AND LEGISLATION - ONTARIO

3530. Bohnen, Linda. "Women workers in Ontario: a socio-legal history," *University of Toronto. Faculty of Law Review*, 31:45-74, 1973.

3531. Business and Professional Women's Clubs of Ontario. *Brief to the Honourable Robert Welsh, Provincial Secretary for Social Development regarding legislation affecting women's employment in Ontario.* Cobourg, Ont., 1974, 11p.

3532. Ontario. Ministry of Labour. Women's Bureau. *Labour law in action: eight case studies about women.* Rev. ed. Toronto, 1980. [14]p.

3533. _____. *Ontario labour legislation of interest to working women.* Revised. Toronto, 1975. 4p.

3534. _____. *Ontario labour legislation of interest to working women.* Rev. ed. Toronto, 1981. [4]p.

3535. _____. *Your rights as a worker in Ontario.* Rev. ed. Toronto, 1981. 15p.

3536. Ontario Status of Women Council. *Brief to the Standing Administration of Justice Committee on Bill 112, The Discriminatory Business Practices Act.* [Toronto], 1978. 5p.

3537. "Ontario's new Women's Equal Employment Opportunity Act went into effect on December 1," *Labour Gazette*, 71:78, Feb. 1971.

LABOUR LAWS AND LEGISLATION - QUEBEC

3538. Bhérer, Jacinthe et Monique Des Rivières. *Lois québécoises discriminatoires a l'égard des femmes.* Québec: Conseil du statut de la femme, 1974. vp.

3539. Confédération des syndicats nationaux. *Les travailleuses et l'accès à la syndicalisation: états généraux II des travailleuses salariées québécoises.* Produit par le comité d'action "accès à la syndicalisation et normes minimales d'emploi". n.p., [1979?] 60p.

3540. Heenan, Roy L. "Women under Quebec labour law," *McGill Law Journal*, 21:594-600, Winter 1975.

LABOUR UNIONS

3541. Acheson, Shelley. "Two 'firsts' for women unionists," *Labour Review* [Ontario Federation of Labour], July-Aug. 1976, p.9.

3542. Attenborough, Susan. *Bargaining for equality.* Ottawa: National Union of Provincial Government Employees, 1982. 70p.

3543. Bachynsky, Valerie. "Women and unions [Conference on equal opportunity and treatment for women workers]," *Perception*, 1:5-6, Mar.-Apr. 1978.

3544. Bagnall, James and Patricia Anderson. "Union interest in maternity leave gathers steam," *Financial Post*, 75:1-2, July 11, 1981.

3545. Baker, Maureen and Mary-Anne Robeson. "Trade union reactions to women workers and their concerns," *Canadian Journal of Sociology*, 6:19-31, Winter 1981.

3546. "Bank unions: when they come, expect changes," *Financial Times*, 65:1, 4, Mar. 21, 1977.

3547. Bannon, Sharleen. "CLC conference: women unionists demand their share," *Labour Gazette*, 76:201-4, Apr. 1976.

3548. _____. "Women unionists demand their share," *Labour Gazette*, 76:201-4, Apr. 1976.

3549. Bourne, Paula. "Women and trade unions," in her, *Women in Canadian society*. Toronto: Ontario Institute for Studies in Education, 1976, pp.103-10.

3550. Briskin, Linda and Linda Yantz, eds. *Union sisters: women in the labor movement.* Toronto: Women's Press, 1984. 424p.

3551. "Building the feminist network: persistent effort and discrete plotting," *Saturday Night*, 93:3-4, Sept. 1978.

3552. Canadian Labour Congress. *Brief no. 440 to the Royal Commission on the Status of Women in Canada.* Ottawa, 1968. 28p.

3553.   _____. *Equal pay for work of equal value | equal opportunity: background paper to report of Committee on Equality of Opportunity and Treatment for Women Workers*. Ottawa, 1980. 12p.

      Report and recommendations of the CLC Working Group on Equal Pay for Work of Equal Value.

3554.   _____. "Equality of opportunity and treatment for women workers; L'égalité de chances et de traitement pour les travailleuses," *Canadian Labour | Travailleur canadien*, 21:2-9, Sept. 1976.

3555.   Canadian Labour Congress. Women's Bureau. *Equal partners for change: women and unions*. Ottawa, 1981.

      Folder, 11 pieces.

3556.   Canadian Union of Public Employees. *Brief no. 437 to the Royal Commission on the Status of Women in Canada*. Ottawa, 1968. 44p.

3557.   _____. *The new status of women in CUPE: a report on past progress and the challenges ahead*. Ottawa: CUPE, 1975. 16p.

      French edition: La nouvelle situation de la femme dans le SCFP.

3558.   _____. *The new status of women in CUPE; a special report approved by the CUPE national convention, September 1971*. [Ottawa, 1971]. 35p.

3559.   _____. *The status of women in CUPE*. Ottawa, 1971. 35p.

3560.   Canadian Union of Public Employees. Education Dept. *Affirmative action: putting a stop to sex discrimination: an outline for locals*. [Ottawa], n.d. 6p.

3561.   Carr, Shirley. "ICFTU Conference," *Canadian Labour*, 20:17-18, Sept. 1975.

3562.   _____. "Women's year - union role," *Canadian Labour*, 20:2-6, 34, June 1975.

3563.   Chaison, Gary N. and P. Andiappan. "Characteristics of female union officers in Canada," *Relations industrielles*, 37(4):765-79, 1982.

3564.   Clark, John. "Canadian Labour Congress: 'You've got a long way to go, Baby!'" *Perception*, 3:18-19, Aug. 1980.

3565.   _____. "Local 31 award sets uneasy precedent on women's wages," *Financial Post*, 72:5, May 13, 1978.

3566.   "CLC program of equality for women workers; Programme d'égalité pour les travailleuses," *Canadian Labour | Travailleur canadien*, 25:8, [English]; 8,[French], May 30, 1980.

3567.   "CLC statement on International Women's Day; Journée internationale de la femme," *Canadian Labour | Travailleur canadien*, 27:6, [English]; 6, [French], Mar. 1982.

3568.   "CLC survey of women in trade unions," *Canadian Labour*, 10:10, June 1965.

3569.   "Collective agreement provisions for women," *Labour Gazette*, 65:518, June 1965.

3570.   Confédération des syndicats nationaux. *La lutte des femmes: pour le droit au travail social: deuxième rapport du comité de la condition féminine, 49e congrès de la CSN, Montréal, juin 1978*. Montréal, 1978. 67p.

3571.   Cornish, Mary. "Women in trade unions," *This Magazine*, 9:8-10, Sept.-Oct. 1975.

3572.   Dofny, Jacques. "Sex and class struggle," trans. by Paul Cappon in Patricia Marchak, ed., *The working sexes: symposium papers on the effects of sex on women at work*. Vancouver: University of British Columbia. Institute of Industrial Relations, 1977, pp.176-94.

      Proceedings of the 3rd annual meeting.

3573.   "Female membership in labour organizations," *Labour Gazette*, 67:186, 197, Mar. 1967.

3574.   "Female union members form 15.4% of total membership," *Labour Gazette*, 66:31, Jan.-Feb. 1966.

3575.   Fisher, Christine. "CLC Ottawa conference: women's battle for equal rights," *Labour Gazette*, 78:199-202, May 1978.

3576.   Gelber, Sylva. "Which side are you on?" *Canadian Labour*, 17:4-6, 16, May 1972.

3577.   _____. "Organized labour and the working woman," in, *Women's Bureau '73*. Ottawa: Canada. Dept. of Labour. Women's Bureau, 1974, pp.16-24.

3578.   _____. "Which side are you on?" in, *Women's Bureau '72*. Ottawa. Canada. Dept. of Labour. Women's Bureau, 1973, pp.7-12.

3579. Geoffroy, Renée and Paule Sainte-Marie. *Attitude of union workers to women in industry*. Royal Commission on the Status of Women in Canada. Study no. 9. Ottawa, 1971. 137p.

3580. Gray, Charlotte. "What will unions do for women in the '80's?" *Chatelaine*, 54:54-5, 85+, May 1981.

3581. Hartman, Grace. "Women and the unions," in Gwen Matheson, *Women in the Canadian mosaic*. Toronto: Peter Martin, 1976, pp.242-55.

3582. _____. "Women in the labour movement; Les femmes dans le mouvement syndical," *Civil Service Review / Revue du service civil*, 46:38+, [English]; 39+, [French], Dec. 1973.

3583. Hickling-Johnston Ltd. *A report on the status of women in the field of collective bargaining*. Report for the Royal Commission on the Status of Women in Canada. Toronto, 1968. 36p.

3584. "ICFTU and women's rights," *Canadian Labour*, 10:14-15, June 1965.

3585. "ILGU Women's Year seminar," *Canadian Labour*, 20:26-7, 36, June 1975.

3586. "ILO convention influences provincial legislation," *Labour Gazette*, 67:350, June 1967.

3587. Landsberg, M. "How trade unions let women down," *Chatelaine*, 44:40, 74-7, Mar. 1971.

3588. Langan, Joy. "BCFL. Women's Rights Committee," *Canadian Labour*, 20:11-12, 34, June 1975.

3589. LaVigna, Claire. "Women in the Canadian and Italian trade union movements at the turn of the century: a comparison," in Caroli Betty Boyd, Robert F. Harney and Lydio F. Tomasi, eds., *The Italian immigrant woman in North America: proceedings of the tenth annual conference of the American Italian Historical Association held in Toronto...* Toronto: Multicultural History Society of Ontario, 1978, pp.32-42.

3590. "L'OIT et la travailleuse," *Canadian Labour*, 10:51, Sept. 1965.

3591. Lowe, Graham S. "Problems and issues in the unionization of female workers: some refections on the case of Canadian bank employees," in Naomi Hersom and Dorothy E. Smith, [eds.], *Women and the Canadian labour force*. Working document. Ottawa: Social Sciences and Humanities Research Council of Canada, 1982, pp.307-42.

3592. "Making it, while women's lib still a baby [Grace Hartman]," *Financial Times of Canada*, 64:20-1, Oct. 20, 1975.

3593. Marchak, Patricia. "Les femmes, le travail et le syndicalisme au Canada," *Sociologie et sociétés*, 6:37-53, mai 1974.

3594. _____. "Women, work, and unions in Canada," *International Journal of Sociology*, 5:39-61, Winter 1975-1976.

3595. _____. "Women workers and white-collar unions," *Canadian Review of Sociology and Anthropology*, 10(2):134-47, 1973.

3596. "McDermott recommends Parliamentary Task Force on the status of women; Besoin d'un groupe de travail sur la situation de la femme," *Canadian Labour / Travailleur canadien*, 26:5, [English]; 5, [French], May 1981.

3597. McFarland, Joan. "Women and unions: help or hindrance," *Atlantis*, 4:48-70, Spring 1979.

3598. Mungall, Constance. "Meet labor leader Shirley Carr: tough, aggressive, caring," *Chatelaine*, 51:48+, Feb. 1978.

3599. "News briefs," *Labour Gazette*, 71:771, Dec. 1971.

3600. Ontario. Ministry of Labour. Women's Bureau. *Women and labour unions*. Toronto, 1973. 7p.

3601. _____. *Women in the labour force. "Labour unions"*. Factsheet, no. 3. Toronto, [1976]. [4]p.

3602. Pappert, Ann. "The union makes us strong," *Quest*, 11:84-7, 90, Oct. 1982.

3603. Parent, Madeleine. "In the business of labor [interview]," *Maclean's*, 93:16b, 16d, Sept. 1, 1980.

3604. "Provisions for women in collective bargaining," *Labour Gazette*, 67:575, Sept. 1967.

3605. Rickenbacker, Louise. "Women in the PSAC; Les femmes de l'AFPC," *Civil Service Review / Revue du service civil*, 48:3-14, Dec. 1975.

3606. Routledge, Janet. "How many bruises make a battered wife?; Le problème des femmes maltraitrées," *Civil Service Review / Revue du service civil*, 53:12-15, [English]; 12-15, [French], Dec. 1980.

3607. Silverman, Peter. "Women on front line in union battlegrounds," *Financial Post*, 75:4, Jan. 3, 1981.

3608. Spinks, Sarah. "Women on strike: Dare and Wardair," *This Magazine*, 7:23-7, May-June 1973.

3609. "The gates should stand open: the ILO looks at woman's world," *Labour Gazette*, 69:18-19, May suppl. 1969.

3610. Townson, Monica. "Organizing women workers," *Labour Gazette*, 75:349-53, June 1975.

3611. "UAW women's programme; Programme féminin des TUA," *Canadian Labour / Le Travailleur canadien*, 20:39-40, [English]; 43-4, [French], Dec. 1975.

3612. United Electrical, Radio and Machine Workers of America. *Brief no. 99 to the Royal Commission on the Status of Women in Canada*. Toronto, 1968. 32p.

3613. Valverde, Mariana. "Union maid, union made," *Broadside*, 2:8-9, 13, Aug.-Sept. 1981.

3614. Vickers, Jill McCalla and Patricia Finn. "'And the winner is - Sally Field for *Norma Rae*':is unionism effective in the fight for women's economic equality?" *Perception*, 3:17-22, July-Aug. 1980.

3615. Wachtel, Eleanor. "SORWUC: the little union that's making big strides for women," *Chatelaine*, 51:22, 97, July 1978.

3616. Watson, Louise. *She was never afraid: the biography of Annie Buller*. Toronto: Progress Books, 1976. 129p.

3617. White, Julie. *Women and unions*. Ottawa: Canadian Advisory Council on the Status of Women, 1980. 131p.

3618. Williams, Jack. "Grace Hartman - a profile," *Labour Gazette*, 76:132-5, Mar. 1976.

3619. _____. "Shirley Carr: a profile," *Labour Gazette*, 75:235-8, Apr. 1975.

3620. "Woman represents CUPE at international conference," *Labour Gazette*, 69:75, Feb. 1969.

3621. "Women in trade unions," *Labour Gazette*, 71:682-5, Oct. 1971.

3622. "Women unionists," *Canadian Labour*, 11:51, Apr. 1966.

3623. "Women workers and the CNTU," *Labour Gazette*, 64:1099, Dec. 1964.

3624. "Women workers discussed at ICFTU Congress," *Labour Gazette*, 65:929, Oct. 1965.

3625. "Women workers growing force in unions," *Globe & Mail*, Apr. 2, 1979, p.B4.

3626. "Women's rights and the newspaper guild," *Labour Gazette*, 71:245, Apr. 1971.

3627. "Working women's 'bill of rights'," *Labour Gazette*, 76:299, June 1976.

LABOUR UNIONS - BRITISH COLUMBIA

3628. Campbell, Marie L. "Unlocking women's experience: a method for using historical sources [British Columbia Royal Commission on Labour Conditions, 1912]," *Our Generation*, 13(3):11-15, 1979.

3629. _____. *Women and trade unions in B.C. 1900-1920: the social organization of sex discrimination*. [Vancouver]: Women's Research Centre, 1978. 26p.

3630. Langan, Joy. "Trade union women's committees; Syndicats et comités féminins," *Canadian Labour / Travailleur canadien*, 21:12-13, 21, [English]; 12-14, [French], Sept. 1976.

3631. Pentland-Smith, Janice. *Provisions for women in B.C. union contracts*. [Vancouver: Women's Research Centre], 1977. 24, [3]p.

3632. Potrebenko, Helen. "Working for women working," *Makara*, 1:22-3, Aug.-Sept. 1976.

3633. Rosenthal, Star. "Union maids: organized women workers in Vancouver 1900-1915," *BC Studies*, 41:36-55, Spring 1979.

3634. Woodward, Joan. "SORWUC: a union for working women; SORWUC: un syndicat pour les femmes au travail mise à jour," *Status of Women News / Statut: Bulletin de la femme*, 5:11-14, [English]; 12-15, [French], Sept. 1978.

146

LABOUR UNIONS - ONTARIO

3635. Adam, Judith. "Toronto gets into the ACTE," *Canadian Labour*, 18:3-5, 24, Mar. 1973.
3636. "OFL Conference on Women Workers," *Canadian Labour*, 11:48, July-Aug.1966.
3637. "OFL Women's Committee sponsors conference," *Labour Gazette*, 66:350, July 1966.
3638. Ontario Federation of Labour. *Brief no. 69 to the Royal Commission on the Status of Women in Canada*. Toronto, 1968. 32p.

LABOUR UNIONS - QUEBEC

3639. Boyer, Ginette. "Une seule lutte," *Relations*, 39:294, Nov. 1979.
3640. Confédération des syndicats nationaux. *Brief no. 347 to the Royal Commission on the Status of Women in Canada*. Montreal, 1968. 49p.
3641. _____. *La lutte des femmes: une lutte permanente, une lutte collective: rapport du comité de la condition féminine de la CSN au 50 ième congrès de la CSN, mai 1980, reçu et amendé par le conseil confédéral du mars 1981*. n.p., 1981. 64p.
3642. _____. *Les travailleuses et l'accès à la syndicalisation: états généraux II des travailleuses salariées québécoises*. Produit par le comité d'action accès à la syndicalisation et normes minimales d'emploi. n.p., [1979?] 60p.
3643. David, Hélène. *La lutte des femmes, combat de tous les travailleurs: rapport du comité de la condition féminine, 47e congrès, Québec, juin 1976 (document 4) tel qu'amendé par le congrès et le conseil confédéral*. 3e ed. n.p.: Confédération des syndicats nationaux, 1979. 72p.
3644. Dion, Suzanne et Gisèle Painchaud. "La participation des femmes dans la vie syndicale agricole," *Resources for Feminist Research*, 11:7-8, Mar. 1982.
3645. Fédération des travailleurs du Québec. *Le combat syndical et les femmes: 14e congrès ... du 1 au 5 déc. 1975*. Montréal, 1975. 47p.
3646. _____. *Travailleuses et syndiquées: rapport du comité FTQ sur la situation de la femme*. Montréal, 1973. 87p. Rapport du 13e congrès du 3 décembre au 7 décembre 1973 à Montréal.
3647. Fortier, Johanne. "Les femmes et leur engagement syndical," *Canadian Women's Studies / Les cahiers de la femme*, 1:54-6, Winter 1978-79.
3648. Gagnon, Mona-Josée. "La femme dans l'ideologie québécoise et dans la C.S.N.: étude ideologique et monographie syndicale." MA thesis, Université de Montréal. Ecole des Relations Industrielles, 1973. 281p.
3649. _____. "Les centrales syndicales et la condition féminine," *Maintenant*, 140:25-7, nov. 1974.
3650. _____. "Les femmes dans le mouvement syndical québécois," *Sociologie et sociétés*, 6:17-36, mai 1974.
3651. _____. "Les femmes dans le mouvement syndical québécois," in Marie Lavigne et Yolande Pinard, *Les femmes dans la société québécoise: aspects historiques*. Montréal: Éditions du boréal express, 1977, pp.145-68.
3652. _____. "Où en sont les femmes dans le mouvement syndical?" *Canadian Women's Studies / Les cahiers de la femme*, 2(2):77-8, 1980.
3653. La Fédération des travailleurs du Québec. *Brief no. 393 to the Royal Commission on the Status of Women in Canada*. Montreal, 1968. 36p. and tables.
3654. Lapointe, Michèlle. "Le syndicat catholique des allumettières de Hull, 1919-1924," *Revue d'histoire de l'Amérique française*, 32:603-28, mars 1979.
3655. Quebec Federation of Labour. *Women's presence in our organization*. Montreal: The Federation, 1973. 87p.
3656. Robertson, Susan E. "Sex roles and politics: a case study." MA thesis. McGill University, 1973. 128pp. (Can. theses, no.15982) Involvement of men and women in library employees' union at Sir George Williams University.
3657. Rouilland, Jacques. *Les travailleurs du coton au Québec 1900-1915*. Montréal: Presses de l'Université du Québec, 1974. 152p.

3658. Roy, Rosaire. "Positions et préoccupations de la Confédération des syndicats nationaux et de la Fédération des travailleurs du Québec sur le travail féminin." MA thèse, Université Laval, 1968. 162p.

3659. Simard, Monique et Carmen Bazzy, eds. *Les femmes à la CSN n'ont pas les moyens de reculer.* 4e Rapport du Comité de la condition féminine CSN. Montréal: Comité de la condition féminine CSN, [1982]. 108p.

3660. Toupin, Louise. "Aux origines de la CEQ: une lutte menée par des femmes," *Ligne directe*, 2:1-8, mars-avr. 1974, suppl.

3661. "Women in the Quebec labour movement," *Labour Gazette*, 73:457-9, July 1973.

LAW (LEGAL PROFESSION)

3662. Adam, Barry D. "Stigma and employability: discrimination by sex and sexual orientation in the Ontario legal profession," *Canadian Review of Sociology and Anthropology*, 18:216-21, May 1981.

3663. Bankier, J. K. "Women and the law school: problems and potential," *Chitty's Law Journal*, 22:171-7, 1974.

3664. Edwards, Val. "Too soon to judge [Bertha Wilson]," *Broadside*, 3:6, Apr. 1982.

3665. Fielding, Joy. "Sisters in law," *Weekend Magazine*, 28:6, 6a-6b, Aug. 26, 1978.

3666. James, Donna. *Emily Murphy.* Toronto: Fitzhenry & Whiteside, 1977. 63p.

3667. MacGill, Elsie Gregory. *My mother the judge: a biography of Helen Gregory MacGill.* Toronto: Peter Martin Associates, 1981. 248p.

3668. Raymond, Valerie. "Female Supreme Court judge?" *Perception*, 4:9-10, Spring-Summer 1981.

3669. Ryval, Michael. "Women in law: ladies no longer in waiting," *Canadian Lawyer*, 1(2):17-22, 1977.

3670. "Survey finds times tougher for law graduates - especially women," *Globe & Mail*, Nov. 27, 1978, p.16.

3671. Wachtel, Eleanor. "Patricia Proudfoot, Federal Judge," *Chatelaine*, 50:12, June 1977.

3672. Wright, John de P. "Admission of women to the bar: an historical note," *The Law Society Gazette*, 16:42-5, 1982.

LEGAL STATUS, LAWS, ETC.

3673. Abella, Rosalie Silberman. "Balancing the scales of justice, the law: then and now," in Sex-Role Stereotyping and Women's Studies Conference, Sept. 28-30, 1978. *Report*. [Toronto]: Ontario. Ministry of Education, [1978], pp.5-20.

3674. Altschul, Susan and Christine Carron. "Chronology of some legal landmarks in the history of Canadian women," *McGill Law Journal*, 21:476-94, Winter 1975.

3675. Anderson, Doris. "The Supreme Court and women's rights," *The Supreme Court Law Review*, 1(1980), pp.457-60.

3676. Bertrand, Marie-Andrée et Réjane Rancourt. "La femme: sujet difficile!" *Maintenant*, 65:169-72, mai 1967.

3677. Bourne, Paula. *Women in Canadian society.* Rev. ed. Toronto: Ontario Institute for Studies in Education, 1978. 158p.

3678. Brent, G. "The development of the law relating to the participation of Canadian women in public life," *University of Toronto Law Journal*, 25:358-70, Fall 1975.

3679. Burke, Angela. "Women: status and statutes," *Canadian Bar Journal*, new ser., 2:1-4, Feb. 1971.

3680. Canada. Advisory Council on the Status of Women. *What's been done?* Assessment of the federal government's implementation of the recommendations of the Royal Commission on the Status of Women. Ottawa, 1974. 40p.

3681. Canada. Co-ordinator, Status of Women. *Status of women in Canada - 1972.* [*La situation de la femme au Canada - 1972*]. [Ottawa: Information Canada, 1972]. 35, 39p.

148

3682. Canada. Dept. of Labour. *Status of women in Canada, 1973. [La situation de la femme au Canada, 1973]*. By the Honourable John C. Munro, Minister of Labour, Minister Responsible for the Status of Women. Ottawa, 1972. 43, 45p.

3683. Canada. Office of the Co-ordinator, Status of Women. *Status of women in Canada. [La situation de la femme au Canada]*. Ottawa, 1975. 56, 58p.

3684. Canadian Advisory Council on the Status of Women. *Background notes on the proposed amendments to the Criminal Code, the Canada Evidence Act and the Parole Act (Bill C-51)*, by Marcia H. Rioux and Joanna L. McFadyen. Ottawa, 1978. 26, 7p.

3685. Canadian Federation of Business and Professional Women's Clubs. *Brief no. 147 to the Royal Commission on the Status of Women in Canada*. Ottawa, n.d. v.p.

3686. "Committee requests equality study," *Labour Gazette*, 66:710, Dec. 1966.

3687. "Could it happen to you?" *Chatelaine*, 47:92-3, Sept. 1974.

3688. Doherty, Janice. "Milestones," *Weekend Magazine*, 28:11, Sept. 30, 1978.

3689. Dombrowski, Lee. "New legislation from our sponsor, the government of Canada," *Branching Out*, 2:20-1, Nov.-Dec. 1975.

3690. Dranoff, Linda Silver. *Women in Canadian law*. Toronto: Fitzhenry & Whiteside, 1977. 112p.

3691. _____. "Ask a lawyer," *Chatelaine*, 53:14, 17, Jan. 1980.

3692. Duncan, Linda. "Human rights: what the law can - and can't - do," *Branching Out*, 4:6-11, May-June 1977.

3693. Eberts, Mary. "The Persons Case," *Chelsea Journal*, 5:235-6, Sept.-Oct. 1979.

3694. _____. "The Person's Case; La cause de la reconnaissance de la personalité juridique de la femme," *Status of Women News / Statut: Bulletin de la femme*, 5:16-18,[English]; 16-18, [French], Mar. 1979.

3695. _____. "The rights of women," in R. St. J. Macdonald and John P. Humphrey, eds., *The practice of freedom: Canadian essays on human rights and fundamental freedoms*. Toronto: Butterworths, 1979, pp.225-49.

3696. Eberts, M. A., ed. *Women and the law: cases and materials*. 2v. Toronto: University of Toronto. Faculty of Law, 1974.
        Collection of various printed and transcript articles prepared and edited for use within the Faculty of Law, University of Toronto. Topics include women in public life, discrimination, criminal law, abortion, employment, family and the legal profession.

3697. Eichler, Margrit. "Social policy concerning women," in Shankar A. Yelaja, ed., *Canadian social policy*. Waterloo: Wilfrid Laurier University Press, 1978, pp.133-46.

3698. Freedman, Samuel. "Law and justice - two concepts or one?" *Manitoba Law Journal*, 7(4):231-48, 1977.

3699. Ginsburg, Marilyn and Gina Quijano. *Canadian women and the law*. Toronto: Osgoode Hall Law School, 1974. 738p.

3700. Holland, Winifred H. and D. Keith McNair. *Unmarried couples: legal aspects of cohabitation*. Toronto: Carswell, 1982. 249p.

3701. Jahn, Penelope and Charles Campbell. *The self-help guide to divorce, children, welfare: an up-to-date handbook on Canadian family law*. Toronto: Anansi, 1976. 108p.

3702. Jain, Harish C. and Peter J. Sloane. *Race, sex and minority group discrimination legislation in North America and Britain*. Working paper series, no. 144. Hamilton, Ont.: McMaster University. Faculty of Business, 1978. 37p.

3703. Kerr, Robert W. "The Canadian Bill of Rights and sex-based differentials in Canadian federal law," *Osgoode Hall Law Journal*, 12:357-87, Oct. 1974.

3704. King, Lynn. "One law for persons: another for women?" *Canada and the World*, 40:16-17, Dec. 1974.

3705. "Law and personhood," in Canadian Research Institute for the Advancement of Women, *Women as persons. [La femme en tant que personne]*. Toronto:Resources for Feminist Research, 1980, pp.76-81.
        Proceedings of the 3rd annual meeting.

3706. Laws, Margaret. "Women: for 50 years 'persons'," *Financial Post*, 73:2, May 5, 1979.

3707. MacDonald, Edythe I. "A view from Ottawa: the role of the federal government as regards the status of women," *McGill Law Journal*, 21:601-14, Winter 1975.

3708. Marchildon, Rudy G. "The 'persons' controversy: the legal aspects of the fight for women senators," *Atlantis*, 6:99-113, Spring 1981.

3709. Masleck, Carolyn. "Bills C-16 and C-72 steps forward in the struggle to end discrimination," *CAUT Bulletin*, 24:5, Sept. 1975.

3710. Morel, André. "La liberation de la femme au Canada: deux itinéraires," *Revue juridique Themis*, no. 5:399-411, 1970.

3711. Morton, F. L. "Sexual equality and the law: a comparative review and analysis of judicial policy-making in the American and Canadian Supreme Courts." Paper presented at The 49th Annual meeting of the Canadian Political Science Association at the University of New Brunswick, Fredericton, N.B., June 9-11, 1977. 47p.

3712. National Association of Women and the Law. "Brief to the Special Joint Committee of the Senate and of the House of Commons on the Constitution of Canada," in the committee's, *Minutes of proceedings and evidence*, no. 22, Dec.9, 1980, pp.50-73.

3713. Réaume, Denise. "Women and the law: equality claims before courts and tribunals," *Queen's Law Journal*, 5:3-45, 1980.

3714. Ritchie, Marguerite E. "Alice through the statutes," *McGill Law Journal*, 21:685-707, Winter 1975.

3715. Robillard, Laurette. *La femme et les lois récentes: implications*. Causerie prononcée devant l'Association interprofessionnelle des specialistes en acquisition de droits immobiliers, oct. 11, 1975. Québec: Québec. Conseil du Statut de la Femme, 1975. 20p.

3716. Ryan, Edward F. "Women and the law," *Civil Service Review*, 49:68-70, May 1976.

3717. _____. "Women and the law; Les femmes et la loi," *Canadian Labour | Travailleur canadien*, 21:16-18; [English]; 17-19, 26, [French], Sept. 1976.

3718. Sauvé, Jeanne. "La femme canadienne: le droit canadien," *Optimum*, 6(1):14-26, 1975.

3719. Schmid, Carol. "The changing status of women in the United States and Canada: an overview," *Sociological Symposium*, 15:1-27, Spring 1976.

3720. "Speech by the Honourable Marc Lalonde on the second reading of the omnibus bill on the status of women (Bill C-16)," in Canada. Parliament. House of Commons, *Debates*, 1st sess., 30th parl., v. 6, 1975, pp.6238-42.

3721. Stone, Olive M. "Canadian women as legal persons: the jubilee of Edwards v. the Attorney-General for Canada," *Alberta Law Review*, 17 (3):331-71, 1979.

3722. "The National Action Committee on the Status of Women in Canada," *New Feminist*, 4(1):18-20, 1973.

3723. Thomas, E. M. "Sisters-in-law," *Law Society Gazette*, 6(4):87-92, 1972.

3724. Wachtel, Eleanor. "The 10 lousiest legal judgements of the seventies," *Chatelaine*, 51:56-7, 114+ , Mar. 1978.

3725. "Women in law: still not equal," *Canada & the World*, 43:5-6, Apr. 1978.

3726. Women's Liberation Movement of Sudbury. "Brief submitted to the Special Joint Committee of the Senate and House of Commons on the Constitution of Canada," in the committee's, *Minutes of proceedings and evidence*, no. 46, Feb. 16, 1971, pp.48-54.

3727. Zucker, Marvin A. and June Callwood. *Canadian women and the law*. Toronto: Copp Clark Co., 1971. 100p.

3728. _____. *The law is not for women: a legal handbook for women*. Toronto: Pitman, 1976. 169p.

3729. Zwarun, Suzanne. "Women's rights: '70's gains, '80's goals," *Chatelaine*, 53:31, 50+, Jan. 1980.

LEGAL STATUS,LAWS,ETC. - ALBERTA

3730. Alberta. Women's Bureau. *A woman's rights*. Rev. ed. Edmonton, 1980. 4p.

3731. _____. *Laws for Albertans*. Revised. [Edmonton] 1974. 38p.

3732. _____. *The juvenile*. Alberta facts. Edmonton, 1973. 1p.

3733. Alberta. Women's Cultural and Information Bureau. *Laws of interest to the women of Alberta*. Revised. [Edmonton], 1968. 24p.

3734. National Association of Women and the Law, Calgary Caucus. *Women and the law: your rights in Alberta*. Calgary, 1978. 36p.
3735. Stone, Olive M. "Canadian women as legal persons: how Alberta combined judicial, executive and legislative powers to win full legal personality for all Canadian Women," *Alberta Law Review*, 17(3):331-71, 1979.

LEGAL STATUS,LAWS,ETC. - BIBLIOGRAPHY

3736. Service, Dorothy Jane. *Women and the law: a bibliography of materials in the University of Toronto Law Library*. 2nd ed. Toronto: n.p., 1978. 105p. Includes text of the 1975 ed.

LEGAL STATUS,LAWS,ETC. - BRITISH COLUMBIA

3737. Bain, Penny and others. *Women and the law*. 2nd ed. Vancouver: Vancouver People's Law School, 1974. 32p.
3738. _____. *Women and the law*. 4th ed. rev. by Gail Bell. [Vancouver]: People's Law School, 1981. 46p.
3739. Beebe, Janet and others. *Update on the status of women in British Columbia*. [Vancouver: Vancouver Status of Women], 1978. 104p.
3740. Jordan, Patricia. *Women and the law in British Columbia*. Victoria, B.C.: Queen's Printer, 1969. 39p.
3741. Ostrowski, Margaret V. *Legal process for battered women*. Rev. and expanded by Leslie Baker. Vancouver: United Way of the Lower Mainland, 1982. 34p.

LEGAL STATUS,LAWS,ETC. - MANITOBA

3742. Akerly, JoAnn and others. *Manitoba women together: a legal handbook*. Winnipeg: Women's Legal Collective, 1972. 47p.
3743. Bubnick, Julie. *Women's place in Manitoba: their legal rights*. Winnipeg: Manitoba. Dept. of Labour. Women's Bureau, 1975. 28p.
3744. Carlyle-Gordge, Peter. "Straightening the eternal triangles," *Maclean's*, 95:26-7, Apr. 12, 1982.

3745. Manitoba. Dept. of Education. Planning and Research Branch. *Manitoba women together: a legal handbook*, by Lois Brown and Sharon Segal. Winnipeg, 1975. 60p.
    First edition by Jo Ann Akerly and others, published 1972.

3746. Manitoba. Dept. of Labour. Women's Bureau. *Women and the law in Manitoba*. Winnipeg, 1975. 28p.
3747. Manitoba. Dept. of the Attorney-General. *Laws of interest to women*. Rev. ed. Winnipeg, 1965. 42p.

LEGAL STATUS,LAWS,ETC. - NEW BRUNSWICK

3748. Fellows, L. *Women and the law in New Brunswick*. Fredericton: Fredericton Women's Action Coalition, 1973. 47p.
3749. New Brunswick. Human Rights Commission. *La femme et la loi*. [Fredericton, 1977?] 32p.
    English edition: *Women and the law in New Brunswick*.

LEGAL STATUS,LAWS,ETC. - NEWFOUNDLAND

3750. St. John's Women's Bureau. *Women and the law in Newfoundland*. 2nd ed. St. John's, Nfld.: Newfoundland Status of Women Council, 1976. 24p.
    1st ed. published 1972.

LEGAL STATUS,LAWS,ETC. - NOVA SCOTIA

3751. Halifax Women's Bureau. *Women and the law in Nova Scotia*. Halifax, 1972. 47p.

3752. Perly, Susan. *Women and the law in Nova Scotia*. Rev. ed. Middleton, N.S.: Resource Education Project, 1976.
    First edition published 1972.
3753. Thibault, Gisele. "The policing of women: welfare legislation in Nova Scotia." MA thesis, Dalhousie University, 1982. (Can. theses, no.53795)
3754. *Understanding the law: a guide for women in Nova Scotia*. Halifax: Nova Scotia Association of Women and the Law, 1981. 32p.
3755. Zonta Club of Halifax. *Legal status of women in Nova Scotia*. Royal Commission on the Status of Women in Canada. Brief no. 433. Halifax, 1968. 3p.

LEGAL STATUS,LAWS,ETC. - ONTARIO

3756. Ontario. Dept. of Labour. Women's Bureau. *Law and the woman in Ontario*. Toronto, 1970. 19p.
3757. Ontario. Ministry of Labour. Women's Bureau. *Law and the woman in Ontario*. New and expanded version. Toronto, 1975. 47p.
3758. _____. *Law and the woman in Ontario*. Rev. ed. Toronto, 1977. 51p.
3759. _____. *Women and the law: rights and responsibilities*. Toronto, 1979. Leaflet.
3760. Poglitsh, Jo-Ann. *Law and the woman in Ontario*. Toronto: Ontario. Dept. of Labour. Women's Bureau, 1967. 16p.

LEGAL STATUS,LAWS,ETC. - PRINCE EDWARD ISLAND

3761. Basiletti, Mari, Donna Greenwood and Beverly Mills Stetson. *Changing times: essays by island women*. Charlottetown: Women's Legal Project of P.E.I., 1977. 67p.

LEGAL STATUS,LAWS,ETC. - QUEBEC

3762. Association féminine d'éducation et d'action sociale. *Comment conjuguer amour et sécurité*. Montréal, 1983. 35p.
3763. Bhérer, Jacinthe. *Historique des lois québécoises touchant les femmes*. Québec: Conseil du statut de la femme, 1974. 24p.
3764. Boucher, Jacques. "L'histoire de la condition juridique et sociale de la femme au Canada français," dans Jacques Boucher et André Morel, *Livre du centenaire du Code civil*, 1-2 ed. Montréal: Presses de l'Université de Montréal, 1970, pp.155-67.
3765. Québec. Conseil du statut de la femme. *Commentaires du Conseil du statut de la femme sur la Charte des droits et libertés de la personne*. Quebec City, 1975. 3p.
3766. _____. *Droit de la famille, droit des femmes?: dossier d'information à l'intention des femmes*. [Québec], 1979. 69p. English edition: Rights of the family, rights of women?: an information tool prepared for women.
3767. Robillard, Laurette. *La femme et les lois recentes: implications*. Causerie prononcée devant l'Association interprofessionnelle des specialistes en acquistion de droits immobiliers, oct. 11, 1975. Québec: Québec. Conseil du statut de la femme. 20p.
3768. Stoddart, Jennifer. "Quebec's legal elite looks at women's rights: the Dorion Commission, 1929-31," in David H. Flaherty, ed., *Essays in the history of Canadian law, vol. I*. Toronto: University of Toronto Press, 1981, pp.323-57.
3769. YWCA Women's Centre. *Women and the law in Quebec*. Montreal, 1975. 32p.

LEGAL STATUS,LAWS,ETC. - SASKATCHEWAN

3770. Saskatchewan. Dept. of Labour. Women's Division. *Legal rights of women in Saskatchewan*. Regina, 1977. [17]p. (Profile 77-0462)
    Contents: Women working in the labour force; Marriage and family; Legal assistance.
3771. Saskatchewan. Law Reform Commission. *Proposals for reform of the law affecting liability between husband and wife and related insurance contracts*. Saskatoon, Sask., 1979. 12p.

152

3772. _____. *Tentative proposals for reform of the law affecting liability between husband and wife and related insurance contracts*. Saskatoon, Sask., 1979. 28p. (Microlog 79-1017)

3773. Saskatoon College of Law. *Women and the law in Saskatchewan*. Saskatoon, Sask., 1976. 47p.

LEGAL STATUS,LAWS,ETC. - YUKON

3774. Gordon, G. Jean. *Brief no. 411 to the Royal Commission on the Status of Women in Canada*. Whitehorse, 1968. 5p.

LEISURE AND RECREATION

3775. Bella, Leslie. "The right to equal play," *Branching Out*, 3:6-7, July-Aug. 1976.

3776. Gilverson, Pamela G. "The female in physical recreation: a study of participation and its relationship to lifestyle." MA thesis, University of Alberta, 1980. 118p. (Can. theses, no.48952)

3777. Hall, Ann. "The task ahead: in leisure," in Canadian Federation of Business and Professional Women's Clubs, *A collection of papers delivered at the National Conference: Women & Work in the 80's: a Decade of Change*. Ottawa: The Federation, 1981, pp.89-96.

3778. Heit, Michael J. and Don Malpass. *Do women have equal play?* [Toronto]: Ontario. Ministry of Culture and Recreation. Sports and Fitness Division, 1975. 12p.

3779. Johnson, Ronald. "Preferences for play areas: age and sex differences in choice of areas for recreation," *CAHPER Journal*, 44:30-5, July-Aug. 1978.

3780. Meissner, Martin. "Sexual division of labour and inequality: labour and leisure," in Marylee Stephenson, *Women in Canada*. Rev. ed. Toronto: General Publishing Co., 1977, pp.160-80.

3781. Meissner, Martin. "Sur la division du travail et l'inégalité des sexes," *Sociologie du travail*, 17:329-50, oct.-déc. 1975.

3782. _____. "Women and inequality: at work - at home," *Our Generation*, 11:59-71, Winter 1976.

3783. Sport and Recreation As It Affects Women Conference. *Sport and recreation as it affects women: conference report, proceedings*. Regina: Saskatchewan. Dept. of Culture and Youth, 1975. 23p.

3784. Theobald, William F. *The female in public recreation: a study of participation and administrative attitudes*. [Toronto]: Ontario. Ministry of Culture and Recreation. Sports and Fitness Division, 1976. 45p.

3785. Welch, Frances. "Dealing with Ms. Fix-it," *Hardware Merchandising*, Nov.-Dec. 1979, pp.28,30-2.

LESBIANS

3786. "At least they have a mutual enemy," *Saturday Night*, 94:4, Mar. 1979.

3787. Bearchell, Chris. "Due to the fact you being a lesbian..." *Body Politic*, no. 45:1, Aug. 1978.

3788. Edwards, Val. "Lesbians in Toronto: the invisible community," *Broadside*, 1:4-5, 14, Sept. 1980.

3789. Fitzgerald, Maureen and Daphne Morrison. "Lesbian conference: agony and audacity," *Broadside*, 2:4, July 1981.

3790. Gosselin, Hélène. "L'impact de la peur du rejet social dans les relations interpersonnelles de la femme homosexuelle." MA thèse, Université de Québec à Montréal, 1980. 175p. (Can. theses, no.47584)

3791. Gottlieb, Amy. "Movement comment," *Broadside*, 1(4):19, [1980].

3792. Ha-Milton, Reina. *Lettre d'amoure de femmes*. Montréal: Éditions du Remue-menage, 1981. 201p.

3793. Hanley, Susan and others. "Lesbianism: knowns and unknowns," in Benjamin Schlesinger, ed., *Sexual behaviour in Canada: patterns and problems*. Toronto: University of Toronto Press, 1977, pp.126-47.

3794. "Lesbian family life," *Chatelaine*, 43:10, Feb. 1970.

3795. Middleton, Kate. "Custody battles - not child's play," *Broadside*, 1(6):8, 1980.

3796. Sangster, Dorothy. "Gay women: a minority report," *Chatelaine*, 50:24, 79-84, July 1977.

3797. Weir, Lorna. "Lesbians against the right," *Broadside*, 2:9, June 1981.

3798. Weir, Lorna and Brenda Steiger. "Lesbian movement: coming together in a hot gym," *Broadside*, 2:7, 14, Aug.-Sept. 1981.

3799. Wyland, Francie. *Motherhood, lesbianism and child custody*. Toronto: Wages Due Lesbians Toronto / Falling Wall Press, 1977. 36p.

LIBERAL PARTY OF CANADA

3800. Liberal Party of Canada. *Affirmative action guidelines for women in the Liberal Party of Canada*. n.p., [1980?] [3]p.

3801. _____. *Woman in Canada*. Ottawa, [1975?]

3802. Liberal Party of Canada. Task Force on the Status of Women. *Final report*. Ottawa, 1972. 19p.

3803. Liberal Party of Canada. Women's Liberal Commission. *Action plan: basic elements and strategies of an affirmative action program for women in the Liberal Party of Canada*. [Ottawa], 1980. Rev. 1982. 6p.

3804. _____. *Background notes on the Women's Liberal Commission*. [Ottawa], 1980. [2]p.

3805. _____. *By-laws*. Ottawa, 1980. 3p.

3806. Trudeau, Pierre E. "Pierre Trudeau on women [interview]," *Canadian Forum*, 60:9-13, Mar. 1981.

LIBRARIANS

3807. Beckman, Margaret. "Woman: her place in the profession," *IPLO Quarterly*, 14:129-34, Apr. 1973.

3808. Bell, Sandra. "Librarians and historical researchers: equal value?" *Status of Women News*, 5:21-2, Summer 1979.

3809. Black, Karen. "Back to the stacks," *Broadside*, 2:9, Dec. 1980-Jan. 1981.

3810. Cheda, Sherrill. "That special little mechanism," *Canadian Library Journal*, 31:422-32, Oct. 1974.

3811. Cheda, Sherrill and others. "Salary differentials of female and male librarians in Canada," *Emergency Librarian*, 5:3-13, Jan.-Feb. 1978.

3812. "For want of a ($600) nail," *Wilson Library Bulletin*, 49:124, Oct. 1974.

3813. Frarey, Carlyle and Carol Learmont. "Placements and salaries, 1974: promise or illusion?" *Library Journal*, 100:1767-74, Oct. 1, 1975.

3814. Gilroy, Marion and Samuel Rothstein, eds. *As we remember it: interviews with pioneering librarians of British Columbia*. Vancouver, B.C.: University of British Columbia. School of Librarianship / Library Development Commission of British Columbia, 1970. 163p.

3815. Hooper, J. "Half a librarian is better than none," *Canadian Literature*, 24:338-40, Jan. 1968.

3816. Klement, Susan. "Feminism and professionalism in librarianship: an interview with Sherrill Cheda," *Canadian Library Journal*, 31:520-8, Dec. 1974.

3817. Kremer, Valerie. "The four-fifths minority continues the struggle," *Feliciter*, 21:3-5, July-Aug. 1975.

3818. "Librarians awarded landmark settlement," *Quill & Quire*, 47:38, Feb. 1981.

3819. Manson, Ruth A. "Let's name names," *Canadian Library Journal*, 32:97-9, Apr. 1975.

3820. "Margaret Beckman: a consultive manager," *Emergency Librarian*, 2:15-17, July-Aug. 1975.

154

3821. Millar, R. "Library school: only singles need apply," *Canadian Library Journal*, 32:221-3, June 1975.

3822. Smart, Anne. "Women ... the 4/5 minority," *Canadian Library Journal*, 32:14-17, Feb. 1975.

3823. Sonnemann, Sabine and Jean L'Espérance. "A case of discrimination," *Canadian Library Journal*, 40:9-12, Feb. 1983.

3824. Wasylycia-Coe, Mary Ann. "Female-male comparison of librarians' careers." MA thesis, University of Waterloo, 1978.

3825. _____. "Profile: Canadian chief librarians by sex," *Canadian Library Journal*, 38:159-63, June 1981.

3826. Zaremba, Eve. "All's not quiet at the library," *Broadside*, 2:4, Oct.-Nov. 1980.

LITERATURE

3827. Allentuck, Marcia. "Resolution and independence in the work of Alice Munro," *World Literature Written in English*, 16:340-3, Nov. 1977.

3828. Anderson, D. "Real women in fiction, where are you?" *Chatelaine*, 44:1, Sept. 1971.

3829. Andersen, Margret. "Innovatrice et conservatrice: deux aspects de l'écriture canadienne au féminin," in *Women's culture: selected papers from the Halifax conference*. Ottawa: Canadian Research Institute for the Advancement of Women, 1982, pp.12-21.

3830. Arnason, David. "Editorial," *Journal of Canadian Fiction*, 4(3):6-8, 1975.

3831. Bagley, Laurie. "Morag Gunn: a Canadian Venus at last?" *Branching Out*, 3:39-40, Feb.-Mar. 1976.

3832. Bailey, Nancy. "Margaret Laurence, Carl Jung and the Manawaka women," *Studies in Canadian Literature*, 2:306-21, Summer 1977.

3833. Bennett, Donna A. "The failure of sisterhood in Margaret Laurence's Manawaka novels," *Atlantis*, 4:103-09, Autumn 1978.

3834. Burns, Jane. "Anne and Emily: L. M. Montgomery's children," *Room of One's Own*, 3(3):37-8, 43-8, 1977.

3835. Burton, Lydia and David Morley. "A sense of grievance: attitudes toward men in contemporary fiction," *Canadian Forum*, 55:57-60, Sept. 1975.

3836. Chawla, Saroj. "Canadian fiction: literature as role exploration, an analysis of novels written by women, 1920-1974." PhD diss., York University, 1981. 337p. (Can. theses, no.51366)

3837. Christ, Carol P. "Margaret Atwood: the surfacing of women's spiritual quest and vision," *Signs: Journal of Women in Culture and Society*, 2:316-30, Winter 1976.

3838. Coderre, Annette-E. "The changing role of women in the French-Canadian and English-Canadian novel." MA thèse, Université de Sherbrooke, 1968. 129p.

3839. Couillard, Marie. "La femme: d'objet mythique à sujet parlant," *Atlantis*, 5:40-50, Fall 1979.

3840. Davidson, Cathy N. "A literature of survivors: on teaching Canada's women writers," *Women Studies Newsletter*, 6:412-5, Fall 1978.

3841. Engel, Marian. "Margaret Laurence: her new book divines women's truths," *Chatelaine*, 47:27, May 1974.

3842. Fairbanks, Carol. "Lives of girls and women on the Canadian and American prairies," *International Journal of Women's Studies*, 2:452-72, Sept.-Oct. 1979.

3843. Fleenor, Juliann E. "Rape fantasies as initiation rite: female imagination in 'Lives of girls and women'," *Room of One's Own*, 4(4):35-49, 1979.

3844. Forsyth, Louise H. "The radical transformation of the mother-daughter relationship in some Canadian writers," *Frontiers*, 6:44-9, Spring-Summer 1981.

3845. Fulton, E. Margaret. "Women in education - changing roles and new challenges," *English Quarterly*, 8:21-32, Winter 1975-76.

3846. Genuist, Monique. "Mille milles et la femme dans *Le nez qui voque*," *Atlantis*, 2:56-63, Spring 1977, Part I.

3847. Gottlieb, Lois C. and Wendy Keitner. "Demeter's daughters, the mother-daughter motif in fiction by Canadian women," *Atlantis*, 3:131-42, Autumn 1977.

3848. _____. "Images of Canadian women in literature and society in the 1970's," *International Journal of Women's Studies*, 2:513-27, Nov.-Dec. 1979.

3849. Grayson, J. Paul. "Male hegemony and the English Canadian novel," *Canadian Review of Sociology and Anthropology*, 20:1-21, Feb. 1983.

3850. Hoy, Helen Elizabeth. "The portrayal of women in recent English-Canadian fiction." PhD diss., University of Toronto, 1977. 410p. (Can. theses, no.36695)

3851. Kreipans-McGrath, Veneranda. "Love and loathing: the role of woman in Irving Layton's vision." MA thesis, Concordia University, 1981. 86p. (Can. theses, no.49638)

3852. Limin, Gloria Hope. "Teaching the theme of women in Canadian prairie fiction." MA thesis, University of Calgary, 1977. 141p. (Can. theses, no.34207)

3853. L'Autre Parole. *Paroles sur "Les fées ont soif"*. Cahier no. 1. [Rimouski, 1979]. [37]p.

3854. MacMillan, Carrie. "Images of women in Canadian English literature," *Chautauqua*, 9:9-10, Apr. 1980.

3855. Masterson, Kathleen Elizabeth. "Women in contemporary Canadian fiction." MA thesis, Bishop's University, 1974. 110p.

3856. McCullough, Elizabeth, ed. *The role of woman in Canadian literature*. Toronto: Macmillan, 1975. 120p.

3857. McKenna, Isobel. "As they really were: women in the novels of Grove," *English Studies in Canada*, 2:109-16, Spring 1976.

3858. _____. "Women in Canadian literature," *Canadian Literature*, no. 62:69-78, Autumn 1974.

3859. McMullen, Lorraine. "Ethnicity and femininity: double jeopardy," *Canadian Ethnic Studies*, 13(1):52-62, 1981.

3860. _____. "Images of women in Canadian literature: woman as hero," *Atlantis*, 2:134-42, Spring 1977, Part II.

3861. _____. "The divided self," *Atlantis*, 5:52-67, Spring 1980.

3862. _____. "Women in Grove's novels," in John Nause, ed., *Grove Symposium, reappraisals*. Canadian Literature Series. Ottawa: University of Ottawa Press, 1974, pp. 67-76.

3863. Miners, Marion Frances. "Women in selected English-Canadian novels, 1954 to 1972." MA thesis, University of Calgary, 1977. 257p. (Can. theses, no.34061)

3864. Mitcham, Allison. "The Canadian matriarch: a study in contemporary French and English-Canadian fiction," *Revue de l'Université de Moncton*, 7:37-42, janv. 1974.

3865. Morley, Patricia. "Engel, Wiseman, Laurence: women writers, women's lives," *World Literature Written in English*, 17:155-64, Apr. 1978.

3866. _____. "Literature engagé," *Branching Out*, 1:30, 43, Mar.-Apr. 1974.

3867. _____. "Margaret Laurence: feminist, nationalist and matriarch of Canadian letters," *Laurentian University Review*, 14:24-33, Feb. 1982.

3868. Onley, Gloria. "Power politics in Bluebeard's castle," *Canadian Literature*, no. 60:21-42, Spring 1974.

3869. Pesando, Frank Joseph. "The women in the prairie novels of Frederick Philip Grove." MA thesis, York University, 1971. 77p.

3870. Plaskow, Judith. "On Carol Christ on Margaret Atwood: some theological reflections," *Signs: Journal of Women in Culture and Society*, 2:331-9, Winter 1976.

3871. Pyke, S. W. "Children's literature: conceptions of sex roles," in Robert M. Pike and Elia Zureik, eds., *Socialization and values in Canadian society*. Vol. 2: *Socialization, social stratification and ethnicity*. Toronto: McClelland & Stewart, 1975, pp.51-73.

3872. Rackowski, Cheryl Stokes. "Women by women: five contemporary English and French Canadian novelists." PhD diss., University of Connecticut, 1978. 308p.

3873. Rankin, Linda Marie. "Sexual roles in the fiction of Alice Munro." MA thesis, University of New Brunswick, 1978. 104p. (Can. theses, no.35642)

3874. Rasporich, Beverly J. "Child-women and primitives in the fiction of Alice Munro," *Atlantis*, 1:5-14, Spring 1976.

3875. Rideout, Elliott Christopher. "The women in the novels of Frederick Philip Grove." MA thesis, University of Alberta, 1969. 104p.

3876.   Rooke, Constance. "A feminist reading of "The Stone Angel"," *Canadian Literature*, 93:26-41, Summer 1982.

3877.   Sanders, Karen E. "Margaret Marshall Saunders: children's literature as an expression of early twentieth century social reform." MA thesis, Dalhousie University, 1978. 161p. (Can. theses, no.38402)

3878.   Scott, Donna Lynn. "Block-and-tackle: multiple roles of women in Canadian and Australian pioneer fiction." MA thesis, Queen's University, 1973. 85p. (Can. theses, no.18548)

3879.   Stewart, Grace. *A new mythos: the novel of the artist as heroine 1877-1977*. St. Alban's, Vt. and Montreal: Eden Press, 1979. 200p. Deals with novels written by American, Canadian, and British women.

3880.   Strong-Boag, Veronica. ""You be sure to tell it like it is': the recovery of Canada's past [review article]," *Journal of Canadian Studies*, 16:217-21, Fall-Winter 1981.

3881.   Tanaszi, Margaret J. "Emancipation of consciousness in Alice Munro's *Lives of girls and women*." MA thesis, Queen's University, 1972. 171p. (Can. theses, no.12335)

3882.   Tausky, Thomas E. *Sara Jeannette Duncan: novelist of empire*. Port Credit: P. D. Meany, 1980. 300p.

3883.   Texmo, Dell. "Image and identity in Margaret Atwood's *The edible woman*," *Atlantis*, 2:65-76, Spring 1977, Part I.

3884.   Thomas, Clara. "Happily ever after: Canadian women in fiction and fact," *Canadian Literature*, 34:43-53, Autumn 1967.

3885.   _____. "Heroinism, feminism and humanism: Anna Jameson to Margaret Laurence," *Atlantis*, 4:19-29, Autumn 1978.

3886.   Tremblay, Anne. "Feminine self-consciousness in the works of Margaret Laurence." MA thesis, McGill University, 1976. 126p. (Can. theses, no.31901)

3887.   Trofimenkoff, Susan Mann. "Nationalism, feminism and Canadian intellectual history," *Canadian Literature*, 83:7-20, Winter 1979.

3888.   Verkruysse, Patricia Louise. "Small legacy of truth: the novels of Nellie McClung." MA thesis, University of New Brunswick, 1975. 225p. (Can. theses, no.27455)

3889.   Verduyn, Christl. "Looking back to Lot's wife," *Atlantis*, 6:38-46, Spring 1981.

3890.   Verduyn, Christl. "L'idée de la découverte de soi dans le roman féminin canadien depuis 1960: étude d'oeuvres québécois et canadiennes-anglaises." PhD diss., Université d'Ottawa, 1979. (Can. theses, no.44165)

3891.   Wilson, Patricia A. "Women of Jubilee: a commentary on female roles in the work of Alice Munro." MA thesis, University of Guelph, 1975. 75p. (Can. theses, no.23630)

3892.   "Women writers of the Commonwealth [Canada]," *World Literature Written in English*, 17:118-217, Apr. 1978, Special issue.

3893.   Wood, Susan. "God's doormats: women in Canadian prairie fiction," *Journal of Popular Culture*, 14:350-9, Fall 1980.

3894.   Yaffe, Phyllis. "Social values in Canadian children's literature," in *Socialization and life skills*. Ottawa: Canadian Teachers' Federation, 1978, pp.25-9.

LITERATURE - BIBLIOGRAPHY

3895.   Anthony, Geraldine. "A bibliography of English drama written by women," *World Literature Written in English*, 17:120-43, Apr. 1978.

3896.   "Bibliography of literature in English by and about women," *Women and Literature*, v.2, 1974- . Annual.
        Includes a section on women in Canadian literature.

3897.   Gottlieb, Lois C. and Wendy Keitner. "Bird at the window: an annotated bibliography of Canadian fiction written by women, 1970-1975," *American Review of Canadian Studies*, 9:3-56, Autumn 1979.

3898.   Hamel, Reginald. *Bibliographie sommaire sur l'histoire de l'écriture féminine au Canada, 1769-1961*. [Montréal]: Université de Montréal, 1974. 134p.

3899.   Linden, Marjorie and Diane Teeple. "The evolving role of Canadian women writers [bibliography]," *Ontario Library Review*, 61:114-31, June 1977.

157

3900. Lister, Rota Herzberg. "Canadian plays in English about older women: a bibliography," *Resources for Feminist Research*, 11:238-40, July 1982.
3901. McIntyre, Sheila. "A bibliography of scholarship on literature by and about Canadian women," *Canadian Newsletter of Research on Women*, 6:99-114, Feb. 1977.
3902. Maranda, Jeanne and Mair Verthuy. "Québec feminist writing," *Emergency Librarian*, 5:2-11, [English]; 12-20 [French], Sept.-Oct. 1977.

LITERATURE, FRENCH - CANADIAN

3903. Aonzo, Jeannine. "La femme dans les romans d'Anne Hébert." MA thèse, McGill University, 1981. (Can. theses, no.54732)
3904. Barrett, Caroline. "La femme et la société dans la littérature sentimentale populaire québécoise, 1940-1960." MA thèse, Université Laval, 1979. 86p. (Can. theses, no.41830)
3905. Barrett, Caroline et Marie-Josée Des Rivières. "La femme dans la littérature populaire québécoise (1945-1966)," *Revue de l'Université d'Ottawa*, 50(1):99-108, 1980.
3906. Boynard-Frot, Janine. "Une lecture féministe des romans du terroir canadien-français de 1860 à 1960," *Possibles*, 4:41-53, automne 1979.
3907. Collet, Paulette. "Les romancières québécoises des années 60 face à la maternité," *Atlantis*, 5:131-41, Spring 1980.
3908. Couillard, Marie. "La femme-écrivain canadienne-française et québécoise face aux idéologies de son temps," *Canadian Ethnic Studies*, 13(1):43-51, 1981.
3909. Couillard-Goodenough, Marie. "La femme et le sacré dans quelques romans québécois contemporains," *Revue de l'Université d'Ottawa*, 50(1): 74-81, 1980.
3910. Crépeau, Jean-François. "L'univers féminin dans l'oeuvre de Marcel Dubé." MA thesis, McGill University, 1974. 143p. (Can. theses, no.20686)
3911. Des Rivières, Marie-Josée. "La représentation de la femme dans le roman populaire 'Les aventures étranges de l'agent IXE-13, l'as des espions canadiens', de Pierre Saurel." MA thèse, Université Laval, 1978. 122p. (Can. theses, no.41410)
3912. Ethier, Pauline. "Monographie du cont-type 590A: l'épouse traîtresse dans la tradition canadienne-française." MA thèse, Université Laval, 1976. 245p. (Can. theses, no.35391)
3913. Fournier, Louise G. "La femme dans les romans d'Yves Thériault." MA thesis, Dalhouse University, 1976. 123p. (Can. theses, no.28881)
3914. Gould, Karen. "Setting words free: feminist writing in Quebec," *Signs: Journal of Women and Culture*, 6:617-42, Summer 1981.
3915. Lafrenière, Suzanne. *Moisette Olier: femme de lettres de la Mauricie*. Hull, Québec: Éditions Asticou, 1980. 224p.
3916. Lequin, Lucie. "Les femmes québécoises ont inventé leurs paroles," *American Review of Canadian Studies*, 9:113-24, Autumn 1979.
3917. Paradis, Suzanne. *Femme fictive, femme réelle: le personnage féminin dans le roman féminin canadien-français 1884-1966*. Québec: Garneau, 1966. 330p.
3918. Pascal, Gabrielle. "La femme dans l'oeuvre de Gabrielle Roy," *Revue de l'Université d'Ottawa*, 50(1):55-61, 1980.
3919. Poulin, Gabrielle. "Romans québécois féminins des années '70: la femme et le pays toujours futurs," *Relations*, 36:347-50, déc. 1976.
3920. Rubinger, Catherine. "Some pioneer women writers of French Canada," *Canadian Women's Studies / Les cahiers de la femme*, 3(1):37-9, 1981.
3921. Smart, Patricia. "La poésie d'Anne Hébert: une perspective féminine," *Revue de l'Université d'Ottawa*, 50(1):62-8, 1980.
3922. ‎_____ "Voices of commitment and discovery: women writers in Quebec," *Room of One's Own*, 4(1/2):7-18, 1978.
3923. Thibaudeau, Huguette. "Les femmes dans l'oeuvre de Claire Martin." MA thesis, University of British Columbia, 1975. 119p. (Can. theses, no.25280)
3924. Trofimenkoff, Susan Mann. "Les femmes dans l'oeuvre de Groulx," *Revue d'histoire de l'Amérique française*, 32:385-98, déc. 1978.
3925. Urbas, Jeannette. "La representation de la femme chez Godbout, Aquin et Jasmin," *Laurentian University Review*, 9:103-13, Nov. 1976.

3926. Urbas, Jeannette. "Le personnage féminin dans le roman canadien-français de 1940 à 1967." PhD diss., University of Toronto, 1971. 583p. (Can. theses, no.38865)

LOBBYING

3927. Alberta Status of Women Action Committee. *Political involvement handbook for Alberta women*. [Edmonton]: Alberta. Women's Bureau, 1978. 79p.
3928. Cameron, Barbara. "OWW: employment strategy for women," *Broadside*, 1(2):9, 1979.
3929. Canadian Advisory Council on the Status of Women. *Sharing the power*. Ottawa, [1980]. Folder. French edition: *Participer au pouvoir*.
3930. Kome, Penney. "Anatomy of a lobby," *Saturday Night*, 98:9-11, Jan. 1983.
3931. Saskatchewan. Dept. of Labour. Women's Division. *For women: problem-solving and action planning kit*. Regina, [1978?] 18, 39p. (Profile 78-0525)
3932. "Women! Rally for action, March 22, Victoria: women's action rally: biggest since the fight for the vote," *Status of Women News*, 2:19, May 1976.

MARRIAGE

3933. Abrioux, Marie-Louise and Harvey W. Zingle. "An exploration of the marital and life satisfactions of middle-aged husbands and wives," *Canadian Counsellor*, 13:85-92, Jan. 1979.
3934. Beyer, Mary Alice and Robert N. Whitehurst. "Value changes with length of marriage: some correlates of consonance and dissonance," *International Journal of Sociology of the Family*, 6:109-20, Spring 1976.
3935. Campbell, Douglas F. and David C. Neice. *Ties that bind: structure and marriage in Nova Scotia*. Port Credit, Ont.: Scribblers' Press, 1979. 207p.
3936. Chamber of Notaries of the Province of Quebec. *Brief no. 387 to the Royal Commission on the Status of Women in Canada*. Montreal, 1968. 41p.
3937. Colbert, Helen. "First-marriage decrement tables for women in Western Canada: 1966," *Journal of Comparative Family Studies*, 7:285-94, Summer 1976.

3938. Day, Marilyn Anne. "Relationships of perceptions of relatives to marriage satisfaction." MEd thesis, University of Alberta, 1974. 31p. (Can. theses, no.18190)
3939. Fisher, Esther. "Economics A, marriage F," *Quest*, 9:38L-38N, 38P+ , Oct. 1980.
3940. Gee, Ellen M. Thomas. "Female marriage patterns in Canada: changes and differentials," *Journal of Comparative Family Studies*, 11:457-73, Autumn 1980.
3941. Gillen, M. "Why are we still brainwashing girls about marriage?" *Chatelaine*, 42:23, 70-2, Dec. 1969.

3942. Guggi, Roswitha. "You are woman," *Weekend Magazine*, 26:4-6, 8-9, May 15, 1976.
3943. Gwyn, Sandra. "The flowering of the two-career marriage," *Saturday Night*, 94:24-9, June 1979.
3944. Harris, Marjorie and Benjamin Schlesinger. "Men and women: where we're at: coming out of the stone age: the myths and the facts separated," *Quest*, 6:24-6, 28, 30, Sept.-Oct. 1977.

3945. Hedlund, David. "An investigation of the marriage encounter program." MEd thesis, University of Alberta, 1980. 209p. (Can. theses, no.48965)
3946. Henshel, Anne-Marie. "Swinging: a study of decision making in marriage," *American Journal of Sociology*, 78:885-91, Jan. 1973.
3947. Hobart, Charles W. *Changing orientations to marriage: a study of young Canadians*. Report to the Royal Commission on the Status of Women in Canada. Edmonton, 1968. 172p.
3948. _____. "Egalitarianism after marriage," in Marylee Stephenson, *Women in Canada*. Toronto: New Press, 1973, pp.138-156.
3949. _____. "Orientations to marriage among young Canadians," *Journal of Comparative Family Studies*, 3:171-93, Autumn 1972.
3950. _____. "Sources of egalitarianism in young unmarried Canadians," *Canadian Journal of Sociology*, 6:261-82, Summer 1981.

3951. Hogervorst, Joann E. "Marital role expectations of adolescent girls." MSc thesis, University of Guelph, 1978. 110p. (Can. theses, no.38938)

3952. Ivison, Carol. "Trends in marriage and illegitimacy: a comparative study of Canada, the provinces and the economic regions of Ontario," in Betty Macleod, ed., *Demography and educational planning*. Monograph series, no. 7. Toronto: Ontario Institute for Studies in Education, 1970, pp.183-204.

3953. Kieren, Dianne K. and Doris R. Badir. "Teaching about marital roles - using research findings to design teaching strategies," *Alberta Journal of Educational Research*, 22:245-53, Sept. 1976.

3954. Labreche, Julianne. "Long-distance marriage: does it work?" *Chatelaine*, 55:60-1, 96-7+ , Apr. 1982.

3955. Laing, Lory and P. Krishnan. "First-marriage decrement tables for males and females in Canada, 1961-1966," *Canadian Review of Sociology and Anthropology*, 13(2):217-28, 1976.

3956. Larivière, Hélène. "Les nouveaux couples," *Le Maclean*, 16:10-12, fév. 1976.

3957. Landsberg, Michele. "Exploding high school girls' marriage fantasies," *Chatelaine*, 48:53, 104-8, Sept. 1975.

3958. Larson, Lyle E., comp. *The Canadian family in comparative perspective*. Scarborough, Ont.: Prentice-Hall, 1976. 481p.

3959. Long, Douglas. "La relation conjugale dans le mariage ouvert sexuellement." MA mémoire, Université du Québec à Montréal, 1980. 188p. (Can. theses, no.47622)

3960. Lupri, Eugen and James Frideres. "The quality of marriage and the passage of time: marital satisfaction over the family life cycle," *Canadian Journal of Sociology*, 6:283-305, Summer 1981.

3961. MacDonald, Dawn. "How wives see their marriage," *Chatelaine*, 45:51, 76, 78-81, Oct. 1972.

3962. Macpherson, Kay. "Some of my best friends are men, but...," *Chatelaine*, 50:20, Oct. 1977.

3963. Magnan, Colette McDuff. "Les relations sexuelles extramaritales chez des femmes québécoises au travail." MA mémoire, Université du Québec à Montréal, 1978. 213p. (Can. theses, no.47625)

3964. Mead, M. "Marriage isn't for every woman," *Continuous Learning*, 4:177-82, July-Aug. 1965.

3965. Meyer, John Peter. "An investigation of the relationship of marital adjustment to need compatibility and role fit in young married couples." MA thesis, University of Western Ontario, 1975. 138p. (Can. theses, no.24615)

3966. Pierzchalski, Paul. "Marital resources: some variables examined." MA thesis, University of Calgary, 1974. 95p. (Can. theses, no.21338)

3967. Ramu, G. N. "The family and marriage in Canada," in G. N. Ramu and Stuart D. Johnson, eds., *Introduction to Canadian society: sociological analysis*. Toronto: Macmillan of Canada, 1976, pp.295-348.

3968. Ramu, G. N., ed. *Courtship, marriage and the family in Canada*. Toronto: Macmillan of Canada, 1979. 219p.

3969. Rich, J. "Has marriage a future?" *Chatelaine*, 43:25, 62-5, Mar. 1970.

3970. Schlesinger, Benjamin, ed. *The Chatelaine guide to marriage*. Toronto: MacMillan, 1975. 218p.

3971. Shorter, Edward. "'Twosies' marriage," *Chatelaine*, 49:57, 98-104, Nov. 1976.

3972. Szala, Karen Victoria. "Clean women and quiet men: courtship and marriage in a Newfoundland fishing village." MA thesis, Memorial University of Newfoundland, 1978. 107p. (Can. theses, no.43187)

3973. Thomas, David. "Whom greed hath joined together," *Maclean's*, 93:16-17, Jan. 5, 1981.

3974. Timson, Judith and Bonnie Palef. "Love and marriage wedded once again," *Maclean's*, 93:46-7, June 30, 1980.

3975. Veevers, J. E. "The child-free alternative: rejection of the motherhood mystique," in Marylee Stephenson, *Women in Canada*. Toronto: New Press, 1973, pp.183-99.

3976.   Veevers, J. E. "The life style of voluntarily childless couples," in Lyle E. Larson, comp., *The Canadian family in comparative perspective*. Scarborough, Ont.: Prentice-Hall, 1976, pp.394-411.

3977.   Wakil, S. Parvez. "Campus mate selection preferences: a cross-national comparison," *Social Forces*, 51:471-6, June 1973.

3978.   Wakil, S. Parvez and E. A. Wakil. "Marriage and family in Canada: a demographic-cultural profile," in K. Ishwaran, *The Canadian family*. Rev. ed. Toronto: Holt, Rinehart and Winston of Canada, 1976, pp.380-407.

3979.   "Weekend poll: what kind of marriages do Canadians want?" *Weekend Magazine*, 28:3, Feb. 11, 1978.

MARRIAGE - BIBLIOGRAPHY

3980.   Nowosielski, Maryna. *Marriage and the family: preliminary check list of National Library holdings. [Mariage et famille: inventaire préliminaire des fonds de la Bibliothèque nationale]*. Ottawa: National Library of Canada / Vanier Institute of the Family, 1980. 130p.

MARRIAGE - HISTORY

3981.   Brown, Jennifer S. H. "Changing views of fur trade marriage and domesticity; James Hargrave, his colleagues, and 'the sex'," *Western Canadian Journal of Anthropology*, 6(3):92-105, 1976.

3982.   Dionne, Hélène. *Les contrats de mariage à Québec (1790-1812)*. National Museum of Man. Mercury series / History division. Paper, no. 29. Ottawa: National Museums of Canada, 1980. 174p.

3983.   Gee, Ellen M. Thomas. "Marriage in nineteenth-century Canada," *Canadian Review of Sociology and Anthropology*, 19:311-25, Aug. 1982.

3984.   Mertens, Walter. "Canadian nuptiality patterns: 1911-1961," *Canadian Studies in Population*, 3:57-71, 1976.

3985.   Rubinger, Catherine. "Marriage and the women of Louisbourg," *Dalhousie Review*, 60:445-61, Autumn 1980.

MARRIAGE,COMMON LAW

3986.   Alberta. Women's Bureau. *Common-law relationships in Alberta*. Edmonton, 1980. 16p. (Microlog 80-1822)

3987.   Gampel, Samuel. "A commentary on 'An analysis of the concepts of the common law marriage and the meretricious union' by B. W. Pritchard, 21 R. F. L. 129," *Reports of Family Law*, 26:271-92, 1977.

3988.   Poulton, Terry. "Lady's not for burning-or is she?" *Maclean's*, 91:45-6, Aug. 21, 1978.

3989.   Poulton, Terry. "Nearly married spouses," *Maclean's*, 92:43, July 30, 1979.

3990.   Pritchard, Bryan W. "An analysis of the concepts of the common law marriage and the meretricious union," *Reports of Family Law*, 21:129-56, 1976.

3991.   Saskatchewan. Dept. of Labour. Women's Division. *Rights of common-law wives or cohabitators*. [Regina, 1978?] [6]p. (Microlog 79-0688)

3992.   Zinck, Cynthia L. "Common law relationships," *Broadside*, 1(9):7, 18, 1980.

MARRIAGE AND MARRIAGE PROPERTY LAW

3993.   Anderson, Doris. "Facing facts on marriage reform," *Chatelaine*, 49:2, July 1976.

3994.   _____. "Marriage contracts: not romantic, but very useful," *Financial Post*, 76:8, May 29, 1982.

3995.   _____. "Two court cases where women lost heavily [editorial]," *Chatelaine*, 47:1, Jan. 1974.

3996.   Aquin, F. "Les conventions entre époux à l'occasion des séparations de fait, des séparations de corps et de divorce," *Cours de perfectionnement du notariat*, 1976, pp.191-212.

3997. Bailey, Stella. "He can break your leg but not your watch," *Branching Out*, 4:5-6, Mar.-Apr. 1977.

3998. _____. "Matrimonial property: what has happened since Murdoch?" *Branching Out*, 3:35-40, Sept.-Oct. 1976.

3999. Bartke, Richard W. "Marital property law reform: Canadian style," *American Journal of Comparative Law*, 25:46-85, Winter 1977.

4000. Bates, Frank. "The presumption of marriage in Canada: its past, present and future," *University of Western Ontario Law Review*, 17:169-83, 1979.

4001. Bernstein, Jack. "Marriage - a tax shelter?" *McGill Law Journal*, 21:631-55, Winter 1975.

4002. Birnie, David A. G. and Josephine Margolis. "Income tax implications of the Family Relations Act of British Columbia," *Canadian Tax Journal*, 27:641-52, Nov.-Dec. 1979.

4003. Bissett-Johnson, Alastair and Winifred H. Holland, eds. *Matrimonial property law in Canada*. Agincourt, Ont.: Burroughs, 1980- . Loose-leaf service.

4004. Brière, Germain. "Régimes matrimoniaux: chroniques régulières," *Revue du Barreau*, 36:414-16, 1976.

4005. Cameron, Silver Donald. "State of the union," *Weekend Magazine*, 27:3, May 7, 1977.

4006. Canada. Advisory Council on the Status of Women. *A definition of equity in marriage*. Ottawa, 1976. 4p.

4007. _____. *Matrimonial property: towards an equal partnership*. [*Les biens conjugaux: vers une association d'égaux*]. 2nd ed. The person papers. Ottawa, 1976. 16, 16p.

4008. Canada. Law Reform Commission. *Family property*. Working paper no. 8. Ottawa: Information Canada, 1975. 45p.

4009. _____. *Studies on family property law*. Ottawa: Information Canada, 1975. 356p.

4010. Canadian Advisory Council on the Status of Women. *Statement on matrimonial property laws in Canada*, prepared by Louise Dulude, update by Ruth Brown. Ottawa, 1978. Update 1979. 23p.

4011. Cantlie, Ronald B. "Effect of change of domicile on property rights of spouses under community of property or marriage contract," in Canadian Bar Association, *Papers presented at the annual meeting, 1967, Quebec City, Quebec*. n.p.: CCH Canadian Ltd., 1968, pp.223-32.

4012. Castel, J.-G. "Choice of law-matrimonial regimes...," *Canadian Bar Review*, 60:180-87, Mar. 1982.

4013. Chapman, F. A. R. *Everything you should know about law and marriage*. Toronto: Pagurian Press, 1971. 163p.

4014. Charron, Camille. "Régimes matrimoniaux: chroniques régulières," *Revue du Barreau*, 39:929-30, 1979.

4015. Cullity, Maurice C. "Family law reform - legislative response!," *Estates and Trusts Quarterly*, 3:129-50, 1976.

4016. _____. "Property rights during the subsistence of marriage," *Canadian Family Law*, 1972, pp.179-281.

4017. Dranoff, Linda Silver. "Ask a lawyer," *Chatelaine*, 54:38, May 1981.

4018. _____. "Ask a lawyer," *Chatelaine*, 52:17, 18, May 1979.

4019. _____. "Ask a lawyer," *Chatelaine*, 52:18, 20, June 1979.

4020. _____. "Ask a lawyer," *Chatelaine*, 52:18, 21, Oct. 1979.

4021. Dulude, Louise. *Outline of matrimonial property laws in Canada (from east and west)*. [*Description des lois canadiennes sur les biens matrimoniaux (le l'est à l'ouest)*]. Ottawa: Canadian Advisory Council on the Status of Women, 1982. 24, 24p. (Microlog 83-3242)

4022. Eng, Susan. "Tax consequences of provincial family law reform legislation," *Canadian Tax Journal*, 26:554-74, Sept.-Oct. 1978.

4023. First National Farm Women's Conference. *Equal partner or "just a wife": farm wives and property law in Canada*. Status of Rural Women Project. [Ottawa], 1980. 27, [19]p. French edition: *Partenaire à part égale ou "rien qu'une femme"*.

4024. Fleishman, Neil. *Counsel for the damned*. Vancouver: Douglas, J. J. Ltd., 1973. 206p.

4025. Ginsburg, Marilyn and Gina Quijano. *Canadian women and the law*. Toronto: Osgoode Hall Law School, 1974. 738p.

4026. Glenn, Jane Matthews. "Tenancy by the entireties: a matrimonial regime ignored," *Canadian Bar Review*, 58:711-36, Dec. 1980.

4027. Gosse, R. "'Hers' and 'his': fair shares for wives and husbands," *Law Society Gazette*, 8:256-72, 1974.

4028. Groffier, E. "La réforme du Droit familial et la condition de la femme au Canada," *McGill Law Journal*, 21:495-517, Winter 1975.

4029. Guay-Archambault, Denyse. "Regards sur le nouveau droit de la famille au Canada anglais et au Québec," *Cahiers de droit*, 22:723-84, 1981.

4030. Hahlo, H. R. "Matrimonial property regimes: yesterday, today and tomorrow," *Osgoode Hall Law Journal*, 11:455-78, Dec. 1973.

4031. Hedley, Max J. "'Normal expectations': rural women without property," *Resources for Feminist Research*, 11:15-17, Mar. 1982.

4032. Héleine, François. "Le contrat de société entre époux d'hier à aujourd'hui," *La Revue juridique Thémis*, 15:357-81, 1980-81.

4033. Hobart, Charles. "Ownership of matrimonial property: a study of practices and attitudes," *Canadian Review of Sociology and Anthropology*, 12:440-52, Nov. 1975.

4034. Holland, Winifred H. and D. Keith McNair. *Unmarried couples: legal aspects of cohabitation*. Toronto: Carswell, 1982. 249p.

4035. Horsford, Patricia A. "Division of Canada Pension Plan credits on termination of marriage," *Reports of Family Law*, 2nd ser., 13:48-58, 1980.

4036. Jacobson, Peter M. "Comment on working paper no. 8 of the Law Reform Commission of Canada: Family property," *Ottawa Law Review*, 8:290-3, 1976.

4037. King, Lynn. *What every woman should know about marriage, separation and divorce*. Toronto: James Lorimer, 1980. 105p.

4038. Major, Henri. *Notes on selected federal statutes recognizing common-law relationships*. Ottawa: Canada. Advisory Council on the Status of Women, 1975. 13p.

4039. Marmer, Jack. "Divorce can threaten a company's survival," *Financial Post*, 75:16, July 18, 1981.

4040. .... "Marriage and business often go hand in hand," *Financial Post*, 75:18, July 25, 1981.

4041. .... "When divorce may cost a business," *Financial Post* 75:1-2, July 11, 1981.

4042. McClean, A. J. "Matrimonial property - Canadian common law style," *University of Toronto Law Journal*, 31:363-435, 1981.

4043. "More common-law cases may reach court," *Financial Post*, 74:4, Dec. 27, 1980.

4044. Murphy, J. David. "The estate planning implications of marital disruptions," *Osgoode Hall Law Journal*, 13:407-38, Oct. 1975.

4045. Ontario Status of Women Council. *Brief to the government of Ontario respecting widows' rights to family property*. [Toronto], 1980. 13p.

4046. Oosterhoff, A. H. "Remedial constructive trusts - matrimonial property disputes - justice and equity or 'palm tree' justice?" *Canadian Bar Review*, 57:356-73, June 1979.

4047. Paris, Erna. "Marriage reform: part one: breaking the tie that binds," *Chatelaine*, 49:39, 95-8, June 1976.

4048. .... "Marriage reform: part two: changing the rules on money, property and chastity," *Chatelaine*, 49:33, 68-70, July 1976.

4049. Payne, Julien D. "Approaches to the economic consequences of marriage breakdown," *Canadian Legal Aid Bulletin*, 4:338-51, 1981.

4050. .... "Family property reform as perceived by the Law Reform Commission of Canada," *Chitty's Law Journal*, 24:289-99, 1976.

4051. Peterson-Dyck, Dawne. "The common law wife: myth or Mrs.?" *Branching Out*, 3:35-8, Apr.-June 1976.

4052. Quijano, Gina. "Matrimonial property law reform in Canada: from separate property to community property with joint management," *Osgoode Hall Law Journal*, 13:381-405, Oct. 1975.

4053. Rioux, Marcia H. *Background notes on matrimonial property rights: a discussion paper*. Revised. Ottawa: Canada. Advisory Council on the Status of Women, Dec. 1974. 40p.

4054. Ryan, Edward. "Family law and human equality," *Atlantis* 1:74-83, Spring 1976.

4055. Secord, Richard Calhoun. "The occupation of the matrimonial home." LLM thesis, University of Alberta, 1979. 249p. (Can. theses, no.43546)

4056. Silverman, Hugh W. "Conflict of laws: some matrimonial problems," *Family Law Review*, 2:103-14, 1979.

4057. Stone, Olive M. "Matrimonial property law: the movement towards equality - separation or community?," *Alberta Law Review*, 16(3):375-87, 1978.

4058. "Summary of the recommendations on matrimonial property," *Advocate*, 33:232-5, 1975.

4059. "The marriage contract," *Financial Times*, 66:41-2, Mar. 13-19, 1978.

4060. Wachtel, Eleanor. "Hers & his," *Homemaker's Magazine*, 17:8-10, 12+ , Mar. 1982.

4061. _____. "50-per-cent solution," *Maclean's*, 93:46-7, June 23, 1980.

4062. Waters, Donovan. "Matrimonial property disputes - resulting and constructive trusts - restitution," *Canadian Bar Review*, 53:366-81, May 1975.

4063. White, Charles A. "Women's rights: rewrite the law?" *Canada and the World*, 39:4-5, May 1974.

4064. "Wife's share more than half, Judge rules," *Globe & Mail*, Mar. 28, 1979, pp.1-2.

4065. "You asked us: coming of age in Canada: young marriage and the law," *Today*, Dec. 19, 1981, p.5.

4066. "You asked us: don't marry your granny, not to mention certain other folks," *Today*, Jan. 9, 1982, p.5

4067. Zinck, Cynthia Hastings. "Marriage contracts: make them and break them," *Broadside*, 1:5, 13, Sept. 1980.

MARRIAGE AND MARRIAGE PROPERTY LAW - ALBERTA

4068. Alberta. Women's Bureau. *Common-law relationships in Alberta*. Edmonton, 1980. 16p. (Microlog 80-1822)

4069. _____. *Ending a marriage: the legal aspects of separation, annulment and divorce*. Edmonton, 1979. 33p.

4070. Bourne, Paula. "Economics of marriage: the case of Irene Murdoch," in her, *Women in Canadian society*. Toronto: Ontario Institute for Studies in Education, 1976, pp.1-24.

4071. "Canadian notes: Mrs. Fiedler's rights," *Time. Can. ed.*, 104:8, July 29, 1974.

4072. Institute of Law Research and Reform, University of Alberta. *Report no. 18 - matrimonial property*. Edmonton: The Institute, 1975. 196p. (Profile 75-0742)

4073. _____. *Working paper - matrimonial property*. Edmonton: The Institute, 1974. (Profile 74-0856)

4074. "Justice: giving and taking away [Mrs. Fiedler's judgement overruled]," *Time. Can. ed.*, 105:9-10, Mar. 10, 1975.

4075. Lown, Peter J. M. "The Matrimonial Property Act, one year of operation," *Alberta Law Review*, 18(2):317-28, 1980.

4076. Lown, Peter J. M. and Frances L. Bendiak. "Matrimonial property - the new regime," *Alberta Law Review*, 17(3):372-422, 1979.

4077. Manley-Casimir, Michael E., L. W. Downey Research Associates Ltd. *Matrimonial property in Alberta: facts and attitudes*. Edmonton: University of Alberta. Institute of Law Research and Reform, 1974. 104p.

   Also published as an appendix to the Institute's, *Working paper - matrimonial property*.

4078. McBean, Jean. *Marriage and family law in Alberta: the rights of husbands, wives, children and common law spouses*. 2nd ed. Vancouver: International Self-Counsel Press, 1980. 203p.

4079. "Murdoch v. Murdoch. Supreme Court of Canada," *Western Weekly Reports*, 1(4):361-84, 1974.

4080. Niven, Michael Bryan. "Matrimonial property and the conflict of laws in Alberta." LLM thesis, University of Alberta, 1977. 183p. (Can. theses, no.34449)

4081. Pollock, Leonard J. "Matrimonial property and trusts: the situation from Murdoch to Rathwell," *Alberta Law Review*, 16(3):357-74, 1978.

4082. Shone, Margaret A. "Principles of matrimonial property sharing: Alberta's new act," *Alberta Law Review*, 17(2):143-87, 1979.

4083. "Women: matrimonial property act [Alberta]," *Native People*, 10:12, Apr. 8, 1977.

4084. Worton, Jean McBean. "Some recent developments in the law of matrimonial property," *Alberta Law Review*, 10:134-43, 1972.

MARRIAGE AND MARRIAGE PROPERTY LAW - BRITISH COLUMBIA

4085. Auxier, Jane. *Marriage & family law in British Columbia: the rights of husbands, wives, children and common-law spouses*. 4th ed. Vancouver: International Self-Counsel Press, 1981. 145p.

4086. Birnie, David. "Income tax implications of the Family Relations Act of British Columbia," *Canadian Tax Journal*, 27:641-52, Nov.-Dec. 1979.

4087. British Columbia. Royal Commission on Family and Children's Law. *Sixth report: report on matrimonial property*. Vancouver, 1975. [95]p. (Profile 75-0371)

4088. Ellis, James. "An income tax perspective on British Columbia marriage agreements," *University of British Columbia Law Review*, 15:153-73, 1981.

4089. Farquhar, Keith B. "Section 8 of the Family Relations Act - an experiment in the exercise of judicial discretion and the distribution of matrimonial property," *University of British Columbia Law Review*, 13(2):169-220, 1979.

4090. _____. "The new matrimonial property legislation in British Columbia: the first year," *University of British Columbia Law Review*, 15(1):1-83, 1981.

4091. Gargrave, Tony. "The Family relations act of British Columbia," Advocate, 38:225-7, 1980.

4092. Harvey, Christopher. "The Family Relations Act, S.B.C. 1978, c.20 or 'With half of my worldly goods I thee endow'," *Advocate*, 37:443-5, 1979.

4093. Schroeder, F. A. "Matrimonial property law reform: evaluating the alternatives," *University of British Columbia Law Review*, 11(1):24-39, 1977.

4094. Vancouver People's Law School. *Matrimony and divorce*. 2nd ed. Vancouver, 1976. 32p.

4095. Woodsworth, K. C., ed. *Settlement of property and maintenance in matrimonial disputes*. Vancouver: University of British Columbia. Centre for Continuing Education, 1971. 113p.

MARRIAGE AND MARRIAGE PROPERTY LAW - MANITOBA

4096. Family Law Review Committee. *Report [on] the Family Maintenance Act and the Marital Property Act*, [submitted by] Myrna Bowman, Rudy Anderson and Ken Houston. n.p., 1978. 23, 56p.

4097. Harvey, Cameron. "Manitoba family law reform legislation and succession," *Manitoba Law Journal*, 9(3):247-53, 1979.

4098. Hoeschen, Susan. "Lyon stumbles over family law [Family Maintenance Act]," *Financial Post*, 72:7, Jan. 7, 1978.

4099. "Howell presents viewpoint on matrimonial property laws," *Free Press Report on Farming*, 97:6, Nov. 30, 1977.

4100. Kostash, Myrna. "Law reform bites the dust in Manitoba," *Chatelaine*, 51:50-1, 112+ , June 1978.

4101. Koulack, Ester and Leona McEvoy. "Family law reform," *Canadian Dimension*, 12:22-3, Sept. 1977.

4102. Koutecky, Teri. "Manitoba's marital law—being against Bill 61 like opposing motherhood," *Free Press Report on Farming*, 97:22, Oct. 5, 1977.

4103. Manitoba. Law Reform Commission. *Reports on family law. Part I - the support obligation. Part II - property disposition*. Winnipeg, 1976. 141p.

4104. "On sharing assets [Manitoba]; text in English and French," *Perception*, 1:9-10, Sept.-Oct. 1977.

4105. "Sees marital law reform as threat to viable farm," *Free Press Report on Farming*, 97:5, Dec. 7, 1977.

4106. "The split decision," *Free Press Report on Farming*, 97:5, Oct. 26, 1977.

MARRIAGE AND MARRIAGE PROPERTY LAW - NEW BRUNSWICK

4107. New Brunswick. Dept. of Justice. Law Reform Division. *Matrimonial property reform for New Brunswick.* [*Réforme du régime des biens matrimoniaux du Nouveau-Brunswick*]. Discussion paper. Frederiction, 1978. 41, 46p. (Profile 78-0554)

4108. Stapleton, Basil D. "Death and property rights in New Brunswick: recent developments," *University of New Brunswick Law Journal*, 30:198-207, 1981.

MARRIAGE AND MARRIAGE PROPERTY LAW - NOVA SCOTIA

4109. Bissett-Johnson, Alastair and D. Campbell. "First appeal decisions on matrimonial property in Nova Scotia," *Reports of Family Law*, 2nd ser., 26:200-8, 1982.

4110. Nova Scotia. Law Reform Advisory Commission. *Development of matrimonial property law in England and Nova Scotia: an historic perspective*, prepared by Lilias M. Toward. Halifax, 1975. 83p.

MARRIAGE AND MARRIAGE PROPERTY LAW - ONTARIO

4111. Anderson, Doris. "At last: legislation to protect wives [editorial]," *Chatelaine*, 47:1, May 1974.

4112. Bala, Nicholas. "Governing relationships by agreement instead of judicial discretion: marriage contracts and cohabitation agreements in Ontario," *Family Law Review*, 3:91-102, 1980.

4113. Bankier, Jennifer. "An act to reform the law respecting property rights and support obligations between married persons and in other family relationships: a critique," *Family Law Review*, 1:33-47, 1978.

4114. Bartke, Richard W. "Ontario Bill 6, or how not to reform marital property rights," *Ottawa Law Review*, 9:321-38, 1977.

4115. Baxter, Ian F. G. "Family law reform in Ontario," *University of Toronto Law Journal*, 25:236-80, Summer 1975.

4116. _____. "Family law reform - Ontario," *Canadian Bar Review*, 55:187-96, Mar. 1977.

4117. Bissett-Johnson, Alastair. "Death and the Matrimonial Property Act," *Reports of Family Law*, 2nd ser., 25:182-92, 1982.

4118. David, Rodica. *Marriage & family law in Ontario: a guide to drafting marriage contracts.* Vancouver: International Self-Counsel Press, 1977. 194p.

4119. David, Rodica. *Marriage & family law in Ontario: a guide to the rights of husbands, wives, children and common-law spouses.* 3d. ed. Vancouver: International Self-Counsel Press, 1982. 204p.
    First edition c. 1975, reprinted 1977; second edition, 1979.

4120. Glenn, Jane Matthews. "Partition - weighing of relative hardship - interrelationship of the Partition Act and the Married Women's Property Act," *Canadian Bar Review*, 54:149-58, Mar. 1976.

4121. Gormely, Sheila. "Parting as a sweeter sorrow: one half for him, the other for her," *Maclean's*, 89:70-1, Nov. 15, 1976.

4122. Greenberg, S. "Ontario's Family Law Reform Act: how it works, what it means," *Perception*, 2:26-9, Jan.-Feb. 1979.

4123. Groffier, Ethel. "La réforme du régime des biens des époux en Ontario," *Revue du notariat*, 81:485-99, 1979.

4124. Holland, Winifred H. "Reform of matrimonial property law in Ontario," *Canadian Journal of Family Law*, 1:3-38, Jan. 1978.

4125. Hughes, Patricia. "The radical/reactionary duality of the Ontario Family Law Reform Act," *Reports of Family Law*, 2nd ser., 27:40-60, 1982.

4126. Jacobson, Peter M. "Recent proposals for reform of family property law in the common law provinces," *McGill Law Journal*, 21:556-88, Winter 1975.

4127. McLeod, James G. "Note on division of non-family assets," *Reports of Family Law*, 2nd ser., 21:439-59, 1981.

4128. McMurtry, R. Roy. "Family law reform in Ontario," *Law Society Gazette*, 10:145-53, 1976.

4129. Monopoli, William. "Family law reform 'bonanza for lawyers'," *Financial Post*, 72:1, 4, May 20, 1978.

4130. Newcombe, Ian P. "Partition actions between spouses in Ontario," *Reports of Family Law*, 28:129-71, 1977.

4131. Ontario Status of Women Council. *Brief to Justice Committee re Bill 140*. [Toronto], 1976. 14p.

4132. Ontario. Law Reform Commission. *Report on family law. Part II, marriage*. Toronto: Ontario. Dept. of Justice, 1970. 64p.

4133. _____. *Report on family law. Part IV, family property law*. Toronto: Ontario. Ministry of the Attorney General, 1974. 219p.

4134. Ontario. Secretariat for Social Development. *"Fair share"*. *Ontario Women's Conference on Family Property Law*. [Toronto], 1974. 47p. (Profile 75-0807)

4135. Rocchi, Rosanne. *Understanding family law reform in Ontario*. Toronto: Coles, 1979. 141p.

4136. Smookler, Kenneth. "In Ontario, beware - you can be hooked without tieing the knot," *Marketing*, 83:18-19, June 12, 1978.

4137. Teasdale, Philip. "Pause for thought on marriage law [Ontario]," *Financial Post*, 70:3, Dec. 18, 1976.

4138. Tennenhouse, Carol. "An examination of section 4 of the (Ontario) Family Law Reform Act, 1978," *Ottawa Law Review*, 11:371-90, 1979.

4139. _____. "An examination of section 4 of the (Ontario) Family Law Reform Act, 1978," *Reports of Family Law*, 2nd ser., 13:251-75, 1980.

MARRIAGE AND MARRIAGE PROPERTY LAW - QUEBEC

4140. Aubry, Jean Pierre. "Ventes et donations entrevifs entre époux," *Revue du notariat*, 79:328-34, 1977.

4141. Auger, Jacques. "La mutabilité du régime matrimonial et la révocabilité des donations par contrat de mariage," *Revue du notariat*, 81:41-8, 1978.

4142. Belanger, A. "La capacité juridique de la femme mariée: le bill 16," *Relations*, no. 292:112-13, avr.; no. 293:146-7, mai; no. 294:173-5, juin 1965.

4143. Bergeron, Jean Guy. "Le praticien et certains aspects du changement conventionnel ou judiciaire d'un régime matrimonial pendant le mariage," *Revue du notariat*, 79:177-201, 1976.

4144. Bisson, Alain-F. et Francois Héleine. "Chronique de droit familial," *Revue générale de droit*, 5(2):333-82, 1974.

4145. Brierley, J. E. C. "Husband and wife in the law of Quebec: a 1970 conspectus," *Canadian Family Law*, 1972, pp.795-844.

4146. _____. "Recent reforms in Quebec matrimonial property law," *Reports of Family Law*, 2:418-28, 1971.

4147. Caparros, Ernest. "La détermination conventionnelle de la contribution des époux aux besoins de la famille," *Cahiers de droit*, 17:603-32, 1976.

4148. _____. *Les lignes de force de l'évolution des régimes matrimoniaux en droits comparé et québécois*. Montréal: Presses de l'Université de Montréal, 1975. 370p.

4149. _____. *Les régimes matrimoniaux au Québec*. 2e éd. Montréal: Wilson & Lafleur / Sorej, 1981. 295p.

4150. Charron, Camille. "Le conjoint survivant et la succession légitime en droit québécois," *Revue de droit*, 8(2):197-336, 1977.

4151. Ciotola, Pierre. "Les conventions matrimoniales au lendemain de la réforme des régimes matrimoniaux," *Cours de perfectionnement du notariat*, 1976, pp.157-90.

4152. Comtois, Roger. "La liquidation de la communauté de meubles et acquêts," *Revue du notariat*, 83:419-43, 1981.

4153. _____. "La liquidation de la séparation de biens," *Revue du notariat*, 84:34-48, 1981.

4154. _____. "La liquidation et le partage de la société d'acquêts," *Revue du notariat*, 83:519-601, 1981.

4155. _____. "Le changement de régime matrimonial et l'intérêt de la famille," *La Revue juridique Thémis*, 15:9-28, 1980-81.

4156. _____. "Le rapport de praticien," *Revue du notariat*, 84:170-77, 1981.

4157. _____. "Les causes de dissolution du régime matrimonial et leurs particularités," *Revue du notariat*, 83:312-48, 1981.

4158. _____. "Les époux communs en biens depuis Le bill 16," dans Germain Brière et autres, *Lois nouvelles*. Montréal: Presses de l'Université de Montréal, 1965, pp.31-50.

4159. _____. "L'interprétation judiciaire de l'article 208 du Code civil," *Revue du notariat*, 80:309-24, 1978.

4160. Crépeau, Paul-A. "Le droit familial du Québec: réalités nouvelles et perspectives d'avenir," *Canadian Bar Review*, 51:169-79, May 1973.

4161. Cuddihy, Margaret. "L'application des lois fiscales aux régimes matrimoniaux," *Revue du notariat*, 82:241-71, 382-426, 1980.

4162. de Mestier du Bourg, Hubert J. M. "Etude comparative des causes et les effets du divorce en droit canadien." DCL thèse, McGill University, 1974. 515p. (Can. theses, no.20773)

4163. Dionne, Hélène. *Les contrats de mariage à Québec (1790-1812)*. National Museum of Man. Mercury series / History Division. Paper, no. 29. Ottawa: National Museums of Canada, 1980. 174p.

4164. Fortin-Houle, Christiane et M. Roy. "L'incidence de la nouvelle loi sur les assurances sur les régimes matrimoniaux," *Cahiers de droit*, 19:431-46, 1978.

4165. Gauthier, G. "Les principes fondamentaux de la réforme des régimes matrimoniaux au Québec — Bill 10," *Canadian Banker*, 77:11-12, 14, Sept.-Oct. 1970.

4166. Goldman, N. P. "How marriage contracts 'set regime' in Quebec," *Financial Post*, 64:13, July 4, 1970.

4167. Groffier, E. "La qualification du régime des biens des époux en droit international privé québécois," *McGill Law Journal*, 22(4):658-65, 1976.

4168. Groffier, Ethel. "Le conjoint survivant dans le projet de Code civil," *Revue du notariat*, 81:117-30, 1978.

4169. _____. "Les droits et les obligations des époux: les régimes matrimoniaux," *Cahiers de droit*, 22:309-23, 1981.

4170. _____. "L'influence de la volonté des époux sur leur régime matrimonial," *Revue de droit*, 7(2):291-318, 1977.

4171. Héleine, François. "Nouveaux propos autour des conflits entre mariage et concubinage: des solutions réalisant un heureux équilibre entre l'économique et le moral," *Revue du Barreau*, 40:463-82, 1980.

4172. Légaré, Michel. "De la rétroactivité ou de la non-rétroactivité du changement de régime matrimonial," *Revue du notariat*, 78:155-60, 1975.

4173. _____. "Institution contractuelle irrévocable et mutation de régime matrimonial," *Revue du notariat*, 79:117-24, 1976.

4174. _____. "Le changement de régime matrimonial: aspects légaux et aspects pratiques," *Revue du notariat*, 80:253-71, 1978.

4175. "Le mariage civil au Québec," *Relations*, no. 314:62-3, mars 1967.

4176. "Le mariage civil du Québec," *Relations*, no. 337:100-1, avr. 1969.

4177. *Les régimes matrimoniaux et le partage dans la séparation et le divorce*. Montréal: Barreau du Québec, 1976. 122p.

4178. Pineau, Jean. *Les régimes matrimoniaux: notions élémentaires*. 2ème éd. Montréal, Qué.: Éditions Thémis, 1976. 149p.

4179. _____. *Mariage, séparation, divorce: l'état du droit au Québec*. Montréal: Presses de l'Université de Montréal, 1976. 289p.

4180. Plamondon, Luc. "A propos de l'article 184 du Code civil," *Revue du notariat*, 82:109-10, 1979.

4181. Québec. Ministère de la justice. Service d'information. *Les régimes matrimoniaux*. [Québec, 1973]. 17p. English edition: *Matrimonial regimes*.

4182. Robinson, Ann. "L'incidence des privilèges et des hypothèques sur le régime légal de la société d'acquêts," *Cahiers de droit*, 22:211-70, 1981.

4183. Ste-Marie, Jean. "Les effets du divorce et de la séparation de corps sur les clauses usuelles des contrats de mariage," *Revue du notariat*, 84:3-33, 1981.

4184. Tétreault, Jean Marie. "Les changements de régimes matrimoniaux," *Cours de perfectionnement du notariat*, 1:205-23, 1975.

4185. Waters, Donovan. "Matrimonial property entitlements and the Quebec conflicts of law," *McGill Law Journal*, 22(2):315-20, 1976.

MARRIAGE AND MARRIAGE PROPERTY LAW - SASKATCHEWAN

4186. Cooper, Ken. "Matrimonial property law in Saskatchewan; the embarrassment of Rathwell," *Saskatchewan Law Review*, 40:185-216, 1976.

4187. "Divorced farm woman [Rathwell] awarded half property," *Free Press Report on Farming*, 98:19, Feb. 1, 1978.

4188. Hewitt, Ron W. "Section 22: The Married Women's Property Act," *Saskatchewan Law Review*, 42:260-73, 1978.

4189. _____. "Section 2: The Married Persons Property Act: an update," *Saskatchewan Law Review*, 43:193-209, 1979.

4190. National Farmers Union. *Submission to the Attorney General of the Province of Saskatchewan on the subject of matrimonial property*. Regina, Sask., 1978. 12p.

4191. Saskatchewan. Law Reform Commission. *Division of matrimonial property: problems within the present law*. First mini-working paper. Saskatoon, Sask., 1974. 23p. (Profile 74-0563)

4192. _____. *Division of matrimonial property: possible solutions to problems within the present law*. Second mini-working paper. Saskatoon, Sask., 1974. 30p. (Profile 74-0714)

4193. _____. *Division of matrimonial property: tentative proposals for reform of matrimonial property law*. Third working paper. Saskatoon, Sask., 1974. 45p. (Profile 74-0714)

4194. _____. *Proposals for a Saskatchewan Matrimonial Homes Act*. Report to the Attorney General. Saskatoon, 1976. 231p. (Profile 76-0828)

4195. _____. *Tentative proposals for an equality of status of married persons act*. Saskatoon, 1981. 68p. (Microlog 82-0297)

4196. "The law as male chauvinist pig," *Time. Can. ed.*, 103:6-8, March 25, 1974.

4197. University of Saskatchewan. Saskatoon Women and Law Committee. *Marriage manual*. Indian Law Series for Women. Saskatoon, [1977?] 11p.

4198. Walen, Gregory G. "Tax implications of Saskatchewan Matrimonial Property Act," *Saskatchewan Law Review*, 45:121-36, 1981.

MARRIED WOMEN - EMPLOYMENT

4199. Allingham, John D. and Byron G. Spence. *Women who work: pt.2. Married women in the labour force: the influence of age, education, childbearing status and residence*. Special labour force studies, Ser. B, no. 2. Ottawa: Dominion Bureau of Statistics, 1968. 21p.

4200. Anderson, D. "How business sees us: witless wives," *Chatelaine*, 43:1, Mar. 1970.

4201. _____. "Men stay home while wives work?" *Chatelaine*, 42:1, Feb. 1969.

4202. _____. "Women, work and husbands," *Chatelaine*, 42:1, Aug. 1969.

4203. Anderson, Patricia. "Business must adjust to needs of changing work force," *Financial Post*, 75:25-6, Apr. 4, 1981.

4204. Apostle, Richard and Don Clairmont. "Income dynamics in the marginal work world," *Atlantis*, 6:47-61, Spring 1981.

4205. Association des femmes diplômées des universités. *La femme mariée face aux études et au travail*. Royal Commission on the Status of Women in Canada. Brief no. 349. Montreal, 1968. 108p.

4206. Bianchi, Maria Teresa Albina. "Causes and consequences of women's working status." MA thesis, Dalhousie University, 1972. 57p. (Can. theses, no.12278)

4207. Bianchi, Maria T. "Correlation of wife's working status," in Satadal Dasgupta, ed., *Structure and change in Atlantic Canada*. PEI community studies report, no. 2. Charlottetown, P.E.I.: University of Prince Edward Island. Dept. of Sociology and Anthropology, 1975, pp.196-205.

4208. Bradbury, Bettina. "The family economy and work in an industrializing city: Montreal in the 1870s," *Canadian Historical Association. Historical Papers*, 1979, pp.71-96.

4209. Canada. Dept. of Labour. Women's Bureau. *Report of a consultation on the employment of women with family responsibilities, February 17, 1965*. Ottawa, 1965. 42p.

4210. _____. "Resolving conflict between employment and family responsibilities: a framework for discussion," in *Sexual equality in the workplace*. Ottawa: Canada. Dept. of Labour. Women's Bureau, 1982, pp.123-38.

4211. Carisse, Colette. "Life plans of innovative women: a strategy for living the feminine role," in Lyle E. Larson, comp., *The Canadian family in comparative perspective*. Scarborough, Ont.: Prentice-Hall, 1976, pp.379-94.

4212. Chappell, Neena L. "Fallacies about women in paid labour," *Atlantis*, 6:18-24, Fall 1980.

4213. Clark, Susan and Andrew S. Harvey. "The sexual division of labour: the use of time," *Atlantis*, 2:46-66, Autumn 1976.

4214. Connelly, M. Patricia. "Canadian women as a reserve army of labour." PhD diss., University of Toronto, 1976. 169p. (Can. theses, no.30337)

4215. _____. "Female labour force participation: choice or necessity," *Atlantis*, 3:40-53, Spring 1978, Part I.

4216. Connelly, Patricia. "The economic context of women's labour force participation in Canada," in John Allan Fry, ed., *Economy, class and social reality: issues in contemporary Canadian society*. Toronto: Butterworths, 1979, pp.206-23.

4217. "Consultation on the employment of women with family responsibilities," *Labour Gazette*, 65:210, 286, Mar. 1965.

4218. "Corporate couples: when it's good it's very good and when it's bad it's horrid," *Financial Times*, 66:21, Apr. 17, 1978.

4219. Cumming, Elaine and others. "Suicide as an index of role strain among employed and not employed married women in British Columbia," *Canadian Review of Sociology and Anthropology*, 12:462-70, Nov. 1975.

4220. Demmler-Kane, Jean. "Multiple migration and the social participation of married women." PhD diss., McMaster University, 1980. 291p. (Can. theses, no.50807)

4221. Derow, Ellan Odiorne. "Married women's employment and domestic labour." PhD diss., University of Toronto, 1977. 474p. (Can. theses, no.36631)

4222. Dreskin, Nathan. "Does it pay a wife to work?" *Reader's Digest (Canada)*, 111:202, 204+, Nov. 1977.

4223. Duvall, Donna. "Women's employment status and mental health." MA thesis, Carleton University, 1980. 148p. (Can. theses, no.49490)

4224. Farid, Z. and Kuyek, J. "Who speaks for working-class women?" *Canadian Dimension*, 10:80-2, June 1975.

4225. Ferguson, Mary Louise. "The role participation and life satisfaction of married women in a rural Ontario community." MSc thesis, University of Guelph, 1981. 146p. (Can. theses, no.52483)

4226. Finlayson, Judith. "Loving and working together," *Homemaker's Magazine*, 13:9-10, 12+, May 1978.

4227. Fox, Bonnie. "The female reserve army of labour: the argument and some pertinent findings," *Atlantis*, 7:45-56, Fall 1981.

4228. _____. "Women's domestic labour and their involvement in wage work: twentieth-century changes in the reproduction of daily life." PhD diss., University of Alberta, 1980. 514p. (Can. theses, no.48944)

4229. Froggatt, Marilyn and Lorraine Hunter. *Pricetag: Canadian women and the stress of success*. Don Mills, Ont.: Nelson Canada, 1980. 198p.

4230. Geoffroy, Renée and Paule Sainte-Marie. *Attitude of union workers to women in industry*. Royal Commission on the Status of Women in Canada. Study no. 9. Ottawa, 1971. 137p.

4231. Gesner, C. "Good morning, Mrs. Smith!" *Atlantic Advocate*, 58:52-3, Jan. 1968.

4232. Gunderson, Morley. "Logit estimates of labour force participation based on census cross-tabulations," *Canadian Journal of Economics*, 10:453-62, Aug. 1977.

4233. Gwyn, Sandra. "The flowering of the two-career marriage," *Saturday Night*, 94:24-9, June 1979.

4234. Héleine, François. "Le droit au travail de la femme mariée ou l'histoire d'une accession à l'indépendance," *Revue générale de droit*, 4:154-79, 1973.

4235. _____. "Le droit au travail de la femme mariée ou l'histoire d'une accession à l'indépendance, pt. II," *Revue générale de droit*, 5(2):298-329, 1974.

4236. "Job and family: measures to help women fulfil a dual role," *Labour Gazette*, 65:1031-4, Nov. 1965.

4237. "Job and family: women in a dual role," *Labour Gazette*, 65:1031-4, Nov. 1965.

4238. Joyce, Libby. "A male chauvinist cure for unemployment: fire the women and send them back home," *Canadian Business*, 51:140, Oct. 1978.

4239. Kehoe, Mary. "Married women in the job market," *Canadian Labour*, 17:7-8, May 1972.

4240. Kieran, Sheila. *The non-deductible woman: a handbook for working wives and mothers*. Toronto: MacMillan, 1970. 107p.

4241. Lachance, Micheline. "Carrière ou bébé, par quoi commencer?" *L'Actualité*, 4:36-8, 10 [ ] [ ] 1979]

4242. Lapierre-Adamcyk, Evelyne. "Activité féminine et fécondité: une enquête au Québec (1971)," *Population*, 33:609-32, mai-juin 1978.

4243. Laws, Margaret. "Coming to grips with superwoman," *Financial Post*, 72:22, June 24, 1978.

4244. Leginsky, Patricia Anne. "Problem solving resources for dual career couples." MSc thesis, University of Alberta, 1980. 163p. (Can. theses, no.44768)

4245. Lowe, Graham S. and Harvey Krahn. *Why wives work: the relative effects of situational and attitudinal factors*. Edmonton area series report, no. 21. Edmonton, Alta.: University of Alberta. Population Research Laboratory / Dept. of Sociology, 1981. 33p.

4246. Lurie, Christine. "Association between marital adjustment and the wife's employment in her profession." MSc thesis, University of Calgary, 1974. 49p. (Can. theses, no.21306)

4247. Luxton, Meg. "Taking on the double day: housewives as a reserve army of labour," *Atlantis*, 7:12-22, Fall 1981.

4248. "Married women in the labour force," *Labour Gazette*, 69:467, Aug. 1969.

4249. Maynard, Fredelle. "New norm: the two-income couple: double the pleasure or double the stress?" *Chatelaine*, 54:39-41, 64+ , June 1981.

4250. McFarlane, Bruce A. "Married life and adaptations to a professional role: married women dentists in Canada," in S. Parvez Wakil, ed., *Marriage, family and society: Canadian perspectives*. Toronto: Butterworth and Co., 1975, pp.359-65.

4251. McIntyre, Margaret R., Ina Graham and Matti Saari. "Anxiety and satisfaction of working vs non-working married women in a northern Ontario community," *Laurentian University Review*, 14:54-61, Feb. 1982.

4252. Meissner, Martin. "No exit for wives: sexual division of labour and the cumulation of household demands," *Canadian Review of Sociology and Anthropology*, 12:424-39, Nov. 1975.

4253. "More married women in the labour force," *Labour Gazette*, 67:685, Nov. 1967.

4254. Nakamura, Alice and Masao Nakamura. "A comparison of the labor force behavior of married women in the U.S. and Canada, with special attention to the impact of income taxes," *Econometrica*, 49:451-89, Mar. 1981.

4255. _____. "Part-time and full-time work behaviour of married women: a model with a doubly truncated dependent variable," *Canadian Journal of Economics*, 15:229-57, May 1983.

4256. Nakamura, Alice and others. *Employment and earnings of married females*. 1971 Census of Canada. Census analytical study. Ottawa: Statistics Canada, 1979. 168p. (Cat. no. 99-760E)

4257. Northcott, Herbert C. *Women, work and health*. Edmonton area series, no. 12. Edmonton: University of Alberta. Dept. of Sociology. Population Research Laboratory, 1979. 13p. (Microlog 80-1490)

4258. _____. "Women, work, and health," *Pacific Sociological Review*, 23:393-404, Oct. 1980.

4259. Ostry, Sylvia. "Labor force participation and childbearing status," in Betty MacLeod, ed., *Demography and educational planning: papers from a conference on implications of demographic factors for educational planning and research*. Toronto: Ontario Institute for Studies in Education, 1970, pp.143-56.

4260. Pool, D. Ian. "Changes in Canadian female labour force participation, and some possible implications for conjugal power," *Journal of Comparative Family Studies*, 9:41-52, Spring 1978.

4261. Ray, Ratna. "Problems of employees with family responsibilities and implications for employers," in Canadian Federation of Business and Professional Women's Clubs, *A collection of papers delivered at the National Conference: Women & Work in the 80's: a Decade of Change*. Ottawa: The Federation, 1981, pp.35-49.

4262. Ribeyron, Marie-Thérèse. "Les amoureux du travail conjugal," *L'Actualité*, 5:46-9, août 1980.

4263. Ross, Aileen D. "Some comments on the home roles of businesswomen in India, Australia and Canada," *Journal of Comparative Family Studies*, 8:327-40, Autumn 1977.

4264. Rosser, M. J. *Married women working part-time in Canada*. Working paper, no. 80-19. Hamilton, Ont.: McMaster University. Dept. of Economics, 1980. 17p.

4265. Schlesinger, B. "Careers," *Chatelaine*, 43:16, Mar. 1970.

4266. _____. "Family patterns are changing with the times," *Canadian Banker & ICB Review*, 82:40-4, May-June, 1975.

4267. Schroter, Candice. "A comparative study of informal social support among employed and non-employed married women." MA thesis, University of Guelph, 1978. 129p. (Can. theses, no.37457)

4268. Sheppard, Mary. "Profiting from equal partnership: demand for skilled professionals and career-minded women is promoting corporate couples," *Maclean's*, 94:50, May 11, 1981.

4269. Skoulas, Nicholas. "Determinants of the participation rate of married women in the Canadian labour force: an econometric analysis." PhD diss., Simon Fraser University, 1973. 162p. (Can. theses, no.15489)

4270. _____. *Determinants of the participation rate of married women in the Canadian labour force: an econometric analysis*. Ottawa: Statistics Canada, 1974. 126p. (Cat. no.71-522)

4271. Spencer, B. G. and D. C. Featherstone. "Why married women are in the labour force," *Canadian Statistical Review*, 45:4-5, 104-5, Apr. 1970.

4272. Spencer, Byron. "Determinants of the labour force participation of married women: a micro-study of Toronto households," *Canadian Journal of Economics*, 6:222-38, May 1973.

4273. Spencer, Byron and Dennis Featherstone. *Married female labour force participation: a micro-study*. Special labour force studies, Ser. B, no. 4. Ottawa: Statistics Canada, 1970. 102p.

4274. _____. "Married women in Canada's labour force," in S. Parvez Wakil, ed., *Marriage, family and society: Canadian perspectives*. Toronto: Butterworth and Company, 1975, pp.341-58.

4275. Stirling, Robert M. *Effect of wife's employment on family relations*. Report for the Royal Commission on the Status of Women in Canada. Calgary, 1968. 56p.

4276. Swan, H. F. "Housewives - an overlooked source of senior executives for government?" *Optimum*, 3(4):19-25, 1974.

4277. Usher, Susan. "Self-esteem in the mature married woman as a function of working status and feminist attitudes." PhD diss., York University, 1977. 141,xliip. (Can. theses, no.33665)

4278. Vincent, Andrea L. and Patricia A. Cox. *Career and family: yours*. Toronto: Career and Family Publications, 1979. 206p.

4279. Wachowich, Elizabeth Louise. "Role competence and marital satisfaction of dual-career couples: a replication study." MSc thesis, University of Alberta, 1979. 151p. (Can. theses, no.40523)

4280. Walsh, William D. "A time series analysis of female labour force participation rates disaggregated by marital status," *Relations industrielles*, 37(2):367-84, 1982; correction, 37(3):703, 1982.

4281. Weir, Tamara and Ronald J. Burke. "Two people, two careers, and *one* relationship! Making it work," *Business Quarterly*, 44:47-53, Spring 1979.

4282. Whittingham, Frank. "Additional and discouraged workers among married women in Canada." PhD diss., Queen's University, 1971. 149p. (Can. theses, no.10681)

4283. Wilson, S. J. *Women, the family and the economy*. Toronto: McGraw-Hill Ryerson, 1982. 176p.

MARRIED WOMEN - LEGAL STATUS,LAWS,ETC.

4284. Auger, Jacques. "La condition juridique de la femme mariée en droit coutumier," *Revue de droit*, 2:99-113, 1971.

4285. Association féminine d'éducation et d'action sociale. *Comment conjuguer amour et sécurité*. Montréal, 1903. 36p.

4286. Bailey, Stella J. "A married woman's right of action for loss of consortium in Alberta," *Alberta Law Review*, 17(3):513-31, 1979.

4287. Baudouin, Jean-Louis. "Examen critique de la réforme sur la capacité de la femme mariée québecoise," *Canadian Bar Review*, 43:393-413, Sept. 1965.

4288. Boucher, Jacques et André Morel, eds. *Livre du centenaire du Code civil*. Vol. 1: *Le droit dans la vie familiale*. Montréal: Presses de l'Université de Montréal, 1970. 302p.

4289. Bourne, Paula. "Economics of marriage: the case of Irene Murdoch," in her, *Women in Canadian society*. Toronto: Ontario Institute for Studies in Education, 1976, pp.1-24.

4290. Boyle, Christine. "Married women - beyond the pale of the law of rape," *Windsor Yearbook of Access to Justice*, 1:192-213, 1981.

4291. "Canadian notes: Mrs. Fiedler's rights," *Time. Can. ed.*, 104:8, July 29, 1974.

4292. Caparros, Ernest. *Les lignes de force de l'évolution des régimes matrimoniaux en droits comparé et québécois*. Montréal: Presses de l'Université de Montréal, 1975. 370p.

4293. Dionne-Bourassa, L. "La femme mariée: évolution récente de sa condition en droit et en fait au Canada," *Colloque international du droit comparé*, 9:273-92, 1971.

4294. Freedman, Frances Schanfield. "The juridical capacity of the married woman in Quebec: in relation to partnership of acquests and recent amendments to the Civil Code," *McGill Law Journal*, 21:518-55, Winter 1975.

4295. "Justice: giving and taking away [Mrs. Fiedler's judgement overruled]," *Time. Can. ed.*, 105:9-10, Mar. 10, 1975.

4296. "La femme et le Code civil: fondements et évolution," *Possibles*, 4:33-9, automne 1979.

4297. McCaughan, Margaret M. *The legal status of married women in Canada*. Carswell's family law series. Toronto: Carswell, 1977. 210p.

4298. Menzies, S. June. "The uncounted hours: the perception of women in policy formulation," *McGill Law Journal*, 21:615-30, Winter 1975.

4299. Midgley, Margaret Morrison. "Legal status of married women in England and Canada." LLM thesis, University of Alberta, 1976. 408p. (Can. theses, no.27706)

4300. Ouellette, Monique. "Droit civil: chroniques régulières," *Revue du Barreau*, 41:279-82, 483-5, 1981.

4301. Réseau d'action et d'information pour les femmes. *Revenu garanti: mémoire pour une formule n'excluant pas les femmes mariées*. Ste-Foy, Québec: Réseau d'action et d'information pour les femmes, 1976. 20p.

4302. Rockett, Eve. "The human stories behind the Irene Murdoch / Helen Rathwell cases," *Chatelaine*, 47:43, 91-4, Sept. 1974.

4303. Rozovsky, Lorne E. "A husband's consent to his wife's abortion," *Dimensions in Health Service*, 57:34, 36, Jan. 1980.

4304. _____. "Can a married women give valid consent?" *Dimensions in Health Service*, 53:8-9, Oct. 1976.

4305. Saskatchewan. Dept. of Labour. Women's Division. *The discarding of Mrs. Hill*. Regina, [1977]. 11p.
    Reprint of article from *Ladies' Home Journal*, Feb. 1976. Includes addendum, Mrs. Hill in Canada.

4306. Saskatchewen. Law Reform Commission. *Tentative proposals for an Equality of Status of Married Persons Act*. Saskatoon, 1981. 68p. (Microlog 82-0297)

4307. Secord, R. C. "Competence and compellability of wives at common law," *Alberta Law Review*, 17(2):313-7, 1979.

4308. "The law as male chauvinist pig," *Time. Can. ed.*, 103:6-8, Mar. 25, 1974.

MASS MEDIA

4309. "ACTRA women on offensive in film, television and radio, watching for bias in content, jobs [symposium]," *Cinema Canada*, no. 92:3, 7, Jan. 1983.

4310. Cadieux, Rita. *The representation of women and the various minorities in broadcasting: a question of balance?* [Ottawa]: Canadian Radio-television and Telecommunications Commission. Research Directorate, 1980. [28]p. and app.
    Prepared for a seminar organized by CRTC on Balance in Broadcasting, Jan. 16-17, 1981, Hull, Quebec.

4311. Canada. Dept. of National Health and Welfare. Office of the Minister of National Health and Welfare and Minister Responsible for the Status of Women. *The media mirage*. An address by the Honourable Marc Lalonde to the Ottawa Women's Canadian Club. Ottawa, 1975. 17p.

4312. Canadian Advisory Council on the Status of Women. *The Status of women and the CBC*. Brief to the Canadian Radio-Television and Telecommunications Commission. Ottawa, 1978. 30p.

4313. Canadian Radio-Television and Telecommunications Commission. *Images of women; report of the Task Force on Sex-Role Stereotyping in the Broadcast Media*. [Ottawa], 1982. 189p.

4314. Carisse, C. *The feminine image: a study of the female subject in the news and of the female character in periodical advertising*. Report to the Royal Commission on the Status of Women in Canada. n.p., 1968. vp.

4315. Geoffroy, Nicole et Geneviève Dubuc. *Les femmes et les médias*. [Québec]:Conseil du statut de la femme. Service de l'information, 1980. 55p.

4316. Malloch, Kati. *Women in the Canadian media*. Basic issues in Canadian mass communication. [Montreal: McGill University, 1973?] 47p.

4317. McDonald, Lynn. "The silenced majority: women and Canadian broadcasting; La majorité silencieuse: les femmes et Radio-Canada," *Status of Women News / Statut: bulletin de la femme*, 6:2-3, 29 [English]; 2-4, [French], Spring 1980.

4318. Preston, Pat. "'Anchorpersons' aren't enough: how the media treat women and what can be done about it," *Perception*, 3:14-16, 18, May-June 1980.

4319. Purdy, Kris. "Fair coverage," *Branching Out*, 5(4): 6-9, 1978.

4320. Robinson, Gertrude Joch. "The future of women in the Canadian media," *McGill Journal of Education*, 12:124-32, Spring 1977.

4321. _____. "Women, media access and social control," in Epstein, Laurily Keir, ed., *Women and the news*. New York: Hastings House Publishers, 1978, pp.87-108.

4322. Shapka, Muriel. *Feminizing influence via the mass media*. Royal Commission on the Status of Women in Canada. Brief no. 60. Los Angeles, Calif., 1968. 7p.

4323. Toeplitz, Jerzy. "Inquiry on participation of women in radio, television and film in four countries (Australia, Canada, United Kingdom and United States)," in *Women in the media*. Paris: UNESCO, 1980, pp.15-80.

4324. Zemel, Carol. "Women and video: an introduction to the community of video," *ArtsCanada*, 30:30-40, Oct. 1973.

MASS MEDIA - BIBLIOGRAPHY

4325. Pulyk, Marcia, comp. *A bibliography of selected articles on women in the mass media*. Ottawa: Canadian Radio-Television Commission. Library, 1975. 43p.

4326. _____. *Bibliography of selected articles on women in the mass media: an update*. Ottawa: Canadian Radio-Television Commission, 1977. [62]p.

MATERNITY AND PARENTAL LEAVE

4327. Bagnall, James and Patricia Anderson. "Union interest in maternity leave gathers steam," *Financial Post*, 75:1-2, July 11, 1981.

4328. Bussy, P. J. "Injustice envers les mères adoptives," *Perception*, 3:37-8, Jan.-Feb. 1980.

4329. Cadwell, Dorothy. "The development of maternity leave in the Civil Service of Canada," in *Report of a consultation on the employment of women with family responsibilities*. Ottawa: Canada. Dept. of Labour. Women's Bureau, 1965, pp.19-22.

4330. Canada. Advisory Council on the Status of Women. *Maternity leave and benefits; a study of federal laws and recent amendments...*, by Elsie Robindaine-Saumure. Ottawa, 1976. 47p.

4331. _____. *Maternity leave, benefits and related issues; ACSW recommendations*. Ottawa, 1976. 5p.

4332. _____. The price of maternity. [*Le coût de la maternité*].The person papers. Ottawa, 1977. 16, 16p.

4333. Canada. Dept. of Labour. Women's Bureau and Economics and Research Branch. *Maternity leave policies*. Ottawa, 1969. 137p.

4334. Canada. Dept. of Labour. Women's Bureau. *Bird's eye view of maternity leave provisions in Canada*. Ottawa, 1981. 10p.

4335. _____. *Maternity and child care leave in Canada*. Ottawa, 1983. 44p.

4336. Canada. Intergovernmental Committee on Women in Employment and Saskatchewan. Dept. of Labour. Women's Division. *Maternity leave in Canada*. [Ottawa]: Canada. Dept. of Labour. Women's Bureau, 1980. 53p.

4337. Canadian Union of Public Employees. Research Dept. *Parental leave and collective bargaining*. Prepared for the Saskatchewan Division Conference on Benefits. [Ottawa], 1981. 56, [11]p.

4338. Confédération des syndicats nationaux. *Travailler et avoir des enfants en santé: le retrait préventif des femmes enceintes ou qui allaitent*. Montréal, 1982. 40p.

4339. Dranoff, Linda Silver. "Ask a lawyer," *Chatelaine*, 52:22, July 1979.

4340. Edmonton Social Planning Council. *Maternity leave in Alberta*. Edmonton: Options for Women, 1975. 9p.

4341. Federation of Women Teachers' Associations of Ontario. *Congé de maternité et congé d'adoption*. Traduit et adapté par l'Association des enseignants franco-ontariens. Toronto, 1978. 28p.

4342. IR Research Services and Labour Canada. *Maternity and related leave*. Collective agreement series, no. 4. Kingston, Ont.: IR Research Publications, 1980. 27p.

4343. Kome, Penney. "Maternity pay?" *Homemaker's Magazine*, 16:92J, May 1981.

4344. "Le bon sens n'est pas la loi," *Commerce*, 82:148, 150, Sept. 1980.

4345. Lepage, Francine et Marie Lavigne. *Les travailleuses face à la maternité*. Québec: Conseil du statut de la femme, 1979. 42p.

4346. List, Wilfred. "An expectant contractual fact of life," *Industrial Management*, Feb. 1982, p.17.

4347. MacFarlane, Stephen J. "Maternity leave: a shelter or sword?" *Health Care*, 22:16, June 1980.

4348. "Maternity leave," *Chatelaine*, 43:10, Feb. 1970.

4349. "Maternity leave benefits in Canada," *Labour Gazette*, 69:466, Aug. 1969.

4350. "Maternity protection for women workers," *Labour Gazette*, 67:299-300, May 1967.

4351. "Maternity protection for working mothers," *Labour Gazette*, 67:351, June 1967.

4352. Ontario. Ministry of Labour. Women Crown Employees Office. *Comparative survey of pregnancy and maternity policies in the provincial governments of Canada and Ontario crown agencies*. [Toronto], 1974. 54p. (Profile 76-0245)

4353. _____. *Maternity leave in the Ontario Public Service*. [Toronto], 1979. Leaflet.

4354. _____. *Summary report of maternity leave in the Ontario Public Service; survey results for 1976-77*; prepared by Dawna Burt and Sharon Peregrine. Toronto, 1978. 39p.

4355. Ontario. Ministry of Labour. Women's Bureau. *Pregnancy leave in Ontario*. Toronto, 1975. Folder.

4356. _____. *Pregnancy leave in Ontario*. Toronto, 1977. Leaflet.

4357. "OPSEU wins nation's best maternity benefits," *Ontario Labour*, Sept.-Oct. 1982, p.13.

4358. "Outgrew her uniform when pregnant, woman wins claim over forced leave," *Globe and Mail*, June 6, 1978, pp.1-2.

4359. O.E.I.C.C. Conference and Canadian Union of Public Employees. Research Dept. *Parental leave: a key bargaining demand for school board workers in Ontario*. [Ottawa], Sept. 1982. 78p.

4360. Potter, Chris. "18 months maternity leave, seniority protected, babies accommodated," *Office Equipment & Methods*, 26:22-3, May 1980.

4361. Simard, Monique et Zaida Nunez. *Pour des congés de maternité payés*. n.p.: [Confédération des syndicats nationaux], 1980. 30p.

4362. "Stewardesses fight sexism," *Canadian Dimension*, 12:10, Sept. 1977.

4363. Woodsworth, Sheila. *Maternity protection for women workers in Canada*. Ottawa: Canada. Dept. of Labour. Women's Bureau, 1967. 63p.

MATERNITY AND PARENTAL LEAVE - BIBLIOGRAPHY

4364. "Paid maternity leave: a selected bibliography," *Labour Topics (Ontario Ministry of Labour Library)*, 5(2):1-4, Feb. 1982.

MEDICAL CARE

4365. Baehre, Rainer. "Victorian psychiatry and Canadian motherhood," *Canadian Women's Studies / Les cahiers de la femme*, 2(1):44-6, 1980.

4366. Cohen, Leah and Constance Backhouse. "Women and health: the growing controversy," *Canadian Women's Studies / Les cahiers de la femme*, 1:4-10, Summer 1979.

4367. Dranoff, Linda Silver. "Ask a lawyer," *Chatelaine*, 53:14, 17, Jan. 1980.

4368. Dyck, Frank J. and others. "Effect of surveillance on the number of hysterectomies in the province of Saskatchewan," *New England Journal of Medicine*, 296:1326-9, June 9, 1977.

4369. Dyck, F. J. and others. "Are hysterectomies necessary?" *Canadian Family Physician*, 22:75-7, Oct. 1976.

4370. Mitchinson, Wendy. "Gynecological operations on the insane," *Archivaria*, 10:125-44, Summer 1980.

4371. Preston, Patricia. "Body politics: are you a casualty?" *Branching Out*, 4:36-7, Sept.-Oct. 1977.

4372. Steinhause, Sandra. "Written in anger," *Canadian Women's Studies / Les cahiers de la femme*, 1:80, Summer 1979.

4373. Talbot, Jocelyne. "Réapproprions nos corps: les femmes contre la supercherie du système médical," dans Rodrigue Bélanger et autres, eds., *Devenirs de femmes*. Cahiers de recherche éthique, no. 8. Montréal: Éditions Fides, 1981, pp.103-110.

176

4374. Vancouver Women's Health Collective. "What women want in health care," *Canadian Family Physician*, 22:21,23, Oct. 1976.

MEDICINE

4375. Amer, Sharon B. "Women in dentistry," *Canada's Health and Welfare*, 24:2-3, Mar. 1966.
4376. Blouin, Jacqueline. "MD comme dans madame," *L'Actualité*, 6:67-8, 70 sept. 1981.
4377. Buck, Ruth Matheson. *The doctor rode side-saddle*. Toronto: McClelland and Stewart, 1974. 175p.
4378. Carver, Cynthia and Susan Berlin. *Proposal for study on productivity of women doctors*. [Toronto: Ontario Status of Women Council], 1978. 8p.
4379. Colwill, Nina Lee and Noralou P. Roos. "Debunking a stereotype: the female medical student," *Sex Roles*, 4(5):717-22, 1978.
4380. Costigliola, Bozica. "Canada's women doctors: challenging medical tradition," *Perception*, 2:14-15, Mar.-Apr. 1979.
4381. Damube, Earl. "All-female obstetrics class," *Chatelaine*, 51:21, Nov. 1978.
4382. "Dental womanpower in Canada," *Labour Gazette*, 66:367, 371, July 1966.
4383. Dixon, Maureen and others. *Women in health administration in Canada*. Toronto: University of Toronto. Dept. of Health Administration, 1980. 91p. and app.
4384. Dubuc, Anne-Marie, Francine L'Heureux, Joanne Baillargeon. "Women and the profession of medical doctor; Les femmes et le métier de médecin," *Status of Women News / Statut: Bulletin de la femme*, 5:24-5, [English]; 18-19, [French], Dec. 1978.
4385. Federation of Medical Women of Canada and Other Canadian Women Physicians. *Brief no. 302 to the Royal Commission on the Status of women in Canada*. Rockliffe, Ontario, 1968. 13p.

4386. Fortier, Lise. "Interview with Dr. Lise Fortier," *Maclean's*, 89:3-4, 6, Dec. 27, 1976.
4387. Gelber, Sylva M. "Sex ghettos in the health professions," in *Women's Bureau '72*. Ottawa: Canada. Dept. of Labour. Women's Bureau, 1973, pp.13-20.
4388. Hacker, Carlotta. "Found women: Canada's first women doctors," *Chatelaine*, 47:17, July 1974.
4389. _____. *The indomitable lady doctors*. Toronto: Clarke Irwin, 1974. 259p.
4390. MacDonald, Eva Mader and Elizabeth M. Webb. "A survey of women physicians in Canada, 1883-1964," *Canadian Medical Association. Journal*, 94:1223-7, June 4, 1966.
4391. McFarlane, Bruce A. "Married life and adaptations to a professional role: married women dentists in Canada," in S. Parvez Wakil, ed., *Marriage, family and society: Canadian perspectives*. Toronto: Butterworth and Company, 1975, pp.359-65.
4392. "Medical womanpower in Canada," *Labour Gazette*, 66:735-6, Dec. 1966.
4393. Pannell, Beverly. "Rx: more women in medicine," *Canadian Women's Studies / Les cahiers de la femme*, 1:30-3, Summer 1979.
4394. "Quebec study shows women physicians have loyalties to medicine and family," *Canadian Medical Association Journal*, 113:1000, Nov. 22, 1975.
4395. Ray, Janet. *Emily Stowe*. Don Mills, Ont.: Fitzhenry and Whiteside, 1978. 63p.
4396. Rooney, Frances. "Elizabeth Bagshaw, M.D.: an interview," *Makara*, 2(3):27-30, [1977?]

4397. Smith, Elizabeth. *'A woman with a purpose': the diaries of Elizabeth Smith, 1872-1884*, edited and introduced by Veronica Strong-Boag. Toronto: University of Toronto Press, 1980. 298p.
4398. Squires, Nicole-marie. "Women have made it - more to follow," *Health Care*, 22:17-21, May 1980.
4399. Stoffman, Judy. "The first lady of birth control [Dr. Elizabeth Bagshaw]," *Weekend Magazine*, 27:8-9, Oct. 1, 1977.
4400. Strong-Boag, Veronica. "Canada's women doctors: feminism constrained," in Linda Kealey, ed., *A not unreasonable claim: women and reform in Canada, 1880s-1920s*. Toronto: Women's Press, 1979, pp.109-29.

4401. Vincent, M. O. "Female physicians as psychiatric patients," *Canadian Psychiatric Association Journal*, 21:461-5, Nov. 1976.

4402. Waxman, Sydell Blossom. "Dr. Emily Stowe: Canada's first female practitioner," *Canada West*, 10:17-23, Spring 1980.

4403. Wilson, Mary Carol. *Marion Hilliard*. Don Mills, Ont.: Fitzhenry & Whiteside, 1977. 63p.

4404. Woods, David. "Women in medicine," *Canadian Family Physician*, May 1970, p.7.

4405. Wright, Bunny. "The healthy careers of women MDs," *Maclean's*, 94:44b, 44d + , May 4, 1981.

MEN

4406. Callwood, June. "Are men obsolete?" *Chatelaine*, 47:33, 50, 52-3, Apr. 1974.

4407. Carbine, Patricia. "Male chauvinism still rampant says Carbine: excerpts from address," *Marketing*, 79:9, Oct. 21, 1974.

4408. Cossman, B. J. "Please, ladies, leave our taverns alone," *Montrealer*, [44]:22-3, Jan.-Feb. 1970.

4409. Edmonds, A. "Why one former 'gentleman' is starting men's lib," *Maclean's*, 83:24e,24g, Oct. 1970.

4410. Gingras, J. B. "Le masculinisme et la famille," *L'Action nationale*, 55:559-65, fév. 1970.

4411. Hartwick, Paul. "What's your MCQ (male chauvinism quotient)?" *Canadian Banker & ICB Review*, 83:40-2, May-June 1976.

4412. Hawley, A. *Men's and women's liberation*. Ottawa: Canadian Union of Students. Secretariat, n.d. 5p.

4413. Hildebrandt, Heather. "Sorry, sisters, women's lib only trades one tyranny for another," *Maclean's*, 84:14, Mar. 1971.

4414. Kieran, Sheila H. "Who's downgrading women? Women," *Maclean's*, 81:18-19, 40-2, Aug. 1968.

4415. Kostash, Myrna. "Rating the Chauvinists on a Richler scale," *Macleans*, 87:75, Jan. 1974.

4416. _____. "Women, groovy men and other myths of liberation," *Maclean's*, 86:84, Feb. 1973.

4417. Leacock, Stephen. "The woman question," in Alan Bowker, ed., *The social criticism of Stephen Leacock*. Toronto: University Of Toronto Press, 1973, pp.52-60.

4418. Payette, Lise. "Un nouveau cri d'alarme de Lise Payette: la société dévore les mâles: une entrevue de Gilles Constantineau," *Magazine Maclean*, 9:cover, 14-16, août 1969.

4419. Ross, A. "Natural superiority of men; with reply," *Maclean's*, 82:22-6, May; 7, July, 1969.

4420. "Scoffs at women's lib," *Atlantic Advocate*, 63:72, July 1973.

4421. Scott, Howard. "Un homme féministe," *Canadian Women's Studies / Les cahiers de la femme*, 2(1):100, 1980.

MENTAL HEALTH

4422. Cooperstock, Ruth. "Women and psychotropic drugs," in Anne MacLennan, ed., *Women: their use of alcohol and other legal drugs: a provincial consultation - 1976*. Toronto: Addiction Research Foundation of Ontario, 1976, pp.83-111.

4423. Corbeil, Christine et autres. *L'intervention féministe: l'alternative des femmes en sexisme au thérapie*. Montréal: Editions coopératives Albert Saint-Martin, 1983. 188p.

4424. Duvall, Donna. "Women's employment status and mental health." MA thesis, Carleton University, 1980. 148p. (Can. theses, no.49490)

4425. D'Arcy, Carl and Janet A. Schmitz. "Sex differences in the utilization of health services for psychiatric problems in Saskatchewan," *Canadian Journal of Psychiatry*, 24:19-27, Feb. 1979.

4426. Guyon, Louise, Roxane Simard et Louise Nadeau. *"Va te faire soigner, t'es malade!"* Montréal: Stanké, 1981. 158p.

4427. New Brunswick Association of Social Workers. *Mental health problems affecting women*. Royal Commission on the Status of Women in Canada. Brief no. 87. Saint John, N.B., 1968. 8p.

4428. Nickels, James B. and Jack Ledger. *Winter, wilderness, and womanhood: explanations or excuses for mental health problems*. Winnipeg: University of Manitoba. Center for Settlement Studies, 1976. 72p. and tables.

4429. Smith, Dorothy E. and Sara J. David, eds. *Women look at psychiatry*. Vancouver: Press Gang Pub., 1975. 199p.

4430. Stark-Adamec, Cannie. "Is there a double standard in mental health research funding as well as a double standard in mental health?" *Ontario Psychologist*, 13:5-16, July 1981.

MICROTECHNOLOGY

4431. Azer, Nadia. "Les femmes et l'informatique," *Relations*, 42:149-50, juin 1982.

4432. Brunet, Lucie. "A la merci des machines-misogynes," *Perception*, 4:21-4, mars-avr. 1981.

4433. Canadian Advisory Council on the Status of Women. *Microtechnology and employment: issues of concern to women*. [*Microtechnologie et emploi: questions d'importance pour les femmes*]. A brief to the Task Force on Micro-Electronics and Employment. Ottawa, 1982. 25, 29p. (Microlog 83-3241)

4434. Communicado Associates. *Towards the integration of women into the high technology labour force in the National Capital Region*. Series B: Changing world of work, no. 1. Ottawa: Canada. Dept. of Labour. Women's Bureau, 1982. 66p.

4435. Humphreys, Elizabeth. *Technological change and the office*. Technical study, no. 17. [Ottawa]: Canada. Task Force on Labour Market Development, 1981. 19p.

4436. Kendall, Brian. "Accession of the superbureaucracy," *Canadian Business*, 51:116-17, 119-20, 122, Apr. 1979.

4437. Levine, G. "All male clerical force may result from automation," *Labour Gazette*, 66:430, Aug. 1966.

4438. McDermott, Patricia. "The new demeaning of work," *Canadian Dimension* 15-16:34-7, Dec. 1981.

4439. Menzies, Heather. *Informatics case studies (Supplementary material to "Women and the Chip")*. Technical study, no. 23. Ottawa: Canada. Task Force on Labour Market Development, 1981. 38p.

4440. _____. *Women and the chip: case studies of the effects of informatics on employment in Canada*. Montreal: Institute for Research on Public Policy, 1981. 98p.

4441. _____. "Women and microtechnology," *Canadian Woman Studies / Les cahiers de la femme*, 3:13-17, Summer 1982.

4442. "Micro processing seen taking jobs from women," *Globe and Mail*, Mar. 31, 1981, p.B2.

4443. "Women and the automated office," *Executive*, 23:60, July 1981.

4444. "Women's traditional jobs predicted to suffer most in technological revolution," *Globe and Mail*, Jan. 17, 1981, p.B1.

4445. Zaremba, Eve. "White-collar blues," *Broadside*, 2:4, Oct.-Nov. 1980.

MICROTECHNOLOGY - BIBLIOGRAPHY

4446. Ford, John and Alan V. Miller. *Women, microelectronics and employment: a selected bibliography*. Rev. ed. Toronto: Ontario. Ministry of Labour Library, 1983. 16p.

MIDDLE AGE

4447. Abrioux, Marie-Louise. "Marital perceptions and life satisfactions of middle-aged husbands and wives." MEd thesis, University of Alberta, 1977. 193p. (Can. theses, no.34276)

4448. Amiel, Barbara. "The mature woman: a new force breaks through," *Maclean's*, 93:41-4, 46, July 7, 1980.

4449. Callwood, June. "Is there radicalization after 40?" *Maclean's*, 86:32-3, 45-6, 48, Jan. 1973.

4450. _____. "Middle-aged women: coming on like gangbusters," *Chatelaine*, 48:52-3, 91-3, 95, 97-9, Mar. 1975.

4451. Davis, Dona Lee. *Blood and nerves: an ethnographic focus on menopause*. Social and economic studies, no. 28. St. John's, Nfld.: Institute of Social and Economic Research, Queen's College, Memorial University of Newfoundland, 1983.

4452. _____. *Women's experience of menopause in a Newfoundland fishing village*. n.p., 1980. 293p.

4453. James, Judith Elaine. "The 'empty nest': an exploratory investigation of a transition within motherhood." MEd thesis, University of Alberta, 1979. 107p. (Can. theses, no.43441)

4454. Lent, Barbara Pauline. "Masculinity - femininity and self-esteem in middle-aged women as a function of age and menopausal status." MA thesis, University of Western Ontario, 1974. 85p. (Can. theses, no.23306)

4455. Snowdon, Annette. "Second life: when the turmoil of their 30s is over, many women find themselves reborn," *The Canadian*, Sept. 23, 1978, pp. 3-5.

MIGRATION

4456. Demmler-Kane, Jean. "Multiple migration and the social participation of married women." PhD diss., McMaster University, 1980. 291p. (Can. theses, no.50807)

4457. Firth, Sophia. *The urbanization of Sophia Firth*. Toronto: Peter Martin, 1974. 271p.

4458. Martin-Matthews, Anne E. "Wives' experiences of relocation: status passage and the moving career." PhD diss., McMaster University, 1980. 337p. (Can. theses, no.46914)

4459. Matthews, Anne Martin. "The Newfoundland migrant wife: a power versus powerless theory of adjustment," *Atlantis*, 2:152-66, Spring 1977, Part II.

MINING

4460. Bonn, Kasandra. "Women in non-traditional mining occupations." MBA thesis, Simon Fraser University, 1977. 64p.

4461. Bottomley, Pamela. "Women's work now includes the diamond drilling field," *Western Miner*, 50:32, June 1977.

4462. Canada. Dept. of Energy, Mines and Resources. Mineral Development Sector. *Women in mining: the progress and the problems*. Mineral policy series, mineral bulletin, MR152. Ottawa, 1976. 17p.

4463. Canada. Dept. of Manpower and Immigration. *Family life through women's eyes: final report*. n.p., [1978]. 84, [21]p.
    Report of a government sponsored project; a survey of Sudbury miners' wives.

4464. Des Rivières, Monique. *Législations canadiennes sur l'emploi féminin dans les mines*. Québec: Conseil du statut de la femme, 1975. [12]p.

4465. "Female miners," *Labour Gazette*, 74:240, Apr. 1974.

4466. Fine, Judylaine. "Go North young woman," *Chatelaine*, 49:53, 117-20, 122, Apr. 1976.

4467. Henson, Jane. "Laborer-teacher tells her tale," *Northern Miner*, 61:B5-B6, Mar. 4, 1976.

4468. "ILO convention influences provincial legislation," *Labour Gazette*, 67:350, June 1967.

4469. Richmond, J. R. "Women in field, mill, labs & offices," *Northern Miner*, 64:B5-B9, Dec. 28, 1978.

4470. Santi, Roberta. "Employment opportunities on the increase," *Northern Miner*, 61:A17-19, Nov. 27, 1975.

4471. Suzanne Veit and Associates Inc. *Women in mining: an exploratory study*. Prepared for B.C. Dept. of Economic Development, B.C. Manpower Sub-committee on North East Coal Developments. Submitted to the Coal Committee of Cabinet. [Victoria], 1976. 114p. and app. (Profile 77-0573)

4472. "Women mineworkers - c'mon mom," *Canadian Mining Journal*, 94(8):47, 1973.

MINORITIES

4473. Bearden, Jim and Linda Jean Butler. *Shadd: the life and times of Mary Shadd Cary*. Toronto: NC Press, 1977. [258]p.

4474. Braithwaite, Rella, comp. and ed. *Black women in Canada*. n.p., [1976]. 70p.

4475. D'Oyley, Enid F. and Rella Braithwaite, eds. *Women of our times*. Toronto: Canadian Negro Women's Association for the National Congress of Black Women, 1973. 40p.

4476. Denis, Ann B. "Femmes: ethnie et occupation au Québec et en Ontario, 1931-1971," *Canadian Ethnic Studies*, 13(1):75-90, 1981.

4477. Early, Mary Two Axe, Zonia Keywan and Helen Potrebenko. "Ethnicity and femininity as determinants of life experience," *Canadian Ethnic Studies*, 13(1):37-42, 1981.

4478. Gelber, Sylva M. "Injustice to one - injustice to all," in, *Women's Bureau '72*. Ottawa: Canada. Dept. of Labour. Women's Bureau, 1973, pp.29-36.

4479. Gipson, Joella H., ed. *Impetus, the black woman: proceedings of the Fourth National Congress of Black Women of Canada*. [*Nouvel essor, la femme noire: procédure du quatrième Congrès national des femmes noires du Canada*. n.p., [1977?]. 54p.

4480. Indra, Doreen M. "Multicultural women's conference," *Canadian Ethnic Studies*, 8(2):103-6, 1976.

4481. Indra, Doreen. "Invisible mosaic: women, ethnicity and the Vancouver press, 1905-1976," *Canadian Ethnic Studies*, 13(1):63-74, 1981.

4482. Juteau-Lee, Danielle and Barbara Roberts. "Ethnicity and femininity: (d') après nos expériences," *Canadian Ethnic Studies*, 13(1):1-23, 1981.

4483. Krawchuk, Peter. "Ukrainian women in early history," *Ukrainian Canadian*, Mar. 1972, pp.15-19.

4484. Maclennan, Susan J. "Hutterite women, work and assistance patterns." MA thesis, University of Calgary, 1978. 75p. (Can. theses, no.39281)

4485. "Minority women and personhood," in Canadian Research Institute for the Advancement of Women, *Women as persons*. [*La femme en tant que personne*]. Toronto: Resources for Feminist Research, 1980, pp.45-9. Proceedings of the 3rd annual meeting.

4486. Prokop, Mary. "Looking back on fifty years [Women's Branches of the Association of United Ukrainian Canadians]," *Ukrainian Canadian*, Mar. 1972, pp.7-14.

4487. Rice, Richard M. "Mothers, daughters and grand-daughters: an examination of the matrilateral bias and related variables in Jews and Icelanders in Canada." MA thesis, University of Manitoba, 1971. 119p. (Can. theses, no.10423)

4488. Sangster, Dorothy. "Sylvia & Kathy Searles—catalysts for the black community," *Chatelaine*, 52:24-5, Feb. 1979.

4489. Shack, Sybil. "Widening horizons," *School Guidance Worker*, 32:42-9, Jan.-Feb. 1977.

4490. Shaheen, Ghazala and Cecilia A. Gonzales. "Clothing practices of Pakistani women residing in Canada," *Canadian Ethnic Studies*, 13(3):120-6, 1981.

4491. Trovato, Frank. "Canadian ethnic fertility," *Sociological Focus*, 14:57-74, Jan. 1981.

4492. Verma, Ravi B. P. "Variations in family size among Canadian women by generation and ethnic group," *International Journal of Comparative Sociology*, 20:293-303, Sept.-Dec. 1979.

MISSIONARIES

4493. Fast, Vera. *Missionary on wheels: Eva Hasell and the Sunday School caravan missions*. Toronto: Anglican Book Centre, 1979. 158p.

4494. Headon, Christopher. "Women and organized religion in mid and late nineteenth century Canada," *Canadian Church Historical Society. Journal*, 20:3-18, Mar.-June 1978.

4495. Klassen, Annie. *Mountains removed*. n.p., 1976. 143p.

4496. Millar, Nancy. "She made all the difference," *United Church Observer*, new ser., 36:28-30, Feb. 1973.

4497. Mitchell, Estelle. *Le soleil brille à minuit*. Montréal: Librairie Beauchemin, 1970. 282p.

4498. Murray, Florence J. *At the foot of Dragon Hill*. New York: E. P. Dutton, 1975. 240p.

MOTHERS

4499. Carson, Susan. "A salute to stay-at-home mothers," *Chatelaine*, 54:68-9, 86+ , Apr. 1981.

4500. Carveth, W. Bruce. "Social support and stress: a study of new mothers." MA thesis, University of Guelph, 1977. 114p. (Can. theses, no.33867)

4501. Chaput, Louise. "L'adaptation chez les belles-mères: analyse de leurs représentation sociales." MA thèse, Université du Québec à Montréal, 1981. 115p. (Can. theses, no.50695)

4502. Dumais, Monique. "Jalons pour une réflexion éthique sur le modèle de la mère dans la société québécoise (1940-1970)," *Cahiers ethicologiques de l'UQUR*, 4:49-67, déc. 1981.

4503. Gerus, Claire. "Motherhood without children: some women walk out on their families. Others have them torn away." *Today*, Nov. 22, 1980, pp.7-9.

4504. Gore, Kenneth G. "Birth order and mother-child interaction in relation to achievement motivation and internal-external locus of control." MA thesis, University of Guelph, 1976. 48p. (Can. theses, no.28074)

4505. Govier, Katherine. "Older mother," *Weekend Magazine*, 29:24-6, May 12, 1979.

4506. Greenglass, Esther R. "A comparison of maternal communication style between immigrant Italian and second-generation Italian women living in Canada," *Journal of Cross-Cultural Psychology*, 3:185-92, June 1972.

4507. Haddock, J. and R. L. Rodensky. *Regent Park Demonstration Project: a descriptive research project examining the effectiveness of a program for abuse-prone mothers. Final report.* Revised. Toronto: Children's Aid Society of Metropolitan Toronto, 1980. 40p. and app.

4508. Landsberg, Michele. "Late motherhood," *Chatelaine*, 50:44-6, 119+ , Oct. 1977.

4509. LeMay, Francine. *La maternité castrée*. Montréal: Parti Pris, 1978. 155p.

4510. Luxton, Meg. "Motherwork: more than a labour of love," *Canadian Women's Studies / Les cahiers de la femme*, 2(1):31-5, 1980.
    Excerpt from *More than a labour of love*.

4511. Ribeyron, Marie-Thérèse. "La grève des ventres," *L'Actualité*, 1:60-1, 64+ , déc. 1976.

4512. Roberts, Wayne. "'Rocking the cradle for the world': the new woman and maternal feminism, 1877-1914," in Linda Kealey, ed., *A not unreasonable claim: women and reform in Canada, 1880s-1920s*. Toronto: Women's Press, 1979, pp.15-45.

4513. Snider, Norman. "Motherhood at mid-career," *Toronto Life*, Apr. 1981, pp.27-31, 49.

4514. "Two things I'd change," *Canadian Women's Studies / Les cahiers de la femme*, 2(1):106-7, 1980.

4515. Uwaegbute, Adaoha C. "Infant feeding practices of Nigerians and Ghanian women living in the Guelph-Kitchener-Waterloo area." MSc thesis, University of Guelph, 1978. 202p. (Can. theses, no.39013)

4516. "*Weekend* poll: mother," *Weekend Magazine*, 28:3, May 13, 1978.

MOTHERS AND DAUGHTERS

4517. Fleming, Martha. "Being friends with my mother: necessary lessons," *Canadian Women's Studies / Les cahiers de la femme*, 2(1):64-6, 1980.

4518. Gottlieb, Lois C. and Wendy Keitner. "Demeter's daughters, the mother-daughter motif in fiction by Canadian women," *Atlantis*, 3:131-42, Autumn 1977.

4519. Govier, Katherine. "Mothers and daughters," *Chatelaine*, 49:40-1, 89-94, June 1976.

4520. Kennedy, Linda Marie. "Mother-daughter relationships and their influence on female sport socialization." MA thesis, University of Alberta, 1975. 217p. (Can. theses, no.26797)

4521. Kostash, Myrna. "A few words on behalf of Mom," *Maclean's*, 88:8, July 1975.

4522. Kennedy, Linda. "Mother-daughter relationships and female sport socialization," *CAHPER Journal*, 43:22-6, Jan.-Feb. 1977.

4523. Light, Beth. "Mothers and children in Canadian history," *Canadian Women's Studies / Les cahiers de la femme*, 2(1):102, 1980.

4524. Maynard, Fredelle. "Can. Kid & Can. Mom 79," *Chatelaine*, 52:29-30, 56-7, Jan. 1979.

4525. Melamed, Lanie and Rosemary Sullivan. "A discovery workshop for mothers and daughters," *Canadian Women's Studies / Les cahiers de la femme*, 2(1):71-2, 1980.

4526. Rice, Richard M. "Mothers, daughters and grand-daughters: an examination of the matrilateral bias and related variables in Jews and Icelanders in Canada." MA thesis, University of Manitoba, 1971. 119p. (Can. theses, no.10423)

4527. Richardson, Kathy and others. "Mothers and daughters," *Weekend Magazine*, 27:4-7, May 7, 1977.

4528. Scrutton, R. Edgar. "Intergenerational value conflicts in the Italian families, Amherstburg, Ontario: a study of mother-daughter responses." MA thesis, University of Windsor, 1978. 100p. (Can. theses, no.37164)

4529. Silverman, Eliane. "In their own words: mothers and daughters on the Alberta frontier," *Frontiers*, 2:37-44, Summer 1977.

4530. Yuzwak, William J. "The effect of setting and mother's education on mother-child interaction." MSc thesis, University of Calgary, 1979. 170p. (Can. theses, no.44656)

MOTHERS - EMPLOYMENT

4531. Adams, David. "Among society's neglected - the working mother," *Canadian Welfare*, 46:18-19, July-Aug. 1970.

4532. Altschul, Susan. "Who's come a long way, baby?" *Maclean's*, 94:6, Jan. 12, 1981.

4533. Antonelli, Marylu. "Impossible situations," *Branching Out*, 1:8-11, Nov.-Dec. 1974.

4534. Bruce, Christopher J. "The effect of young children on female labor force participation rates: an exploratory study," *Canadian Journal of Sociology*, 3:431-9, Fall 1978.

4535. Canada. Dept. of Labour. Women's Bureau. *Report of a consultation on the employment of women with family responsibilities, February 17, 1965*. Ottawa, 1965. 42p.

4536. Canada. Dept. of Labour. Women's Bureau. *Working mothers and their child-care arrangements*. Ottawa, 1970. 58p.

4537. Carson, Susan. "The working mother blues," *Weekend Magazine*, 27:4-7, Feb. 19, 1977.

4538. "Consultation on the employment of women with family responsibilities," *Labour Gazette*, 65:210, 286, Mar. 1965.

4539. Carson, Susan. "When new mothers go back to work," *Chatelaine*, 54:66-7, 82+, Sept. 1981.

4540. Davidson, Jane. "Will companies become baby-sitters, too?" *Financial Post*, 66:1, 8, July 15, 1972.

4541. Fancy, Gail P. "Working mothers and private day nurseries: with special emphasis on day care as a service for pre-school children." MSW thesis, University of Toronto, 1965. 133p.

4542. Gill, A. "Lament for wasted resource: homestuck mothers," *Financial Post*, 60:1-2, Oct. 15, 1966.

4543. Gold, Dolores. "Full-time employment of mothers in relation to their ten-year old children," *Atlantis*, 2:98-105, Spring 1977, Part II.

4544. Gold, Dolores and Charlene Berger. "Problem-solving performance of young boys and girls as a function of task appropriateness and sex identity," *Sex Roles*, 4(2):183-93, 1978.

4545. Gold, Dolores and David Andres. "Comparisons of adolescent children with employed and nonemployed mothers," *Merrill-Palmer Quarterly*, 24(4):243-54, 1978.

4546. _____. "Developmental comparisons between ten-year-old children with employed and nonemployed mothers," *Child Development*, 49:75-84, Mar. 1978.

4547. _____. "Maternal employment and child development at three age levels," *Journal of Research and Development in Education*, 10(4):20-9, 1977.

4548. _____. "Maternal employment and development of ten-year-old Canadian francophone children," *Canadian Journal of Behavioural Science*, 12(3):233-40, 1980.

4549. _____. "Relations between maternal employment and development of nursery school children," *Canadian Journal of Behavioural Science*, 10(2):116-29, 1978.

4550. Gold, Dolores, David Andres and Jacqueline Glorieux. "The development of Francophone nursery-school children with employed and nonemployed mothers," *Canadian Journal of Behavioural Science*, 11(2):169-73, 1979.

4551. Gray, Charlotte. "A mother's dilemma: returning to work," *Chatelaine*, 56:36, Dec. 1983.

4552. Hedley, R. Alan and Susan M. Adams. "Mom in the labour force, verdict: not guilty," *Perception*, 6:28-9, Sept.-Oct. 1982.

4553. Hétu, Renée. "Les mères en emploi et la garde de leurs enfants: une étude des dispositions prises par un groupe de mères au travail (paroisses St-Henri et St-Irénée) pour assurer la garde de leurs enfants pendant leurs heures ouvrées." MA thesis, Université de Montréal, 1966. 95p.

4554. Jones, Laura, Fiona McCall, and Ellen Powers. "Mothering at the workplace," *Canadian Women's Studies / Les cahiers de la femme*, 2(1):9-12, 1980.

4455. Kappel, Bruce Edwin. "Self-esteem among the children of working mothers." MA thesis, University of Waterloo, 1972. 109p.

4556. Kieran, Sheila. *The non-deductible woman: a handbook for working wives and mothers*. Toronto: MacMillan, 1970. 107p.

4557. Kostash, Myrna. "Coming back from motherhood," *Macleans*, 88:8, Aug. 1975.

4558. Lashuk, Maureen Grace Wilson. "Effects of role conflict on employed mothers: an empirical investigation and sociology of knowledge interpretation of its study." MA thesis, University of Calgary, 1970. 118p. (Can. theses, no.6116)

4559. Lashuk, Maureen Wilson and George Kurian. "Employment status, feminism, and symptoms of stress: the case of a Canadian prairie city," *Canadian Journal of Sociology*, 2:195-204, Spring 1977.

4560. Li, Selina. *Options for single mothers*. Project Child Care working paper, no. 4. Toronto: Project Child Care, 1978. 44p. (Microlog 80-3317)
   "Project Child Care is jointly sponsored by the Children's Day Care Coalition and the Social Planning Council of Metropolitan Toronto."

4561. Manitoba. Dept. of Labour. Women's Bureau. *Mothers in the labour force: their child care arrangements*. Winnipeg, 1974. [39]p. and app. (Profile 75-0198)

4562. Marra, Glenna. "When mothers work: their need for child care services." MA thesis, Dalhousie University, 1977. 147p. (Can. theses, no.36137)

4563. "Maternal employment and child development," *Canada's Mental Health*, 27:25, Sept. 1979.

4564. McIntyre, Eilene Lifsha Goldberg. "The provision of day care in Ontario: responsiveness of provincial policy to children at risk because their mothers work." PhD diss., University of Toronto, 1979. 349p.

4565. Propper, Alice. "The relationship of maternal employment and sex to adolescent's parental relationships and participation in household tasks and leisure activities," in K. Ishwaran, ed., *Childhood and adolescence in Canada*. Toronto: McGraw-Hill Ryerson, 1979, pp.161-76.

4566. Quiggin, Betty. "Run mother run, see mother run," *Canadian Welfare*, 43:48, May-June 1967.

4567. Racicot, Colette et Marie Tellier. "La participation de la mère de famille à la vie active." MA thése, Université de Montréal, 1973. 289p.

4568. Roberts, Imla. "The dual role of career woman and mother," *Canadian Training Methods*, 13:31-2, Oct. 1980.

4569. Stevens, Gillian and Monica Boyd. "The importance of mother: labor force participation and intergenerational mobility of women," *Social Forces*, 59:186-99, Sept. 1980.

4570. University Women's Club of Regina. *Working mothers in Regina and their child care arrangements: a study*. n.p., 1975. 57p.

4571. Usher, Sarah. "Is there really a choice? The need for life skills counselling with female adolescents," *School Guidance Worker*, 33:35-8, May-June 1978.

4572. Vincent, Andrea L. and Patricia A. Cox. *Career and family: yours*. Toronto: Career and Family Pub., 1979. 206p.

4573. "Working mothers' child care study released," *Canadian Welfare*, 46:23, July-Aug. 1970.

4574. "Working mothers and their child care arrangements in Canada, 1973," *Labour Force* [*Statistics Canada*], 31:83-91, Sept. 1975.

MUNICIPAL EMPLOYEES

4575. Edmonton. Task Force on the Status of Women in the Edmonton Civic Service. *Report*. Edmonton, 1978. 41p.
4576. Hamilton Status of Women Committee. *Equality of opportunity: a report on opportunities for women employed by the Corporation of the City of Hamilton*. Hamilton, Ont., 1980. 16p. (Microlog 82-0794)
4577. Ottawa, Ont. International Women's Year Task Force. *The status of women employed by the City of Ottawa and the Regional Municipality of Ottawa-Carleton: a report of the International Women's Year Task Force*. [Ottawa, 1976]. 150p.

MUSIC

4578. Anthony, George. "Anne Murray," *Chatelaine*, 48:28, 80-2, Jan. 1975.
4579. Batten, Jack. "Bye-bye Brunhild," *Maclean's*, 87:82, 84, Oct. 1974.
4580. _____. "New sounds," *Chatelaine*, 49:46-9, 118-22, Nov. 1976.
4581. Brotman, Ruth C. *Pauline Donalda: the life and career of a Canadian prima donna*. n.p., 1975. 125p.

4582. Cooke, Esther, comp. *Canadian women in music: a bibliography of Canadian women composers and artists in the Alfred Whitehead Memorial Library*. Sackville, N.B.: Alfred Whitehead Memorial Library, 1975. 8p.
4583. Eastman, Sheila Jane. "Barbara Pentland: a biography." MMus thesis, British Columbia, 1974. 187p. (Can. theses, no.22069)
4584. Gillen, Mollie. "Maureen Forrester: Canada's superstar," *Chatelaine*, 45:49, 96-8, 100, Sept. 1972.
4585. Goddard, Peter. "Maureen Forrester is one magnificent woman," *Chatelaine*, 51:12, 14, Feb. 1978.
4586. LeBlanc, L. "Flipside of Anne Murray," *Maclean's*, 87:86-8, Nov. 1974.
4587. Lemay, Jacqueline. "Le monde de la chanson - comment quatre femmes ont pris place dans l'industrie du disque," *Canadian Women's Studies / Les cahiers de la femme*, 1:66-8, Spring 1979.
4588. Malka. "Face to face: Joni Mitchell in conversation with Malka," *Maclean's*, 87:28-9, 66, 70, June 1974.
4589. Livingstone, David. "The magnificent McGarrigles," *Chatelaine*, 56:66, 223+ , Oct. 1983.

4590. Marshall, Kye. "Canadian women composers: breaking the sound barrier," *Broadside*, 2:19, Dec. 1980-Jan. 1981.
4591. Masters, Philinda. "Heather Bishop: more than meets the ear," *Broadside*, 1(1):15, [1979].
4592. Montagnes, Anne. "A musical ménage à trois: stars Tyson, Forrester and Julien," *Performing Arts in Canada*, 12:17-19, Fall 1975.
4593. Murphy, Johnny. "Total dedication required: climb to fame easing for women in country music," *Music Scene*, 305:10-11, Jan.-Feb. 1979.
4594. "Rock'n' roll's leading lady [Joni Mitchell]," *Time. Can. ed.*, 104:59-62, Dec. 16, 1974.
4595. Roberts, Agnes. "A view from the violin section," *Canadian Women's Studies / Les cahiers de la femme*, 1:64-5, Spring 1979.
4596. Rooney, Frances. "The Montréal Women's Symphony," *Atlantis*, 5:70-82, Fall 1979.
4597. Ross, Beverley. "Daisy Debolt," *Branching Out*, 2:6-8, May-June 1975.
4598. Swan, Susan. "The woman as musicmaker: classical music," *Communiqué*, no. 8:14, 16, 47, May 1975.
4599. White, Nancy. "Woman as musicmaker: popular music," *Communiqué*, no. 8:15, 17, 48, May 1975.

NAMES, PERSONAL - LAW

4600. Alberta. Women's Bureau. *Changing your name*. Rev. ed. Edmonton, 1981. 5p.
4601. Bankier, J. K. "Change of name and the married woman," *Canadian Patent Reporter*, new ser., 13:76-85, 1974.
4602. ----------. "Change of name and the married woman," *Chitty's Law Journal*, 21:302-6, 1973.
4603. Brandt, Caryl. "Commentary: the name game," *Branching Out*, 2:46, Sept.-Oct. 1975.
4604. British Columbia. Royal Commission on Family and Children's Law. *Eleventh report. Change of name*. Vancouver, 1975. [17]p. (Profile 75-0692)
4605. Cullis, T. E. "Why should a wife change her name?" *Chatelaine*, 48:32, 122, Dec. 1975.
4606. Dranoff, Linda Silver. "Ask a lawyer: what's in a name?" *Chatelaine*, 52:17, 20, Jan. 1979.
4607. Dundass, Helen. "Suffragettes wanted," *Branching Out*, 5(4):4-5, 1978.
4608. Lord, Catherine. "Veuillez étiqueter vos bagages et votre femme!" *Le Maclean*, 16:44, août 1976.
4609. Monette, Lise. *Rapport d'analyse sur les difficultés rencontrées par les femmes mariées quant à l'utilisation de leur nom de naissance*. Québec: Conseil du statut de la femme, 1974. 5p.
4610. Mungall, Constance. *Changing your name in Canada: how to do it legally*. Vancouver: International Self-Counsel Press, 1977. 132p.
4611. Ontario. Law Reform Commission. *A woman's name: a study paper for the Ontario Law Reform Commission*. Toronto, 1975. 33p.
4612. Ontario. Law Reform Commission. *Report on changes of name*. Toronto: Ontario. Ministry of the Attorney General, 1976. 51p.
4613. Ontario. Law Reform Commission. *Report on the change of name act*. Toronto: Ontario. Dept. of Justice, 1971. 9p.
4614. Pask, E. Diane. "Bill 28: An Act to amend the Change of Name Act," *Saskatchewan Law Review*, 41:177-93, 1977.

NATIVE WOMEN

4615. B.C. Native Women's Society. *Socio-economic development and Indian women*. Presented to Mr. John Munro, Minister of Indian and Inuit Affairs. n.p., 1980. [5]p.
4616. Belfry, Ron. "Boost in the arm for Native women," *Native People*, 15:12, May 14, 1982.
4617. Bursey, Maureen. "Maria Campbell: putting the pieces together," *Branching Out*, 7(1):6-7, 1980.
4618. Campbell, Maria. *Half-breed*. Toronto: McClelland & Stewart, 1973. 157p.
4619. Canadian Religious Conference. *Brief no. 313 to the Royal Commission on the Status of Women in Canada*. Ottawa, n.d. 44p.
4620. Chalifoux, Thelma. "Native women running for office," *Native People*, 13:9, Oct. 3, 1980.
4621. Chartrand, Larry. "Women against patriation," *Native People*, 14:1-2, Mar. 20, 1981.
4622. Cheda, Sherrill. "Indian women: an historical example and a contemporary view," in Marylee Stephenson, *Women in Canada*. Toronto: New Press, 1973, pp.58-70.
4623. Cheda, Sherrill. "To be an Indian and a woman," *Indian-Eskimo Association of Canada Bulletin*, 12(3): (n.p.), Apr. 1971.
4624. Dubec, Bernice. *Native women and the criminal justice system; an increasing minority*. [Thunder Bay, Ont.]: Ontario Native Women's Association, 1982. 50p. and app.
4625. Goodwill, Jean. "Indian women can work together regardless of their status," *Indian News*, 16:5, Dec. 1973.
4626. "Indian women plan to organize," *Indian News*, 14(9):5, 1972.
4627. "Indian women were equal in own society," *Native People*, 9:4, Nov. 26, 1976.
4628. Jamieson, Kathleen. "Multiple jeopardy: the evolution of a native women's movement," *Atlantis*, 4:157-78, Spring 1979, Part II.
4629. ----------. "Sisters under the skin: an exploration of the implications of feminist-materialistic perspective research," *Canadian Ethnic Studies*, 13(1):130-43, 1981.

4630. Labarge, Dorothy. "Femme traditionnelle, femme nouvelle," *North*, 22:8-11, Oct. 1975.

4631. Lee, Bobbi. *Bobbi Lee: Indian rebel: struggles of a native Canadian woman*. v.1. Recorded and edited by Don Barnett and Rick Sterling. Richmond, B.C.: LSM Information Center, 1975. 123p.

4632. "Mary Two-Axe-Early moves first resolution at national conference of Indian women," *Indian News*, 15:12, Feb. 1973.

4633. McIntyre, Mary Margaret. "Attitudes of Indian and non-Indian girls." MA thesis, University of Calgary, 1974. 115p. (Can. theses, no.21310)

4634. Munro, Mary. "Pangnirtung women carvers," *North*, 22:46-9, Oct. 1975.

4635. Myers, Marybelle. "Remembering," *North*, 22:26-9, Oct. 1975. Eskimo women's crafts workshop.

4636. _____. "Reveil culturel chez les femmes de l'Arctique québécois," *North*, 22:22-5, Oct. 1975.

4637. "Native women feel slighted," *Native People*, 15:1-2, Mar. 19, 1982.

4638. Native Women's Association of Canada. "Brief to the Special Joint Committee of the Senate and of the House of Commons on the Constitution of Canada," in the committee's *Minutes of proceedings and evidence*, no. 17, Dec. 2, 1980, pp.63-81.

4639. "Native women's steering committee meet in Winnipeg to discuss unity," *Indian News*, 16:7, Sept. 1973.

4640. Palliser, Annie. "Annie, jeune Inuk en transition," *North*, 22:50-1, Oct. 1975.

4641. "Pride means survival," *Native People*, 13:9, Nov. 28, 1980.

4642. "Program for women latest Peigan activity," *Native People*, 9:15, June 4, 1976.

4643. Romaniuk, A. "Increase in natural fertility during the early stages of modernization: Canadian Indians case study, *Demography*, 18.137-72, May 1901.

4644. Serre, Michèle. "La femme indienne et l'économie - condition mineure, problème majeur," *Canadian Woman Studies / Les cahiers de la femme*, 3:73-5, Summer 1982.

4645. "Teacher says Indian women were always equal," *Native People*, 9:8, Nov. 19, 1976.

4646. Willis, Jane. *Geniesh: an Indian girlhood*. Toronto: New Press, 1973. 199p.

NATIVE WOMEN - BIBLIOGRAPHY

4647. Jamieson, Kathleen. *Native women in Canada: a selected bibliography*. Ottawa: Social Sciences and Humanities Research Council of Canada, [1983]. 49p.
    "Prepared in conjunction with the Regional Workshop on Women in the Canadian Economy held at Simon Fraser University, September 11, 1982."

4648. McNiven, Jean. "La femme et le Nord," *North / Nord*, 22:62-3, Sept.-Oct. 1975.

NATIVE WOMEN,EASTERN CANADA

4649. "Indian women continue protest [Tobique reserve, New Brunswick]," *Native People*, 10:3, Sept. 16, 1977.

4650. Mah, Angela. "Nova Scotia women combat social problems," *Native People*, 10:7, June 3, 1977.

4651. "The plight of women on the Tobique, N.B. reserve," *Status of Women News*, 4:11, Mar. 1978.

4652. Whitehead, Ruth Holmes. "Christina Morris: Micmac artist and artist's model," *Material History Bulletin*, 3:1-14, Spring 1977.

NATIVE WOMEN - EMPLOYMENT

4653. "Action not just words...," *Native People*, 9:16, Mar. 26, 1976.

4654. Boyd, M. *Occupational attainment of native born Canadian women: results from the 1973 Canadian National Mobility Study*. Working paper, no. 77-26. Madison: University of Wisconsin. Center for Demography and Ecology, 1977. 42p.

4655. British Columbia Native Women's Society and Native Outreach for Women. *Presentation and recommendations to the Parliamentary Task Force on Employment Opportunities for the 80's*. n.p., 1980. 4p.

4656. Bruneau, L. "Women want equal employment opportunities at Esso plant," *Native People*, 12:1-2, Feb. 9, 1979.

4657. Canada. Employment and Immigration Commission and Native Women's Association of Canada. Working Group on Native Women's Employment. *Native women - labour force development*. [Ottawa]: Canada. Dept. of Employment and Immigration, 1981. 32, [46]p.

4658. Chartrand, Larry. "Help for women seeking work [Native Women Pre-Employment Training program]," *Native People*, 14:7, Mar. 13, 1981.

4659. _____. "Native women's network established," *Native People*, 15:3, May 14, 1982.

4660. _____. "Pre-employment course added [Slave Lake Friendship Centre]," *Native People*, 14:7, July 31, 1981.

4661. "'Good to get back to bush,' says Fort Chip woman," *Native People*, 9:4, June 11, 1976.

4662. Mah, Angela. "Doris Cardinal - Native homemaker," *Native People*, 10:6-7, Feb. 4, 1977.

4663. _____. "Women and employment," *Native People*, 12:12, Sept. 28, 1979. Re. Native Women Pre-Employment Training program.

4664. McGrath, Judy. "Arctic design for an exclusive market," *North / Nord*, 22:2-7, Sept.-Oct. 1975.

4665. "Native women: doubly disadvantaged workers," *Canadian Woman Studies / Les cahiers de la femme*, 3:70-2, Summer 1982.

4666. Van Kirk, Sylvia. "Thanadelthur," *Canadian Women's Studies / Les cahiers de la femme*, 3(1):62-5, 1981.

NATIVE WOMEN - HISTORY

4667. Brown, Jennifer. *Strangers in blood: fur trade company families in Indian country*. Vancouver: University of British Columbia Press, 1980. 255p.

4668. Brown, Jennifer S. H. "Company men and native families: fur trade social and domestic relations in Canada's Old Northwest." PhD diss., University of Chicago, 1976.

4669. Burtin. *Bienheureuse Kateri Tekakwitha vierge iroquoise: 1656-1680*. St.-Jovite, Québec: Editions Magnificat, 1980. 111p.

4670. Carpenter, Jock. *Fifty dollar bride: Marie Rose Smith, a chronicle of Métis life in the 19th century*. Sidney, B.C.: Gray's Pub., 1977. 160p.

4671. Lavallee, Mary Ann. "Yesterday's Indian women," *Tawow*, 1:6-7, Spring 1970.

4672. Leacock, Eleanor. "Montagnais women and the Jesuit program for colonization," in Mona Etienne and Eleanor Leacock, eds., *Women and colonization: anthropological perspectives*. New York: Praeger, 1980, pp.25-42.

4673. McElroy, Ann. "The negotiation of sex-role identity in Eastern Arctic culture change," *Western Canadian Journal of Anthropology*, 6(3):184-200, 1976.

4674. Robinson, Helen Caister. *Mistress Molly, the brown lady: a portrait of Molly Brant*. Toronto: Dundurn Press, 1980. 160p.

4675. Van Kirk, Sylvia. "Women in between: Indian women in fur trade society," *Western Canadian Historical Association. Historical Papers*, pp.30-47, 1977.

NATIVE WOMEN - LEGAL STATUS

4676. Anderson, Doris. "Two court cases where women lost heavily [editorial]," *Chatelaine*, 47:1, Jan. 1974.

4677. Applegarth, Larry. "Treaty women against IRIW," *Native People*, 13:1-2, May 23, 1980.

4678. B.C. Native Women's Societies. *Policy paper as adopted at their special meeting on May 13th, 1978*. Kamloops, B.C., 1978. [5]p.

4679. B.C. Native Women's Society. *Position paper on Indian self-government*. n.p., 1983. 4p.

188

4680. Bourne, Paula. "Status of native women: case of Jeanette Lavell," in her, *Women in Canadian society*. Toronto: Ontario Institute for Studies in Education, 1976, pp.111-31.

4681. Canada. Advisory Council on the Status of Women. *Indian women and the Indian Act*. Ottawa, 1976. 10p.

4682. Canada. Dept. of Indian and Northern Affairs. *The elimination of sex discrimination from the Indian Act*. [*Élimination de la discrimination selon le sexe dans le loi sur les Indiens*]. Ottawa, 1982. 21, 23p. (Microlog 82-4623)

4683. Canada. Parliament. House of Commons. Standing Committee on Indian Affairs and Northern Development. Sub-committee on Indian Women and the Indian Act. *Minutes of proceedings and evidence*. no. 1-5, Sept. 1-20, 1982.

4684. _____. "First report," in the committee's, *Minutes of proceedings and evidence*. no. 58, Sept. 20, 1982, pp.5-50.

4685. Cardinal, Harold. "Native women and the Indian Act," in Jean Leonard Elliott, ed., *Two nations, many cultures: ethnic groups in Canada*. Scarborough, Ont.: Prentice-Hall, 1979, pp.44-50.

4686. "Citizens minus," *Canada & the World*, 46:14, Nov. 1980.

4687. Couture, Suzette. "A question of status," *Today*, Nov. 29, 1980, pp.5-7.

4688. Dingman, Elizabeth. "Indian women - the most unequal in Canada!" *Chatelaine*, 46:38-9, 78, 80-2, Feb. 1973.

4689. "Exemptions from [Indian] Act," *Native People*, 14:1-2, July 31, 1981.

4690. "Fairweather says Indian women can't be protected by rights act," *Globe & Mail*, Feb. 16, 1978, p.W2.

4691. "First National Conference on Indian Rights for Indian Women," *Forgotten People*, 2:10-11, 16, Jan. 1973.

4692. Fish, Karen. "Native women fight unique battle," *Native People*, 10:6, 12, July 8, 1977.

4693. Folster, David. "Ancient injustice revisited," *Maclean's*, 91:13, Sept. 20, 1901.

4694. "Gladue lashes out at Buchta," *Native People*, 15:7, Mar. 26, 1982.

4695. "Government fence sitting on Indian Act changes," *Native People*, 14:1-2, Dec. 4, 1981.

4696. Hughes, Lorraine. "Fight over Native women's rights continue," *Native People*, 12:1-2, Sept. 28, 1979.

4697. _____. "IRIW demands changes," *Branching Out*, 5(3):4, 1978.

4698. Hunt, Constance. "Fishing rights for Inuit women," *Branching Out*, 4:6-7, Mar.-Apr. 1977.

4699. "Indian act on hold," *Native People*, 13:5, July 18, 1980.

4700. Indian Rights for Women Group. "Brief to the Special Joint Committee of the Senate and of the House of Commons on the Constitution of Canada," in the committee's *Minutes of proceedings and evidence*, no. 17, Dec. 2, 1980, pp.83-103.

4701. "Indian rights for Indian women," *Native People*, [6(10)]:10, [1978].

4702. "Indian women's rights," *Native People*, 13:6, Apr. 11, 1980.

4703. Jamieson, Kathleen. "Battling expulsion," *Report on Confederation*, 2:5-8, Nov. 1978.

4704. _____. *Indian women and the law in Canada: citizens minus*. Ottawa: Canada. Advisory Council on the Status of Women, 1978. 108p.

4705. Jamieson, Kathleen Macleod. "Human rights: Indian women need not appeal," *Branching Out*, 6(2):11-13, 1979.

4706. Mah, Angela. "Native woman's rights," *Native People*, 10:5, Apr. 1, 1977.

4707. _____. "Party line," *Native People*, 10:6, Nov. 18, 1977.

4708. Matas, D. "Indian women's rights," *Manitoba Law Journal*, 6:195-209, 1974.

4709. Miner, Valerie. "Indian women and the Indian Act," *Saturday Night*, 89:28-31, Apr. 1974.

4710. Mohawk Women of Caughnawaga. "'The least members of our society'," *Canadian Women's Studies / Les cahiers de la femme*, 2(2):64-6, 1980.

4711. Nahanee, Theresa. "Why some Indian women are more equal than others," *Chatelaine*, 49:28, Apr. 1976.

4712. "No closer to problem," *Native People*, 14:12, Nov. 6, 1981.

4713. "No compensation," *Native People*, 14:2, Oct. 23, 1981.

4714. "Non status Indian women fear outcome of Caughnawaga eviction dispute," *Native People*, 10:8-9, Sept. 30, 1977.

4715. "On John Munro's offer, no action taken [Indian Act]," *Native People*, 13:1-2, Dec. 19, 1980.

4716. "Regaining Indian status: a decade of struggle," *Today*, Nov. 29, 1980, p.7.

4717. Richardson, Karen. "No Indian women...no Indian nation," *Ontario Indian*, 4:10-12, May 1981.

4718. "Rights violated [United Nations Human Rights Committee Report]," *Native People*, 14:2, Sept. 11, 1981.

4719. Roy, Laurent and others. "Opinion poll: Indian rights," *Native People*, 12:7, Sept. 28, 1979.

4720. Roy, Laurent. "Jean Michael fights for justice," *Native People*, 10:1-2, Sept. 2, 1977.

4721. Sanders, Douglas. "Indian women: a brief history of their roles and rights," *McGill Law Journal*, 21:656-72, Winter 1975.

4722. Sanders, D. E. "Indian Act: status of Indian woman on marriage to person without Indian status," *Saskatchewan Law Review*, 38:243-9, 1974.

4723. Schrieber, Dorothy. "Indian woman defends Joe Dion," *Native People*, 12:1-2, Oct. 5, 1979.

4724. Séguin, Claire. "Essai sur la condition de la femme indienne au Canada," *Recherches amerindiennes au Québec*, 10(4):251-60, 1981.

4725. *Selected documents in the matter of Lovelace versus Canada pursuant to the International Covenant on Civil and Political Rights*. [Fredericton: New Brunswick. Human Rights Commission], 1981. 165p. (Microlog 82-1615)

4726. Smith-Cassill, Clarence. "Laws of status," *Native People*, 12:4, Sept. 7, 1979.

4727. Stanley, F. "BC Native Women's special meeting," *Native People*, 12:7, Dec. 21, 1979.

4728. "Status of Indian woman married to non-Indian disputed: Jeannette Corbiere Lavell," *Labour Gazette*, 74:66-8, Jan. 1974.

4729. University of Saskatchewan. Saskatoon Women and Law Committee. *Marriage manual*. Indian Law Series for Women. Saskatoon, [1977?] 11p.

4730. Whyte, John D. "Lavell case and equality in Canada," *Queen's Quarterly*, 81:28-42, Spring 1974.

NATIVE WOMEN,NORTHERN CANADA

4731. Briggs, Jean L. "Eskimo women: makers of men," in Carolyn J. Matthiasson, ed., *Many sisters: women in cross-cultural perspective*. New York: Free Press, 1974, pp.261-304.

4732. Brizinski, Peggy Martin. "Les femmes dans le Nord: problématique et devenir," *Recherches amerindiennes au Québec*, 10(4):261-8, 1981.

4733. Burgess, Helen. "Women north," *North*, 15:36-43, Jan.-Feb. 1968.

4734. Canada. Dept. of Indian and Northern Affairs. *Arctic women's workshop*. Ottawa, 1974. 92p.

4735. Canada. Dept. of Indian and Northern Affairs. Indian and Inuit Affairs Program. Research Branch. *Demographic profile of registered Indian women*. [Ottawa], 1979. 31p.

4736. Canada. Dept. of the Secretary of State. *Native Women's Program; discussion paper*. [*Programme des femmes autochtones; document de travail*]. [Ottawa], 1980. 11p.

4737. _____.*Speaking together: Canada's native women*. Ottawa, 1975. 126p. French edition: *A nous la parole: les femmes autochtones du Canada*.

4738. Cardinal, Shirley and others. "Women's job on the trapline," *Native People*, 13:9, Dec. 19, 1980.

4739. Chalifoux, Thelma. "Women migrate to Slave Lake," *Native People*, 13:7, May 2, 1980.

4740. Cruikshank, Julie. *Athapaskan women: lives and legends*. National Museum of Man. Mercury series / Canadian Ethnology Service paper, no. 57. Ottawa: National Museums of Canada, 1979. 202p.

4741. _____. "Becoming a woman in Athapaskan society: changing traditions on the Upper Yukon River," *Western Canadian Journal of Anthropology*, 5(2):1-14, 1975.

190

4742.   _____. "Matrifocal families in the Canadian North," in K. Ishwaran, ed., *The Canadian family*. Rev. ed. Toronto: Holt, Rinehart and Winston of Canada, 1976, pp.105-19.

4743.   _____. "Native women in the North: an expanding role," *North*, 18:1-7, Nov.-Dec. 1971.

4744.   _____. "The role of northern Canadian Indian women in social change." MA thesis, University of British Columbia, 1969. 139p.

4745.   French, Alice. *My name is Masak*. Winnipeg: Peguis Publishers, 1976. 110p.

4746.   Hancock, Lyn. "A good woman in the North," *North / Nord*, 22:12-15, Sept.-Oct. 1975.

4747.   Hinds, Margery. "Mina," *Beaver*, 307:20-4, Winter 1976.

4748.   Hudson, Douglas Ridley. "The historical determinants of social organization: a study of Northwest Athabascan matriliny." MA thesis, McMaster University, 1972. 185p.

4749.   Labarge, Dorothy. "Femme traditionnelle, femme nouvelle," *North / Nord*, 22:8-11, Sept.-Oct. 1975.

4750.   Labrador Inuit Association. *Labradoriub Tachangata Arnangit Katimasimaningit. Northern Labrador Women's Conference*. Nain, Nfld., 1978. 154p.

4751.   Lambert, Carmen. "Rapports asymétriques entre Indiennes et Blancs dans le Nord canadien," *Canadian Review of Sociology and Anthropology*, 12(4):417-23, 1975.

4752.   Withdrawn.

4753.   Marvin, Schiff. "Ruby Angrna'naaq: Inuit co-op manager," *Chatelaine*, 49:22-3, Oct. 1976.

4754.   Matthiasson, John S. "Northern Baffin Island women in three cultural periods," *Western Canadian Journal of Anthropology*, 6(3):201-12, 1976.

4755.   McAlpine, Phyllis J. and Nancy E. Simpson. "Fertility and other demographic aspects of the Canadian Eskimo communities of Igloolik and Hall Beach," *Human Biology*, 48:113-38, Feb. 1976.

4756.   McElroy, Ann. "Canadian Arctic modernization and change in female Inuit role identification," *American Ethnologist*, 2:662-86, Nov. 1975.

4757.   Munro, Mary and others. "Pangnirtung women carvers," *North / Nord*, 22:46-9, Sept.-Oct. 1975.

4758.   Nicholls, Roy. "Arctic women's workshop photo story," *North*, 21:10-13, Sept.-Oct. 1974.

4759.   Palliser, Annie. "Annie, jeune Inuk en transition," *North / Nord*, 22:50-1, Sept.-Oct. 1975.

4760.   "Women/North," *North*, 12:25-32, Sept.-Oct. 1965.

NATIVE WOMEN, ONTARIO

4761.   Fels, Julie, *Ontario native women: a perspective*. Thunder Bay, Ont.: Guide Printing & Publishing for the Ontario Native Women's Association, 1980. 125p.

4764.1 Landes, Ruth. *The Ojibwa woman*. New York: AMS Press, 1969. 247p. First published 1938.

4762.   Freedman, Catherine Jan. "Anduhyaun: a Toronto residence for Canadian Indian girls migrating to the city for retraining." MA thesis, York University, 1974. 105p. (Can. theses, no.30902)

4763.   George, Gary. "Millie Redmond adds personal touch to [Anduhyaun] centre for Native women," *Native People*, 9:5, Apr. 16, 1976.

4764.   Hudson, Grace. "Participatory research by Indian women in Northern Ontario remote communities," *Convergence*, 13(1/2):24-33, 1980.

4765.   Ontario Native Women's Association. *Resource manual*. Thunder Bay, Ont., May 1981. 24p.

4766.   _____. *What does the future hold for native women - aboriginal entitlement?* by Priscilla A. Simard. Thunder Bay, Ont.: Guide Printing & Publishing, 1982. Report of a conference, 1982.

4767.   Simard, Priscilla. *Nations within a nation: an aboriginal right?* Report on the [Ontario Native Women's Association] Conference Proceedings, Nov. 12-14, 1982. Thunder Bay: Ontario Native Women's Association, 1983. 67p.

4768. Vanderburgh, Rosamond M. "Tradition and transition in the lives of Ojibwa women," *Resources for Feminist Research*, 11:218-20, July 1982.

4769. Vanderburgh, R. M. *I am Nokomis, too: the biography of Verna Patronella Johnston*. Don Mills: General, 1977. 247p.

4770. ‒‒‒‒‒. "Southern Ojibwa of Ontario," *Canadian Newsletter of Research on Women*, 7:14-17, Nov. 1978.

NATIVE WOMEN - ORGANIZATIONS

4771. Chartrand, Larry. "VANWS fight for rights," *Native People*, 15:12, May 14, 1982.

4772. Mah, Angela. "Native Women's Association of Canada holds meeting," *Native People*, 10:7, Feb. 18, 1977.

4773. ‒‒‒‒‒. "Party line [VANWS]," *Native People*, 10:7, Feb. 4, 1977.

4774. Nanimahoo, Carmel. "Indian rights for Indian women," *Native People*, 12:13, Apr. 27, 1979.

4775. Newborn, Terry. "Revision of Indian Act - IRIW's priority," *Native People*, 11:1-2, Nov. 10, 1978.

4776. O'Murcada, L. "IRIW and Treaty women disagree," *Native People*, 13:7, June 20, 1980.

4777. "Regina [Native] women's groups battle for basic rights," *Native People*, 9:14, June 16, 1976.

4778. Semotiuk, Craig. "Native Women's Association of Canada meet," *Native People*, 10:12-13, July 22, 1977.

4779. Thompson, Martin. "Board calls for dissolution: controversy hits IRIW," *Native People*, 14:1-2, July 10, 1981.

4780. ‒‒‒‒‒. "IRIW funds suspended," *Native People*, 14:1-2, Aug. 7, 1981.

4781. ‒‒‒‒‒. "Sec of State checking IRIW," *Native People*, 14:1-2, Oct. 9, 1981.

4782. ‒‒‒‒‒. "Secretary of State gives IRWA a week," *Native People*, 14:7, Sept. 18, 1981.

4783. ‒‒‒‒‒. "Secretary of State requests audit," *Native People*, 14:2, July 10, 1981.

4784. ‒‒‒‒‒. "Spring conference set for VANWS," *Native People*, 15:2, Mar. 26, 1982.

4785. "VANWS hires project officer," *Native People*, 12:8, Dec. 21, 1979.

NATIVE WOMEN, QUEBEC

4786. Larivière, H. "Quand les femmes se prennent en mains," *Perception*, 5:14-15, 29, Nov.-Dec. 1981.

4787. Myers, Marybelle. "Remembering," *North / Nord*, 22:26-9, Sept.-Oct. 1975.

4788. ‒‒‒‒‒. "Réveil culturel chez les femmes de l'Arctique québécois," *North / Nord*, 22:22-5, Sept.-Oct. 1975.

4789. Preston, Sarah. "Let the past go: a life history narrated by Alice Jacob." MA thesis, McMaster University, 1982. 208p.

4790. Sioui, Monique. "Monique Sioui: une autochtone très engagée dans les luttes [entrevue]," *Perception*, 5:26-7, Nov.-Dec. 1981.

NATIVE WOMEN - SEX ROLE

4791. Cruikshank, Julie and June Lotz. *The changing role of Canadian Indian women*. Report for the Royal Commission on the Status of Women in Canada, from the Canada Research Center for Anthropology. Ottawa, 1968. 71p.

4792. Gonzalez, Ellice Becker. "The changing economic roles for MicMac men and women: an ethnohistorical analysis." PhD. diss., State University of New York at Stony Brook, 1979. 326p. (UM, 79-14445)

4793. Matthiasson, John S. "Northern Baffin Island women in three cultural periods," *Western Canadian Journal of Anthropology*, 6(3):201-12, 1976.

4794. McElroy, Ann. "Canadian Arctic modernization and change in female Inuit role identification," *American Ethnologist*, 2:662-86, Nov. 1975.

4795. ‒‒‒‒‒. "The negotiation of sex-role identity in Eastern Arctic culture change," *Western Canadian Journal of Anthropology*, 6(3):184-200, 1976.

4796. Meadows, Mary Lea. "Adaptation to urban life by native Canadian women." MA thesis, University of Calgary, 1981. 156p. (Can. theses, no.52414)

4797. Walters, Cyril Maurice. "Indian children's perception of sex roles." MEd thesis, University of Alberta, 1970. 104p.

NATIVE WOMEN,WESTERN CANADA

4798. Blackman, Margaret B. "The changing status of Haida women: an ethnohistorical and life history approach," in Donald N. Abbott, ed., *The world is as sharp as a knife*. Victoria, B.C.: British Columbia Provincial Museum, 1981, pp.65-77.

4799. Brass, Eleanor. "Women take on street patrol [Regina Native Women's Residence Resource Centre]," *Native People*, 9:3, Jan. 23, 1976.

4800. Brettle, Paul. "Haven for Native families [Regina Native Women's Residence Resource Centre]," *Native People*, 10:6, Mar. 4, 1977.

4801. Chalifoux, Thelma. "Native women in politics [Alberta]," *Native People*, 13:5, Oct. 17, 1980.

4802. Clatworthy, Stewart J. *Issues concerning the role of native women in the Winnipeg labour market*. Technical study, no. 5. Ottawa: Canada. Task Force on Labour Market Development, 1981. 14p. and app.

4803. Community Task Force on Maternal and Child Health. *Manitoba native Indian mother and child: a discussion paper on a high risk population*. Winnipeg, Man., 1981. 45p.

4804. Keetley, K. *Native teen pregnancy and parenting: a problem in perspective*. Vancouver: Social Planning and Review Council of British Columbia, 1981. 48p.
        Project sponsored by Health and Welfare Canada, Health Promotions Branch,

4805. McCord, Joanne. "Alberta first Native appointment: Maria Campbell new writer-in-residence at university," *Native People*, 12:1-2, Sept. 28, 1979.

4806. McManus, Patricia R. "Problems of the isolated and non-isolated Indian female students in Manitoba." MEd thesis, University of Manitoba, 1970. 80p.

4807. Mitchell, Marjorie Ruth. "Women, poverty and housing: some consequences of hinterland status for a coast Salish Indian reserve in metropolitan Canada."PhD diss., University of British Columbia, 1976. 428p. (Can. theses, no.29898)

4808. Mitchell, Marjorie. "The Indian Act: social and cultural consequences for native Indian women on a British Columbia reserve," *Atlantis*, 4:179-88, Spring 1979, Part II.

4809. "Native women's rights," *Native People*, 14:2, Oct. 9, 1981.

4810. Neilson, Kathryn Elizabeth. "The delinquency of Indian girls in British Columbia: a study in socialization." MA thesis, University of British Columbia,1969. 85p.

4811. Nelms, Joyce Ethel. "The Indian woman and household structure in Mill Creek, British Columbia." MA thesis, University of Victoria, 1974. 84p. (Can. theses, no.29040)

4812. "Saskatchewan Indian women meet," *Indian News*, 11:6, Nov. 1968.

4813. "Saskatchewan Indian women speak out," *Indian News*, 11:7, Apr. 1968.

4814. Shipley, Nan. *Report on the status of the Indian and Métis women of Manitoba*. Report for the Royal Commission on the Status of Women in Canada. n.p., 1968. 21p.

4815. Scott-Brown, Joan M. "Stoney ethnobotany: an indication of cultural change amongst Stoney women of Morley, Alberta." MA thesis, University of Calgary, 1977. 194p. (Can. thesis, no.34081)

4816. Speare, Jean E., ed. *The days of Augusta*. Vancouver: J. J. Douglas, 1973. 79p.

4817. Thomas, W. D. S. "Maternal mortality in native British Columbia Indians, a high-risk group," in Carl F. Grindstaff and others, eds., *Population issues in Canada*. Toronto: Holt, Rinehart & Winston, 1971, pp.54-60.

4818. Van Raalte, Sharon. "Inuit women and their art," *Communiqué*, no. 8:21-3, May 1975.

4819. Voice of Alberta Native Women's Society. *Report of the Voice of Alberta Native Women's Society, Foster Care Project*. [Edmonton]: Alberta. Dept. of Social Services and Community Health, [1977]. 21p. and app. (Profile 77-0489)

NEW DEMOCRATIC PARTY

4820.   Bashevkin, Sylvia. "In a man's world? Women and the Ontario NDP," *Canadian Forum*, 61:34, 42, Feb. 1982.

4821.   Kidd, Varda. "Sexism prevailed at the NDP convention," *Canadian Dimension*, 8:7-9, June 1971.

4822.   Maeots, K. "Women and the N.D.P.," *Canadian Dimension*, 7:26-9, Apr. 1971.

4823.   "NDP program for economic equality for women; Programme NDP d'égalité économique pour les femmes," *Canadian Labour / Travailleur canadien*, 24:6, [English]; 6, [French], May 11, 1979.

4824.   New Democratic Party. *Women in Canada: in society, in public life, in the NDP*. Ottawa: New Democratic Party, 1971. 16p.

4825.   New Democratic Party of Ontario. *Resolution passed at the 1970 Provincial Convention: liberation of women R-223*. 14p.

NUNS

4826.   Alexandre, Marie-Jeanne. *Les religieuses enseignantes dans le système d'éducation du Québec*. Québec: Institut supérieur des sciences humaines, Université Laval, 1977. 137p.

4827.   Cimichella, André-M. *Marguerite Bourgeoys, lumière sur notre ville*. Montréal: Editions Jésus Marie et notre temps, 1974. 71p.

4828.   D'Allaire, Micheline. "Origine sociale des religieuses de l'Hôpital-Général de Québec (1692-1764)," *Revue d'histoire de l'Amérique française6r, 23:559-81, mars 1970*.

4829.   _____. *"Les prétentions des religieuses de l'Hôpital-Général de Québec sur le palais épiscopal (1692-1764)," Revue d'histoire de l'Amérique française*, 23:559-81, mars 1970.

4829.   _____. "Les prétentions des religieuses de l'Hôpital-Général de Québec sur le palais épiscopal de Québec," *Revue d'histoire de l'Amérique française*, 23:53-67, juin 1969.

4831.   _____. "Taking the veil in Montreal, 1840-1920: an alternative to marriage, motherhood and spinsterhood." PhD diss., University of Toronto, 1981. 324p.

4832.   Dawson, Joyce Taylor. "A note on research in progress: the needlework of the Ursulines of early Quebec," *Material History Bulletin*, 5:73-80, Spring 1978.

4833.   Dumais, Monique. "Les défis d'être une femme religieuse," *Possibles*, 4:147-54, automne 1979.

4834.   _____. "Les religieuses des femmes spéciales," *Communauté chrétienne*, no. 95:485-90, sept.-oct. 1977.

4835.   _____. "Les religieuses, leur contribution à la société québécoise," *Canadian Women's Studies / Les cahiers de la femme*, 3(1):18-20, 1981.

4836.   Dumont-Johnson, Micheline. "Les communautés religieuses et la condition féminine," *Recherches sociographiques*, 19:79-102, janv.-avr. 1978.

4837.   Duval, Germaine. *Par le chemin du roi, une femme est venue: Marie-Rose Dürocher, 1811-1849*. Montréal: Ed. Bellarmin, 1982. 398p.

4838.   Ebacher, Roger. *La religieuse animatrice de paroisse: informations et réflexions sur le diocèse d'Amos*. L'Église du Québec, 5. Montréal: Fides, 1978. 85p.

4839.   Fitts, Mary Pauline. *Hands to the needy: Blessed Marguerite d'Youville, apostle to the poor*. Garden City, N.Y.: Doubleday, 1971. 332p.

4840.   Jean, Marguerite. *Evolution des communautés religieuses de femmes au Canada de 1639 à nos jours*. Montréal: Fides, 1977. 324p. Published version of the author's PhD dissertation, Université Saint-Paul, 1974.

4841.   Jordan, Mary. *De ta soeur, Sara Riel*. Sante-Boniface, Man.: Éditions des Plaines, [1980?] 180p.

4842.   King, Dennis. *The Grey Nuns and the Red River Settlement*. Agincourt, Ont.: Book Society of Canada, 1980. 76p. Juvenile level book.

4843.   Lambert, Thérèse. *Marguerite Bourgeoys, èducatrice, 1620-1700: mère d'un pays et d'une église*. Montréal: Les Editions Bellarmin, 1978. 137p.

4844. Lee, Danielle Juteau. "Les religieuses du Québec: leur influence sur la vie profession-nelle des femmes, 1908-1954," *Atlantis*, 5:22-33, Spring 1980.

4845. Légaré, Jacques. "Les religieuses au Canada: leur évolution numérique entre 1965 et 1980," *Recherches sociographiques*, 10:7-21, janv.-avr. 1969.

4846. Lessard, Marc-André et Jean-Paul Montminy. "Les religieuses du Canada: âge, re-crutement et persévérance," *Recherches sociographiques*, 8:15-48, janv.-avr. 1967.

4847. McGuire, Rita. *Marguerite d'Youville: a pioneer for our times: a biography based on the life and times of Marguerite d'Youville, Foundress of the Sisters of Charity (Grey Nuns) of Montreal*. Ottawa: Novalis, 1982. 309p.

4848. Piche, R. "Value survey among women in religious orders throughout Alberta." MA thesis, University of Alberta, 1968. 110p.

4849. Proulx, Marcienne. "L'action sociale de Marie Gérin-Lajoie, 1910-1925." MA mémoire, Université de Sherbrooke, 1976. 127p. (Can. theses, no.27019)

4850. Small, Helen Francis. "Changes in traditional norms of enclosure: a study of the secularization of religious women." PhD diss., McMaster University, 1973. 498p. (Can. theses, no.19459)

4851. Ward-Harris, E. D. *A nun goes to the dogs: a biography of Mother Cecilia Mary, O.S.B.* Rev. ed. Victoria, B.C.: Sono Nis Press, 1977. 136p.

NURSING

4852. "A day to remember," *Canadian Nurse*, 77:4, May 1981.

4853. Alderson, Henrietta Jane. *Twenty-five years a-growing: the history of the School of Nursing, McMaster University*. Hamilton, Ont.: McMaster University, 1976. 333p.

4854. Allemang, Margaret May. "Nursing education in the United States and Canada 1873-1950: leading figures, forces, views on education." PhD diss., University of Washington, 1974. 316p.

4855. Beamish, Rahnom. *Fifty years a Canadian nurse: devotion, opportunities and duty*. New York: Vantage Press, 1970. 344p.

4856. Bellamy, Marjory. "Beyond the call of duty," *Manitoba Pageant*, 20:13-17, Summer 1975.

4857. Blaker, Gloria. "Some of us are more equal than others," *Canadian Nurse*, 76:6, May 1980.

4858. Cockerill, Art. "Ready aye ready: three decades of British women in Newfoundland and Labrador," *North / Nord*, 23:22-7, May-June 1976.

4859. "Is there sex discrimination in health care?" *Canadian Nurse*, 71:15-18, Dec. 1975.

4860. Kelly, Nora. *Quest for a profession: the history of the Vancouver General Hospital School for Nursing*. Vancouver: Vancouver General Hospital School of Nursing Alumnae Associa-tion, 1973. 174p.

4861. MacLeod, Donna Jean. "A study of nursing students from a feminist perspective." MA thesis, University of Calgary, 1976. 113p. (Can. theses, no.30551)

4862. "Messieurs, Les infirmières ne sont plus ce qu'elles étaient," *Canadian Women's Studies / Les cahiers de la femme*, 1:15-16, Winter 1978-1979.

4863. Mitchell, Samuel. *A woman's profession, a man's research*. [Edmonton: Alberta Associa-tion of Registered Nurses / University of Calgary], 1971. 318p.

4864. Nevitt, Joyce. *White caps and black bands: nursing in Newfoundland to 1934*. St. John's: Jesperson Printing Ltd., 1978. 278p.

4865. Nicholson, Gerald W. L. *Canada's nursing sisters*. Toronto: A. M. Hakkert, 1975. 272p.

4866. Pepperdene, Barbara J. "The occupation of nursing and careers: a study of the careers of diploma and degree nurses," PhD diss., University of Toronto, 1974. 401p. (Can. theses, no.27944)

4867. Pinnell, Lynn Ellen. "Perceptions of stress among hospital nursing staff." MN thesis, University of Alberta, 1979. 147p. (Can. theses, no.40482)

4868. "Professions and personhood," in Canadian Research Institute for the Advancement of Women, *Women as persons*. [*La femme en tant que personne*]. Toronto: Resources for Feminist Research, 1980, pp.61-9.

      Proceedings of the 3rd annual meeting.

4869. Ray, Marilyn Anne. "An applied anthropological study of role behavior within the profession of nursing within the complex institution of the hospital." MA thesis, McMaster University, 1978, 174p.

4870. Sloan, Harriet J. T. "Nursing in the Canadian Armed Forces," *Canadian Nurse*, 62:23-5, Nov. 1966.

4871. Street, Margaret M. *Watch-fires on the mountains: the life and writings of Ethel Johns*. Toronto: University of Toronto Press, 1973. 336p.

4872. Strilaeff, Florence. "Turnover of nurses in hospitals: a study of a service organization." PhD diss., University of Toronto, 1974. 287p. (Can. theses, no.27984)

4873. Tunis, Barbara Logan. *In caps and gowns: the story of the school for graduate nurses McGill University, 1920-1964*. Montreal: McGill University Press, 1966. 154p.

OCCUPATIONAL RE-TRAINING

4874. Canadian Committee on Learning Opportunities for Women. *Cutbacks to training allowances and out-reach programs: their impact on women*. [n.p.], 1979. 35p.

      Brief presented to representatives of the Liberal Party, New Democratic Party and the Progressive Conservative Party.

4875. Chartrand, Larry. "Help for women seeking work [Native Women Pre-Employment Training program]," *Native People*, 14:7, Mar. 13, 1981.

4876. _____. "Pre-employment course added [Slave Lake Friendship Centre]," *Native People*, 14:7, July 31, 1981.

4877. Cooper, Jack Edward. "An analysis and evaluation of a multi-agency rehabilitation program for disadvantaged women." MA thesis, Simon Fraser University, 1972. 173p. (Can. theses, no.12564)

4878. De Pauw, Karen. "Training women for non-traditional occupations." MA thesis, Concordia University, 1980. 144p. (Can. theses, no.49598)

4879. Lewington, Jennifer. "Ottawa may liberate more women for job training," *Financial Post*, 68:9, Jan. 1974.

4880. Mah, Angela. "Women and employment," *Native People*, 12:12, Sept. 28, 1979. Re. Native Women Pre-Employment Training program.

4881. Marsden, L. R. "Canadian economic and sociological trends: implications for counselling," *School Guidance Worker*, 30:5-11, May-June 1975.

4882. Ontario. Ministry of Colleges and Universities. *Women into trades and technology: a training profile*. [Toronto], 1982. 156, 9p. (Microlog 82-4713)

ORGANIZATIONS

4883. Adamson, Nancy and Kathy Arnup. "A committee for all seasons [International Women's Day Committee]," *Broadside*, 3:4, Mar. 1982.

4884. Anderson, D. M. "Desegregating the woman scene," *Chatelaine*, 42:1, June 1969.

4885. Bell, Sandra. "Women for Political Action," *Broadside*, 1(4):8, [1980].

4886. Bruhy, Billie Jo. "The Flaming Apron women's craft store: an experience through the collectivity." MA thesis, Sir George Williams University, 1973. 73p. (Can. theses, no.20604)

4887. Canada. Dept. of the Secretary of State. Women's Programme. *Pressure for change: the role of Canadian women's groups*. Ottawa, 1974. 23p.

      Notes prepared for discussion at the United Nations International Seminar, Sept. 7, 1974.

4888. Canada. Dept. of the Secretary of State. Women's Programme. *Women and voluntarism: a stimulus paper*. Ottawa, 1975. 9p.

4889. Collectif. "Comment lutter au bas de l'échelle," *Possibles*, 4:167-73, automne 1979.

4890. Collectif. "D'où vient et où va le Regroupement des femmes québécoises," *Possibles*, 4:109-12, automne 1979.

4891. Cooper, Pat. "Women as advocates in their communities," *Atlantis*, 4:121-27, Spring 1979, Part II.

4892. Corbet, Elise A. "Woman's Canadian Club of Calgary," *Alberta History*, 25:29-36, Summer 1977.

4893. Corkery, Mary. "Canadian Committee on Learning Opportunities for Women," *Broadside*, 1(1):8, [1979].

4894. Duckworth, Muriel and Peggy Hope-Simpson. "Voice of Women Dialogue," *Atlantis*, 6:168-76, Spring 1981.

4895. Durden, Vivienne. *The YWCA: its role in relation to serious personal problems of girls and women*. Toronto: Young Women's Christian Association of Canada, 1965. 56p.

4896. _____. *The YWCA: it's role in relation to serious personal problems of girls and women*. Toronto: Young Women's Christian Association of Canada, 1965. 56p.

4897. Elkin, Frederick and Catherine McLean. "Pressure towards cooperation in voluntary association: the YMCA and YWCA in Canada," *Journal of Voluntary Action Research*, 5:16-26, Jan. 1976.

4898. Erickson, Mary Anne. "Prime Time: aid for women's middle years," *Branching Out*, 6(4):12, 1979.

4899. Federated Women's Institutes of Canada. *Report of national convention*. 10th, 1970. Ottawa. Annual.

4900. *Feminist Services Training Programme: a Youth Job Corps project*, sponsored by the Women's Programme, Department of the Secretary of State. n.d. [5]p.

4901. Foster, Nigel. "A story no woman could ever write [Toronto Women's Ad and Sales Club]," *Marketing*, 81:2, Feb. 16, 1976.

4902. Fraser, Janet and Eileen Hendry, eds. *Womens' networks in Canada*. Vancouver: University of British Columbia. Centre for Continuing Education, [1983?] 230, [10]p.
    Based on the Proceedings of the First National Womens' Network Conference June 3-5, 1982.

4903. Gagnon, Claude-Lyse. "Crafts, cuisine, and Québec culture [Les Cercles de Fermières]," *Review (Imperial Oil)* 63(6):20-3, 1979.

4904. Gervais, Solange. "L'Association féminine d'éducation et d'action sociale - un mouvement qui s'adapte," *Relations*, 37:24-5, janv. 1977.

4905. Grescoe, Audrey. "Women's networks," *Homemaker's Magazine*, 15:70-2, 74+ , Apr. 1980.

4906. Home, Alice Marian. "Change in women's consciousness-raising groups: a study of four types of change and of some factors associated with them." DSW diss., University of Toronto, 1978. 310p. (Can. theses, no.38744)

4907. _____. "A study of change in women's consciousness-raising groups," *Canadian Journal of Social Work Education*, 6(2/3):7-24, 1980.

4908. "How Laura built a lobby [National Action Committee on the Status of Women]," *Saturday Night*, 93:4, Sept. 1978.

4909. Imperial Order Daughters of the Empire. *Brief no. 311 to the Royal Commission on the Status of Women in Canada*. Toronto, 1968. 75p.

4910. Kessler, Gail. "Time out for friendship," *Branching Out*, 1:33-4, Mar.-Apr. 1974.

4911. Labreche, Julianne. "Women's pressure groups: what's their role in the '80s?" *Chatelaine*, 55:33, 72+ , July 1982.

4912. Lancaster, Jan. "British Columbia Federation of Women," *Canadian Women's Studies / Les cahiers de la femme*, 2(2):35-6, 1980.

4913. Lavoie, Stella. "Les Cercles de Fermières de la province de Québec dans la région," *Revue d'histoire du Bas Saint-Laurent*, 5:24-6, déc. 1978.

4914. Leduc, Chantal. "YWCA de Montréal," *Canadian Women's Studies / Les cahiers de la femme*, 2(2):44, 1980.

4915. Lord, Catherine. "RAIF: outil de la contestation féministe," *L'Actualité*, 2:80, oct. 1977.

4916. Macmillan, Moira. "Beyond jam making," *New Society*, 48:768-9, June 28, 1979.

4917. McCart, Joyce. "Counting the YWCA," *Branching Out*, 2:8-10, Sept.-Oct. 1975.

4918. Mah, Angela. "Party line [Alberta Status of Women Action Committee]," *Native People*, 10:12, Apr. 22, 1977.

4919. Mann, Brenda. "Canadian Research Council for the Advancement of Women," *Branching Out*, 3:7-8, July-Aug. 1976.

4920. Maranda, Jeanne. "Des féministes avant l'heure?" *Canadian Women's Studies / Les cahiers de la femme*, 3(1):56-7, 1981. Re. les Cercles des fermières.

4921. Marchessault-Lussier, Lucie. "Une agent d'éducation populaire pas comme les autres [AFEAS]," *Canadian Woman Studies / Les cahiers de la femme*, 3:88-9, Summer 1982.

4922. Marsden, Lorna and others. "NAC annual meeting, April 23-26, Ottawa: programme, President's report, background materials," *Status of Women News*, 2:7-16, May 1976.

4923. McGee, Arlee D. "Federated Women's Institutes gather," *Atlantic Advocate*, 73:72-4, Sept. 1982.

4924. Morgan, Joanna. "Julie Strickley, President / Canadian Housewives Register," *Chatelaine*, 50:12, Mar. 1977.

4925. Morris, Cerise. "'Determination and thoroughness': the movement for a Royal Commission on the Status of Women in Canada," *Atlantis*, 5:1-21, Spring 1980.

4926. Morrison, Suzanne. "Women: career route rough," *Journal (The Board of Trade of Metropolitan Toronto)*, Christmas 1977, pp.43-5.

4927. National Action Committee on the Status of Women. "Annual meeting and conference, March 18-21, 1977, Ottawa: proposals arising from workshops: women and family law," *Status of Women News*, 3:9-12, [English]; 13-16, [French], May 1977.

4928. Newfoundland Status of Women Council. *A history and celebration of 10 years of feminism (1972-1982)*. St. John's, Nfld., 1982. 35p.

4929. Ontario Status of Women Council. *Women's groups and services in Metropolitan Toronto*. Toronto, 1981. 17p.

4930. Picard-Pilon, Louise. "Être femme et autonome: le défi de l'AFEAS," *Possibles*, 4:131-5, automne 1979.

4931. "Recognition - as time goes by: [Women's Advertising and Sales Club of Winnipeg]," *Marketing*, 83:24, Apr. 24, 1978.

4932. "Resolutions: National Action Committee annual meeting, Ottawa, March, 1978; CNA résolutions 1978," *Status of Women News / Statut: Bulletin de la femme*, 4:21-4, [English]; 21-4, [French], June 1978.

4933. Ricks, Frances A. and Sandra W. Pyke. "Women in voluntary social organizations," *Ontario Psychologist*, 5(2):48-55, 1973.

4934. Robillard, Laurette. "Réflexions à l'occasion du 10ième anniversaire de la fondation de la Fedération des femmes du Québec," *Status of Women News*, 3:11, July 1976.

4935. Sadoway, Geri. "TACWL [Toronto Area Caucus of Women and the Law]," *Broadside*, 3:8, Dec. 1981-Jan. 1982.

4936. Savoie, Marie. "Le RAIF et le changement social," *Possibles*, 4:155-61, automne 1979.

4937. Sorensen, J. "West: support for businesswomen," *Financial Post*, 75:7, Sept. 26, 1981.

4938. Steele, Betty. "Women's groups are coming back [IODE]," *Atlantic Advocate*, 63:34-5, 38-9, 41, Feb. 1973.

4939. Tasaka, Karen Joy. "A study of selected nonformal educational programs for rural women in Alberta and their relationship to clientele needs." MSc thesis, University of Alberta, 1978. 190p. (Can. theses, no.36486)

4940. "The National Action Committee on the Status of Women in Canada," *New Feminist*, 4:18-20, Mar. 1973.

4941. Walton, Jo Anne. "Organizing lobbies for tradeswomen," *Perception*, 4:9-10, Jan.-Feb. 1981.

4942. "WAVAW: the way we were," *Broadside*, 3:19, Nov. 1981.

4943. Willman, Gwen. "Report: NAC annual meeting Ottawa," *Status of Women News*, 3:4-8, July 1976.

4944. Wilson, L. J. "Educating the Saskatchewan farmer: the educational work of the Saskatchewan Grain Growers' Association [and Women's Grain Growers' Association]," *Saskatchewan History*, 31:20-33, Winter 1978.
4945. "Women executives organize," *Journal (The Board of Trade of Metropolitan Toronto)*, Easter 1977, pp.25-6, 28-9.

ORGANIZATIONS - DIRECTORIES

4946. Canada. Secretary of State. *Directory of Canadian women's groups*. Ottawa, 1975. 498p.
4947. Canada. Secretary of State. Women's Programme. *Listing of women's groups, Canada*. 3rd ed., 1981- .
       Previous editions: *Directory of Canadian women's groups*. 1st, 1975; 2nd, 1977.
4948. Conseil du statut de la femme. *Répertoire des groupes de femmes du Québec*. Montréal: Consult-Action, 1980. 233p.
4949. Hamilton-Wentworth. Community Information Service. *Women's organizations in Hamilton-Wentworth*, updated by Ontario Experience '79 summer students and United Steelworkers of America. Hamilton, Ont., 1979. 14p.
4950. Hudak, Ladislas. *A directory of main women's cultural group organizations in Canada*. Rev. & enl. ed. Ottawa: Canada. Dept. of the Secretary of State. Research and Documentation Division. Citizenship Branch, 1973. 53p.
4951. Québec. Conseil du statut de la femme. *Repértoire des groupes de femmes du Québec*. [Québec], 1979- . Annual.
4952. Vancouver Women's Network. *The Women's Network directory*. [Vancouver, 1983-]. Continues Vancouver Women's Network directory.

ORGANIZATIONS - HISTORY

4953. Alberta Mennonite Women in Mission. *History of Alberta Mennonite women in Mission: 1947-1977*. Coaldale, Alta., 1978. 128p.
4954. Bamman, Haley. "The Ladies Benevolent Society of Hamilton, Ontario: form and function in mid-nineteenth century urban philanthropy," in *Canadian social history project: interim report no. 4*. Toronto: Ontario Institute for Studies in Education. Dept. of History and Philosophy, 1972, pp.161-217.
4955. Buchynsky, Vera, ed. [*The 25 year endeavor: Ukrainian Catholic Women's League of Canada in Manitoba*]. Winnipeg, Man.: Ukrainian Catholic Women's League (Canada) Winnipeg Archeparchy, 1973. 216p.
4956. Campbell, R. Philip. *Challenging years 1894-1979; 85 years of the Council of Women in Saint John*. [Saint John, N.B.: n.p., 1981?]
4957. Canadian Women's Christian Temperance Union. *Centennial mosaic 1874-1974*. Toronto, [1977?] 55p.
4958. Clarke, Mary Eileen. "The Saint John Women's Enfranchisement Association, 1894-1919." MA thesis, University of New Brunswick, 1979. 168p. (Can. theses, no.43881)
4959. Clifford, Betty and others, ed. *Women's Auxiliary to the West Coast General Hospital, 1913-1978*. Port Alberni, B.C.: Women's Auxiliary to the West Coast General Hospital, 1978. 56p.

4960. Earl, Marion R. *A history of the Local Council of Women (in affiliation with National Council of Women of Canada) of Kingston*. n.p., 1975. 42p.
4961. Forbes, Elizabeth. *With enthusiasm and faith: history of the Canadian women's clubs - 1930-1972*. Ottawa: Canadian Federation of Business and Professional Women's Clubs, 1974. 170p.
4962. Harshaw, Josephine. *When women work together: a history of the Young Women's Christian Association in Canada, 1870-1966*. Toronto: Ryerson Press, 1966. 209p.
4963. Jarvis, Julia. "The founding of the girl guide movement in Canada, 1910," *Ontario History*, 62:213-19, 1970.
4964. Kerr, Vivian. *A flame of compassion: a history of the Provincial Council of Women of Ontario*. Toronto: T. H. Best, 1967. 134p.

4965. Kertland, May G. *I.O.D.E.: the third twenty-five years 1950-75*. Don Mills, Ont.: T.H. Best Printing Co., 1975. 129p.

4966. Lavigne, Marie, Yolande Pinard and Jennifer Stoddart. "La Fédération Nationale Saint-Jean-Baptiste et les revendications féministes au début du XXe siècle," *Revue d'histoire de l'Amérique française*, 29:353-73, déc. 1975.

4967. MacPherson, Kay and Meg Sears. "The Voice of Women: a history," in Gwen Matheson, *Women in the Canadian mosaic*. Toronto: Peter Martin, 1975, pp.70-89.

4968. Manitoba Women's Institute. *The great human heart: a history of the Manitoba Women's Institute, 1910-1980*. Winnipeg, 1980. 143p.

4969. Manley, John. "Women and the left in the 1930's: the case of the Toronto CCF Women's Joint Committee," *Atlantis*, 5:100-19, Spring 1980.

4970. Mitchinson, Wendy L. "Aspects of reform: four women's organizations in nineteenth century Canada." PhD diss., York University, 1977. 349p. (Can. theses, no.30928)
    Examines church missionary societies, Y.W.C.A., Woman's Christian Temperance Union and the National Council of Women.

4971. _____. "The Woman's Christian Temperance Union: a study in organization," *International Journal of Women's Studies*, 4:143-56, Mar.-Apr. 1981.

4972. _____. "The YWCA and reform in the nineteenth century," *Histoire sociale / Social History*, 12:368-84, May 1979.

4973. Panabaker, Katherine Marks. *The story of the girl guides in Ontario*. [Toronto]: Girl Guides of Canada. Ontario Council, [1966]. 118p.

4974. Pedersen, Diana L. "Keeping our good girls good: the Young Women's Christian Association of Canada, 1870-1920. MA thesis, Carleton University, 1981. (Can. theses, no.55626)

4975. Powell, Mary Patricia. "Response to the depression: three representative women's groups in British Columbia." MA thesis, University of British Columbia, 1967. 115p.

4976. Prokop, Mary. "Looking back on fifty years [Women's Branches of the Association of United Ukrainian Canadians]," *Ukrainian Canadian*, Mar. 1972, pp.7-14.

4977. Reeve, Phyllis. *The history of the University Women's Club of Vancouver, 1907-1982*. [Vancouver]: University Women's Club of Vancouver, 1982. 102p.

4978. Reid, Diane and others. *A bridge to the future: a history of the Council of Women of Ottawa and area*. [*Un pont vers l'avenir: l'historique du Conseil des femmes d'Ottawa et de la région*]. [Ottawa]: Regional Municipality of Ottawa-Carleton, 1976. 78, 68p.

4979. "Report on the Home for Young Women Seeking Employment, Halifax 1870," *Atlantis*, 5:196-99, Spring 1980.

4980. Robinson, Helen Caister. *Decades of caring: the Big Sister story*. Toronto: Dundurn Press, 1979. 156p.

4981. Robinson, Jo. *Faculty Women's Club: sixty years of friendship and service, 1917-1977: a brief history*. Vancouver: University of British Columbia. Faculty Women's Club, 1977. 34p.

4982. Strong-Boag, Veronica Jane. "The parliament of women: the National Council of Women of Canada, 1893-1929." PhD. diss., University of Toronto, 1975. (Can. theses, no.31347)

4983. _____. *The parliament of women: The National Council of Women of Canada 1893-1929*. Canada. National Museum of Man. Mercury series / History Division paper, no. 18. Ottawa: National Museums of Canada, 1976. 492p.

4984. Stuart, Elizabeth. *100th Anniversary of Osgoode Baptist Women's Missionary Society*. Vernon, Ont.: Osgoode Twp. Historical Society and Museum, 1981. 30p.

4985. Thompson, Retta. *Synoptic view of the Woman's Christian Temperance Union, 1913-1973*. 3rd ed. Saskatoon: Early Mailing Service Ltd., 1975. 58p.

4986. Thorpe, Wendy Lisbeth. "Lady Aberdeen and the National Council of Women of Canada: a study of a social reformer in Canada, 1893-1898." MA thesis, Queen's University, 1972. 158p. (Can. theses, no.13044)

4987. *Through the years, part II; the Women's Institutes of Prince Edward Island, 1963-1979*. Summerside, P.E.I.: Williams and Crue, 1980. 97p.

4988. Trevelyan, Margot. "'Be prepared!' For what?; 'Toujours prête!' A quoi? (Girl Guides)" *Status of Women News / Statut: Bulletin de la femme*, 5:8-9, [English]; 8-9, [French], Fall 1979.
4989. University Women's Club of Toronto. *75 years in retrospect: University Women's Club of Toronto, 1903-1978*. Toronto: UWCT, [1978]. 109p.
4990. Vineberg, Ethel. *The history of the National Council of Jewish Women of Canada*. Montreal, 1967. 84p.
4991. Wilson, L. J. "Educational role of the United Farm Women of Alberta," *Alberta History*, 25:28-36, Spring 1977.
4992. Young Women's Christian Association of Canada. *The YWCA in Canada: more than 100 years of women working together*. Toronto: YWCA of Canada, [1978]. 2p.
4993. *Women as achievers in Canadian history*. Toronto: YWCA of Canada, 1979-1980. Series of pamphlets: 1. Adelaide Hoodless 2. Emma Kaufman 3. Marion Royce, Agnes Roy, Margaret Smith.
4994. Zaremba, Eve. "'Y' and why not?" *Broadside*, 2:4, June 1981.

PARTI QUÉBÉCOIS

4995. Fournier, Francine. "Quebec women and the Parti Québécois," in Marlene Dixon, Susanne Jones and Pauline Vaillancourt, eds., *Quebec and the Parti Québécois*. San Francisco: Synthesis Pub., 1978, pp.60-3.
4996. Fraser, Graham. "Backseat drivers who won't let up," *Maclean's*, 91:31, Nov. 13, 1978.
4997. Hamilton, Roberta. "Sexual politics," *Canadian Forum*, 59:27-9, Feb. 1980.
4998. *La femme au Québec*. Les Québécois, no. 1. Montréal: Éditions du Parti québécois, 1974. 63p.

PART-TIME EMPLOYMENT

4999. Bayefsky, Evelyn. "Part time work: policies for women (and men)," *Canadian Woman Studies / Les cahiers de la femme*, 3:81-3, Summer 1982.
5000. Canada. Commission of Inquiry into Part-Time Work. *Part-time work in Canada*. Ottawa: Canada. Dept. of Labour, 1983. 218p.
    Includes material relevant to women.
5001. Canada. Dept. of Labour. Economics and Resources Branch and Canada. Dept. of Labour. Women's Bureau. *Part-time employment in retail trade*. Ottawa, 1969. 66p.
5002. Canada. Dept. of Labour. Women's Bureau. *Women and part-time work in Canada*. Ottawa, 1966. 18p.
5003. Canadian Advisory Council on the Status of Women. *Part-time work, part-time rights*. [*Travail à temps partiel avantages restreints*]. Brief presented to the Commission of Inquiry into Part-time Work. Ottawa, 1982. 36, 39p. (Microlog 83-3244)
5004. Canadian Advisory Council on the Status of Women. *Part-time work: a review of the issues*. Brief to the Advisory Council of Employment and Immigration Canada. Ottawa, 1980. 28p.
5005. Carpentier, Renée. "Les femmes et le temps partiel," *Relations*, 43:29-32, janv.-fév. 1983.
5006. "Disadvantages of working part-time," *Labour Gazette*, 69:386-7, July 1969.
5007. Duffy, Ann and Wendy Weeks. "Women part-time workers and the needs of capital," *Atlantis*, 7:23-35, Fall 1981.
5008. "Experiment in part-time employment for married women," *Labour Gazette*, 68:406, July 1968.
5009. Glowinsky, Ruth. "The best of both worlds. Job-sharing: a new concept in part-time work," *Canadian Women's Studies / Les cahiers de la femme*, 1:36-7, Winter 1978-1979.
5010. Hooper, J. "Half a librarian is better than none," *Canadian Literature*, 24:338-40, Jan. 1968.
5011. "Le travail à temps partiel: un miroir déformant," *Perception*, 5:6, Apr. 1982.

201

5012. Manitoba. Dept. of Labour. Women's Bureau. *Women and part-time employment*. Winnipeg, 1982. 51p.

5013. Mungall, Constance. "Part-time jobs as good as full-time, only shorter?" *Chatelaine*, 50:37, 51, 55-8, Jan. 1977.

5014. Nakamura, Alice and Masao Nakamura. "Part-time and full-time work behaviour of married women: a model with a doubly truncated dependent variable," *Canadian Journal of Economics*, 15:229-57, May 1983.

5015. New Brunswick. Advisory Council on the Status of Women. *Part-time work: liberation or exploitation?*. Prepared by Susan LeBlanc. Halifax, 1982. 16, [14]p.
Submission to the Commission of Enquiry into Part-Time Work.

5016. "OECD releases study of part-time employment," *Labour Gazette*, 68:638, Nov. 1968.

5017. Ontario Status of Women Council. *Brief on part-time employment*. [Toronto], 1982. 10p.

5018. "Part-time work [Department of Labour study]," *Labour Gazette*, 76:634-5, Dec. 1976.

5019. Rosser, M. J. *Married women working part-time in Canada*. Working paper, no. 80-19. Hamilton, Ont.: McMaster University. Dept. of Economics, 1980. 17p.

5020. Saskatchewan. Dept. of Labour. Women's Division. *Part-time work*. Regina, 1978. 4p.

5021. Shaver, Fran. "Le travail à temps partiel: les femmes y perdent toujours," *Perception*, 6:7-8, Nov.-Dec. 1982.

5022. Simpkins, Joan and others. *A study of part-time employment*. Winnipeg: Manitoba. Dept. of Labour. Women's Bureau / Planning and Priorities Committee of Cabinet Secretariat, 1976. 39p. (Profile 77-0277)

5023. Weeks, Margaret Wendy. "Part-time work in Canada: a study of ideology and implications for women." MA thesis, McMaster University, 1977. 322p. (Can. theses, no.36570)

5024. "Women's Bureau report on women and part-time work," *Labour Gazette*, 66:710, Dec. 1966.

PART-TIME EMPLOYMENT - BIBLIOGRAPHY

5025. Bayefsky, Evelyn. "Women and the status of part-time work: a review and annotated bibliography," *Ontario Library Review*, 61:87-106, June 1977.

5026. _____. "Women and the status of part-time work, a review and annotated bibliography," *Ontario Library Review*, 58:124-41, June 1974.

5027. "Women and part-time work: a selected bibliography," *Labour Topics (Ontario Ministry of Labour Library)*, 5(7):1-3, July 1982.

PENSIONS AND RETIREMENT

5028. Anderson, Doris. "Three good ideas we can't afford to cut," *Chatelaine*, 49:2, May 1976.

5029. Aubert, Lucienne. "Les femmes et la retraite," *Cahiers québécois de demographie*, 8:99-106, avr. 1979.

5030. Begin, Monique. "Women and pensions in Canada. [La femme et le pensionne]," in Canadian Federation of Business and Professional Women's Clubs, *A collection of papers delivered at the National Conference: Women & Work in the 80's: a Decade of Change*. Ottawa: The Federation, 1981, pp.139-63.

5031. Bernard, Gaston. "Participation des femmes au régime; Female participation in the plan," *Bulletin statistique / Régime de rentes du Québec*, 8:x-xxii, juin 1974.

5032. Brown, David. "Sex discrimination in pension plans," *Dalhousie Law Journal*, 4:189-200, Oct. 1977.

5033. Bursey, Maureen. "Divorced and widowed homemakers denied pension," *Branching Out*, 6(3):6-7, 1979.

5034. Cameron, Carmen. *Women and aging: towards tomorrow*. St. John's, Nfld.: Newfoundland Status of Women Council, 1981. 16p.

5035. Canada Pension Plan Advisory Committee. *More effective participation of homemakers in the Canada Pension Plan: majority and minority reports*. [Submitted] to Minister of National Health and Welfare. [Ottawa], 1983. 41, 7p. (Microlog 83-3264)
Includes French edition.

5036. _____. *Participation of housewives in the Canada Pension Plan*. Report to the Honourable Marc Lalonde, Minister of National Health and Welfare. n.p., 1974. 21p.

5037. Canada. Advisory Council on the Status of Women. *ACSW recommendations concerning the participation of homemakers in the Canada and Quebec Pension Plans*. Ottawa, 1976. 4p.

5038. Canada. Dept. of National Health and Welfare. *Better pensions for Canadians: focus on women*. [*De meilleures pensions pour les Canadiens: la part des femmes*]. Ottawa, 1982. 18, 19p.

5039. Canadian Advisory Council on the Status of Women. *Pension reform for women: a discussion paper*. [*Les femmes et la réforme des régimes de pensions*]. Ottawa, 1981. 19, 22p. (Microlog 83-3235)

5040. Collins, Kevin. *Women and pensions*. Ottawa: Canadian Council on Social Development, 1978. 254p.

5041. De Blois, Carole. "Les femmes collaboratrices et le Régime de rentes du Québec," *Bulletin statistique / Régime de rentes du Québec*, 14:vii-xiii, déc. 1980.

5042. Dranoff, Linda Silver. "Ask a lawyer," *Chatelaine*, 54:38, Sept. 1981.

5043. Dulude, Louise. "Justice économique pour les femmes âgées; Who needs pensions? Women do!" *Canadian Woman Studies / Les cahiers de la femme*, 3:9-12, [French]; 31-3, [English], Summer 1982.

5044. _____. *Pension reform with women in mind*. Ottawa: Canadian Advisory Council on the Status of Women, 1981. 111p. and app. (Microlog 83-3236)

5045. _____. "What are you going to live on when you are old?; Les femmes et les pensions ou de quoi allez-vous vivre quand vous serez vieille?" *Status of Women News / Statut: Bulletin de la femme*, 5:4-5, [English]; 4-5, [French], Mar. 1979.

5046. _____. "Women and pensions," in Social Planning Council of Metropolitan Toronto, *Pensions: passport to poverty. Can we afford our elderly?* Toronto: The Council, 1979, pp.38-30.

5047. Elliott, Jean Leonard. "Pensions and poverty: the health of elderly women," *Atlantis*, 4:44-50, Spring 1979, Part II.

5048. _____. "Retirement without tears: the report of the Special Senate Committee on Retirement Age Policies [review]," *Atlantis*, 5:216-18, Spring 1980.

5049. Filion, Jean-Paul. "Les causes de l'invalidité chez les femmes; The causes of disability among women," *Bulletin statistique / Régime de rentes du Québec*, 10:vii-xiii, [French]; xxi-xxvii [English], sept. 1976.

5050. Frappier, Georges. "Unisex mortality tables," *CAUT Bulletin*, 24:19-20, Oct. 1975.

5051. Gelber, Sylva M. "Equality in pensions for working women," in, *Women's Bureau '73*. Ottawa: Canada. Dept. of Labour. Women's Bureau, 1974, pp.39-43.

5052. Grabner, Karen. "Will divorce sunder pension payments?" *Financial Post*, 71:17, May 28, 1977.

5053. Horsford, Patricia A. "Division of Canada Pension Plan credits on termination of marriage," *Reports of Family Law*, 2nd ser., 13:48-58, 1980.

5054. "Housewives should be eligible for pension plan: Trudeau says," *Globe & Mail*, Apr. 28, 1979, p.1.

5055. Lalonde, Marc. "Discussion paper on housewives and the Canada Pension Plan," in Canada. House of Commons. Standing Committee on Health. Welfare and Social Affairs, *Minutes of proceedings*, Apr. 4, 1974, Appendix E, pp.26-36.

5056. Landau, Reva. "From paupers to pensioners," *Broadside*, 4:3, 10, Oct. 1982.

5057. Lord, Catherine. "La révolte des vieilles dames pas indignes," *L'Actualité*, 1:90, déc. 1976.

5058. Major, Henri. *Background notes on the proposed amendments to the Canada Pension Plan (Bill C-49)*. Ottawa: Canadian Advisory Council for the Status of Women, 1977. 19p.

5059. Manitoba. Pension Commission. *Sister, will you have a dime?: women and pensions*. Winnipeg, [1980?] 40p. (Microlog 83-2641)

5060. Menzies, S. June. *Recommendation concerning the inclusion of housewives in the Canada Pension Plan*. Ottawa: Canada. Advisory Council on the Status of Women, 1975. 8p.

5061.   _____. *The Canada Pension Plan and women: a discussion paper*. Ottawa: Canada. Advisory Council on the Status of Women, 1975. 18p.

5062.   National Action Committee on the Status of Women. *The economic outlook*. Presentation to the Cabinet of the Government of Canada. Ottawa, 1978. 17p.

5063.   _____. *Women and pensions: brief*. Toronto, 1982. 21p.

5064.   National Council of Women of Canada. *Proposals for pension reform: the 1983 report of the National Council of Women of Canada*. [Ottawa], 1983. 37p.

5065.   _____. *The financial situation of older women: report on a survey of opinion*. Ottawa, 1979. 14p.

5066.   New Brunswick. Advisory Council on the Status of Women. *Pensions - a new deal for women: submission to the Law Amendments Committee concerning the Pension Benefits Standards Act*, prepared by Susan Shalala. Moncton, 1981. 24p.

5067.   _____. *Retirement in New Brunswick, the woman's perspective*, prepared by Pamela Easterbrook. [Moncton], 1980. 21p.

5068.   "Pension credits for women at home," *Canadian Welfare*, 50:25-6, July-Aug., 1974.

5069.   "Pensions for housewives," *IR Research Reports*, 3:17, July-Aug. 1979.

5070.   Rhodes, Ann. "Women: still the losers in pensions," *Chatelaine*, 55:53, 199-200+ , May 1982.

5071.   Ross, David. "Les femmes et les pensions," *Perception*, 5:33, June 1982.

5072.   Saskatchewan. Dept. of Labour. Women's Division. *Pensions and women*. Regina, 1979. 13p.

5073.   "Sex discrimination challenged in money-purchase pension plan," *Globe & Mail*, Dec. 12, 1978, p.B6.

5074.   Sutton, May. "Widowhood: a keynote address: the facts of life," *Status of Women News*, 5:6-8, Mar. 1979.

5075.   Townson, Monica. "Canada's women: riding a treadmill to poverty," *Canadian Business Review*, 7:22-9, Spring 1980.

5076.   _____. "Women and pensions: the reward for a lifetime's service is poverty," *Perception*, 3:14-17, Jan.-Feb. 1980.

5077.   "Women and retirement," in *Retirement without tears; a report of the Special Senate Committee on Retirement Age Policies*. Ottawa, 1979, pp.87-95.

5078.   "Women and the provision of retirement income," in Ontario. Royal Commission on the Status of Pensions in Ontario, *Report. Vol. III: Design for retirement*. [Toronto], 1980, pp.115-39.

5079.   "Women workers seen easing pension burden," *Globe & Mail*, June 20, 1980, p.9.

5080.   Wood, Jean. "Equal payouts for men and women, please," *Benefits Canada*, 5:14, 16, Sept.-Oct. 1981.

PENSIONS AND RETIREMENT - BIBLIOGRAPHY

5081.   Swanick, M. Lynne Struthers. *Women and pensions: a checklist of publications*. Public administration series, no.P-273. Monticello, Ill.: Vance Bibliographies, 1979. 9p.

PERIODICALS

5082.   Anderson, Doris. "Women's magazines in the 1970's," *Canadian Women's Studies / Les cahiers de la femme*, 2(2):15-16, 1980.

5083.   Batt, Sharon. "Feminist publishing: where small is not so beautiful," *Status of Women News*, 6:12-13, Spring 1980.

5084.   Becker, Mary. "The outdoors is her business," *Status of Women News*, 6:14-15, Spring 1980.
            Re: Sheila Kaighin, editor of *Outdoor Canada*.

5085.   Carrier, Micheline. "Monsieur dehors, madame à la cuisine," *Canadian Women's Studies / Les cahiers de la femme*, 1:42-3, Summer 1979.

5086.   Cohen, Yolande. "L'histoire des femmes au Québec (1900-1950)," *Recherches sociographiques*, 21:339-45, sept.-déc. 1980.

5087. Cole, Susan G. "Breakthrough doesn't," *Broadside*, 1:7, Sept. 1980.

5088. Coulombe, Danielle. "La femme des années trente: image dans *Châtelaine* et les pages féminines du *Country guide* et de la *Revue moderne*, 1929-1939." MA thèse, Université d'Ottawa, 1981. (Can. theses, no.53209)

5089. Desforges, Louise. "Le féminisme et ses impasses: l'exemple des 'Têtes de pioche'," *Stratégie*, 15/16:89-97, automne-hiver 1976-1977.

5090. Dupré, Louise. "L'écriture féminine dans ' Les herbes rouges'," *Revue de l'Université d'Ottawa*, 50(1):89-94, 1980.

5091. Fahmy-Eid, Nadia. "La presse féminine au Québec (1890-1920): une pratique culturelle et politique ambivalente," in Yolande Cohen, *Femmes et politique*. Montréal: Le Jour, 1981, pp.101-15.

5092. Gottlieb, Lois C. and Wendy Keitner. "Images of Canadian women in literature and society in the 1970's," *International Journal of Women's Studies*, 2:513-27, Nov.-Dec. 1979.

5093. Harris, Marjorie. "50 golden years of Chatelaine, 1928-1978," *Chatelaine*, 51:43-55, Mar. 1978.

5094. Jean, Michèle. "Les Têtes de pioche (1976-1979): une expérience de presse féministe radicale," *Statut: Bulletin de la femme*, 6:9, printemps 1980.

5095. Kirkwood, Hilda. "Women in the Forum 1945-1946," *Canadian Forum*, 55:29-30, Sept. 1975.

5096. Kome, Penney. "Homemaker's," *Canadian Women's Studies / Les cahiers de la femme*, 2(2):17, 1980.

5097. Kostash, Myrna. "The feminist press - is anyone out there listening?" *Chatelaine*, 48:24, 107, Mar. 1975.

5098. Lambert, Anne. "Images for sale: how Eaton's saw us," *Branching Out*, 4:30-3, Mar.- Apr. 1977.

5099. McCallum, Pamela. "World without conflict: magazines for working class women," *Canadian Forum*, 55:42-4, Sept. 1975.

5100. Michener, W. "Reflections in a paper mirror, looking for the new woman in magazines," *Saturday Night*, 80:35-8, Nov. 1965.

5101. Pelrine, Eleanor Wright. "Whatchamacallit and why," *Content*, no. 85:8-30, May 1978. Controversy re. renaming section of Globe and Mail to 'Women's Globe and Mail'.

5102. Robinson, Gertrude Joch. "Changing Canadian and US magazine portrayals of women and work: growing opportunities for choice," in Marianne Grewe-Partsch and Gertrude J. Robinson, eds., *Women, communication, and careers*. Communication research and broadcasting, no. 3. Munich: K. G. Saur, 1980, pp.93-113.

5103. Rymell, Heather. "Images of women in the magazines of the '30s and '40s," *Canadian Women's Studies / Les cahiers de la femme*, 3(2):96-9, 1981.

5104. Stoffman, Judy. "The importance of being Doris [Anderson]," *Weekend Magazine*, 28:8-10, Mar. 4, 1978.

5105. "The lifestyle of women's pages: calling them people, family, living and you," *Content*, no. 85:11, May 1978.

5106. "The Makara menagerie," *Makara*, 2:18-23, Spring 1977.

5107. Valois, Jocelyne. "La presse féminine et le rôle social de la femme," *Recherches sociographiques*, 8:351-75, sept.-déc. 1967.

5108. Vipond, Mary. "Image of women in Canadian mass circulation magazines in the 1920's," *Modernist Studies*, 1(3):5-13, 1974-75.

5109. _____. "The image of women in mass circulation magazines in the 1920s," in Susan Mann Trofimenkoff and Alison Prentice, eds., *The neglected majority: essays in Canadian women's history*. Toronto: McClelland and Stewart, 1977, pp.116-24.

5110. Wilson, Susannah Jane Foster. "The relationship between mass media content and social change in Canada: an examination of the image of women in mass circulating Canadian magazines 1930-1970." PhD diss., University of Toronto, 1977. 319p. (Can. theses, no.36871)

5111.   Wilson, Susannah J. "Sex-role socialization and the mass media in Canada: a study of employment characteristics of magazine heroines," in J. Ross Eshleman and Juanne N. Clarke, eds., *Intimacy, commitments, and marriage: development of relationships*. Boston: Allyn and Bacon, 1978, pp.79-86.

5112.   .... "The changing image of women in Canadian mass circulating magazines, 1930-1970," *Atlantis*, 2:33-44, Spring 1977, Part II.

5113.   Wolfe, Margie. "Feminist publishing in Canada," *Canadian Women's Studies / Les cahiers de la femme*, 2(2):11-14, 1980.

5114.   Wyman, Georgina. "The day women took over the Toronto Globe," *Branching Out*, 1:22-3, 39-40, Mar.-Apr. 1974.
        Re. special woman's edition of the Globe (Toronto) Apr. 18, 1895.

PHARMACY

5115.   Empey, Charlotte. "Women in pharmacy," *Drug Merchandising*, 59:20-3, Jan. 1978.

5116.   .... "Women in pharmacy: breaking new ground," *Drug Merchandising*, 59:39-41, May, 1978.

5117.   .... "Women in pharmacy: hard work and a sense of humour," *Drug Merchandising*, 59:44-5, Mar. 1978.

5118.   Hornosty, Roy W. "Implications of feminism for the profession of pharmacy in Canada," *International Journal of Women's Studies*, 3:183-206, Mar.-Apr. 1980.

5119.   "Increase in percentage of women pharmacists," *Canadian Pharmaceutical Journal*, 110:32, June 1977.

5120.   Kelly, Terry. "Women in pharmacy," *Chatelaine*, 54:48, Oct. 1981.

5121.   "Pharmacy today: women in pharmacy," *Canadian Pharmaceutical Journal*, 113:255-68, Aug. 1980.

5122.   "Women in pharmacy: faith is her cornerstone," *Drug Merchandising*, 59:44-5, Aug. 1978.

5123.   "Women in pharmacy - Ontario study says community pharmacy still the first choice," *Drug Merchandising*, 54:38, Sept. 1973.

5124.   "Women in pharmacy: the changing face of pharmacy," *Drug Merchandising*, 59:32,34, Oct. 1978.

PHOTOGRAPHY

5125.   Bersianik, Louky and others. *Au fond des yeux: 25 Québècoises qui écrivent*. Montréal: Nouvelle optique, 1981. 110p. Collection of photographs.

5126.   Canada. National Film Board. Still Photography Division. *National Film Board of Canada salutes International Women's Year 1975*. Ottawa, 1975. 192p. Collection of photographs.

5127.   Cobb, Myrna and Sher Morgan. *Eight women photographers of British Columbia, 1860-1978*. Victoria: Camosun College. Applied Communication Program, 1978. 97p.

5128.   McMaster, Susan. "St. Joan in silken armour," *Branching Out*, 3:7-10, Feb.-Mar. 1976.

5129.   Verthuy, Maïr. "Au fond des yeux," *Canadian Woman Studies / Les cahiers de la femme*, 3:75, Spring 1982.

5130.   Wilks, Claire Weissman. *The magic box: the eccentric genius of Hannah Maynard*. Toronto: Exile Editions, 1980. 149p.

5131.   .... "The eccentric genius of Hannah Maynard," *Saturday Night*, 95:35-40, Nov. 1980.

PHYSICAL FITNESS

5132.   Castle, Cheryl R. "The performance of educable mentally handicapped girls on the Canada fitness award / CAHPER fitness-performance test." MA thesis, University of Alberta, 1978. 76p. (Can. theses, no.43367)

5133.   Conger, P. R. and others. "Age and sex performance variation of the CAHPER fitness performance II test," *CAHPER Journal*, 49:12-16, Sept.-Oct. 1982.

5134. Edwards, Peggy, ed. *Growing together: demonstration fitness and lifestyle projects for low-income women*. Ottawa: Canadian Public Health Association / Fitness and Amateur Sport Canada, 1981. 29, 31p.

5135. Massicotte, Denis. "Physiological effects on older women of a 30 week physical conditioning program," *CAHPER Journal*, 47:31-8, July-Aug. 1981.

PIONEERS

5136. Alberta. Women's Bureau. *Pioneer women of the west*. Alberta facts. Edmonton, n.d. 7p.

5137. Allison, Susan. *A pioneer gentlewoman in British Columbia: the recollections of Susan Allison*. Edited and introduced by Margaret A. Ormsby. Vancouver: University of British Columbia Press, 1976. 210p.

5138. Bailey, Mary C. "Reminiscences of a pioneer," *Alberta Historical Review*, 15:17-25, Autumn 1967.

5139. Caswell, Maryanne. *Pioneer girl*. Toronto: McGraw-Hill Ryerson, 1979. ca 100p. Originally published 1964.

5140. Coburn, Judith and Margaret Wolfe. *A harvest yet to reap: a history of prairie women. Teacher's guide*. Toronto: Women's Press, 1979. 47p.

5141. Duncan, Joy, ed. *Red seige wives*. [n.p.]: Centennial Book Committee [R.C.M.P.], 1974. 249p.

5142. Eaton, Sara. *Lady of the backwoods: a biography of Catherine Parr Traill*. Toronto: McClelland & Stewart, 1969. 175p.

5143. Forbes, Elizabeth. *Wild roses at their feet: pioneer women of Vancouver Island*. Vancouver: British Columbia Centennial '71 Committee, 1971. 147p.

5144. Fowler, Marian. "Portrait of Susan Sibbald, writer and pioneer," *Ontario History*, 66:51-64, Mar. 1974.

5145. _____. *The embroidered tent: five gentlewomen in early Canada, Elizabeth Simcoe, Catharine Parr Traill, Susanna Moodie, Anna Jameson, Lady Dufferin*. Toronto: Anansi, 1982. 239p.

5146. Fredrickson, Olive A. *The silence of the north*. Leicester, Eng.: Ulverscroft, 1978. 357p. French edition: *Une femme dans le Grand Nord*.

5147. Gowanlock, Theresa. *Two months in the camp of Big Bear: the life and adventures of Theresa Gowanlock and Theresa Delaney*. Reprint of the 1885 ed. New York: Garland Pub., 1976. 141p.

5148. Head, Gertrude. *Saga of a homesteader*. n.p., 1977. 72p.

5149. Healy, W. J. *Women of Red River: being a book written from the recollections of women surviving from the Red River era*. Rev. ed. Winnipeg: Peguis Pub., 1977. 274p. First edition published 1923.

5150. Holmes, Peggy. *It could have been worse*. Toronto: Collins, 1980. 190p.

5151. Hopkins, Monica. *Letters from a lady rancher*. Calgary: Glenbow Museum, 1981. 172p.

5152. Inderwick, Mary. "A lady and her ranch," *Alberta Historical Review*, 15:1-9, Autumn 1967.

5153. Jackel, Susan, ed. *A flannel shirt and liberty: British emigrant gentlewomen in the Canadian west, 1880-1914*. Vancouver: University of British Columbia Press, 1982. 229p.

5154. Johnson, Jean L. "The homestead at Rabbit Creek," *Canadian Women's Studies / Les cahiers de la femme*, 3(1):21-5, 1981.

5155. Keywan, Zonia. "Women who won the west," *Branching Out*, 2:17-19, Nov.-Dec. 1975.

5156. Latham, Barbara. "Nation building on Vancouver Island," *Canadian Women's Studies / Les cahiers de la femme*, 3(1):58-9, 1981.

5157. Light, Beth and Alison Prentice, eds. *Pioneer and gentlewomen of British North America, 1713-1867*. Documents in Canadian women's history, no. 1. Toronto: New Hogtown Press, 1980. 245p.

5158. MacEwan, Grant. *...And mighty women too: stories of notable western Canadian women*. Saskatoon, Sask.: Western Producer Prairie Books, 1975. 275p.

5159. Metcalf, Vicky. *Catherine Schubert*. Don Mills, Ont.: Fitzhenry & Whiteside, 1978. 62p.

5160. Murphy, Emily F. *Janey Canuck in the West*. Heritage books, no. 2. Toronto: McClelland and Stewart, 1975. 223p.

5161. O'Brien, Mary Sophia. *Journals of Mary O'Brien: 1828-1838*, edited by Audrey S. Miller. Toronto: MacMillan of Canada, 1968. 314p.

5162. Polowy, Hannah. "The role of the pioneer woman in family life," *Ukrainian Canadian*, Mar. 1972, pp.20-1.

5163. Purdy, Harriet and David Gagan. "Pioneering in the North-West Territories: Harriet Johnson Neville, 1882-1905," *Canada: an Historical Magazine*, 2:1-64, June 1975.

5164. Rasmussen, Linda and others. *A harvest yet to reap: a history of prairie women. Teacher's guide*. Toronto: Women's Press, 1976. 240p.

5165. Roberts, Barbara Ann. "Susanna Moodie: the exiled princess as empire builder." MA thesis, Simon Fraser University, 1977. 248p. (Can. theses, no.35969)

5166. Robinson, Charlotte Gourlay. *Pioneer profiles of New Brunswick settlers*. Belleville, Ont.: Mika Pub. Co., 1980. 221p.

5167. Rouslin, Virginia Watson. "The intelligent woman's guide to pioneering in Canada," *Dalhousie Review*, 56:319-35, Summer 1976.

5168. Smith, Margot and Carol Pasternak, eds. *Pioneer women of Western Canada*. Curriculum series, no. 32. Toronto: Ontario Institute for Studies in Education, 1978. 134p.

5169. Thomas, Clara. *Love and work enough: the life of Anna Jameson*. Toronto: University of Toronto Press, 1967. 252p.

5170. Van Kirk, Sylvia. *"Many tender ties": women in fur-trade society in western Canada, 1670-1870*. Winnipeg: Watson & Dwyer Pub., [1980]. 302p.

5171. Vincens, Simone. *Madame Montour et son temps*. Montréal: Québec/Amérique, 1979. 331p.

5172. Vinohradova, Mary. "Recollections of a pioneer woman," *Ukrainian Canadian*, Mar. 1972, pp.22-4.

5173. Woywitka, Anne B. "A Roumanian pioneer," *Alberta Historical Review*, 21:20-7, Autumn 1973.

POETRY

5174. Dunn, Margo. "Valancy Crawford: the lifestyle of a Canadian poet," *Room of One's Own*, 2(1):11-19, 1976.

5175. Godard, Barbara. "Nicole Brossard: amantes and la mer," *Broadside*, 2:14-15, Apr. 1981.

5176. Keller, Betty. *Pauline, a biography of Pauline Johnson*. Vancouver: Douglas & McIntyre, 1981. 317p.

5177. Keeler, Judy. "An interview with P. K. Page," *Canadian Forum*, 55:33-5, Sept. 1975.

5178. Livesay, Dorothy. "Dorothy Livesay: a bluestocking remembers [interview]," *Branching Out*, 7(1):18-21, 1980.

5179. _____. *40 women poets of Canada*. Montreal: Ingluvin Publications, 1971. 141p.

5180. _____. "Livesay's Choice," *Canadian Dimension*, 10:15-16, June 1975.

5181. _____. *Right hand, left hand*. Erin, [Ont.]: Press Porcepic, 1977. 280p.

5182. Mallinson, Anna Jean. "Versions and subversions: formal strategies in the poetry of contemporary Canadian women." PhD diss., Simon Fraser University, 1981. 277p.(Can. theses,no.51042)

5183. "Margaret Atwood: the woman as poet," *Communiqué*, no. 8:9-11, 45-6, May 1975.

5184. Marshall, Tom. "Major Canadian poets IV: Margaret Avison," *Canadian Forum*, 58:20-3, Mar. 1979.

5185. Sequin, Lucie. "Nicole Brossard: les mots-étreintes," *Canadian Women's Studies / Les cahiers de la femme*, 1:56-9, Spring 1979.

5186. Shain, Merle. "Some of our best poets are ... women," *Chatelaine*, 45:48-50, 103-7, Oct. 1972.

5187. Van Steen, Marcus. *Pauline Johnson, her life and work*. Toronto: Hodder and Stoughton, 1965, 1973 printing. 279p.

5188. Zimmerman, C. D. and S. C. Zimmerman. "Remember Dorothy?" *Canadian Forum*, 60:33-4, Sept. 1980.
5189. Zimmerman, S. "Livesay's houses," *Canadian Literature*, no. 61:32-45, Summer 1974.

POLICE FORCE

5190. "Board orders Ottawa police to let women re-apply," *Globe & Mail*, Jan. 22 1970, p.13.
5191. Bourne, Paula. "The case of Lois Beckett," in her, *Women in Canadian society*. Toronto: Ontario Institute for Studies in Education, 1976, pp.63-86.
5192. Breen, L. "Riding with the Redcoats: a psychologist on patrol in "D" division," *RCMP Quarterly*, 43(2):29-33, 1978.
5193. "Female police," *Labour Gazette*, 74:457-8, July 1974.
5194. Johnson, Eve. "Evelyn Daisy Le Sueur, or whatever happened to all those marching women," *Makara*, 1:28-31, Feb.-Mar. 1976.
5195. Martin, M. A. "Police personnel administration survey. Part 2," *Canadian Police College Journal*, 2(2):248-55, 1978.
5196. "Policewomen, why not?" *Royal Canadian Mounted Police Gazette*, 37(7/8):2-8, [1975?]
5197. Primeau, Liz. "They always get their person," *Ottawa Journal Weekend Magazine*, 25:1-9, Mar. 15, 1975.
5198. Prindiville, Joanne. *Report on women in policing in British Columbia*. Abridged version. [Vancouver]: British Columbia Police Commission, 1975. 47p.
5199. Roberts, Patricia J. "The policewoman - a personal view," *Canadian Police Chief*, 66:33-5, July 1977.
5200. Sandrock, Tom. "Les femmes dans la police," *Canadian Police Chief*, 67:27-8, 36, Apr. 1978.
5201. "The first woman troop," *Royal Canadian Mounted Police Gazette*, 37(7/8):10-11, [1975?]
5202. "Women police: the early years," *Canadian Police Chief*, 68(3):45-51, 1979.

POLITICAL SCIENCE

5203. Brody, M. Janine. "Women in political science: report on the status of women in the discipline," *Resources for Feminist Research*, 11:341-7, Nov. 1982.
5204. Lamont, Michèle. "De quelques subtilités hiérarchiques au sein de la science politique au Québec: le cas des sexes," *Resources for Feminist Research*, 11:339-40, Nov. 1982.
5205. "La science politique et les femmes: textes de communications présentées...Congrès de la Société québécoise de science politique...Montréal, le 14 mai 1982," *Resources for Feminist Research*, 11:334-40, Nov. 1982.
5206. Simard, Carolle. "La science politique et les femmes," *Resources for Feminist Research*, 11:334-5, Nov. 1982.
5207. Tahon, Marie-Blanche. "Repère: la production étudiante sur les femmes en science politique," *Resources for Feminist Research*, 11:335-7, Nov. 1982.
5208. Vaillancourt, Germaine et Francine Paquin. "Introduction à la politique...un regard féminin," *Resources for Feminist Research*, 11:337-8, Nov. 1982.

POLITICIANS

5209. Alain, Guilbert. "Albanie Morin: député et femme libérée," *Actualité*, 13:26-28, nov. 1973.
5210. Alberta. Women's Bureau. *Women in Canadian politics*. Alberta facts. Edmonton, 1975. 8p.

5211. Anderson, D. M. "As Judy saw it," *Chatelaine*, 42:3, Mar. 1969.
5212. _____. "Five good women MPs now and more tomorrow? [editorial]," *Chatelaine*, 46:1, Jan. 1973.
5213. Armstrong, Alvin. *Flora MacDonald*. Don Mills, Ont.: J. M. Dent & Sons (Canada), 1976. 217p.

5214. Batt, Sharon. "The radical tradition of Rosemary Brown," in, *Branching Out*, 2:16-17, 46, July-Aug. 1975.

5215. Beirne, Anne. "Women in provincial politics: part 5: Quebec," *Chatelaine*, 55:38-9, 50+ , July 1982.

5216. Bertrand, Réal. *Thérèse Casgrain*. Montréal: Lidec, 1981. 63p.

5217. Brodie, M. Janine and Jill McCalla Vickers. *Canadian women in politics: an overview*. CRIAW papers, no. 2. Ottawa: Canadian Research Institute for the Advancement of Women, 1982. 46, 14p.

5218. Brown, Rosemary. "Running a feminist campaign," *Branching Out*, 4:16-18, Nov.-Dec. 1977.

5219. Burgess, Jean. "'Power is not electoral'," *Branching Out*, 4:14-15, Nov.-Dec. 1977.

5220. Butler, Richard W. and Susan Phillips. "Women at city hall," in G. R. Wekerle, R. Peterson and D. Morley, eds., *New space for women*. Boulder: Westview Press, 1980, pp.273-86.

5221. Casgrain, Thérèse F. *Une femme chez les hommes*. Montréal: Éditions du Jour, 1971. 296p.

5222. _____. *Woman in a man's world*, translated by Joyce Marshall. [Toronto]: McClelland and Stewart, 1972. 192p.
French edition: Une femme chez les hommes.

5223. Charney, Ann. "Thérèse Casgrain: enfant terrible at 78," *Maclean's*, 87:37, 52-6, Sept. 1974.

5224. Chartrand, Simonne Monet. "Thérèse Casgrain: 'Il y a tant à faire, il ne faut pas abandonner'," *Relations*, 41:327, déc. 1981.

5225. Clarkson, Adrienne. "The female style in politics," in William Kilbourn, ed., *Guide to the peaceable kingdom*. Toronto: Macmillan, 1970, pp.185-7.
Re. Judy LaMarsh, 'Bird in a gilded cage'.

5226. Conroy, Mary M. "A woman in politics," *Chatelaine*, 46:32, 98, 100-2, Apr. 1973.

5227. Cormack, Barbara. *Perennials and politics: the life story of Hon. Irene Parlby*. Sherwood Park, Alta.: Professional Print, [1968]. 160p.

5228. Darveau-Cardinal, Jacqueline. "'Une femme chez les hommes' ou Thérèse-F. Casgrain, femme politique, canadienne française," *Forces*, no. 18: 46, 1972.

5229. Davidson, True. "The gentle heroine: Thérèse F. Casgrain," in her, *Golden strings*. Toronto: Griffin House, 1973, pp.35-47.

5230. Dutil, Denis et Mair Verthuy. "Femmage [Thérèse Casgrain]," *Canadian Women's Studies / Les cahiers de la femme*, 2(2):24-6, 1980.

5231. Fergusson, C. Bruce. *Alderman Abbie Lane of Halifax*. Windsor, N.S.: Lancelot Press, 1976. 40p.

5232. Festeau, Hélène. "Des voix de femmes dans un choeur d'hommes [Jean Sauvé]," *Châtelaine*, 14:26-7, 46, mars 1973.

5233. "Flora a Thatcher matcher?" *Canada and the World*, 40:10, May 1975.

5234. Forsyth, Carolyn June. "'Whatever my sex, I'm no lady': Charlotte Whitton, politician; welfare pioneer," *Makara*, 2(4):27-31.

5235. Fotheringham, Allan. "The pure left politics of Rosemary Brown," *Saturday Night*, 90:31-4, July-Aug. 1975.

5236. Frève, Claire, Sylvia Park and Wendy Lawrence. "City women: women in municipal politics; Les femmes et la politique municipale," *Status of Women News / Statut: Bulletin de la femme*, 5:17-19, [English]; 16-18, [French], Summer 1979.

5237. Gleason, Marie. "How sweet it sounds," *Atlantic Advocate*, 64:15, Feb. 1974. Re. Dorothy Wyatt, first woman mayor of St. Johns.

5238. Gray, Charlotte. "Women in provincial politics: part 6: Atlantic provinces," *Chatelaine*, 55:54-5, 121-2+ , Aug. 1982.

5239. _____. "10 women MPs: a new breed," *Chatelaine*, 52:62-3, Oct. 1979.

5240. Guggi, Anita. "Steady increase of women in [local] government," *Civic*, 33:6, 47, Sept. 1981.

210

5241. Guilbert, Alain. "Albanie Morin: député et femme libérée," *Actualité*, 13:26-8, nov. 1973.

5242. Gwyn, Sandra. "Flora," *Saturday Night*, 90:17-23, June 1975.

5243. Haggan, Hilary and Denise Ledoux. *Women in parliament and the provincial legislatures*. Ottawa: Library of Parliament. Information and Reference Branch, 1983. 58p.

5244. Hobbs, Lisa. "Are the PC's (and Canada) ready for Flora MacDonald?" *Chatelaine*, 49:37, 76, 78, 80-1, Feb. 1976.

5245. _____. "Why is Rosemary running?" *Chatelaine*, 48:30, 73-5, 77-8, July 1975.

5246. Horne, H. Shirley. "Frances Perry [Mayor]: breaking new ground for women,"*Atlantic Advocate*, 70:40-1, May 1980.

5247. Hynes, Maureen. "'We need a national network of power brokers'," *Branching Out*, 4:9-11, Nov.-Dec. 1977. Interview with Laura Sabia.

5248. Jackson, R. "First woman speaker [Senate]," *Atlantic Advocate*, 63:17-18, Apr. 1973.

5249. Jameson, Sheilagh. "Give your other vote to the sister," *Alberta Historical Review*, 15:10-16, Autumn 1967.

5250. Kane, Becky. "Agnes MacPhail: first woman M.P.,"*Status of Women News*, 2:4-6, May 1976.

5251. Kieran, Sheila. "(Woman) doctor in the house [Bette Stephenson]," *Chatelaine*, 49:47, 99-103, Sept. 1976.

5252. Kirkland-Casgrain, Claire. "A woman in politics, my own story," *Chatelaine*, 48:37, 66+, Mar. 1975.

5253. Kohn, Walter S. G. "The Canadian House of Commons," in his *Women in national legislatures: a comparative study of six countries*. New York: Praeger, 1980, pp.113-34.

5254. Kome, Penney. "Hard hats & flowers [Judy Erola]," *Homemaker's Magazine*, 17:75-6, 78+ , Sept. 1982.

5255. Konantz, Gail. *Edith Rogers*. Winnipeg. Peguis Publishers, 1981. 52p.

5256. Kostash, Myrna. "Iona Campagnolo: is there life after Ottawa?" *Chatelaine*, 53:38-9, 108+ , Sept. 1980.

5257. Labreche, Julianne. "Monique Bégin: the politician people like," *Chatelaine*, 54:56-7, 97+ , Feb. 1981.

5258. _____. "Women in provincial politics: part 4: Ontario," *Chatelaine*, 55:52-3, 170+ , June 1982.

5259. LaMarsh, Judy. *Memoirs of a bird in a gilded cage*. Toronto: McClelland and Stewart, 1969. 367p.

5260. Lawrence, Judith and Jean Wilson. "Anne Johnston [Toronto City Council]," *Broadside*, 2:7, Oct.-Nov. 1980.

5261. Lister, Joan. "Joan Neiman: the Senate's one-woman demolition squad,"*Impetus*, Sept. 1974, pp.9, 15-16, 18, 26.

5262. "Liberal senator Muriel Fergusson of Fredericton has been appointed Speaker of the Senate," *Atlantic Advocate*, 63:55, Feb. 1973.

5263. MacGregor, Roy. "The honorable Flora," *Maclean's*, 92:17-21, Sept. 3, 1979.

5264. McKeown, Robert. "The determined Miss Pauline Jewett," *Weekend Magazine*, 24:7-10, Oct. 12, 1974.

5265. Manitoba. Dept. of Education. *Manitoba women in politics*. Poster series notes. [Winnipeg], 1979. 47p. (Microlog 80-1294) Notes to accompany a series of posters.

5266. Marchand, Philip. "Judy Erola: the one-woman energy resource who's minister of state for mines," *Chatelaine*, 54:52-3, 146+ , Apr. 1981.

5267. Melnyk, Helen. "The lady was a politician [Irene Parlby]," *Branching Out*, 6(4):14-17, 1979.

5268. Monté, Denyse. *On l'appelle toujours...Lise*. Montréal: La Presse, 1975. 214p.

5269. Morier, Roger. "Style and substance: the career of Charlotte Whitton," *Canadian Women's Studies / Les cahiers de la femme*, 3(1):66-72, 1981.

5270. "Our Ms. Chatelaine 1974 is Jean Fowlow of Stephenville, Newfoundland,"*Chatelaine*, 47:43, 89-90, May 1974.

5271. Payette, Lise. *Le pouvoir? Connais pas!* Montréal: Québec/Amérique, 1982. 212p.

5272. Preston, Patricia. "'You have to run for yourself'," *Branching Out*, 4:12-13, Nov.-Dec. 1977. Interview with Maria Eriksen of Calgary.

5273. Prodanou, Anna. "Women in Territorial politics," *Chatelaine*, 55:34, 185-6+ , Sept. 1982.

5274. Rabkin, Brenda. "A galaxy of women mayors," *Chatelaine*, 53:42-3, 112+ , Aug. 1980.

5275. Robb, Jim. "Monique Bégin: the reluctant politician," *Perception*, 3:27-31, May-June 1980.

5276. Robertson, Heather. "A woman for our time [Flora MacDonald]," *Canadian Magazine*, May 3, 1975, pp.2-4, 7.

5277. _____. "Flora, the red Tory, or, Ms. MacDonald as Prime Minister," *Maclean's*, 87:120, Nov. 1974.

5278. Rooke, Patricia T. and R. L. Schnell. "'An idiot's flowerbed' - a study of Charlotte Whitton's feminist thought, 1941-50," *International Journal of Women's Studies*, 5:29-46, Jan.-Feb. 1982.

5279. Ross, Val. "Getting clout: what are our women politicians doing for you?" *Chatelaine*, 51:45-7, 66+ , May 1978.

5280. Ross, Val. "The honourable Flora," *Chatelaine*, 53:36-7, 57+ , Jan. 1980.

5281. Sangster, Dorothy. "Ottawa's dedicated new mayor, Marion Dewar," *Chatelaine*, 52:28+ , May 1979.

5282. Schendlinger, Mary. "From Vancouver East to Ottawa central [interview with Marg Mitchell, Federal NDP candidate for Vancouver East]," *Makara*, 3(2):21-2, [1978?]

5283. Taylor, James A. "Brenda Robertson: a woman worth watching," *United Church Observer*, new ser. 36:26-8, 44, Sept. 1972.

5284. Vastel, Michel. "La femme de 18 milliards [Monique Bégin]," *L'Actualité*, 6:27-33, août 1981.

5285. "Women in politics," *Journal (The Board of Trade of Metropolitan Toronto)*, Easter 1977, pp.29-31.

5286. "Women in politics: a conversation with Pauline Jewett," *Canadian Business Review*, 2:17-19, Summer 1975.

5287. "Women with political clout," *Financial Post*, 65:BC11, Mar. 13, 1971.

5288. Wright, J. F. C. *The Louise Lucas story. This time tomorrow*. Montreal: Harvest House, 1965. 137p.

5289. Zwarun, Suzanne. "Women in provincial politics: part 1: British Columbia," *Chatelaine*, 55:58-9, 85+ , Mar. 1982.

5290. _____. "Women in provincial politics: part 2: Alberta," *Chatelaine*, 55:64-5, 178+ , Apr. 1982.

5291. _____. "Women in provincial politics: part 3: Manitoba & Saskatchewan," *Chatelaine*, 55:60-1, 130+ , May 1982.

POLITICIANS' WIVES

5292. Beirne, Anne. "Backstage: referendum: women who live in different worlds," *Maclean's*, 93:4, May 12, 1980.

5293. Buxton, Bonnie. "Meet Maureen McTeer" *Chatelaine*, 49:52, 117-23, Oct. 1976.

5294. Callwood, June. "Margaret's first hurrah," *Maclean's*, 87:4, 6-10, Aug. 1974.

5295. Cochrane, Felicity. *Margaret Trudeau: the prime minister's runaway wife*. Scarborough, Ont.: New American Library of Canada, 1978. 173p.

5296. Gotlieb, Sondra. "Dare a political wife be a real person?" *Chatelaine*, 50:49, 76-8, Jan. 1977.

5297. Holt, Simma. *The other Mrs. Diefenbaker*. Toronto: Doubleday Canada, 1982. 378p.

5298. Johnson, Arthur. *Margaret Trudeau*. Markham, Ont.: PaperJacks, 1977. 210p.

5299. Labreche, Julianne. "Lucille Broadbent: portrait of a very political wife," *Chatelaine*, 55:58, 104+ , Apr. 1982.

5300. Marchand, Philip. "Margaret Trudeau: life after Pierre," *Chatelaine*, 55:52-3, 101+ , Feb. 1982.

5301. Paterson, Sheena and Mary C. McEwan. "Margaret Trudeau's struggle for identity: victor or victim?" *Chatelaine*, 50:32-3, 91-3, Aug. 1977.

5302. Reynolds, Louise. *Agnes: the biography of Lady Macdonald*. Toronto: Samuel Stevens, 1979. 229p.

5303. Roberts, Barbara. "'They drove him to drink'... Donald Creighton's, MacDonald and his wives," *Canada: an Historial Magazine*, 3:51-64, Dec. 1975.

5304. Rossiter, Sean. "Will the real Maureen McTeer please stand up?" *Chatelaine*, 52:36-7, 114+ , Feb. 1979.

5305. Trudeau, Margaret. *Beyond reason*. New York. Paddington Press, 1979. 256p.

POLITICS

5306. "A modesty of Ms.P.s," *Time. Can. ed.*, 100:12-14, Oct. 23, 1972.

5307. Alberta Status of Women Action Committee. *Political involvement handbook for Alberta women*. [Edmonton]: Alberta. Women's Bureau, 1978. 79p.

5308. Anderson, Doris. "Let's desegregate the Commons [editorial]," *Chatelaine*, 45:1, Oct. 1972.

5309. _____. "Let's put women into politics [editorial]," *Chatelaine*, 45:1, Oct. 1972.

5310. _____. "More women MP's. How significant? [editorial]," *Chatelaine*, 47:1, Sept. 1974.

5311. _____. "MPs who care and the MPs who don't [editorial]," *Chatelaine*, 45:1, May 1972.

5312. _____. "Now is the time for all good women to come to the aid of themselves [editorial]," *Chatelaine*, 47:1, Feb. 1974.

5313. _____. "105 good reasons why women should be in parliament," *Chatelaine*, 44:1, Oct. 1971.

5314. Archibald, Linda and others. "Sex biases in newspaper reporting: press treatment of municipal candidates," *Atlantis*, 5:177-84, Spring 1980.

5315. Assheton-Smith, Marilyn. "Women and politics in Western Canada: a socio-political study." Working draft of paper presented at the 14th Annual Meeting of the Western Association of Sociology and Anthropology, Banff, Dec. 29-31, 1973. 10p.

5316. Bashevkin, Sylvia B. "Women's participation in the Ontario political parties, 1971-1981," *Journal of Canadian Studies*, 17:44-54, Summer 1982.

5317. Beeby, Deen. "Women in the Ontario C.C.F., 1940-1950," *Ontario History*, 74:258-83, Dec. 1982.

5318. Beirne, Anne. "Backstage: referendum: women who live in different worlds," *Maclean's*, 93:4, May 12, 1980.

5319. _____. "Blossoming of the Yvettes," *Maclean's*, 93:26, Apr. 21, 1980.

5320. Black, Jerome H. and Nancy E. McGlen. "Changing patterns of political participation between Canadian men and women, 1965-1974." Paper presented at the 49th Annual meeting of the Canadian Political Science Association, University of New Brunswick, Fredericton, N.B., June 9-11, 1977. 36p.

5321. _____. "Male-female political involvement differentials in Canada, 1965-1974," *Canadian Journal of Political Science*, 12:471-97, Sept. 1979.

5322. Black, Naomi. "A further note about women in Canadian political science," *Resources for Feminist Research*, 8:5, Nov. 1979.

5323. _____. "Changing European and North American attitudes towards women in public life," *Journal of European Integration*, 1(2):221-40, 1978.

5324. _____. "Women in Canadian political science," *Resources for Feminist Research*, 8:36-8, Mar. 1979.

5325. Boyd, Rosamonde R. "Women and politics in the U.S. and Canada," *Annals of the American Academy of Political and Social Science*, 375:52-7, Jan. 1968.

5326. Brent, G. "Development of the law relating to the participation of Canadian women in public life," *University of Toronto Law Journal*, 25:258-70, 1975.

5327. Brodie, M. Janine and Jill McCalla Vickers. "Gates, gatekeepers and women legislative candidates in Canada: a preliminary investigation." Paper presented at the 50th Annual meeting of the Canadian Political Science Association, University of Western Ontario, London, Ont., May 31, 1978. 41p.

5328. Brodie, M. Janine. "The recruitment of Canadian women provincial legislators, 1950-1975," *Atlantis*, 2:6-17, Spring 1977, Part I.

5329. _____. "The recruitment of men and women political party activists in Ontario: a four variable model." MA thesis, University of Windsor, 1976. 194p. (Can. theses, no.29116)

5330. Brown, Heather, comp. "Women candidates running," *Broadside*, 1(4):10, [1980].

5331. Brown, Rosemary. "A new kind of power," in Gwen Matheson, *Women in the Canadian mosaic*. Toronto: Peter Martin, 1976, pp.288-98.

5332. Burt, Sandra D. "The political participation of women in Ontario." PhD diss., York University, 1981. 335p. (Can. theses, no.51364)

5333. _____. "Women's perceptions of politics: some implications for behavioral research." Paper presented at the 51st Annual meeting of the Canadian Political Science Association, Saskatoon, Sask., May 30, 1979. 35p.

5334. Canada. Library of Parliament. Research Branch. *Canadian women in public life*. [Ottawa] 1966. 34p.

5335. Canadian Advisory Council on the Status of Women. *Sharing the power*. Ottawa, [1980]. Folder.

5336. Charney, Ann. "The passionate quest of Quebec's separatist women," *Chatelaine*, 52:54-5, 146+ , Mar. 1979.

5337. Clarke, Harold D. and Allan Kornberg. "Moving up the political escalator: women party officials in the United States and Canada," *Journal of Politics*, 41:442-77, May 1979.

5338. Cochrane, Jean. *Women in Canadian politics*. Rev ed. Markham,Ont.: Fitzhenry and Whiteside Limited, 1983.

5339. Cohen, Yolande, ed. *Femmes et politique*. Montréal: Le Jour, 1981. 227p.

5340. Eichler, Margrit. "Sex equality and political participation of women in Canada: some survey results," *International Review of Sociology*, 15:49-75, Apr.-Dec. 1979.

5341. Engel, Joan J. *The 'persons case', 50th anniversary Oct. 18, 1929-Oct. 18, 1979*. Edmonton: Alberta. Women's Bureau, 1979. 28p. (Microlog 80-1592)
        Learning kit prepared for application to Grades 8B and 10A Social Studies programs.

5342. "Federal party platforms on women: excerpts from NAC's assessment," *Canadian Forum*, 59:10, Sept. 1979.

5343. Fédération des femmes du Québec. *La participation politique des femmes du Québec*. Royal Commission on the Status of Women in Canada. Study no. 10. Ottawa: Information Canada, 1971. 166p.

5344. Ferrante, Angela. "The prime of Iona Campagnolo," *Chatelaine*, 56:53, 70, 72, 74, May 1983.

5345. Fisher, Douglas. "All men had better find the right answer to 'why not?'," *Executive*, 17:66, Apr. 1975.

5346. Fotheringham, Allan. "Female sex in public life," *Maclean's*, 95:80, Nov. 22, 1982.

5347. _____. "Shall they join the ladies?" *Maclean's*, 94:64, Feb. 23, 1981.

5348. _____. "Where are the women in the House?," *Maclean's*, 94:72, Dec. 14, 1981.

5349. Fournier, Francine. "Les femmes et la vie politique au Québec,"dans Marie Lavigne et Yolande Pinard, *Les femmes dans la société québécoise: aspects historiques*. Montréal: Éditions du Boréal Express, 1977, pp.169-90.

5350. Frum, B. "Insiders' tips on how to get women elected," *Chatelaine*, 44:38, Oct. 1971.

5351. _____. "Why there are so few women in Ottawa," *Chatelaine*, 44:33, 110+ , Oct. 1971.

5352. Gray, Charlotte. "Women in politics, 1980: the new backroom girls," *Chatelaine*, 53:25-9, 60+ , July 1980.

5353. "Inside politics," *Makara*, 1:13-16, Dec. 1975.

214

5354. Ion, Caroline, ed. *Women in local government: an OCLG study project*. Toronto: Ontario Conference on Local Government, 1974. 115p.

5355. Istona, Mildred. "The vote is not enough," *Chatelaine*, 52:2, May 1979.

356. Jean, Michèle et Marie Lavigne. "Le phénomène des Yvettes: analyse externe," *Atlantis*, 6:17-23, Spring 1981.

5357. Kome, Penney. "Her honor, the mayor," *Homemaker's Magazine*, 15:6-8, 10+ , June 1980.

5358. Kopinak, Kathryn Mary. "Sex differences in Ontario political culture." PhD diss., York University, 1978. 208p. (Can. theses, no.36993)

5359. Lacelle, Nicole. "Minding our PQ's," *Broadside*, 1(8):10, 1980.

5360. Lamothe, Jacqueline et Jennifer Stoddart. "Les Yvettes ou: comment un parti politique traditionnel se sert encore une fois des femmes," *Atlantis*, 6:10-16, Spring 1981.

5361. Landsberg, Michele. "105 potential women MP's," *Chatelaine*, 44:33-7, 110, Oct. 1971.

5362. _____. "Why we still need more women MP's," *Chatelaine*, 45:32, 36, 38, 112-13, Oct. 1972.

5363. _____. "Women in politics: good news and bad," *Chatelaine*, 47:37, 73-6, Apr. 1974.

5364. Langevin, Liane. *Ms...ing: women in Canadian federal politics*. Ottawa: Canada. Advisory Council on the Status of Women, 1977. 60p.

5365. _____. "Women in politics: legislative behaviour of female members of parliament in Canada." MA research essay, Institute of Canadian Studies, Carleton University, 1977. 83p.

5366. Lavigne, Marie et Michèle Jean. "40 ans de vote...et après," *La Gazette des femmes*, 2:8-10, Apr. 1980.

5367. Lawrence, Wendy and Naomi Black. "Political participation by Canadian women; Participation politique des Canadiennes," *Status of Women News / Statut: Bulletin de la femme*, 5:13, [English]; 13, [French], Summer 1979.

5368. Laws, Margaret. "Fewer women up front but more become backroom boys," *Financial Post*, 73:13, May 5, 1979, suppl.

5359. Light, Beth. "The National Council of Women, government centralization, and the 1917 federal election campaign." MA major research paper, York University, 1975. 34p.

5370. MacInnis, Grace. "Women and politics," *Parliamentarian*, 53:8-12, Jan. 1972.

5371. Macpherson, Kay. "Four per cent is no solution," *Canadian Forum*, 59:9-10, Sept. 1979.

5372. Manley, John. "Women and the left in the 1930's: the case of the Toronto CCF Women's Joint Committee," *Atlantis*, 5:100-19, Spring 1980.

5373. Marchildon, Rudy G. "The 'persons' controversy: the legal aspects of the fight for women senators," *Atlantis*, 6:99-113, Spring 1981.

5374. Maroney, Heather Jon. "Sexual politics in Quebec: the structure and dynamics of class, national and sex oppression." MA thesis, McMaster University, 1978. 308p. (Can. theses,no.46913)

5375. McCall-Newman, Christina. "Women and political power: what's holding us back?" *Chatelaine*, 55:58, 86+ , Dec. 1982.

5376. McDowell, Linda. "Some women candidates for the Manitoba legislature," *Historical and Scientific Society of Manitoba. Transactions*, 32:5-20, 1975-1976.

5377. Moisan, Lise. "Quebec: a view from inside: yes, but... ," *Broadside*, 1(8):11, 1980.

5378. New Democratic Party. *Women in Canada: in society, in public life, in the NDP*. Ottawa: New Democratic Party, 1971. 16p.

5379. Newman, C. "Body politic in Ottawa - women are either babes or blobs," *Chatelaine*, 43:20, Sept. 1970.

5380. Ontario. Ministry of Treasury, Economics and Intergovernmental Affairs and Ontario Conference on Local Government. *Women and local government ... a beginning*. Toronto, 1975. 25p.

5381. Paris, Erna. "Women's status - how the MPs rate you," *Chatelaine*, 45:28-9, 102, 104-6, 108, 110-13, May 1972.

5382. Pelletier, Gérard. "Jouez avec le feu: un grain du poivre," *Châtelaine*, 15:2, janv. 1974.

5383. Pike, Lois. "Participation of women in the Canadian political process." MA thesis, University of Guelph, 1972. 128p.

5384. "Polity and personhood," in Canadian Research Institute for the Advancement of Women, *Women as persons. [La femme en tant que personne]*. Toronto: Resources for Feminist Research, 1980, pp.52-60.
Proceedings of the 3rd annual meeting.

5385. Robb, W. "Women in politics," *Canadian Business*, 41:11-12, Mar. 1968.

5386. Roberts, Barbara. "Women in politics," in Lynda Turner, comp., *Woman in Canadian society*. [New Westminster, B.C.: Douglas College, 1972], pp.30-42.

5387. Ross, Val. "Getting clout: what are our women politicians doing for you?" *Chatelaine*, 51:45-7, 66+ , May 1978.

5388. Roycroft, Marilyn M. "Political socialization of women in Canada." MA thesis, University of Waterloo, 1973. 145p.

5389. Sabia, Laura. "Women and politics," in Ann B. Shteir, ed., *Women on women*. Toronto: York University, 1978, pp.29-42.

5390. Sauvé, Jeanne and Lise Bacon. "Women, politics and the civil service," *Canadian Banker and ICB Review*, 82:32-5, May-June 1975.

5391. "Sexual politics Canadian-style," in Solange Chaput-Rolland and Gertrude Laing, *Face to face*. Toronto: New Press, 1972, pp.44-51.

5392. Stein, David Lewis and Erna Paris. "Politics & power: why do women lag?" *Chatelaine*, 51:22, 122, June 1978.

5393. Stewart, Walter. "You've come a short way, baby," *Maclean's*, 88:8, May 1975.

5394. Tardy, Evelyne et autres. *La politique, un monde d'hommes?: une étude sur les mairesses au Québec*. Cahiers du Québec, no. 70. Montréal: Hurtubise H M H, 1982. 111p.

5395. Thomson, Aisla Margaret. "Women and Canadian politics: a critique of the 'Adam's Rib' approach to political science." MA thesis, Queen's University, 1977. 163p. (Can. theses, no.34662)

5396. "Towards a Canadian feminist party," *Atlantis*, 5:142-5, Fall 1979.

5397. Van der Gracht, Deb. "OWL women politically wise," *Branching Out*, 6(1):5, 1979.

5398. Van Herk, Aritha. "Editorial: feminism: wallflower in party politics," *Branching Out*, 6(2):2, 1979.

5399. Vickers, Jill McCalla and M. Janine Brodie. "Canada," in Joni Lovenduski and Jill Hills, eds., *The politics of the second electorate: women and public participation*. London: Routledge and Kegan Paul, 1981, pp.52-82.
For extended treatment, see Brodie and McCalla, *Canadian women in politics: an overview*. 1982.

5400. Vickers, Jill McCalla. "Where are the women in Canadian politics?" *Atlantis*, 3:40-51, Spring 1978, Part II.

5401. Vickers, J. McCalla. *A preliminary statistical map of female candidacies in federal and provincial elections 1951-74*. Ottawa: Canada. Secretary of State, 1975. 21p.
Prepared for seminar, "Women and Politics", Mar. 10-12, 1975.

5402. _____. *Private lives and public responsibilities: Canadian women in politics*. Ottawa: Canada. Secretary of State, 1975. 18p.
Prepared for seminar, "Women and Politics", Mar. 10-12, 1975.

5403. Wallace, Catherine. "What would the suffragists think of our voting record?" *Chatelaine*, 47:32, Nov. 1974.

5404. Wallace, Joan. "Missing in action - women in politics; Absentes des grandes débats du jour - les femmes et la vie politique," *Status of Women News / Statut: Bulletin de la femme*, 4:3-4, [English]; 3-4, [French], June 1978.

5405. Weppler, Doreen. "Early forms of political activity among white women in British Columbia, 1880-1925." MA thesis, Simon Fraser University, 1971. 146p. (Can. theses, no.10294)

5406. "Why she wants a minister for women [British Columbia]," *Financial Post*, 67:39, Mar. 17, 1973.

5407. Women for Political Action. *Women in politics: national conference 1973*. [*Femme dans la vie politique: conférence nationale 1973*]. Toronto, [1975]. 66, 68p.
5408. "Women in politics: a conversation with Pauline Jewett," *Canadian Business Review*, 2:17-19, Summer 1975.
5409. Wyman, Georgina. "Pauline Jewett: an interview," *Branching Out*, 1:20-3, 38, Sept.-Oct. 1974.

POLITICS - BIBLIOGRAPHY

5410. Evans, Gwynneth, comp. *Women in federal politics: a bio-bibliography*. Edited by Marion C. Wilson. Ottawa: National Library of Canada, 1975. 81p.
5411. Feldman, Wendy A. "Women in Canadian politics since 1945: a bibliography," *Resources for Feminist Research*, 8:38-42, Mar. 1979.
5412. Swanick, M. Lynne Struthers. *Women in Canadian politics and government: a bibliography*. Council of Planning Librarians. Exchange bibliography, no. 697. Monticello, Ill.: Council of Planning Librarians, 1974. 29p.

POPULATION

5413. Canadian Broadcasting Corporation. Research Dept. *Attitudes of Canadians to certain aspects of population growth*. Ottawa, 1971.
5414. Norland, J. A. *The age-sex structure of Canada's population: a compendium of selected data. Annotated updates and addenda based on the 1976 census*. Ottawa: Statistics Canada, 1979. 17p.
5415. Yam, J. *The age-sex structure of Canada's population: a compendium of selected data*. Statistics Canada. Analytical and technical memorandum, no. 9. Ottawa: Statistics Canada, 1974. 57p.

PORNOGRAPHY

5416. Engel, Marian and others. "What price censorship?" *Branching Out*, 6(4):5-8, 1979.
5417. Fulford, Robert. "Freedom, pornography, and violence against women," *Saturday Night*, 94:14, 18, Mar. 1979.
5418. McCormack, Thelma. "Passionate protests: feminists and censorship," *Canadian Forum*, 59:6-8, Mar. 1980.
5419. National Action Committee on the Status of Women. *Discussion paper on pornography*, prepared by Jillian Ridington. [Toronto], 1983. 21p. and app.
5420. Robertson, Jennifer. *Pornography and its effects: a survey of recent literature*. Toronto: Ontario Status of Women Council, [1979]. 28, 2p.
5421. Stickney, Mercia and others. *Survey: women's community standard on sexually-explicit material publicly available and promoted as entertainment*. Burnaby, B.C.: B.C. Public Interest Research Group, 1983.
5422. Wachtel, Eleanor. "Our newest battleground: pornography," *Branching Out*, 6(3):33-7, 1979.
         For commentary and reply Marian Engel above.

POSTAGE STAMPS

5423. "Feminist stamps issued by Canada Post," *Broadside*, 2:10, Mar. 1981.
5424. Fitzpatrick, Helen. "Feminist philately," *Branching Out*, 3:38-40, July-Aug. 1976.

POVERTY

5425. Adams, I. "Real poor in Canada are women," *Chatelaine*, 42:42-3, 109-12, Apr. 1969.
5426. Arel, Louise. "Être pauvre parce que femme et âgée," *Perception*, 4:36-7, Jan.-Feb. 1981.

5427. Canadian Council on Social Development. *Women in need: a sourcebook*. Ottawa: Canadian Council on Social Development, 1976. 92p.
 French edition: Pauvre et seule.
5428. McCallan, N. J. and Katherine Roback. *An ordinary life: life histories of women in the urban core of Vancouver*. CRIAW working papers. Sponsored by the Canadian Research Institute for the Advancement of Women. n.p., n.d. 36p. and app.
5429. National Council of Welfare. *Women and poverty*. Ottawa, 1979. 59p. and app.
5430. Schull, Christiane. "Bag ladies," Today, Apr. 25, 1981, pp.15-16.
5431. Townson, Monica. "Canada's women: riding a treadmill to poverty," *Canadian Business Review*, 7:22-9, Spring 1980.

PREGNANCY

5432. Adler, Cathy and Shirley Congdon. *An overview of teenage pregnancy and parenthood in British Columbia: a paper released to promote public discussion*. Vancouver: Social Planning and Review Council of British Columbia, 1980. 101p.
5433. Briedis, Catherine. "Marginal deviants: teenage girls experience community response to premarital sex and pregnancy," *Social Problems*, 22:480-93, Apr. 1975.
5434. Canadian Institute of Child Health. *Prenatal information in Canada: resources available on a national basis 1981: major findings and recommendations*. Ottawa: CICH, 1981. 80p.
5435. Community Task Force on Maternal and Child Health. *Manitoba native Indian mother and child: a discussion paper on a high risk population*. Winnipeg, Man., 1981. 45p.
5436. Lambert, John Thomas. "The internalized other: identity change over the course of pregnancy." MA thesis, McMaster University, 1975. 149p.
5437. McKilligan, Helen R. "Deliveries in teenagers at a Newfoundland general hospital," *Canadian Medical Association. Journal*, 118:1252-4, May 20, 1978.
5438. Orton, Maureen Jessop and Ellen Rosenblatt. *Adolescent birth planning needs: Ontario in the eighties*. n.p.: Planned Parenthood Ontario, 1981. 84p.
5439. Roy, Monique. "Ça n'arrive qu'aux autres," *Canadian Women's Studies / Les cahiers de la femme*, 2(1):4-5, 1980.
5440. S.O.S. grossesse. *Listening*. [*Femmes à l'écoute*]. Charlesbourg, Québec: S.O.S. grossesse, 1976. 11,12p.
5441. Stone, Sharon H. and Kenneth E. Scott. "The unwanted pregnancy," *Canadian Medical Association. Journal*, 111:1093, 1096-7, Nov. 16, 1974.
5442. Thomas, Eleanor. "Maternity and narcotic addiction," *Canada's Mental Health*, 23:13-16, Sept. 1975, Suppl.

PRESS

5443. Archibald, Linda and others. "Sex biases in newspaper reporting: press treatment of municipal candidates," *Atlantis*, 5:177-84, Spring 1980.
5444. Boyer, Ginette. "Le colloque sur les femmes et l'information: à quand un regard-femme sur le monde?" *Relations*, 41:326, déc. 1981.
5445. Canadian Women's Press Club. *Brief no.94 to the Royal Commission on the Status of women in Canada*. Toronto, 1968. 5p.
5446. Carisse, Colette. "Images of woman's action," in Clio Presvelou and Pierre de Bie, eds., *Images and counter-images of young families*. [Louvain: Secretariat of the International Scientific Commission on the Family], 1970, pp.155-68.
5447. Indra, Doreen. "Invisible mosaic: women, ethnicity and the Vancouver press, 1905-1976," *Canadian Ethnic Studies*, 13(1):63-74, 1981.
5448. Ingram, Marta and Ceta Ramkhalawansingh. "Women and the politics of culture in the mass media: a survey of five Canadian newspapers, 1979," *Resources for Feminist Research*, 8:86-9, Nov. 1979.
5449. McRae, Earl. "Don't women know how lucky they are to be singled out?" *The Canadian*, Feb. 18, 1978, p.24.

5450. Pineau-Ouellet, Ghislaine. "Les femmes vues à travers les journaux rimouskois," *Revue d'histoire du Bas Saint-Laurent*, 5:14-21, déc. 1978.

5451. *Sexism and the newspapers*. Ottawa: Ontario Press Council, 1978. 26p.

PRISONS AND PRISONERS

5452. *B.C. federal women: an alternative proposal: report on a consultation, June 1979*. Vancouver: Elizabeth Fry Society of British Columbia, [1979?] 30, 30p.

5453. "Behind the pink steel door," *Time Canada*, 104:14-15, Dec. 9, 1974.

5454. Berner, Geri. "Both sides now," *Branching Out*, 2:6-7, Jan.-Feb. 1975.

5455. Berzins, Lorraine and Sheelagh Cooper. "The political economy of correctional planning for women: the case of the bankrupt bureaucracy," *Canadian Journal of Criminology*, 24:399-416, Oct. 1982.

5456. "Better treatment, opportunity urged for women behind bars," *Globe & Mail*, Feb. 5, 1979, p.5.

5457. British Columbia. Royal Commission on the Incarceration of Female Offenders. *Report*. Vancouver, 1978. 176, [18]p. Commissioner: Patricia A. Proudfoot.

5458. Canada. Joint Committee to Study Alternatives for the Housing of the Federal Female Offender. *Report*. [Canada. Comité mixte chargé d'étudier les possibilités de logement pour les détenues sous responsabilité fédérale. *Rapport*.] [Ottawa: Canada. Dept. of the Solicitor General. Correctional Service of Canada], 1978. 39, 40p.

5459. Canada. National Advisory Committee on the Female Offender. *Report*.[Ottawa]: Canadian Penitentiary Service. Public Affairs Division / National Parole Service, 1977. 74p.

5460. Canada. Public Service Commission. *A study of the existing sex restrictions in the correctional group CX(COF-LUF-STI): un unnotional and controversial issue*. [Ottawa], 1977. 67, 75p. Report of a Committee. Includes French text under title: Étude sur les restrictions d'ordre sexuel dans le groupe des services correctionnels CX(COF-LUF-STI): une question fort controversée.

5461. Canadian Advisory Council on the Status of Women. *Women in prison: expanding their options*. Brief presented to the Strategic Planning Committee on the Future of Correctional Service of Canada. Ottawa, 1980. 20p.

5462. Clark, Donna. "Our sisters' keepers [interview]," *Broadside*, 1(6):10-11, 1980.

5463. Dunn, Sheelagh. "Prisonwomen: sex discrimination in Canada's only federal prison for women," *Perception*, 4:33-6, Spring-Summer 1981.

5464. Fournier, Suzanne. "Women in prisons: organizing behind bars," *Makara*, 1:2-8, Dec. 1975.

5465. Gillan, Mary Ellen. "Female prisoners and the inmate code." MA thesis, University of Alberta, 1976. 99p. (Can. theses, no.27651)

5466. Gillan, Mary E. "Female prisoners: are you ready to accept them in your community?" *Branching Out*, 2:16-19, May-June 1975.

5467. Gilroy, Joan. "Facing the outside: the views of women prisoners." MA thesis, University of Toronto, 1974. 113p.

5468. Hartnagel, Timothy F. and Mary Ellen Gillan. "Female prisoners and the inmate code," *Pacific Sociological Review*, 23:85-104, Jan. 1980.

5469. Kirkaldy, Anne D. *Incarcerated women in British Columbia provincial institutions*. [Victoria]: British Columbia. Ministry of the Attorney-General. Corrections Branch. Program Evaluation and Data Systems, 1978. 102p. (Profile 78-0820)

5470. Lambert, Leah R. and Patrick G. Madden. *The adult female offender before-during-after incarceration*. Vanier Centre research report, no. 3. Toronto: Ontario. Ministry of Correctional Services, 1975. 114p. (Profile 76-0416)

5471. _____. "The adult female offender: the road from institution to community life," *Canadian Journal of Criminology and Corrections*, 18:319-31, Oct. 1976.

5472. _____. *Vanier Centre for Women. Research report no. 1. An examination of the social milieu*. [Toronto]: Ontario. Ministry of Correctional Services, 1974. 59p. and app.

5473. _____. *Vanier Centre for Women. Research report no. 2. Length of time in Vanier, attitudes and first year recidivism*. [Toronto]: Ontario. Ministry of Correctional Services, 1974. 8p.

5474. Landreville, Pierre. "Population carcérale féminine au Canada," *Canadian Journal of Corrections*, 11(1):1-25, 1969.

5475. Lawson, Darlene. "Home on the range," *Broadside*, 3:30-1, May 1982.

5476. Martin, Eva. "Women in Toronto Don jail," *Ontario Library Review*, 60:54-5, Mar. 1976.

5477. Masters, Philinda. "Straightening out the kinks," *Broadside*, 1(2):1, 1979.

5478. Ontario. Ministry of Correctional Services. *Vanier Centre for Women*. [Toronto], reprinted 1977. Leaflet.

5479. "Prison freedom - women in crumbling building fight to stay where they can have sex, drugs, alcohol," *Globe & Mail*, Mar. 1, 1979, pp.1, 4.

5480. Rockett, Eve. "British Columbia: a woman's place is in the jail," *Maclean's*, 92:17-18, July 30, 1979.

5481. Rogers, Sally and Catherine Carey. *Child-care needs of female offenders; a comparison of incarcerates and probationers*. [Toronto]: Ontario. Ministry of Correctional Services. Planning and Research Branch, 1979. 36p.

5482. Rosenbluth, Vera. "Women in prison," in Marylee Stephenson, *Women in Canada*. Toronto: New Press, 1973, pp.71-89.

5483. Ross, Robert R., Claudia Currie and Barbara Krug-McKay. *The female offender: treatment and training*. [Toronto]: Ontario. Ministry of Correctional Services. Planning and Research Branch, 1980. 105p.

5484. Watson, Catherine Margaret. "Women prisoners and modern methods of prison control: a comparative study of two Canadian women's prisons." PhD diss., McGill University, 1981.

5485. Whitney, Beverley. "Word from the inside," *Broadside*, 1(6):10, 1980.

5486. "Women in corrections - reality is now [correctional personnel]," *Discussion*, 3:7-10, Sept. 1975.

5487. "Women in prison: the human rights connection; Les femmes incarcérées: décision de la Commission canadienne des droits de la personne," *Liaison*, 8:16-21, Mar. 1982.

PROGRESSIVE CONSERVATIVE PARTY OF CANADA

5488. Ontario Progressive Conservative Association of Women. *The constitution of the Ontario Progressive Conservative Association of Women*. [Toronto, Ont.], 1980. 4p.

5489. Progressive Conservative Party of Canada. *The Progressive Conservative program for women in Canada*. Discussion paper, no. 7, Society and the individual. n.p., 1974. 3p.

PROSTITUTION

5490. Amiel, Barbara. "The politics of prostitution - devaluing the sexual mystery," *Maclean's*, 93:42, Aug. 11, 1980.

5491. Bedford, Judy. "Prostitution in Calgary, 1905-1914," *Alberta History*, 29:1-11, Spring 1981.

5492. Bourne, Paula. "Prostitution," in her, *Women in Canadian society*. Toronto: Ontario Institute for Studies in Education, 1976, pp.25-30.

5493. Browne, A. "Changes to Criminal Code brand everyone a whore," *Perception*, 2:38, Mar.-Apr. 1979.

5494. Budgen, Mark. "British Columbia: selling teen sex on trendy street," *Maclean's*, 93:29, May 12, 1980.

5495. "Ces demoiselles des petites annonces, masseuses à domicile," *Le Magazine Maclean*, 10:7-8, juill., 1970.

5496. Cooper, Joy. "Red lights in Winnipeg," *Manitoba Historical and Scientific Society. Transactions*, Feb. 16, 1971, pp.61-74.

5497. Coupland, Michael W. "Antecedents of juvenile prostitution: a test of social control theory." MA thesis, Simon Fraser University, 1979. 122p. (Can. theses, no.44880)

220

5498. Cummer, Denise. "The oldest profession survives; Le plus ancien métier du monde survit," *Liaison*, 8:9-13, Jan. 1982.

5499. Forbes, G. A. *Street prostitution in Vancouver's west end*. [Vancouver]: Vancouver Police Board and Vancouver City Council, [1977]. 22p.

5500. Gray, J. H. "Ces dames des prairies: extrait de 'Red lights on the prairies'," *Le Maclean*, 11:50-2, 53-4, nov. 1971.

5501. _____. "Prairie chickens: excerpt from 'Red lights on the prairies'," *Maclean's*, 84:37-9, 64+ , Nov. 1971.

5502. Gray, James. *Red lights on the prairies*. Toronto: MacMillan, 1971. 207p.

5503. Greber, Dave. "Tricky proposition for the mayors," *Maclean's*, 95:46-7, May 24, 1982.

5504. Grescoe, Paul. "Vancouver: hustling's bustling," *Maclean's*, 91:27-8, May 1, 1978.

5505. Hawreliak, Sylvia. "Roll over, woman," in Lynda Turner, comp., *Woman in Canadian society*. [New Westminster, B.C.: Douglas College, 1972], pp.131-4.

5506. Kaminski, Helena and others. "Exchange," *Canadian Dimension*, 13(2):54-6, [1978]. Commentaries on Anne Mclean's article below.

5507. Kennedy, William J. "Perceived parental behaviors and belief systems of prostitutes." PhD diss., University of Alberta, 1978. 111p. (Can. theses, no.40199)

5508. Kohlmeyer, Klaus Kim. "An ethnographic study of street prostitution in Vancouver, British Columbia." MA thesis, Simon Fraser University, 1982. (Can. theses, no.53448)

5509. Labreche, Julianne and Robert Stall. "A nod is as good as a wink," *Maclean's*, 92:25, Mar. 12, 1979.

5510. LaMothe, Dennis M. "Female heterosexual prostitution and love deficit." PhD diss., University of Alberta, 1979. 100p. (Can. theses, no.40443)

5511. Lapalme, M. "Le film de la prostitution à Montréal," *Le Magazine MacLean*, 6:2, déc. 1966.

5512. Layton, Monique. *Prostitution in Vancouver (1973-1975): official and unofficial reports*. Vancouver: British Columbia. Police Commission, 1975. 265p. (Profile 76-0186).

5513. _____. "Street women and their verbal transactions: some aspects of the oral culture of female prostitute drug addicts." PhD diss., University of British Columbia, 1978. 264p. (Can. theses, no.37662)

5514. _____. "The ambiguities of the law or the street-walker's dilemma," *Chitty's Law Journal*, 27:109-20, 1979.

5515. Levy, Harold J. "The law and prostitution: the girls win again," *Canadian Lawyer*, 2(6):14-15, 1978.

5516. Limoges, Thérèse. *La prostitution à Montréal: comment, pourquoi certaines femmes deviennent prostituées*. Montréal: Editions de l'Homme, 1967. 125p.

5517. McLean, Anne. "Snuffing out snuff: feminists react on Yonge Street," *Canadian Dimension*, 12(8):20-3, [1978]. For commentaries see Helena Kaminski above.

5518. Newman, Frances and Paula J. Caplan. "Juvenile female prostitution as gender consistent response to early deprivation," *International Journal of Women's Studies*, 5:128-37, Mar.-Apr. 1982.

5519. Prus, Robert and Styllianos Irini. *Hookers, rounders and desk clerks: the social organization of the hotel community*. Toronto: Gage, 1980. 279p.

5520. Street Haven at the Crossroads. *Brief no. 205 to the Royal Commission on the Status of Women in Canada*. Willowdale, Ont., 1968. v.p.

5521. Stuckey, Johanna. "A feminist looks at prostitution," in Benjamin Schlesinger, ed., *Sexual behaviour in Canada: patterns and problems*. Toronto: University of Toronto Press, 1977, pp.194-200.

5522. Texier, Catherine and Marie-Odile Vézina. *Profession: prostituée: rapport sur la prostitution au Québec*. n.p.: Éditions Libre expression, 1978. 354p.

5523. Toronto. City Council. Special Committee, Places of Amusement. *Report and recommendations*. Toronto: City of Toronto, 1977. 175p.

5524. Yaga, Baba. "Committee Against Street Harassment: dykes and hookers fight back," *Body Politic*, no. 57:22, Oct. 1979.

Numbering resumes at 5543.

PSYCHOLOGY

5543. Adamec, Cannie Stark and Martin Graham. "The complexity of attitudes toward women: II. Perception of societal attitudes and associated tension," *International Journal of Women's Studies*, 1:503-16, Sept.-Oct. 1978.

5544. Ames, Elinor W. "The status of women in Canadian psychology: a case study of women in science," *International Journal of Women's Studies*, 4:431-40, Sept.-Oct. 1981.

5545. Anderson, Dianne. "Psychosocial correlates of locus of control expectancies in female children." PhD diss., University of Alberta, 1976. 164p. (Can. theses, no.27600)

5546. Bell, Lorna E. "Effects of sex of juror, sex of defendant, and sex of victim on the decisions of simulated jurors." MA thesis, University of Windsor, 1979. 94p. (Can. theses, no.41930)

5547. Berger, Charlene. "Psychological characteristics of anglophone and francophone initial and repeat aborters and contraceptors." PhD diss, Concordia University, 1978. 205p. (Can. theses, no.38528)

5548. Blackwell, Jacqueline E. "Psychological androgyny, expectancy for success and causal attributions for a success or failure performance outcome in women." MA thesis, York University, 1977. 146p. (Can. theses, no.33626)

5549. Brunet, Dominique. *La femme expliquée: l'histoire d'un truquage*. Montréal: Le Jour, 1982. 185p.

5550. Burwell, Elinor J. "Issues in the education and training of women in Canadian psychology," *Canadian Psychological Review*, 18:34-45, Jan. 1977.

5551. Byrne, Patrick Niall. "Stage and sex differences in moral and ego development prior and consequent to independence training." PhD diss., University of Toronto, 1973. 85p. and app.

5552. Canadian Psychological Association. "Guidelines for therapy and counselling with women," *Canadian Psychological Review*, 21:185-6, Oct. 1980.

5553. Canadian Psychological Association. Committee on the Status of Women. Calgary Subcommittee. *Guidelines for therapy and counselling with women*. Ottawa: The Association, 1980. 12p.

5554. Canadian Psychological Association. Task Force on the Status of Women in Canadian Psychology. "Report of the Task Force... ," *Canadian Psychological Review*, 18:3-18, Jan. 1977.

5555. Caplan, Paula J. and Georgina White. "Current themes in Canadian feminist psychology," *Resources for Feminist Research*, 11:295-306, Nov. 1982.

5556. Carveth, W. Bruce. "Social support and stress: a study of new mothers." MA thesis, University of Guelph, 1977. 114p. (Can. theses, no.33867)

5557. Cooke, Sharon W. "A comparison of identity formation in preadolescent girls and boys." MA thesis, Simon Fraser University, 1979. 93p. (Can. theses, no.41136)

5558. "Counselling and personhood," in Canadian Research Institute for the Advancement of Women, *Women as persons*. [*La femme en tant que personne*]. Toronto: Resources for Feminist Research, 1980, pp.110-118.
Proceedings of the 3rd annual meeting.

5559. CPA Committee on the Status of Women. "Women and psychology: beyond the CPA Task Force Report," *Ontario Psychologist*, 13:18-19, Apr. 1981.

5560. Crombie, Gail. "Women's attributions for achievement: an examination of within-sex differences." MA thesis, Concordia University, 1978. 91p. (Can. theses, no.38545)

5561. Cust, Marlene. "Self-actualization and psychological androgyny in a sample of university women." PhD diss., University of Alberta, 1978. 152p. (Can. theses, no.40119)

5562. DeLuca, Rayleen V. and Manly N. Spigelman. "Effects of models on food intake of obese and non-obese female college students," *Canadian Journal of Behavioural Science*, 11(2):124-9, 1979.

5563. Dubin, Gloria Louise Joachim. "Nursing, leadership and the women's liberation movement." MScN thesis, University of British Columbia, 1976. 70p. (Can. theses, no.29824)

5564. Durden, Vivienne. *The YWCA: it's role in relation to serious personal problems of girls and women*. Toronto: Young Women's Christian Association of Canada, 1965. 56p.

222

5565. Egger, Larry Robert. "The effects of a training program designed for the contemporary woman, on attitudes toward self, children and child-bearing." MSc thesis, University of Calgary, 1978. 123p. (Can. theses, no.42000)

5566. Fiske, D. Heather. "Sex role and self-esteem in adolescence." MA thesis, University of Guelph, 1979. 102p. (Can. theses, no.41715)

5567. Froggatt, Marilyn and Lorraine Hunter. *Pricetag: Canadian women and the stress of success*. Don Mills, Ont.: Nelson Canada, 1980. 198p.

5568. Fullerton, Timothy. "Evaluation of the competence of authors as a function of the author's gender, the sex-relatedness of the article and the sex of the evaluator." MA thesis, University of Manitoba, 1974. 106p. (Can. theses, no.20860)

5569. George, Janet M. "Self-concept and personality in women as a function of traditional-nontraditional career choice and sex-role attitudes." MA thesis, University of Windsor, 1980. 105p. (Can. theses, no.49211)

5570. Gold, Dolores and Charlene Berger. "Problem-solving performance of young boys and girls as a function of task appropriateness and sex identity," *Sex Roles*, 4(2):183-93, 1978.

5571. Goldberg, Joel O. "Defensive styles and women's reactions to discrimination." MA thesis, University of Waterloo, 1981. 86p. (Can. theses, no.49780)

5572. Grafstein, Rina. "Menstruation and sexuality: an attitudinal survey," *Canadian Women's Studies / Les cahiers de la femme*, 3(2):14-16, 1981.

5573. Graham, Martin and Cannie Stark Adamec. "The complexity of attitudes toward women: I. Personal attitudes and their sources," *International Journal of Women's Studies*, 1:482-502, Sept.-Oct. 1978.

5574. Gray, Charlotte. "Raging female hormones in the courts: several cases boost legal recognition for premenstrual syndrome as a factor in female crime," *Maclean's*, 94:46-7, 10, June 15, 1981.

5575. Gray, Vicky A. "The image of women in psychology textbooks," *Canadian Psychological Review*, 18:46-55, Jan. 1977.

5576. Greenglass, Esther. "The psychology of women; or the high cost of achievement," in Marylee Stephenson, *Women in Canada*. Toronto: New Press, 1973, pp.108-18.

5577. Hatt, Linda Lou. "The perception of assertive women." MSc thesis, University of Alberta, 1980. (Can. theses, no.43427)

5578. Hawrylko, Rosalie. "Sex-role identity and self-esteem in college women." MA thesis, Simon Fraser University, 1972. 83p.

5579. Henderson, Jule and John Briere. "Sexism and sex roles in letters of recommendation to graduate training in psychology," *Canadian Psychological Review*, 21:75-80, Apr. 1980.

5580. Henriksen, Sheila P. "Personality and deviance: a study of female prisoners and welfare recipients." MA thesis, Queen's University, 1972. 120p. and app. (Can. theses, no.15012)

5581. Hyatt, Patricia M. "Sex roles, self-esteem and level of depression in university students." MA thesis, Simon Fraser University, 1980. 68p. (Can. theses, no. 51023)

5582. Irwin, Kathleen Florence. "Self-injurious behaviour among adolescent girls in residential treatment." MSW thesis, University of Windsor, 1979. 197p. (Can. theses, no.41950)

5583. Jacobs, Bryna. "Sex differences in psychiatric diagnosis and treatment." MA thesis, McMaster University, 1980. 234p. (Can. theses, no.46884)

5584. Kalin, Rudolf and Brian A. Grant. "Sex differences in employment - experiences of 1976 Canadian graduates in psychology," *Canadian Psychological Review*, 22:238-46, July 1981.

5585. Kennedy, William J. "Perceived parental behaviors and belief systems of prostitutes." PhD diss., University of Alberta, 1978. 111p. (Can. theses, no.40199)

5586. Kimball, Meredith M. "Women and success: a basic conflict?" in Marylee Stephenson, *Women in Canada*. Toronto: New Press, 1973, pp.118-35.

5587. Kirsh, Sharon L. "Emotional support systems of working-class women." PhD diss., University of Toronto, 1981. (Can. theses, no.53089)

5588. Korabik, Karen. "Sex-role orientation and leadership style," *International Journal of Women's Studies*, 5:329-37, Sept.-Oct. 1982.

5589. Langlais, Nicole. "Comment le sentiment de culpabilité restreint la femme dans son développement vocationnel," *Orientation professionnelle*, 14:128-37, été 1978.

5590. Lanktree, Cheryl B. "The effects of sex of subject, sex preference, sex of experimenter and sex-typed instructions on preschoolers' task performance." MA thesis, University of Guelph, 1977. 47p. (Can. theses, no.31063)

5591. Lehman, Carol L. "The sex roles and life styles of married women in relation to mental health indices of the California Psychological Inventory (CPI)." PhD diss., University of Ottawa, 1979. 226p. (Can. theses, no.48572)

5592. Loughner-Gillin, Cheryl. "Sex of the therapist: an exploration of competence attributions as a function of therapist's gender." PhD diss., University of Windsor, 1981. 92p. (Can. theses, no.51202)

5593. Luce, Sally R. "Sex differences in achievement attributions: patterns and processes." PhD diss., Carleton University, 1980. 93p. and tables. (Can. theses, no.44417)

5594. Luce, Sally R. and Barbara Wand. "Sex differences in referrals to a rehabilitation facility for the physically disabled: a research note," *Canadian Psychological Review*, 18:92-5, Jan. 1977.

5595. Lumsden, Barbara L. "Women's dependency: the interrelationship of structure and ideology." MA thesis, University of Guelph, 1981. 118p. (Can. theses, no.52521)

5596. MacDonald, Ann Clarice. "Selected motivational aspects of clothing conformity and compartmentalization among female university students." MSc thesis, University of Guelph, 1977. 127p.

5597. Mackey, Betty Ann. "The effect of transactional analysis on self-concept in adolescent women." MSc thesis, University of Calgary, 1978. 67p. (Can., theses, no.37301)

5598. McCarron, Mary L. "Personality characteristics as affected by variable stress situations in wives of alcoholics." MA thesis, University of Regina, 1977. 89p. (Can. theses, no.33451)

5599. Meikle, Stewart. "The psychological effects of hysterectomy," *Canadian Psychological Review*, 18:128-41, Apr. 1977.

5600. Mills, Catherine Estelle. "An experiment concerning the effects of sex of the teacher, sex of the student and participation in a sex-roles course on teachers predictions of academic success and failure." MA thesis, Dalhousie University, 1979. 160p. (Can. theses, no.44292)

5601. Miscisco, Daniel Robert. "The influence of distinct coaching styles on personality and sportsmanship attitudes of elementary age girls playing competitive basketball." MPE thesis, University of British Columbia, 1976. 165p. (Can. theses, no.29907)

5602. Myers, Anita M. "The psychological measurement of masculinity-femininity: cultural definitions and self-ratings." PhD diss., York University, 1981. (Can. theses, no.44503)

5603. Noonan, Barrie A. "Toward an existential approach to therapy with women." PhD diss., University of Alberta, 1981. 99p. (Can. theses, no.49052)

5604. Nuechterlein, Dorothea I. Allwardt. "The self and the mid-course correction: the mature woman's return to school." MA thesis, Queen's University, 1977. 182p. (Can. theses, no.37533)

5605. Olmsted, Marion. "Anorexic-normal differences and predictors of concern with dieting in college women." MA thesis, University of Guelph, 1981. 110p. (Can. theses, no.52544)

5606. Pfeifer, Patricia. "Personality differences between male and female MBA students." [MBA thesis, Concordia University, 1977]. 42p. and app.

5607. Piccolo, Ornella. "Menstrual-cycle distress: a study of its relation to feminine identity and sexual inhibition." PhD diss., University of Windsor, 1981. (Can. theses, no.53404)

5608. Pyke, Sandra W. "Selected characteristics of the female psychologist in the labour force," *Canadian Psychological Review*, 18:23-33, Jan. 1977.

5609. Pinnell, Lynn Ellen. "Perceptions of stress among hospital nursing staff." MN thesis, University of Alberta, 1979. 147p. (Can. theses, no.40482)

5610. Posluns, Elaine. "The change process of women becoming liberated from sex-role stereotypes." PhD diss., University of Toronto, 1981. (Can. theses, no.53140)

224

5611. "Psychology and personhood," in Canadian Research Institute for the Advancement of Women, *Women as persons. [La femme en tant que personne]*. Toronto: Resources for Feminist Research, 1980, pp.87-93.
Proceedings of the 3rd annual meeting.

5612. Pyke, Sandra W. "Selected characteristics of the female psychologist in the labour force," *Canadian Psychological Review*, 18:23-33, Jan. 1977.

5613. Pyke, S. W. and C. Stark-Adamec. "Canadian feminism and psychology: the first decade," *Canadian Psychological Review*, 22:38-54, Jan. 1981.

5614. Raphael, Dennis. "An investigation into aspects of identity status of high school females." PhD diss., University of Toronto, 1975. 237p. (Can. theses, no.32869)

5615. _____. "Identity status in high school females," *Adolescence*, 13:627-41, Winter 1978.

5616. _____. "Sequencing in female adolescents' consideration of occupational, religious and political alternatives," *Adolescence*, 14:73-80, Spring 1979.

5617. Ricks, Frances A. and others. "The status of women and men in Canadian psychology academia," *Canadian Psychological Review*, 21:109-15, July 1980.

5618. Ross, Hazel Miriam. "Women and wellness: defining, attaining and maintaining health in Eastern Canada." PhD diss., University of Washington, 1982. 393p.

5619. Semkow, Verna-Jean Amell. "Locus of control and outcome expectancy: a complementary model of women's attributions to failure." PhD diss., University of Ottawa, 1980. 188p. (Can. theses, no.48451)

5620. Shershen, Eugene D. "Shading in the H-T-P: its relationship to situationally specific anxiety and other variables in a male and female Canadian university sample." PhD diss., University of Ottawa, 1976. 214p.

5621. Sherwin, Barbara Brender and others. "Mood and behaviour changes in menopausal women receiving gonadal hormones or placebo," in Cannie Stark-Adamec, ed., *Sex roles: origins, influences and implications for women*. Montreal: Eden Press, 1980, pp.190-205.

5622. Smith, Gerald P. "Psychological androgyny and attitudes toward feminism in relation to the perception of dominance and sexuality." PhD diss., University of Windsor, 1981. (Can. theses, no.53409)

5623. Spricer, Rosa. "Adulthood: developmental tasks of adult women." PhD diss., University of Alberta, 1981. 233p. (Can. theses, no.51587)

5624. Stark-Adamec, Cannie and J. Martin Graham. "Resource people: the results of a CPA-IGWAP survey," *Resources for Feminist Research*, 9:78-86, July 1980.

5625. Stark-Adamec, Cannie, ed. *Sex roles: origins, influences and implications for women*. Montreal: Eden Press, 1980. 238p.
Canadian Psychological Association, Interest Group on Women and Psychology - Proceedings of the Inaugural Institute.

5626. Thew, Carol Larson. *The role of mothers and firstborn female siblings in teaching and encouraging language skills*. ERIBC report, no. 79:4. n.p.: Educational Research Institute of British Columbia, [1979]. 33p. (Microlog 79-2015)

5627. Thomas, Gregory Charles. "The relationship between personality and performance of Canadian women intercollegiate basketball players." MPE thesis, University of British Columbia, 1977. 85p. (Can. theses, no.34965)

5628. Towson, Shelagh M. J. and Mark P. Zanna. "Toward a situational analysis of gender differences in aggression," *Sex Roles*, 8(8):903-14, 1982.

5629. Usher, Sarah. "Self-esteem in the mature married woman as a function of working status and feminist attitudes." PhD diss., York University, 1977. 141,[42]p. (Can. theses, no.33665)

5630. Vandonselaar, Kodyn Herman. "Characteristics of women in 'a second look' program." MEd thesis, University of Alberta, 1978. 99p. (Can. theses, no.36491)

5631. Vickers, Joan. "Sex and age differences in attitude toward the concepts "male", "female", "male athlete", "female athlete". MSc thesis, University of Calgary, 1976. 91p. (Can. theses, no.30590)

5632. Vingilis, Evelyn. "Feeling states and the menstrual cycle," in Cannie Stark-Ademec, ed., *Sex roles: origins, influences and implications for women*. Montreal: Eden Press, 1980, pp.206-16.

5633.   _____. "Feeling-states and the menstrual cycle." PhD diss., York University, 1978. 135, [34]p. (Can. theses, no.37025)

5634.   Williams, Tannis MacBeth and others. "Some factors affecting women's participation in psychology in Canada," *Canadian Psychological Review*, 21:97-108, July 1980.

5635.   Willis, Kathleen Diane. "The effects of sex of audience and degree of evaluation on task performance of women assessed on fear of success." MA thesis, University of Victoria, 1977. 64p. (Can. theses, no.34135)

5636.   Wood, H. Diane. "Predicting behavioural types in preadolescent girls from psychosocial development and friendship values." PhD diss., University of Windsor, 1976. 125p. (Can. theses, no.29249)

5637.   Woodman, Marion. *The owl was a baker's daughter: obesity, anorexia nervosa, and the repressed feminine: a psychological study*. Studies in Jungian psychology, no. 4. Toronto: Inner City Books, 1980. 139p.

5638.   Woolsey, Lorette. "Psychology and the reconciliation of women's double bind: to be feminine or to be fully human," *Canadian Psychological Review*, 18:66-78, Jan. 1977.

5639.   Yee, Paul H. N. "Sex stereotypes: their effects on impression formation and evaluation." PhD diss., University of Toronto, 1981. (Can. theses, no.53185)

RADIO BROADCASTING

5640.   Blashill, Lorraine. "Where are all the women? One is doing a man's work on an ENG crew at CBC," *Broadcaster*, 38:38, Aug. 1979.

5641.   Cochrane, Jean. *Kate Aitken*. Don Mills, Ont.: Fitzhenry & Whiteside, 1979. 63p.

5642.   Edwards, Alyn. "You have to learn to take the 'No's'," *Broadcaster*, 37:30, June 1978.

5643.   Fraser, Sylvia. "Getting down to basics with Betty Kennedy," *Chatelaine*, 48:55, 82, 84-6, 88-9, Sept. 1975.

5644.   "Humber College sets up radio advisory group," *Marketing*, 81:11, Feb. 16, 1976.

5645.   Landsberg, Michele. "Barbara Frum," *Chatelaine*, 46:44-5, 88-91, Apr. 1973.

5646.   Paré, Jean. "La Chronique: attention femmes au travail," *Le Maclean*, 15:8, 10, avr. 1975.

5647.   Robertson, Heather. "Keep plugging Barbara Frum," *Macleans*, 88:32-5, June 1975.

5648.   _____. "The first lady of radio [Margaret Lyon]," *Saturday Night*, 96:13-14, Jan. 1981.

5649.   Rockett, Eve. "So Judy LaMarsh, what are you up to now?" *Chatelaine*, 46:42-3, 98-9, Oct. 1973.

5650.   Women for Political Action - Ontario Committee on the Status of Women. *Brief to the Canadian Radio and Television Commission concerning the Canadian Broadcasting Corporation and its policies and attitudes with regard to women*. Submitted Feb. 1, 1974. 82p.

RAPE

5651.   "Athletic support in court," *Broadside*, 2:2, Apr. 1981.

5652.   Beirne, Anne. "Marital rape," *Chatelaine*, 55:61, 176+ , Nov. 1982.

5653.   Bliss, Janet. "Lady Beware - this pamphlet is not about rape," *Branching Out*, 6(3):5-6, 1979.

5654.   Bourne, Paula. "Rape," in her, *Women in Canadian society*. Toronto: Ontario Institute for Studies in Education, 1976, pp.30-44.

5655.   Boyle, Christine. "Married women - beyond the pale of the law of rape," *Windsor Yearbook of Access to Justice*, 1:192-213, 1981.

5656.   _____. "Section 142 of the Criminal Code: a Trojan Horse?," *Criminal Law Quarterly*, 23:253-65, 1981.

5657.   Bray, Ruth M. *Sexual assault in Canada*. Toronto: University of Toronto. Guidance Centre, 1980. 56p.

5658.   British Columbia. Police Commission. Rape Prevention Project. *Rape prevention: resource manual*. [Victoria, 1978]. [90]p. (Microlog 80-0859) Manual produced to accompany the film, "This film is about rape."

226

5659.   Bruce, Jean. "Our 'new' rape law: already out-of-date?" *Chatelaine*, 49:11, Oct. 1976.
5660.   Canada. Advisory Council on the Status of Women. *Rape and sexual assault. [Après le viol, l'humiliation]*. 2nd ed. The person papers. Ottawa, 1976. 16, 16p.
5661.   _____. *Rape and sexual assault. [Le viol et les agressions sexuelles]*. Fact sheet no. 4. Ottawa, [1981] 6p.
5662.   Carrier, Micheline. "La femme, objet de violence," *Perception*, 4:30-3, Sept.-Oct. 1980.
5663.   CARSA. Niagara Region Sexual Assault Centre. *Sexual assault: information and issues.* [Niagara Falls, Ont.: CARSA, 1978?] 45p.
5664.   Catton, Katherine. "Evidence regarding the prior sexual history of an alleged rape victim; its effect on the perceived guilt of the accused," *University of Toronto Faculty of Law Review*, 33:165-80, 1975.
5665.   "Changes in rape law introduced," *Canadian Welfare*, 51:23-4, Sept.-Oct. 1975.
5666.   Chapman, Terry L. "Rape in Alberta: an overview," *Canadian Women's Studies / Les cahiers de la femme*, 3(2):85-7, 1981.
5667.   Chase, Gillean. "Ontario Provincial Police report, 1979," *Canadian Women's Studies / Les cahiers de la femme*, 1:74-5, Summer 1979.
5668.   Clark, Lorenne. "Rape - position paper prepared for the National Action Committee," *Status of Women News*, 4:11-15, Nov. 1977.
5669.   Clark, Lorenne and Linda Duncan. "Follow-up," *Branching Out*, 3:41, 44, July-Aug. 1976.
5670.   Clark, Lorenne M. G. "Group rape in Vancouver and Toronto," *Canada's Mental Health*, 28:9-12, June 1980.
5671.   _____. "Rape in Toronto: psychosocial perspectives on the offender," in Benjamin Schlesinger, ed., *Sexual behaviour in Canada: patterns and problems*. Toronto: University of Toronto Press, 1977, pp. 177-94.
5672.   Clark, Lorenne M. G. and Debra J. Lewis. *Rape: the price of coercive sexuality*. Toronto: Women's Press, 1977. 222p.
5673.   Cohen, Leah and Constance Backhouse. "Putting rape in its (legal) place," *Maclean's*, 93:6, June 30, 1980.
5674.   Collette-Carrière, R. "La victimologie et le viol: un discours complice," *Criminologie*, 13(1):60-79, 1980.
5675.   "Decisions on sentencing: offences against the person," *Criminal Law Quarterly*, 17(4):343-5, 1975.
5676.   Dick, Jane. "Are we paranoid?" *Branching Out*, 3:30-1, Feb.-Mar. 1976.
5677.   Duncan, Linda. "Rape logic: hit 'em where it hurts," *Branching Out*, 3:28-30, Feb.-Mar. 1976. For commentary and reply Lorenne Clark and Linda Duncan above.
5678.   Geller, Sheldon H. "The sexually assaulted female: innocent victim or temptress?" *Canada's Mental Health*, 25:26-8, Mar. 1977.
5679.   Gibson, Lorne Randall. "Rape: victims, offenders and facilitating situations." MA thesis, University of Manitoba, 1978. 179p.
5680.   Gibson, Lorne, Rick Linden and Stuart Johnson. "A situational theory of rape," *Canadian Journal of Criminology*, 22:51-65, Jan. 1980.
5681.   Giroux, Jocelyn and others. "Les causes de viol entendues dans le district judiciaire de Montréal entre 1975 et 1978: une enquête rétrospective," *Canadian Journal of Criminology*, 23:173-90, Apr. 1981.
5682.   Goldsberry, Nancy. *Rape in British Columbia; a report to the Ministry of the Attorney-General, [Justice Development Commission]*. Victoria, 1979. 232p. (Microlog 79-1870)
5683.   Gray, Elizabeth. "Courting regression on rape," *Maclean's*, 93:44-5, July 28, 1980.
5684.   Jackman, Nancy. "Bill C-53 law reflects values," *Canadian Woman Studies / Les cahiers de la femme*, 3:120, Summer 1982.
5685.   Johnson, Stuart D. and others. "Alcohol as a contributing factor in forcible rape," in Robert A. Silverman and James J. Teevan, eds., *Crime in Canadian society*. 2d ed. Toronto: Butterworths, 1980, pp.290-7.
5686.   Jonas, George. "Rape and marriage are not like horse and carriage," *Canadian Lawyer*, 3(2):10-11, 1979.

5687. Kasinsky, Renée Goldsmith. "Rape: a normal act?" *Canadian Forum*, 55:18-22, Sept. 1975.

5688. _____. "Rape: the social control of women," in William K. Greenaway and Stephen L. Brickey, eds., *Law and social control in Canada*. Scarborough, Ont.: Prentice-Hall, 1978, pp.59-69.

5689. _____. "The rise and institutionalization of the anti-rape movement in Canada," in Mary A. B. Gammon, ed., *Violence in Canada*. Toronto: Methuen, 1978, pp.151-67.

5690. Kinnon, Dianne. *Report on sexual assault in Canada*. Ottawa: Canadian Advisory Council on the Status of Women, 1981. 87, [4]p.

5691. Kostash, Myrna. "Are we winning the war against rape?" *Chatelaine*, 54:55, 112+ , Sept. 1981.

5692. _____. "Profile of the rapist as an ordinary man," *Maclean's*, 88:45-8, Apr. 1975.

5693. _____. "Rape: machismo's secret police? Questions and more questions," *This Magazine*, 9:26-7, May-June 1975.

5694. _____. "Rape! When our courts deal with the ultimate rip-off, it's the victims who are often guilty until proven innocent," *Maclean's*, 88:62-71, Mar. 1975.

5695. Lacerte-Lamontagne, Céline. "L'article 142 du Code criminel et les victimes de viol," *Revue du Barreau*, 40:448-62, 1980.

5696. Lacerte-Lamontagne, Célyne et Yves Lamontagne. *Le viol: acte de pouvoir et de colère*. Montréal: La Presse, 1980. 132p.

5697. Lalonde, Claire. "Les médecins et la société: confronté par le viol," *Canadian Medical Association. Journal*, 115:278-80, Aug. 7, 1976.

5698. Landau, Reva and Lois Lowenberg. "Legal lies legalize rape," *Broadside*, 2:8, 20, Mar. 1981.

5699. Lebourdais, E. "Rape victims: unpopular patients," *Dimensions in Health Service*, 53:12-14, Mar. 1976.

5700. Levine, Sylvia and Joseph Koenig, eds. *Why men rape: interviews with convicted rapists*. Toronto: Macmillan of Canada, 1980. 184p.

5701. Lewis, T. J. "Recent proposals in the criminal law of rape: significant reform or semantic change?" *Osgoode Hall Law Journal*, 17:445-58, Aug. 1979.

5702. Lowenberger, Lois and Reva Landau. "A rape by any other name... ," *Broadside*, 3:3, Aug. 1982.

5703. McCaldon, R. J. "Rape," in C. L. Boydell, C. F. Grindstaff and P. C. Whitehead, eds., *Deviant behaviour and societal reaction*. Toronto: Holt, Rinehart & Winston, 1972, pp.546-70.

5704. McFadyen, Joanna. "Inter-spousal rape: the need for law reform," in John M. Eekelaar and Sanford N. Katz, eds., *Family violence: an international and interdisciplinary study*. Toronto: Butterworths, 1978, pp.193-8.

5705. McTeer, Maureen. "Rape and the Canadian legal process," in Mary A. B. Gammon, ed., *Violence in Canada*. Toronto: Methuen, 1978, pp.135-50.

5706. Miller, Joni E. "Rape: violation by the Criminal Code," *Broadside*, 2:5, 21, Dec. 1980-Jan. 1981.

5707. Nelson, Susan Hess. "An experimental study concerning jury decisions in rape trials," *Criminal Reports*, 3rd ser., 1:265-83, 1978.

5708. _____. "Jurors' verdicts in a mock rape trial experiment: a social learning approach." PhD diss., Carleton University, 1979. 178p. (Can. theses, no.49524)

5709. Olson, Ruth A. "Rape - an 'un-Victorian' aspect of life in Upper Canada," *Ontario History*, 68:75-9, June 1976.

5710. Ontario. Provincial Secretariat for Justice. *Helping the victims of sexual assault*. [Toronto, 1979]. 93p.

5711. _____. *Information for the victims of sexual assault*. n.p.: Provincial Secretariat for Justice, [19 ?]. 14p.

5712. Ottawa Rape Crisis Centre. *Study of health care practices for rape and sexual assault victims in select Ottawa-area hospital emergency units*, Carol A. B. Blackwell, evaluator & research consultant. CRIAW working paper. Sponsored by Canadian Research Institute for the Advancement of Women. Ottawa, 1979. 5p.

5713. Phillips, M. "Understanding patients charged with rape," *Dimensions in Health Service*, 55:22-4, Dec. 1978.

5714. Posner, Michael. "Rape: the word may go, the violence remains [Bill C-52]," *Maclean's*, 91:56-7, May 29, 1978.

5715. Price, Vern. "Rape victims - the invisible patients," *Canadian Nurse*, 71:29-34, Apr. 1975.

5716. "Raped by honest belief," *Broadside*, 2:5, Dec. 1980-Jan. 1981.

5717. Ribeyron, Marie-Thérèse. "Le viol," *Le Maclean*, 15:24-8, août. 1975.

5718. Rioux, Marcia. *When myths masquerade as reality: a study of rape*. Discussion paper. Ottawa: Canada. Advisory Council on the Status of Women, 1975. 74p.

5719. Roberts, Barbara. "No safe place: the war against women," *Our Generation*, 15:7-26, Spring 1983.

5720. Russell, Mary. "Rape victims and police reporting," *Canada's Mental Health*, 28:14-16, June 1980.

5721. Schneider, Elizabeth M. and others. "Representation of women who defend themselves in response to physical or sexual assault," *Family Law Review*, 1:118-32, 1978.

5722. Scutt, J. A. "Fraud and consent in rape: comprehension of the nature and character of the act and its moral implications," *Criminal Law Quarterly*, 18:312-24, 1976.

5723. Stein, David Lewis and Erna Paris. "Can a woman be raped by her husband?" *Chatelaine*, 51:36, 188, Nov. 1978.

5724. Timson, Judith. "Vancouver: the crime of the year," *Maclean's*, 90:16-17, Sept. 5, 1977.

5725. Toronto Rape Crisis Centre. *Rape; the crime against women*. 2nd ed. Toronto, 1977. [35]p.

5726. *Viol: sexualité masculine et société phallocratique*. St. Jérôme, Qué.: Éditions Raisons de femmes, 1980. 10p.

RAPE - BIBLIOGRAPHY

5727. Clark, Lorenne M. G. and Simon Armstrong. *A rape bibliography; with special emphasis on rape research in Canada. [Bibliographie sur le viol; et plus particulièrement sur la recherche au Canada dans ce domaine]*. [Ottawa]: Canada. Ministry of the Solicitor General. Communication Division, 1979. 130p. (Microlog 80-1379)

    Based on *Forcible rape: bibliography*, compiled by Duncan Chappell, Gilbert Geis and Faith Fogarty. Revised and updated with the addition of a section on rape research in Canada.

RAPE CRISIS CENTRES

5728. Erickson, Mary Anne. "Relief centre funds denied [Victoria]," *Branching Out*, 5(3):4-5, 1978.

5729. Kasinsky, Renée Goldsmith. "The rise and institutionalization of the anti-rape movement in Canada," in Mary A. B. Gammon, ed., *Violence in Canada*. Toronto: Methuen, 1978, pp.151-67.

5730. Lockherst, Augusta et Raymonde Lincourt. "Bilan du Centre d'aide [aux victimes] du viol," *Canadian Women's Studies / Les cahiers de la femme*, 2(2):95-6, 1980.

5731. Lord, Catherine. "Un centre anti-bêtise [Québec]," *L'Actualité*, 2:14, fév. 1977.

5732. Perreault, Yvette. "Anti-rape movement in Canada," *Broadside*, 1(1):8, [1979].

5733. Robinson, G. Erlick. "Establishment of a rape crisis centre," *Canada's Mental Health*, 23:10-12, Sept. 1975, suppl.

5734. Robinson, G. Erlick and others. "The establishment of a rape crisis centre," in Benjamin Schlesinger, ed., *Sexual behaviour in Canada: patterns and problems*. Toronto: University of Toronto Press, 1977, pp.194-200.

5735. Vance, Joanie. "The experience of rape crisis centres," *Atlantis*, 4:133-40, Spring 1979, Part II.

REMARRIAGE

5736. Kuzel, Paul and P. Krishnan. "Changing patterns of remarriage in Canada, 1961-1966," *Journal of Comparative Family Studies*, 4:215-24, Autumn 1973.

5737. Osachoff, Carolynn Dee. "Remarriage as family reorganization: the remarried woman." MSW thesis, University of Toronto, 1968. 188p. and app. (Can. theses, no.17802)

5738. Paris, Erna Newman. "Second marriages: for better or for worse?" *Chatelaine*, 50:45, 74+ , Dec. 1977.

5739. Peters, John F. "A comparison of mate selection and marriage in the first and second marriages in a selected sample of the remarried divorced," in George Kurian, ed., *Cross-cultural perspectives of mate selection and marriage*. Contributions in family studies, no. 3. Westport, Conn.: Greenwood Press, 1979, pp.417-26.

5740. Schlesinger, Benjamin. "Remarriage as family reorganization for divorced persons: a Canadian study," *Journal of Comparative Family Studies*, 1:101-18, Autumn 1970.

5741. _____. "The adjustment process in remarriages: a Canadian experience," *Australian Social Work*, 25:5-15, Sept. 1972.

5742. _____. "The single woman in second marriages," *Social Science*, 49:104-9, Spring 1974.

5743. _____. "Women and men in second marriages," in S. Parvez Wakil, ed., *Marriage, family and society: Canadian perspectives*. Toronto: Butterworth and Company, 1975, pp.317-33.

5744. Schlesinger, Benjamin and Alex Macrae. "Remarriages in Canada: statistical trends," *Journal of Marriage and the Family*, 32:300-3, May 1970.

RESOURCE COMMUNITIES

5745. Barclay, Nancy and others. *Adequacy of selected goods and services as evaluated by homemakers in a resource frontier community*. Series 2: Research report, no. 18. Winnipeg: University of Manitoba. Center for Settlement Studies, 1974. 111p.

5746. Krahn, Harvey, John Gartrell and Lyle Larson. "The quality of family life in a resource community," *Canadian Journal of Sociology*, 6:307-24, Summer 1981.

5747. Langin, Susan Esther. "Resource development and new towns: a women's perspective." MA thesis, University of British Columbia, 1981. 167p. (Can. theses, no.55057)

5748. Luxton, Meg. "Opening the North: women in primary resource communities," *Status of Women News*, 6:7, 14, Winter 1979-80.

5749. Nadeau, Denise. "Women and self-help in resource-based communities," *Resources for Feminist Research*, 11:65-7, Mar. 1982.

5750. Nickels, James B. and Jack Ledger. *Winter, wilderness, and womanhood: explanations or excuses for mental health problems*. Winnipeg: University of Manitoba. Center for Settlement Studies, 1976. 72p. and tables.

5751. Northern British Columbia Women's Task Force. *Report on single industry resource communities*. Kitimat, B.C., Fraser Lake, B.C., Mackenzie, B.C., 1977. 100p.
    Includes Kitimat report, by Tamitik Status of Women; Fraser Lake report, by Gina Baker; Mackenzie report, by Joan Koturski.

5752. Vlassoff, Carol and J. W. Gartrell. *Frontier fertility: a study of Fort McMurray families*. Discussion paper, no. 21. [Edmonton, Alta.: University of Alberta. Population Research Laboratory], 1980. 27p. (Microlog 80-4536)

RETAILING

5753. Bossen, Marianne. *Patterns of manpower utilization in Canadian department stores*. Royal Commission on the Status of Women in Canada. Study no. 3. Ottawa, 1971. 105p.

5754. Davis, Curt. "You've gotta have heart," *Marketing*, 86:10, Jan. 5, 1981.

5755. Dowling, Deborah. "Working women weigh in," *Financial Post*, 73:32, Mar. 31, 1979.

5756. Paddy, Victor. "Making it in a man's world: women in the jewellery business," *Canadian Jeweller*, 100:88-9, Oct. 1979.

230

5757. Paris, Erna. "Looking for a dead-end job? For a start, try department stores and supermarkets," *Chatelaine*, 46:41, 113-15, 118-19, Nov. 1973.

5758. Praskey, Sally. "Working women: limitless potential for success [in hardware & building supply industries]," *Hardware Merchandising*, Aug. 1982, pp.8-11.

5759. Skinner, Hank. "Selling: face it, women are loaded with skills," *Marketing*, 83:18, May 22, 1978.

5760. Turnbull, Andy. "Female touch helps hockey," *Sporting Goods Canada*, 6:29-32, Nov.-Dec. 1978.

5761. Welch, Frances. "Dealing with Ms. Fix-it," *Hardware Merchandising*, Nov.-Dec. 1979, pp.28,30-2.

5762. "Woman top salesperson at Toyota dealership," *Canadian Automotive Trade*, 58:32, Feb. 1976.

5763. "Working women vs stay-at-homes," *Volume Retail Merchandising*, 31:7, Apr. 1979.

ROYAL COMMISSION ON THE STATUS OF WOMEN

5764. "A la Commission d'enquête la FTQ recommande une société juste pour la femme," *Canadian Labour*, 13:62, June 1968.

5765. Anderson, D. "Report: making women more equal," *Chatelaine*, 44:1, Feb. 1971.

5766. Anderson, Doris. "Women's rights: long road to equality," *Canada & the World*, 46:14-15, Nov. 1980.

5767. Bird, Florence. *Anne Francis: an autobiography*. Toronto: Clarke Irwin, 1974. 324p.

5768. ----------. "The great decade for Canadian women," *Current History*, 72:170-2, 179-180, Apr. 1977.

5769. Campbell, C. "Le rapport de la Commission royale d'enquête sur le statut de la femme au Canada," *Relations*, no. 347:86, mars 1970.

5770. ----------. "Une clé pour la comprehension du rapport," *Relations*, no. 358:85, mars 1971.

5771. Canada. Advisory Council on the Status of Women. *What's been done?* Assessment of the federal government's implementation of the recommendations of the Royal Commission on the Status of Women. Ottawa, 1974. 40p.

5772. Canada. Royal Commission on the Status of Women in Canada. *Report*. Ottawa, 1970. 488p.

5773. Canadian Advisory Council on the Status of Women. *10 years later: an assessment of the federal government's implementation of the recommendations made by the Royal Commission on the Status of Women*. Ottawa, 1979. 72p.

5774. Canadian Association for Adult Education. *What's in it? (A) study guide ... based on the final report of the Royal Commission on the Status of Women in Canada*. Ottawa: National Council of Women of Canada, in co-operation with la Fédération des femmes du Québec, 1970. 48p.

5775. Edmonds, A. "Cheer up, girls, help is on the way," *Maclean's*, 81:9-11, 52+, Jan. 1968.

5776. Fédération des femmes du Québec. *Guide de discussion et résumé du rapport de la Commission royale d'enquête sur la situation de la femme au Canada*. Montreal, 1971. 46p.

5777. Francis, Anne. "Action from the blueprint: the Royal Commission on the Status of Women," *Canadian Business Review*, 2:2-5, Summer 1975.

5778. Hynna, Martha. "Some are more equal than others," *Canada and the World*, 40:14-15, Dec. 1974.

5779. Jewett, P. "Where were the men when Canada set out to find what makes life tough for its women?" *Maclean's*, 81:12, Dec. 1968.

5780. Knox, D. N. "Liberté, êgalité, maternité," *Atlantic Advocate*, 59:29-30, Aug. 1969.

5781. Lane, G. "Canadian report on the status of women: packed with dynamite," *Christian Century*, 88:345, Mar. 17, 1971.

5782. Larkin, J. "Status of Women Report: fundamental questions remain unanswered," *Canadian Dimension*, 7:6-8, Jan.-Feb. 1971.

5783. "Let them think, let them act," *Labour Gazette*, 71:164-70, Mar. 1971.

5784. Marchak, Patricia. "A critical review of the Status of Women Report," *Canadian Review of Sociology and Anthropology*, 9(1):73-85, 1972.

5785. Marcotte, M. "En marge du Rapport Bird: la femme devant l'avortement," *Relations*, no. 358:81-5, mars 1971.

5786. _____. "Etre femme aujourd'hui," *Relations*, no. 357:47-50, fév. 1971.

5787. Morris, Cerise Darlene. "No more than simple justice: the Royal Commission on the Status of Women and social change in Canada." PhD diss., McGill University, 1982.

5788. Morris, Cerise. "'Determination and thoroughness': the movement for a Royal Commission on the Status of Women in Canada," *Atlantis*, 5:1-21, Spring 1980.

5789. Morton, E. H. "Raising the status of Canadian women," *Queen's Quarterly*, 78:304-7, Summer 1971.

5790. "National commissions on the status of women," *Labour Gazette*, 68:151, Mar. 1968.

5791. "Newfoundland report," *Atlantic Advocate*, 62:61-2, Jan. 1972.

5792. Newman, C. "Some awkward truths about women that the Royal Commission missed," *Chatelaine*, 44:14, Mar. 1971.

5793. _____. "What's so funny about the Royal Commission on the Status of Women?" *Saturday Night*, 84:21-4, Jan. 1969.

5794. "No working women on Royal Commission," *Canadian Labour*, 12:26, Mar.1967.

5795. "Opinions of experts on women in business," *Canadian Business*, 44:46, Sept. 1971.

5796. Rothman, Betsy. "Women in Canada," *Social Education*, 35:617-19, Oct. 1971.

5797. Sauvé, J. "Commentaires sur la Commission royale sur la situation de la femme au Canada," *Canadian Banker*, 78:30-3, Jan.-Feb. 1971.

5798. Schlesinger, Benjamin. "Status of women in Canada: summary of commission recommendations," *Family Coordinator*, 20:253-8, July 1971.

5799. Speirs, R. "Will this woman change your life?" *Chatelaine*, 42:32, 52-3, July 1969.

5800. Status of Women Council [of British Columbia]. *Brief prepared for presentation to the British Columbia Liberal Party Caucus meeting in Vancouver on April 10, 1972.* n.p. 8p.

5801. "Where are the recommendations of yesteryear?" *Branching Out*, 1:25-8, June-July, 1974.

5802. "Women's Commission," *Canadian Labour*, 16:17, Jan. 1971.

RURAL WOMEN

5803. Beatty-Guenter, Patricia Diane. "Women's roles and the urban-rural continuum." MA thesis, University of Victoria, 1980. 64p. (Can. theses, no.49386)

5804. Canada. Council on Rural Development Canada. *Rural women: their work, their needs and their role in rural development*. Ottawa: Minister of Supply and Services Canada, 1979. 106p.

5805. Canada. Dept. of the Secretary of State. Women's Programme. *Summary of issues: rural women*. Ottawa, 1975. 10p.

5806. Cape, Elizabeth. "Aging women in rural society: out of sight, out of mind," *Resources for Feminist Research*, 11:214-5, July 1982.

5807. Cavanagh, Judy. "The plight of women farmworkers," *Resources for Feminist Research*, 11:6-7, Mar. 1982.

5808. Crocker, Olga L. "Stress of farm women related to the changing economy," *Resources for Feminist Research*, 11:182-4, Mar. 1982.

5809. Dion, Suzanne et Gisèle Painchaud, "La participation des femmes dans la vie syndicale agricole," *Resources for Feminist Research*, 11:7-8, Mar. 1982.

5810. Ferguson, Mary Louise. "The role participation and life satisfaction of married women in a rural Ontario community." MSc thesis, University of Guelph, 1981. 146p. (Can. theses, no.52483)

5811. Grant, Debra Ann. "Social isolation and loneliness among new rural women." MA thesis, University of Guelph, 1981. 104p. (Can. theses, no.52490)

5812. Hayford, Alison. "Different routes to different places," *Resources for Feminist Research*, 11:17-19, Mar. 1982.

5813. Hedley, Max J. "'Normal expectations': rural women without property," *Resources for Feminist Research*, 11:15-17, Mar. 1982.

5814. Hulbert, Winifred. "Rural reflections," *Branching Out*, 2:20-1, July-Aug. 1975.

5815. Jacques, Lysane. "Status of rural women project (Summer 1980) [review]," *Resources for Feminist Research*, 11:184-5, Mar. 1982.

5816. Johnson, Joanna. "Women living in isolated areas," *Atlantis*, 4:300-5, Spring 1979, Part II.

5817. Lapping, Joyce K. and Mark B. Lapping. "Rural women's work: a note on the C.C.R.D. study on Canadian rural women [review]," *Resources for Feminist Research*, 11:54-5, Mar. 1982.

5818. Lavoie, Stella. "Les Cercles de fermières de la province de Québec dans la région," *Revue d'histoire du Bas Saint-Laurent*, 5:24-6, déc. 1978.

5819. Maranda, Jeanne. "Des féministes avant l'heure?" *Canadian Women's Studies / Les cahiers de la femme*, 3(1):56-7, 1981. Re. les Cercles des fermières.

5820. Morissette, Yvonne Rialland. *Le passé conjugé au présent: Cercles de fermières, historique 1915-1980*. [Laval?, Québec]: Editions Pénélope, 1980. 249p.

5821. Paltiel, Freda L. "Rural women in the seventies," *Living*, 2:13-14, Winter 1974.

5822. Pattillo, Margaret. "Education and vocational training of rural women,"in, *The family in the evolution of agriculture*. Ottawa: Vanier Institute of the Family, 1968, pp.32-46.

5823. Tasaka, Karen Joy. "A study of selected nonformal educational programs for rural women in Alberta and their relationship to clientele needs." MSc thesis, University of Alberta, 1978. 190p. (Can. theses, no.36486)

5824. Zaleski, Halina. "Women in production co-operatives: unique problems - special benefits," *Resources for Feminist Research*, 11:24-5, Mar. 1982.

RURAL WOMEN - BIBLIOGRAPHY

5825. Cebotarev, E. A. and others. "An annotated bibliography on women in agriculture and rural societies; Canada," *Resources for Feminist Research*, 11:93-100, Mar. 1982.

SCHOLARSHIPS

5826. *Canadian directory of funding sources for research for women*. Ottawa: Canadian Research Institute for the Advancement of Women [1982]- . Annual.

5827. "Women and scholarships," *Labour Gazette*, 66:577-8, Oct. 1966.

SCHOOL ADMINISTRATION

5828. Asper, Linda B. "Factors affecting the entry of women teachers into administrative positions of the Manitoba public school system." MA thesis, University of Manitoba, 1974. 193p. (Can. theses, no.18060)

5829. Brown, Daniel J. "The financial penalty of the sex talent inversion in Canadian education," *Interchange*, 12(1):69-77, 1981.

5830. Brown, Lois. "Career patterns of male and female elementary principals." MA thesis, University of Calgary, 1979. 104p. (Can. theses, no.44554)

5831. Cairns, Kathleen V. "Women and school administration," *Journal of Educational Thought*, 9:165-75, Dec. 1975.

5832. Caverly, Laurie J. "Women in administration - getting there is more than half the battle," *Challenge in Educational Administration*, 16(4):6-8, 1978.

5833. Gosse, Stella-Marie Rideout. "The status of women in educational administration: a comparative analysis of variables by sex and by rank." MEd thesis, Memorial University of Newfoundland, 1975. 180p. (Can. theses, no.27548)

5834. Hrynyk, N. P. "A teacher organization point of view: women in administration," *Challenge in Educational Administration*, 19(2):31-4, 1980.

5835. Lambert, Ruth Carolyn. "A comparison of the value systems of male and female administrators and female teachers on Prince Edward Island." MEd thesis, University of Alberta, 1980. 193p. (Can. theses, no.49006)

5836. Lupini, Dante. "Women in administration - where are they?" Address delivered to the 52nd Convention of the Canadian Education Association, Toronto, Sept. 1975. 11p.

5837. _____. "Women in administration - where are they?" *Education Canada*, 15:17-22, Winter 1975.

5838. McIntosh, Janet. "In conflict with tradition: women in education administration," *Educational Courier*, 45:18-20, Oct. 1974.

5839. McKinnon, Donald Findlay. "A study of selected group attitudes toward the employment of women as educational administrators." MA thesis, University of Victoria, 1974. 77p. (Can. theses, no.29036)

5840. Morgan, Jacqueline. "Perceived communication activities and effectiveness of male and female elementary school principals." MEd thesis, University of Alberta, 1977. 220p. (Can. theses, no.32035)

5841. Nixon, Mary and L. R. Gue. "Professional role orientation of women administrators and women teachers," *Canadian Administrator*, 15:[1]-5, Nov. 1975.

5842. _____. "Women administrators and women teachers: a comparative study," *Alberta Journal of Educational Research*, 21:196-206, Sept. 1975.

5843. Nixon, Mary and Nicholas Hrynyk. *Women in school administration*. Edmonton: Alberta Teachers' Association, 1973. 34p.

5844. Nixon, Mary. "Focus on Alberta: women in administration," *Challenge in Educational Administration*, 19(2):19-30, 1980.

5845. _____. "No females need apply: fact or fiction?" *ATA Magazine*, 52:11-14, Jan.-Feb. 1972.

5846. _____. "Women administrators and women teachers: a comparative study." PhD diss., University of Alberta, 1975. 316p. (Can. theses, no.24104)

5847. _____. "Women in administration: focus on Alberta," *Administrator (Manitoba)*, 4:22-32, Summer 1980.

5848. _____. "Women in educational administration," *Saskatchewan Educational Administrator*, 10:5-9, June 1978.

5849. Poelzer, Irene. "Unprincipaled women: the Saskatchewan case," *Atlantis*, 1:113-18, Fall 1975.

5850. _____. "Women and administration: the statistical story," *Saskatchewan Bulletin*, 42:4-5, Sept. 15, 1975.

5851. Robillard, Elaine. "Women administrators in Alberta community colleges." MEd thesis, University of Alberta, 1979. 189p. (Can. theses, no.43537)

5852. Russell, Connie. "Still few women in educational administration," *Challenge in Educational Administration*, 18(1):7-9, 1978.

5853. Stokes, Shirley. "Career patterns of women elementary school principals in Ontario." MA thesis, University of Toronto, 1974. 298p. and app.

5854. "Women principals: how did they get there?" *Education B.C.*, 3:[3], June-July 1975.

SCIENCE AND TECHNOLOGY

5855. Dotto, Lydia. "A woman's place is in the lab," *Quest*, 12:40j-v, Apr. 1983.

5856. Dunbar, Moira. "Women in science: how much progress have we really made?" *Science Forum*, 6:13-15, Apr. 1973.

5857. Erickson, Gaalen, Lynda Erickson and Sharon Haggerty. *Gender and mathematics / science education in elementary and secondary schools*. Victoria: British Columbia. Ministry of Education. Information Services, 1980.

5858. Goodings, Sidlofsky, Goodings and Associates. *Female engineering technicians and technologists*. [Toronto]: Ontario. Ministry of Colleges and Universities, 1975. 78, [9]p.

5859. Gray, Charlotte. "Women who are meeting the great computer challenge," *Chatelaine*, 56:96-7, 200+ , Oct. 1983.

5860. Irvine, D. M. "Food technology: a new career for women," *Labour Gazette*, 67:638-9, Oct. 1967.

5861. Lasvergnas-Grémy, Isabelle. "Pratiques réticulaires et inscription de la différence dans l'institution scientifique," *Sociologie et sociétés*, 13:83-93, oct. 1981.

5862. Momsen, Janet Henshall. "Women in Canadian geography," *Canadian Geographer*, 24:177-83, Summer 1980.

5863. Morgan, Joanna. "Margaret Wilson space physicist," *Chatelaine*, 50:14, Jan. 1977.
5864. Morrison, Carolyn. "Options for women in geography: some experiences shared," *Canadian Geographer*, 26:360-6, Winter 1982.
5865. Pinet, Janine. "La femme et la science," *Atlantis*, 3:96-115, Spring 1978, Part II.
5866. Science Council of Canada. *Who turns the wheel?* Compiled by Janet Ferguson. Ottawa, 1981. 136p.
      Proceedings of a workshop on the science education of women in Canada.
5867. Science Council of Canada. Science and Education Committee. *The science education of women in Canada: a statement of concern. [Les femmes et l'enseignement des sciences au Canada: déclaration]*. Ottawa: Minister of Supply and Services, 1982. 4, 4p.
5868. Scott, Joan Pinner. "Science subject choice and achievement of females in Canadian high schools," *International Journal of Women's Studies*, 4:348-61, Sept.-Oct. 1981.
5869. "Sexism in science creates special woes," *Globe & Mail*, Sept. 3, 1981, p.T1.
5870. Sheinin, Rose. "The rearing of women for science, engineering and technology," *Journal of Women's Studies*, 4(4):339-47, 1981.
5871. Stinson, Jane. *Technological change and working women*. Prepared for the Organized Working Women Conference on Women and Employment, Feb. 20-22, 1981. [Ottawa]: Canadian Union of Public Employees. Research Dept., 1981. 37p.
5872. Warskett, George. "The choice of technology and women in the paid work force," in Naomi Hersom and Dorothy E. Smith, [eds.], *Women and the Canadian labour force*. Working document. Ottawa: Social Sciences and Humanities Research Council of Canada, 1982, pp.133-64.

SECRETARIES

5873. Anderson, Doris. "Secretaries: the great legal put down,"*Chatelaine*, 47:1, Nov. 1974.
5874. Association of Administrative Assistants or Private Secretaries. *Brief no. 149 to the Royal Commission on the Status of Women in Canada*. Toronto, 1968. v.p.
5875. Canada. Treasury Board Secretariat. Personnel Policy Branch. *Secretaries in the public service. [Les secrétaires dans la fonction publique]*. Ottawa, 1976. 37, 38p. and app.
5876. Carroll, Joy. "Ladies in waiting," *Weekend Magazine*, 29:4-10, Apr. 21, 1979.
5877. Duval, Thérèse. *99.9% des femmes au travail finissent toujours par dire "O.K. boss"*. Montréal: Éditions Libre expression, 1978. 294p.
5878. Hoek, Margaretha. "A descriptive study of women enrolled in the office careers programmes at selected community colleges." MA thesis, University of Victoria, 1978. 126p. (Can. theses, no.39399)

5879. Justus, Marian. "A descriptive study of the female nonpersisters enrolled in the office careers programs at Douglas College between 1976-1979." MA thesis, Simon Fraser University, 1981. 127p. (Can. theses, no.51028)
5880. Kendall, Brian. "Ascension of the supersecretary," *Canadian Business*, 51:116-17, 119-20, 122, Apr. 1979.
5881. Lowe, Graham S. "Women, work and the office: the feminization of clerical occupations in Canada, 1901-1931," *Canadian Journal of Sociology*, 5:361-81, Fall 1980.
5882. McLaren, Peter. "Blue-eyed mistress of the keys," *Canadian Woman Studies / Les cahiers de la femme*, 3:44-7, Summer 1982.
5883. Messier, Monique. "L'employée de bureau, cette inconnue," *Commerce*, 72:48-52, fév. 1970.

5884. Paris, Erna. "Why secretaries get mad," *Chatelaine*, 47:25, 42, 44-7, June 1974.
5885. Parry, David. "Timely death of your girl Friday: she's after more of your money - and your job," *Impetus*, May 1974, pp.24-6, 39+ .
5886. Smith, M. Elizabeth. "'Boss-secretary teams' a source of executive talent," *Canadian Personnel and Industrial Relations Journal*, 17:52-4, May 1970.
5887. "The ideal secretary: 6 bosses day-dream" *Canadian Secretary*, Sept. 1976, pp.18-20.
5888. "The original secretaries were monks (because they could read and write)," *Canadian Secretary*, Sept. 1976, pp.6-7.

5889.   "The upward-mobile WP secretary: unlearning the 'go-fer' route," *Office Equipment &*
        Methods, 21:33-4, 36, July 1975.

SEPARATION AND SEPARATED WIVES

5890.   Annesley, Pat. "Separated wives tell how they cope," *Chatelaine*, 45:45, 80, 82, 84, 88,
        Sept. 1972.
5891.   Bala, Nicholas. "Consequences of separation for unmarried couples: Canadian de-
        velopments," *Queen's Law Journal*, 6:72-149, 1980.
5892.   Cook, David and others. "Separation and divorce in Canada: can we get closer to
        accurate data?" *Canadian Journal of Public Health*, 70:271-4, July - Aug. 1979.
5893.   Garrison, Ada M. "Money to grow on," *Canadian Women's Studies / Les cahiers de la
        femme*, 2(1):69, 1980. Re. Bill 59.
5894.   Mayrand, Albert. "La séparation de fait et ses effets principaux," *Revue générale de droit*,
        8(1):7-31, 1977.
5895.   McVey, Wayne W. and Barrie W. Robinson. "Separation in Canada: new insights
        concerning marital dissolution," *Canadian Journal of Sociology*, 6:353-66, Summer 1981.
5896.   Robinson, Joan. "Splitting up is hard to do," *Chatelaine*, 50:47, 94-8, Oct. 1977.
5897.   Todres, Rubin. "Runaway wives: an increasing North American phenomenon," *Family
        Coordinator*, 27:17-21, Jan. 1978.
5898.   Wanless, Janet L. "Support systems and the transitional process of the recently separated
        woman." MSc thesis, University of Guelph, 1982. 125p. (Can. theses, no.55580)
5899.   Zinck, Cynthia Hastings. "Separate but equal?" *Broadside*, 2:13, 25, Oct.-Nov. 1980.

SEX

5900.   Briedis, Catherine. "Marginal deviants: teenage girls experience community response to
        premarital sex and pregnancy," *Social Problems*, 22:480-93, Apr. 1975.
5901.   Cameron, Stevie. "Why do married women cheat?" *Chatelaine*, 55:58-9, 138+ , May
        1982.
5902.   Carrier, Micheline. "Le discours sur la sexualité," dans Rodrigue Bélanger et autres,
        eds., *Devenirs de femmes*. Cahiers de recherche éthique, no. 8. Montréal: Éditions Fides,
        1981, pp.77-88.
5903.   Crépault, Claude. "Attitudes et comportements sexuels masculins et féminins: con-
        tribution empirique à l'étude comparative des sexes." PhD diss., Université de
        Montréal, 1973. 463p.
5904.   Crépault, Claude et Robert Gemme. *La sexualité prémaritale: étude sur la différenciation
        sexuelle des jeunes adultes québécois*. Montréal: Presses de l'Université du Québec, 1975.
        204p.
5905.   Delehanty, Rosalyn. "An investigation of the relationship between assertiveness, sex-
        role values, fantasy, sexual beliefs and sexual satisfaction in females." MEd thesis,
        University of Alberta, 1980. (Can. theses, no.48928)
5906.   Goldfield, Evelyn. "A woman is a sometime thing: sexual liberation: for whom and for
        what?" in Bryan Finnigan, *Making it: the Canadian dream*. Toronto: McClelland and
        Stewart, 1972, pp.42-60.
5907.   Henshel, Anne-Marie. "Swinging: a study of decision making in marriage," *American
        Journal of Sociology*, 78:885-91, Jan. 1973.
5908.   Herold, Edward S. and Marilyn Shirley Goodwin. "Premarital sexual guilt and con-
        traceptive attitudes and behavior," *Family Relations*, 30:247-253, Apr. 1981.
5909.   Herold, Edward S. and Roger E. Thomas. "Sexual and contraceptive attitudes and
        behavior of high school and college females," *Canadian Journal of Public Health*,
        69:311-14, July-Aug. 1978.
5910.   Hobart, Charles. "Sexual permissiveness in young English speaking and French speak-
        ing Canadians," *Journal of Marriage and the Family*, 34:292-303, May 1972.
5911.   _____. "Social context of morality standards among anglophone Canadian students,"
        Journal of Comparative Family Studies, 5:26-40, Spring 1974.

5912. Hobart, Charles W. "Youth and sex expression," in K. Ishwaran, ed., *The Canadian family*. Rev. ed. Toronto: Holt, Rinehart and Winston of Canada, 1976, pp.418-36.

5913. Le Riche, N. and J. Howard. *A survey of teenage attitudes to sex and contraception in Kingston*. Kingston, Ont.: Queen's University. Dept. of Community Medicine, 1974. 62p.

5914. Mann, W. E. *Canadian trends in premarital behaviour*. Council for Social Service. Bulletin no. 198. Toronto: Anglican Church of Canada, 1967.

5915. _____. "Non conformist sexual behavior on the Canadian campus," in his, *Deviant behaviour in Canada*. Toronto: Social Science Publishers, 1968, pp.300-9.

5916. _____. "Sex at York University," in W. E. Mann, ed., *The underside of Toronto*. Toronto: McClelland and Stewart, 1970, pp.158-74.

5917. Miralles-Nobell, Teresa. "Attitudes sexuelles de la population dans le Montréal métropolitain." PhD diss., Université de Montréal, 1971. 282p.

5918. Neiger, Stephen. "Some new approaches in treating the anorgasmic woman," in Benjamin Schlesinger, ed., *Sexual behaviour in Canada: patterns and problems*. Toronto: University of Toronto Press, 1977, pp.95-106.

5919. Perron, Marie et Jean Perron. *Amour et sexualité des Québécoises*. Montréal: Québécor, 1981. 140p.

5920. "Sexuality and personhood," in Canadian Research Institute for the Advancement of Women, *Women as persons*. [*La femme en tant que personne*]. Toronto: Resources for Feminist Research, 1980, pp.70-5. Proceedings of the 3rd annual meeting.

5921. Wollison, Mary Anne. *Affairs: the secret lives of women*. Don Mills, Ont.: Musson, 1982. 180p.

5922. Young, Connie. *Sex, sexuality and our changing society*. Social problems in Canada, no. 4. Toronto, Ont.: University of Toronto. Faculty of Education. Guidance Centre, 1975. 60p.

SEX CRIMES

5923. Allen, Charlotte Vale. *Daddy's girl*. Toronto: McClelland and Stewart, 1980. 255p.

5924. Canada. Advisory Council on the Status of Women. *Rationalization of sexual offences in the Criminal Code; ACSW recommendations*. Ottawa, 1976. 9p.

5925. Canada. Dept. of Justice. *Information paper: sexual offences against the person and the protection of young persons*. [*Document d'information: infractions sexuelles contre la personne et protection des jeunes*]. Revised. Ottawa, 1980. 43p.

5926. Canada. Law Reform Commission. *Report on sexual offences*. [*Rapport sur les infractions sexuelles*]. Report, no. 10. Ottawa, 1978. 56, 60p.

5927. _____. *Sexual offences*. [*Infractions sexuelles*]. Working paper, no. 22, Criminal law. Ottawa, 1978. 66, 72p.

5928. Canadian Advisory Council on the Status of Women. *Background notes on the proposed amendments to the Criminal Code in respect of indecent assault (Bill C-52)*, by Marcia H. Rioux and Joanna L. McFadyen. Ottawa, 1978. 27p.

5929. _____. *Background notes on the proposed amendments to the Criminal Code, the Canada Evidence Act and the Parole Act (Bill C-51)*, by Marcia H. Rioux and Joanna L. McFadyen. Ottawa, 1978. 26, 7p.

5930. Cannon, Margaret. "Oldest taboo - newest outrage," *Broadside*, 3:5, Nov. 1981.

5931. Cooper, Ingrid K. "Decriminalization of incest - new legal-clinical responses," in John M. Eekelaar and Sanford N. Katz, eds., *Family violence: an international and interdisciplinary study*. Toronto: Butterworths, 1978, pp.518-28.

5932. Rioux, Marcia. *The web of the law: a study of sexual offences in the Canadian Criminal Code*. Ottawa: Canada. Advisory Council on the Status of Women, 1975. 29p.

5933. Waisberg, Barbara. "A group for incest survivors," *Canadian Women's Studies / Les cahiers de la femme*, 3(2):84, 1981.

SEX DIFFERENCES

5934. Ambert, Anne-Marie. *Sex structure*. 2d rev. ed. Don Mills, Ont.: Longman Canada, 1976. 248p.

5935. Bélanger, Claire. "Une différence sexuelle de comportement linguistique: la production verbale au niveau quantitatif chez les filles et les garçons," *Canadian Women's Studies / Les cahiers de la femme*, 2(1):108-11, 1980.

5936. Birnbaum, Dana Wolfe. "Preschoolers' stereotypes about sex differences in emotionality: an investigation of possible etiologies." Phd diss., Carleton University, 1978. 163p. (Can. theses, no.44392)

5937. Buckley, Patrick G. "Perceived sex differences in social situations." MA thesis, University of Guelph, 1976. 287p.

5938. Colwill, Nina. "Women in business: on evaluating the research," *Business Quarterly*, 47:19-21, Dec. 1982.

5939. Cooke, Sharon W. "A comparision of identity formation in preadolescent girls and boys." MA thesis, Simon Fraser University, 1979. 93p. (Can. theses, no.41136)

5940. Cox, Marlene Joan. "A cross-cultural study of sex differences found in drawings by Canadian Inuit and American children." EdD diss., Illinois State University, 1979. 174p.

5941. Greenglass, Esther R. *A world of difference: gender roles in perspective*. Toronto: John Wiley & Sons, 1982. 356p.

5942. Johns, Nick. "A study of the sex-differentiated characteristics of members of the Canadian Association of Social Workers." MSW thesis, University of Toronto, 1966. 176p. (Can. theses, no.22761)

5943. Johnson, Ronald. "Preferences for play areas: age and sex differences in choice of areas for recreation," *CAHPER Journal*, 44:30-5, July-Aug. 1978.

5944. Millar, Garnet, Sharon Coté and Glenna Moorey. "Grade eight girls out-perform boys in language arts and mathematics," *Special Education in Canada*, 54:17-18, Fall 1979.

5945. Pfeifer, Pat and Stanley J. Shapiro. "Mistress of Business Administration: male and female candidates: are there personality differences?" *Canadian Women's Studies / Les cahiers de la femme*, 1:17-19, Fall 1978.

5946. Precosky, Catherine G. "Sex differences in response to a competitive situation." MA thesis, Lakehead University, 1980. 91p. (Can. theses, no.47497)

5947. Pyke, Sandra W. "Androgyny: a dead end or a promise?" in Cannie Stark-Adamec, ed., *Sex roles: origins, influences and implications for women*. Montreal: Eden Press, 1980, pp.20-32.

5948. Robitaille, David F. "A comparison of boys' and girls' feelings of self-confidence in arithmetic computation," *Canadian Journal of Education*, 2(2):15-22, 1977.

5949. Sawada, Daiyo, Alton T. Olson and Sol E. Sigurdson. "Sex differences in mathematics learning in a Canadian setting," *Canadian Journal of Education*,6(2):5-19, 1981.

5950. Shershen, Eugene D. "Shading in the H-T-P: its relationship to situationally specific anxiety and other variables in a male and female Canadian university sample." PhD diss., University of Ottawa, 1976. 214p.

5951. Smye, Marti Diane and Jeri Dawn Wine. *A comparison of female and male adolescents' social behaviors and cognitions: a challenge to the assertiveness literature*. GROW paper no. 11. Toronto: Ontario Institute for Studies in Education. Group for Research on Women, [1977?] 31p.

5952. Stelmaschuck, Marian Adele. "The gifted in school: does sex make a difference?" MEd thesis, University of Alberta, 1980. 249p. (Can. theses, no.44825)

5953. Turrittin, Anton H., Paul Anisef and Neil J. MacKinnon. "Gender differences in educational achievement: a study of social inequality," *Canadian Journal of Sociology*, 8:395-419, Fall 1983.

5954. Vernon, Philip E. "Sex differences in personality structure at age 14," *Canadian Journal of Behavioural Science*, 4(4):283-97, 1972.

SEX ROLE

5955. Aitchison, Douglas Wayne. "Sexism and sexual discrimination." PhD diss., University of Waterloo, 1978. 150p. (Can. theses, no.36196)

5956. Ambert, Anne-Marie. *Sex structure*. 2d rev. ed. Don Mills, Ont.: Longman Canada, 1976. 248p.

5957. Anderson, D. M. "Men stay home while wives work?" *Chatelaine*, 42:1, Feb. 1969.

5958. Barnhorst, Sherrie. "Female delinquency and the role of women," *Canadian Journal of Family Law*, 1:254-73, Apr. 1978.

5959. Beatty-Guenter, Patricia Diane. "Women's roles and the urban-rural continuum." MA thesis, University of Victoria, 1980. 64p. (Can. theses, no.49386)

5960. Beaulne, Trudy Lynn. "Sex-stereotyped behavioral flexibility for feminine, masculine and androgynous females." MA thesis, University of Guelph, 1981. 158p. (Can. theses, no.48672)

5961. Belanger, J. "It's high time women stopped searching for meaning — and started cooking like Granny used to," *Maclean's*, 79:44, Feb. 19, 1966.

5962. Berens, Anne E. "Sex-role stereotypes and the development of achievement motivation," *Ontario Psychologist*, 5(2):30-5, 1973.

5963. Bird, Barbara Jean. "Differences in achievement motivation in women: the sex-role orientation of the situation." MA thesis, University of Western Ontario, 1972. 113p. (Can. theses, no.12518)

5964. Birnbaum, Dana Wolfe. "Preschoolers' stereotypes about sex differences in emotionality: an investigation of possible etiologies." Phd diss., Carleton University, 1978. 163 p. (Can. theses, no.44392)

5965. Boyd, Monica. "English-Canadian and French-Canadian attitudes toward women: results of the Canadian gallup polls," *Journal of Comparative Family Studies*, 6:153-169, Autumn 1975.

5966. Cairns, Kathleen Vivian Osborne. "Motivation to avoid success, sex-role stereotyping and same-sex affiliation." PhD diss., University of Calgary, 1974.204p. (Can. theses, no.21247)

5967. Campbell, C. "La femme doit humaniser la société," *Relations*, no. 336:80-3, mars 1969.

5968. Canada. Dept. of Employment and Immigration. Public Affairs. *Eliminating sex-role stereotyping: editorial guidelines for Employment and Immigration Canada communications*. Ottawa, 1983. 22, 22p.
    Includes French edition.

5969. Canada. Dept. of National Health and Welfare. Policy Research and Long Range Planning (Welfare). *The changing dependence of women: roles, beliefs and inequality*. [*La dependance changeante de la femme: rôles, croyances et inégalité*]. Social security research reports. Research report, no. 5. Ottawa, 1978. 45, 49p.

5970. Carisse, Colette. "Life plans of innovative women: a strategy for living the feminine role," in Lyle E. Larson, comp., *The Canadian family in comparative perspective*. Scarborough, Ont.: Prentice-Hall, 1976, pp.379-94.

5971. Carment, D. W. "Effects of sex-role in a maximizing difference game: a replication in Canada," *Journal of Conflict Resolution*, 18:461-72, Sept. 1974.

5972. Cassie, J. B. and others. *Sex-role stereotyping: incidence and implications for guidance and counselling of students*. OISE project, 5616-80. Toronto: Ontario Institute for Studies in Education, 1980. 193p.

5973. Chabot-Ferland, Francine. "Sexualité féminine, une dépendance," *Maintenant*, no. 117:28-32, juin-juill. 1972.

5974. Chekki, Dan A. "The changing roles of women in Canada," *Sociologia Internationalis*, 14(1/2):201-20, 1976.

5975. Colwill, Nina Lee and Noralou P. Roos. "Debunking a stereotype: the female medical student," *Sex Roles*, 4(5):717-22, 1978.

5976. *Condition féminine, condition masculine*. Québec: Université du Québec, Télé-université, 1980. 226, [160]p.

239

5977. Corporation des psychologues de Québec. *Brief no. 428 to the Royal Commission on the Status of Women in Canada*. Montreal, 1968. 43p.

5978. Crawford, Susan M. Heffernan. "Demographic, behavioural, and social psychological predictors of women's role aspirations." MSc thesis, University of Guelph, 1977. 265p. (Can. theses, no.37397)

5979. Cumming, Elaine and others. "Suicide as an index of role strain among employed and not employed married women in British Columbia," *Canadian Review of Sociology and Anthropology*, 12:462-70, Nov. 1975.

5980. Cust, Marlene. "Self-actualization and psychological androgyny in a sample of university women." PhD diss., University of Alberta, 1978. 152p. (Can. theses, no.40119)

5981. De Man, Anton F. and Rejeanne Benoit. "Self-esteem in feminist and nonfeminist French-Canadian women and French-Canadian men," *Journal of Psychology*, 111:3-8, May 1982.

5982. Doyle, James A. "Study of the relationships between mental health, field dependency and attitudes toward the female's role." PhD diss., University of Saskatchewan, 1973. 213p. (Can. theses, no.16849)

5983. Eaton, Warren O., Donna Von Bargen, and James G. Keats. "Gender understanding and dimensions of preschooler toy choice: sex stereotype versus activity level," *Canadian Journal of Behavioural Science*, 13(3): 203-9, 1981.

5984. Edwards, John R. and J. E. Williams. "Sex-trait stereotypes among young children and young adults: Canadian findings and cross-national comparisons," *Canadian Journal of Behavioural Science*, 12(3): 210-20, 1980.

5985. Eichler, Margrit. *The double standard: a feminist critique of feminist social science*. New York: St. Martin's Press, 1980. 151p.

5986. _____. "Sex-role attitudes of male and female teachers in Toronto," *Interchange*, 10(2):2-14, 1979/80.

5987. Fisher, Margaret Ada. "Sex-role socialization and female sport participation." MEd thesis, University of New Brunswick, 1976. 122p. (Can. theses, no.30399)

5988. Garigue, Philippe. *La vie familiale des Canadiens français*. Montréal: Presses de l'Université de Montréal, 1970. 143p.

5989. Gaskell, Jane. "Sex-role ideology of working class girls," *Canadian Review of Sociology and Anthropology*, 12:453-61, Nov. 1975.

5990. Gelber, Sylva. "New role of women," *Labour Gazette*, 69:314-16, 322, June 1969.

5991. Gelber, Sylva M. "New role of women," in, *Women's Bureau '69*. Ottawa: Canada. Dept. of Labour, Women's Bureau, 1970, pp.7-21.

5992. George, Janet M. "Self-concept and personality in women as a function of traditional-nontraditional career choice and sex-role attitudes." MA thesis, University of Windsor, 1980. 105p. (Can. theses, no.49211)

5993. Gibbins, Roger, J. Rick Ponting and Gladys Symons. "Attitudes and ideology: correlates of liberal attitudes towards the role of women," *Journal of Comparative Family Studies*, 9:19-40, Spring 1978.

5994. Gingras, J. B. "Les blessures infligées aux deux sexes par le masculinisme," *L'Action nationale*, 59:465-71, janv. 1970.

5995. _____. "Feminisme ou masculinisme: le rêve masculin et le rêve féminin," *L'Action nationale*, 59:255-60, nov. 1969.

5996. Gold, Dolores and David Andres. "Relations between maternal employment and development of nursery school children," *Canadian Journal of Behavioural Science*, 10(2):116-29, 1978.

5997. Gold, Dolores. "Full-time employment of mothers in relation to their ten-year old children," *Atlantis*, 2:98-105, Spring 1977, Part II.

5998. Greenglass, Esther R. *A world of difference: gender roles in perspective*. Toronto: John Wiley & Sons, 1982. 356p.

5999. Groulx, Lionel. "Sexismes et service social: point de vue historique et empirique," *Canadian Journal of Social Work Education*, 6(2/3):59-80, 1980.

240

6000. Guay, Chantal. "Comment le changement de rôle chez la femme peut entraîner un rajustement des rôles dans la relation conjugale," *Orientation professionnelle*, 14:138-44, été 1978.

6001. Guse, Linda L. "Vulnerability to external influence, gender, sex-role identity, and model gender as variables." PhD diss., University of Manitoba, 1981. 86p. (Can. theses, no.50930)

6002. Hall, M. Ann. *Sport, sex roles and sex identity*. CRIAW papers, no. 1. Ottawa: Canadian Research Institute for the Advancement of Women, 1981. 41p.

6003. Hall, O. "Gender and the division of labour," *Office Administration*, 11:74, Sept. 1965.

6004. Hanif, Muhammad. "Separation trends: a functional analysis of changing dynamics in relationships." MA thesis, University of Windsor, 1977. 85p. (Can. theses, no.33195)

6005. Harrison, Donna J. "The perceived image of the female athlete in relation to other female social roles." MA thesis, University of Alberta, 1978. 116p. (Can. theses, no.40172)

6006. Henshel, Ann-Marie. *Sex structure*. Don Mills, Ont.: Longman, 1973. 165p.

6007. Irigaray, Luce. *Le corps-à-corps avec la mére*. Montréal: Éditions de la Pleine lune, 1981. 89p.

6008. Istona, Mildred. "You, me & the next generation," *Chatelaine*, 51:4, July 1978.

6009. Jabes, Jak. "Causal attributions and sex-role stereotypes in the perceptions of women managers," *Canadian Journal of Behavioural Science*, 12(1):52-63, 1980.

6010. _____. *Sex-role stereotypes and success attributions of women and men managers as perceived by women managers*. Working Paper, no. 78-12. Ottawa: University of Ottawa. Faculty of Management Science, 1978. 33p.

6011. Jack, Deloris A. and George Fitzsimmons. "Sex role stereotyping in first grade and pre-vocational junior high school students: an attitudinal study," *Canadian Counsellor*, 13:206-10, July 1979.

6012. Jeffery, Gary Herbert. "Parental sex-role differentiation of young children." PhD diss., University of Alberta, 1975. 178p. (Can. theses, no.24067)

6013. Kahn, Sharon E. "Sex-role attitudes: who should raise consciousness?" *Sex Roles*, 8(9):977-85, 1982.

6014. Kieran, Tom and Diane Kieran. "Sex role biases: we can escape them? [interview]," *Branching Out*, 5(1):16-17, 1978.

6015. Kinley, Donald Albert. "Sex-role learning of grade one students." MEd thesis, University of Alberta, 1966. 151p.

6016. Kinzel, Mary Kathleen. "A study of the influence of sex-role stereotypes on marriage counsellors' personal and clinical evaluations of their clients." MA thesis, University of Regina, 1974. 272p. (Can. theses, no.23642)

6017. Korabik, Karen. "Sex-role orientation and leadership style," *International Journal of Women's Studies*, 5:329-37, Sept.-Oct. 1982.

6018. Koziol, Carol Ann. "Role conflict in female athletes." MPEd thesis, University of New Brunswick, 1980. 111p. (Can. theses, no.47757)

6019. Lambert, Ronald D. *Sex role imagery in children: social origins of mind*. Royal Commission on the Status of Women in Canada. Study no. 6. Ottawa, 1971. 156p.

6020. Landau, Barbara. "Women pushing for job equality - but old attitudes won't die; digest of address," *Financial Post*, 71:18, Feb. 26, 1977.

6021. Landsberg, Michèle. "Young women in the post-lib era," *Chatelaine*, 50:47, 114+ , Nov. 1977.

6022. Lashuk, Maureen Wilson and George Kurian. "Employment status, feminism, and symptoms of stress: the case of a Canadian prairie city," *Canadian Journal of Sociology*, 2:195-204, Spring 1977.

6023. Levine, Helen. "On women and on one woman," in Anne MacLennan, ed., *Women: their use of alcohol and other legal drugs: a provincial consultation - 1975*. Toronto: Addiction Research Foundation of Ontario, 1976, pp.21-43.

6024. Loo, Robert and Pamela Logan. "Investigations of the Attitudes Toward Women Scale in western Canada," *Canadian Journal of Behavioural Science*, 9(2):201-4, 1977.

6025. Lysons, H. "Role models have changed from fantasy to reality," *Branching Out*, 5(1):30-2, 1978.

6026. Mackie, Marlene. "Gender relations," in Robert Hagedorn, ed., *Sociology*. 2d ed. Toronto: Holt, Rinehart & Winston, 1983, pp.91-121.

6027. Mainemer, Nathan. "Sex roles and intimate relationships." MA thesis, University of Regina, 1977. 132p. (Can. theses, no.33453)

6028. "Male-female behavior on the job. A round table discussion," *ICB Review*, 5:6-8, Summer 1972.

6029. Meyer, John Peter. "An investigation of the relationship of marital adjustment to need compatibility and role fit in young married couples." MA thesis, University of Western Ontario, 1975. 138p. (Can. theses, no.24615)

6030. Moudgil, Ranvir. "Changes in sex-role identity among Ugandan Asians in Canada," *State University of New York, Buffalo. Occasional Papers in Anthropology*, no. 1:123-31, Apr. 1979.

6031. Myers, Anita M. "Psychological androgyny and its relationship to contraceptive use." MA thesis, York University, 1977. 90p. (Can. theses, no.33647)

6032. Myhr, Ronald Peder. "Sex-role and counsellor evaluation." PhD diss., University of Toronto, 1976. 151p. (Can. theses, no.30350)

6033. Nemiroff, Greta. "Eduquer les femmes en vue de la maturité," *Critère*, no. 9:52-67, juin 1973.

6034. Ontario. Ministry of Education. *Changing roles in a changing world; a resource guide focusing on the female student*. [Toronto, 1976]. 24p.

6035. Paquette, Lucie. *Rôles familiaux et planification des naissances en milieu défavorisé urbain québécois*. Laboratoire de recherches sociologiques. Rapports de recherches. Cahier 5. Québec: Université Laval. Dept. de sociologie, Faculté des sciences sociales, 1974. xxii, 313p.

6036. Pearl, Brian. "Empirical testing of social learning theories of sex role identification." MA thesis, York University, 1974. 138p. (Can. theses, no.20021)

6037. Plowman, Shirley. "Woman's place in the home?" *Labour Gazette*, 75:245-6, Apr. 1975.

6038. Prefontaine, Marielle. "Women's role orientation in three types of French Canadian educational institutions." PhD diss., Cornell University, 1969. 154p. (UM69-10,462)

6039. Proulx, Monique Cecile. "Personal, family and institutional factors associated with attitudes toward women's roles among French-Canadian college students." PhD diss., Michigan State University, 1976. 143p. (UM, 77-5871)

6040. Pyke, Sandra W. "Sex role socialization in the school system," in Richard A. Carlton, *Education, change and society*. Toronto: Gage, 1977, pp.426-38.

6041. Richardson, Ann. "An evaluation of the effectiveness of a course in sex role stereotyping and the socialization process." MA thesis, University of British Columbia, 1979. 173p. (Can. theses, no.42723)

6042. Ricks, Frances and Sandra Pyke. "Teacher perceptions and attitudes that foster or maintain sex role differences," *Interchange*, 4(1):26-33, 1973.

6043. Robertson, Susan E. *Sex roles and politics: a case study*. MA thesis, McGill University, 1973. 128p. (Can. theses, no.15982)

6044. Roper, Julie Faye. "Masculinity, femininity or androgyny: teacher reactions to chil-drens' androgynous or sex-typed characteristics." MEd thesis, University of New Brunswick, 1979. 124p. (Can. theses, no.43934)

6045. Ross, Valerie. "She stoops-grovels!-to conquer," *Maclean's*, 88:67, Dec. 15, 1975.

6046. Russell, Susan Jessie. "Sex role socialization in the high school: a study of the perpetua-tion of patriarchal culture." PhD diss., University of Toronto, 1978. 307p. (Can. theses, no.38828)

6047. _____. "Women and equality: a study of the effect of sex structure on the educational aspirations of women." MA thesis, Carleton University, 1973. 164p.

6048. Schmidt, Lanalee Carol. "Sex role attitudes and changing life styles of professional women." PhD diss., University of Alberta, 1973. 250p. (Can. theses, no.15335)

6049. Schneider, Frank W. and Larry M. Coutts. "Teacher orientations towards masculine and feminine: role of sex of teachers and sex composition of school," *Canadian Journal of Behavioural Science*, 11(2): 99-111, 1979.

242

6050. Schreiber, E. M. "The social bases of opinions on woman's role in Canada," *Canadian Journal of Sociology*, 1:61-74, Spring 1975.

6051. Sex-Role Stereotyping and Women's Studies Conference, Sept. 28-30, 1978, Toronto. *Report*. [Toronto]: Ontario. Ministry of Education / Ontario Association for Curriculum Development, [1978]. 130p.

6052. Sexton, Christine S. "Career orientation, sex role orientation, and perceived equity as factors affecting marital power." PhD diss., University of Manitoba, 1979. 165p. (Can. theses, no.40048)

6053. Shack, Sybil. "He takes out the garbage," *School Guidance Worker*, 31:44-9, Sept.-Oct. 1975.

6054. "She stoops - grovels! - to conquer," *Maclean's*, 88:67, Dec. 15, 1975.

6055. Sheinin, Rose. "The rearing of women for science, engineering and technology," *Journal of Women's Studies*, 4(4):339-347, 1981.

6056. Short, Judith-Ann Catherine. "The effect of the sex-role orientation of the situation on the arousal of the motive to avoid success in women." MA thesis, University of Western Ontario, 1973. 134p. (Can. theses, no.14975)

6057. Simmons, Alan B. "The socialization of sex-roles and fertility ideals: a study of two generations in Toronto," *Journal of Comparative Family Studies*, 7:255-71, Summer 1976.

6058. Smyth, Frances E. "The relationship of maternal employment and current field of study to certain sex-role attitudes of male and female university students." PhD diss., University of Ottawa, 1979. 251p. (Can. theses, no.44151)

6059. Stacy, Stanley. "Perceptions of male and female success in sex-linked occupations in relation to the sex of subject and the stance of spouse: impressions of conflicts, consequences, and attributions." MA thesis, Concordia University, 1976. 65p. (Can. theses, no.28470)

6060. Stanton-Jean, M. "Liberté, égalité—féminité: allocution," *Relations*, no. 297:262-3, sept. 1965.

6061. Stark-Adamec, Cannie, ed. *Sex roles: origins, influences and implications for women*. Montreal: Eden Press, 1980. 238p. Canadian Psychological Association, Interest Group on Women and Psychology - Proceedings of the Inaugural Institute.

6062. Stoppard, Janet Mary. "Personality characteristics in gender stereotypes and sex roles." PhD diss., Queen's University, 1976. 227p. (Can. theses, no.30225)

6063. Synge, Jane. "The sex factor in social selection processes in Canadian education," in Richard A. Carlton, *Education, change and society*. Toronto: Gage, 1977, pp.298-310.

6064. Toews, Lorette K. "Self-hatred in college women: sex-role stereotypes and same-sex affiliation." PhD diss., University of Alberta, 1973. 286p. (Can. theses, no.16156)

6065. Tomeh, Aida K. "Sex roles in a cross-cultural perspective - Canada," in her, *Family and sex roles*. Toronto: Holt, Rinehart and Winston of Canada, 1975, pp.75-83.

6066. Trotter, Beth Sherran. "A study of the relationships between sex-role stereotypes, mental health and attitudes toward women's roles." MA thesis, University of Regina, 1974. 153p. (Can. theses, no.21193)

6067. Trudeau, P. E. *The evolving role of the Canadian woman: an address by Prime Minister the Right Honourable P. E. Trudeau*. Statements and speeches no. 71/9. Ottawa: Canada. Dept. of External Affairs. Information Division, 1971. 8p.

6068. Tudiver, Judith G. "Parents and the sex-role development of the preschool child," in Cannie Stark-Adamec, ed., *Sex roles: origins, influences and implications for women*. Montreal: Eden Press, 1980, pp.33-49.

6069. Tuohimaa, Anne. "Sex role adjustment and alcoholism in women." MA thesis, University of Windsor, 1980. 142p. (Can. theses, no.49254)

6070. Turner, Jean and Alan B. Simmons. "Sex roles and fertility: which influences which?" *Canadian Studies in Population*, 4:43-60, 1977.

6071. Walsh, Richard T. and John R. Schallow. "The experimenter as a sex-role model in sex-role stereotyping," *Canadian Journal of Behavioural Science*, 9(4):305-14, 1977.

6072. Waterman, Diane C. "Sex roles and career goals of university women." MA thesis, University of British Columbia, 1977. 166p. (Can. theses, no.34975)

6073. Woolsey, Lorette. "Psychology and the reconciliation of women's double bind: to be feminine or to be fully human," *Canadian Psychological Review*, 18:66-78, Jan. 1977.

6074. Woolsey-Toews, L. "Sex-roles, self-hatred and sisterhood," *Atlantis*, 1:24-37, Fall 1975.

6075. Young, Connie. *Sex, sexuality and our changing society*. Social problems in Canada, no. 4. Toronto, Ont.: University of Toronto. Faculty of Education. Guidance Centre, 1975. 60p.

6076. Young, Filson A. "Sex-role stereotyping in career counselling: effects of differences in sex of counsellor and sex of client." PhD diss., University of Toronto, 1973. 122p. (Can. theses, no.26092)

SEX ROLE STEREOTYPING IN EDUCATION

6077. Brett, Joyce. "What's that honey? Sex role stereotyping," *Challenge in Educational Administration*, 18(1):10-15 1978.

6078. Canadian Teachers' Federation. *Challenge '76: sexism in schools*. Report of the Proceedings of the C.T.F. workshop on the status of women in education [Ottawa, Jan. 1976]. Ottawa, 1976. 102p.

6079. Caron, Anita. "Femmes, sexisme et éducation morale," dans Rodrigue Bélanger et autres, eds., *Devenirs de femmes*. Cahiers de recherche éthique, no. 8. Montréal: Éditions Fides, 1981, pp.69-76.

6080. Dagg, Anne Innis. "Letter to the editor," *Canadian Women's Studies / Les cahiers de la femme*, 1:113, Summer 1979.

6081. Dunnigan, Lise. *L'école 'sexiste' c'est quoi?* [Québec]: Conseil du statut de la femme, 1974. 15p.

6082. Federation of Women Teachers' Associations of Ontario. *Challenging the double standard*. [Toronto]: The Federation, May 1978. 59p.

6083. Gaskell, Jane. "Stereotyping and discrimination in the curriculum: sex," in H. A. Stevenson and J. D. Wilson, eds., *Precepts, policy and process: perspectives on contemporary Canadian education*. London, Ont.: Alexander, Blake Associates, 1977, pp.268-74.

6084. Kincaid, Pat J. "Response to 'A sexy topic': sex stereotyping imprisons boys and girls," *Orbit*, 11:10, Feb. 1980.

6085. Nova Scotia Confederation of University Faculty Associations. Status of Women Committee. *Her and his: language of equal value*, by Wendy R. Katz. Halifax: NSCUFA, 1981. 52p.

6086. Pyke, Sandra W. "Sex-role socialization in the school system," in Richard A. Carlton and others, eds., *Education, change and society: a sociology of Canadian education*. Toronto: Gage, 1977, pp.426-38.

6087. Richer, Stephen. "Sex-role socialization and early schooling," *Canadian Review of Sociology and Anthropology*, 16(2):195-205, 1979.

6088. Russell, Susan. "Learning sex roles in the high school," *Interchange*, 10(2):57-66, 1979/80.

6089. _____. "School kids: does sex determine their future roles in society?" *Perception*, 2:27-9, July-Aug. 1979.

6090. Storey, John. "'Dick does' and 'Jane watches': sex-role stereotyping in the curriculum," *Interchange*, 10(2):15-19, 1979/80.

6091. Synge, Jane. "The sex factor in social selection processes in Canadian education," in Richard A. Carlton and others, eds., *Education, change and society: a sociology of Canadian education*. Toronto: Gage, 1977, pp.298-310.

6092. Wine, Jeri Dawn. *School sex role socialization: female children's rights*. Toronto: Ontario Institute for Studies in Education, 1978. 26p.

SEX ROLE STEREOTYPING IN TEXTBOOKS

6093. Adamchick, Tom. "Desexing Ontario civil service training material," *Canadian Personnel and Industrial Relations Journal*, 24:27-9, Nov. 1977.

244

6094. Atnikov, Pamela and others. *A study of social studies text books approved for use in Manitoba schools*. Winnipeg: Manitoba Human Rights Commission, 1971.

6095. Batcher, Elaine and others. *... And then there were none*. Toronto: Federation of Women Teachers' Associations of Ontario, 1975. 22p.

6096. British Columbia. Dept. of Education. Educational Programs. Provincial Advisory Committee on Sex Discrimination. *Equal treatment of the sexes: guidelines for educational materials*. Victoria, B.C., 1974. 8p.

6097. Centrale de l'enseignement du Québec. *Stéréotypes sexistes dans l'éducation: unité et solidarité*. 25e congrès de la Centrale de l'enseignement du Québec, 23-27 août, 1976. 36p.

6098. Chadwick, J. and others. *Brief on the presentation of girls and women in the primary and elementary curriculum of Newfoundland*. St. John's: Newfoundland Status of Women Council, 1975. 19p.

6099. Cheda, S. "Non-sexist books: sliding down the iceberg," *Branching Out*, 5(1):28-9, 1978.

6100. Cheda, Sherrill. "See Dick run, see Jane sit," *Chatelaine*, 45:40, 52, 55-7, Dec. 1972.

6101. _____. "Sex roles in children's books," *The New Feminist*, 2:1-3, Oct. 1971.

6102. Cullen, Linda. "The books ... ," *Branching Out*, 1:8-11, 41, Sept.-Oct. 1974.

6103. _____. *A study into sex stereotyping in Alberta elementary school textbooks*. [Edmonton: Alberta. Dept. of Education], 1972. 28p.

6104. "Discrimination?" *Atlantic Advocate*, 67:54, Dec. 1976.

6105. Dunnigan, Lise. *Analyse des stéréotypes masculins et féminins dans les manuels scolaires au Québec*. Québec City: Québec. Conseil du statut de la femme, 1975. 188p.

6106. "Getting older, yes. But getting better? The women's question in the schools [excerpt Globe and Mail, Jan. 1976 and Apr. 19, 1976]," *This Magazine*, 10:11-12, June-July 1976.

6107. Goundrey, Jane and others. *Bias in Newfoundland textbooks: an evaluation of English, history and geography texts used in grades 7-11 of the Newfoundland School System, 1975-6*. St. John's: Memorial University. Faculty of Education, 1976. 92p.

6108. Gray, Vicky A. "The image of women in psychology textbooks," *Canadian Psychological Review*, 18:46-55, Jan. 1977.

6109. Inkster, Brenda. " ... the kids," *Branching Out*, 1:15, 41, Sept.-Oct. 1974.

6110. Jeanmart, Monique. *"Le discours sur la différenciation sexuelle dans cinq manuels scolaires québécois."* MA thèse, Université de Montréal, 1975. 149p.

6111. Kaplan, Harriett. "Sex typing in textbooks used in the Saskatoon public schools," *Canadian Newsletter of Research on Women*, 2:10-12, Feb. 1973.

6112. Ladan, C. J. and D. Hodgins Miller. "Jane's prerogative: mediocrity," *English Quarterly*, 8:31-42, Spring-Summer 1975.

6113. Lord, Catherine. "Comment on abêtit nos filles," *L'Actualité*, 1:20, sept. 1976.

6114. Lorimer, Rowland and Margaret Long. "Sex-role stereotyping in elementary readers," *Interchange*, 10(2):25-45, 1979/80.

6115. Malone, Patricia. "Learning about women in junior high," *Chatelaine*, 48:32, Oct. 1972.

6116. Marsden, Lorna. "Criteria for the identification of sex-role stereotyping in educational materials, methods and programs," in Sex-Role Stereotyping and Women's Studies Conference, Sept. 28-30, 1978. *Report*. [Toronto]: Ontario. Ministry of Education, [1978], pp.29-35.

6117. Nett, Emily M. "Gender and the Canadian introductory sociology textbook," *Atlantis*, 7:127-33, Fall 1981.

6118. Newfoundland Status of Women Council. *Brief on the presentation of girls and women in the primary and elementary curriculum of Newfoundland*. [St. John's], 1975. 20p.

6119. Nova Scotia Confederation of University Faculty Associations. Status of Women Committee. *Her and his: language of equal value*, by Wendy R. Katz. Halifax: NSCUFA, 1981. 52p.

6120. Nova Scotia. Human Rights Commission. *Sexism in school textbooks*. n.p., [1976?] 98p. (Profile 77-0182)

6121.   _____. *Textbook analysis: Nova Scotia*. [Halifax], 1974. 115p.

6122.   Ontario. Interministerial Textbook Committee. *Report to the Deputy Minister of Education and Deputy Minister of Labour*, June 1972.

6123.   Ontario Status of Women Council. *About face: towards a more positive image of women in textbooks*. Toronto, 1974. 11p.

6124.   Preston, Patricia. "Our language arts texts teach sex discrimination," in Lynda Turner, comp., *Woman in Canadian society*. [New Westminster, B.C.: Douglas College, 1972], pp.11-16.

6125.   Saskatchewan. Human Rights Commission. *Sex bias in primary readers: a content analysis of primary reading textbooks used in Saskatchewan schools*. Saskatoon: Saskatchewan Human Rights Commission, 1974. 78p.

6126.   Venton, Anne, Ross Traub and Ellen Campbell. *Stereotyping in elementary school readers*. Toronto: Ontario Institute for Studies in Education. Educational Evaluation Centre, [1977?] 60p.

6127.   Women for Non-sexist Education. *Confronting the stereotypes: handbook on bias at the primary level*. Winnipeg: Manitoba Human Rights Commission / Manitoba. Dept. of Education, 1977. 125p.

6128.   Wood, Beverly A. "Pink and blue text books - the price we pay," *Newfoundland Teachers' Association Journal*, 1:11-19, Fall 1980.

6129.   Wright, Vicki. "Hidden messages: expressions of prejudice," *Interchange*, 7(2):54-62, 1976/77.

SEX ROLE STEREOTYPING IN TEXTBOOKS -BIBLIOGRAPHY

6130.   Manitoba. Dept. of Education. Curriculum Services. *Resource materials presenting positive female images*. Curriculum support series. [Winnipeg], 1979. 42p. (Microlog 80-1279)

6131.   Ontario. Ministry of Labour. Women's Bureau. *Bibliography: sex stereotyping in children's books, the media, and elementary education*. Toronto, 1974. 5p.

SEXUAL HARASSMENT

6132.   Anderson, Doris. "How employers can help thwart sexual harassment," *Financial Post*, 76:8, Jan. 2, 1982.

6133.   Attenborough, Susan. *Sexual harassment at work*. Rev. and reprinted. Ottawa: National Union of Provincial Government Employees, 1981. 31p.

6134.   Backhouse, Constance and Leah Cohen. *The secret oppression: sexual harassment of working women*. Toronto, Ont.: MacMillan Co., 1978. 208p.
          Also published under the title: Sexual harassment on the job: how to avoid the working woman's nightmare. Englewood Cliffs, N.J.: Prentice-Hall, 1981.

6135.   Bagnall, James. "The name of the game is power," *Financial Post*, 72:20, May 6, 1978.

6136.   "BCGEU contract bans sexual harassment; Un contrat du SFPCB proscrit le harcèlement sexuel," *Canadian Labour / Travailleur canadien*, 26:6, [English]; 6, [French], June-July-Aug. 1981.

6137.   Bradbury, Patricia. "Working women unite," *Quill & Quire*, 45:30, Feb. 1979.

6138.   Burstyn, Varda. "Sexual harassment on the job," *Canadian Dimension*, 15:9-11, Dec. 1980.

6139.   B.C. Federation of Labour. Women's Rights Committee / Women's Research Centre. *Sexual harassment in the workplace; a discussion paper*. [Burnaby, B.C.], Mar. 1980. 42p.

6140.   Canadian Association of University Teachers. *CAUT guidelines on professional ethics and professional relationships. Appendix II: abuse of professional authority: sexual harassment*. Ottawa, C.A.U.T., 1982. 4, 6p.

6141.   Canadian Human Rights Commission. *Sexual harassment.* [*Harcèlement sexuel*]. Background paper, by Shelagh M'Gonigle. [Ottawa], 1981. 16, 17p.

6142.   "Council passes interim guidelines on sexual harassment," *University Affairs*, 22:9, June-July 1981.

6143.   Cram, Kathy. *Sexual harassment in the workplace: an occupational health hazard: a study of sexual harassment in North-Western Ontario.* Thunder Bay: Thunder Bay Committee on Sexual Harassment / Northern Women's Centre, 1980. 76p.

6144.   Cuddy, Pat L. "I'm a damn good machinist," *Canadian Dimension*, 15:46-9, Feb. 1981.

6145.   Gray, Elizabeth. "Heading them off at the passes," *Maclean's*, 94:26-7, Apr. 6, 1981.

6146.   Johnson, Theresa. "Sexual harassment in the workplace; Le harcèlement sexuel au travail," *Civil Service Review / Revue du service civil*, 53:8-9, 11, [English]; 9-11, 23, [French], Dec. 1980.

6147.   Oberman, Edna. "Hands off! Sexual harassment is serious business," *B.C. Business Magazine*, 9:13-14, Sept. 1981.

6148.   Preston, Patricia. "Give in - he wins; refuse - you lose: sexual harassment in the office," *Branching Out*, 4:19-21, July-Aug.1977.

6149.   _____. "Sexual harassment in the workplace; Le harcèlement sexuel au travail," *Status of Women News / Statut: Bulletin de la femme*, 5:2-5, [English]; 2-5, [French], Sept. 1978.

6150.   Rovan, Rhonda. "Sexual harassment, *Chatelaine*, 51:16, 18, Aug. 1978.

6151.   Saskatchewan. Advisory Council on the Status of Women. *Sexual harassment in the workplace: an information guide for employees and employers.* Prepared [in co-operation with the] Women's Division, Dept. of Labour. Saskatoon, 1980. [4]p.

6152.   "Sexual advances on the job," *Globe & Mail*, Aug. 31, 1978, p.T1.

6153.   "Sexual harassment & the working woman," *Financial Times*, 67:1, Jan.8, 1979.

6154.   Shore, Valerie. "Sexual harassment: prevention is better," *University Affairs*, 2:2-4, Mar. 1981.

6155.   Sim, Victor W. "Strickler dismissal upheld," *CAUT Bulletin*, 27:5-6, Dec. 1980.

6156.   "The secret oppression: sexual harassment is a serious problem," *Financial Times*, 67:10,11, Jan. 8, 1979.

6157.   York University. Presidential Advisory Committee on Sexual Harassment. *Final report.* Downsview, Ont., 1982. [8]p.

6158.   _____. *Preliminary report of the Presidential Committee on Sexual Harassment, York University, September 1980.* [Downsview, Ont.: York University], 1980. 15p.

SEXUAL HARASSMENT -BIBLIOGRAPHY

6159.   Miller, Alan V. *Sexual harassment of women in the workplace: a bibliography with special emphasis on Canadian publications.* Public administration series: bibliography, P-801. Monticello, Ill.: Vance Bibliographies, 1981. 22p.

6160.   "Sexual harassment [bibliography], pt. 1-3," *Labour Topics (Ontario Ministry of Labour Library)*, v.l(6), June 1978; 2(2), Feb. 1979; 3(6), June 1980.

6161.   "Sexual harassment - legal aspects: a bibliography, part 4," *Labour Topics (Ontario Ministry of Labour Library)*, 5(3), Mar. 1982.

6162.   Storrie, Kathleen and Pearl Dykstra. "Bibliography on sexual harassment," *Resources for Feminist Research*, 10:25-32, Dec. 1981-Jan. 1982.

SINGLE WOMEN

6163.   Anderson, Karen. "Heeeere's...supersingle!," *Chatelaine*, 51:43, 110+ , Dec. 1978.

6164.   Brisson, Marcelle et Louise Poissant. *Célibataire, pourquoi pas?* Québec: Serge Fleury, 1981. 200p.

6165.   Chandler, Verna. "A study of single women who turn to the Y.W.C.A. for help." MSW thesis, University of Toronto, 1964 (c1975). 127p. (Can. theses, no.22742)

6166.   Deathe, Donald George and Julie Sibley Farrell. "Affiliation and achievement needs of never-married women thirty and over." MSW thesis, University of Windsor, 1979. 197p. (Can. theses, no.41941)

6167.   Duval, Thérèse. *Madame ou mademoiselle? Vivre seule dans une société pour couples.* [n.p.]: Libre expression, 1977. 156p.

6168. Hamilton Regional Women's Research Collective. *The single women's book*. [Hamilton, Ont.], 1975. 73p.

6169. Hindbo, Ester and Micheline Kisner. "Aspects of life experience of mature single women." MSW thesis, University of Calgary, 1975. 154p.

6170. Kostash, Myrna. "The single-girl rip-off," *Chatelaine*, 47:29, 55-8, Feb. 1974.

6171. Lovell, Verna Louise. "Still single: an ethnography of having-never-married." MA thesis, University of British Columbia, 1978. 115p. (Can. theses, no.40690)

6172. "Never-married women," *Canadian Welfare*, 44:13, Nov.-Dec. 1968.

6173. Ross, Val. "Couple assumption," *Chatelaine*, 51:42-3, 104+ , Dec. 1978.

6174. Slopen, Beverley. "On being successfully single," *Chatelaine*, 50:45, 62-6, Apr. 1977.

SINGLE -PARENT FAMILY

6175. Alberta. Women's Bureau. *The single parent*. Edmonton, 1982. 42p.

6176. Alexander, Gay, Betty Campbell and Gilda Jubas. *Self acceptance, substance use and sole support mothers in Toronto: an examination of the relationship*. n.p., [1978?] 57p. and app.
    Funded by Non-Medical Use of Drugs Directorate, Health and Welfare Canada.

6177. Arseneau, Mona and others. "Mothers of one-parent families." MA thesis, Maritime School of Social Work, 1971. 111p.

6178. Burke, Mary-Lynn. "Perspectives," *Branching Out*, 2:30-3, 42, May-June 1975.

6179. Canada. Advisory Council on the Status of Women. *New directions for public policy: a position paper on the one-parent family*, by S. June Menzies. Ottawa, 1976. 29p.

6180. Canada. Statistics Canada. *Characteristics of parents in lone parent families*. Canada. 1976 Census. Families, v. 4. Ottawa, 1978. [42]p. (Cat. no. 93-824)

6181. _____. *Lone parent families*. Canada. 1976 Census. Supplementary bulletins: housing and families. Ottawa, 1978. [151]p. (Cat. no. 93-833)

6182. Canadian Advisory Council on the Status of Women. *One-parent family; ACSW principles and recommendations*. Ottawa, 1977. 4p.

6183. Canadian Council on Social Development. *The one-parent family: report of an inquiry on one-parent families in Canada*. Ottawa, 1971. 167p.

6184. Carson, Susan. "Surviving as a single parent," *Chatelaine*, 54:80-1, 100+ , Nov. 1981.

6185. Edmonton. Social Services. Social Planning Section. *The one-parent family in Edmonton; report of a study looking at the conditions and needs of one-parent families and the services available*. Edmonton, 1975. 103p. and app. (Profile 76-0704)

6186. Emile, Gary. "No husband needed," *Native People*, 13:3, May 16, 1980.

6187. "Femmes et chefs de famille," *Canadian Women's Studies | Les cahiers de la femme*, 2(1):41, 1980.

6188. Guyatt, Doris E. *The one-parent family in Canada*. Ottawa: Vanier Institute of the Family, 1971. 148p.
    French edition: *La famille à parent unique au Canada*.

6189. Heath, Jean. *Lone parent families in Canada and British Columbia: an analysis based on 1971 and 1976 census data*. Vancouver: British Columbia. Ministry of Education. Division of Continuing Education, 1980. 39p.

6190. Hetherington, E. "Girls without fathers," *Chatelaine*, 46:29, 49-51, Aug. 1973.

6191. Hood, Nancy E. "One parent families - their housing needs." MA thesis, University of British Columbia, 1976. 98p. (Can. theses, no.28710)

6192. Humphreys, Carolyn Ann. "Single mothers: an investigation of their experience as single-parents." PhD diss., University of Toronto, 1980. 450p. (Can. theses, no.43658)

6193. James, Jean M. *Family benefits mothers in Metropolitan Toronto*. Research report, no. 2. Toronto: Ontario. Ministry of Community and Social Services. Research and Planning Branch, 1973. 219p.

6194. Jerusalem, Carol. "Single mothers and the just society," *Perception*, 6:7, 9, Jan.-Feb. 1983.

6195. Knight, Bryan M. *Enjoying single parenthood*. Toronto: Van Nostrand Reinhold, 1980. 170p.

248

6196. Knive-Ingraham, Kathleen Dorothy. "The impact of the Contemporary Woman: Options and Opportunities Program on single mothers' perceptions of family functioning." MSc thesis, University of Calgary, 1980. 79p. (Can. theses, no.49315)

6197. Kunin, Roslyn. "To work or not to work?" *Canadian Welfare*, 48:16-20, July-Aug. 1972.

6198. Laberge, Diane, Jeannine Lawless et Rollande V. Bédard. *Évaluation des besoins des familles monoparentales du comté de Portneuf*. n.p.: Carrefour FM Portneuf, 1979. 120p.

6199. Langstone, Mike. *Study of single parents: summary and analysis of the six month stage*. Toronto: Children's Aid Society of Metropolitan Toronto, 1974. 18p.

6200. Li, Selina. *Options for single mothers*. Project Child Care working paper, no. 4. Toronto: Project Child Care, 1978. 44p. (Microlog 80-3317)
    "Project Child Care is jointly sponsored by the Children's Day Care Coalition and the Social Planning Council of Metropolitan Toronto."

6201. MacKenzie, Joan. "My battle to be a stay-at-home mother," *Chatelaine*, 48:85, 93-7, Oct. 1975.

6202. Marsot, Ghislaine. "Famille monoparentale," *Canadian Women's Studies / Les cahiers de la femme*, 2(1):39-41, 1980.

6203. Metro Agencies Action Committee. Work Group. *Facts for advocacy*. [Toronto, 1982?] v.p. (Microlog 83-2855)
    "A project designed to identify and explore the conditions which block women on family benefits moving from economic dependence to independence."

6204. National Council of Welfare. *One in a world of two's: a report by the National Council of Welfare on one-parent families in Canada*. Ottawa, 1976. 41p.

6205. Newlands, Elizabeth. "A study of self-concept in women as heads of one-parent families." MSW thesis, Memorial University of Newfoundland, 1978. 186p. (Can. theses, no.38645)

6206. Orton, Jeanne D. "Mothers who are breadwinners: an exploration of the lives of a group of sole-support women." MA thesis, University of Toronto, 1975. 90p.

6207. Rosensweig, Donna. "Women and children last," *Broadside*, 3:8, Feb. 1982.

6208. Schlesinger, Benjamin. *Families: Canada*. Toronto: McGraw-Hill Ryerson, 1979. 193p.

6209. _____. "Family patterns are changing with the times," *Canadian Banker & ICB Review*, 82:40-5, May-June 1975.

6210. _____. *One-parent families in Canada*. Social problems in Canada, no. 2. Toronto, Ont.: University of Toronto. Faculty of Education. Guidance Centre, 1974. 44p.

6211. _____. "Parents without partners," *Canadian Welfare*, 42:231-35, Nov. 1966.

6212. _____. *The one-parent family: perspectives and annotated bibliography*. 4th ed. Toronto: University of Toronto Press, 1978. 224p.

6213. _____. "The widowed as a one-parent family unit," *Social Science*, 46:26-32, Jan. 1971.

6214. _____. *One in ten: the single parent in Canada*. Toronto: University of Toronto. Guidance Centre. Faculty of Education, 1979. 151p.

6215. Silversides, Ann. "Catch-22 of single parents on welfare," *Maclean's*, 93:54, 57-8, Nov. 17, 1980.

6216. Soper, Mary. "Housing for single-parent families: a women's design," in G. R. Wekerle, R. Peterson and D. Morley, eds., *New space for women*. Boulder: Westview Press, 1980, pp.319-32.

6217. Strong-Boag, Veronica. "'Wages for housework': mothers' allowances and the beginnings of social security in Canada," *Journal of Canadian Studies*, 14:24-34, Spring 1979.

6218. Tapp, John L. "Parents without partners." MSW thesis, University of Toronto, 1963 [c1976]. 196p. (Can. theses, no.27519)

6219. Tcheng-Laroche, Françoise and Raymond H. Prince. "Middle income, divorced female heads of families: their lifestyles, health and stress levels," *Canadian Journal of Psychiatry*, 24:35-42, Feb. 1979.

6220. Tcheng-Laroche, Françoise. "Yesterday wife and mother, today head of household," *Canada's Mental Health*, 26:6-9, Sept. 1978.

6221. The Minus Ones, Winnipeg. *Women alone with dependent children*. Royal Commission on the Status of Women in Canada. Brief no. 146. Winnipeg, 1968. 18p. and app.

6222. Wilkinson, Shelagh. "Mother's rights," *Canadian Women's Studies | Les cahiers de la femme*, 2(1):58-9, 1980.

SINGLE - PARENT FAMILY -BIBLIOGRAPHY

6223. Schlesinger, Benjamin. *The one-parent family: perspectives and annotated bibliography*. 4th ed. Toronto: University of Toronto Press, 1978. 224p.

SOCIAL WORK

6224. Canadian Association of Schools of Social Work. Task Force on the Status of Women in Social Work Education. *The status of women in social work education: brief to the Canadian Association of Schools of Social Work*. Prepared by Gillian Walker. [Ottawa, n.p.], 1977. 29, 33p. (Microlog 79-0068)

6225. _____. *The status of women in social work education: a preliminary brief to the Canadian Association of Schools of Social Work from the C.A.S.S.W. Task Force on the Status of Women in Social Work Education*. n.p., 1976.

6226. Cummings, Joan E. "Sexism in social work: the experience of Atlantic social work women," *Atlantis*, 6:62-79, Spring 1981.

6227. Dobrowolsky, Sonia A. "A study of women in social work: their aspirations to administrative positions and attitudes toward discrimination." MSW thesis, University of Windsor, 1975. 91p. (Can. theses, no.29137)

6228. Gelber, Sylva. "Social work and the status of women; Les travailleurs sociaux et la situation de la femme," *Social Worker*, 41:193-7, [English]; 198-203, [French], Autumn 1973.

6229. Gelber, Sylva M. "Social workers and the status of women," in, *Women's Bureau '73*. Ottawa: Canada. Dept. of Labour. Women's Bureau, 1974, pp.7-15.

6230. Gripton, James. "Sexism in social work: male takeover of a female profession," *Social Worker*, 42:78-89, Summer 1974.

6231. Groulx, Lionel et Charlotte Poirier. "Les pionnières en service social: nouveau métier féminin dans le champ philanthropique," in *Women's culture: selected papers from the Halifax conference*. Ottawa: Canadian Research Institute for the Advancement of Women, 1982, pp.34-46.

6232. Groulx, Lionel. "Sexismes et service social: point de vue historique et empirique," *Canadian Journal of Social Work Education*, 6(2/3):59-80, 1980.

6233. Jeffery, Bonnie L. and Martha Wiebe. "Women, work & welfare: the Saskatchewan perspective," *Social Worker*, 50:117-18, 135-7, Fall 1982.

6234. Johns, Nick. "A study of the sex-differentiated characteristics of members of the Canadian Association of Social Workers." MSW thesis, University of Toronto, 1966. 176p. (Can. theses, no.22761)

6235. Legault, Gisèle. "Une expérience d'enseignement de la condition féminine en service social," *Canadian Journal of Social Work Education*, 6(2/3):93-105, 1980.

6236. Michalski, Andrzej B. "Essex County social workers: their attitudes toward women." MSW thesis, University of Windsor, 1976. 187p. (Can. theses, no.29198)

6237. Montgomery, Frances L. "One of our pioneers: Jane B. Wisdom 1884-1975; Un de nos pionniers: Jane B. Wisdom 1884-1976]," *Social Worker*, 43:130, [English]; 131, [French], Fall 1975.

6238. Olyan, Sidney. "The feminization of the John Howard Society in Ontario: a case example," *Canadian Journal of Social Work Education*, 6(2/3):81-91, 1980.

6239. Proulx, Marcienne. "L'action sociale de Marie Gérin-Lajoie, 1910-1925." MA mémoire, Université de Sherbrooke, 1976. 127p. (Can. theses, no.27019)

6240. Stolar, G. Elaine. "Occupational mobility: male-female variants in the social work profession," *Social Worker*, 41:204-10, Autumn 1973.

6241. Thring, Beverley R. "Homemaking responsibilities as a factor influencing a mother's educational plans." MA thesis, University of Toronto, 1966. 127p.

6242. White-Tanabe, Patricia Anne. "Social work as a women's profession: image and reality," *Atlantis*, 4:222-30, Spring 1979, Part II.
6243. Women's Counselling Collective. *Report of a research project, sponsored by the Women's Faculty and Staff Group of the Maritime School of Social Work*. [Halifax, N.S.], 1981. 58p. and app. A-D.
6244. Wren, Derdri. "Fear of success and some of its correlates in female graduate social work students." Research paper submitted for Social Work 608 and 630, University of British Columbia, April 1975. 125p.

SOCIALIZATION

6245. Ashby, Gail. "The child I was," in Bryan Finnigan, *Making it: the Canadian dream*. Toronto: McClelland and Stewart, 1972, pp.1-12.
6246. Berens, Anne Elizabeth. "The socialization of achievement motives in boys and girls." PhD diss., York University, 1972. 224p. (Can. theses, no.15681)
6247. Dagenais, Huguette. "Représentations des rapports hommes-femmes chez les adolescents québécois," dans Rodrigue Bélanger et autres, eds., *Devenirs de femmes*. Cahiers de recherche éthique, no. 8. Montréal: Éditions Fides, 1981, pp.147-68.
6248. Kee, Y. T. "Don't raise your daughter to behave 'like a lady!'" *Business Quarterly*, 40:4-5, 7-8, Spring 1975.
6249. Kimball, Meredith. "Socialization of women: a study in conflict," in S. Parvez Wakil, ed., *Marriage, family and society: Canadian perspectives*. Toronto: Butterworth, 1975, pp.189-201.
6250. Richer, Stephen. "Sex-role socialization and early schooling," *Canadian Review of Sociology and Anthropology*, 16(2):195-205, 1979.
6251. Spinks, Sarah. "Sugar'n spice," in Bryan Finnigan, *Making it: the Canadian dream*. Toronto: McClelland and Stewart, 1972, pp.22-35.

SOCIOLOGY

6252. Burnet, Jean. "Minorities I have belonged to," *Canadian Ethnic Studies*, 13(1):24-36, 1981.
6253. Christiansen-Ruffman, Linda. "Positions for women in Canadian sociology and anthropology," *Society*, 3:9-12, Sept. 1979.
6254. Connelly, M. Patricia and Linda Christiansen-Ruffman. "Women's problems: private troubles or public issues?" *Canadian Journal of Sociology*, 2:167-78, Spring 1977.
6255. Dagenais, Huguette. "Quand la sociologie devient action: l'impact du féminisme sur la pratique sociologique," *Sociologie et sociétés*, 13:49-65, oct. 1981.
6256. Khosla, Renu Chopra. "A Canadian perspective on the Hindu woman: a study in identity transformation." MA thesis, McMaster University, 1980. 154, ivp. (Can. theses, no.50842)
6257. Laurin-Frenette, Nicole. "Présentation: les femmes dans la sociologie," *Sociologie et sociétés*, 13:3-18, oct. 1981.
6258. Maroney, Heather Jon. "Sexual politics in Quebec: the structure and dynamics of class, national and sex oppression." MA thesis, Mcmaster University, 1978. 308p. (Can. theses, no.46913)
6259. Stanko, Elizabeth A. "What's a nice girl like you doing in a place like this?" *Crime and/et Justice*, 7/8(3/4):220-5, 1981.
6260. Tyndale, Eleanor. "The status of women and women's studies in Canadian colleges," *Society*, 5:11-13, May 1981.

STRIKES

6261. "Birth of the 'kitchen economists' [Sudbury]," *Financial Post*, 73:3, May 19, 1979.
6262. Cuthbertson, Wendy. "Fleck: the unionization of women," *Canadian Women's Studies / Les cahiers de la femme*, 1:71-2, Winter 1978-1979.

251

6263. Dumas, Evelyn. "Les grèves de la guenille," dans sa, *Dans le sommeil de nos os: quelques grèves au Québec de 1934 à 1944*. Montréal: Lemeac, 1971, pp.43-75.

6264. Hynes, Maureen. "Cheap labour," *Branching Out*, 5(3): 5, 1978.

6265. Kates, Joanne. "Report from Canada: they stopped typing - and stopped the country: Trudeau's new constitution," *Ms*, 10:77-80, Aug. 1981.

6266. Posner, Judith. "YUSA strike report - ladies last: the 6% solution," *Canadian Women's Studies / Les cahiers de la femme*, 1:64-5, Winter 1978-1979.

6267. Sangster, Joan. "The 1907 Bell Telephone strike: organizing women workers," *Labour / Le Travailleur*, 3:109-30, 1978.

6268. Sodoway, Geraldine. "Immigrant workers championed," *Branching Out*, 6(2): 4-5, 1979.

6269. Spinks, Sarah. "Women on strike: Dare and Wardair," *This Magazine*, 7:23-7, May-June 1973.

6270. Tolmie, Ellen. "Fleck - profile of a strike," *This Magazine*, 12:22-9, Oct. 1978.

6271. _____. "The Fleck Women: a victory for workers and a victory for women," *Canadian Women's Studies / Les cahiers de la femme*, 1:69-70, Winter 1978-1979.

STUDENT ASPIRATIONS

6272. Brinkerhoff, Merlin B. "Women who want to work in a man's world: a study of the influence of structural factors on role innovativeness," *Canadian Journal of Sociology*, 2:283-303, Summer 1977.

6273. Clark, Sheila Elizabeth. "Attitudes toward women's roles and career choices of high school girls." MA thesis, Dalhousie University, 1977. 119p. (Can. theses, no.36057)

6274. Fahmy-Pomerleau, Pauline. "Égalité et dépendance ou l'impossible aspiration des adolescentes," in Yolande Cohen, *Femmes et politique*. Montréal: Le Jour, 1981, pp.81-100.

6275. Gagnon, Rosette, Louise Biron et Marie-Andrée Bertrand. *Aspirations et délinquance révélée chez les adolescentes. Rapport no. 3*. Montréal: Université de Montréal. Groupe de Recherche sur l'inadaptation juvénile, 1980. 198p.

6276. Humphreys, Linda. "Women of tomorrow," *Chatelaine*, 53:26, 162+ , Mar. 1980.

6277. "Les adolescentes face à l'amour et à la société," dans, *La femme au Québec*. Les Québécois, no. 1. Montréal, Qué.: Editions du Parti québécois, 1974, pp.48-54.

6278. Lindell, Susan Howard. "Role expectations of adolescent women (16-18)," *Canadian Woman Studies / Les cahiers de la femme*, 4:67-70, Fall 1982.

6279. Russell, Susan Jessie. "Women and equality: a study of the effect of sex structure on the educational aspirations of women." MA thesis, Carleton University, 1973. 164p.

6280. Russell, Susan. "School kids: does sex determine their future roles in society?" *Perception*, 2:27-9, July-Aug. 1979.

6281. Waterman, Diane C. "Sex roles and career goals of university women." MA thesis, University of British Columbia, 1977. 166p. (Can. theses, no.34975)

SUCCESS, FEAR OF

6282. Cairns, Kathleen Vivian Osborne. "Motivation to avoid success, sex-role stereotyping and same-sex affiliation." PhD diss., University of Calgary, 1974.204p. (Can. theses, no.21247)

6283. Leblanc, Christine M. "Fear of success in sport among female basketball players and female swimmers." MA thesis, University of Alberta, 1976. 88p. (Can. theses, no.30736)

6284. Rubin, Berte. "Beyond the fear of success: observations on women's fears," in Cannie Stark-Adamec, ed., *Sex roles: origins, influences and implications for women*. Montreal: Eden Press, 1980, pp.139-47.

6285. Syrotuik, Janice Letitia. "Fear of success in sport among adolescent girls." MA thesis, University of Alberta, 1975. 117p.

6286. Wilensky, Marshall. "An investigation of the motive to avoid success in high school students." MA thesis, University of Toronto, 1974. 62p.

6287. Wren, Derdri. "Fear of success and some of its correlates in female graduate social work students." Research paper submitted for Social Work 608 and 630, University of British Columbia, 1975. 125p.

SUFFRAGE

6288. Assheton-Smith, Marilyn. "Political women in the west," *Branching Out*, 1:7-9, 29, June-July 1974.

6289. Bacchi, Carol. "Divided allegiances: the response of farm and labour women to suffrage," in Linda Kealey, ed., *A not unreasonable claim: women and reform in Canada, 1880s-1920s*. Toronto: Women's Press, 1979, pp.89-107.

6290. _____. *Liberation deferred?: the ideas of the English-Canadian suffragists, 1877-1918*. Toronto: University of Toronto Press, 1983. 203p.

6291. _____. "Liberation deferred: the ideas of the English-Canadian suffragists, 1877-1918," *Histoire sociale / Social History*, 10:433-4, Nov. 1977.

6292. _____. "Race regeneration and social purity: a study of the social attitudes of Canada's English-speaking suffragists," *Histoire sociale / Social History*, 11:460-74, Nov. 1978.

6293. Bacchi, Carol Lee. "Liberation deferred: the ideas of the English-Canadian suffragists, 1877-1918." PhD diss., McGill University, 1976. 445p. (Can. theses, no.35678)

6294. Bacchi-Ferraro, Carol Lee. "The ideas of the Canadian suffragists, 1890-1920." MA thesis, McGill University, 1970. 168p. (Can. theses, no.9849)

6295. Clarke, Mary Eileen. "The Saint John Women's Enfranchisement Association, 1894-1919." MA thesis, University of New Brunswick, 1979. 168p. (Can. theses, no.43881)

6296. Cleverdon, Catherine L. *The woman suffrage movement in Canada*. 2nd ed. Introduction by Ramsay Cook. Toronto: University of Toronto Press, 1974. 324p.
   1st edition published 1950.

6297. Garner, John. "Minors, women and Indians," in his, *The franchaise and politics in British North America 1755-1867*. Ottawa: University of Toronto Press, 1969, pp.155-60.

6298. Geller, Gloria. "The Wartimes Elections Act of 1917 and the Canadian women's movement," *Atlantis*, 2:88-106, Autumn 1976.

6299. Gesner, Claribel. "Women and elections," *Atlantic Advocate*, 62:39-40, June 1972.

6300. Gorham, Deborah. "English militancy and the Canadian suffrage movement," *Atlantis*, 1:83-112, Fall 1975.

6301. _____. "Flora MacDonald Denison; Canadian feminist," in Linda Kealey, ed., *A not unreasonable claim: women and reform in Canada, 1880s-1920s*. Toronto: Women's Press, 1979, pp.47-70.

6302. _____. "Singing up the hill," *Canadian Dimension*, 10:26-38, June 1975.

6303. _____. "The Canadian suffragists," in Gwen Matheson, *Women in the Canadian mosaic*. Toronto: Peter Martin, 1976, pp.23-55.

6304. Hale, Linda Louise. "The British Columbia woman suffrage movement, 1890-1917." MA thesis, University of British Columbia, 1977. 156p. (Can. theses, no.34829) Includes appendix, "Biographies of the British Columbia woman suffrage leaders, 1890-1917."

6305. Lavigne, Marie, and others. "The Fédération Nationale Saint-Jean-Baptiste and the women's movement in Quebec," in Linda Kealey, ed., *A not unreasonable claim: women and reform in Canada, 1880s-1920s*. Toronto: Women's Press, 1979, pp.71-87.

6306. Menzies, June. "Votes for Saskatchewan's women," in Norman Ward and Duff Spafford, eds., *Politics in Saskatchewan*. Don Mills, Ont.: Longmans Canada Ltd., 1968, pp.78-92.

6307. Paul, Norma Joan. "The quiet suffragists," *Atlantic Advocate*, 73:42-4, Jan. 1983.

6308. Stoddart, Jennifer. "The woman suffrage bill in Quebec," in Marylee Stephenson, *Women in Canada*. Toronto: New Press, 1973, pp.90-106.

6309. Tennyson, Brian D. "Premier Hearst, the war and votes for women," *Ontario History*, 57:115-21, Sept. 1965.

6310. Thompson, John H. "'The beginning of our regeneration': the Great War and Western Christian Reform Movements," *Canadian Historical Association. Historical Papers*, 1972. pp.227-245.

6311. Trifiro, Luigi. "La crise de 1922 dans la lutte pour le suffrage féminin au Québec." MA thesis, Université de Sherbrooke, 1976. 113p. (Can. theses, no.29305)

6312. _____. "Une intervention à Rome dans la lutte pour le suffrage féminin au Québec (1922)," *Revue d'histoire de l'Amérique française*, 32:3-18, juin 1978.

6313. Trofimenkoff, Susan Mann. "Henri Bourassa and 'the woman question'," in Susan Mann Trofimenkoff and Alison Prentice, eds., *The neglected majority: essays in Canadian women's history*. Toronto: McClelland and Stewart, 1977, pp.104-15.

6314. Voisey, Paul. "The 'votes for women' movement," *Alberta History*, 23:10-23, Summer 1975.

6315. "WSPU deputation to Prime Minister Borden, 1912," *Atlantis*, 5:188-95, Spring 1980.

SUICIDE

6316. Bigras, Julien and others. "Suicidal attempts in adolescent girls: a preliminary study," *Canadian Psychiatric Association. Journal*, 11(suppl.):S275-82, 1966.

6317. Cumming, Elaine and others. "Suicide as an index of role strain among employed and not employed married women in British Columbia," *Canadian Review of Sociology and Anthropology*, 12:462-70, Nov. 1975.

6318. Ornstein, Michael D. "The impact of marital status, age and employment on female suicide in British Columbia," *Canadian Review of Sociology and Anthropology*, 20:96-100, Feb. 1983.

SUPPORT (DOMESTIC RELATIONS)

6319. Anderson, Doris. "Should alimony be cut off? [editorial]," *Chatelaine*, 48:2, Oct. 1975.

6320. Barnett, Jim. "Alimony and maintenance payments; Pension alimentaire et allocations indemnitaires," *CA Magazine*, 112:65-70, June 1979.

6321. Bhardwaj, Vijay K. "An outline of the matrimonial and child support insurance plan: a new law of maintenance," *Reports of Family Law*, 28:295-309, 1977.

6322. Binks Rice, Mary Jane and De Sousa, M. L. "Comments on working paper no. 12 of the Law Reform Commission of Canada: maintenance on divorce," *Ottawa Law Review*, 8:345-57, 1976.

6323. Bowman, C. Myrna. *Practical tools to improve interprovincial enforcement of maintenance orders after divorce: a study paper*. Modernization of statutes series. Ottawa: Law Reform Commission, 1980. 50p.

    French edition: *L'exécution interprovinciale des ordonnances de soutien après le divorce - solutions pratiques*.

6324. Canada. Law Reform Commission. *Enforcement of maintenance obligations. [Exécution des ordonnances de soutien]*. Study paper, family law, prepared by Edward F. Ryan. [Ottawa], 1976. 47, 53p.

6325. _____. *Maintenance on divorce*. Working paper no. 12. Ottawa: Information Canada, 1975. 40p.

6326. Canadian Institute for Research. *Matrimonial support failures: reasons, profiles and perceptions of individuals involved*. Vol. 1: *Summary report*. Vol.2: *Technical reports*. Edmonton, Alta.: University of Alberta. Institute of Law Research and Reform, 1981.

6327. Connon, Jane A. "Conduct and spousal support in Ontario," *Family Law Review*, 2:253-59, 1979.

6328. Cooper, Jennifer. "The new concept of spousal relations in the Family Maintenance Act," *Manitoba Law Journal*, 9(4):435-44, 1979.

6329. Dawe, Carolyn. "Section 60(b) of the Income Tax Act: an analysis and some proposals for reform," *Queen's Law Journal*, 5:153-69, 1980.

6330. Drache, Arthur. "Ex-spouse's free rent was not deductible," *Financial Post*, 73:33, Oct. 20, 1979.

6331. Drache, Arthur. "Tax break possible for alimony," *Financial Post*, 73:29, June 30, 1979.

6332. Dranoff, Linda Silver. "Ask a lawyer," *Chatelaine*, 52:16, Apr. 1979.

6333. _____. "Ask a lawyer," *Chatelaine*, 53:18, 20, Oct. 1980.

6334. _____. "Ask a lawyer," *Chatelaine*, 54:24, 26, Nov. 1981.

6335. Family Law Review Committee. *Report* [on] *the Family Maintenance Act and the Marital Property Act*, [submitted by] Myrna Bowman, Rudy Anderson and Ken Houston. n.p., 1978. 23, 56p.

6336. Ferguson, T. M. "Divorce is sad enough, but the taxman's rules manage to make it even sadder," *Canadian Business*, 52:154, May 1979.

6337. Foster, Henry H. and D. J. Freed. "Alimony: dum casta and smart women," *Family Law Review*, 1:26-32, 1978.

6338. Hawkes, Cheryl. "The bills of divorcement: how to ease the pain," *Canadian Business*, 55:153, Oct. 1982.

6339. Hunsley, Terrance M. "Impressions," *Perception*, 5:4, June 1982.

6340. Kloppenburg, Cheryl. "The enforcement of maintenance," *Saskatchewan Law Review*, 40:217-37, 1976.

6341. Komar, Roman Nicholas. "The enforcement of support arrears; a history of alimony, maintenance and the myth of the one-year rule," *Reports of Family Law*, 19:129-91, 1975.

6342. Kondo, Vickie A. "No-fault maintenance for spouses," *Canadian Journal of Family Law*, 1:57-86, Jan. 1978.

6343. "Maintenance on divorce," *Canadian Welfare*, 51:22-3, Sept.-Oct. 1975.

6344. Manitoba. Law Reform Commission. *Reports on family law. Part I - the support obligation. Part II - property disposition*. Winnipeg, 1976. 141p.

6345. _____. *Working paper on family law: part I - the support obligation; part II - property disposition*. Winnipeg, 1975. 63p. (Profile 75-0196)

6346. Mazel, Annie. "Pension alimentaire et pratique judiciaire d'appel en matière de di-vorce," *La Revue juridique Thémis*, 11:311-34, 1976.

6347. Ontario. Law Reform Commission. *Report on family law. Part VI, support obligations*. Toronto: Ontario. Ministry of the Attorney General, 1975. 251p.

6348. Payne, Julien D. "Maintenance rights and obligations: a search for uniformity," *Family Law Review*, 1:2-25, 91-107, 185-203, 1978.

6349. _____. "The relevance of conduct to the assessment of spousal maintenance under the Family Law Reform Act," *Family Law Review*, 3:103-119, 1980.

6350. Poulton, Terry. "Nearly married spouses," *Maclean's*, 92:43, July 30, 1979.

6351. Rivet, Michèle. "L'analyse des 'sommes globales' en matière de divorce à travers la jurisprudence canadienne," *Canadian Bar Review*, 58:58-102, Mar. 1980.

6352. Ryan, Edward F. "Maintenance obligations in a new legal concept of marriage," *Reports of Family Law*, 21:1-11, 1976.

6353. Saskatchewan. Law Reform Commission. *Family maintenance between husband and wife; background paper*. Saskatoon, 1975. 31p. (Profile 76-0827)

6354. _____. *Tentative proposals for an Enforcement of Maintenance Orders Act*. Saskatoon, 1982. 100, xiiip. (Microlog 82-2891)

6355. Steel, Freda M. "The award of maintenance subsequent to decree nisi: a question of jurisdiction or discretion?," *Reports of Family Law*, 2nd ser., 19:33-70, 1981.

6356. Suzuki, Barbara A. F. "Income tax consequences of separation and divorce," *Canadian Journal of Family Law*, 2:33-62, Jan. 1979.

6357. Tennenhouse, Carol. "An examination of section 4 of the (Ontario) Family Law Reform Act, 1978," *Ottawa Law Review*, 11:371-90, 1979.

6358. University of Alberta. Institute of Law Research and Reform. *Working paper - matrimonial support*. Edmonton: The Institute, 1974. 117p. (Profile 74-0856)

6359. _____. *Matrimonial support*. Report no. 27. Edmonton, Alta., 1978. 246p.

6360. Wachtel, Andy and Brian E. Burtch. *Excuses; an analysis of court interaction in show cause enforcement of maintenance orders*. Vancouver: United Way of the Lower Mainland. Social Planning and Research, 1981. 69p. and app. (Microlog 82-1041)
         Joint research project with the British Columbia Ministry of Attorney General, Policy Planning Division, Research and Evaluation Unit.

6361. Walmsley, Ann. "Tracing the escape routes of errant spouses: the knotty problem of collecting maintenance payments," *Maclean's*, 94:52-3, Feb. 23, 1981.

6362. Woodsworth, K. C., ed. *Settlement of property and maintenance in matrimonial disputes*. Vancouver: University of British Columbia. Centre for Continuing Education, 1971. 113p.

6363. Ziff, Bruce. "Maintenance claims in divorce actions: Goldstein revisited," *Family Law Review*, 2:186-91, 1979.

TAXATION

6364. Barnett, Jim. "Alimony and maintenance payments. Pension alimentaire et allocations indemnitaires," *CA Magazine*, 112:65-70, June 1979.

6365. Bernstein, Jack. "Marriage - a tax shelter?" *McGill Law Journal*, 21:631-55, Winter 1975.

6366. Birnie, David A. G. and Josephine Margolis. "Income tax implications of the Family Relations Act of British Columbia," *Canadian Tax Journal*, 27:641-52, Nov.-Dec. 1979.

6367. B'nai B'rith Women District 22. *Taxation submission*. Royal Commission on the Status of Women in Canada. Brief no. 107. Toronto, n.d. 20p.

6368. Canada. Advisory Council on the Status of Women. *Background study on women and the personal income tax system*, by Louise Dulude. Ottawa, 1976. 49p.

6369. _____. *Taxation untangled. [L'impôt démystifié]*. The person papers. Ottawa, 1977. 16, 16p.

6370. _____. *Annotated recommendations on women and taxation*. Ottawa, 1978. 15p.

6371. Cuddihy, Margaret. "L'application des lois fiscales aux régimes matrimoniaux," *Revue du notariat*, 82:241-71, 382-426, 1980.

6372. Dawe, Carolyn. "Section 60(b) of the Income Tax Act: an analysis and some proposals for reform," *Queen's Law Journal*, 5:153-69, 1980.

6373. Denega, Michael. "Women can take advantage of tax laws," *Benefits Canada*, 5:41-2, Sept.-Oct. 1981.

6374. Drache, Arthur. "Tax break possible for alimony," *Financial Post*, 73:29, June 30, 1979.

6375. Dulude, Louise B. "Joint taxation of spouses - a feminist view," *Canadian Taxation*, 1:8-12, Winter 1979.

6376. Ellis, James. "An income tax perspective on British Columbia marriage agreements," *University of British Columbia Law Review*, 15(1):153-73, 1981.

6377. Hartle, Douglas G. *Taxation of the incomes of married women*. Royal Commission on the Status of Women in Canada. Study no. 5. Ottawa, 1971. 88p.

6378. Manitoba Bar Association. *Brief no. 80 to the Royal Commission on the Status of Women in Canada*. Winnipeg, n.d. 6p.

6379. "New ruling allows split in husband-wife [farm] income," *Farm and Country*, 42:M4, June 20, 1978.

6380. Rhodes, Ann. "How our Income Tax Act zaps women," *Chatelaine*, 56:64, 122+ , Aug. 1983.

6381. "Sex discrimination and the income tax act," *CGA Magazine*, 13:20-1, Feb. 1979.

6382. "Status of Women Commission: OFL proposes tax allowances for working mothers," *Canadian Labour*, 11:59, June 1968.

6383. Suzuki, Barbara A. F. "Income tax consequences of separation and divorce," *Canadian Journal of Family Law*, 2:33-62, Jan. 1979.

6384. "Tax burden on working wives: outdated and unfair," *Macleans*, 79:4, Dec. 3, 1966.

TEACHING

6385. Alexandre, Marie-Jeanne. *Les religieuses enseignantes dans le système d'éducation du Québec*. Québec: Institut supérieur des sciences humaines, Université Laval, 1977. 137p.

6386. Alphonsus, Sister Mary. "Life on Baccalieu: the reminiscences of the last teacher there, (Miss) Margaret Noonan," *Newfoundland Quarterly*, 75(3):10-12, Christmas 1979.

6387. Andersen, Marion. "Together is best: women in education [Saskatchewan]," *Chelsea Journal*, 5:87-8, Mar.-Apr. 1979.

6388. Azer, Nadia. "'Désormais...', les femmes de la C.E.C.M.... ," *Relations*, 40:167, juin 1980.

6389. Black, Naomi. "Politics and the woman teacher," *Challenge in Educational Administration*, 19(1):5-8, 1979.

6390. Boland, J. A. Heidi. "Whatever happened to the dedicated teacher?" *Branching Out*, 2:34, 46, Jan.-Feb. 1975.

6391. Bulcock, Jeffrey and others. *Women teachers in Newfoundland and Labrador 1972: a statistical description*. St. John's: Memorial University of Newfoundland, 1973. 151p.

6392. Cairns, Kathleen Vivian Osborne. "Motivation to avoid success, sex-role stereotyping and same-sex affiliation." PhD diss., University of Calgary, 1974. 204p. (Can. theses, no.21247)

6393. Cairns, Kathleen V. "Women and school administration," *Journal of Educational Thought*, 9:165-75, Dec. 1975.

6394. Canadian Teachers' Federation. *Brief no. 301 to the Royal Commission on the Status of Women in Canada*. Ottawa, 1968. 17p.

6395. _____. *Socialization and life skills: report of the proceedings of the Canadian Teachers' Federation workshop on the Status of Women in Education held in Winnipeg, Manitoba, November 6-8, 1977*. Ottawa: Canadian Teachers' Federation, 1978. 59p.
        French edition: *La socialisation et les aptitudes à la vie*.

6396. _____. *Teacher-worker-person, an integrated lifestyle: a report of the CTF Status of Women Conference, Jan. 18-20, 1981*. Ottawa, 1981. 36p.

TEACHING

6397. Centrale de l'enseignement du Québec. *Condition féminine*. xxive Congrès de la Corporation des enseignants du Québec / le Congrès de la Centrale de l'enseignement du Québec. [Québec]: La Centrale, [1974] 52p.

6398. _____. *Les absentes n'ont pas tous les torts...: la participation syndicales des membres féminins de la C.E.Q*. [Sainte-Foy, Québec]: C.E.Q., Service des communications, 1978. 16p.

6399. _____. *Le droit au travail pour toutes les femmes: défis d'aujourd'hui, réalités de demain: rapport du XXVIIe congrès général, Québec*. n.p., 1980. 43p.

6400. Corporation des enseignants du Québec et Centrale de l'enseignement du Québec. *Condition féminine: XXIVième congrès de la Corporation des enseignants du Québec: 1er congrès de la Centrale de l'enseignement du Québec*. Québec: CEQ, 1974. 52p.

6401. Coulter, Rebecca. "Strathcona women have never looked back," *ATA Magazine*, 55:26-7, Jan.-Feb. 1975.

6402. Davies, Rhona. "Career expectations of female teachers in British Columbia," *Atlantis*, 6:202-7, Spring 1981.

6403. Eichler, Margrit. "Sex-role attitudes of male and female teachers in Toronto," *Interchange*, 10(2):2-14, 1979/80.

6404. Fagan, Lenora Perry and others. "Declining enrolments: implications for women teachers," *Newfoundland Teachers' Association. Journal*, 70:6-10, Fall 1981.

6405. Fédération canadienne des enseignants. *Enseignante - employée - personne: un mode de vie intégré: compte rendu de la conférence de la FCE sur la situation de la femme du 18 au 20 janvier 1981 - Montréal*. Ottawa, 1981. 36p.
        English edition: *Teacher - worker - person, an integrated lifestyle*.

6406. Federation of Women Teachers' Associations of Ontario. *Brief no. 342 to the Royal Commission on the Status of Women in Canada*. Toronto, 1968. 39p.

6407. _____. *Brief to the Commission on Declining Enrolment*. Toronto, 1978. 80p.

6408. _____. *Dear teacher*. Toronto: The Federation, 1978. 51p.

6409. Fulton, E. Margaret. "Women in education - changing roles and new challenges," *English Quarterly*, 8:21-32, Winter 1975-76.

6410. Gagnon, Marie. "Le comité Laure-Gaudreault: les femmes dans l'enseignement," *Possibles*, 4:115-21, automne 1979.

6411. Gold, Sylvia. "The status of women in education. Where we are - where we're going," *Newfoundland Teachers' Association. Bulletin*, 22:7-11, Nov. 28, 1978.

6412. Guillet, Raymond D. "The status of women in administrative positions in the province of Ontario." EdD diss., Wayne State University, 1982. 144p.

6413. Handelman, Esther. "Differential socialization by female elementary school teachers." MA thesis, Concordia University, 1977. 94p. (Can. theses, no.34694)

6414. "If you think you've come a long way, baby, you aren't teaching school," *This Magazine*, 8:19, June 1974.

6415. Jackson, Robert, Saud Quazi and Wayne Burtnyk. *Mobility of secondary school teachers in Ontario by sex and by board, 1966-67 to 1977-78*. Commission on Declining School Enrolments in Ontario. Statistical appendix, no. 3. Toronto: Ontario. Commission on Declining School Enrolments in Ontario, 1978. 89p.

6416. L'Alliance des professeurs de Montréal. *Brief no. 434 to the Royal Commission on the Status of Women in Canada*. Montreal, 1968. 38p. and app.

6417. Lambert, Ruth Carolyn. "A comparison of the value systems of male and female administrators and female teachers on Prince Edward Island." MEd thesis, University of Alberta, 1980. 193p. (Can. theses, no.49006)

6418. MacIsaac, Mary Elizabeth. "Factors affecting women's decisions to seek administrative positions in education." MEd thesis, Dalhousie University, 1978. 109p. (Can. theses, no.44277)

6419. Manitoba Teachers' Society. *Brief no. 372 to the Royal Commission on the Status of Women in Canada*. Winnipeg, 1968. 7p.

6420. Mathien, Julie. "Women teachers: a long hard fight for equality," *Community Schools*, Oct. 1972, pp.14-16.

6421. McConaghy, T. W. "Women in teaching [editorial]," *ATA Magazine*, 55:2-3, Jan.-Feb. 1975.

6422. Muir, Pearl. "Teaching ability is not a matter of sex," *ATA Magazine*, 55:9-14, Jan.-Feb. 1975.

6423. Newfoundland. Dept. of Education. Division of School Services. *Statistical presentation for the Minister's Advisory Committee on Women's Issues in Education*. [St. John's], 1980. 53p. (Microlog 80-3460)

6424. Nixon, Mary and L. R. Gue. "Professional role orientation of women administrators and women teachers," *Canadian Administrator*, 15:[1]-5, Nov. 1975.

6425. _____. "Women administrators and women teachers: a comparative study," *Alberta Journal of Educational Research*, 21:196-206, Sept. 1975.

6426. Nixon, Mary. "Women administrators and women teachers: a comparative study." PhD diss., University of Alberta, 1975. 316p. (Can. theses, no. 24104)

6427. North York Board of Education. Ad Hoc Committee Respecting the Status of Women in the North York System. *Interim report no. 2*. [Willowdale, Ont.], 1975. [16]p.
Published as Appendix C in *Minutes of North York Board of Education*, [1975?].

6428. North York Board of Education. Office of the Director of Education. *Affirmative action and women's studies report*. [Willowdale, Ont.], 1982. [14]p. and app. A & B.

6429. _____. *Affirmative Action*. [Willowdale, Ont.], 1981. [8]p.
Appendix A, Positive action plan; Appendix B, Affirmative action program in North York.

6430. Novogrodsky, M. "Sorry girls, that's the way it is," *Community Schools*, May 1972, pp.18-19.

6431. Reich, Carol and Helen La Fountaine. *The effect of sexism on the career development of teachers*. Report of the Ontario Secondary School Teachers' Federation, Task Force on Women. [Toronto]: OSSTF. Provincial Communications Office, 1975. [103], xxiip.

6432. _____. *The effects of sex on careers within education: implications for a plan of action*. [Toronto: Ontario Institute for Studies in Education. Group for Research on Women, 1976]. 37p. and app.

6433. _____. "The effects of sex on careers within education: implications for a plan of action," *Canadian Journal of Education*, 7(2):64-84, 1982.

6434. Robertson, Cheryl. "Concerns facing women in the education force [Status of Women Conference]," *Newfoundland Teachers' Association. Bulletin*, 22:[18-23], Dec. 19, 1978.

6435. Shack, Sybil. *Armed with a primer: a Canadian teacher looks at children, schools, and parents*. Toronto: McClelland and Stewart, 1965. 181p.

6436. _____. *The two-thirds minority: women in Canadian education*. Toronto: University of Toronto. Faculty of Education. Guidance Centre, 1973. 128p.

6437. _____. *Women in Canadian education*. The Quance lectures in Canadian education. Toronto: Gage Educational Pub., 1975. 95p.

6438. "Shop teacher's sex sets her back," *Globe & Mail*, Aug. 31, 1978, pp.1-2.

6439. Sigurjonsson, Kay. "The hard part begins: new directions for the women's movement," in *Socialization and life skills*. Ottawa: Canadian Teachers' Federation, 1978, pp.1-11.

6440. Smith, Dorothy E. and others. *Working paper on the implications of declining enrolment for women teachers in public elementary and secondary schools in Ontario*. Working paper, no. 24. Toronto: Ontario. Commission on Declining School Enrolments in Ontario, 1978. 81p.

6441. St. John, Clinton. "Opinion of parents on certain behaviours of women teachers and other employed women," *Ontario Journal of Educational Research*, 8:23-33, Autumn 1965.

6442. Stokes, Shirley. *The shortest shadow: a descriptive study of the members of the Federation of Women Teachers' Associations of Ontario*. [Toronto]: Federation of Women Teachers' Associations of Ontario, [1969]. 120p. and app.

6443. Taylor, Connie. "The new masculinization of the teaching profession," *Canadian Women's Studies / Les cahiers de la femme*, 2(2):16-7, 1980.

6444. Toupin, Louise. "Aux origines de la CEQ: une lutte menée par des femmes," *Ligne directe*, 2:1-8, mars-avr. 1974, suppl.

6445. Tremblett, Gwen. "NTA status of women committee," *Newfoundland Teachers' Association. Bulletin*, 21:5-6 Mar. 14, 1978.

6446. Vancouver Women's Caucus. *Women teachers and the education process, or, 'It's something you can always fall back on'*. Victoria, B.C.: Social Science Research, [1969?] 3p.

6447. Whalen-Way, Audrey. "The determinants of the probability of women teachers expressing an interest in educational administration." MEd thesis, Memorial University of Newfoundland, 1978. 118p. (Can. theses, no.36914)

TEACHING - HISTORY

6448. Bryans, Wendy E. "Virtuous women at half the price: the feminization of the teaching force and early women teacher organizations in Ontario." MA thesis, University of Toronto, 1974. 125p.

6449. Campbell, Helen Richards. *From chalk dust to hayseed*. Belleville, Ont.: Mika Pub. Co., 1975. 116p.

6450. Delta Kappa Gamma Society. Alpha Chapter, Edmonton, Alta. *Sketches of women pioneer educators of Edmonton*. [Edmonton]: Alpha Chapter, Zeta Province of the Delta Kappa Gamma Society, 1972. 50p.

6451. French, Doris. *High button bootstraps: Federation of Women Teachers' Associations of Ontario: 1918-1968*. Toronto: Ryerson Press, 1968. 205p.

6452. Goodwin, Theresa. "Recollections and reminiscences of an English school marm in Saskatchewan," *Saskatchewan History*, 27:103-8, Autumn 1974.

6453. Khosla, Punam, Laura King, and Linda Read. *The unrecognized majority: a history of women teachers in British Columbia*. Edited by Patricia Gibson. [Vancouver, B.C.: British Columbia Teachers' Federation, 1979]. 54, [7]p.

6454. Kojder, Apolonja Maria. "The Saskatoon Women Teachers' Association: a demand for recognition," *Saskatchewan History*, 30:63-74, Spring 1977.

6455. Létourneau, Jeannette. *Les écoles normales de filles au Québec*. Montréal: Fides, 1981. 239p. Published edition of the author's PhD. diss., "Les écoles normales de jeunes filles au Québec, 1836-1974." Université d'Ottawa, 1979.

6456. Prentice, Alison. "The feminization of teaching," in Susan Mann Trofimenkoff and Alison Prentice, eds., *The neglected majority: essays in Canadian women's history*. Toronto: McClelland and Stewart, 1977, pp.49-65.

6457. Prentice, Alison, "The feminization of teaching in British North America and Canada, 1845-1875," *Social History*, 8:5-20, May 1975.

6458. Purcell, Myrtle. "What was it like to teach in the 1920's?" *Community Schools*, Oct. 1972, p.13.

6459. "Reminiscences of a pioneer teacher," in E. Blanche Norcross, ed., *Nanaimo retrospective: the first century*. Nanaimo, B.C.: Nanaimo Historical Society, 1979, pp.47-8.

TELEVISION

6460. Amiel, Barbara. "Banning the word 'stewardess' will not win women equality," *Maclean's*, 93:58, Sept. 8, 1980.

6461. Batten, Jack. "Miss modesty: understanding CTV's Carole Taylor, the especially nice celebrity," *Maclean's*, 86:44-5, 104, 106, 108-9, Nov. 1973.

6462. Canadian Broadcasting Corporation. Task Force on the Status of Women. *Women in the C.B.C.* Ottawa, 1975. x, 196p.

6463. Caron, André H. and Chantal Mayrand. *The presence, role and image of women in prime time on the French television network of the CBC*. Submitted to the Office of the Coordinator, Portrayal of Women, CBC. Ottawa: Canadian Broadcasting Corporation, 1982. 24, 24p. (Microlog 82-4182)
    Includes French edition.

6464. Caron, Margaret Ann. "Sex stereotyping in Canadian television." PhD diss., University of Regina, 1978. 343p. (Can. theses, no.39060)

6465. Clarkson, Adrienne. "Woman at large: watching TV grow up," *Chatelaine*, 47:30, Dec. 1974.

6466. "Community and personhood," in Canadian Research Institute for the Advancement of Women, *Women as persons*. [*La femme en tant que personne*]. Toronto: Resources for Feminist Research, 1980, pp.49-51.
    Proceedings of the 3rd annual meeting.

6467. Deslongchamps, Ginette. "Le rôle de la femme dans les téléromans," *Relations*, no. 384:203-5, juill.-août, 1973.

6468. Eddie, Christine. "L'évolution des personnages féminins de 'Rue des Pignons'." MA thèse, Université Laval, 1979. 112p. (Can. theses, no.43126)

6469. Frum, B. "Television: the social problem of women," *Saturday Night*, 82:38, 41, June 1967.

6470. Gould, Allan M. "CTV's Pam Wallin: a skyrocket from Saskatchewan," *Chatelaine*, 56:60-1, 102+ , Apr. 1983.

6471. _____. "Women in TV: new power behind the scenes," *Chatelaine*, 56:86-7, 182+ , Nov. 1983.

6472. Grills, Lee. "The portrayal of women on CTV," *Status of Women News*, 6:9, Spring 1980.

6473. Katz, Bill. "The television program preferences of working women," *Stimulus*, Nov.-Dec. 1982, pp.30-1.

6474. _____. "Working women and television," *Stimulus*, Oct. 1982, pp.24-5.

6475. Kilbourn, E. "T.V. note: the single girl ... [review]," *Canadian Forum*, 44:235-6, Jan. 1965.

6476. Klassen, Rita. "A content analysis of women's roles in TV ads in Ontario." Undergraduate thesis, University of Guelph, Dept. of Consumer Studies, 1977. 43p.

6477. Landsberg, Michèle. "Joan Watson our mild-mannered star," *Chatelaine*, 50:36, 40, 44, Nov. 1977.

6478. _____. "TV women: how they're doing in male-chauvinist TV-land," *Chatelaine*, 47:39, 85-7, May 1974.

6479. Lawrence, Wendy. "Broadcasting: educational TV producer Barbara Barde: filming women in the foreground," *Status of Women News*, 6:4-5, Spring 1980.

6480. Méar, Annie. "L'image de la femme à la télévision: proposition d'un modèle d'analyse," *Communication et information*, 3:102-8, automne 1979.

6481. _____. "Ravissante idiole: la femme dans les média," *Perception*, 3:28-9, Jan.-Feb. 1980.

6482. Mehr, Martin. "Progress on role stereotype issue [CRTC Task Force on Sex Role Stereotyping in the Broadcast Media]," *Financial Post*, 74:12, Apr. 5, 1980.

6483. National Action Committee on the Status of Women. *Portrayal of women in C.B.C. television*. Brief to the Canadian Radio-Television and Telecommunications Commission. [Toronto], 1978. 21p.

6484. _____. *The portrayal of women in CTV television*. Brief to the Canadian Radio-Television and Telecommunications Commission. [Toronto], 1978. 9p.

6485. Paris, Erna. "Diane Stapley: on the brink of the big time," *Chatelaine*, 49:36, 41, 96-7, Nov. 1976.

6486. Pyke, S. W. and J. C. Stewart. "This column is about women: women and television," *Ontario Psychologist*, 6:66-9, Dec. 1974.

6487. Read, Merilyn. "Women in television," *Chatelaine*, 54:54, 56+ , Dec. 1981.

6488. Réseau d'action et d'information pour les femmes. *Lettre-mémoire au Conseil de la radiodiffusion et des télécommunications canadiennes sur les stéréotypes sexistes*. Québec, 1980. 3p.

6489. _____. *L'image de la femme véhiculée par Radio-Canada: mémoire présenté au colloque du 22 et 23 février 1979 à Ottawa pour la Société Radio-Canada*. Québec, 1979. 44p.

6490. Ribeyron, Marie-Thérèse. "L'école des femmes," *Le Maclean*, 16:35-9, janv. 1976.

6491. Ross, M. J. "Television [commercials]," *Saturday Night*, 80:41-2, May 1965.

6492. Ruff, Kathleen. "Kathleen Ruff: passionate commitment and no apologies," *Branching Out*, 7(1):32-6, 1980.

6493. Spears, George and Kasia Seydegart. *The presence, role and image of women in prime time on the English television network of the CBC*. Submitted to the Office of the Co-ordinator, Portrayal of Women, CBC. Ottawa: Canadian Broadcasting Corporation, 1982. 25, 25p. (Microlog 82-4183)
    Contents: Pt. 1, Content analysis; Pt. 2, The viewer's perception. Includes French edition.

6494. Swartzen, Judy and others. "How women are presented in the media," *Canadian Women's Studies / Les cahiers de la femme*, 3(2):21, 1981.

6495. Thibault, Andrée. "L'image de la femme à la télévision," *Canadian Women's Studies/Le cahiers de la femme*, 2(2):79, 1980.

6496. Trevelyan, Margot. "The CBC and women: a progress report; Radio-Canada et les femmes: quelles nouvelles?" *Status of Women News / Statut: Bulletin de la femme*, 6:10-11, [English]; 6-7, [French]; Spring 1980.

6497. Van Der Gracht, Deb. "NAC brief [to Canadian Radio-Television and Telecommunications Commission] hits CBC," *Branching Out*, 6(1):5, 1979.

6498. Wolfe, Morris. "Television: a propaganda machine for male supremacy," *Saturday Night*, 89:43, Apr. 1974.

6499. Women for Political Action and Ontario Committee on the Status of Women. *Brief to the Canadian Radio and Television Commission concerning the CanadianBroadcasting Corporation and its policies and attitudes with regard to women*. Submitted Feb. 1, 1974. 82p.

6500. "Women's stereotypes 'offensive'," *Globe & Mail*, Sept. 2, 1982, p.3.

TEMPERANCE

6501. Bliss, J. M. "Neglected radicals, [WCTU]," *Canadian Forum*, 50:16-17, Apr.-May 1970.

6502. Canadian Women's Christian Temperance Union. *Centennial mosaic 1874-1974*. Toronto, [1977?] 55p.

6503. McGovern, Marcia A. "The Woman's Christian Temperance Union movement in Saskatchewan, 1886-1930: a regional perspective of the International White Ribbon Movement." MA thesis, University of Regina, 1977. 260p. (Can. theses, no.36954)

6504. Mitchinson, Wendy. "The WCTU: 'for God, home and native land': a study in nineteenth century feminism," in Linda Kealey, ed., *A not unreasonable claim: women and reform in Canada, 1880s-1920s*. Toronto: Women's Press, 1979, pp.151-67.

6505. _____. "The Woman's Christian Temperance Union: a study in organization," *International Journal of Women's Studies*, 4:143-56, Mar.-Apr. 1981.

6506. Sheehan, Nancy M. "The WCTU on the Prairies, 1886-1930: an Alberta-Saskatchewan comparison," *Prairie Forum*, 6:17-33, Spring 1981.

THEATRE

6507. Colette, Paulette. "La quarantaine âge de l'abdication ou du renouveau pour la femme, dans le théâtre de Marcel Dubé," *Canadian Drama*, 5:144-63, Fall 1979.

6508. Dennison, Holly. "Director, Holly Dennison [interview]," *Broadside*, 2:14, July 1981.

6509. "Feminist theatre," *Homemaker's Magazine*, 16:46-8, 50+ , Apr. 1981.

6510. Forsyth, Louise. "First person feminine singular: monologues by women in several modern Quebec plays," *Canadian Drama*, 5:189-203, Fall 1979.

6511. Hendry, J. C. "8 women at the top in theatre," *Chatelaine*, 42:31-3, June 1969.

6512. Kaplan, Beth. "Women in theatre," *Communiqué*, no. 8:30-1, 50-1, May 1975.

6513. King, Deirdre. "Domination and resistance: women playwrights in Québec," *Canadian Forum*, 61:44, 46, Sept.-Oct. 1981.

6514. Lafon, Dominique. "L'image de la femme dans le théâtre québécois," *Revue de l'Université d'Ottawa*, 50(1):148-52, 1980.

6515. Mathews-Klein, Yvonne and Ann Pearson. "A stage of seven women: feminist theatre in Québec," *Branching Out*, 3:17-19, Sept.-Oct. 1976.

6516. Pelletier, Pol. "Petite histoire du théâtre de femmes au Québec," *Canadian Women's Studies / Les cahiers de la femme*, 2(2):85-7, 1980.

6517. "Petite histoire... ," *Possibles*, 4:175-87, automne 1979.

6518. _____. "Talking to Pol Pelletier [interview]," *Fireweed*, 7:88-96, Summer 1980.

6519. Smith, Patricia Keeney. "When the subject is women," *Performing Arts in Canada*, 16:26-8, Winter 1979.

6520. Tisseyre, Michelle. "Women at the footlights," *Imperial Oil Review*, 59(5):3-7, 1976.

6521. Worthington, Bonnie. "Ryga's women," *Canadian Drama*, 5:139-43, Fall 1979.

TRANSITIONAL HOUSING

6522. Allen, Catherine. "Refuge from the storm: transitional housing for battered women," *Habitat*, 25(4):2-4, 1982.

6523. Barnsley, Jan and others. *Review of Munroe House; second stage housing for battered women*. Vancouver: Women's Research Centre, 1980. 35, [46]p.

6524. Canada. Dept. of the Secretary of State. Women's Programme. *Transition houses for women*. Ottawa, 1978. 39p.
    Includes speech by Gene Errington "Family violence - is it a woman's problem?" given at the Symposium on Family Violence, Vancouver, Mar. 1977.

6525. Cools, Anne. "Emergency shelter; the development of an innovative women's environment," in G. R. Wekerle, R. Peterson and D. Morley, eds., *New space for women*. Boulder: Westview Press, 1980, pp.311-18.

6526. Gould, Gail and others. *Transient women in Metropolitan Toronto*. Toronto: Traveller's Aid Society of Toronto, 1976. 87p. (Urban Canada, 77-4187)

6527. Handelman, Mark and Wendy Ward. *Battered women: emergency shelter and the law*. Windsor, Ont.: University of Windsor. Faculty of Law. Community Law Program, 1976. 69p. and app.

6528. Lynn, Shirley. "Transition houses: an important service for women," *Canadian Women's Studies / Les cahiers de la femme*, 1:88, Fall 1978.

6529. MacLeod, Flora. *Transition house: how to establish a refuge for battered women*. Vancouver: United Way of the Lower Mainland. Social Planning and Research, 1982. 118p.
6530. "Maisons de transition: une problématique non-théorique," *Canadian Women's Studies / Les cahiers de la femme*, 1:90, Fall 1978.
6531. Ridington, Jillian Botham. "Women in transition: a study of Vancouver Transition House as agent of change." MA thesis, University of British Columbia, 1977. 139p. (Can. theses, no.34934)
6532. Roberts, Owen. "Crisis centre for battered women [Cold Lake, Alberta]," *Native People*, 15:6, Apr. 16, 1982.
6533. Rooney, Frances. "Vancouver Transition House," *Canadian Women's Studies / Les cahiers de la femme*, 1:91, Fall 1978.
6534. Torrance Consulting Ltd. *Policy study respecting emergency shelters for women*. Prepared for Alberta. Dept. of Social Services and Community Health. Camrose, Alta.: n.p., 1980. 43p.
6535. "Women in Transition," *Broadside*, 1(7):8, 1980.
6536. Young Women's Christian Association of Canada. *Crisis housing information*. Coordinated by Donna Hunter. Toronto: YWCA of Canada, 1978. 55p.

UNEMPLOYMENT

6537. Armstrong, Pat. "Women and unemployment," *Atlantis*, 6:1-16, Fall 1980.
6538. Armstrong, Pat and Hugh Armstrong. *Job creation and unemployment for Canadian women*. CRIAW working papers. Vanier College, Montreal, Quebec, 1980. 46p.
      Prepared for the NATO Symposium "Women and the World of Work", Portugal, Aug. 4-8, 1980. Funded in part by the Canadian Research Institute for the Advancement of Women.
6539. _____. "Job creation and unemployment for Canadian women," in Anne Hoiberg, ed., *Women and the world of work*. New York: Plenum Press, 1982, pp.129-52.
6540. _____. "Job creation and unemployment for Canadian women," in Naomi Hersom and Dorothy E. Smith, [eds.], *Women and the Canadian labour force*. Working document. Ottawa: Social Sciences and Humanities Research Council of Canada, 1982, pp.209-55.
6541. Cameron, Barbara. "OWW: employment strategy for women," *Broadside*, 1(2):9, 1979.
6542. Cousineau, Jean-Michel. "Impact du salaire minimum sur le chômage des jeunes et des femmes au Québec," *Industrial Relations*, 34(3):403-17, 1979.
6543. Della Valle, P. A. and B. Meyer. "Changes in relative female male unemployment: a Canadian-United States comparison," *Industrial Relations*, 31(3):417-33, 1976.
6544. Eady, Mary. "Sex and unemployment; Sexe et chômage," *Canadian Labour / Travailleur canadien*, 22:6-7, [English]; 6-7, 12, [French], Dec. 1977.
6545. Gelber, Sylva M. "Unemployment and the woman worker: the facts," *Canadian Newsletter of Research on Women*, 7:10-12, July 1978.
6546. Leaper, Richard John. "Female labor force attachment: an analysis of unemployment rates in the United States and Canada." PhD diss., Duke University, 1976. 183p. (UM, 76-8757)
6547. Robinson, H. L. "A secondary majority: the hidden unemployed," *Canadian Forum*, 57:15-18, Oct. 1977.
6548. _____. "Unemployment in 1977: unemployment among women is higher than among men," *Canadian Newsletter of Research on Women*, 7:12-13, July 1978.
6549. Swan, Carole. "Women and unemployment; Les femmes et le chômage," *Status of Women News / Statut: bulletin de la femme*, 5:18-19, [English]; 19-20 [French], Sept. 1975.
6550. Tangri, Beverly. "Women and unemployment," *Atlantis*, 3:85-95, Spring 1978, Part II.
6551. White, Julie. "Women: the first fired," *Canadian Dimension*, 12(8):32-3, [1978].

UNEMPLOYMENT INSURANCE

6552. Alexander, Judith A. "Unemployment insurance: indemnity for whom?" *Atlantis*, 4:180-88, Spring 1979.

6553. Cohen, Marjorie. "Unemployment insurance: the high price of equality," *Canadian Woman Studies / Les cahiers de la femme*, 3:34-6, Summer 1982.

6554. "Could be refused job benefits if breast-feeding, woman told," *Globe & Mail*, Apr. 15, 1981, pp.1-2.

6555. National Action Committee on the Status of Women. *The impact of the proposed amendments to the Unemployment Insurance Act on women workers*. [Toronto], 1978. 18p. Brief to the House of Commons Standing Committee on Labour, Manpower and Immigration, Nov. 27, 1978.

6556. Townson, Monica. "Women and the economic crisis," *Branching Out*, 7(1):9-11, 1980.

UNIVERSITIES AND COLLEGES

6557. "A profile of women in Canadian universities," *University Affairs*, 13:6-7, Jan. 1972.

6558. Adam, June. *A profile of women in Canadian universities*. Ottawa: Association of Universities and Colleges of Canada, 1971. 98p.

6559. Andersen, Margret. "Economics and sex roles in academe," *CAUT Bulletin*, 24:6-8, Sept. 1975.

6560. Association of Universities and Colleges of Canada. *Report of the Committee on the Status of Women in Universities on the Progress made by AUCC member institutions regarding the status of women*. Ottawa, 1976. 38p.

6561. _____. *Status of women in Canadian universities 1975*. Ottawa, 1975. vp.
    Background paper for the AUCC Annual Meeting, Ottawa, Oct. 29-30, 1975.

6562. _____. *Women and the universities*. Ottawa, 1975. 98p.
    Proceedings of the Annual Business Meeting and Conference, Ottawa, Oct. 27-30, 1975.

6563. Canadian Association of Women Deans and Advisors. *Report on a survey taken in 1973 of women deans, counsellors and advisors in Canadian universities and colleges*. n.p., 1974. 41p.
    Data compiled by Isobel Mackay, Assistant Dean of Women, University of Waterloo.

6564. Carleton University Women's Centre. Handbook Committee. *Surviving: a woman's guide to Carleton University (and life!)*. Carleton University Women's Centre Handbook 81/82. Ottawa, 1981. 40p.

6565. "Council passes interim guidelines on sexual harassment," *University Affairs*, 22:9, June-July 1981.

6566. Fédération des associations des professeurs de universités du Québec. *La situation de la femme dans les universités québécoises*. Montréal: FAPUQ, 1978. 20p.

6567. Gane, Margaret Drury. "Dr. Margaret Fulton: feminist in academe," *Chatelaine*, 53:25, 28-9, Feb. 1980.

6568. Gillett, Margaret. "The majority minority: women in Canadian universities," *Canadian and International Education*, 7:42-50, June 1978.

6569. _____. *We walked very warily: a history of women at McGill*. Montreal: Eden Press Women's Publications, 1981. 476p.

6570. Gillett, Margaret and others. *A survey of teaching and research on women at McGill*. Report to Principal Robert E. Bell. [Montreal]: n.p., 1976. 46p.

6571. Imbeault, Marie-Andrée. "Le monde des femmes: Laval passe à l'action," *University Affairs*, 22:5-6, Mar. 1981.

6572. Lewis, Lesley V. *Women and the colleges of applied arts and technology*. Toronto: Ontario. Ministry of Colleges and Universities, 1975. 176p.

6573. Masleck, Carolyn. "Discrimination and traditional patterns evident in studies of Ontario colleges and universities," *CAUT Bulletin*, 24:7-8, Oct. 1975.

6574. _____. "Status of women: collective bargaining may be key to improvement," *CAUT Bulletin*, 24:6, Oct. 1975.

6575. McIntyre, Gail. *Women and Ontario universities*. [Toronto]: Ontario. Ministry of Colleges and Universities, 1975. 145p.

6576. McLeod, E. M. *A study of child care services at Canadian universities*. Ottawa: Association of Universities and Colleges of Canada, 1975. 44p. (Canedex 76-0007)

6577. Momsen, Janet Henshall. "Women in Canadian geography," *Canadian Geographer*, 24:177-83, Summer 1980.

6578. National Conference on Women in Colleges and Universities. *Women in colleges and universities: report on the third national conference, York University, Toronto, 1974.* n.p., [1974?] 52p.

6579. Robillard, Elaine. "Women administrators in Alberta community colleges." MEd thesis, University of Alberta, 1979. 189p. (Can. theses, no.43537)

6580. "Second progress report on status of women is encouraging," *University Affairs*, 17:7, Dec. 1976.

6581. Shore, Valerie. "A miracle at the Mount," *University Affairs*, 21:5-6, Oct. 1980.

6582. _____. "Sexual harassment: prevention is better," *University Affairs*, 22:2-4, Mar. 1981.

6583. Statistics Canada and Association of Universities and Colleges of Canada. *Women in Canadian universities: a statistical compendium.* [Ottawa?], 1975. 165p.

6584. Stephenson, Patricia. *Hidden voices: the life experiences of women who have worked and studied at Queen's University.* Kingston, Ont.: Queen's University. Office of the Dean of Women, 1980. 60p.
    Catalogue of abstracts of oral history recordings; a student group project extending over four years (1976-1980).

6585. Sullivan, Nancy. "Status of women in the university: progress is being made," *University Affairs*, 16:2-4, Oct. 1975.

6586. Symons, Gladys L. "Equality of opportunity in American and Canadian graduate education: a comparison of gender differences," *Alberta Journal of Educational Research*, 26:96-112, June 1980.

6587. Tausig, Christine. "Women's gains being lost," *University Affairs*, 22:40, Jan. 1981.

6588. Vickers, Jill McCalla and June Adam. *But can you type? Canadian universities and the status of women.* CAUT monograph series. Toronto: Clarke, Irwin & Co. / Canadian Association of University Teachers, 1977. 142p.

6589. Williams, Tannis M. "Canadian childrearing patterns and the response of universities to women as childbearers and childrearers," *Canada's Mental Health*, 23:6-9 Sept. 1975, suppl.

6590. Woodcock, Lynda and Nancy Sullivan. "National meeting looks at status of women in the universities," *University Affairs*, 16:2, 4-5, Dec. 1975.

6591. Wyman, Georgina. "Pauline Jewett: an interview," *Branching Out*, 1:20-3, 38, Sept.-Oct. 1974.

6592. York University. Presidential Advisory Committee on Sexual Harassment. *Final Report.* Downsview, Ont., 1982. [8]p.

6593. _____. *Preliminary report of the Presidential Committee on Sexual Harassment, York University, September 1980.* [Downsview, Ont.: York University], 1980. 15p.

UNIVERSITIES AND COLLEGES - STATUS OF WOMEN REPORTS

6594. Acadia University. Committee on the Status of Women. *Report on the status of women at Acadia University: presented to President J.M.R. Beveridge, February 1978.* [Wolfville, N.S.: Committee on the Status of Women at Acadia University, 1978]. 38p. and tables.

6595. Alberta. University. Senate. Task Force on the Status of Women. *Report on academic women.* Edmonton Alta., 1975. 69p.

6596. Association of Universities and Colleges of Canada. *Second report of the Committee on the Status of Women in Universities on the progress made by AUCC member institutions regarding the status of women.* Ottawa, 1977. 120p.

6597. Boyd, Monica. *Rank and salary differentials in the 1970's: a comparison of male and female full-time teachers in Canadian universities and colleges.* Ottawa: Association of Universities and Colleges of Canada, 1979. 59p.
    French edition: *Écarts dans les traitements et les rangs au cours des années 1970: comparaison entre les professeurs du sexe féminin en emploi à plein temps dans les universités et collèges du Canada.*

6598. British Columbia. University. President's Ad Hoc Committee to Study the Report on the Status of Women at UBC. *A comparative study of the success rates of male and female applicants for admission to graduate studies at UBC, 1973-74*. Vancouver, 1974.

6599. British Columbia. University. President's Ad Hoc Committee which considered 'A report on the status of women at the University of British Columbia' with particular reference to employed staff. *Final report*. Vancouver, 1973. 37p.

6600. Calgary. University. Committee on the Status of Women. *Status of women, University of Calgary. Part 1: faculty*. Calgary, 1977. 26p.

6601. Calgary. University. Presidential Advisory Committee on the Status of Women. *Report: Part II: students*. Calgary, 1977. 18p.

6602. Daigle, Joanne et Jennifer Stoddart. "La situation des femmes à l'Université du Québec à Montréal en 1980." Mise à jour du mémoire présenté en 1978 par les professeurs du Groupe Interdisciplinaire pour l'enseignement et la recherche sur la condition des femmes à l'Université du Québec à Montréal. Montréal, [1980?] [65]p.

6603. Dalhousie University. Committee on the Status of Women. *Report. Phase 1: full-time faculty*. [Halifax, N.S.], 1979. 8p. Published as special edition of [Dalhousie] *University News*, Jan. 1979.

6604. Day, Shelagh. *Report on the status of women at the University of British Columbia, 1973*. Vancouver: Talonbooks, 1973. 100p.

6605. Finn, Patricia A. *Report on the status of women at Carleton University (students and support staff)*. Ottawa, [1975?] 43p.

6606. Guelph. University. President's Task Force on the Status of Women. *Report*. Guelph, Ont., 1975. 58p.

6607. Humber College of Applied Arts and Technology. *Report on the status of women employees*. Rexdale, Ont., 1974. 31p.

6608. Lakehead University. Office of the President and Lakehead University Faculty Association's Committee on the Status of Women. *Report on the status of the female full-time academic staff, 1975/76*. [Thunder Bay, Ont.], 1976. 15p.

6609. Lakehead University. Personnel Dept. *Report of the status of non-academic (Schedule 2) women employees at Lakehead University*. [Thunder Bay, Ont.], 1976. 25p.

6610. Laurentian University. *Report of the Status of Women Committee*. [Sudbury, Ont.: Laurentian University, 1980]. 12p.

6611. Manitoba. University. Committee on Representation of Women on Search and Appointment Committees. *Report*. [Winnipeg, Man.], 1977. 7p. and app.

6612. Manitoba. University. Faculty Association. Status of Women Committee. *Report no. 1*. Winnipeg, 1974. vp.

6613. McGill University. Senate Committee on Discrimination as to Sex in the University. *Report*. Montreal, 1970. 43p.

6614. McMaster University. *Status of women at McMaster University*. A report and petition of the group for equal rights at McMaster. Hamilton, Ont., 1971. 22p.

6615. McMaster University. Equal Rights Review and Coordinating Committee. *Report to Senate*. Hamilton, Ont., 1973. 13p.

6616. _____. *Report to Senate*. Hamilton, Ont., 1976. 37p. and app.

6617. McMaster University. President's Committee to Review McMaster's Personnel Policies and Practice Relative to Equal Rights. *First Report*. Hamilton, Ont., 1972. 5p.

6618. Memorial University of Newfoundland. Faculty Association. *A report on sex discrimination in faculty salaries, 1973-74*. St. Johns, Nfld., 1974. 69p.

6619. _____. *Sex discrimination in faculty salaries, 1973-74: a further analysis*. St. John's, Nfld., 1975. 19p.

6620. Montréal. Université. Association des cadres et professionels. Comité d'étude sur la situation de la femme cadre ou professionelle à l'Université de Montréal. *Rapport*. Montréal, 1978. 87, 15p.

6621. Montréal. Université. Comité permanent sur le statut de la femme à l'Université. *Y a-t-il discrimination à l'endroit des femmes professeurs a l'Université de Montréal?* par Marie-Andrée Bertrand. [Montreal, 1979]. 12p.

6622. Mount Allison University. President's Committee on the Status of Women. *Report*. Sackville, N.S., 1975. 45p.

6623. New Brunswick. University. Task Force on the Status of Women at U.N.B. *The status of women at U.N.B.: task force report to the president*. Fredericton, N.B., 1979. 99p.

6624. Ohm, V. "They're beginning to see the light...but changing the system is a slow process [report on the status of women at UBC]," *UBC Alumni Chronicle*, 31:5-11, Autumn 1975.

6625. Ottawa. University. Rector's Committee on the Status of Women Professors. *Report*. Ottawa, 1976. 52, [9]p.

6626. Payton, L. C. *Status of women in the Ontario universities*. Report to Council of Ontario Universities, June 1975. 21p.

6627. Pelletier, Jacqueline and others. *Interim report on the status of women employees at Algonquin College. [Rapport intérimaire sur la situation des femmes employées au Collège Algonquin]*. Ottawa: Algonquin College, 1977. 33, 33p.

6628. Prince Edward Island. University. President's Advisory Committee on the Status of Women in the University. *Interim report*. [Charlottetown, June 1976]. 5p.

6629. Queen's University. Association of Women Teaching at Queen's. *Report and recommendations ... on the Recommendations of the Principal's report on the status of women at Queens*. Kingston, Ont., 1975. 7p.

6630. Queen's University. Office of the Principal. *Report on actions taken on recommendations of the report of the Principals Committee on the Status of Women at Queen's University*. Kingston, Ont., 1975. 21p.

6631. Queen's University. Principal's Advisory Review Committee on the Status of Women. *The status of women at Queen's, 1979: the report of the Principal's Advisory Committee on the Status of Women at Queen's*. Kingston, Ont., 1979. 18p.
   Published as a supplement to *Queen's Gazette*, V.12, no.10, Mar. 11, 1980.

6632. Queen's University. Principal's Committee on the Status of Women. *Report*. Kingston, Ont., 1975. 32p.
   Published as a supplement to *Queen's Gazette*, v.6, no. 9, Feb. 28, 1974.

6633. Regina. University. President's Committee on the Status of Women. *Report*. Regina, Sask., 1975. 94p.

6634. Regina. University. President's Committee on the Status of Women. Sample Survey and Data Bank Unit. *Matched pairs study*. Regina, Sask., 1977. 65p.

6635. Saskatchewan. University. University Studies Group. *University of Saskatchewan full-time faculty matched pair study*. Saskatoon, Sask., 1976. 9, [4]p.

6636. Seneca College of Applied Arts and Technology. President's Task Force on Affirmative Action. *Report on equality of opportunity. (Part 1: employees)*. Willowdale, Ont., 1978. 178p.

6637. _____. *Report on equality of opportunity. (Part II: students)*. [Willowdale, Ont., 1978?] 82p.

6638. Shepherd, Marian M. *York University: statistical results of a survey of the members of the professional and managerial group*. Downsview, Ont.: York University, 1978. 19p.

6639. Sherbrooke. Université. Comité permanent de l'AUCC pour la situation de la femme à l'université. *Rapport*. Sherbrooke, Quebec, 197? 11p.

6640. Simon Fraser University. Office of the Academic Vice-President. *Women at Simon Fraser University*, by Lolita Wilson. Burnaby, B.C., 1972. 21p.

6641. Simon Fraser University. President's Continuing Committee on the Status of Women at Simon Fraser University. *Progress report*. Burnaby, B.C., 1977. 154p.

6642. Toronto. University. Committee on Employment Conditions of Full Time Women Faculty. *Report*. Toronto, 1974.

6643. Toronto. University. Office of the Provost. Committee on Employment Conditions of Full-Time Women Faculty. *Report*. Toronto, 1974. 13p.

6644. Toronto. University. Task Force to Study the Status of Non-Academic Women at the University of Toronto. *Preliminary* [Final] *report*. Toronto, 1975. 4p.
   Published as a supplement to the *University of Toronto Bulletin*, Mar. 21, 1975.

6645. Trent University. Presidential Advisory Committee on the Status of Women. *Faculty and librarians' salaries*. Peterborough, Ont., 1975. 29p.

6646. _____. *Interim report on women staff*. Peterborough, Ont., 1975. 31p.

6647. Université du Québec à Montréal. Groupe interdisciplinaire pour l'enseignement et la recherche sur la condition des femmes. *La situation des femmes à l'Université du Québec à Montréal*. Montréal, [1978]. 43p.

6648. Université Laval. Comité d'étude sur la condition féminine à l'Université Laval. *L'Université Laval au féminin: rapport du Comité d'étude sur la condition féminine à l'Université Laval*. [Québec: n.p., 1980?] 297p.

6649. University of Western Ontario. President's Advisory Committee on the Status of Women. *Report*. London, Ont., 1975. 31p.
      Published as a supplement to *Western News*, Sept. 18, 1975.

6650. University of Western Ontario. President's Advisory Committee on Women's Salaries (Academic). *Report*. London, Ont., 1975. 4p.
      Published as a supplement to *Western News*, Oct. 30, 1975.

6651. Victoria. University. *Status of women report*. [Victoria, B.C.], 1975. 19p.
      Unofficial report.

6652. Waterloo. University. President's Advisory Committee on Equal Rights for Women and Men. *Report*. Waterloo, Ont., 1973. 8p.
      Published as a supplement to the *University of Waterloo Gazette*, Nov. 1973.

6653. Windsor. University. Faculty Association Sub-Committee on the Status of Women Academics. *Report*, prepared by Nancy Parsons Dickie. Windsor, Ont., 1974.

6654. Windsor. University. Faculty Association Sub-Committee on the Status of Women Faculty. *Report*. Windsor, Ont., 1975.

6655. Windsor. University. President's Committee on Equal Rights. *Report*. Windsor, Ont., 1976. 3p.

6656. Winnipeg. University. *Report on the status of women*. Winnipeg, Man. 1977.

6657. York University. Adviser to the President on the Status of Women. *Report on the Adviser's work during the period 1 July 1975 to 30 June 1977*, prepared by Jane Banfield Haynes. Downsview, Ont., 1977.

6658. York University. Presidential Committee to Review Salaries of Full-Time Faculty Women. *Report*. Downsview, Ont., 1976. 25p.

6659. York University. President's Committee on Staff Compensation and Personnel Policies. *Final report*. Downsview, Ont., 1975. 59p.
      Includes report by Senate Task Force on the Status of Women at York.

6660. York University. Senate Committee on Part-Time Faculty. *Report*. [Downsview, Ont.], 1976. 11p.

6661. York University. Senate. Task Force on the Status of Women at York University. *Report to the Senate at its meeting on Feb. 27, 1975*. [Downsview, Ont., 1975]. 299p.

6662. York University. Senate Task Force on the Status of Women. *Full-time faculty salary report*. [Downsview, Ont.], 1975. 101p.

UNIVERSITY AND COLLEGE TEACHING

6663. Ambert, Anne-Marie and Gladys Symons Hitchman. "A case study of status differential: women in academia," in Anne-Marie Ambert, *Sex structure*. 2d rev. ed. Don Mills, Ont.: Longman Canada, 1976, pp.113-46.

6664. Andersen, Margret. "Economics and sex roles in academe," *CAUT/ACPU Bulletin*, 24:6-8, Sept. 1975.

6665. _____. "Status of women academics in Canada," *CAUT/ACPU Bulletin*, 22:8-9, 14-15, June 1974.

6666. Archer, Maureen. "Women - a minority group in the academic profession," *Branching Out*, 1:21, 24, Mar.-Apr. 1974.

6667. _____. "Women as a minority group in the academic profession." PhD diss., Acadia University, 1975.

6668. Baker, Maureen. "Academic queen bees," *Atlantis*, 1:84-93, Spring 1976.

268

6669. Black, Naomi. "A further note about women in Canadian political science," *Resources for Feminist Research*, 8:5, Nov. 1979.

6670. _____. "Women in Canadian political science," *Resources for Feminist Research*, 8:36-8, Mar. 1979.

6671. Bowen, Norma. "The academic woman and the Canadian university," *University Affairs*, 14:2-3, July 1973.

6672. Bowen, Norma V. "Women in Ontario universities," *CAUT/ACPU Bulletin*, 24:13, Sept. 1975.

6673. Boyd, Monica. *Rank and salary differentials in the 1970's: a comparison of male and female full time teachers in Canadian universities and colleges*. Ottawa: Association of Universities and Colleges of Canada, 1979. 59p.

6674. Burnet, Jean. "Minorities I have belonged to," *Canadian Ethnic Studies*, 13(1):24-36, 1981.

6675. Canadian Association of Schools of Social Work. Task Force on the Status of Women. *The status of women in social work education: a preliminary brief to the Canadian Association of Schools of Social Work from the C.A.S.S.W. Task Force on the Status of Women in Social Work Education*. n.p., 1976.

6676. "Corrective action is long overdue," *University Affairs*, 16:17, June 1975.

6677. Dagenais, Huguette. "Les femmes et le pouvoir," *Canadian Women's Studies / Les cahiers de la femme*, 2(2):53-5, 1980.

6678. "Discrimination against women still common in universities," *CAUT/ACPU Bulletin*, 23:4, Feb. 1975.

6679. Gelber, Sylva M. "Discriminatory practices in the universities and a proposed role for the Canadian Federation of University Women," in, *Women's Bureau '70*. Ottawa: Canada. Dept. of Labour. Women's Bureau, 1971, pp.15-19.

6680. Gillett, Margaret. "Sexism in higher education," *Atlantis*, 1:68-81, Fall 1975.

6681. Hall, Ann, Jane Cameron and Debbie Shogan. *Women in athletic administration at Canadian universities*. Report of a National Conference sponsored by the Faculty of Physical Education and Recreation, University of Alberta, May 15-17, 1981. 60p.

6682. Hersom, Naomi. "Women in academia: a time for change," *ATA Magazine*, 52:10-13, Sept.-Oct. 1971.

6683. Jewett, Pauline and others. *Status of women in Canadian universities*. Royal Commission on the Status of Women in Canada. Brief no. 443. Ottawa, 1971. 39p.

6684. Kostash, Myrna. "Why does a pretty girl like you need a PhD?" *Maclean's*, 88:14, May 1975.

6685. Macdonald, Lynn and Marcia Lenglet. "The status of women at McMaster University," in Marylee Stephenson, *Women in Canada*. Toronto: New Press, 1973, pp.227-44.
　　　Reprint of paper prepared for presentation to the university Senate.

6686. Mackie, Marlene. "Students' perceptions of female professors," *Journal of Vocational Behavior*, 8:337-48, June 1976.

6687. Masleck, C. "Status of women: collective bargaining may be key to improvement," *CAUT Bulletin*, 24:6, Oct. 1975.

6688. Maxwell, Mary Percival. "Germaine Greer or the Apparatchiks: elitist vs pressure group models for women academics," *CAUT Bulletin*, 25:8-9, Sept. 1977.

6689. Perticaro, Barbara. "The relative statuses of academic men and women at York University." MA thesis, York University, 1975. 95, [23]p. (Can. theses, no.23572)

6690. Pinet, Janine. "La femme et la science," *Atlantis*, 3:96-115, Spring 1978, Part II.

6691. Ricks, Frances A. and others. "The status of women and men in Canadian psychology academia," *Canadian Psychological Review*, 21:109-15, July 1980.

6692. Robson, R. A. H. *A comparison of men's and women's salaries and employment fringe benefits in the academic profession*. Royal Commission on the Status of Women in Canada. Study no. 1. Ottawa, 1971. 39p.

6693. "Salary anomalies by sex [University of Toronto]," *Labour Gazette*, 75:333-4, June 1975.

6694. Schrank, William E. "Sex discrimination in faculty salaries: a case study," *Canadian Journal of Economics*, 10:411-33, Aug. 1977.

6695. Semas, Phillip. "Canada's female academics wary of affirmative action," *Chronicle of Higher Education*, 11:3, Nov. 10, 1975.

6696. "Status of women academics," in Ontario Confederation of University Faculty Associations, *Brief to the Ontario Council on University Affairs*. Toronto, 1975, pp.30-5 and app.II.

6697. Swartz, Shirley. "Things do happen in the groves of academe," *Branching Out*, 3:6-10, Sept.-Oct. 1976.

6698. Tyndale, Eleanor. "The status of women and women's studies in Canadian colleges," *Society*, 5:11-13, May 1981.

6699. Vickers, Jill. "Women in the universities," in Gwen Matheson, *Women in the Canadian mosaic*. Toronto: Peter Martin, 1976, pp.198-240.

6700. "Women faculty members in Canadian universities," *Labour Gazette*, 67:7, Jan. 1967.

6701. "Women in higher education: special report," *CAUT Bulletin*, 24:6-26, Sept. 1975.

UNIVERSITY GRADUATES

6702. Cockburn, Patricia. *Women university graduates in continuing education and employment: an exploratory study initiated by the Canadian Federation of University Women, 1966*. Toronto: Canadian Federation of University Women, 1967. 196p.

6703. Devereaux, M. S. and Edith Rechnitzer. *Higher education - hired? Sex differences in employment characteristics of 1976 postsecondary graduates*. Ottawa: Statistics Canada. Projections Section. Education, Science and Culture Division, 1980. 212p.

6704. Farine, Avigdor. "La formation universitaire et l'emploi des femmes au Canada," *Orientation professionnelle*, 14:105-17, été 1978.

6705. Gelber, Sylva M. "Highly qualified manpower policies and the Canadian woman graduate: what price discrimination?" in, *Women's Bureau '69*. Ottawa: Canada. Dept. of Labour. Women's Bureau, 1970, pp.27-31.

6706. "Harvard brags of women grads from Canada," *Globe & Mail*, Mar. 28, 1979, p.12.

6707. Levine, Sybil and Christine Magraken. "Trending towards equality," *Financial Post*, 72:20, Feb. 11, 1978.

6708. Marsden, Lorna and others. "Female graduates: their occupational mobility and attainments," *Canadian Review of Sociology and Anthropology*, 12:385-405, Nov. 1975.

6709. Peal, Emma. "Women MBAs: the new elite?" *Journal (The Board of Trade of Metropolitan Toronto)*, Spring 1978. pp.38-9.

6710. Ryten, Eve. "Our best educated women," *Canadian Business Review*, 2:12-16, Summer 1975.

6711. "The real world of a woman MBA," *Journal (The Board of Trade of Metropolitan Toronto)*, Spring 1978, pp.40-2.

6712. Wilson, I. "Seminar on continuing education for women university graduates, York University," *Continuous Learning*, 4:221-2, Sept.-Oct. 1965.

6713. Zur-Muehlen, Max von and Mary Sue Devereaux. *Past and present graduation trends at Canadian universities and implications for the eighties with special emphasis on women and on science graduates*. [Ottawa: Statistics Canada], 1982. 88p.

UNIVERSITY STUDENTS

6714. Burwell, Elinor J. "Issues in the education and training of women in Canadian psychology," *Canadian Psychological Review*, 18:34-45, Jan. 1977.

6715. Côté, Françoise. "La femme dans les universités québécoises," *University Affairs*, 16:5, Oct. 1975.

6716. Cyr, Johanne Saint. "Les femmes se retrouvent a l'université à plus fort pourcentage dans les secteurs dit féminins: interrogations," *Orientation professionnelle*, 14:150-61, été 1978.

6717. Dandurand, Pierre and others. *Les études universitaires au féminin: (situation des étudiantes dans les universités québécoises avec référence particulière au cas de l'Université Laval)*. Montréal: Université de Montréal. Departement de sociologie, 1980. 116p.

270

6718. Denis, Ann B. "Educational aspirations of Montreal post-secondary students: ethnic, sex and social class differences," in Jean Leonard Elliott, ed., *Two nations, many cultures: ethnic groups in Canada*. Scarborough, Ont.: Prentice-Hall, 1979, pp.86-98.

6719. Doucet-Bouchard, Pauline. "Les aspirations professionnelles de niveau universitaire." MA thesis, Université Laval, 1969. 130p. and app.

6720. Gray, Elizabeth. "Heading them off at the passes," *Maclean's*, 94:26-7, Apr. 6, 1981.

6721. Hitchman, Gladys Symons. "Occupational decision-making, career aspirations and preparation for labour force participation: the case of male and female doctoral candidates," in Patricia Marchak, ed., *The working sexes: symposium papers on the effects of sex on women at work*. Vancouver: University of British Columbia. Institute of Industrial Relations, 1977, pp.110-36.

6722. _____. "The professional socialization of women and men in two Canadian graduate schools." PhD diss., York University, 1976. 346p. (Can. theses, no.26639)

6723. Laforce, Jocelyne et Francine Séguin. "Étudiante '65," *Maintenant*, 41:170-1, mai 1965.

6724. Leduc, Constance. "Les orientations des femmes à l'Université de Montréal en 1949-50 et en 1974-75," *Canadian and International Education*, 7:51-8, June 1978.

6725. Mackay, Isobel. *A report on women taking part-time degree courses at the University of Waterloo*. Waterloo, Ont.: University of Waterloo, 1973. 85p.

6726. McDonald, Marci. "4 Rhodes scholars: young, brilliant, female," *Chatelaine*, 51:54-5, 85+, May 1978.

6727. Mehra, Nim. *Enrollment patterns and academic performance of women students at the University of Alberta: a summary report*. Edmonton, Alta.: University of Alberta. Office of Institutional Research and Planning, 1978. 53p.

6728. Munz, Diane and others. "Contraceptive knowledge and practice among undergraduates at a Canadian university," *American Journal of Obstetrics and Gynecology*, 124:499-505, Mar. 1, 1976.

6729. Pfeifer, Pat and Stanley J. Shapiro. "Mistress of Business Administration: male and female candidates: are there personality differences?" *Canadian Women's Studies / Les cahiers de la femme*, 1:17-19, Fall 1978.

6730. Pfeifer, Patricia. "Personality differences between male and female MBA students." [MBA thesis, Concordia University, 1977]. 42p. and app.

6731. Pinet, Janine. "La femme et la science," *Atlantis*, 3:96-115, Spring 1978, Part II.

6732. Ricks, Frances A. and others. "The status of women and men in Canadian psychology academia," *Canadian Psychological Review*, 21:109-15, July 1980.

6733. Smyth, Frances E. "The relationship of maternal employment and current field of study to certain sex-role attitudes of male and female university students." PhD diss., University of Ottawa, 1979. 251p. (Can. theses, no.44151)

6734. Sutherland, Sharon L. "The unambitious female: women's low professional aspirations," *Signs*, 3:774-94, Summer 1978.

6735. Symons, Gladys. "Can women translate education into occupational mobility?" *University Affairs*, 19:16-18, July 1978.

6736. _____. "Stress in graduate school: some male-female comparisons." Paper presented at the Canadian Sociology and Anthropology Association Annual Meeting, Fredericton, N.B., June 1977. 18p.

7377 Toews, Lorette K. "Self-hatred in college women: sex-role stereotypes and same-sex affiliation." PhD diss., University of Alberta, 1973. 286p. (Can. theses, no.16156)

6738. University of British Columbia. Women's Office. Women's Research Collective. *Voices of women students*. Vancouver, 1974. 58p.

6739. Wakil, S. Parvez. "Campus mate selection preferences: a cross-national comparison," *Social Forces*, 51:471-6, June 1973.

6740. Wener, D. and W. D. Cairns. *Historical enrolment trends and GPA distributions for male and female students 1970-71 to 1978-79*. IRP project no. 79.19. Edmonton: University of Alberta. Office of Institutional Research and Planning, 1980. 14p.

6741. Williams, Tannis MacBeth and others. "Some factors affecting women's participation in psychology in Canada," *Canadian Psychological Review*, 21:97-108, July 1980.

6742. Wren, Derdri. "Fear of success and some of its correlates in female graduate social work students." Research paper submitted for Social Work 608 and 630, University of British Columbia, April 1975. 125p.

UNMARRIED COUPLES

6743. Clarke, Juanne. "Unmarried marrieds: a study of middle class unmarried couples living together." MA thesis, York University, 1971. 126p. and app.
6744. Delisle, Michel. "Autonomie et couple non marié." MA thèse, Université du Québec à Montréal, 1976. 72p. (Can. theses, no.41522)
6745. Fels, Lynn. *Living together: unmarried couples in Canada*. Toronto: Personal Library, 1981. 208p.
6746. Groffier, Ethel. "Les époux de fait dans le droit civil du Québec," in John M. Eekelaar and Sanford N. Katz, eds., *Marriage and cohabitation in contemporary societies: areas of legal, social and ethical change: an international and interdisciplinary study*. Toronto: Butterworths, 1980, pp.235-44.
6747. Holland, Winifred H. and D. Keith McNair. *Unmarried couples: legal aspects of cohabitation*. Toronto: Carswell, 1982. 249p.
6748. Lazure, Jacques. *Le jeune couple non marié: une nouvelle forme de révolution sexuelle*. Montréal: Presses de l'Université du Québec, 1975. 476p.
6749. Leclerc, Marie. *Mieux vivre à deux*. 2e éd. Québec: Conseil du statut de la femme, 1979. 38p.
6750. O'Hoski, John J. "The legal recognition of domestic contracts: the experience of Ontario," in John M. Eekelaar and Sanford N. Katz, eds., *Marriage and cohabitation in contemporary societies: areas of legal, social and ethical change: an international and interdisciplinary study*. Toronto: Butterworths, 1980, pp.228-34.

UNMARRIED MOTHERS

6751. Adler, Cathy and Shirley Congdon. *An overview of teenage pregnancy and parenthood in British Columbia: a paper released to promote public discussion*. Vancouver: Social Planning and Review Council of British Columbia, 1980. 101p.
6752. "Adolescent pregnancies: position paper - Canadian Home Economics Association," *Canadian Home Economics Journal*, 31:167-70, Summer 1981.
6753. "Adolescent pregnancy and sexuality - a matter of public responsibility," *Canadian Pharmaceutical Journal*, 114:143-4, Apr. 1981.

6754. Anderson, Joan and Sharon L. Ogden. "Twenty fatherless families," *Canadian Welfare*, 51:14-15, July-Aug. 1975.
6755. Billung-Meyer, Jo. "Forsaken children," *Canadian Woman Studies / Les cahiers de la femme*, 4:27-9, Fall 1982.
6756. _____. "The single mother: can we help?" *Canadian Nurse*, 75:26-8, Nov. 1979.
6757. Borchelt, David. "Adolescent mothers: an alternative to welfare," *Perception*, 6:30-1, Sept.-Oct. 1982.
6758. Callwood, June. "Jessie's: young moms & thriving babies," *Canadian Woman Studies / Les cahiers de la femme*, 4:37-8, Fall 1982.
6759. Carson, Susan. "A mother at 15," *Today*, Nov. 1, 1980, pp.6-7.
6760. _____. "Too many pregnancies too soon," *Reader's Digest (Canada)*, 115:69-72, Nov. 1979.

6761. Claman, A. David, Barry J. Williams and L. Wogan. "Reaction of unmarried girls to pregnancy," *Canadian Medical Association. Journal*, 101:328-34, Sept. 20, 1969.
6762. Community Task Force on Maternal and Child Health. *Adolescent pregnancy in Manitoba: current status, future alternatives*. Winnipeg, Man., 1981. 96p.
6763. Guyatt, Doris Elsie. "Adolescent pregnancy: a study of pregnant teenagers in a suburban community in Ontario." DSW diss., University of Toronto, 1976. 304p. (Can. theses, no.35036)

6764. Hackett, John and Diana Barza. "The clinical management of the unwed mother," *Laval médical*, 42:83-90, janv. 1971.

6765. Hedderwick, William and Kathryn Pelkey. *Study of single (unmarried) parents in the community*. Toronto: Children's Aid Society of Metropolitan Toronto, 1975. 19p.

6766. Ivison, Carol. "Trends in marriage and illegitimacy: a comparative study of Canada, the provinces and the economic regions of Ontario," in Betty Macleod, ed., *Demography and educational planning*. Monograph series, no. 7. Toronto: Ontario Institute for Studies in Education, 1970, pp.183-204.

6767. Keetley, K. *Native teen pregnancy and parenting: a problem in perspective*. Vancouver: Social Planning and Review Council of British Columbia, 1981. 48p.
       Project sponsored by Health and Welfare Canada, Health Promotions Branch.

6768. Kome, Penney. "New help for teenage mums [Jessie's Centre, Toronto]," *Homemaker's Magazine*, 17:102, 104, Oct. 1982.

6769. Lightman, Ernie S. and Benjamin Schlesinger. "Non-married mothers in maternity homes," *Social Worker*, 48:39-40, Spring 1980.

6770. MacDonnell, Susan. "A teenage pregnancy epidemic?" *Canadian Nurse*, 75:22-3, Nov. 1979.

6771. _____. "The teen pregnancy explosion," *Perception*, 3:12, Nov.-Dec. 1979.

6772. _____. *Vulnerable mothers, vulnerable children; a follow-up study of unmarried mothers who kept their children*. Halifax: Nova Scotia. Dept. of Social Services. Policy, Planning and Research Division, 1981. 325p.

6773. MacKay, Harry. "Les enfants dans une société en changement," *Perception*, 5:29, 69, June 1982.

6774. _____. "Meeting young mothers on their home ground," *Perception*, 5:8-9, Nov.-Dec. 1981.

6775. Mahon, Barbara M. "Educational alternatives for the pregnant schoolgirl." MA thesis, University of Calgary, 1976. 113p. (Can. theses, no.30554)

6776. Maranda, Jeanne. "Pénitentes hier - monoparentales aujourd'hui," *Canadian Woman Studies / Les cahiers de la femme*, 4:25-6, Fall 1982.

6777. Massé, Jacqueline C., Micheline St-Arnaud et Marie-Marthe T.-Brault. *Les jeunes mères célibataires: l'influence du milieu sur la décision de garder l'enfant ou de le faire adopter*. Montréal: Presses de l'Université de Montréal, 1981. 150p.

6778. Maynard, Fredelle. "Teen-age mothers: a nationwide dilemma," *Chatelaine*, 55:91, 126+ , Oct. 1982.

6779. Poulos, Susan. *Problem inventory of single mothers*. Vancouver: Children's Aid Society of Vancouver, B.C., 1969. 17p.

6780. Pozsonyi, Judith. *A longitudinal study of unmarried mothers who kept their first-born children*. London, Ont.: Family and Children's Services of London and Middlesex, 1973. 64p.

6781. Purdy, Margaret. "Vulnerable mothers, vulnerable children," *Perception*, 6:20-2, Sept.-Oct. 1982.

6782. Rabkin, Brenda. "Despair that breeds despair," *Maclean's*, 92:37-8, Feb. 5, 1979.

6783. Rodd, Catherine. "Lending a helping hand to the teenage parent," *Maclean's*, 95:46, Jan. 18, 1982.

6784. Ross, Anne. *Teenage mothers / teenage fathers*. Toronto: Personal Library, 1982. 128p.

6785. Rossé, Glen Peter. "The unmarried minor mother: the need for new policies and new programs." MA thesis, Dalhousie University, 1978. 143p. (Can. theses, no.44335)

6786. Schlesinger, Benjamin. "The unmarried mother who keeps her child," *Social Worker*, 44:108-13, Winter 1976.

6787. Stanleigh, Judy. "Ripple effect," *Broadside*, 2:18, Apr. 1982.

6788. Toumishey, Laura Hope. "Punishing the pregnant innocents: single pregnancy in St. John's, Newfoundland." MSc thesis, Memorial University of Newfoundland, 1978. 148p. (Can. theses, no.38658)

6789. Ward, W. Peter. "Unwed motherhood in nineteenth-century English Canada," *Canadian Historical Association. Historical Papers*, 1981, pp.34-56.

6790. Woolner, Susan. "Child mother: the Catch-22 of being an adolescent single parent," *Perception*, 3:10-11, 13, Nov.-Dec. 1979.

URBAN PROBLEMS

6791. Canada. Ministry of State for Urban Affairs. *Metropolitan Canada women's views of urban problems*. Ottawa: Information Canada, 1976. 29p.
6792. Cihocki, Mary K. "Women's travel patterns in a suburban development," in G. R. Wekerle, R. Peterson and D. Morley, eds., *New space for women*, Boulder: Westview Press, 1980, pp.151-63.
6793. Croteau, Mary J. and Wendy Zink. *Women's concerns about the quality of life in Winnipeg*. Winnipeg: University of Winnipeg. Institute of Urban Studies, 1975. 53 [15]p.
6794. National Workshop on the Concerns of Women in Shaping the Urban Environment. *Proceedings*, by Nan Griffiths and N.C.C. Women's Task Force. Ottawa: National Capital Commission, 1975. 42p.

   Cover title: *Women in the urban environment. [La femme en milieu urban].*

6795. Pollowy, Anne-Marie. *Études des problèmes et préoccupation des femmes à l'égard de la qualité de la vie dans le milieu urbain de Montréal*. Montréal: Université de Montréal. Centre de recherches et d'innovation urbaines, 1975. 138p.

   Prepared for the Minister of State for Urban Affairs.

6796. Wekerle, Gerda. "Urban planning: making it work for women; La planification urbaine; comment la mettre au service des femmes," *Status of Women News / Statut: Bulletin de la femme*, 6:2-4, 11, [English]; 2-5, [French], Winter 1979-80.
6797. Wekerle, Gerda R. and Novia Carter. "Urban sprawl: the price women pay," *Branching Out*, 5(3): 12-14, 1978.
6798. *Women's concerns about the quality of life in the city of Calgary*. Submitted to the Ministry of State and Urban Affairs. [Ottawa]: Canada. Ministry of State and Urban Affairs, 1975. 56p.

VOCATIONAL ASPIRATIONS

6799. Breton, Raymond. *Social and academic factors in the career decisions of Canadian youth*. Ottawa: Information Canada, 1972. 612p.
6800. Brinkerhoff, Merlin B. "Women who want to work in a man's world: a study of the influence of structural factors on role innovativeness," *Canadian Journal of Sociology*, 2:283-303, Summer 1977.

6801. Bubnick, Julie and others. *Vocational and educational aspirations of high school youth*. Winnipeg: Manitoba. Dept. of Labour. Women's Bureau, 1976. 218p. (Profile 77-0096)
6802. "Career aspirations," *Labour Gazette*, 78:391-2, Sept. 1978.
6803. "Career choice, advancement and personhood," in Canadian Research Institute for the Advancement of Women, *Women as Persons. (La femme en tant que personne]*. Toronto: Resources for Feminist Research, 1980, pp.25-33.

   Proceedings of the 3rd annual meeting.

6804. Cassie, J. B. and others. *Sex-role stereotyping: incidence and implications for guidance and counselling of students*. OISE project, 5616-80. Toronto: Ontario Institute for Studies in Education, 1980. 193p.

6805. Coffin, Susan Dianne. "Sex differences in educational aspirations of Newfoundland youth: the effects of family, school and community variables." MEd thesis, Memorial University of Newfoundland, 1976. 111p. (Can. theses, no.31391)
6806. Crealock, Carol. "The influence of 'fear of success' and 'need for achievement' on the vocational aspirations of male and female high school students," *Canadian Counsellor*, 14:32-5, Oct. 1979.
6807. Davies, Rhona. "Career expectations of female teachers in British Columbia," *Atlantis*, 6:202-7, Spring 1981.

274

6808.	Denis, Ann B. "Educational aspirations of Montreal post-secondary students: ethnic, sex and social class differences," in Jean Leonard Elliott, ed., *Two nations, many cultures: ethnic groups in Canada*. Scarborough, Ont.: Prentice-Hall, 1979, pp.86-98.

6809.	Doucet-Bouchard, Pauline. "Les aspirations professionnelles de niveau universitaire." MA thesis, Université Laval, 1969. 130p. and app.

6810.	Fahmy-Pomerleau, Pauline. "Aspirations prédominantes et aspirations professionnelles des adolescentes de Québec," *Orientation professionnelle*, 8:366-73, hiver 1972.

6811.	_____. "Égalité et dépendance ou l'impossible aspiration des adolescentes," in Yolande Cohen, *Femmes et politique*. Montréal: Le Jour, 1981, pp.81-100.

6812.	Gagnon, Rosette, Louise Biron et Marie-Andrée Bertrand. *Aspirations et délinquance révélée chez les adolescentes. Rapport no. 3*. Montréal: Université de Montréal. Groupe de Recherche sur l'inadaptation juvénile, 1980. 198p.

6813.	Gaskell, Jane. "Sex inequalities in education for work: the case of business education," *Canadian Journal of Education*, 6(2):54-72, 1981.

6814.	Geller, Gloria. "Role aspirations and life-style orientations of school women." MA thesis, University of Toronto, 1973.

6815.	Glaze, Avis. "Factors which influence career choice and future orientations of females: implications for career education." EdD diss., University of Toronto, 1979. 215p. (Can. theses, no.50267)

6816.	_____. and Dormer Ellis. "Ontario girls' career aspirations and expectations," *Orbit*, 11:19-22, June 1980.

6817.	Hitchman, Gladys Symons. "Occupational decision-making, career aspirations and preparation for labour force participation: the case of male and female doctoral candidates," in Patricia Marchak, ed., *The working sexes: symposium papers on the effects of sex on women at work*. Vancouver: University of British Columbia. Institute of Industrial Relations, 1977, pp.110-36.

6818.	Kahn, Sharon E. "Psychological barriers to the occupational success of mature women," *Canadian Counsellor*, 13:211-14, July 1979.

6819.	_____. and Alana S. Schroeder. "Counsellor bias in occupational choice for female students," *Canadian Counsellor*, 14:156-9, Apr. 1980.

6820.	Langlais, Nicole. "Comment le sentiment de culpabilité restreint la femme dans son développement vocationnel," *Orientation professionnelle*, 14:128-37, été 1978.

6821.	Leith, Nancy Louise. "The effect of exposure to film-mediated career information of traditionally defined male occupations on the vocational interest level of girls." MEd thesis, University of Alberta, 1977. 67p. (Can. theses, no.34407)

6822.	Leith, Nancy and George Fitzsimmons. "An evaluation of the vocational readiness package for girls: a solution to one problem," *Canadian Counsellor*, 13:18-22, Oct. 1978.

6823.	Lerch, Renate. "Female job segregation 'is beginning in school'," *Financial Post*, 74:14, Oct. 4, 1980.

6824.	Maxwell, Mary Percival and James D. Maxwell. "Women, religion, and achievement aspirations: a study of private school females," in Robert M. Pike and Elia Zureik, eds., *Socialization and values in Canadian Society*. Vol.2: *Socialization, social stratification and ethnicity*. Toronto: McClelland & Stewart, 1975, pp.104-28.

6825.	Maynard, Fredelle. "Can. Kid & Can. Mom 79," *Chatelaine*, 52:29-30, 56-7, Jan. 1979.

6826.	McCarrey, Michael W., Shirley Edwards and Robert Jones. "The influence of ethnolinguistic group membership, sex and position level on motivational orientation of Canadian anglophone and francophone employees," *Canadian Journal of Behavioural Science*, 9(3):274-82, 1977.

6827.	Murray, Michael A. and Tom Atkinson. "Gender differences in correlates of job satisfaction," *Canadian Journal of Behavioural Science*, 13(1):44-52, 1981.

6828.	Pyke, Sandra W. and Faye Weisenberg. "Desired job characteristics for males and females," *Canadian Counsellor*, 10:185-91, July 1976.

6829.	Richardt, Joan Marie. "The relationship of four dimensions of career orientation to the vocational maturity of grade twelve girls." MA thesis, University of British Columbia, 1979. 108p. (Can. theses, no.46252)

6830. Romm, Tsilia. "Interaction of vocational and family factors in the career planning of teenage girls - a new developmental approach," *Interchange*, 11(1):13-24, 1980/81.
6831. Russell, Susan. "Learning sex roles in the high school," *Interchange*, 10(2):57-66, 1979/80.
6832. Sayer, Lynda Anne. "Career awareness of grade nine girls: evaluation of treatment programs." PhD diss., University of Toronto, 1980. 332p. (Can. theses, no.47152)
6833. Snider, Nancy Jay. "Women's vocational commitment and the SVIB-W." MSc thesis, University of Calgary, 1973. 95p. (Can. theses, no.17065)
6834. Sutherland, Sharon L. "The unambitious female: women's low professional aspirations," *Signs*, 3:774-94, Summer 1978.
6835. Tannis, Wendy Bunt. "An analysis of the effects of social class, mother's working status, mother's occupation and mother's education on the educational and occupational aspirations of female grade ten students in an Ontario community." MA thesis, University of Windsor, 1972. 115p. (Can. theses, no.14792)
6836. University of British Columbia. Women's Office. Women's Research Collective. *Voices of women students*. Vancouver, 1974. 58p.

6837. Wand, Barbara. "Sex differences in educational aspirations and academic performance in high school students," *Atlantis*, 3:99-111, Autumn 1977.
6838. Wasserman, David. "Personality and vocational choice of adolescent girls." MSc thesis, University of Calgary, 1974. 69p. (Can. theses, no.21366)
6839. Waterman, Diane C. "Sex roles and career goals of university women." MA thesis, University of British Columbia, 1977. 166p. (Can. theses, no.34975)

VOCATIONAL ASPIRATIONS - BIBLIOGRAPHY

6840. Ontario. Ministry of Labour. Women's Bureau. *Selected bibliography: factors in the career choice of female students*. Toronto, 1974. 8p.

VOCATIONAL GUIDANCE

6841. Andresen, Susan A. *Introduction to Non-traditional Occupations Program (INTO) evaluation: expanding women's career options*. [London, Ont.: Women's Workshop, Continuous Learning Project, 1981].175p. (Microlog 82-3760) Study funded by Ontario Ministry of Colleges and Universities.

6842. Canada. Dept. of Labour. Women's Bureau. *Do you know where you are going?* Ottawa, 1980. [12]p.
6843. Carson, Jean E., comp. *"Facts/fantasies/futures": a conference held by the University Women's Club of Winnipeg*. [Winnipeg: University Women's Club of Winnipeg, 1976?] 119p.
6844. Clarke, Marnie A. "Women in transition: the change process," *Ontario Library Review*, 59:236-41, Dec. 1975.

6845. Council of Associations of University Student Personnel Services. *Brief no. 426 to the Royal Commission on the Status of Women in Canada*. n.p., n.d. 28p.
6846. Dunnigan, Lise. *L'orientation des filles en milieu scolaire*. Résultats d'un sondage effectué en automne 1976 auprès des conseillers d'orientation... Québec: Conseil du statut de la femme, 1977. 37p.
6847. Dvorak, Leona and Bev Siller. *Evaluation of the Pre-Trades Training Program for Women (February - May 1979), Regina*. [Regina: Regina Plains Community College], 1979. 32, [23]p.

6848. Ewing, Marjorie. "Increased career awareness for girls: an experimental course," *School Guidance Worker*, 30:34-9, Nov.-Dec. 1974.
6849. Francis, Anne. "Let's stop wasting women's potential," *Canadian Counsellor*, 7:218-31, Oct. 1973.
6850. Gagnon, Lysiane. "Un jeu [Vire-vie] qui déniaise," *L'Actualité*, 3:20 mai 1978.

276

6851. Hicks, M. Ellen. "The task ahead: in education and training," in Canadian Federation of Business and Professional Women's Clubs, *A collection of papers delivered at the National Conference: Women & Work in the 80's: a Decade of Change*. Ottawa: The Federation, 1981, pp.73-6.

6852. Ironside, Anne. *Women's access centres: a proposal*. Discussion paper 03/79. [Victoria]: British Columbia. Ministry of Education, Science and Technology, 1979. 40p.

6853. Johnson, Valerie M. "Fighting (nervously) the sexual sterotypes: for high school girls, liberation is still an exotic idea," *Saturday Night*, 89:23-6, Jan. 1974.

6854. Kainola, May Ann and Margie Bruun-Meyer. *Making changes: employment orientation for immigrant women*. Toronto: Cross Cultural Communication Centre, 1982. 136p. and app.

6855. Krakauer, Renate. *Career development workshop for women: outline*. Toronto: Ontario. Ministry of Labour. Women's Bureau, 1978. 20p. and app.

6856. Landsberg, Michele. "Exploding high school girls' marriage fantasies," *Chatelaine*, 48:53, 104-8, Sept. 1975.

6857. Lester, Tanya. "Growing up female: the high school woman's career," *Canadian Dimension*, 14:24-6, May 1980.

6858. Lindell, Susan Howard. "Behind closed doors," *Canadian Woman Studies / Les cahiers de la femme*, 4:76-8, Fall 1982.

6859. Manuel, Philip A. "View from my bridge," *School Guidance Worker*, 31:35-9, Sept.-Oct. 1975.

6860. Marsden, L. R. "Canadian economic and sociological trends: implications for counselling," *School Guidance Worker*, 30:5-11, May-June 1975.

6861. Maynard, Rona. "Why can't we give high-school girls the career guidance they need?" *Chatelaine*, 56:77, 182+ , Oct. 1983.

6862. McCreary, Gillian and Patricia Pitsel. *Life options for young women: tomorrow's dreams begin today: workbook*. Regina: Saskatchewan. Dept. of Labour. Women's Division, 1978. 64p.

6863. Morris, Joan. "What to do until androgyny comes: on counselling girls in the new decade," *School Guidance Worker*, 35:13-17, Nov.-Dec. 1979.

6864. Ontario. Ministry of Education. *Changing roles in a changing world: a resource guide focusing on the female student*. [Toronto, 1976] 24p.

6865. Ontario. Ministry of Labour. Women's Bureau. *Evaluation research of the Introduction to Non-Traditional Occupations program*, by Lynn Dzeoba. [Toronto], 1979. 24p.

6866. Quigley, Jocelyne. *Pre-trade training for women*. [Winnipeg, Man.: Red River Community College], 1979. 19, [19]p.

6867. Regina Plains Community College. *Report on Pre-Trades Training for Women (February-May '79)*. Regina, 1979. 58p.

6868. Sayer, Liz and Dormer Ellis. "The wheel of fortune or the love boat," *Orbit*, 12:21-3, Oct. 1981.

6869. Sayer, Lynda Anne. "Career awareness of grade nine girls: evaluation of treatment programs." PhD diss., University of Toronto, 1980. 332p. (Can. theses, no.47152)

6870. Schroeder, Alana Shirley. "Counsellor bias in occupational choice for female students." MA thesis, University of British Columbia, 1975. 112p. (Can. theses, no.42735)

6871. Shack, Sybil. "He takes out the garbage," *School Guidance Worker*, 31:44-9, Sept.-Oct. 1975.

6872. Shields, Barbara A. "Androgyny is here: on counselling girls now," *School Guidance Worker*, 27:28-33, Nov.-Dec. 1971.

6873. Status of Women Council of British Columbia. *An investigation of counselling in Vancouver secondary schools*. Vancouver, n.d. 4p.

6874. Usher, Sarah. "Is there really a choice? The need for life skills counselling with female adolescents," *School Guidance Worker*, 33:35-8, May-June 1978.

6875. Wolfe, Sandra J. "Development and evaluation of vocational counselling program for high school girls." MEd thesis, University of Alberta, 1977. 132p. (Can. theses, no.34521)

6876. Women's Employment Counselling. *No need to just pretend: new work choices for women*. Corner Brook, Nfld.: Canada. Dept. of Employment and Immigration / Corner Brook Status of Women Council, [1982]. 24p.

6877. Woodcock, Penelope Jane Robinson. "The facilitation of career awareness in grade ten girls." MSc thesis, University of Calgary, 1977. 83p. (Can. theses, no.34270)

6878. Young, Filson A. "Sex-role stereotyping in career counselling: effects of differences in sex of counsellor and sex of client." PhD diss., University of Toronto, 1973. 122p. (Can. theses, no.26092)

VOCATIONAL GUIDANCE - BIBLIOGRAPHY

6879. Ontario. Ministry of Labour. Women's Bureau. *Selected bibliography: the counsellor's role in the career counselling of female students*. Toronto, 1973. 8p. Addendum May 1974. 1p.

VOLUNTEER WORK

6880. Canadian Association of Hospital Auxiliaries. *Brief no. 91 to the Royal Commisssion on the Status of Women in Canada*. Ottawa, n.d. 8p.

6881. Conklin, Elizabeth Nancy. "Women's voluntary associations in French Montreal: a study of changing institutions and attitudes." PhD diss., University of Illinois at Urbana, 1972. 308p. (UM73-9909)

6882. Hamilton Women's Services Central Training. *Volunteer training manual*. Hamilton, [1981]. 37p. and app.

6883. Howarth, Joyce and Susan Secord. *The female volunteer: a survey conducted in the province of Alberta, Canada*. [Edmonton: Queen's Printer for the Province of Alberta], 1974. 38, xxip. (Profile 74-0879)
      Submitted to the Honourable Miss Hunley, Minister responsible for the Alberta Women's Bureau.

6884. I.O.D.E. *Brief no. 311 to the Royal Commission on the Status of Women in Canada*. Toronto, 1968. 75p.

6885. Junior League of Montreal. *Brief no. 333 to the Royal Commission on the Status of Women in Canada*. Montreal, n.d. 15p.

6886. La Société d'étude et de conferences. *Brief no. 152 to the Royal Commission on the Status of Women in Canada*. Montreal, 1968. 23p.

6887. Ricks, Frances A. and Sandra W. Pyke. "Women in voluntary social organizations," *Ontario Psychologist*, 5(2):48-55, 1973.

6888. Steele, Betty. "Women's groups are coming back," *Atlantic Advocate*, 63:34-5, 38-9, 41, Feb. 1973.

WAGES

6889. Agarwal, Naresh C. and Harish C. Jain. "Pay discrimination against women in Canada: issues and policies," *International Labour Review*, 117:169-77, Mar.-Apr. 1978.

6890. _____. *Pay discrimination against women in Canada: issues and policies*. Working paper series, no. 143. Hamilton, Ont.: McMaster University. Faculty of Business, 1978. 9p.

6891. "AIB to review its rollback of agreement that gave catch-up pay to women workers," *Globe & Mail*, May 19, 1977, p.F9.

6892. "Are wages the ultimate compensation?" *Labour Gazette*, 74:353-6, May 1974.

6893. Boyd, Monica and Elizabeth Humphreys. *Labour markets and sex differences in Canadian incomes*. Discussion paper, no. 143. Ottawa: Economic Council of Canada, 1979. 81p.

6894. _____. "Sex differences in Canada: incomes and labour markets," in *Reflections on Canadian incomes: selected papers presented at the Conference on Canadian Incomes, May 10-12, 1979*. Ottawa: Economic Council of Canada, 1980, pp.401-20.

6895. Boyd, Monica. *Rank and salary differentials in the 1970's: a comparison of male and female full time teachers in Canadian universities and colleges*. Ottawa: Association of Universities and Colleges of Canada, 1979. 59p.

6896. Burgham, Catherine. "The great summer job rip-off," *Chatelaine*, 48:24, Sept. 1975.

278

6897. "Canada flunks world test on women's wages," *Ontario Labour*, Sept.-Oct. 1980, p.12.

6898. Carroll, Michael P. "The gap between male and female income in Canada," *Canadian Journal of Sociology*, 5:357-60, Fall 1980.

6899. Cheda, Sherrill and others. "Salary differentials of female and male librarians in Canada," *Emergency Librarian*, 5:3-13, Jan.-Feb. 1978.

6900. Cinman, I. "Peer evaluation salary study results in adjustments for women," *CAUT Bulletin*, 25:5, Apr. 1977.

6901. Connelly, M. Patricia. "The economic context of women's labour force participation in Canada," in Patricia Marchak, ed., *The working sexes: symposium papers on the effects of sex on women at work*. Vancouver: University of British Columbia. Institute of Industrial Relations, 1977, pp.10-27.

6902. _____. "Women workers and the family wage in Canada," in Anne Hoiberg, ed., *Women and the world of work*. New York: Plenum Press, 1982, pp.223-37.

6903. "Council says 40% of wives earn more than husbands," *Globe & Mail*, May 17, 1979, p.T2.

6904. David-McNeil, J. "Disparité des salaires masculins et féminins au Canada," *L'Actualité économique*, 40:469-81, oct.-déc. 1964.

6905. De Sève, Michel et Marlen Carter. "Les inégalités salariales entre les travailleurs féminins et masculins: effet de qualification ou effet de statut?" *Recherches sociographiques*, 21:253-82, sept.-déc. 1980.

6906. "Economics and personhood," in Canadian Research Institute for the Advancement of Women, *Women as persons*. [*La femme en tant que personne*]. Toronto: Resources for Feminist Research, 1980, pp.94-102.
    Proceedings of the 3rd annual meeting.

6907. Fox, Bonnie. "The female reserve army of labour: the argument and some pertinent findings," *Atlantis*, 7:45-56, Fall 1981.

6908. Fox, Bonnie J. and John Fox. "Effects of women's employment on wages," *Canadian Journal of Sociology*, 8:319-28, Summer 1983.

6909. Gelber, Sylva M. "Compensation of women," in, *Women's Bureau '74*. Ottawa: Canada. Dept. of Labour. Women's Bureau, 1975, pp.7-16.

6910. _____. "Economic and academic status of women in relation to their male colleagues," in, *Women's Bureau '74*. Ottawa: Canada. Dept. of Labour. Women's Bureau, 1975, pp.39-44.

6911. Goyder, John C. "Income differences between the sexes: findings from a national Canadian survey," *Canadian Review of Sociology and Anthropology*, 18(3):321-42, 1981.

6912. Gunderson, Morley. "Decomposition of the male/female earnings differential: Canada 1970," *Canadian Journal of Economics*, 12:479-85, Aug. 1979.

6913. _____. "Male-female wage differentials and the impact of equal pay legislation," *Review of Economics and Statistics*, 57:462-9, Nov. 1975.

6914. _____. *The male-female earnings gap in Ontario: a summary*. [Toronto]: Ontario. Ministry of Labour. Research Branch, 1982. 23p. (Microlog 82-2600)

6915. _____. *Time pattern of male-female wage differentials: Ontario 1946-71*. Working Paper, no. 75-09. Toronto: University of Toronto. Faculty of Management Studies, 1975. 18p.

6916. _____. "Time pattern of male-female wage differentials: Ontario 1946-71," *Industrial Relations*, 31(1):57-71, 1976.

6917. Hird, Richard. *Characteristics of low-wage workers in Ontario*. Report no. 7. Toronto: Ontario. Ministry of Labour. Research Branch, 1974. 30p.

6918. Holmes, R. A. "Male-female earnings differentials in Canada," *Journal of Human Resources*, 11:109-17, Winter 1976.

6919. Hossie, Helen. "Women in the work force," *Manitoba Business Review*, 1(4):8-10, May 1976.

6920. Istona, Mildred. "Man-size wages for women," *Chatelaine*, 54:4, Jan. 1981.

6921. Kuch, Peter and Walter Haessel. *An analysis of earnings in Canada*. Census analytical study. Ottawa: Statistics Canada, 1979. 212p. (Catalogue no. 99-758E)
    Chapter 6, Empirical analysis of female earnings; Chapter 7, Effects of sex and marital status on distribution of wages and salaries.

6922. "Male-female median salaries in Canadian universities 1971-72 and 1974-75," *CAUT Bulletin*, 24:12, Sept. 1975.

6923. Marchak, Patricia. "Les femmes, le travail et le syndicalisme au Canada," *Sociologie et sociétés*, 6:37-53, mai 1974.

6924. "Men are still pulling in bigger bucks," *Marketing*, 84:19, Apr. 9, 1979.

6925. Nakamura, Alice and others. *Employment and earnings of married females*. 1971 Census of Canada. Census analytical study. Ottawa: Statistics Canada, 1979. 168p. (Cat. no. 99-760E)

6926. Ontario Status of Women Council. *Brief to the General Government Committee on Bill 3, An Act to Amend the Employment Standards Act*. [Toronto], 1980. 8p. and table.

6927. Ornstein, Michael D. *Gender wage differentials in Canada: a review of previous research and theoretical framework*. Discussion paper series. Series A: equality in the workplace, no. 1. Ottawa: Canada. Dept. of Labour. Women's Bureau, 1982. 57p. (Microlog 83-0723)

6928. Réseau d'action et d'information pour les femmes. *Revenu garanti: mémoire pour une formule n'excluant pas les femmes mariées*. Ste-Foy, Québec: Réseau d'action et d'information pour les femmes, 1976. 20p.

6929. Robb, Roberta Edgecombe. "Earning differentials between males and females in Ontario, 1971," *The Canadian Journal of Economics*, 11:350-9, May 1978.

6930. Robson, R. A. H. *A comparison of men's and women's salaries and employment fringe benefits in the academic profession*. Royal Commission on the Status of Women in Canada. Study no. 1. Ottawa, 1971. 39p.

6931. Rosenfeld, Rachael A. "Sex difference in socioeconomic achievement: an overview of findings and explanations," in *Reflections on Canadian incomes: selected papers presented at the Conference on Canadian Incomes, May 10-12, 1979*. Ottawa: Economic Council of Canada, 1980, pp.383-99.

6932. "Salary anomalies by sex [University of Toronto]," *Labour Gazette*, 75:333-4, June 1975.

6933. Saskatchewan. Dept. of Labour. Research and Planning Division. *Occupational wage rates by sex: Saskatchewan 1977*. [Regina], 1977. 71p. (Profile 77-0911)

6934. Schrank, William E. "Sex discrimination in faculty salaries: a case study," *Canadian Journal of Economics*, 10:411-33, Aug. 1977.

6935. Shapiro, Daniel M. and Morton Stelcner. *Earnings determination: the role of language and sex: Quebec 1970*. Working paper, no. 1981-1. Montreal: Concordia University. Dept. of Economics, 1981. 223p.

6936. _____. *Language legislation and male-female earnings differentials in Quebec*. Working paper, no. 1981-2. Montreal: Concordia University. Dept. of Economics, 1980. 23p.

6937. _____. "Language legislation and male-female earnings differentials in Quebec," *Canadian Public Policy*, 8:106-13, Winter 1982.

6938. _____. "Male-female earnings differentials and the role of language in Canada, Ontario, and Quebec, 1970," *Canadian Journal of Economics*, 14:341-8, May 1981.

6939. _____. *Male-female earnings differentials within the public and private sectors Canada and Québec, 1970*. Working paper, no. 1980-2. Montreal: Concordia University. Dept. of Economics, 1980. 20p.

6940. Silverman, Peter. "Controls help to maintain the wage gap," *Financial Post*, 71:25, Oct. 15, 1977.

6941. Slanders, Ann. "Why should we women be the sacrificial lambs?" *Office Equipment and Methods*, 21:16, Nov. 1975.

6942. Stelcner, Morton and Daniel M. Shapiro. *The decomposition of the male/female earnings differential: Québec, 1970*. Working paper, no. 1980-3. Montreal: Concordia University. Dept. of Economics, 1980. 32p.

6943. "The earnings gap between men & women," *IR Research Reports*, 4:10-12, Dec. 1979.

6944. Townson, Monica. "Money matters," *Canadian Woman Studies / Les cahiers de la femme*, 3:20-4, Summer 1982.

6945. "Wage discrimination in British Columbia," in Lynda Turner, comp., *Woman in Canadian society*. [New Westminster, B.C.: Douglas College, 1972], pp.97-8.

280

6946. Walmsley, P.Y. and M. Ohtsu. "Wage discrimination against women: an assessment of the use of job evaluation in the measurement of sex-based wage discrimination." [Paper presented at the 16th annual meeting of the Canadian Industrial Relations Association, May 1979. 30p.]

WELFARE

6947. Canadian Advisory Council on the Status of Women. *Discussion paper on federal income security programs for families with children*, by Louise Dulude. Ottawa, 1980. 10p.
6948. "In the beginning was Charlotte [Whitton]... ," *Canadian Welfare*, 51:14-15, Mar.-Apr. 1975.
6949. James, Jean M. *Family benefits mothers in Metropolitan Toronto*. Research report, no. 2. Toronto: Ontario. Ministry of Community and Social Services. Research and Planning Branch, 1973. 219p.
6950. Kitchen, Brigitte. "Women and the social security system in Canada," *Atlantis*, 5:89-99, Spring 1980.
6951. Kunin, Roslyn. "To work or not to work," *Canadian Welfare*, 48:16-20, July-Aug. 1972.
6952. Larsen, Carolyn and Lorna Cammaert. *A follow-up study on contemporary women: a group counselling program for women on assistance*. Calgary: University of Calgary. Student Counselling Services, 1975. 27p. and app.
6953. Maas, Alex. "Whose family benefits?" *Broadside*, 1(2):10-11, 1979.
6954. Metro Agencies Action Committee. Work Group. *Facts for advocacy*. [Toronto, 1982?] v.p. (Microlog 83-2855)

·"A project designed to identify and explore the conditions which block women on family benefits moving from economic dependence to independence."
6955. Munro, Don. R. "The care of the dependent poor in Ontario, 1891-1921: a study of the impact of social change on the organization of welfare services in Ontario for the dependent poor, especially the unemployed, the aged and the mother raising children by herself, between 1891-1921." MSW thesis, University of Toronto, 1966 [1977]. 171p. (Can. theses, no.31294)
6956. New Brunswick. Advisory Council on the Status of Women. *'One step forward, two steps back'*, A submission to the Parliamentary Task Force on Federal-Provincial Fiscal Arrangements, prepared by Susan Shalala. Moncton, 1981. 18p.
6957. Rook, Patricia T. and R. L. Schnell. "Charlotte Whitton and the 'babies for export' controversy 1947-48," *Alberta History*, 30:11-16, Winter 1982.
6958. _____. "Charlotte Whitton meets 'The Last Best West': the politics of child welfare in Alberta," *Prairie Forum*, 6:143-62, Fall 1981.
6959. Rosensweig, Donna. "Women and children last," *Broadside*, 3:8, Feb. 1982.
6960. Silversides, Ann. "Catch-22 of single parents on welfare," *Maclean's*, 93:54, 57-8, Nov. 17, 1980.
6961. Strong-Boag, Veronica. "Canada's early experience with income supplements: the introduction of mothers' allowances," *Atlantis*, 4:35-43, Spring 1979, Part II.
6962. Struthers, James. "A profession in crisis: Charlotte Whitton and Canadian social work in the 1930s," *Canadian Historical Review*, 62:169-85, June 1981.
6963. Thibault, Gisele. "The policing of women: welfare legislation in Nova Scotia." MA thesis, Dalhousie University, 1982. (Can. theses, no.53795)
6964. "Women on welfare want to work," *Canadian Welfare*, 46:27, Nov.-Dec. 1970.

WIDOWS

6965. Alberta. Women's Bureau. *When you're alone: helping you cope with widowhood*. Rev. ed. Edmonton, 1980. 12p.
6966. Elias, Brenda M. "Residential environment and social adjustment among older widows." MSc thesis, University of Guelph, 1978. 119p. (Can. theses, no.37404)
6967. Eustace, David F. "Three widows," *Life Insurance in Canada*, 4:6, 8, 48-9, 54, May-June 1977.

6968. Gould, Allan B. "When widows step into their husbands' shoes," *Chatelaine*, 56:78-9, 97+ , Dec. 1983.

6969. Harrison, Brian R. "Fertility differentials and living arrangements of older widows," in his *Living alone in Canada: demographic and economic perspectives, 1951-1976*. Ottawa: Statistics Canada, 1981, pp.41-50. (Cat. no. 98-811)

6970. Hunsberger, Emily J. "Social and work involvement of middle-aged women within the first three years of widowhood." MSc thesis, University of Manitoba, 1973. 65p. (Can. theses, no.17330)

6971. Lazarus, Ena. "Widows helping widows; Entraide communautaire pour les veuves et veufs," *Status of Women News / Statut: Bulletin de la femme*, 5:9, [English]; 8, [French], Mar. 1979.

6972. Matthews, Anne Martin. "Review essay: Canadian research on women as widows: a comparative analysis of the state of the art," *Resources for Feminist Research*, 11:227-30, July 1982.

6973. _____. "Women and widowhood," in Victor W. Marshall, *Aging in Canada: social perspectives*. Toronto: Fitzhenry & Whiteside, 1980, pp.145-53.

6974. Ontario Status of Women Council. *Brief to the government of Ontario respecting widow's rights to family property*. [Toronto], 1980. 13p.

6975. Sawyer, Deborah C. "Wife after death: to be prepared she needs more than a will," *Canadian Business*, 55:122-3, Jan. 1982.

6976. Schlesinger, Benjamin. "The crisis of widowhood in the family circle," *Essence*, 1(3):147-57, 1977.

6977. _____. "The widowed as a one-parent family unit," *Social Science*, 46:26-32, Jan. 1971.

6978. Sutton, May. "Widowhood: a keynote address: the facts of life," *Status of Women News*, 5:6-8, Mar. 1979.

6979. Vachon, Mary L. Suslak. "Identity change over the first two years of bereavement: social relationships and social support in widowhood." PhD diss., York University, 1979. 282p. (Can. theses, no.42147)

6980. Wylie, Betty Jane. "Beyond the veil," *The Canadian*, Aug. 6, 1977, pp.8-10.

WOMEN - ALBERTA

6981. Alberta. Citizens' Advisory Board. *Interim report on the status of women in Alberta, made to the Honourable Miss W. H. Hunley*. [Edmonton, 1972]. 45p.

6982. Blackburn, John. "A woman's work is never done," in his, *Land of promise*. Toronto: MacMillan of Canada, 1970, pp.169-75.

6983. Darmah Associates. *Joint initiatives: a goal for women and government in Alberta: a submission to Executive Council of the Province of Alberta*. [Edmonton]: Alberta Status of Women Action Committee, 1976. 75p.

6984. Grescoe, Paul. "Wild rose country," *Today*, July 19, 1980, pp.9-12.

6985. Johnson, Joanna. "Women living in isolated areas," *Atlantis*, 4:300-5, Spring 1979, Part II.

6986. Schulz, Linda Z. "Feminism, down on the farm," *Branching Out*, 6(1): 37-8, 1979.

6987. Sheppard, June. "Women of Edmonton: the pattern breakers," *Chatelaine*, 48:32-3, 66-7, 70-1, Apr. 1975.

WOMEN - ALBERTA - HISTORY

6988. Alberta Mennonite Women in Mission. *History of Alberta Mennonite Women in Mission: 1947-1977*. Coaldale, Alberta, 1978. 128p.

6989. Boyd, Helen. "Growing up privileged in Edmonton," *Alberta History*, 30:1-10, Winter 1982.

6990. Corbet, Elise Elliott. "Alberta women in the 1920's: an inquiry into four aspects of their lives." MA thesis, University of Calgary, 1979. 176p. (Can. theses, no.41995)

6991. Cox, Barbara J. *Summer of childhood*. n.p.: B.J. Cox, 1978. 96p.

6992. Duncan, Joy, ed. *Red seige wives*. [n.p.]: Centennial Book Committee [R.C.M.P.], 1974. 249p.

6993. Ferguson, Ted. "Emily Murphy, the forgotten feminist," *Chatelaine*, 50:20, May 1977.
6994. Hogg, Carol. "Women of Calgary: the pattern breakers," *Chatelaine*, 49:44-6, 114-16, Apr. 1976.
6995. Jameson, Sheilagh S. "Give your other vote to the sister," *Alberta Historical Review*, 15:10-16, Autumn 1967.
6996. _____. "Women in the Southern Alberta ranch community: 1881-1914," in Henry C. Klassen, ed., *The Canadian West: social change and economic development*. Calgary: University of Calgary / Comprint Pub., 1977, pp.63-78.
6997. Jones, David C. "'From babies to buttonholes': women's work at agricultural fairs," *Alberta History*, 29:26-32, Autumn 1981.
6998. McCrum, Elizabeth M., ed. *Letters of Louisa McDougall, 1878-1887*. Provincial Archives of Alberta. Occasional paper, no. 1. Edmonton: Alberta Culture, Historical Resources Division, 1978. 91p.
6999. Philip, Catherine. "The fair, frail flowers of western womanhood," in Anthony W. Rasporich and Henry C. Klassen, eds., *Frontier Calgary: town, city and region, 1875-1914*. Calgary: University of Calgary / McClelland and Stewart West, 1975, pp.114-23.
7000. Pippa. "Three who led the way [Nellie McClung, Helen Smith and Christine Meikle]," *ATA Magazine*, 55:38-9, Jan.-Feb. 1975.
7001. Sanderson, Kay. *One hundred years of Alberta women*. [Calgary, Alta: Alberta Historical Resources Foundation, 1982?] 25p. (Microlog 83-3400)
        Brief biographies
7002. Silverman, Eliane Leslau. "Preliminaries to a study of women in Alberta, 1890-1929," *Canadian Oral History Association. Journal*, 3(1):22-6, 1978.
7003. Silverman, Eliane. "In their own words: mothers and daughters on the Alberta frontier," *Frontiers*, 2:37-44, Summer 1977.
7004. Wilson, L. J. "Educational role of the United Farm Women of Alberta," *Alberta History*, 25:28-36, Spring 1977.
7005. Woywitka, Anne B. "A pioneer woman in the labour movement," *Alberta History*, 26:10-16, Winter 1978.

WOMEN - ATLANTIC PROVINCES - HISTORY

7006. Pierson, Ruth. "Women's history: the state of the art in Atlantic Canada," *Acadiensis*, 7:121-31, Autumn 1977.
7007. Prentice, Alison. "Writing women into history: the history of women's work in Canada," *Atlantis*, 3:72-84, Spring 1978, Part II.

WOMEN - BRITISH COLUMBIA

7009. Beebe, Janet and others. *Update on the status of women in British Columbia*. [Vancouver: Vancouver Status of Women], 1978. 104p.
7010. Hobbs, Lisa. "Women of Vancouver: the pattern breakers," *Chatelaine*, 46:48-51, 96, Nov. 1973.
7011. Status of Women Council of Vancouver. *Two-fold proposal to improve the status of women in the province of British Columbia*. Brief presented to the Honourable David Barrett, Oct. 1972. 16p.
7012. Vancouver Status of Women Council. *Status anyone?* Vancouver, 1972. 42p.
7013. Weiss, Star. "Quadra Island's quiet revolution," *Chatelaine*, 54:54, 96+ , Nov. 1981.
7014. Women's Research Centre. *Beyond the pipeline: a study of the lives of women and their families in Fort Nelson, British Columbia, and Whitehorse, Yukon Territory; and an identification of their socio-economic concerns resulting from the proposed construction ... .* [Vancouver, B.C.], 1979. 252, [26]p.
7015. _____. *Energy development and social institutions: community research from the perspective of women in northern communities impacted by the Alaska Highway Gas Pipeline*. Papers presented at The Human Side of Energy: 2nd International Forum, University of Alberta, August 16-19, 1981. 35p.

WOMEN - BRITISH COLUMBIA - HISTORY

7016. Forbes, Elizabeth. *Wild roses at their feet: pioneer women of Vancouver Island*. Vancouver: British Columbia Centennial '71 Committee, 1971. 147p.

7017. Gould, Jan. *Women of British Columbia*. Saanichton, B.C.: Hancock House Publishers, 1975. 221p.

7018. Kloppenborg, Anne, ed. "Women in our past: a brief history of the status of women in British Columbia," *Urban Reader*, 3(4), May 1975.

7019. Latham, Barbara and Cathy Kess, eds. *In her own right: selected essays on women's history in B.C.* Victoria, B.C.: Camosun College, 1980. 302p.

7020. Powell, Mary Patricia. "Response to the depression: three representative women's groups in British Columbia." MA thesis, University of British Columbia, 1967. 115p.

7021. Reeve, Phyllis. *The history of the University Women's Club of Vancouver, 1907-1982*. [Vancouver]: University Women's Club of Vancouver, 1982. 102p.

7022. Storrs, Monica. *God's galloping girl: the Peace River diaries of Monica Storrs, 1929-1931*, edited and introduced by W. L. Morton. Vancouver: University of British Columbia Press, 1979. 307p.

7023. "Women in our past: a brief history of the status of women in British Columbia," *Urban Reader*, 3:4-11, May 1975.

7024. Wozney, Christine. "Extra ordinary women in history," *Canadian Women's Studies / Les cahiers de la femme*, 3(1):87-9, 1981.

WOMEN - CANADA

7026. Abbott, George. *George Abbott's women of Canada*. Photographed by Gordon Hay. Geneva: Rotovision S.A., 1980. 202p.
       Consists mainly of photographs of women in the field of the arts.

7027. Anderson, Doris. "Editorial," *Canadian Woman Studies / Les cahiers de la femme*, 3:3-4, Summer 1982.

7028. _____. "How to help women help society," *Chatelaine*, 43:1, Aug. 1970.

7029. _____. "Progress in the world of women," *Chatelaine*, 42:1, May 1969.

7030. _____. "Women: a chance for a choice?" *Chatelaine*, 42:1, Oct. 1969.

7031. _____. "The women's movement is alive and kicking," *Chatelaine*, 50:2, Aug. 1977.

7032. Anglican Church of Canada. Commission on Women's Work. *Brief no. 52 to the Royal Commission on the Status of Women in Canada*. Toronto, 1968. 19p.

7033. Arnopoulos, Sheila and others. *To see ourselves: five views on Canadian women*. Ottawa: Canada. Privy Council Office. International Women's Year Secretariat, 1975. 225p.
       Contents: The non-professional working woman; A personal look at the homemaker today; Professional working woman; Disadvantaged woman; The young woman.

7034. Barnes, Angela. "The voice of women [interviews]," *Journal (The Board of Trade of Metropolitan Toronto)*, Easter 1977, pp.34-44.

7035. Bird, Florence. *Options unlimited: women in our developing society*. Fredericton: University of New Brunswick. Dept. of Public Relations and Development, 1975. 18p.

7036. _____. "Progress for Canadian women [1967-1977]," *Civil Service Review*, 50:21-4, Dec. 1977.

7037. Bourne, Paula. *Women in Canadian society*. Toronto: Ontario Institute for Studies in Education, 1976. 158p.

7038. Brown, Rosemary. "Women and the economy: bleak prospects," *Perception*, 2:31-3, Nov.-Dec. 1978.

7039. Burton, Jane. "Studies on the status of Canadian women," *Labour Gazette*, 76:377-80, July 1976. Re. Gail Cook's, *Opportunity for choice: a goal for women in Canada*.

284

7040. Campbell, C. "L'avilissement de la femme," *Relations*, no. 323:146-14-16, janv. 1968.
7041. _____. "L'evolution de la femme," *Relations*, no. 320:267-8, oct. 1967.
7042. _____. "La femme 'dans les limbes'," *Relations*, no. 341-234-7, sept. 1969.
7043. _____. "La femme doit humaniser la société," *Relations*, no. 336:80-3, mars 1969.
7044. _____. "Ma vie de femme," *Relations*, no. 318:206-7, juill.-août 1967.
7045. Canada. Co-ordinator, Status of Women. *Status of women in Canada, 1972*. [*La situation de la femme au Canada, 1972*]. [Ottawa: Information Canada, 1972]. 35, 39p.
7046. Canada. Office of the Co-ordinator, Status of Women. *Status of women in Canada*. [*La situation de la femme au Canada*]. Ottawa, 1975. 56, 54p.
7047. Canada. Dept. of External Affairs. *Women in Canada*. Rev. Reference paper, no. 99. Ottawa, 1973. 7p.
7048. Canada. Dept. of External Affairs. External Information Programs Division. *Women in Canada*. Reference series. Prepared by Canada. Dept. of Labour. Women's Bureau. Ottawa, 1980. 7p.
7049. Canada. Dept. of Labour. *Status of women in Canada, 1973*. [*La situation de la femme au Canada, 1973*]. By the Honourable John C. Munro, Minister of Labour, Minister Responsible for the Status of Women. Ottawa, 1972. 43, 45p.
7050. Canada. Federal-Provincial-Territorial Conference of Ministers Responsible for the Status of Women. [*Public documents*]. Ottawa, 1982. vp.
7051. Canada. Minister Responsible for the Status of Women. *Notes for an address by the Honourable Lloyd Axworthy, Minister Responsible for the Status of Women to the United Nations Decade for Women: Equality, Development and Peace, Copenhagen, July 15, 1980*. [Ottawa, 1980]. 16p.
7052. Canada. Privy Council Office. International Women's Year Secretariat. *Women in Canada*. 2nd ed. Prepared by Decision Marketing Research Ltd. Ottawa: Canada. Office of the Co-ordinator, Status of Women, [1976]. 256p.
7053. Canadian Federation of Business and Professional Women's Clubs. *Memorandum presented to the Right Honourable Lester B. Pearson, Prime Minister of Canada on Monday, February 21, 1966*. Ottawa, 1966. 26p.
7054. _____. *Memorandum presented to the Right Honourable Pierre Elliott Trudeau, Prime Minister of Canada*. Ottawa, 1973. 23p.

7055. Canadian Federation of University Women. *Brief no. 192 to the Royal Commission on the Status of Women in Canada*. Sudbury, Ont., n.d. 27p. and app.
7056. "Canadian women: a long way to go," *Time. Can. ed.*, 99:14-18, Mar. 20, 1972.
7057. Cartlidge, Thora and Sharon Batt. "Our readers on the women's movement [survey]," *Branching Out*, 6(1):18-21, 1979.
7058. Catholic Women's League of Canada. *Brief no. 56 to the Royal Commisssion on the Status of Women in Canada*. Cornwall, Ont., n.d. 21p.
7059. Chekki, Dan A. "The changing roles of women in Canada," *Sociologia Internationalis*, 14(1/2):201-20, 1976.
7060. Communist Party of Canada. Central Executive Committee. *Brief no. 126 to the Royal Commission on the Status of Women in Canada*. Toronto, 1968. 21p.
7061. *Condition féminine, condition masculine*. Québec: Université du Québec, Télé-université, 1980. 226, [160]p.
7062. Congress of Canadian Women. *Brief no. 139 to the Royal Commission on the Status of Women in Canada*. Toronto, 1968. 32p.
7063. Daly, M. "How women in power keep other women powerless," *Maclean's*, 83:38-41, Mar. 1970.
7064. Dickman, Thelma. "Women: sister you never had it so good," *Maclean's*, 87:10, Sept. 1974.
7065. Eichler, Margrit. "Sociology of feminist research in Canada," *Signs*, 3:409-22, Winter 1977.
7066. Fédération des femmes canadiennes-françaises. *La part des femmes, il faut la dire*. Ottawa, 1981. 151p.
    Brief interviews with French-Canadian women.

7067. Fitzgerald, Maureen, Connie Guberman and Margie Wolfe, eds. *Still ain't satisfied! Canadian feminism today*. Toronto: Women's Educational Press, 1982. 318p.

7068. Fremes, Ruth. *The Canadian woman's almanac*. Toronto: Methuen, 1978. 272p.

7069. Frum, Barbara. "Great dames: interviews," *Maclean's*, 86:32-8, 68, Apr. 1973.
      Re. Alice Munro, Peggy Sellers, Andrée Pelletier, Shirley Gibson, Lorraine Monk, Molly Bobak.

7070. Gelber, Sylva M. "Canada's international posture on the status of women," in *Women's Bureau '71*. Ottawa: Canada. Dept. of Labour. Women's Bureau, 1972, pp.29-36.

7071. _____. "What do women want?" in *Women's Bureau, '70*. Ottawa: Canada. Dept. of Labour. Women's Bureau, 1971, pp. 7-14.

7072. _____. "Women's responsibility in the search for equality of rights," in *Women's Bureau '72*. Ottawa: Canada. Dept. of Labour. Women's Bureau, 1973, pp.21-8.

7073. Gray, Charlotte. "Baby boom women: high hopes, uncertain prospects," *Chatelaine*, 56:50-1, 68-70, Aug. 1983.

7074. _____. "25 women to watch," *Chatelaine*, 53:32-5, Jan. 1980.

7075. Griffiths, N. E. S. *Penelope's web: some perceptions of women in European and Canadian society*. Toronto: Oxford University Press, 1976. 249p.

7076. Hawley, A. *Men's and women's liberation*. Ottawa: Canadian Union of Students. Secretariat, n.d. 5p.

7077. Hughes, D. O. "Sexual politics and social change," *Canadian Forum*, 50:277-9, Nov.-Dec. 1970.

7078. Imperial Order Daughters of the Empire. *Brief no. 311 to the Royal Commission on the Status of Women in Canada*. Toronto, 1968. 75p.

7079. *International women's day supplement*. [Ottawa]: Canadian University Press, [1979]. ca 300p.

7080. "Joint brief on status of women," *Canadian Labour*, 11:32, Dec. 1966.

7081. Johnson, Valerie Miner. "Meet Miss Canada: or, the rape of Cinderella," *Saturday Night*, 88:15-20, Feb. 1973.

7082. Kieran, Sheila H. "Who's downgrading women? Women," *Maclean's*, 81:18-19, 40-2, Aug. 1968.

7083. Lalonde, Marc. *Notes for an address to the Women's Canadian Club of Toronto*. Ottawa: Canada. Dept. of National Health and Welfare, 1975. 18p.

7084. Landsberg, Michele. *Women and children first: a provocative look at modern Canadian women at work and at home*. Toronto: MacMillan of Canada, 1982. 239p.

7085. League for Socialist Action. *The status of women in Canada*. Royal Commission on the Status of Women in Canada. Brief no. 163. Toronto: Crescent Publications, 1969. 4p.

7086. Liberal Party of Canada. Task Force on the Status of Women. *Final Report*. Ottawa, 1972. 19p.

7087. Martineau, B. "Thoughts about the objectification of women," *Take One*, 3:15-18, Nov.-Dec. 1970.

7088. Manuel, Philip A. "View from my bridge," *School Guidance Worker*, 31:35-9, Sept.-Oct. 1975.

7089. Matheson, Gwen, ed. *Women in the Canadian mosaic*. Toronto: Peter Martin, 1976. 353p.

7090. McGibbon, Pauline. "Women's Year: a hopeful milestone," *Canadian Business Review*, 2:1, Spring 1975.

7091. Michener, W. "Anything he can do, she can do better," *Saturday Night*, 84:24-6, Jan. 1969.

7092. "Minister announces plan of action [address by Marc Lalonde]," *Information - Status of Women*, 2(2):1-2, 4, 6, [English]; 1, 3, 5 [French], 1978.

7093. Moscarello, Rebeka. "Thoughts on the status of women," *Canada's Mental Health*, 20:30-5, Jan.-Feb. 1972.

7094. Mungall, Constance. "10 most powerful women in Canada," *Chatelaine*, 50:54-5, 102+ , Dec. 1977.

286

7095. Morissette, Y. R. *Brief no. 322 to the Royal Commission on the Status of Women in Canada.* [*Expo*]. Montreal, 1968. 22p.

7096. National Council of Women of Canada. *Brief no. 131 to the Royal Commission on the Status of Women in Canada.* Ottawa, 1968. 22p.

7097. New Democratic Party. *Women in Canada: in society, in public life, in the NDP.* Ottawa: New Democratic Party, 1971. 16p.

7098. Nunes, Maxine. *The lace ghetto.* Toronto: New Press, 1972. 152p.

7099. Paris, Erna. "Women's status - how the MPs rate you," *Chatelaine*, 45:28-9, 102, 104-6, 108, 110-3, May 1972.

7100. Pelrine, Eleanor Wright. "IWY postscript with Dr. Katie Cooke," *Chatelaine*, 50:26, 60-2, Feb. 1977.

7101. Phillips, M. "Lives of girls and women [interviews]," *Maclean's*, 88:22-5, Feb. 1975.

7102. "Progress report on the status of women," *Labour Gazette*, 74:200-2, Mar. 1974.

7103. Rae, Jane. "Today's woman: a description," *Stimulus*, May-June 1978, pp.20-1.

7104. Reeves, John. "Celebration of women," *Chatelaine*, 48:68-72, Oct. 1975.

7105. Rhodes, A. "She's putting women back in chains," *Financial Post*, 65:32, Jan. 23, suppl.1971.

7106. Ross, Valerie. "The champs: women who won in 1977," *Chatelaine*, 51:34-5, Jan. 1978.

7107. Saskatoon Women's Calendar Collective. *Herstory: a Canadian women's calendar, 1975.* Toronto: Canadian Women's Educational Press, 1974. 150p. Annual.

7108. Schmid, Carol. "The 'changing' status of women in the United States and Canada," *McMaster University. Sociology of Women Programme. Occasional Papers*, no. 1, Spring 1977, pp.231-65.

7109. Schreiber, E. M. "The social bases of opinions on woman's role in Canada," *Canadian Journal of Sociology*, 1:61-74, Spring 1975.

7110. "Status of women: where is it at?" *Labour Gazette*, 73:382-4, June 1973.

7111. Stephenson, Marylee ed. *Women in Canada.* Toronto: New Press, 1973. 331p.

7112. _____. ed. *Women in Canada.* Rev. ed. Don Mills, Ont.: General Publishing Co., 1977. 368p.

7113. Stienecker, Sandy. "The changing role of women," in Anne MacLennan, ed., *Women: their use of alcohol and other legal drugs: a provincial consultation - 1976.* Toronto: Addiction Research Foundation of Ontario, 1976, pp.3-19.

7114. "The status of women today and tomorrow," *Bank Canadian National. Monthly Bulletin*, 7:1-4, Jan. 1976.

7115. Tisseyre, Michelle A. *L'encyclopédie de la femme canadienne.* Montréal: Messageries du Saint-Laurent, 1966. 1056p.

7116. Trudeau, P. E. *The evolving role of the Canadian woman: an address by the Prime Minister, the Right Honourable P. E. Trudeau, Mar. 3, 1971.* Statements and speeches, no. 71/9. Ottawa: Canada. Dept. of External Affairs. Information Division, 1971. 8p.

7117. Turner, Lynda E. *Woman in Canadian society.* [New Westminster, B.C.: Douglas College, 1972]. 208p.
Collection of reprints from periodicals, books, papers, etc.

7118. *Women in society*, by Wayne Sproule and others. Toronto: Maclean Hunter Learning Materials Co., 1971. 52p.

7119. "Women 75 Canada. Chatelaine salutes Canadian women for Women's Year 1975," *Chatelaine*, 48:34-5, Jan. 1975.

7120. Wyman, Georgina. "Pauline Jewett: an interview," *Branching Out*, 1:20-3, 38, Sept.-Oct. 1974.

7121. Young Women's Christian Association of Canada. *Brief no. 160 to the Royal Commission on the Status of Women in Canada.* Toronto, 1968. 55p. and app.

WOMEN - CANADA - BIBLIOGRAPHY

7122. Banks, May. *Material relating to women in the Reference Collection, Dana Porter Arts Library, University of Waterloo.* Waterloo: The Library, 1975. 22p.

7123. Canada. Dept. of the Secretary of State. Library. *Women: a selective bibliography of the holdings of the Library*, prepared by Charlene Elgee. [Ottawa], 1978. 36p.

7124. Canada. Dept. of the Secretary of State. Women's Programme. *Women's resource catalogue. [Catalogue de références de la femme]*. Ottawa, 1982. 73, 64p.

7125. Dallaire, Marie. *Liste bibliographique thème condition féminine*. Montréal: Corporation professionnelle des travailleurs sociaux du Québec, 1982. 10p.

7126. Eichler, Margrit and Lynne Primrose. "A bibliography of materials on Canadian women - pertinent to the social sciences and published between 1950 and 1970," in Marylee Stephenson, *Women in Canada*. Toronto: New Press, 1973, pp.291-326.

7127. Eichler, Margrit, Jennifer Newton, and Lynne Primrose. "A bibliography of materials on Canadian women - pertinent to the social sciences and published between 1950 and 1975," in Marylee Stephenson, *Women in Canada*. Rev. ed. Toronto: General Publishing Co., 1977, pp.275-368.

7128. Farrar, Mary, comp. *Women's Resource Area: a bibliography*. [Welland, Ont.: Niagara College. Women's Rsource Area], 1981. [21]p.

7129. Hauck, Philomena. *Sourcebook on Canadian women*. Ottawa: Canadian Library Association, 1979. 111p.

7130. Hood, D. D. and others. *Women in the Canadian culture: a selected bibliography*. Waterloo: W.O.M.E.N. Education News, [1976?] Looseleaf.
    Contents: Dramatic arts; Historical contributions of women; Labour force; Law; Literature; Media; Music; People and society; Politics; Science; Sexism in education; Sex roles and stereotypes; Sports.

7131. Light, Beth and Alison Prentice. *Recent publications in Canadian women's history*. Canadian women's history series, no. 2. Toronto: Ontario Institute for Studies in Education. Dept. of History and Philosophy of Education. Women in Canadian History Project, 1977. 36p.

7132. Light, Beth and Veronica Strong-Boag. *True daughters of the north: Canadian women's history: an annotated bibliography*. OISE bibliography series, no. 5. Toronto: Ontario Institute for Studies in Education, 1980. 210p.

7133. Light, Beth. "Recent publications in Canadian women's history," *Canadian Women's Studies / Les cahiers de la femme*, 3(1):114-17, 1981.

7134. *On the status of women in Canada: a bibliography of bibliographies, with selected materials on related subjects (1970-1975)*. [Ottawa]: Canada. Dept. of National Health and Welfare. Departmental Library Services, 1975. 8p.

7135. Ontario. Ministry of Education. *Girls and women in society; resource list*. [Toronto, 1977]. 21p.

7136. Pierson, Ruth and Beth Light. "Women in the teaching and writing of Canadian history," *History and Social Science Teacher*, 17:83-95, Winter 1982.

7137. Royal Commission on the Status of Women in Canada. *Bibliography*. Ottawa, 1968. 42p.

7138. Samson, Marcelle Germain. *Des livres et des femmes: bibliographie*. Québec: Conseil du statut de la femme, 1978. 254p.

7139. Seifert, Carol. "An inventory of articles concerning women in the Canadian Magazine, 1883-1919," *Resources for Feminist Research*, 8:56-67, July 1979.

7140. Stevens, Alta Mae and Linda McDowell. "Filling in the picture: resources for teaching about women in Canada," *History and Social Science Teacher*, 14:7-14, Fall 1978.

7141. Swanick, Lynne Struthers. *A checklist of Canadian federal, provincial and municipal government publications of special significance for women*. Exchange bibliography, no. 1118. Monticello, Ill.: Council of Planning Librarians, 1976. 20p.

7142. University of British Columbia. Women's Resources Centre. *Annotated bibliography for women's studies for high school students*. Vancouver: University of British Columbia. Women's Resources Centre / Daytime Program, Centre for Continuing Education, 1976. 126p.

7143. Waterloo. University. Library. Lady Aberdeen Collection. *A catalogue of the Lady Aberdeen Library on the history of women in the University of Waterloo Library donated by the National Council of Women of Canada*, compiled by Jane Britton. University of Waterloo Library bibliography, no. 7. Waterloo, Ont.: University of Waterloo Library, 1982. 237p.

7144. Young Women's Christian Association (Montreal). Roles of Women Study Committee. *Bibliography*. Rev. ed. Montreal, 1966. 47p.

WOMEN - CANADA - HISTORY

7145. Andrews, Margaret W. "Review article: attitudes in Canadian women's history, 1945-1975," *Journal of Canadian Studies*, 12:69-78, Summer 1977.

7146. Andersen, Margaret, comp. *Mother was not a person*. 2nd ed. Montreal: Content Publishers Ltd. / Black Rose Books, 1974. 253p.

7147. Bacchi, Carol. "Race regeneration and social purity: a study of the social attitudes of Canada's English-speaking suffragists," *Histoire sociale / Social History*, 11:460-74, Nov. 1978.

7148. Bassett, John M. *Elizabeth Simcoe: first lady of Upper Canada*. Don Mills, Ont.: Fitzhenry & Whiteside, 1974. 61p. French edition: *Elisabeth Simcoe: la première dame du Haut-Canada*.

7149. Bassett, John M. and A. Roy Petrie. *Laura Secord: a Canadian heroine*. Don Mills, Ont.: Fitzhenry & Whiteside, 1974. 61p.

7150. Buckley, Suzann. "British female emigration and imperial development: experiments in Canada, 1885-1931," *Hecate*, 3(2):26-40, 1977.

7151. Conrad, Margaret. "'No discharge in this war': a note on the history of women and aging," *Resources for Feminist Research*, 11:216-18, July 1982.

7152. Cook, Ramsay and Wendy Mitchinson, eds. *The proper sphere: woman's place in Canadian society*. Toronto: Oxford University Press, 1976. 334p.
    Includes articles on the following topics: legal rights, education, work, organizations, morality and suffrage.

7153. Corrective Collective. *She named it Canada: because that's what it was called*. 3rd rev. ed. Vancouver: Press Gang Publishers, 1972. 80p.

7154. Durham, Louise Elizabeth Grey. *Letters and diaries of Lady Durham*, edited by Patricia Godsell. n.p.: Oberon Press, 1979. 203p.

7155. Federation of Women Teachers' Associations of Ontario. *The visible woman: a history of women and of women's rights in Canada*, by Beryl Fox with Annette Cohen and Jean Cochrane. [Toronto]: The Federation, n.d. [22]p.

7156. Fox, Beryl and Annette Cohen. *Visible woman: a history of women and of women's rights in Canada*. n.p.: Federation of Women Teachers' Associations of Ontario, [1975?] [21]p.

7157. Gorham, Deborah. "Singing up the hill," *Canadian Dimension*, 10:26-38, June 1975.

7158. Hawken, Ann. "The image of the new woman at work in Canada, 1890-1915," *Canadian Woman Studies / Les cahiers de la femme*, 3:59, Summer 1982.

7159. Hotchkiss, Ron. "Women in the 1920's: becoming persons," *Canada & the World*, 46:12-13, Nov. 1980.

7160. Johnston, Jean. *Wilderness women: Canada's forgotten history*. Toronto: Peter Martin, 1973. 242p.

7161. Labarge, Margaret Wade, Micheline D. Johnson and Margaret E. MacLellan. *Cultural tradition and political history of women in Canada*. Royal Commission on the Status of Women in Canada. Study no. 8. Ottawa: Information Canada, 1971. v.p.

7162. Lenskyj, Helen. "Social change affecting women in urban Canada, 1890-1930, and its impact upon immigrant women in the labour force." MA thesis, University of Toronto, 1980. 152p.

7163. L'Espérance, Jeanne. *The widening sphere: women in Canada, 1870-1940*. [*Vers des horizons nouveaux: la femme canadienne de 1870 à 1940*]. [Ottawa]: Public Archives Canada, 1982. 65p.

7164. Light, Beth and Alison Prentice, eds. *Pioneer and gentlewomen of British North America, 1713-1867*. Documents in Canadian women's history, no. 1. Toronto: New Hogtown Press, 1980. 245p.

7165. Light, Beth and Veronica Strong-Boag. *True daughters of the North: Canadian women's history: an annotated bibliography*. OISE bibliography series, no. 5. Toronto: Ontario Institute for Studies in Education, 1980. 210p.

7166. Lischke-McNab, Ute and David McNab. "Petition from the backwoods [Catharine Parr Traill]," *Beaver*, 308:51-7, Summer 1977.

7167. MacKenzie, Suzanne. *Women and the reproduction of labour power in the industrial city: a case study*. Brighton, Eng.: University of Sussex. Urban and Regional Studies, 1980. 172p.

7168. "Milestones," *Canada & the World*, 46:22, Nov. 1980.

7169. National Council of Women of Canada. *Women of Canada: their life and work*. [Montreal]: National Council of Women of Canada, 1975. 442p. Reprint of the 1900? ed.
    French edition: *Les femmes du Canada*.

7170. Pitters-Caswell, Marian Irene. "Woman's participation in sporting activities as an indicator of femininity and cultural evolution in Toronto, 1910 to 1920." MHK thesis, University of Windsor, 1975. 194p. (Can. theses, no.29223)

7171. MacLellan, Margaret. "History of women's rights in Canada," *Status of Women News*, 1(2):16-20, 1974.

7172. McKenzie, Ruth. *Laura Secord: the legend and the lady*. Toronto: McClelland and Stewart, 1971. 142p.

7173. Ray, Janet. *Towards women's rights*. Focus on Canadian history series. Toronto: Grolier, 1981. 96p.
    Secondary school level.

7174. Read, Daphne, ed. *The great war and Canadian society: an oral history*. Toronto: New Hogtown Press, 1978. 223p.

7175. Schmid, Carol. "The changing status of women in the United States and Canada: an overview," *Sociological Symposium*, 15:1-27, Spring 1976.

7176. Strong-Boag, Veronica. "'You be sure to tell it like it is': the recovery of Canada's past [review article]," *Journal of Canadian Studies*, 16:217-21, Fall-Winter 1981.

7177. Trofimenkoff, Susan Mann and Alison Prentice. *The neglected majority: essays in Canadian women's history*. Toronto: McClelland and Stewart, 1977. 192p.

7178. Turner, Wesley. "80 stout and healthy looking girls," *Canada: an Historical Magazine*, 3:37-49, Dec. 1975.

7179. Van Kirk, Sylvia. "Women and the fur trade," *Beaver*, Outfit 303:4-21, Winter 1972.

7180. Zaremba, Eve, comp. *Privilege of sex: a century of Canadian women*. Toronto: Anansi, 1974. 173p.

WOMEN - LABRADOR

7181. Campbell, Lydia. "Sketches of a Labrador life, [1893-1894]," *Canadian Women's Studies / Les cahiers de la femme*, 3(1):4-9, 1981.

7182. Goudie, Elizabeth. *Woman of Labrador*. Toronto: Peter Martin Associates, 1973. 166p.

7183. Lawrence, Judith. "Elizabeth Goudie: how life was in that time," *Broadside*, 1(9):6, 1980.

7184. Saunders, Doris. "A daughter of Labrador," *Canadian Women's Studies / Les cahiers de la femme*, 2(1):105, 1980.

7185. St. John's Local Council of Women. *Remarkable women of Newfoundland and Labrador*. St. John's, Nfld.: Valhalla Press Canada, 1976. 78p.

WOMEN - MANITOBA

7186. Balderstone, Helen and others. *Women in the community*. Winnipeg: Manitoba. Dept. of Labour. Women's Bureau, 1975. 98p. (Profile 77-0097)

7187. Croteau, Mary J. and Wendy Zink. *Women's concerns about the quality of life in Winnipeg.* Winnipeg: Institute of Urban Studies, University of Winnipeg, 1975. 53, [15]p.

7188. Luxton, Margaret. "Why women's work is never done: a case study from Flin Flon, Manitoba of domestic labour in industrial capitalist society." PhD diss., University of Toronto, 1978. 364p. (Can. theses, no.38766)

7189. Luxton, Meg. "Motherwork: more than a labour of love," *Canadian Women's Studies / Les cahiers de la femme*, 2(1):31-5, 1980.
    Excerpt from *More than a labour of love*.

WOMEN - MANITOBA - BIBLIOGRAPHY

7190. Atmikov, Pam and others. *Out from the shadows: a bibliography of the history of women in Manitoba.* [Winnipeg]: Manitoba Human Rights Commission, 1975. 64p.

WOMEN - MANITOBA - HISTORY

7191. Francis, Alice Katharine. *From Ty Mawr to Two Bar.* Brandon, Man.: A.K. Francis, 1975. 136p.

7192. Healy, W. J. *Women of Red River: being a book written from the recollections of women surviving from the Red River era.* Rev. ed. Winnipeg: Peguis Pub., 1977. 274p.
    First edition c. 1923, republished 1970.

7193. Manitoba Women's Institute. *The great human heart: a history of the Manitoba Women's Institute, 1910-1980.* Winnipeg, 1980. 143p.

7194. Manitoba. Dept. of Cultural Affairs and Historical Resources. *E. Cora Hind.* Winnipeg, 1982. 9p. (Microlog 82-3234)

7195. McDowell, Linda. "Harriet Dick - a lady ahead of her time?" *Manitoba Pageant*, 20:11-13, Summer 1975.

7196. Peterkin, Audrey and Margaret Shaw. *Mrs. Doctor: reminiscences of Manitoba doctors' wives.* Winnipeg: Prairie Publishing Co., 1976. 168p.

7197. Saint-Pierre, Annette. "Les Manitobaines et l'argent," *Canadian Women Studies / Les cahiers de la femme*, 3:26-7, Summer 1982.

7198. Smith, Marilyn. *Women in Manitoba history - herstory research and biographies.* Winnipeg: Manitoba. Dept. of Tourism, Recreation and Cultural Affairs. Historic Resources Branch, 1974. 42p.

WOMEN - NEW BRUNSWICK

7199. Breau, Alice. "Situation de la femme acadienne," *Canadian Woman Studies / Les cahiers de la femme*, 3:37-8, Summer 1982.

7200. Lemieux, Thérèse et Gemma Caron. *Silhouettes acadiennes.* n.p.: [Fédération des dames d'Acadie], 1981. 374p.

7201. McGee, Arlee. "A grandmother to three thousand people: New Brunswick's equivalent to Mother Theresa," *Atlantic Advocate*, 71:18-21, 23, Mar. 1981.

7202. Mungall, Constance. "Pattern-breakers of New Brunswick," *Chatelaine*, 50:30-3, 49-51, July 1977.

7203. New Brunswick. Advisory Council on the Status of Women. *Annual report.* 1st, 1978/79- . (Microlog 80-0940)

7204. New Brunswick. Executive Council. *Government of New Brunswick plan of action on the status of women.* [Fredericton], 1980. 11p.

7205. New Brunswick. Interdepartmental Committee on the Role of Women in the New Brunswick Economy and Society. *Report.* [Fredericton, N.B.], 1975. 169p. (Profile 76-0068)

7206. Sealy, Nanciellen. "Acadian women: economic development, ethnicity, and the status of women," in Jean Leonard Elliott, ed., *Two nations, many cultures: ethnic groups in Canada.* Scarborough, Ont.: Prentice-Hall, 1979, pp.123-35.

7207. Swanick, M. Lynne. "Women in New Brunswick: bibliography," *Emergency Librarian*, 2:19-21, Dec. 1974.

WOMEN - NEW BRUNSWICK - HISTORY

7208. Robinson, Charlotte Gourlay. *Pioneer profiles of New Brunswick settlers*. Belleville, Ont.: Mika Pub. Co., 1980. 221p.

WOMEN - NEWFOUNDLAND

7209. Antler, Ellen. "The economics of 'home economics': a Newfoundland example," *Resources for Feminist Research*, 11:19-20, Mar. 1982.

7210. Benoit, Cecilia. "The poverty of mothering: a case study of women in a Newfoundland community." MA thesis, Memorial University of Newfoundland, 1982. (Can. theses, no.53316)

7211. Canadian Federation of University Women, Grand Falls Branch. *A study of the economic status of women in Newfoundland*. Royal Commission on the Status of Women in Canada. Brief no. 77. Grand Falls, Newfoundland, n.d. 8p.

7212. Canadian Federation of University Women of St. John's, Newfoundland. *Brief no. 209 to the Royal Commission on the Status of Women in Canada*. St. John's, Newfoundland, 1968. 18p.

7213. Davis, Dona Lee. *Blood and nerves: an ethnographic focus on menopause*. Social and economic studies, no. 28. St. John's, Nfld.: Institute of Social and Economic Research, Queen's College, Memorial University of Newfoundland, 1983.

7214. _____. *Women's experience of menopause in a Newfoundland fishing village*. n.p., 1980. 293p.

7215. Gleason, Marie. "Women in Newfoundland fishing communities...they had to be pretty good skippers themselves... ," *Atlantic Advocate*, 66:51-2, Mar. 1976.

7216. Goundrey, Shirley. *A history of the Newfoundland Status of Women Council from April 1972-January 1975*. [St. John's], 1975. 20p.

7217. Hiscock, Pamela Ruth. "A report on the development of two instructional units on women of Newfoundland and Labrador entitled Mary Southcott and Georgina Stirling." MEd thesis, University of Newfoundland, 1982. (Can. theses, no.53330)

7218. Manuel, Ella. "Ella Manuel: a person in her own right [interview]," *Broadside*, 2:5, Feb. 1981.

7219. Miller, Ann. "Narration and life history of a Newfoundland woman." MA thesis, McMaster University, 1981. 197p. (Can. theses, no.54184)

7220. Murray, Hilda Chaulk. *More than fifty percent: woman's life in a Newfoundland outport, 1900-1950*. Memorial University of Newfoundland folklore and language publications monograph series, no. 2. [St. John's]: Breakwater Books, 1979. 160p.

7221. Murray, Hilda, E. L. "The traditional role of women in a Newfoundland fishing community." MA thesis, Memorial University of Newfoundland, 1972. 319p. (Can. theses, no.11896)

WOMEN - NEWFOUNDLAND - HISTORY

7222. Harrington, Michael Francis. "Ann Hulan: a Newfoundland pioneer," *Atlantic Advocate*, 71:39-41, Jan. 1981.

7223. McCarthy, Michael. "Role of the woman in Newfoundland history," *Newfoundland Teachers' Association. Journal*, 65:34-47, Summer 1974.

7224. O'Neill, Paul. "Jezebels and the just (women in Newfoundland 1500-1800)," *Newfoundland Quarterly*, 76:25-30, Dec. 1980.

7225. St. John's Local Council of Women. *Remarkable women of Newfoundland and Labrador*. St. John's, Nfld.: Valhalla Press Canada, 1976. 78p.

WOMEN - NORTHWEST TERRITORIES

7226. Leishman, H. *The status of women, Northwest Territories*. Yellowknife: Indian-Eskimo Association of Canada, Northwest Territories, n.d.

7227. Northwest Territories. [Dept. of Planning and Evaluation]. *International Women's Year community relations programs*. [Yellowknife, 1975]. 112p. (Profile 77-0815)

WOMEN - NOVA SCOTIA

7228. Bruce, Harry. "Women of Halifax: the pattern breakers," *Chatelaine*, 47:38-9, 77-9, Dec. 1974.
7229. Maritime School of Social Work. Women's Group. *Singly more; a handbook for women working with women*. [Halifax, N.S., 1977]. 58p.
7230. Nova Scotia. Advisory Council. *Status of Women. Implementation report: what has happened to the ninety-five recommendations contained in the Nova Scotia Task Force Report on the Status of Women in 1976*. [Halifax], 197?. (Microlog 81-2116)
7231. Nova Scotia. Task Force on the Status of Women. *Herself: report of the Nova Scotia Task Force on the Status of Women*. [*Elle-même: rapport de la Commission d'enquête sur le statut de la femme en Nouvelle Écosse.*) Halifax, 1976. 91p.

WOMEN - NOVA SCOTIA - HISTORY

7232. Blakeley, Phyllis R. "And having a love for people [Elizabeth O. M. P. Doane]," *Nova Scotia Historical Quarterly*, 5:167-76, June 1975.
7233. Stirling, Lilla. *In the vanguard: Nova Scotia women, mid-twentieth century*. Windsor, N.S.: Lancelot Press, 1976. 72p.
7234. Colchester Historical Museum, comp. *Colchester women*. Truro, N.S.: Colchester Historical Museum, 1978. 92p.
7235. Gérin, Pierre M. "Une femme à la recherche et à la défense de l'identité acadienne à la fin du XIXe siècle, Marichette," *Revue de l'Université de Moncton*, 11:17-26, mai 1978.
7236. MacHab-de Viles, Georgina and Pieter J. de Viles. "Subsistence agriculture, wage labour and the definition of women's roles: a Cape Breton example," *Resources for Feminist Research*, 11:8-10, Mar. 1982.
7237. Ross, Beatrice Spence. "Adaptation in exile: Loyalist women in Nova Scotia after the American Revolution." PhD diss., Cornell University, 1981. 376p. (UM, 81-10998)

WOMEN - ONTARIO

7238. Blanchard, Don. "Why not?" *CA Magazine*, 110:11, May 1977.
7239. Chambers, Patricia. *Women's resource manual*. St. Thomas, Ont.: Young Women's Christian Association, 1978. 64p.
7240. Ontario. Office of the Provincial Secretary for Social Development. *Equal opportunity for women in Ontario: a plan for action*. Toronto, 1973. 73p. (Profile 73-0373)
7241. Ontario Status of Women Council. *Annual report*. 1st, 1974- . (Profile 75-0051)
7242. Pelletier, Jacqueline. "Les Franco-Ontariennes," *Canadian Women's Studies / Les cahiers de la femme*, 2(2):60-3, 1980.
7243. Redmond, Sarah and Eileen Turcotte. "Women of Ottawa: the pattern breakers," *Chatelaine*, 47:26-9, 42-3, 45, Aug. 1974.
7244. Toronto. Mayor's Task Force on the Status of Women in Toronto. *Final report*. Toronto, 1975. 146p. and app. (Profile 76-0263)
7245. Whissel-Tregonning, Marguerite. *Kitty, le gai pinson: résumé de la vie d'une pionnière du nord de l'Ontario écrit en français-canadien*. Sudbury, Ont.: Prise de parole, 1978. 218p.

WOMEN - ONTARIO - HISTORY

7246. Bell, Lily M. and Kathleen E. Bray. *Women of action: St. Catharines and area, 1876-1976*. St. Catharines: Published for the Local Council of Women for International Women's Year 1975 and St. Catharines Centennial 1976, 1976. 134p.
7247. Cake, Sharon. *Eminent women of Grey County*. Owen Sound, Ont.: Grey County Historical Society, 1977. 133p.

7248. Carter, Charles Ambrose and Thomas Melville Bailey, eds. *The diary of Sophia MacNab*. 2nd. ed. rev. Hamilton, Ont.: W.L. Griffin, 1974. 88p.

7249. Corbett, Gail. *Portraits: Peterborough area women past and present*. Peterborough: Portraits' Group, 1975. 206p.

7250. Dyer, Brenda and others. *Outstanding women of Oxford County*. Woodstock, Ont.: Oxford County Board of Education, 1979.

7251. Greenland, Cyril. "Mary Edwards Merrill, 1858-1880: 'the psychic'", *Ontario History*, 68:81-92, June 1976.

7252. Katz, Michael B. "On the condition of women 1851-1861 [Hamilton]," in, *Canadian Social History Project: Interim report no. 4; working paper no. 29*. Toronto: Ontario Institute for Studies in Education, Dept. of History and Philosophy, 1972, pp.16-25.

7253. Kolasiewicz, Sarah. "Outstanding women of Oxford County," *Canadian Women's Studies / Les cahiers de la femme*, 3(1):50-1, 1981.

7254. Roberts, Wayne. "Six new women: a guide to the mental map of women reformers in Toronto," *Atlantis*, 3:145-64, Autumn 1977.

7255. Shortt, Elizabeth Smith. *'A woman with a purpose': the diaries of Elizabeth Smith 1872-84*. Edited by Veronica Strong-Boag. Toronto: University of Toronto Press, 1980.

7256. Tivy, Louis. *Your loving Anna: letters from the Ontario frontier*. Toronto: University of Toronto Press, 1972. 120p.

7257. Trow, Susan. *Coming out: six generations of women*. Toronto: Art Gallery of Ontario, 1978. 40p.
    Photographs with accompanying text.

7258. Van Norman, Catherine Bell. *Catherine Bell Van Norman: her diary, 1850*. Burlington, Ont.: Burlington Historical Society, 1981. 61p.

7259. "Women" in Barbara M. Wilson, ed., *Ontario and the first world war, 1914-1918: a collection of documents*. Toronto: Champlain Society, 1977, pp. lxxxv - xciv [Introduction]: pp. 101-47 [Documents].

WOMEN - PRINCE EDWARD ISLAND

7260. Basiletti, Mari, Donna Greenwood and Beverly Mills Stetson. *Changing times: essays by island women*. Charlottetown: Women's Legal Project of P.E.I., 1977. 67p.

7261. Clark, Marlene-Russell. "Women and the Island heritage," in Harry Baglole, ed., *Exploring island history: a guide to the historical resources of Prince Edward Island*. Belfast, P.E.I.: Ragweed Press, 1977, pp.119-24.

7262. Mungall, Constance. "Pattern-breakers of Prince Edward Island," *Chatelaine*, 49:48-50, 74-8, May 1976.

7263. Prince Edward Island. Advisory Council on the Status of Women. *Annual report*. 1st, 1975/76- .

7264. Prince Edward Island. Provincial Advisory Committee on the Status of Women in the Province of Prince Edward Island. *Report*. Charlottetown, 1973. 192p.

7265. Zonta Club of Charlottetown, comp. *Outstanding women of Prince Edward Island*. Charlottetown, P.E.I., 1981. 163p.

WOMEN - QUEBEC

7266. Association féminine d'éducation et d'action sociale. *Dans l'histoire...des femmes aussi...au Saguenay-Lac-St-Jean*. 2 vols. Chicoutimi, Qué.: Éditions Science moderne, 1978-1980.

7267. _____. *Participation de la femme dans la société et dans l'église*. Montréal: Secrétariat général de l'A.F.E.A.S., 1974.

7268. Beattie, Margaret. "La politique d'ensemble. 'Pour les Québécoises: égalité et indépendance' du Conseil du Statut de la Femme du Québec... ," *Resources for Feminist Research*, 9:32-4, Nov. 1980.

7269. Bertrand, Marie-Andrée. "La Québecoise entre hier et demain," *Forces*, no. 45:3-15, 1978.

294

7270. Bhérer, Jacinthe et Monique des Rivières. *Statistiques diverses sur les femmes du Québec*. Québec: Conseil du statut de la femme, 1974. 15p.

7271. Bouchard, Laurette. *Courtepointe d'une grand-mère*. Hull, Québec: Éditions Asticou, 1981. 89p.

7272. Carisse, Colette et Joffre Dumazedier. *Les femmes innovatrices: problèmes post-industriels d'une Amérique francophone, le Québec*. Paris: Éditions du Seuil, 1975. 283p.

7273. Centre de recherche sur la femme. *Analyse socio-économique de la ménagère québécoise*, par Carmell Benoit et autres. Montréal, 1972. 287p.

7274. Charney, Ann. "Quebec: no more 'happiness' schools," *Ms*, 4:27-30, Mar. 1976.

7275. ----------. "The passionate quest of Quebec's separatist women," *Chatelaine*, 52:54-5, 146+ , March 1979.

7276. Cloutier, Renée et autres. *Femmes et cultures au Québec: un avant-projet de chantier*. Institut québécois de research sur la culture. Documents préliminaires, no. 3. Québec: Institut québécois de recherche sur la culture, 1982. 105p.

7277. Cohen, Yolande, ed. *Femmes et politique*. Montréal: Le Jour, 1981. 227p.

7278. Conklin, Elizabeth Nancy. "Women's voluntary associations in French Montreal: a study of changing institutions and attitudes." PhD diss., University of Illinois at Urbana, 1972. 308p. (UM73-9909)

7279. Corporation des enseignants du Québec et Centrale de l'enseignement du Québec. *Condition féminine: XXIVième congrès de la Corporation des enseignants du Québec: 1er congrès de la Centrale de l'enseignement du Québec*. Québec: CEQ, 1974. 52p.

7280. Dagenais, Huguette. "L'evolution des Québécoises en période de luttes féministes," *Atlantis*, 4:146-56, Spring 1979, Part II.

7281. Danylewycz, Marta and Jacinthe Fraser. "Les femmes au Québec: quelques récents développements," *Canadian Newsletter of Research on Women*, 7:62-8, Nov. 1978.

7282. Denatie, Francine. "La femme dans la vie économique et sociale du Québec," *Forces*, no. 27:15-22, 1974.

7283. Descôteaux, Aurore Dessureault et Yolande Buist Bordeleau, comp. *Passé et présent au féminin*. Trois-Rivières, Québec: Éditions du Bien Public, 1979. 174p.

7284. Dolment, Marcelle and Marcel Barthe. *La femme au Québec*. Montréal: Presses Libres, 1973. 158p.

7285. Duguay, Diane et Gaétane Leblanc. *Femmes traditionnelles ou modernes: Chandler-Nouvelle*. Rimouski, Québec: Collège de Rimouski, 1975. 105p.

7286. Duguay, Marie-Anne. *Lettres d'une paysanne à son fils*, compilé par Jeanne L'Archevêque-Duguay. Montréal: Leméac, 1977. 214p.

7287. Dumais, Monique. "Face à l'actualité: égalité et indépendance," *Relations*, 38:323, déc. 1978.

7288. ----------. "Sages-femmes demandées," dans Rodrigue Bélanger et autres, eds., *Devenirs de femmes*. Cahiers de recherche éthique, no. 8. Montréal: Éditions Fides, 1981, pp.9-17.

7289. *Figures du temps de nos grand'mères*. Sainte-Anne-de-la-Pérade, Qué.: Éditions du Bien Public, 1976. 39p.

7290. Fortier-Langlois, Suzanne et autres. *Personnalités féminines: Sita Riddez, Marguerite Paquet, Gertrude Néron, Edouardina Dupont, Jeanne L'Archevêque-Duguay*. Chicoutimi: Editions Science moderne, 1975. 176p.

7291. Fournier, Francine. "Le Québec de 1978 et les femmes," *Resources for Feminist Research*, 8:28-9, Mar. 1979.

7292. Fournier, Gaétane et Sylvia Morin. *Des femmes au pouvoir*. Sherbrooke, Québec: Éditions Sherbrooke, 1978. 119p.

7293. Gelber, Sylva M. "Quebec's contribution to the status of women in Canada," in, *Women's Bureau '73*. Ottawa: Canada. Dept. of Labour. Women's Bureau, 1974, pp.44-51.

7294. Germain, Nicole, pseud. et Liette Desjardins. *La femme émancipée*. Montréal: Éditions de l'Homme, 1971, 119p.

7295. Germain, Nicole. *Sachons nous débrouiller*. Montréal: Québécor, 1980. 117p.

7296. Gervais, Solange Fernet. "Regroupement des femmes au Québec," *Resources for Feminist Research*, 11:64-5, Mar. 1982.

7297. Granger, D. and Adamcyk La Pierre. "Les taux d'activité chez les québécoises francophones," *Population et famille*, 34(1):1-27, 1975.

7298. Gratton-Boucher, Marie. "Pour les Québecoises: égalité et indépendance, un lieu de réflexion théologique," *Relations*, 39:149-54, mai 1979.

7299. G.R.A.F.S. *Nous, notre santé, nos pouvoirs*. Montréal: Éditions coopératives Albert Saint-Martin, 1983. 204p.

7300. Houle, Ghislaine. "La situation de la femme au Québec," *Bibliothèque nationale de Québec. Bulletin*, sept. 1974, pp.12-3.

7301. "In memorium: Madeleine G. Dubuc, Fédération des femmes du Québec," *Canadian Women's Studies / Les cahiers de la femme*, 3(1):118, 1981.

7302. Jean, Michèle. "Les Québécoises, ont-elles une histoire?" *Forces*, no. 27:4-14, 1974.

7303. Jean, Michèle et Marie Lavigne ed. *Québécoises du 20e siècle*. Montréal: Éditions du Jour, 1974. 303p.

7304. _____. "Le phénomène des Yvettes: analyse externe,"*Atlantis*, 6:17-23, Spring 1981. tis, 6:17-23, Spring 1981.

7305. _____. "Condition féminine et féminisme au Québec: ou en sommes-nous?" *Communauté chrétienne*, no. 95:441-9, sept.-oct. 1977.

7306. "La condition economique des femmes au Québec. Collection études et dossiers, la documentation Québécoise, Ministère des communications, éditeur officiel du Québec; Québec 1978, recense par Monique B. Boulanger," *Orientation professionnelle*, 14:181-2, été 1978.

7307. *La condition féminine, janvier 1977 à avril 1979*. [Textes sélectionnés par le] Centre de documentation, Ministère des communications. [Québec: Éditeur officiel du Québec, 1979]. 415p.

7308. *La femme au Québec*. Les Québécois, no. 1. Montréal: Editions du Parti québécois, 1974. 63p.

7309. LaFleur, Manon. *Témoignage d'une québécoise*. [Montréal: Éditions québécoises, 1972]. 94p.

7310. Le Moyne, Jean. "Woman and French-Canadian civilization," in her, *Convergence: essays from Quebec*. Toronto: Ryerson Press, 1966, pp.59-90.

7311. *La recherche sur les femmes au Québec: compte rendu d'un colloque interdisciplinaire tenu à Montréal les 12 et 13 mai 1979*. Québec: U.Q.A.M. Comité de publication du colloque organisé par le Groupe interdisciplinaire sur la condition des femmes / Conseil du statut de la femme, 1980. 129p.

7312. Lafontaine, Danielle. "Profondeur historique et dimension politique de la cause des femmes," dans Rodrigue Bélanger et autres, eds., *Devenirs de femmes*. Cahiers de recherche éthique, no. 8. Montréal: Éditions Fides, 1981, pp.21-38.

7313. Lamothe, Jacqueline et Jennifer Stoddart. "Les Yvettes ou: comment un parti politique traditionnel se sert encore une fois des femmes," *Atlantis*, 6:10-16, Spring 1981.

7314. Lavigne, Marie et autres. *Travailleuses et féministes: les femmes dans la société québécoise*. Études d'histoire du Québec, no. 13. Montréal: Boréal express, 1983. 430p.

7315. *Les têtes de pioche: journal des femmes*. Montréal: Éditions du Remue-ménage, 1980. 207p.

7316. MacDonald, Dawn. "Women of Montreal: the pattern breakers," *Chatelaine*, 47:30-1, 66-8, Feb. 1974.

7317. Magloire Chancy, Adéline. *L'analphabétisme chez les femmes immigrantes haitiennes*. [Montréal]: Librairie de l'Université de Montréal, [1981?] 168p.

7318. *Manifeste des femmes québécoises*, par un groupe de femmes de Montréal. [Montréal]: L'Étincelle, [1971]. 58p.

7319. Maranda, Jeanne. "Madame Justine Lacoste-de Gaspé Beaubien," *Canadian Women's Studies / Les cahiers de la femme*, 1:57-9, Summer 1979.

7320. Marchand, Azilda. "Les femmes au foyer hier et demain," *Canadian Women's Studies / Les cahiers de la femme*, 2(2):46-8, 1980.

7321. Maroney, Heather Jon. "Sexual politics in Quebec: the structure and dynamics of class, national and sex oppression." MA thesis, McMaster University, 1978. 308p. (Can. theses, no.46913)

7322. Meunier-Tardif, Ghislaine. *Vies des femmes*. Montréal: Libre expression, 1981. 199p.

7323. Mirza, Hayat. "L'avenir, au féminin pluriel!" *McGill Journal of Education*, 16:131-40, Spring 1981.

7324. Moisan, Lise. "Quebec: a view from inside: yes, but... ," *Broadside*, 1(8):11, 1980.

7325. Morissette, Brigitte. "Treize femmes à la recherche des femmes," *Le Maclean*, 12:18-19, 46-8, oct. 1972.

7326. Muir, Margaret. "Professional women and network maintenance in French- and an English-Canadian fishing village," *Atlantis*, 2(2):45-55, Spring 1977, Part II.

7327. O'Leary, Véronique et Louise Toupin, [eds.]. *Québécoises deboutte! Tome 1: une anthologie de textes du Front de libération des femmes (1969-1971) et du Centre des femmes (1972-1975)*. Montréal: Les Éditions du Remue-ménage, 1982. 212p.

7328. Pelletier-Baillargeon, Hélène. "Femmes d'ici," in her, *Le Pays légitime*. Ottawa: Leméac, 1979, pp.143-69.

7329. _____. "La Québécoise et l'église," *Communauté chrétienne*, no. 95:450-62, sept.-oct. 1977.

7330. Pestieau, Caroline. "Women in Quebec," in Gwen Matheson, *Women in the Canadian mosaic*. Toronto: Peter Martin, 1976, pp.56-69.

7331. Québec. Conseil du statut de la femme. *Carrefour 75: rapport des tables-rondes*. Québec, 1975. 24p.

7332. _____. *Pour les Québécoises: égalité et indépendance*, par Denis Turcotte. Québec: Éditeur officiel du Québec, 1978. 335p. and app. A-F. (Microlog 79-0699)
   Contents: La socialisation; Les différences biologiques; La famille; Le marché du travail; Le loisir; La création artistique; Le pouvoir.

7333. _____. *Rapport annuel*. Québec: Québec. Editeur officiel du Québec, 1973-74- .

7334. Québec. Ministère de l'éducation. *Les actions du ministère de l'éducation dans le dossier de la condition féminine: dossier synthèse*. [Québec], 1980. 26p.

7335. Québec. Ministère des communications. Centre de documentation. *Le statut de la femme: réstrospective 1976*. [Québec]: Ministère des communications, 1977. 241p.

7336. Québec. Secrétariat d'état a la condition féminine. *État des actions gouvernementales en matière de condition féminine, 1979/1980-* . Québec, 1980- . Annuel.
   English edition: Action taken by the government with regard to the status of women. Later called, Report on government action with regard to the status of women.

7337. "Rapport de L'OFAO: femmes et famille," *Canadian Women's Studies / Les cahiers de la femme*, 2(1):29-30, 1980.

7338. Réseau d'action et d'information pour les femmes. *Le livre rouge de la condition féminine et critique de la politique d'ensemble du Conseil du statut de la femme contenue dans "Pour les Québécoises: égalité et indépendance"*. Sillery, Qué., 1979. 67, 263p.

7339. Robillard, Laurette Champigny. "Pour les Québécoises: égalité et indépendance," *Commerce*, 81:88-90, 92+ , mai 1979.

7340. Université du Québec à Montréal. Laboratoire sur la répartition et la securité du revenu / Québec. Conseil du statut de la femme. *La condition économique des femmes au Québec*. Vol.1: *L'exposé de la question*. Vol.2: *L'évaluation de la réponse apportée par l'État*. Québec: Éditeur officiel du Québec, 1978.

7341. Vézina-Parent, Monique. "La participation de la femme au pouvoir écononique," dans Rodrigue Bélanger et autres, eds., *Devenirs de femmes*. Cahiers de recherche éthique, no. 8. Montréal: Éditions Fides, 1981, pp.123-30.

7342. Victor, Jean-Louis et Denise Roussel. *Des québécoises d'aujourd'hui se racontent: amour, sexualité, spiritualité*. Montréal: Presses Sélect, 1978. 246p.

7343. Weitz, Margaret Collins. "An introduction to "Les Québécoises"," *Contemporary French Civilization*, 5:105-129, Fall 1980.

WOMEN - QUEBEC - BIBLIOGRAPHY

7344. Bégin, Diane, Francine Harel-Giasson, Marie-Françoise Marchis-Mouren. *Portraits de Québécoises gestionnaires: une bibliographie annotée*. Rapport de recherche, no. 82-07. Montréal: Université de Montréal. École des hautes études commerciales, 1982. 64p.

7345. Houle, Ghislaine. *La femme au Québec*. Montréal: Québec. Ministère des affaires culturelles, 1975. 228p.

7346. Maranda, Jeanne and Mair Verthury. "Québec feminist writing; Les écrits féministes au Québec," *Emergency Librarian*, 5:2-11, [English]; 12-20, [French], Sept.-Oct. 1977.

7347. Québec. Conseil du statut de la femme. *Les Québécoises: guide bibliographique suivi d'une filmographie*. Québec: Editeur officiel du Québec, 1976. 160p.

7348. St.-Pierre, Nicole et Ginette Ruel. *Bibliographie sélective sur la condition des femmes*. Québec: Québec. Ministère des affaires sociales, 1981. 16p.

7349. Weitz, Margaret Collins. "An introduction to 'Les Québécoises'," *Contemporary French Civilization*, 5:105-129, Fall 1980.

WOMEN - QUEBEC - HISTORY

7350. Association féminine d'éducation et d'action sociale. *Pendant que les hommes travaillaient, les femmes elles...: 266 fiches biographiques de femmes qui ont marqué le Québec entre 1820 et 1950*. Montréal: Guérin, [1978?]. 405p.

7351. Auger, Geneviève et Raymonde Lamothe. *De la poêle à frire à la ligne de feu: la vie quotidienne des québécoises pendant la guerre '39-'45*. Montréal: Boréal express, 1981. 232p.

7352. Beaudoin, Marie-Louise. *Les premières et les filles du roi à Ville-Marie*. 2e éd. rév. et corr. Montréal: Les Soeurs de la Congrégation de Notre-Dame, Maison Saint-Gabriel, 1971. 95p.

7353. Bradbury, Bettina. "The family economy and work in an industrializing city: Montreal in the 1870s," *Canadian Historical Association. Historical Papers*, 1979, pp.71-96.

7354. Chartrand, Simonne Monet. *Ma vie comme rivière: récit autobiographique*. Vol.1: *1919-1942*. Vol.2: *1939-1949*. Montréal: Éditions du Remue-ménage, 1981-82.

7355. Cross, D. Suzanne. "La majorité oubliée: le rôle des femmes à Montréal au 19e siècle," dans Marie Lavigne et Yolande Pinard, *Les femmes dans la société québécoise: aspects historiques*. Montréal: Éditions du Boréal express, 1977, pp.33-59.

7356. _____. "The neglected majority: the changing role of women in 19th century Montreal," *Histoire sociale/Social History*, 6:202-23, Nov. 1973.

7357. _____. "The neglected majority: the changing role of women in 19th Century Montreal," in Susan Mann Trofimenkoff and Alison Prentice, eds., *The neglected majority: essays in Canadian women's history*. Toronto: McClelland and Stewart, 1977, pp.66-86.

7358. D'Allaire, Micheline. "Jeanne Mance à Montréal en 1642: une femme d'action qui force les événements," *Forces*, 23:38-46, 2e trimestre, 1973.

7359. Danylewycz, Marta. "Taking the veil in Montreal, 1840-1920: an alternative to marriage, motherhood and spinsterhood." PhD diss., University of Toronto, 1981. 324p.

7360. Desjardins, Paul. *La vie toute de grâce de Jeanne Mance: fondatrice de l'Hôtel-Dieu de Montréal et première infirmière laïque*. Montréal: Les Éditions Bellarmin, 1979. 188p.

7361. Dionne, Hélène. *Les contrats de mariage à Québec (1790-1812)*. National Museum of Man. Mercury series / History division. Paper, no. 29. Ottawa: National Museums of Canada, 1980. 174p.

7362. Douville, Raymond. *Nos premières mères de famille: les "filles du roi" aux origines de Sainte-Anne*. Trois Rivières, Qué.: Éditions du Bien Public, 1976. 46p.

7363. Dumais, Monique. "Jalons pour une réflexion éthique sur le modèle de la mère dans la société québécoise (1940-1970)," *Cahiers ethicologiques de l'UQAR*, 4:49-67, déc. 1981.

7364. _____. "Les femmes et la religion dans les écrits de langue française au Québec," *Atlantis*, 4:152-62, Spring 1979.

7365. _____. "Perspectives pour les femmes telles que proposées par un évêque entre 1928-1950," *Revue d'histoire du Bas Saint-Laurent*, 5:33-6, déc. 1978.

7366. Dumas, Silvio. *Les filles du roi en Nouvelle-France: étude historique avec répertoire biographique*. Cahiers d'histoire, no. 24. Québec: La Société historique de Québec, 1972. 382p.

7367. Dumont-Johnson, Micheline. "Découvir la mémoire des femmes," dans Rodrigue Bélanger et autres, eds., *Devenirs de femmes*. Cahiers de recherche éthique, no. 8. Montréal: Éditions Fides, 1981, pp.51-65.

7368. Dumont, Micheline et autres. *L'histoire des femmes au Québec depuis quatre siècles*. Montréal: Quinze, 1982. 521p.

7369. Fadette. *Journal d'Henriette Dessaulles, 1874-1880*. Montréal: Éditions Hurtubise, 1971. 325p.

7370. Forster, Jan. "Marie LaTour, Canada's unknown heroine," *Chatelaine*, 45:34-5, 68-70, May 1972.

7371. Foulché-Delbosc, Isabel. "Women of Three Rivers: 1651-63," in Susan Mann Trofimenkoff, and Alison Prentice, eds., *The neglected majority: essays in Canadian women's history*. Toronto: McClelland and Stewart, 1977, pp.14-26.

7372. Gagnon, Mona-Josée. "La femme dans l'ideologie québécoise et dans la C.S.N.: étude ideologique et monographie syndicale." MA thesis, Université de Montréal. École des Relations Industrielles, 1973. 281p.

7373. _____. *Les femmes vues par le Québec des hommes: 30 ans d'histoire des ideologies, 1940-1970*. Montréal: Éditions du Jour, 1974. 159p.

7374. Gillett, Margaret. "Leacock and the ladies of R.V.C.," *McGill Journal of Education*, 16:121-9, Spring 1981.

7375. Girouard-Décarie, Jeanne. "La fermière canadienne-française," *Québec-Histoire*, 2:32-6, hiver 1973.

7376. Guilde familiale du Domaine St-Sulpice, Victor Barbeau et François-Albert Angers. *Hommage à Berthe Chaurès-Louard, 1889-1968*. n.p., 1982. 60p.

7377. Jean, Michèle. *Québécoises du 20e siècle: les étapes de la libération féminine au Québec, 1900-1974*. Montréal: Quinze, 1977. 303p.

7378. Labarge, Margaret W., Micheline D. Johnson and Margaret E. MacLellan. *Cultural tradition and political history of women in Canada*. Royal Commission on the Status of Women in Canada. Study no. 8. Ottawa, 1971. v.p.

7379. Lacoursière, Jacques. "La Québécoise, trop tôt libérée," *Maintenant*, 140:20-4, nov. 1974.

7380. Lanctôt, Gustave. *Filles de joie ou filles du roi: étude sur l'émigration féminine en Nouvelle-France*. Montréal, Éditions du Jour, 1966. 160p.

7381. Lavigne, Marie et Yolande Pinard. *Les femmes dans la société québécoise: aspects historiques*. Études d'histoire du Québec, no. 8. Montréal: Éditions du Boréal express, 1977. 214p.

7382. Lavigne, Marie. "The Fédération Nationale Saint-Jean-Baptiste and the women's movement in Quebec," in Linda Kealey, ed., *A not unreasonalbe claim: women and reform in Canada, 1880s-1920s*. Toronto: Women's Press, 1979, pp.71-87.

7383. Lavigne, Marie, Yolande Pinard et Jennifer Stoddart. "La Fédération nationale Saint-Jean-Baptiste et les revendications féministes au début du 20e siecle," dans Marie Lavigne et Yolande Pinard, *Les femmes dans la société québécoise: aspects historiques*. Montréal: Éditions du Boréal express, 1977, pp.89-108.

7384. Lee, Danielle Juteau. "Les religieuses du Québec: leur influence sur la vie professionnelle des femmes, 1908-1954," *Atlantis*, 5:22-33, Spring 1980.

7385. Lord, Catherine. "L'histoire des Québécoises," *L'Actualité*, 3:18, mai 1978.

7386. Maroney, Heather Jon. "Sexual politics in Quebec: the structure and dynamics of class, national and sex oppression." MA thesis, McMaster University, 1978. 308p. (Can. theses, no.46913)

7387. Morissette, Yvonne Rialland. *Le passé conjugé au présent: Cercles de fermières, historique 1915-1980*. [Laval?, Québec]: Editions Pénélope, 1980. 249p.

7388. Noel, Jan. "New France: les femmes favorisées," *Atlantis*, 6:80-98, Spring 1981.

7389. Pinard, Yolande. "Les débuts du mouvement des femmes," dans Marie Lavigne et Yolande Pinard, *Les femmes dans la société québécoise: aspects historiques*. Montréal: Éditions du Boréal express, 1977, pp.61-87.

7390. Pineau-Ouellet, Ghislaine. "Les femmes vues à travers les journaux rimouskois," *Revue d'histoire du Bas Saint-Laurent*, 5:14-21, déc. 1978.

7391. Plamondon, Lilianne. "Une femme d'affaires en Nouvelle-France, Marie-Anne Barbel." MA thèse, Université Laval, 1976.

7392. Plamondon, Lilianne. "Une femme d'affaires en Nouvelle-France: Marie-Anne Barbel, veuve Fornel," *Revue d'histoire de l'Amérique française*, 31:165-85, sept. 1977.

7393. Racicot, Colette et Marie Tellier. "La participation de la mère de famille à la vie active." MA thèse, Université de Montréal, 1973. 289p.

7394. Reeves-Morache, Marcelle. *Les Québécoises de 1837-1838*. Montréal: Éditions A. St-Martin / Société nationale populaire du Québec, 1975. 27p.

7395. Thivierge, Nicole. *Histoire de l'enseignement ménager-familial au Québec 1882-1920*. Québec: Institut québécois de recherche sur la culture, 1982. 475p.

7396. Trofimenkoff, S. M. "Henri Bourassa and the 'woman question'," *Journal of Canadian Studies*, 10:3-11, Nov. 1975.

7397. Trofimenkoff, Susan Mann. "Henri Bourassa et la question des femmes," dans Marie Lavigne et Yolande Pinard, *Les femmes dans la société québécoise: aspects historiques*. Montréal: Editions du Boréal express, 1977, pp.109-24.

7398. _____. "Les femmes dans l'oeuvre de Groulx," *Revue d'histoire de l'Amérique française*, 32:385-98, déc. 1978.

WOMEN - SASKATCHEWAN

7399. Annesley, Pat. "Women of Saskatoon: the pattern breakers," *Chatelaine*, 48:46-8, 94-6, Feb. 1975.

7400. Boechler, M. A. *Dawn to dusk*. [Spiritwood, Sask.: n.p., 1979]. 53p.

7401. Hynd, Arleen and Mary Rocan. *Saskatchewan women '73. Task force report on the status of women in Saskatchewan*. [Regina], 1973. 54p. and app. (Profile 74-0562)

7402. Kohl, Seena B. *Working together: women and family in southwestern Saskatchewan*. Toronto: Holt, Rinehart and Winston of Canada, 1976. 139p.

7403. Saskatchewan. Advisory Council on the Status of Women. *Annual report*. 1st, 1974/75 - .

7404. Saskatchewan. Dept. of Labour. Women's Division. *The status of women in Saskatchewan: summary Dec. 31, 1976*. Regina, [1977]. 13p. (Profile 77-0462)

7405. Saskatchewan. Office of the Co-ordinator, Status of Women. *Interim report for the period Jan. 1, 1974 to May 1, 1975*. [Regina], 1975. 35p.

7406. Saskatoon Business and Professional Women's Club. *Some outstanding women: they made Saskatoon a better community*. Saskatoon: University of Saskatchewan Print Services, [1976?] 60p.

WOMEN - SASKATCHEWAN - HISTORY

7407. Binnie-Clark, Georgina. *Wheat and woman*. With an introduction by Susan Jackel. Toronto: University of Toronto Press, 1979. xxxvii, 313p.

7408. Duncan, Joy, ed. *Red seige wives*. [n.p.]: Centennial Book Committee [R.C.M.P.], 1974. 249p.

7409. McGovern, Marcia A. "The Woman's Christian Temperance Union movement in Saskatchewan, 1886-1930: a regional perspective of the International White Ribbon Movement." MA thesis, University of Regina, 1977. 260p. (Can. theses, no.36954)

7410. Menzies, June. "Votes for Saskatchewan's women," in Norman Ward and Duff Spafford, eds., *Politics in Saskatchewan*. Don Mills, Ont.: Longmans Canada Ltd., 1968, pp.78-92.

7411. Saskatchewan. Dept. of Labour. Women's Division. *Notable Saskatchewan women 1905-1980*. [Regina, 1980]. 33p. (Microlog 80-3405)

7412. _____. *Saskatchewan women 1905-1980*. [Regina, 1980]. 73p. (Microlog 80-3404)
        Collection of short, illustrative excerpts from various sources.

7413. Savage, Candace. *Foremothers: personalities and issues from the history of women in Saskatchewan*. n.p., [1975]. 99p.

7414. Skarsgard, Anne. "Violet McNaughton: Saskatchewan's forgotten crusader," *Chatelaine*, 52:148-50, Dec. 1979.

WOMEN - WESTERN CANADA - HISTORY

7415. Batt, Sharon. "Who is Erma Stocking?" *Branching Out*, 1:12-16, Nov.-Dec. 1974.

7416. Brown, Jennifer S. H. "Changing views of fur trade marriage and domesticity; James Hargrave, his colleagues, and 'the sex'," *Western Canadian Journal of Anthropology*, 6(3):92-105, 1976.

7417. Collins, Jessie. "Heroines at home; Elizabeth Gaines Llewellen (1892-1972)," *Makara*, 3: 2-4, Fall 1978.

7418. Fairbanks, Carol. "Lives of girls and women on the Canadian and American prairies," *International Journal of Women's Studies*, 2:452-72, Sept.-Oct. 1979.

7419. MacEwan, J. W. Grant. *...And mighty women too: stories of notable western Canadian women*. Saskatoon; Sask.: Western Producer, 1975. 300p.

7420. MacLeod, Margaret Arnett, ed. *The letters of Letitia Hargrave*. New York: Greenwood Press, 1969. 310p.

7421. Peter, Karl and Ian Whitaker. "The changing roles of Hutterite women," *Prairie Forum*, 7:267-77, Fall 1982.

7422. Thompson, Arthur N. "The wife of the missionary," *Canadian Church Historical Society. Journal*, 15:35-44, June 1973.

7423. Van Kirk, Sylvia. *"Many tender ties": women in fur-trade society in western Canada, 1670-1870*. Winnipeg: Watson & Dwyer Pub., [1980]. 302p.

7424. _____. "The impact of white women on fur trade society," in Susan Mann Trofimen-koff and Alison Prentice, eds., *The neglected majority: essays in Canadian women's history*. Toronto: McClelland and Stewart, 1977, pp.27-48.

7425. Van Kirk, Sylvia M. "The role of women in the fur trade society of the Canadian West, 1700-1850." PhD diss., University of London. Queen Mary College, 1975.

7426. Woywitka, Anne B. "Homesteader's woman," *Alberta History*, 24:20-4, Spring 1976.

WOMEN - YUKON

7427. Badley, Jo-Ann and others. *Yukon women*. [Whitehorse]: Yukon Status of Women Council, 1975. 192p.

7428. Black, Martha Louise. *My ninety years*. Anchorage, Alaska: Alaska Northwest Pub., 1976. 166p.

7429. Women's Research Centre. *Beyond the pipeline: a study of the lives of women and their families in Fort Nelson, British Columbia, and Whitehorse, Yukon Territory; and an identification of their socio-economic concerns resulting from the proposed construction ... .* [Vancouver, B.C.], 1979. 252, [26]p.

7430. Yukon Territorial Government. Dept. of Social Welfare. *Brief no. 415 to the Royal Commission on the Status of Women in Canada*. Whitehorse, 1968. 7p.

WOMEN'S BUREAUS

7431. Bannon, Sharleen. "The Women's Bureau is 21," *Labour Gazette*, Anniversary Issue - 1975, pp.629-31.

7432. "B.C. third province to set up Women's Bureau," *Labour Gazette*, 66:295, June 1966.

7433. Canada. Dept. of Labour. *Increased funding and staff resources for the Women's Bureau, Labour Canada*. Discussion paper. [Ottawa], 1980. 23p.

7434. _____. Women's Bureau. *Women's Bureau '69-* . Ottawa: Queen's Printer, 1970-75. Annual.

7435. Fédération des femmes du Québec. *Mémoire présenté à l'Honorable Robert Bourassa, premier ministre du Québec*. Montréal, 1971. [18]p.

7436. Fraser, Sylvia. "Laura Sabia: not exactly mom and apple pie [Ontario Women's Bureau]," *Chatelaine*, 48:54-5, 98, 100, 102-4, 106, Nov. 1975.

7437. Gillen, M. "Woman who knows about women [Canada Women's Bureau]," *Chatelaine*, 43:38, 93-6, Oct. 1970.

7438. "Manitoba Women's Bureau," *Canadian Labour*, 20:25, June 1975.

7439. Ontario. Ministry of Labour. Women's Bureau. *Ontario Women's Bureau, what, why, how*. Revised. 1975. Folder.

7440. Poglitsh, J. A. "Role of a women's bureau: Ontario," *Labour Gazette*, 67:18, 20-1, Jan. 1967.

7441. Royce, M. V. "Role of a women's bureau: Canada," *Labour Gazette*, 67:18-20, Jan. 1967.

7442. _____. "Women's Bureau," *Canadian Labour*, 10:5-9, June 1965.

7443. "The public and private Sylvia Gelber [Canada Women's Bureau]," *Branching Out*, 2:14-17, Sept.-Oct. 1975.

7444. "Twentieth anniversary of Women's Bureau; Vingtième anniversaire du Bureau de la main-d'oeuvre féminine," *Civil Service Review / Revue du Service Civil*, 48:21-2, [English]; 22-3, [French], Mar. 1975.

7445. Waddell, C. "Role of a women's bureau: British Columbia," *Labour Gazette*, 67:19, 21, Jan. 1967.

7446. Wensel, Joan. "The Alberta Women's Bureau: a community development approach." MA thesis, University of Alberta, 1977. 174p. (Can. theses, no.32088)

7447. "Women at work: members of the family and community," *Women's Bureau Bulletin*, no. 16, Nov. 1965.

WOMEN'S CENTRES

7448. Brass, Eleanor. "Women take on street patrol [Regina Native Women's Residence Resource Centre]," *Native People*, 9:3, Jan. 23, 1976.

7449. Brettle, Paul. "Haven for Native families [Regina Native Women's Residence Resource Centre]," *Native People*, 10:6, Mar. 4, 1977.

7450. Callbeck, C. "From travelling van to women's centre [Charlottetown]," *Atlantic Advocate*, 66:67-8, Oct. 1975.

7451. Carlyle-Gordge, Peter. "A building of one's own," *Maclean's*, 92:17, Mar. 26, 1979.

7452. Enns, Helga M. and Bev Le Francois. *Story of a women's centre*. [Port Coquitlam, B.C.: Port Coquitlam Area Women's Centre], 1979. 117p.

7453. Helmers, D. *A study of the developmental program of the Women's Overnight Shelter, Edmonton: January 23, 1970-May 23, 1973*. Edmonton: Edmonton Women's Shelter, 1973. 78, [37]p.

7454. Kreps, B. "Hotline on women: Woman's Place, Montreal," *Chatelaine*, 47:16, Feb. 1974.

7455. Le François, Bev and Helga Martens Enns. *Story of a women's centre*. n.p. [Vancouver]: Press Gang, 1979. 117p.

7456. Michaud, Janice. "Solid brick, solid asset [Women's Building]," *Branching Out*, 6(1):6, 1979.

7457. Ottawa Women's Centre. *Ottawa women's resource handbook*. Ottawa: The Centre, 1976. 71p.

7458. Smith, Bruna. "Centro femminile: a source of help to immigrant women," *Multiculturalism*, 1(1):18-21, 1977.

7459. Van Luven, Lynne. "Holding pattern may spell end [Women's Place]," *Branching Out*, 6(1):6-7, 1979.

7460. Willick, Liz and Sue Berlove. *Building the movement: from one women's centre to another*. Kitchener: K-W Women's Place, 1975. 30p.

7461. Working Women (formerly Women's Community Employment Centre). *A report on the research and development phase*. Submitted to Secretary of State. [Toronto], 1975. 39p. and app.

WOMEN'S LIBERATION MOVEMENT

7462. Alderdice, Kate, ed. *Women's liberation in Canada*. Toronto: Pathfinder Press, 1975. 23p.

7463.   Anderson, Doris. "The women's movement is alive and kicking," *Chatelaine*, 50:2, Aug. 1977.

7464.   _____. "Woman's work is never done," *Today*, Jan. 9, 1982, pp.6-7.

7465.   Auger, Jeanette and Jill Thomas. *Liberated views: observations on the Women's Liberation Movement*. Vancouver: University of British Columbia. Dept. of Anthropology and Sociology, 1975. 32p.

7466.   Brown, Heather. "New times / new tactics," *Broadside*, 1(1):5, 18, [1979].

7467.   "Building the feminist network: persistent effort and discreet plotting," *Saturday Night*, 93:3-4, Sept. 1978.

7468.   Cartlidge, Thora and Sharon Batt. "Our readers on the women's movement [survey]," *Branching Out*, 6(1):18-21, 1979.

7469.   Cheda, Sherrill. "Not a very funny story: review article," *Canadian Dimension*, 10:50-2, June 1974.

7470.   Dewar, Elaine. "Beyond sisterhood," *Weekend Magazine*, 27:6-8, 10-11, Apr. 2, 1977.

7471.   Fairley, Margaret. "Domestic discontent," *Canadian Forum*, 55:31-2, Sept. 1975.
        First published in Canadian Forum, Dec. 1920.

7472.   Fitzgerald, Maureen. "Toronto International Women's Day Committee," *Canadian Women's Studies / Les cahiers de la femme*, 2(2): 33-4, 1980.

7473.   Furness, Eric. "A man's view of liberation," *Canada and the World*, 40:22, Dec. 1974.

7474.   Goldfield, Evelyn and others. "Why women's lib?" in Bryan Finnigan, *Making it: the Canadian dream*. Toronto: McClelland and Stewart, 1972, pp.557-62.

7475.   *Guide to the B.C. women's movement*. Vancouver: Western Canadian Women's News, 1975. 27p.

7476.   Hildebrandt, Heather. "Sorry, sisters, women's lib only trades one tyranny for another," *Maclean's*, 84:14, Mar. 1971.

7477.   Home, Alice Marian. "Change in women's consciousness-raising groups: a study of four types of change and of some factors associated with them." DSW diss., University of Toronto, 1978. 310p. (Can. theses, no.38744)

7478.   Kostash, Myrna. "The spirit is still willing but the flesh is bone-tired," *Maclean's*, 88:8, Sept. 1975.

7479.   Kreps, Bonnie. *Guide to the women's movement in Canada: a Chatelaine cope-kit*. Toronto: Chatelaine, [1973?] 43p.

7480.   MacPherson, Kay. "The seeds of the seventies," *Canadian Dimension*, 10:39-41, June 1975.

7481.   McDonald, Lynn. "Evolution of the women's movement in Canada," *Branching Out*, 6(1):39-43, 1979; correction 6(2):3, 1979.

7482.   McKee, Liz. "Counterpoint: a woman's view of liberation," *Canada and the World*, 40:23, Dec. 1974.

7483.   Manuel, Philip A. "View from my bridge," *School Guidance Worker*, 31:35-9, Sept.-Oct. 1975.

7484.   Radio, Vera. "Community development, social movement and feminism." MA thesis, University of Alberta, 1974. 160p. (Can. theses, no.21947)

7485.   Ricks, Francie and others. "Women's liberation: a case study of organizations for social change," *Canadian Psychologist*, 13:30-9, Jan. 1972.

7486.   Sigurjonsson, Kay. "The hard part begins: new directions for the women's movement," in *Socialization and life skills*. Ottawa: Canadian Teachers' Federation, 1978, pp.1-11.

7487.   Smith, Dorothy E. "Where there is oppression there is resistance," *Branching Out*, 6(1):10-15, 1979.

7488.   Stein, David Lewis and Erna Paris. "Has feminism fizzled out?" *Chatelaine*, 51:24, July 1978.

7489.   Stephenson, Marylee. "Being in women's liberation: a case study in social change." PhD diss., University of British Columbia, 1975. 307p. (Can. theses, no.25998)

7490.   _____. "Housewives in women's liberation: social change as role-making," in her *Women in Canada*. Toronto: New Press, 1973, pp.245-60.

7491. Teather, Lynne. "The feminist mosaic," in Gwen Matheson, *Women in the Canadian mosaic*. Toronto: Peter Martin, 1976, pp.300-46.
7492. "The inside track," *Saturday Night*, 93:3-6, Sept. 1978.
7493. Vancouver Women's Caucus. *The women's liberation movement: an introduction*. Victoria, B.C.: Social Science Research, 1969. 6p.
7494. "*Weekend* poll: women's lib," *Weekend Magazine*, 29:3, Mar. 3, 1979.
7495. "We've both come a long way [editorial]," *Canadian Personnel and Industrial Relations Journal*, 22:9-10, Mar. 1975.
7496. White, Charles A. "The quiet revolution," *Canada and the World*, 40:12-13, Dec. 1974.
7497. "Why should a woman be more like man?" *Marketing*, 79:34, Apr. 8, 1974.
7498. *Women unite!* Toronto: Canadian Women's Educational Press, 1972. 191p.

WOMEN'S LIBERATION MOVEMENT - QUEBEC

7499. Centre de formation populaire. *Le mouvement des femmes au Québec*. Montréal, 1981. 88p.
7500. Cousineau, Lea. "Les Québécoises [interview]," *Canadian Dimension*, 13(1):31-4, [1978].
7501. Gagnon, Lysiane. "En douceur et mine de rien: le women's lib version québécoise," *Maintenant*, 140:12-15, nov. 1974.
7502. Godin, Pierre et Micheline Lachance. "La guerre n'est pas finie," *L'Actualité*, 3:19-22, 24, sept. 1978.
7503. Jean, Michèle. "Condition féminine et féminisme au Québec: où en sommes-nous?" *Communauté chrétienne*, no. 95:441-9, sept.-oct. 1977.
7504. _____. "Two decades of feminism in Quebec: 1960-1979," *Fireweed*, 5/6:189-93, Winter 1979/80 and Spring 1980.
7505. Lanctôt, Martine. "La genèse et l'évolution du mouvement de libération des femmes à Montréal, 1969-1979." MA thèse, Université du Québec à Montréal, 1980. 207p. (Can. theses, no.50744)
7506. O'Leary, Véronique et Louise Toupin, [eds]. *Québécoises deboutte! Tome 1: une anthologie de textes du Front de libération des femmes (1969-1971) et du Centre des femmes (1972-1975)*. Montréal: Les Éditions du remue-ménage, 1982. 212p.

WOMEN'S RESOURCE CENTRES

7507. Deschamps, Johanne. "Le pouvoir de la connaissance ou 'si l'on pouvait se comprendre'," in Naomi Hersom and Dorothy E. Smith, [eds.], *Women and the Canadian labour force*. Working document. Ottawa: Social Sciences and Humanities Research Council of Canada, 1982, pp.523-44.
7508. Forman, Freida. "Women's resource centres - Canada," *Emergency Librarian*, 5:9-16, May-June 1978.
7509. Ironside, Anne. *Women's access centres: a proposal*. Discussion paper 03/79. [Victoria]: British Columbia. Ministry of Education, Science and Technology, 1979. 40p.
7510. James, Alice. "The Women's Resources Centre - 1974." MA thesis, University of British Columbia, 1975. 85p. (Can. theses, no.25886)
7511. Peltz, Barbara. "YWCA women's resource centre," *Broadside*, 1(7):8, 1980.
7512. Thom, Patricia, Anne Ironside and Eileen Hendry. "The Women's Resources Centre: an educational model for counselling women," *Adult Leadership*, 24:129-32, Dec. 1975.

WOMEN'S STUDIES

7513. Adler, Iris. "High school women's studies: a working model," *This Magazine*, 10:14-15, Aug.-Sept. 1976.
7514. Anderson, Ann Leger. "On teaching women's history," *Resources for Feminist Research*, 8:9-10, July 1979.
7515. Anderson, Letty. "Women in the economy: a women's studies course," *Canadian Woman Studies / Les cahiers de la femme*, 3:57, Summer 1982.

304

7516. Andersen, Margret. "New subject: women's studies," *McGill Journal of Education*, 9:67-76, Spring 1974.

7517. Brandt, Gail Cuthbert. "The teaching of women's past in the present and the future: some comments," *Resources for Feminist Research*, 8:8-9, July 1979.

7518. British Columbia Teachers' Federation. *Lesson aid: women in history*. Vancouver, 1982. 24p.

7519. British Columbia. Dept. of Education. *Resource guide for women's studies for high school students*. [Victoria, B.C.], [1975?] 89p.

7520. Canada. Dept. of the Secretary of State. Women's Programme. *Perspectives on women; study guide on the status of women*. [Ottawa], 1978. Folder.

7521. *Canadian directory of funding sources for research for women*. Ottawa: Canadian Research Institute for the Advancement of Women, [1982]- . Annual.

7522. Centennial College. *Centennial College conference on women's studies in the community colleges, Toronto, Ontario, February 1977*. [Scarborough, Ont., 1977]. 22p.

7523. Cohen, Yolande. "La recherche universitaire sur les femmes au Québec (1921-1980): répertoire de thèses de maîtrise et de doctorat déposées dans les Universités du Québec," *Resources for Feminist Research*, 10:7-24, Dec. 1981-Jan. 1982.

7524. Conrad, Margaret R. "Women's studies in Canada," *Dalhousie Review*, 60:438-44, Autumn 1980.

7525. Danglewicz, Marta, Jacinthe Fraser and Carol Zavitz. "Women's studies Canada 1978," *Canadian Newsletter of Research on Women*, 7(4):17-46, 1978.

7526. Dumont-Johnson, Micheline. "Peut-on faire l'histoire de la femme?" *Revue d'histoire de l'Amérique francaise*, 29:421-8, déc. 1975.

7527. Eichler, Margrit. "Sociological research on women in Canada," *Canadian Review of Sociology and Anthropology*, 12:474-81, Nov. 1975.

7528. _____. "Sociology of feminist research in Canada," *Signs*, 3:409-22, Winter 1977.

7529. _____. *Towards a sociology of feminist research in Canada*. First draft (Feb. 1977). [Toronto], 1977. 60p. Published as Ontario Institute for Studies in Education. Group for Research on Women. Paper no. 6?

7530. _____. *Towards a sociology of feminist research in Canada*. First draft (Feb. 1977). [Toronto], 1977. 60p. Published as Ontario Institute for Studies in Education. Group for Research on Women. Paper no. 6?

7531. Fellman, Anita Clair. "Please may I have some more? Requests for further work in Canadian women's history," *Resources for Feminist Research*, 8:11-13, July 1979.

7532. "FemLit comes to academe," *Saturday Night*, 93:5, Sept. 1978.

7533. Gillett, Margaret and others. *A survey of teaching and research on women at McGill*. Report to Principal Robert E. Bell. [Montreal]: n.p., 1976. 46p.

7534. Gillett, Margaret. "Women's studies at McGill: has anything happened?" *Social Sciences in Canada*, 4(4):12-3, 1976.

7535. Kane, Becky and Margot Smith. "Women's kit," *Orbit*, 5:10-12, Oct. 1974.

7536. Kincaid, Pat. "Long term effects of women's studies," *School Guidance Worker*, 31:25-7, Sept.-Oct. 1975.

7537. _____. "Women's studies at the Toronto Board," *Ontario Education Dimensions*, 9:4-5, Oct. 1975.

7538. Lafontaine, Danielle. "La recherche scientifique, et la cause des femmes," in Yolande Cohen, ed., *Femmes et politique*. Montréal: Le Jour, 1981, pp.119-37.

7539. Legault, Gisèle. "Une expérience d'enseignement de la condition féminine en service social," *Canadian Journal of Social Work Education*, 6(2/3):93-105, 1980.

7540. Limin, Gloria Hope. "Teaching the theme of women in Canadian prairie fiction." MA thesis, University of Calgary, 1977. 141p. (Can. theses, no.34207)

7541. Lord, Catherine. "La nouvelle école des femmes," *L'Actualité*, 3:88, déc. 1978.

7542. Mann, Brenda. "Canadian Research Council for the Advancement of Women," *Branching Out*, 3:7-8, July-Aug. 1976.

7543. Marsden, Lorna. "Some problems of research on women in the Canadian labour force," *Atlantis*, 2:116-24, Spring 1977, Part I.

7544. Mitchinson, Wendy. "The historiography of Canadian women's history," *Conference Group in Women's History. Newsletter*, 4:16-21, Jan. 1979.

7545. Moore, Catherine, Sylvia Van Kirk and Susan Bazilli. "Courses on Canadian women's history / Histoire des femmes au Québec et Canada - études féminines," *Resources for Feminist Research*, 8:15-19, July 1979.

7546. Morgan, Joanne. "Report. The first summer Institute in Women's Studies, Concordia University, 1974," *McGill Journal of Education*, 10:97-8, Sept. 1975.

7547. Morgan, Kathryn Pauly. "'Philosophy of human sexuality and how I teach it'," *Canadian Women's Studies / Les cahiers de la femme*, 3(2):72-5, 1981.

7548. Morris, Eileen. "Case against women's studies," *ATA magazine*, 56:10-13, Sept.-Oct. 1975.

7549. Murdoch, Sarah. "'We're not here for rap sessions'," *Canadian Women's Studies / Les cahiers de la femme*, 3(1):52-4, 1981.

7550. Nemiroff, Greta Hofmann. "Women's body image," *Canadian Women's Studies / Les cahiers de la femme*, 3(2):36-9, 1981.

7551. Newton, Jennifer L. "Theory for the grass roots," *Branching Out*, 5(2):2, 1978.

7552. Nyquist, Mary E. "Teaching from a feminist platform: sexism and political reality," *School Guidance Worker*, 31:13-20, Sept.-Oct. 1975.

7553. Ontario Educational Communications Authority. *Women's studies: a multimedia approach*. Toronto, 1977. 122p.

　　　Joint project of Centennial College of Applied Arts and Technology and the Ontario Educational Communications Authority.

7554. _____. *Women's studies: video resource catalogue*. Toronto, 1979. 116p.

7555. Ontario. Ministry of Education. *Girls and women in society: resource list*. [Toronto, 1977]. 21p.

7556. _____. *Sex-role stereotyping and women's studies; a resource guide for teachers including suggestions, units of study and resource lists*. [Toronto, 1978]. 87p.

7557. Pierson, Ruth and Beth Light. "Women in the teaching and writing of Canadian history," *History and Social Science Teacher*, 17:83-95, Winter 1982.

7558. Pierson, Ruth. "Women's history: the state of the art in Atlantic Canada," *Acadiensis*, 7:121-31, Autumn 1977.

7559. Prentice, Alison. "Writing women into history: the history of women's work in Canada," *Atlantis*, 3:72-84, Spring 1978, Part II.

7560. "Research and personhood," in Canadian Research Institute for the Advancement of Women, *Women as persons. [La femme en tant que personne]*. Toronto: Resources for Feminist Research, 1980, pp.119-30.

　　　Proceedings of the 3rd annual meeting.

7561. Roberts, Barbara. "Seeing is believing: audio-visual aids in Canadian women's history," *Resources for Feminist Research*, 8:37-8, July 1979.

7562. "Share-in on women's studies," *Ontario Education Dimensions*, 9:6, Apr. 1975.

7563. Simon Fraser University. Academic Planning Committee. *Women's studies program*. Vancouver, 1975. 89p.

7564. Siu, Bobby. "The great leap inward: a critique of Canadian studies of women's movements." Prepared for the Annual meeting of the Canadian Sociology and Anthropology Association, University of Saskatchewan, Saskatoon, June 1-4, 1979. 50p.

7565. Staton, Pat. "A decade of women's studies," *Canadian Women's Studies / Les cahiers de la femme*, 2(2):58-9, 1980.

7566. Stevens, Alta Mae and Linda McDowell. "Filling in the picture: resources for teaching about women in Canada," *History and Social Science Teacher*, 14:7-14, Fall 1978.

7567. Strong-Boag, Veronica. "Graduating into women's history," *Resources for Feminist Research*, 8:10-11, July 1979.

7568. "Studying women as persons," in Canadian Research Institute for the Advancement of Women, *Women as persons. [La femme en tant que personne]*. Toronto: Resources for Feminist Research, 1980, pp.82-6.

　　　Proceedings of the 3rd annual meeting.

7569. Trofimenkoff, Susan Mann. "Fashions in feminism: reflections on a resource guide [Sex-role stereotyping and women's studies: a resource guide for teachers]," *Canadian Forum*, 59:15-17, Aug. 1979.

7570. Van Daele, Christa. "Women's studies: time for a grass roots revival," *Branching Out*, 5(1):8-11, 1978.

7571. Verthuy, Mair. "An institute for women's studies," *Canadian Women's Studies / Les cahiers de la femme*, 1:159-60, Fall 1978.

7572. _____. "Le premier Institut des études de la femme," *Canadian Women's Studies / Les cahiers de la femme*, 1:39-40, Fall 1978.

7573. _____. "Survey of women's studies in Canadian universities and community colleges." Paper presented at the meeting of Experts on Research and Teaching Related to Women: Evaluation and Prospects, Unesco, Paris, 5-8 May 1980. 6p.

7574. Wekerle, Gerda, Rebecca Peterson and David Morley. "Trial balloon: the story of a course," *Branching Out*, 5(3):26-9, 1978.

7575. Wilson, Frances. "The new subject: women's studies," in Gwen Matheson, *Women in the Canadian mosaic*. Toronto: Peter Martin, 1976, pp.182-96.

YOUTH

7576. Bouchard, Louise. "Aie - j'suis menstruée," *Canadian Woman Studies / Les cahiers de la femme*, 4:4-7, Fall 1982.

7577. Cowell, Carol A. "Wilful exposure to unwanted pregnancy," *Canadian Medical Association. Journal*, 111:1045, 1047, Nov. 16, 1974.

7578. Dagenais, Huguette. "Représentations des rapports hommes-femmes chez les adolescents québécois," dans Rodrigue Bélanger et autres, eds., *Devenirs de femmes*. Cahiers de recherche éthique, no. 8. Montreal. Éditions Fides, 1981, pp.147-60.

7579. Landsberg, Michele. "Young women in the post-lib era," *Chatelaine*, 50:47, 114+ , Nov. 1977.

7580. Maynard, Fredelle. "Can. Kid & Can. Mom 79," *Chatelaine*, 52:29-30, 56-7, Jan. 1979.

7581. _____. "Tammy turns 11," *Chatelaine*, 52:31, 57+ , Jan. 1979.

7582. Raphael, Dennis. "An investigation into aspects of identity status of high school females." PhD diss., University of Toronto, 1975. 237p. (Can. theses, no.32869)

7583. _____. "Identity status in high school females," *Adolescence*, 13:627-41, Winter 1978.

7584. _____. "Sequencing in female adolescents' consideration of occupational, religious and political alternatives," *Adolescence*, 14:73-80, Spring 1979.

AUTHOR INDEX

Aaron, Dorothy. : 165
Abbott, George. : 7026
Abella, Rosalie Silberman. : 2807, 2808, 3673
Abernathy, Thomas J. and Margaret E. Arcus. : 1893
Abrahamson, U. : 1972
Abrioux, Marie-Louise. : 3270, 4447
Abrioux, Marie-Louise and Harvey W. Zingle. : 3933
Abu-Laban, Sharon McIrvin and Baha Abu-Laban. : 350
Acadia University. Committee on the Status of Women. : 6594
Acheson, Shelley. : 2499, 3541
Acton, Janice, Penny Goldsmith and Bonnie Shepard, eds. : 2403
Adam, Barry D. : 3662
Adam, Judith. : 3635
Adam, June. : 6558
Adamchick, Tom. : 6093
Adamec, Cannie Stark and Martin Graham. : 5543
Adams, David. : 1612, 4531
Adams, David W. : 99
Adams, I. : 5425
Adams, Janet. : 2391
Adams, Scott. : 100
Adamson, Nancy and Kathy Arnup. : 2977, 4883
Addy, Cenovia. : 1014
Adler, Cathy and Shirley Congdon. : 5432, 6751
Adler, Hans J. and Oli Hawrylyshyn. : 3225
Adler, Iris. : 7513
Agarwal, N. C. : 2502
Agarwal, Naresh C. and Harish C. Jain. : 2500, 2501, 6889, 6890
Agger, Ellen. : 554, 3118
Aitchison, Douglas Wayne. : 1730, 5955
Aitken, John. : 555
Akerly, JoAnn and others. : 3742
Alain, Guilbert. : 5209

Alberro, Ana and Gloria Montero. : 3312, 3313
Albert, Richard G. : 2503

Alberta. Citizens' Advisory Board. : 6981
Alberta. Dept. of Manpower and Labour. Research Divison. : 2357
Alberta. Provincial Archives. : 409, 410
Alberta. University. Senate. Task Force on the Status of Women. : 6595
Alberta. Women's Bureau. : 1169, 1894, 2598, 2995, 3391, 3468, 3526, 3730, 3731, 3732, 3986, 4068, 4069, 4600, 5136, 5210, 6175, 6965

Alberta Mennonite Women in Mission. : 4953, 6988
Alberta Status of Women Action Committee. : 3927, 5307

Alcoholism and Drug Dependency Commission of New Brunswick. Research and Evaluation Division. : 381, 1990
Alderdice, Kate, ed. : 7462
Alderson, Henrietta Jane. : 4853
Alexander, Gay, Betty Campbell and Gilda Jubas. : 1986, 6176
Alexander, Judith A. : 6552
Alexandre, Marie-Jeanne. : 4826, 6385
Allain, Marie-Hélène. : 446
Allaire, Émilia (Boivin). : 849, 850
Allemang, Margaret May. : 4854

Allen, Catherine. : 6522
Allen, Charlotte Vale. : 851, 5923
Allen, Patrick. : 3, 4
Allentuck, Marcia. : 3827
Alliance des professeurs de Montréal. : 6416
Allingham, John D. : 2151, 2152
Allingham, John D. and Byron G. Spence. : 4199
Allison, Susan. : 852, 5137
Allodi, Mary. : 447
Alperovitz, Cath and Women's Research Centre. : 1666
Alphonsus, Sister Mary. : 6386
Althoff, Roly. : 1491
Altschul, Susan. : 4532
Altschul, Susan and Christine Carron. : 3674
Ambert, Anne-Marie. : 1895, 5934, 5956
Ambert, Anne-Marie and Gladys Symons Hitchman. : 6663
Amer, Sharon B. : 4375
Ames, Elinor W. : 5544
Amiel, Barbara. : 5, 1973, 4448, 5490, 6460
Andersen, Margaret. : 1752, 3829, 6559, 6664, 6665, 7146, 7516
Andersen, Marion. : 6387
Anderson, Ann Leger. : 7514
Anderson, Ann Leger and Patricia Marie Chuchryk. : 411
Anderson, D. : 101, 2599, 2896, 2897, 3828, 4200, 4201, 4202, 5765, 7028, 7029, 7030
Anderson, D. M. : 3078, 3079, 4884, 5211, 5212, 5957
Anderson, Dianne. : 5545
Anderson, Doris. : 102, 262, 1342, 1343, 1613, 1896, 2600, 2601, 2602, 2153, 3407, 3408, 3675,
    3993, 3994, 3995, 4111, 4676, 5028, 5082, 5308, 5309, 5310, 5311, 5312, 5313, 5766, 5873,
    6132, 6319, 7027, 7031, 7463, 7464,
Anderson, Helen. : 3393
Anderson, Joan and Sharon L. Ogden. : 6754
Anderson, Karen. : 6163
Anderson, Letty. : 7515
Anderson, Patricia. : 168, 4203
Andresen, Susan A. : 1212, 6841
Andrews, H. T. G., ed. : 2809
Andrews, Margaret W. : 7145
Angers, Maurice. : 1015, 3271
Anglican Church of Canada. Commission on Women's Work. : 7032
Anglican Church of Canada. General Synod Task Force on the Ordination of Women to the
    Priesthood. : 1299
Annesley, Pat. : 1083, 5890, 7399
Anschutz, Martha. : 2154
Anthony, George. : 4578
Anthony, Geraldine. : 3895
Antler, Ellen. : 7209
Antonelli, Marylu. : 3080, 4533
Aonzo, Jeannine. : 3903
Apostle, Richard and Don Clairmont. : 1791, 4204
Appel, David. : 1897
Applegarth, Larry. : 4677
Aquin, F. : 3996
Arbour, Rose-Marie et Suzanne Lemerise. : 448
Archer, Maureen. : 1753, 6666, 6667
Archevêché de Montréal. : 1300

Archibald, Kathleen. : 1344, 1345
Archibald, Linda and others. : 5314, 5443
Arel, Louise. : 351, 5426
Arès, Richard. : 2748, 3018, 3019
Armatage, Kay. : 3081, 3082, 3083
Armstrong, Alvin. : 5213
Armstrong, Hugh and Pat Armstrong. : 2155
Armstrong, Pat. : 1959, 2161, 6537
Armstrong, Pat and Hugh Armstrong. : 1792, 2155, 2156, 2157, 2158, 2159, 3226, 6538, 6539, 6540
Armstrong, Patsy Lauraine. : 2160
Arnason, David. : 3830
Arnold, Robert, Cyril Greenland and Marylen Wharf. : 1016
Arnopoulos, Sheila and others. : 7033
Arnopoulos, Sheila McLeod. : 2162, 3314
Arseneau, Mona and others. : 6177
Ash, Stephen B. : 3115, 3394
Ashby, Gail. : 6245
Ashley, Mary Jane and others. : 382
Asper, Linda. : 1754
Asper, Linda B. : 5828
Assheton-Smith, Marilyn. : 5315, 6288
Association des femmes diplômées des universités (Montréal). : 2097, 2426, 2475, 4205
Association féminine d'éducation et d'action sociale. : 853, 854, 1301, 3762, 4285, 7266, 7267, 7350
Association of Administrative Assistants or Private Secretaries. : 5874
Association of Universities and Colleges of Canada. : 6560, 6561, 6562, 6596
Atcheson, Beth. : 3204
Atkins, J. Louise. : 1213
Atnikov, Pam and others. : 7190
Atnikov, Pamela and others. : 6094
Attenborough, Susan. : 2163, 3542, 6133
Attorney General of Manitoba. : 2810
Atwood, Margaret. : 689, 690, 691
Aubert, Lucienne. : 2000, 5029
Aubry, Jean Pierre. : 4140
Audet, Bernard. : 1974
Auger, Geneviève et Raymonde Lamothe. : 7351
Auger, Jacques. : 4141, 4284
Auger, Jeanette and Jill Thomas. : 7465
Auxier, Jane. : 4085
Avard, Phyllis. : 263
Axford, R. W. : 2463
Axworthy, Lloyd. : 264, 2164
Ayim, Maryann. : 2603
Ayling, Vera. : 426
Azer, Nadia. : 4431, 6388
B.C. Federation of Labour. Women's Rights Committee / Women's Research Centre.: 6139
B.C. Native Women's Societies.: 4678
B.C. Native Women's Society.: 4615, 4679
B.C. Teachers' Federation.: 1756
Baar, E. : 1614
Bacave, Christiane et Michèle Jean. : 2119
Bacchi, Carol. : 2863, 6289, 6290, 6291, 6292, 7147
Bacchi, Carol Lee. : 6293

Bacchi-Ferraro, Carol Lee. : 6294

Bachynsky, Valerie. : 3543

Backhouse, Constance and Leah Cohen. : 6134

Backhouse, Constance and others. : 774

Bacon, Hugh M. : 136

Badiet, Patricia. : 383, 1987

Badley, Jo-Ann and others. : 7427

Baehre, Rainer. : 4365

Bagley, Laurie. : 3831

Baglow, John and Louise Dulude. : 103

Bagnall, James. : 265, 6135

Bagnall, James and Patricia Anderson. : 3544, 4327

Bailey, Mary C. : 5138

Bailey, Nancy. : 3832

Bailey, Stella. : 2811, 3997, 3998

Bailey, Stella J. : 4286

Bain, George. : 1347

Bain, Penny and others. : 3737, 3738

Bains, Amar. : 2864

Baker, Marilyn. : 449

Baker, Maureen. : 6668

Baker, Maureen and Mary-Anne Robeson. : 3545

Bala, Nicholas. : 2812, 4112, 5891

Balakrishnan, T. R. and others. : 7

Balakrishnan, T. R., G. E. Ebanks and C. F. Grindstaff. : 3020

Balakrishnan, T. R., J. F. Kantner and J. D. Allingham. : 1017, 3021

Balderstone, Helen and others. : 663, 1452, 7186

Bamman, Haley. : 4954

Bank of Montreal. : 2165

Bankier, J. K. : 3663, 4601, 4602

Bankier, Jennifer. : 4113

Banks, May. : 7122

Bannerman, Jean (MacKay). : 855

Bannon, Sharleen. : 1795, 2166, 3143, 3409, 3410, 3547, 3548, 7431

Barber, Marilyn. : 1960, 3376

Barclay, Nancy and others. : 5745

Baril, Joan. : 3315

Baril, Michèle. : 1433

Barling, Marion. : 3084

Barndt, Deborah, Ferne Cristall and Dian Marino. : 3316

Barnes, Angela. : 1170, 7034

Barnett, Jim. : 6320, 6364

Barnhorst, Sherrie. : 3474, 5958

Barnsley, Jan and others. : 6523

Barrett, Caroline. : 3904

Barrett, Caroline et Marie-Josée Des Rivières. : 3905

Barrett, Cindy. : 556

Barrett, Michael and Malcolm Fitz-Earle. : 8

Barriault, Rachel and Shirley Hawes. : 1214

Barry, Francine. : 2427

Bartke, Richard W. : 3999, 4114

Basford, Ron. : 2813

Basha, Rosemary. : 2392

Bashevkin, Sylvia. : 4820

Bashevkin, Sylvia B. : 5316

Basiletti, Mari, Donna Greenwood and Beverly Mills Stetson. : 3761, 7260
Bassett, Isabel. : 856, 2604, 2996
Bassett, John M. : 857, 7148
Bassett, John M. and A. Roy Petrie. : 7149
Batcher, Elaine and others. : 6095
Bates, Frank. : 4000
Batt, Sharon. : 557, 3085, 5083, 5214, 7415
Batten, Elizabeth and others. : 2393
Batten, J. : 2898
Batten, Jack. : 9, 558, 4579, 4580, 6461
Bauchman, Rosemary. : 692
Baudouin, Jean-Louis. : 4287
Bawden, Anne. : 450
Baxter, Ian F. G. : 2814, 4115, 4116
Bayefsky, Anne. : 1731
Bayefsky, Evelyn. : 2360, 4999, 5025, 5026,
Bazilli, Susan. : 3119
B.-Dandurand, Renée. : 2752
Beamish, James and Arthur Gans. : 2815
Beamish, Rahno M. : 858, 4855
Bearchell, Chris. : 3787

Bearden, Jim and Linda Jean Butler. : 4473
Beattie, Jessie L. : 859, 693
Beattie, Margaret. : 2428, 7268
Beatty-Guenter, Patricia Diane. : 5803, 5959
Beaudoin, Marie-Louise. : 7352
Beaujot, Roderic Paul. : 1018
Beaulieu, Lucien A. : 2749
Beaulieu, Michel. : 1898
Beaulne, Trudy Lynn. : 5960
Beaupré, Gerard. : 2816
Becker, Jane. : 2661
Becker, Mary. : 1085, 5084
Beckman, Margaret. : 3807
Bedford, Judy. : 5491
Beebe, Janet and others. : 3739, 7009
Beeby, Deen. : 5317
Bégin, Diane, Francine Harel-Giasson, Marie-Françoise Marchis-Mouren. : 1155, 7344

Begin, Monique. : 352, 5030
Beirne, Anne. : 775, 5215, 5292, 5318, 5319, 5652
Belanger, A. : 4142
Bélanger, Claire. : 5935
Belanger, J. : 5961
Belfry, Ron. : 3144, 4616
Béliveau, Pierre. : 104
Bell Telephone Co. of Canada. : 2167
Bell, Garry L. : 776
Bell, Lily M. and Kathleen E. Bray. : 860, 7246
Bell, Linda. : 2464
Bell, Lorna E. : 1557, 5546
Bell, Sandra. : 2504, 3808, 4885
Bella, Leslie. : 1615, 3775
Bellamy, Marjory. : 4856
Bellingham, Susan. : 412
Belton, Ted. : 3395

Black, Karen. : 1961, 3809
Black, Martha Louise. : 866, 7428
Black, Naomi. : 2120, 5322, 5323, 5324, 6669, 6670, 6389
Blackburn, John. : 6982
Blackman, Margaret B. : 4798
Blackridge, Persimmon. : 451
Blackwell, Jacqueline E. : 5548
Blakeley, Phyllis R. : 7233
Blaker, Gloria. : 2506, 4857
Blanchard, Don. : 7238
Blashill, Lorraine. : 5640
Bliss, J. M. : 6501
Bliss, Janet. : 5653
Blouin, Jacqueline. : 4376
B'nai B'rith Women District 22. : 6367
Bobak, Molly Lamb. : 452
Bode, Carolyn. : 1723
Bode, Carolyn, Larraine Brown and Mary Ann Kelly, eds. : 1724

Bodnar, Ana and Marilee Reimer. : 3318
Boechler, M. A. : 867, 7400
Boggs, Jean S. : 453
Bohémier, A. : 2818
Bohnen, Linda. : 2405, 3530
Boileau, Jacqueline. : 2663, 2664
Boivin, Aurélien et Kenneth Landry. : 3443
Boivin, Micheline. : 1019, 3272
Boland, J. A. Heidi. : 6390
Bonn, Kasandra. : 4460
Borchelt, David. : 6757
Borgman, A. E. and A. Ansara. : 2900
Bosher, John F. : 2750
Bossen, M. and Associates. : 3124
Bossen, Marianne. : 751, 752, 753, 5753
Bottomley, Pamela. : 4461
Bouchard, Danielle. : 1962
Bouchard, Laurette. : 868, 7271
Bouchard, Louise. : 7576
Bouchard, Micheline. : 2483
Boucher, Jacques. : 3764
Boucher, Jacques et André Morel, eds. : 2819, 4288
Boucher, Marie Gratton. : 1302
Boughton, Noelle. : 454
Boulet, Jac-André and Laval Lavallée. : 2168, 2361

Bouma, Gary D. and Wilma J. Bouma. : 1020
Bourne, Paula. : 13, 2507, 2508, 3549, 3677, 4070, 4289, 4680, 5191, 5492, 5654, 7037
Bow, Jane. : 560
Bowen, Norma. : 6671
Bowen, Norma V. : 6672
Bowen, Sally and others. : 2077
Bower, Anne. : 2665
Bowman, C. Myrna. : 6323
Bowman, Phylis. : 427
Boyce, Eleanor. : 455
Boyce, R. M. and R. W. Osborn. : 14, 15
Boyd, Helen. : 6989

Boyd, M. : 1173, 4654

Boyd, Monica. : 664, 1171, 1172, 1755, 1899, 2751, 3319, 3320, 5965, 6597, 6673, 6895

Boyd, Monica and Deirdre Gillieson. : 16

Boyd, Monica and Elizabeth Humphreys. : 2169, 2170, 6893, 6894

Boyd, Rosamonde R. : 5325

Boyer, Ginette. : 1303, 1304, 3639, 5444

Boyle, Christine. : 4290, 5655, 5656

Boynard-Frot, Janine. : 3906

Bracher, Michael D. and P. Krishnan. : 2800

Bracher, Michael David. : 1021

Bradbury, Bettina. : 4208, 7353

Bradbury, Patricia. : 6137

Bradley, Christine Felecia. : 1280

Braid, Kate. : 1215, 1216, 1217, 1218, 2366

Braid, Kathleen. : 1219

Braithwaite, Rella, comp. and ed. : 4474

Brand, Johanna and Ester Koulack. : 2978

Brandt, Caryl. : 4603

Brandt, Gail Cuthbert. : 1435, 7517

Brass, Eleanor. : 4799, 7448

Bratton, Robert D. : 561

Bray, Ruth M. : 5657

Breau, Alice. : 7199

Breen, L. : 5192

Breen, Mary Catherine. : 562

Brent, G. : 3678, 5326

Breton, Raymond. : 6799

Brett, Joyce. : 6077

Brett, Kathrine Beatrice. : 1975

Brettle, Paul. : 4800, 7449

Brickman, Julie. : 456

Briedis, Catherine. : 5433, 5900

Brien, Jasmine. : 2001

Brien, Pat. : 1092

Brière, Germain. : 1900, 2820, 4004

Brierley, J. E. C. : 4145, 4146

Brigden, Beatrice. : 2954

Briggs, Jean L. : 4731

Briggs, Margaret. : 1093

Brinkerhoff, Merlin and Eugen Lupri. : 3273

Brinkerhoff, Merlin B. : 6272, 6800

Briskin, Linda and Linda Yantz, eds. : 3550

Brisson, Marcelle et Louise Poissant. : 6164

British Columbia. Apprenticeship Training Programs Branch. : 1220, 2002

British Columbia. Dept. of Education. : 7519

British Columbia. Dept. of Education. Educational Programs. Provincial Advisory Committee on Sex Discrimination. : 6096

British Columbia. Ministry of Education. Post-Secondary Dept. : 1509, 2079

British Columbia. Police Commission. Rape Prevention Project. : 5658

British Columbia. Royal Commission on Family and Children's Law. : 4087, 4604

British Columbia. Royal Commission on the Incarceration of Female Offenders. : 5457

British Columbia. Task Force on Women's Issues. : 268, 1411

British Columbia. University. President's Ad Hoc Committee to Study the Report on the Status of Women at UBC. : 6598

British Columbia. University. President's Ad Hoc Committee which considered 'A report on the status of women at the University of British Columbia' with particular reference to employed staff.: 6599

British Columbia Native Women's Society and Native Outreach for Women. : 4655

British Columbia Teachers' Federation. : 7518

Brizinski, Peggy Martin. : 4732

Brodie, M. Janine. : 5203, 5328, 5329

Brodie, M. Janine and Jill McCalla Vickers. : 5217, 5327

Brossard, Nicole. : 696

Brotman, Ruth C. : 869, 4581

Brown, Caree Rozen and Marilyn Levitt Hellinger. : 665

Brown, Catherine. : 413

Brown, Daniel J. : 5829

Brown, David. : 5032

Brown, Dick. : 2666

Brown, Heather. : 2988, 2989, 5330, 7466

Brown, Ian. : 1094

Brown, Jennifer. : 4667

Brown, Jennifer S. H. : 3981, 4668, 7416

Brown, Lois. : 5830

Brown, M. Jennifer. : 2121

Brown, Rosemary. : 5218, 5331, 7038

Brown, Sharon. : 3412

Browne, A. : 5493

Bruce, Christopher J. : 4534

Bruce, Harry. : 7228

Bruce, Jean. : 5659

Bruhy, Billie Jo. : 4886

Bruneau, L. : 4656

Brunelle, Heather. : 1658

Brunet, Dominique. : 5549

Brunet, Lucie. : 4432

Brunet-Weinmann, Monique. : 457, 458, 459, 460, 537

Bryans, Wendy E. : 6448

Bryant, Lee. : 385

Bubnick, Julie. : 3743

Bubnick, Julie and others. : 6801

Buchanan, Roberta. : 1901

Buchynsky, Vera, ed. : 4955

Buck, Ruth Matheson. : 4377

Buckley, Patrick G. : 5937

Buckley, Suzann. : 1281, 1282, 3377, 7150

Budgen, Mark. : 5494

Buhrmann, Hans G. and Robert D. Bratton. : 563

Bulcock, Jeffrey and others. : 6391

Bureau, Yvon. : 754

Burgess, Catherine. : 461

Burgess, Helen. : 4733

Burgess, Jean. : 5219

Burgham, Catherine. : 6896

Burke, Angela. : 3679

Burke, Mary-Lynn. : 6178

Burke, Ronald and Tamara Weir. : 3274

Burnet, Jean. : 6252, 6674

Burnford, Sheila. : 870

Canada. Advisory Council on the Status of Women. : 106, 269, 1022, 1023, 1157, 1902, 2172, 3125, 3133, 3209, 3210, 3680, 4006, 4007, 4330, 4331, 4332, 4681, 5037, 5660, 5661, 5771, 5924, 6179, 6368, 6369

Canada. Commission of Employment and Immigration. : 2466

Canada. Commission of Inquiry into Part-Time Work. : 5000

Canada. Co-ordinator, Status of Women. : 270, 3681, 7045

Canada. Council on Rural Development. : 5804

Canada. Dept. of Employment and Immigration. : 271, 1174

Canada. Dept. of Employment and Immigration. Public Affairs. : 5968

Canada. Dept. of Energy, Mines and Resources. Mineral Development Sector. : 4462

Canada. Dept. of External Affairs. : 7047

Canada. Dept. of External Affairs. External Information Programs Division. : 7048

Canada. Dept. of Indian and Northern Affairs. : 4682, 4734

Canada. Dept. of Indian and Northern Affairs. Indian and Inuit Affairs Program. Research Branch. : 4735

Canada. Dept. of Industry, Trade and Commerce. Small Business Secretariat. : 1095

Canada. Dept. of Justice. : 5925

Canada. Dept. of Justice. Committee on the Operation of the Abortion Law. : 107

Canada. Dept. of Labour. : 272, 273, 1349, 2173, 3682, 7049, 7433

Canada. Dept. of Labour. Economics, and Resources Branch and Canada. Dept. of Labour. Women's Bureau. : 5001

Canada. Dept. of Labour. International Labour Affairs Branch. : 2509

Canada. Dept. of Labour. Women's Bureau and Economics and Research Branch. : 4333

Canada. Dept. of Labour. Women's Bureau. : 1175, 1617, 2174, 2175, 2176, 2177, 3495, 3496, 3497, 4209, 4210, 4334, 4535, 4536, 5002, 6842, 7434

Canada. Dept. of Manpower and Immigration. : 2753, 4463

Canada. Dept. of National Health and Welfare. : 274, 1350, 1618, 1619, 1620, 2606, 3145, 5038

Canada. Dept. of National Health and Welfare. Departmental Library Services. : 1958

Canada. Dept. of National Health and Welfare. Equal Opportunities for Women Program. : 275, 1351

Canada. Dept. of National Health and Welfare. Fitness and Amateur Sport. : 569

Canada. Dept. of National Health and Welfare. National Day Care Information Centre. : 1663

Canada. Dept. of National Health and Welfare. Office of the Minister of National Health and Welfare and Minister Responsible for the Status of Women. : 170, 2607, 4311

Canada. Dept. of National Health and Welfare. Planning and Evaluation Branch. Welfare Research Division. : 1716

Canada. Dept. of National Health and Welfare. Policy Research and Long Range Planning (Welfare). : 2178, 5969

Canada. Dept. of the Secretary of State. : 3146, 3413, 4736, 4737

Canada. Dept. of the Secretary of State. Library. : 7123

Canada. Dept. of the Secretary of State. Multiculturalism Directorate. : 3321, 3322

Canada. Dept. of the Secretary of State. Women's Programme. : 4887, 4888, 5805, 6524, 7124, 7520

Canada. Dept. of Transport. Canadian Marine Transportation Administration. : 1176, 1223, 2484

Canada. Employment and Immigration Commission. Affirmative Action Program. : 276, 1732, 3498

Canada. Employment and Immigration Commission and Native Women's Association of Canada. Working Group on Native Women's Employment. : 4657

Canada. Federal-Provincial-Territorial Conference of Ministers Responsible for the Status of Women. : 7050

Canada. Fitness and Amateur Sport. Women's Program. : 570, 571

Canada. Intergovernmental Committee on Women in Employment and Saskatchewan. Dept. of Labour. Women's Division. : 4336

Canada. Joint Committee to Study Alternatives for the Housing of the Federal Female Offender. : 5458

Canadian Federation of University Women, Grand Falls Branch. : 7211
Canadian Human Rights Commission. : 2511, 6141
Canadian Human Rights Commission. Task Force on Equal Pay. : 2512
Canadian Institute for Research. : 6326
Canadian Institute of Child Health. : 5434
Canadian Labour Congress. : 2513, 3552, 3553, 3554
Canadian Labour Congress. Women's Bureau. : 2182, 3555
Canadian Psychological Association. : 1511, 5552
Canadian Psychological Association. Committee on the Status of Women. Calgary Subcommittee. : 5553
Canadian Psychological Association. Task Force on the Status of Women in Canadian Psychology. : 5554
Canadian Radio-Television and Telecommunications Commission. : 172, 4313
Canadian Religious Conference. : 4619
Canadian Teachers' Federation. : 1177, 1757, 6078, 6394, 6395, 6396

Canadian Union of Public Employees. : 286, 2183, 2184, 3556, 3557, 3558, 3559
Canadian Union of Public Employees. Education Dept. : 285, 1814, 3560
Canadian Union of Public Employees. Research Dept. : 4337
Canadian Welfare Council. : 1717
Canadian Welfare Council. Research Branch. : 1664
Canadian Women's Christian Temperance Union. : 4957, 6502
Canadian Women's Press Club. : 5445
Cannon, Margaret. : 5930
Cantlie, Ronald B. : 4011
Caparros, Ernest. : 4147, 4148, 4149, 4292
Cape, Elizabeth. : 355, 5806
Caplan, Paula J. and Georgina White. : 5555
Carbine, Patricia. : 4407
Cardinal, Harold. : 4685
Cardinal, Shirley and others. : 4738
Carey, Patricia. : 2866, 2990
Carisse, C. : 4314
Carisse, Colette. : 2756, 4211, 5446, 5970
Carisse, Colette and Joffre Dumazedier. : 2757, 7272
Carleton University Women's Centre. Handbook Committee. : 6564
Carliner, Geoffrey, Christopher Robinson and Nigel Tomes. : 3023
Carlyle-Gordge, Peter. : 3134, 3744, 7451
Carmel, Alan. : 2187, 2188
Carment, D. W. : 5971
Caron, André H. and Chantal Mayrand. : 6463
Caron, Anita. : 6079
Caron, Margaret Ann. : 6464
Carpenter, Jock. : 4670
Carpentier, Renée. : 5005
Carr, Robert. : 2823
Carr, Shirley. : 3561, 3562
Carrara, Angelo. : 1025
Carrier, Micheline. : 5085, 5662, 5902
Carroll, Joy. : 5876
Carroll, Michael P. : 6898
CARSA. Niagara Region Sexual Assault Centre. : 5663
Carson, J. J. : 1375
Carson, Jean E., comp. : 6843
Carson, Susan. : 1376, 1805, 2667, 4499, 4537, 4539, 6184, 6759, 6760
Carter, Charles Ambrose and Thomas Melville Bailey, : 873, 7248

Cartlidge, Thora and Sharon Batt. : 7057, 7468
Carver, Cynthia and Susan Berlin. : 4378
Carver, Virginia. : 388
Carveth, W. Bruce. : 4500, 5556
Casgrain, T. F. : 2612
Casgrain, Thérèse F. : 874, 5221, 5222
Cash, Gwen. : 3444
Cassels, Derek. : 3166
Cassie, J. B. and others. : 5972, 6804
Castel, J.-G. : 4012
Castelli, Mireille D. : 2824
Castle, Cheryl R. : 5132
Caswell, Maryanne. : 5139
Catholic Women's League of Canada. : 7058
Catton, Katherine. : 5664
Cavanagh, Judy. : 2189, 5807
Caverly, Laurie J. : 5832
Cebotarev, E. A. and others. : 5825
Centennial College. : 7522
Centrale de l'enseignement du Québec. : 2431, 2432, 6097, 6397, 6398, 6399

Centrale de l'enseignement du Québec et Confédération des syndicats nationaux. : 2430
Centre de formation populaire. : 7499
Centre de planification familiale. : 1051
Centre de recherche sur la femme. : 3228, 7273
Cercle des femmes journalistes. : 875, 3445
Chabot-Ferland, Francine. : 5973
Chadourne, Michèle. : 784
Chadwick, J. and others. : 6098
Chaison, Gary N. and P. Andiappan. : 3563

Chalifoux, Thelma. : 4620, 4739, 4801
Chalkley, Hugh. : 2190
Chalmers, J. W. : 876, 2053
Chamber of Notaries of the Province of Quebec. : 3936
Chambers, Patricia. : 7239
Chambre des Notaires de la Province de Québec. : 1924
Champagne, Lyse. : 3135
Chan, Kwok Bun. : 785
Chandler, Verna. : 6165
Chapman, F. A. R. : 1905, 4013
Chapman, Terry L. : 5666
Chappell, Neena L. : 4212
Chappell, Neena L. and Betty Havens. : 356, 3167
Chappell, Neena Lane. :2192
Chappell, Neenah. : 357
Chaput, Louise. : 4501
Charlesworth, Maxine A. : 1178
Charney, Ann. : 2902, 5223, 5336, 7274, 7275
Charron, Camille. : 3387, 4014, 4150
Chartrand, Larry. : 1467, 4621, 4658, 4659, 4660, 4771, 4875, 4876
Chartrand, Simonne Monet. : 877, 5224, 7354
Chase, Gillean. : 5667
Chawla, Saroj. : 3836
Cheda, S. : 6099
Cheda, Sherrill. : 2746, 2904, 3810, 4622, 4623, 6100, 6101, 7469
Cheda, Sherrill, and others. : 3811, 6899

Cheda, Sherrill, Johanna Stuckey, and Maryon Kantaroff. : 2903
Chekki, Dan A. : 5974, 7059
Chenier, Nancy Miller. : 3211
Cheung, K. W. : 108
Chiasson, Gail. : 173
Children's Aid Society of Vancouver, B.C. : 2758
Chimbos, Peter D. : 1572, 1573, 3275
Chisholm, Elspeth and Patricia Thorvaldson. : 3088
Chisholm, Marjorie. : 3229
Christiansen-Ruffman, Linda. : 1758, 6253
Christ, Carol P. : 3837
Chruscinski, Theresa. : 2514
Chuchryk, Patricia Marie. : 2905
Cihocki, Mary K. : 6792
Cimichella, André-M. : 878, 4827
Cinman, I. : 6900
Ciotola, Pierre. : 4151
Citizen's Committee on Children. Committee of the Day Care Section. : 1623
Claman, A. David, Barry J. Williams and L. Wogan. : 6761
Clark, Donna. : 5462
Clark, John. : 287, 1377, 2515, 3564, 3565
Clark, Lorenne. : 5668
Clark, Lorenne and Linda Duncan. : 5669
Clark, Lorenne M. G. : 5670, 5671
Clark, Lorenne M. G. and Debra J. Lewis. : 5672
Clark, Lorenne M. G. and Simon Armstrong. : 5727
Clark, Marlene-Russell. : 7261
Clark, Sheila Elizabeth. : 6273
Clark, Susan and Andrew S. Harvey. : 3230, 4213
Clark, Wayne. : 1906
Clarke, Allan B. : 21
Clarke, Harold D. and Allan Kornberg. : 5337
Clarke, Juanne. : 6743
Clarke, Marnie A. : 1512, 2467, 6844
Clarke, Mary Eileen. : 4958, 6295
Clarkson, Adrienne. : 5225, 6465
Clatworthy, Stewart J. : 2387, 4802
Clements, George. : 1492, 2759
Cleverdon, Catherine L. : 6296
Clifford, Betty and others, ed. : 4959
Cloutier, Renée et autres. : 2906, 7276
Cloutier-Cournoyer, Renée. : 1026, 1027, 3276
Cobb, Myrna and Sher Morgan. : 5127
Coburn, Judith and Margaret Wolfe. : 5140
Cochrane, Felicity. : 879, 5295
Cochrane, Jean. : 880, 3168, 3446, 5338, 5641
Cochrane, Jean, Abby Hoffman, and Pat Kincaid. : 572
Cockburn, Patricia. : 6702
Cockburn, Patricia and Yvonne R. Raymond. : 2197
Cockerill, Art. : 4858
Codère, Clarisse. : 3435
Coderre, Annette-E. : 3838
Coffey, Mary Anne. : 1808
Coffin, Susan Dianne. : 2122, 6805
Cohen, J. : 2198

Cohen, Leah. : 1179, 1225, 1226
Cohen, Leah and Constance Backhouse. : 4366, 5673
Cohen, Marcy and others. : 1667
Cohen, Marjorie. : 2199, 2615, 2907, 6553
Cohen, Shaughnessy M. : 2200
Cohen, Shaughnessy Murray. : 1180
Cohen, Yolande. : 5086, 5339, 7277, 7523
Colbert, Helen. : 3937
Colby, Marion. : 3277
Colchester Historical Museum. : 7234
Cole, Peter. : 1028
Cole, Susan G. : 786, 5087
Cole, Susan G. and others. : 1163
Colette, Paulette. : 6507
Collard, Eileen. : 1976, 1977
Collectif. : 3499, 4889, 4890
Collet, Paulette. : 3907
Collette-Carrière, R. : 5674
Collins, Catherine. : 3436
Collins, Jessie. : 7417
Collins, Kevin. : 5040
Collins, Winston. : 1378
Collishaw, Neil. : 3024
Collison, Robert. : 109
Colwill, Nina. : 1809, 5938
Colwill, Nina Lee and Noralou P. Roos. : 4379, 3973
Comité de lutte pour l'avortement libre et gratuit. : 22
Comité pour la planification des naissances de Gaspé. : 1029
Communicado Associates. : 4434
Communist Party of Canada. Central Executive Committee. : 7060
Community Information Centre of Metropolitan Toronto. : 1677
Community Task Force on Maternal and Child Health. : 3169, 4803, 5435, 6762

Comtois, Roger. : 4152, 4153, 4154, 4155, 4156, 4157, 4158, 4159
Condon, Richard G. : 3025
Confédération des syndicats nationaux. : 1810, 1811, 2433, 3539, 3570, 3640, 3641, 3642, 4338
Confédération des syndicats nationaux. Comité de condition féminine. : 1812
Confédération des syndicats nationaux et le Syndicat canadien de la fonction publique. : 1705
Conger, P. R. and others. : 5133
Congrès des relations industrielles de l'Université Laval. : 2202
Congress of Canadian Women. : 7062
Conklin, Elizabeth Nancy. : 6881, 7278
Connelly, M. Patricia. : 2203, 2204, 2205, 2362, 4214, 4215, 6901, 6902

Connelly, M. Patricia and Linda Christiansen-Ruffman. : 2616, 6254
Connelly, Patricia. : 2206, 2979, 2980, 4216
Connon, Jane A. : 6327
Conrad, Joyce D. : 2397
Conrad, Margaret. : 358, 414, 7151
Conrad, Margaret R. : 7524
Conroy, Mary M. : 5226
Conseil du Statut de la femme. : 4948
Constantineau, G. : 1813
Constantineau, Gilles. : 23
Cook, David and others. : 1907, 5892
Cook, Gail. : 1815, 2006, 2207, 2208, 2760
Cook, Jane T. and Jane Widerman. : 1096

Cook, Janet McLaren. : 881
Cook, Judith K. : 1030
Cook, Ramsay. : 882, 3447
Cook, Ramsay and Wendy Mitchinson. : 7152
Cooke, Esther, comp. : 4582
Cooke, Katie. : 3414
Cooke, Sharon W. : 5557, 5939
Cools, Anne. : 6525
Cooper, Ingrid K. : 5931
Cooper, Jack Edward. : 2209, 4877
Cooper, Jennifer. : 6328
Cooper, Joy. : 5496
Cooper, Joy and others. : 1412
Cooper, Ken. : 4186
Cooper, Margaret. : 3089
Cooper, Pat. :4891
Cooperstock, Ruth. : 1991, 1992, 1993, 1994, 1995, 4422
Copp, Terry. : 2434
Coquatrix, Nicole. : 1283
Corbeil, Christine et autres. : 2908, 4423
Corbet, Elise A. : 4892
Corbet, Elise Elliott. : 6990
Corbett, Gail. : 883, 7249
Corkery, Mary. : 4893
Cormack, Barbara. : 884, 5227
Corne, Sharon. : 463
Cornell, Bonnie. : 1379, 1380

Corner Brook Status of Women Council. : 1181
Cornish, Mary. : 3571
Corporation des enseignants du Québec et Centrale de l'enseignement du Québec. : 1706, 6400, 7279
Corporation des psychologues de Québec. : 5977
Corrective Collective. : 2373, 7153
Cossman, B. J. : 4408
Costigliola, Bozica. : 787, 4380
Couillard, Marie. : 3839, 3908
Couillard-Goodenough, Marie. : 3909
Coulombe, Danielle. : 5088
Coulter, J. M. : 2007
Coulter, Rebecca. : 6401
Council of Associations of University Student Personnel Services. : 6845
Coupland, Michael W. : 3477, 5497
Courchesne, Ginette. : 885, 3448
Courtney, Alice. : 174
Courtney, Alice E. and Thomas W. Whipple. : 175, 176, 177

Cousineau, Jean-Michel. : 6542
Cousineau, Lea. : 7500
Couture, Suzette. : 4687
Cowell, Carol A. : 1031, 7577
Cox, Barbara J. : 886, 6991
Cox, Marlene Joan. : 5940
CPA Committee on the Status of Women. : 5559
Craig, Sheri. : 178, 1494
Cram, Kathy. : 6143
Crawford, Susan M. Heffernan. : 5978

Crealock, Carol. : 6806
Crean, Susan. : 464
Creighton, Helen. : 698, 887
Crépault, Claude. : 5903
Crépault, Claude et Robert Gemme. : 5904
Crépeau, Jean-François. : 3910
Crépeau, Paul-A. : 4160
Crocker, Olga L. : 5808
Crombie, Gail. : 5560
Cross, D. Suzanne. : 7355, 7356, 7357
Croteau, Mary J. and Wendy Zink. : 6793, 7187
Cruikshank, Julie. : 4740, 4741, 4742, 4743, 4744
Cruikshank, Julie and June Lotz. : 4791
Cuddihy, Margaret. : 4161, 6371
Cuddy, Pat L. : 6144
Cullen, Linda. : 6102, 6103
Cullis, T. E. : 4605
Cullity, M. C. : 4016
Cullity, Maurice C. : 2825, 4015
Cummer, Denise. : 5498
Cumming, Elaine and others. : 4219, 5979, 6317
Cummings, Joan E. : 1816, 6226
Cunningham, Charnie and Laurel Limpus. : 2761
Cunningham, John. : 888
Curley, Bill · 180
Cust, Marlene. : 5561, 5980
Cuthbertson, Wendy. : 6262
Cyr, Johanne Saint. : 6716
Côté, Françoise. : 6715
Dagenais, Huguette. : 6247, 6255, 6677, 7280, 7578
Dagg, Anne Innis. : 6080
Daigeler, Hanow. : 1305
Daigle, Johanne. : 2435
Daigle, Joanne et Jennifer Stoddart. : 6602
Dale, Patricia. : 2210
Daley, Pat. : 1537, 2516
Dalhousie University. Committee on the Status of Women. : 6603
Dallaire, Marie. : 7125
D'Allaire, Micheline. : 4828, 4829, 7358
Daly, Janis. : 1605
Daly, M. : 7063
Damude, Earl. : 24, 110, 4381
Damude, Earle. : 137
Dandurand, Pierre and others. : 6717
Danglewicz, Marta, Jacinthe Fraser and Carol Zavitz. : 7525
Dansereau, J. : 2085
Danson, Barney. : 428
Danylewycz, Marta. : 2955, 4830, 4831, 7359
Danylewycz, Marta and Jacinthe Fraser. : 7281
Danziger, Kurt. : 3323
D'Arcy, Carl and Janet A. Schmitz.: 4425
Darling, Martha. : 2211
Darmah Associates. : 6983
Darveau-Cardinal, Jacqueline. : 5228
Davey, Ian E. : 2054

David, Hélène. : 1817, 3643
David, Rodica. : 4118, 4119
David, Sarah Joy. : 1514
David-McNeil, J. : 6904
Davids, Leo. : 2762
Davidson, Cathy N. : 3840
Davidson, Jane. : 1097, 1625, 2517, 4540
Davidson, Margaret Rutherford, ed. : 890
Davidson, True. : 891, 892, 5229
Davidson-Palmer, Judith. : 2668
Davies, Rhona. : 6402, 6807
Davies, Sarah. : 2212
Davis, Curt. : 181, 182, 5754
Davis, Dona Lee. : 4451, 4452, 7213, 7214
Davis, Gayle R. : 465
Davis, N. H. W. : 2406
Davison, James D. : 894, 2056
Davison James Doyle. :893, 2055
Dawe, Carolyn. : 6329, 6372
Dawson, Joyce Taylor. : 4832
Day, Helen and Josephine Budgell. : 573
Day, Marilyn Anne. : 3938
Day, Shelagh. : 6604
Day, Sonia. : 756
de Blicquy, Lorna. : 1227
De Blois, Carole. : 5041
De Koninck, Maria. : 788
De Man, Anton F. and Rejeanne Benoit. : 5981
de Mestier du Bourg, Hubert J. M. : 1908, 4162

De Pauw, Karen. : 1228, 4878
De Schepper, Gladys. : 3324
De Sève, Michel et Marlen Carter. : 1424, 6905
De Sinçay, Beatrice. : 668, 1032
De Valk, Alphonse. : 111
De Villiers, Marq. : 1164, 1381, 3416
Dean, Joanna and Jannie Edwards. : 1284
Dean, Loral. : 3170
Deane, Marie and others. : 683, 3090
Deathe, Donald George and Julie Sibley Farrell. : 6166
Decore, Anne Marie. : 2213
DeJordy, Micheline. : 3478
DeKoninck, Maria, Francine Saillant et Lise Dunningan. : 3171

Delaney, M. : 3091
Delehanty, Rosalyn. : 5905
Deleury, Edith et M. Rivet. : 2826
Delisle, Gertrude. : 2057
Delisle, Lucie. : 2468
Delisle, Mary Ann. : 3279
Delisle, Michel. : 6744
Della Valle, P. A. and B. Meyer. : 6543
Delta Kappa Gamma Society. Alpha Chapter, Edmonton, Alta. : 6450
Delta Kappa Gamma Society. Delta Chapter. : 1734
DeLuca, Rayleen V. and Manly N. Spigelman. : 3172, 5562
Demmler-Kane, Jean. : 4220, 4456
Dempsey, Lotta. : 895, 3449

Doyon, Helen and Pat Hacker. : 1515
Drache, Arthur. : 6330, 6331, 6374
Drake, Robin. : 1098
Dranoff, Linda Silver. : 575, 792, 1718, 1735, 1911, 2520, 3259, 3388, 3389, 3690, 3691, 4017, 4018, 4019, 4020, 4339, 4367, 4606, 5042, 6332, 6333, 6334
Dreskin, Nathan. : 4222
Drobot, Eva. : 3450
Dubec, Bernice. : 1576, 4624
Dubin, Gloria Louise Joachim. : 2909, 5563
Dubuc, Anne-Marie, Francine L'Heureux, Joanne Baillargeon. : 4384
Dubuc, C. : 2618
Duchesne, Louis. : 3026
Duckworth, Muriel and Peggy Hope-Simpson. : 4894
Duff, Diane Marie. : 1912
Duffy, Ann and Wendy Weeks. : 5007
Duguay, Diane et Gaétane Leblanc. : 7285
Duguay, Marie-Anne. : 899, 7286
Dulude, Louise. : 113, 359, 1736, 3126, 4021, 5043, 5044, 5045, 5046
Dulude, Louise B. : 6375
Dumais, Monique. : 1307, 1308, 1309, 1310, 4502, 4833, 4834, 4835, 7287, 7288, 7363, 7364, 7365
Dumas, Evelyn. : 6263
Dumas, Silvio. : 7366
Dumont, Hélène. : 114
Dumont, Micheline et autres. : 7368
Dumont, Monique. : 3397
Dumont-Henry, Suzanne. : 1737
Dumont-Henry, Suzanne et Michèle Jean. : 2086
Dumont-Johnson, Micheline. : 1707, 4836, 7367, 7526
Dunbar, Moira. : 5856
Duncan, Joy. : 5141, 6992, 7408
Duncan, Linda. : 290, 2521, 3692, 5677
Duncan, Muriel. : 1311
Dundass, Helen. : 4607
Dunlop, John. : 27
Dunn, Margo. : 5174
Dunn, Sheelagh. : 5463
Dunnigan, Barbara. : 3280
Dunnigan, Lise. : 6081, 6105, 6846
Dunphy, Jill. : 1818, 2671
Dupont, Claire. : 2216
Dupont, Théodora. : 900
Dupré, Louise. : 5090
Durden, Vivienne. : 4895, 4896, 5564
Durham, Louise Elizabeth Grey. : 901, 7154
Dussault, Hélène. : 2827
Dutil, Denis et Mair Verthuy. : 5230
Duval, Germaine. : 902, 4837
Duval, Thérèse. : 2217, 5877, 6167
Duvall, Donna. : 4223, 4424
Duvall, Donna and Alan Booth. : 3173, 3260
Dvorak, Leona and Bev Siller. : 6847
Dyck, F. J. and others. : 3174, 4369
Dyck, Frank J. and others. : 4368
Dyer, Brenda and others. : 7250

Feldhammer, Louis. : 2011

Feldman, Wendy A. : 5411

Fellman, Anita Clair. : 7531

Fellows, L. : 3748

Fels, Julie. : 4761

Fels, Lynn. : 6745

Feltmate, Peggy. : 2059

Ferguson, Edith. : 3331

Ferguson, Mary Louise. : 4225, 5810

Ferguson, T. M. : 6336

Ferguson, Ted. : 906, 3000, 3451, 6993

Fergusson, C. Bruce. : 907, 5231

Fernet-Martel, Florence. : 361

Ferrante, Angela. : 5344

Ferrence, Roberta G. : 390

Ferrence, Roberta G. and Paul C. Whitehead. : 1998

Festeau, Hélène. : 5232

Festy, M. Patrick. : 3027

Fielding, Joy. : 3665

Filion, Jean-Paul. : 3175, 5049

Fillmore, Cathy. : 3480

Fine, Judylaine. : 2913, 4466

Finlayson, Judith. : 3284, 4226

Finn, Ed. : 2533

Finn, Patricia A. : 6605

First National Farm Women's Conference. : 186, 1539, 2802, 2868, 2869, 2870, 2871, 4023

Firth, Sophia. : 909, 4457

Fischer, Linda. : 2012

Fish, Karen. : 2622, 4692

Fisher, Christine. : 2534, 2535, 3575

Fisher, Douglas. : 5345

Fisher, Esther. : 2124, 3939

Fisher, J. : 1495

Fisher, John. : 187, 188, 189

Fisher, Margaret Ada. : 576, 5987

Fiske, D. Heather. : 5566

Fitts, Mary Pauline. : 910, 4839

Fitzgerald, Maureen. : 7472

Fitzgerald, Maureen and Daphne Morrison. : 3789

Fitzgerald, Maureen, Connie Guberman and Margie Wolfe. : 2914, 7067

Fitzpatrick, Helen. : 1313, 5424

Fleck, J. C. : 116

Fleenor, Juliann E. : 3843

Fleisher, Pat. : 471

Fleishman, Neil. : 1913, 4024

Fleming, Martha. : 4517

Fleming, Thomas S. : 794

Fletcher, Susan and Leroy O. Stone. : 362, 363, 3261, 3262

Fodden, Simon. : 1719

Foley, Christine. : 1496, 2956

Folster, David. : 4693

Forbes, Elizabeth. : 4961, 5143, 7016

Forbes, G. A. : 5499

Forbes, Rosalind. : 2675

Ford, John and Alan V. Miller. : 4446

Ford, Judy and Ellen McDonald. : 472
Forman, Freida. : 7508
Forster, Jan. : 7370
Forsyth, Carolyn June. : 5234
Forsyth, Louise. : 6510
Forsyth, Louise H. : 3844
Fortier, Johanne. : 3647
Fortier, Lise. : 4386
Fortier-Langlois, Suzanne et autres. : 911, 7290
Fortin, Carrier. : 2439
Fortin, Gerald. : 2872

Fortin, J. N. and others. : 1036
Fortin-Houle, Christiane et M. Roy. : 4164
Foster, Henry H. and D. J. Freed. : 6337
Foster, Nigel. : 4901
Fotheringham, Allan. : 5235, 5346, 5347, 5348
Foulché-Delbosc, Isabel. : 7371
Fournier, Francine. : 2440, 4995, 5349, 7291
Fournier, Gaétane et Sylvia Morin. : 2441, 2676, 7292
Fournier, Jean-Pierre. : 577
Fournier, Louise G. : 3913
Fournier, Suzanne. : 5464
Fowler, Marian. : 912, 5144, 5145
Fox, Beryl and Annette Cohen. : 2623, 7156
Fox, Bonnie. : 2982, 3234, 4227, 4228, 6907
Fox, Bonnie J. and John Fox. : 2224, 6908
Fox, John and Timothy F. Hartnagel. : 1577, 1578

Francis, Alice Katharine. : 913, 7191
Francis, Anne. : 296, 914, 3001, 5777, 6849
Francis, Daniel. : 3452
Frankel, Vivian. : 701
Frappier, Georges. : 5050
Frarey, Carlyle and Carol Learmont. : 3813
Fraser, Graham. : 4996
Fraser, Janet and Eileen Hendry. : 4902
Fraser, Joan. : 1825
Fraser, Judy. : 391
Fraser, Karen. : 1102
Fraser, Sylvia. : 1414, 5643, 7436
Fraser, Winnie. : 392
Frazee, Rowland. : 758, 1826
Frederickson, Margaret C. : 2125
Fredrickson, Olive A. : 915, 5146
Freedman, Catherine Jan. : 4762
Freedman, Frances Schanfield. : 4294
Freedman, Lisa and Susan Ursel. : 795
Freedman, Samuel. : 3698
Freeland, Halyna. : 1275
Freeman, Beverly A. : 33
Freeman, Jody. : 2442
Freitag, Walter. : 1314
Fremes, Ruth. : 7068
French, Alice. : 916, 4745
French, Doris. : 6451
French, William. : 702, 703

332

Frenette, Lyse. : 3028
Frenette, Lyse et Suzanne Messier. : 364
Frewer, Barry. : 429
Friedenberg, E. Z. : 117
Froggatt, Marilyn and Lorraine Hunter. : 4229, 5567
Frosst, Sandra and Wendy Thomson. : 1914
Frum, B. : 2915, 5350, 5351, 6469
Frum, Barbara. : 7069
Frève, Claire, Sylvia Park and Wendy Lawrence. : 5236
Fulford, Robert. : 5417
Fullerton, Timothy. : 5568
Fulton, E. Margaret. : 3845, 6409
Furness, Eric. : 7473
G.R.A.F.S. : 2919, 7299
Gabor, Agota. : 796
Gabriel, Lynn. : 393
Gagné, Christiane Bérubé. : 2088
Gagnon, Claude-Lyse. : 4903
Gagnon, Jacques. : 2624
Gagnon, Lysiane. : 1425, 6850, 7501
Gagnon, Marie. : 6410
Gagnon, Mona-Josée. : 2225, 3648, 3649, 3650, 3651, 3652, 7372, 7373
Gagnon, Rosette, Louise Biron et Marie-Andrée Bertrand. : 3481, 6275, 6812
Gallagher, Diane May. : 2226, 3029
Galloway, Priscilla. : 1760
Gumpel, Samuel. : 3907
Gane, Margaret Drury. : 3002, 6567
Gargrave, Tony. : 2828, 4091
Garigue, Philippe. : 2766, 3285, 5988
Garneau, Hélène. : 1427

Garner, John. : 6297
Garr, Allen. : 1315
Garrison, Ada M. : 5893
Gaskell, Jane. : 2015, 2016, 2017, 2228, 2229, 5989, 6083, 6813
Gaskell, Jane S. : 2013
Gaskell, Jane S. and Marvin Lazerson. : 2014, 2227
Gaudet, Bérengère. : 2829
Gaulin, Hélène Caron. : 2767
Gauthier, G. : 4165
Gauthier, Gilles. : 1436
Gauthier, Kathleen. : 1827
Gauthier, Linda. : 2677

Gay, Richard. : 3093
Gee, Ellen M. Thomas. : 3030, 3940, 3983
Gee, Ellen Margaret Thomas. : 2768
Geering, Jacqueline. : 3094
Geirsson, Freya. : 704, 1739, 1761, 1830, 1831, 2230, 2231, 2537, 2625, 2626, 3235, 3236, 3399, 3503, 3504, 3577, 3578
Gelber, Sylva. : 1832, 3505, 3576, 5990, 6228
Gelber, Sylva M. : 1828, 1829, 1833, 2126, 3127, 4387, 4478, 5051, 5991, 6229, 6545, 6679, 6705, 6909, 6910, 7070, 7071, 7072, 7293
Gellatly, C. and N. K. Thompson. : 2627
Geller, Gloria. : 3483, 6298, 6814
Geller, Gloria Rhea. : 3482
Geller, Sheldon H. : 5678

Godin, Pierre et Micheline Lachance. : 7502

Gold, Dolores. : 4543, 5997

Gold, Dolores and Charlene Berger. : 4544, 5570

Gold, Dolores and David Andres. : 4545, 4546, 4547, 4548, 4549, 5996

Gold, Dolores, David Andres and Jacqueline Glorieux. : 4550

Gold, Sylvia. : 6411

Goldberg, Joel O. : 1741, 5571

Goldenberg, S. : 1541

Goldenberg, Shirley B. : 2234. 3507

Goldfield, Evelyn. : 5906

Goldfield, Evelyn and others. : 7474

Goldfield, Evelyn, Sue Munaker, and Naomi Weisstein. : 2918

Goldman, N. P. : 4166

Goldman, Pearl. : 798

Goldsberry, Nancy. : 5682

Goliger, Gabriella. : 3263

Goneau, Marilyn. : 2679

Gonzalez, Ellice Becker. : 4792

Good, D. B. :1233

Gooding, Wayne. : 1104

Goodings, Sidlofsky, Goodings and Associates. : 1184, 5858

Goodman, E. :2235, 2680

Goodman, Eileen. : 1836, 2681

Goodwill, Jean. : 4625

Goodwin, Theresa. : 6452

Gordon, G. Jean. : 3774

Gordon, Margie and Shelly Gavignan. : 120

Gordon, Marie. : 799

Gordon, Sheldon E. : 298, 759

Gore, Kenneth G. : 4504

Gorham, Deborah. : 919, 2957, 3453, 4504, 6300, 6301, 6302, 6303, 7157

Gormely, Sheila. : 4121

Gosse, R. : 4027

Gosse, Stella-Marie Rideout. : 5833

Gosselin, Hélène. : 1428, 2444, 3790

Gostick, Kim. : 2538

Gotlieb, Sondra. : 5296

Gottlieb, Amy. : 3791

Gottlieb, Lois C. and Wendy Keitner. : 3847, 3848, 3897, 4518, 5092

Goudie, Elizabeth. : 920, 7182

Gould, Allan B. : 6968

Gould, Allan M. : 579, 2682, 3454, 6470, 6471

Gould, Gail and others. : 6526

Gould, Jan. : 7017

Gould, Karen. : 3914

Goundrey, Jane and others. : 6107

Goundrey, Shirley. : 7216

Gourgues, Jules-Henri. : 1038

Govier, Katherine. : 395, 1105, 3455, 4505, 4519

Gowanlock, Theresa. : 5147

Goyder, John C. : 6911

Grabner, Karen. : 5052

Graff, Linda L. : 2874, 2875

Grafstein, Rina. : 5572

Graham, Martin and Cannie Stark Adamec. : 5573

Guse, Linda L. : 6001
Guyatt, Doris E. : 6188
Guyatt, Doris Elsie. : 141, 6763
Guyon, Louise, Roxane Simard et Louise Nadeau. : 4426
Gwyn, Sandra. : 474, 475, 1109, 3943, 4233, 5242
Gzowski, Peter. : 583
Hacker, Carlotta. : 922, 3456, 4388, 4389
Hackett, John and Diana Barza. : 6764
Haddock, J. and R. L. Rodensky. : 4507
Hagan, John and Nancy O'Donnel. : 1584
Haggan, Hilary and Denise Ledoux. : 5243
Hahlo, H. R. : 1916, 4030
Haist, Dianne. : 2597, 2747
Hale, Linda Louise. : 415, 6304
Haliburton, Jane. : 121
Haliburton, Jane C. : 3206
Halifax Women's Bureau. : 2398, 2399, 3751
Hall, Ann. : 584, 3777
Hall, Ann, Jane Cameron and Debbie Shogan. : 585, 6681
Hall, Audrey. : 3207
Hall, M. Ann. : 588, 589, 590, 591, 648, 6002

Hall, M. Ann and Dorothy A. Richardson. : 586
Hall, M. Ann and Patricia A. Lawson. : 587
Hall, Margaret Ann. : 647
Hall, O. : 1839, 2237, 6003
Hallet, Mary E. : 1316
Hamel, Réginald. : 923, 3457, 3898
Ha-Milton, Reina. : 3792
Hamilton, Roberta. : 4997
Hamilton Regional Women's Research Collective. : 6168
Hamilton Status of Women Committee. : 4576
Hamilton Women's Services Central Training. : 6882

Hamilton-Wentworth. Community Information Service. : 4949
Hancock, Lyn. : 4746
Handelman, Esther. : 2020, 6413
Handelman, Mark and Wendy Ward. : 6527
Handfield, M. : 2021
Hanif, Muhammad. : 1917, 6004
Hanley, Susan and others. : 3793
Hannell, Lesley. : 802
Hannley, Lynn and Marsha Mitchell. : 3264
Hansen, Barbara. : 760
Hardy, Allison Taylor. : 3138
Harel, Louise. : 2628
Harel-Giasson, Francine et Marie-Françoise Marchis-Mouren. : 152
Harrington, Michael Francis. : 7222
Harris, M. : 1978
Harris, Marjorie. : 192, 301, 476, 1110, 1446, 2470, 2471, 2684, 5093
Harris, Marjorie and Benjamin Schlesinger. : 2770, 3944
Harris, S. : 1918
Harrison, Brian, R. :3265, 3266, 6979
Harrison, Donna J. : 592, 6005
Harshaw, Josephine. : 4962
Hart, L. B. : 2685
Hartle, Douglas G. : 6377

Hartman, Grace. : 1840, 3581, 3582
Hartnagel, Timothy F. : 1585
Hartnagel, Timothy F. and Mary Ellen Gillan. : 5468
Hartwick, Paul. : 761, 4411
Harvey, Cameron. : 2832, 4097
Harvey, Christopher. : 4092
Harvey, Dona. : 3458
Harvey, Julien. : 1317
Harvor, Beth. : 707
Haslam, P. : 1586
Haslam, Phyllis G. : 1587
Hastings, Jane and Judith Lawrence. : 1469
Haswell, Geof. : 431
Hatt, Linda Lou. : 5577
Hauck, Philomena. : 7129
Hauser, Anne M. and June N. Wilton. : 803
Hawken, Ann. : 7158
Hawkes, Cheryl. : 122, 1919, 6338
Hawley, A. : 2921, 4412, 7076
Hawley, Brendan, ed. : 2486
Hawreliak, Sylvia. : 5505
Hawrylko, Rosalie. : 5578
Hawrylyshyn, Oli. : 3239
Hayford, Alison. : 5812
Hayman, Sasha. : 478
Hayman, Sasha and Joan Barfoot. : 477

Head, Gertrude. : 924, 5148
Headon, Christopher. : 1318, 4494
Heald, Tim. : 3139
Healy, W. J. : 5149, 7192
Heath, Brian. : 193
Heath, David S. : 142
Heath, Jean. : 6189
Hedderwick, William and Kathryn Pelkey. : 6765
Hedley, Max J. : 2876, 4031, 5813
Hedley, R. Adams and Susan M. Adams. : 4552
Hedlund, David. : 3288, 3945

Heenan, Roy L. : 3540
Heiman, Trudie. : 479
Heit, Michael J. and Don Malpass. : 3778
Héleine, François. : 4032, 4171, 4234, 4235
Helmers, D. : 7453
Henderson, Jule and John Briere. : 1764, 5579
Henderson, Karen. : 1236
Hendry, J. C. : 6511
Henriksen, Sheila P. : 1588, 5580
Henripin, Jacques. : 3033, 3034, 3035
Henripin, Jacques and Jacques Légaré. : 3036
Henripin, Jacques et Evelyne Lapierre-Adamcyk. : 2771
Henry, Ann. : 925, 3459
Henshel, Anne-Marie. : 3946, 5907, 6006
Henson, Jane. : 4467
Hepworth, H. Philip. : 39, 1041
Hepworth, P. : 1632
Hepworth, Philip. : 1631

Herman, Sheryl Frances. : 3177, 3289
Herold, Edward S. : 1042
Herold, Edward S. and Lynne M. Samson. : 1043
Herold, Edward S. and Marilyn R. Goodwin. : 1044
Herold, Edward S. and Marilyn Shirley Goodwin. : 1045, 1046, 5908
Herold, Edward S. and Roger E. Thomas. : 1047, 5909
Hersom, Naomi. : 6682
Hersom, Naomi and Dorothy E. Smith. : 2238, 2239, 2241
Hersom, Naomi and Lucy Scott. : 2240
Herzog, Carol. : 1633, 1634, 1680
Hetherington, E. : 6190
Hétu, Renée. : 1708, 4553
Hewett, Adlyn M. : 2833
Hewitt, Ron W. : 4188, 4189
Hibbert, Joyce, ed. : 3379
Hickling-Johnston Ltd. : 2242, 3583
Hicks, M. Ellen. : 6851
Hildebrandt, Heather. : 4413, 7476
Hill, Christina Maria. : 2243
Hill, Mary W. : 366
Hillmer, Sandra. : 3418
Hilts, Daniel. : 1447
Hindbo, Ester and Micheline Kisner. : 6169
Hinds, Margery. : 4747
Hipwell, Anne. : 1542
Illid, Richard. . 0917
Hiscock, Pamela Ruth. : 2022, 7217
Hitchman, Gladys Symons. : 2127, 6721, 6722, 6817
Hobart, Cathy. : 480, 481, 482
Hobart, Charles. : 4033, 5910, 5911
Hobart, Charles W. : 3947, 3948, 3949, 3950, 5912
Hobbs, Lisa. : 1277, 5244, 5245, 7010
Hoek, Margaretha. : 2089, 2472, 5878
Hoeschen, Susan. : 2686, 4098
Hoffman, Abby. : 593, 594, 595, 649
Hogervorst, Joann E. : 3951
Hogg, Carol. : 6994
Holland, Winifred H. : 4124
Holland, Winifred H. and D. Keith McNair. : 3700, 4034, 6747
Hollobon, J. : 2244
Holman, Roy Paul. : 596
Holmberg, R. : 1048
Holmes, Barry. : 1237, 2546
Holmes, Peggy. : 926, 5150
Holmes, R. A. : 6918
Holt, Simma. : 927, 5297
Home, Alice. : 4907
Home, Alice Marian. : 4906, 7477
Home Economics International Development Workshop, Halifax, N.S., 1979. : 3220
Hood, D. D. and others. : 7130
Hood, Nancy E. : 6191
Hooper, J. : 3815, 5010
Hopkins, Monica. : 928, 5151
Horlick, Sharon Debra. : 804
Horna, Jarmila L. A. : 3333

Horne, H. Shirley. : 5246
Hornosty, Roy W. : 5118
Horsford, Patricia A. : 4035, 5053
Hosek, Chaviva. : 1470, 2629
Hossie, Helen. : 2245, 6919
Hotchkiss, Ron. : 7159
Houle, Ghislaine. : 7300, 7345
Hovius, Berend. : 2834
Howard, Paul. : 3290
Howarth, Joyce and Susan Secord. : 6883
Howell, Shelley and Margaret Malone. : 2246, 3334
Hoy, Helen Elizabeth. : 3850
Hrynyk, N. P. : 5834
Hudak, Ladislas. : 4950
Hudson, Douglas Ridley. : 4748
Hudson, Grace. : 4764
Hughes, D. O. : 7077
Hughes, Jane. : 196
Hughes, Lorraine. : 4696. 4697

Hughes, Patricia. : 4125
Hulbert, Winifred. : 5814
Humber College of Applied Arts and Technology. : 2023, 2090, 6607
Humphreys, Carolyn Ann. : 6192
Humphreys, Elizabeth. : 4435
Humphreys, Linda. : 6276
Hunsberger, Emily J. : 6970
Hunsley, Terrance M. : 6339
Hunt, Constance. : 4698
Hunt, J. Doris. : 483
Hunt, Keith. : 3508
Hunter, Marlene E. : 40
Huot, François. : 597
Hustvedt, Eric. : 1113
Hyatt, Patricia M. : 5581
Hynd, Arleen and Mary Rocan. : 7401

Hynes, Maureen. : 598, 2958, 2993, 5247, 6264
Hynna, Martha. : 5778
I.O.D.E. : 6884
Imbeault, Marie-Andrée. : 6571
Imperial Order Daughters of the Empire. : 4909, 7078
Inderwick, Mary. : 5152
Indian Rights for Women Group. : 1471, 4700
Indra, Doreen. : 4481, 5447
Indra, Doreen M. : 4480
Ingram, Marta and Ceta Ramkhalawansingh. : 5448
Inkster, Brenda. : 6109
Innes, Eva. : 2547
Innis, Mary (Quayle). : 929
Institute of Law Research and Reform, University of Alberta. : 4072, 4073
Ion, Caroline, ed. : 5354
IR Research Services and Labour Canada. : 4342
Irigaray, Luce. : 6007
Ironside, Anne. : 2024, 6852, 7509
Irvine, D. M. : 1238, 5860
Irving, Howard H. : 1920, 2835

Kome, Penney. : 1473, 1474, 1475, 1476, 2631, 2690, 4343, 5096, 5254, 5357
Konantz, Gail. : 939, 5255
Kondo, Vickie A. : 6342
Kopinak, Kathryn Mary. : 5358
Korabik, Karen. : 5588, 6017
Korchinsky, Nestor Nick. : 651
Kostash, Myrna. : 48, 711, 2474, 2926, 4100, 4415, 4416, 4521, 4557, 5097, 5256, 5691, 5692, 5693, 5694, 6170
Kostash, Myrna and others. : 940
Koulack, Ester and Leona McEvoy. : 4101
Koutecky, Teri. : 2879, 4102
Kowalski, Edita. : 305, 2255, 2691, 2692
Kozak, John Francis. : 368
Koziol, Carol Ann. : 602, 6018
Krahn, Harvey, John Gartrell and Lyle Larson. : 2777, 5746
Krakauer, Renate. : 1522, 2094, 2129
Krashinsky, Michael. : 1681
Krawchuk, Peter. : 4483
Kremer, E. J. and E. A. Synan. : 49
Kreps, Bonnie. : 2927, 3097
Krishnamoni, Devaki. : 50
Kronby, Malcolm. : 2840

Kronby, Malcolm C. : 2839
Krossel, Martin. : 763
Krotki, K. J. and S. A. McDaniel. : 51
Krotz, Larry. : 1320
Kryzanowski, Lawrence and Elizabeth Bertin-Boussu. : 1543
Kunin, Roslyn. : 6197
Kuzel, Paul and P. Krishnan. : 5736
Kyriazis, Natalie. : 3040, 3041
Kyriazis, Natalie and J. Henripin. : 3042
Labarge, Dorothy. : 4630, 4749
Laberge, Diane, Jeannine Lawless and Rollande V. Bédard. : 6198
Labrador Inuit Association. : 4750
Labreche, Julianne. : 4911, 5257, 5258, 5299
Labreche, Julianne and Catherine Fox. : 433
Labreche, Julianne and Robert Stall. : 5509
Lacelle, Claudette. : 1969, 2377
Lacelle, Élisabeth J. : 1321
Lacelle, Nicole. : 5359
Lacerte-Lamontagne, Céline. : 5695

Lacerte-Lamontagne, Célyne et Yves Lamontagne. : 5696
Lachance, Micheline. : 2778, 4241
Lachapelle, Réjean. : 3044
Ladan, C. J. and D. Hodgins Miller. : 6112
Ladan, C. J. and Maxine M. Crooks. : 2095
Lafon, Dominique. : 6514
Laframboise, Philippe. : 941
Lafrenière, Suzanne. : 942
Lalonde, Claire. : 5697
Lalonde, Marc. : 1049, 5055
Lalonde, Michele. : 204
LaMarsh, Judy. : 943, 5259
Lambert, Anne. : 1979, 5098
Lambert, Carmen. : 4751

Lambert, John Thomas. : 5436
Lambert, Leah and Patrick Madden. : 5472, 5473
Lambert, Leah R. and Patrick G. Madden. : 1589, 1590, 5470, 5471
Lambert, Ronald D. : 6019
Lambert, Ruth Carolyn. : 5835, 6417
Lambert, Thérèse. : 944, 4843
Lamont, Michèle. : 5204
LaMothe, Dennis M. : 5510
Lamothe, Jacqueline et Jennifer Stoddart. : 5360
Lamy, Suzanne. : 712
Lancaster, Jan. : 4912
Landau, Barbara. : 1591, 1845, 6020
Landau, Reva. : 5056
Landau, Reva and Lois Lowenberg. : 5698
Landes, Ruth. : 4764.1
Landreville, Pierre. : 5474
Landsberg, Michèle. : 489, 2928, 3098, 3129, 4508, 5361, 5362, 5363, 5645, 6021, 6477, 6478
Lane, G. : 5781
Lane, Grace. : 1322
Lange, Linda. : 1641
Langevin, Liane. : 5364, 5365
Langin, Susan Esther. : 5747
Langlais, Nicole. : 5589
Langstone, Mike. : 6199
Lanken, Dane. : 205
Lanktree, Cheryl R. : 5500
Lapalme, M. : 5511
Lapierre-Adamcyk, Evelyne. : 3045, 3047, 4242
Lapierre-Adamcyk, Evelyne et Nicole Marcil-Gratton. : 1050
Laplante, Germaine. : 945
Laplante, Michelle. : 684
Lapping, Joyce K. and Mark B. Lapping. : 5817
Larivière, H. : 4786
Larkin, J. : 5782
Larouche, Ginette. : 808
Larsen, Carolyn and Lorna Cammaert. : 1523
Larson, Doris. : 490, 491
Larson, Lyle E. : 2779
Lashuk, Maureen Grace Wilson. : 4558
Lashuk, Maureen Wilson and George Kurian. : 4559, 6022
Lasvergnas-Grémy, Isabelle. : 5861
Latham, Barbara. : 5156
Laurence, Margaret. : 713
Laurin-Frenette, Nicole. : 6257
Lautard, Emile Hugh. : 1189
Lauzon, Sylvie. : 1387
Lavallee, Mary Ann. : 4671
Lavigne, Marie and Jennifer Stoddart. : 2447, 2448, 2449, 2450
Lavigne, Marie et Michèle Jean. : 5366
Lavigne, Marie, and others. : 2451, 6305
Lavigne, Marie, Yolande Pinard and Jennifer Stoddart. : 2960, 4966
Lavoie, Stella. : 4913, 5818
Lawrence, Judith and Jane Hastings. : 1477
Lawrence, Judith and Jean Wilson. : 5260
Lawrence, Karen. : 714, 715

Lawrence, Wendy. : 1457, 6479

Lawrence, Wendy and Naomi Black. : 5367

Lawrence, William J. : 143

Laws, Margaret. : 434, 1166, 1388, 1846, 2555, 2693, 2961, 4243, 5368

Lawson, Darlene. : 1592, 5475

Layton, Monique. : 1593, 5512, 5513, 5514

Layton, Nancy. : 603

Lazar, Frances E. : 160

Lazar, Morty M. : 1323

Le Bourdais, E. : 123

Le Riche, N. and J. Howard. : 1052, 5913

Le Rougetel, Katy. : 2378

Leacock, Eleanor. : 4672

Leacock, Stephen. : 4417

Leah, Ronnie. : 1682

Leaper, Richard John. : 2257, 6546

Leblanc, Christine M. : 6283

Leblanc, Claudette. : 2929

LeBlanc, L. : 4586

Leblond, Georges. : 52

LeBourdais, E. : 2930, 5699

Leduc, Chantal. : 4914

Lee, Betty. : 306, 1190, 2694

Lee, Bobbi. : 4631

Lee, Danielle Juteau. : 4844

LeFeuvre, Joan. : 809

Légaré, Jacques. : 3046, 4845

Légaré, Michel. : 4172, 4173, 4174

Legault, Gisèle. : 6235

Legendre, Anne Carmelle. : 1324, 2061

Leginsky, Patricia Anne. : 4244

Lehman, Carol L. : 5591

Leith, Nancy Louise. : 1191

LeMay, Francine. : 4509

Lemay, Jacqueline. : 4587

Lemieux, Lucien. : 2062

Lemieux, Thérèse et Gemma Caron. : 946

Lemoine, Christine. : 491

Lennon, Elizabeth Shilton. : 1847

Lenskyj, Helen. : 2379

Lent, Barbara Pauline. : 4454

Leonard, Anne Hewitt. : 2368

Lepage, Francine et autres. : 2452

Lepage, Francine et Marie Lavigne. : 4345

Lequin, Lucie. : 716

Lerch, Renate. : 1118, 2695

Leslie, Susan. : 604

L'Espérance, Jeanne. : 2063

Lessard, Marc-André et Jean-Paul Montminy. : 4846

Lester, Tanya. : 1240

Létourneau, Jeannette. : 6455

Lever, Bernice. : 717

Levine, G. : 2259, 4437

Levine, Helen. : 1524, 6023

Levine, Sybil and Christine Magraken. : 1119

Makabe, Tomoko. : 1929
Makward, Christiane. : 720
Malka. : 4588
Mallinson, Anna Jean. : 5182
Malloch, Kati. : 4316
Malmo-Levine, Cheryl Lynne. : 2935
Malone, Patricia. : 6115
Man, Angela. : 2559
Manitoba. Dept. of Education. : 5265
Manitoba. Dept. of Education. Curriculum Services. : 6130
Manitoba. Dept. of Labour. Women's Bureau. : 1672, 2558, 4561, 5012
Manitoba. Dept. of the Attorney-General. : 2842, 2843
Manitoba. Law Reform Commission. : 4103, 6344, 6345
Manitoba. Pension Commission. : 5059
Manitoba. Task Force on Equal Opportunities in the Civil Service of Manitoba. : 1413
Manitoba Bar Association. : 6378
Manitoba Teachers' Society. : 6419
Manitoba Women's Institute. : 4968
Manley, John. : 4969, 5372
Manley-Casimir, Michael E., L. W. Downey Research Associates Ltd. : 4077
Mann, Brenda. : 765, 4919
Mann, Brenda and Peat O'Neil. : 609
Mann, W. E. : 5914, 5915, 5916
Manson, Freda. : 1686
Maranda, Jeanne. : 496, 497, 4920, 5819
March, Kem. : 721
Marchak, M. Patricia. : 2267
Marchak, Patricia. : 5784
Marchand, Philip. : 57, 1326, 1327, 5266, 5300

Marchessault-Lussier, Lucie. : 2803, 4921
Marchildon, Rudy G. : 5373
Marcil-Gratton, Nicole. : 1056
Marcotte, M. : 1930, 5785, 5786
Marcotte, Marcel. : 58, 59, 60, 61, 62
Marcus, Robert J. : 63
Marmer, Jack. : 2804, 2805, 2806
Marney, Jo. : 1501
Maroney, Heather Jon. : 2936, 2984, 5374, 6258

Marra, Glenna. : 1676, 4562
Marsden, L. R. : 4881
Marsden, Lorna. :6116
Marsden, Lorna and Edward Harvey. : 2132
Marsden, Lorna and others. : 2268, 4922
Marsden, Lorna R. : 2269, 2270, 2560
Marshall, Kye. : 4590
Marshall, Tom. : 5184
Marsot, Ghislaine. : 6202
Martel, Suzanne. : 722
Martens, Debra. : 3120
Martin, Claire. : 954, 955
Martin, Eva. : 5476
Martin, Jane. : 498
Martin, Louis. : 64
Martin, M. A. : 5195
Martin-Matthews, Anne E. : 4458

Martineau, Barbara. : 3100, 3101, 3102, 3103
Marvin, Schiff. : 4753
Massicotte, Denis. : 5135
Masters, Philinda. : 1546, 4591, 5477
Matas, D. : 4708
Matheson, Gwen. : 3006
Matheson, Gwen and V. E. Lang. : 3007, 3008
Mathews, Catherine and Marnie Shea. : 348
Mathews-Klein, Yvonne. : 3104
Mathews-Klein, Yvonne and Ann Pearson. : 6515
Mathien, Julie. : 6420
Matthew, Barbara A. : 2410
Matthews, Anne Martin. : 4459
Matthiasson, John S. : 4754, 4793
Maxwell, Denise. : 1244
Maynard, Fredelle. : 4249, 4524
Mayo, Susan and Susan Holtz. : 2494
Mayrand, Albert. : 5894
Mazel, Annie. : 6346
McAlpine, Phyllis J. and Nancy E. Simpson. : 3049, 4755
McArthur, John. : 2697
McArthur, Laura. : 65
McBean, Jean. : 2844, 4078
McCaldon, R. J. : 1596, 5703
McCall-Newman, Christina. : 5375
McCallan, N. J. and Katherine Roback. : 956, 5428
McCallum, Pamela. : 5099
McCarron, Mary L. : 398, 5598
McCart, Joyce. : 610, 4917
McCaughan, Margaret M. : 4297
McClung, M. G. : 723, 957
McClung, Nellie. : 724, 958, 3009
McConaghy, T. W. : 6421
McConnell, Wanda. : 2780
McCord, Joanne. : 725, 4805
McCormack, Thelma. : 5418
McCoubrey, James. : 206
McCreary, Gillian, Beverly Lambert and Jeff Jones. : 1195
McDaniel, Susan A. and Karol J. Krotki. : 66
McDermott, Patricia. : 4438
McDonald, David and Lauren Drewery. : 611, 959
McDonald, L. : 2985
McDonald, Lynn. : 1479, 2133, 2561, 2562, 4317
McDonald, Marci. : 2937
McDonnell, Kathleen. : 1288, 1931
McDonough, Peggy. : 2634
McDougall, Anne. : 499, 960
McDowell, Linda. : 961, 5376
McElroy, Ann. : 4673, 4756, 4794, 4795
McFadden, Fred. : 612, 962
McFadyen, Joanna. : 5704
McFarlane, Bruce A. : 4250, 4391
McGee, Arlee D. : 4923
McGibbon, Pauline. : 1123
McGill University. Industrial Relations Centre. : 2271

Morissette, Yvonne Rialland. : 5820
Morley, Patricia. :3867
Morneau, François. : 2700
Morris, Cerise. : 4925, 5788
Morris, Cerise Darlene. : 5787
Morrison, Carolyn. : 5864
Morrison, Suzanne. : 210, 539, 1853, 1854, 2565, 2701, 2702, 2703, 2704, 4926
Morrison, T. R. : 2782, 2965
Morrissey, Mary and others. : 211, 675
Morton, E. H. : 5789
Morton, F. L. : 2635
Moudgil, Ranvir. : 3348, 6030
Mount Saint Vincent University. Art Gallery. : 505
Muir, Margaret. :3251, 7326
Muir, Pearl. : 6422
Mungall, Constance. : 1126, 1196, 4610, 5013
Munro, Don R. : 6955
Munro, Mary. : 506, 4634
Munro, Mary and others. : 4757
Munz, Diane and others. : 1061, 6728
Murdoch, Sarah. : 7549
Murphy, Emily F. : 969, 5160
Murphy, J. David. : 4044
Murphy, Johnny. : 4593
Murphy, Pat. : 1439, 3349
Murray, Florence J. : 970, 1109
Murray, Hilda Chaulk. : 7220
Murray, Hilda E. L. : 7221
Murray, Joan. : 507
Murray, Michael A. and Tom Atkinson. : 6827
Muse, A. : 154
Myers, Anita M. : 1062, 5602, 6031
Myers, Anita M. and Hilary M. Lips. : 614
Myers, Marybelle. : 4635, 4636, 4787, 4788
Myette, J. M. : 1855
Myhr, Ronald Peder. : 1528, 6032
Myrtle, Jeanne-Marie. : 2705
Nadeau, Denise. : 1529, 5749
Nadeau, Elaine. : 1197
Nadeau, J. R. : 2280
Nahanee, Theresa. : 4711
Naidoo, Josephine C. : 3350, 3351
Naissance-Renaissance. : 1292
Nakamura, Alice and Masao Nakamura. : 4254, 4255, 5014
Nakamura, Alice and others. : 4256, 6925
Nanimahoo, Carmel. : 4774
Narayana, Hélène. : 508
Nash, Joanna. : 540

National Action Committee on the Status of Women. : 1391, 1480, 2281, 2636, 2846, 4927,
    5062, 5063, 5419, 6483, 6484, 6555
National Association of Women and the Law. : 1481, 3712
National Association of Women and the Law, Calgary Caucus. : 3734
National Association of Women and the Law. Victoria Caucus. : 3117
National Conference of Women in Trades. 1st, Sept. 26-8, 1980. : 1245
National Conference on Women and Sport. : 615

Oliver, Carole. : 125
Ollsen, Andree. : 3426
Olmsted, Marion. : 3191, 5605
Olson, Ruth A. : 5709
Olyan, Sidney. : 6238
O'Malley, Martin. : 619
O'Murcada, L. : 4776
O'Neill, Paul. : 7224
O'Neill, Peat. : 1127
Onley, Gloria. : 3868
Ontario. Advisory Council on Equal Opportunity for Women. : 321
Ontario. Civil Service Commission and Ontario. Women Crown Employees Office. : 1415
Ontario. Dept. of Labour. Women's Bureau. : 1199, 2291, 2412, 2413, 3756
Ontario. Interministerial Textbook Committee. : 6122
Ontario. Joint Task Force on Immigrant Women, September 1979. : 3357
Ontario. Law Reform Commission. : 2848, 4132, 4133, 4611, 4612, 4613, 6347
Ontario. Legislative Assembly. Standing Committee on Social Development. : 821
Ontario. Ministry of Colleges and Universities. : 1248, 1249, 4882
Ontario. Ministry of Community and Social Services. : 1689
Ontario. Ministry of Community and Social Services. Advisory Council on Day Care. : 1690
Ontario. Ministry of Consumer and Commercial Relations. : 1549
Ontario. Ministry of Correctional Services. : 5478
Ontario. Ministry of Culture and Recreation. Office of the Women's Advisor. : 322, 1416
Ontario. Ministry of Education. : 2036, 6034, 6864, 7135, 7555, 7556
Ontario. Ministry of Health. Health Education, Promotion Unit and Ontario Interagency Council on Smoking and Health. : 3191.1
Ontario. Ministry of Labour. : 2571
Ontario. Ministry of Labour. Office of the Executive Coordinator, Women's Programs. : 323, 1417
Ontario. Ministry of Labour. Research Branch. : 2037, 2414
Ontario. Ministry of Labour. Women Crown Employees Office. : 324, 325, 1418, 1419, 1420, 1421, 1422, 1423, 4352, 4353, 4354
Ontario. Ministry of Labour. Women's Bureau. : 326, 327, 349, 1200, 1250, 1251,1691, 1858, 2135, 2288, 2417, 2418, 2419, 2420, 2421, 2706, 3157, 3532, 3533, 3534, 3535, 3600, 3601, 3757, 3758, 3759, 4355, 4356, 6131, 6840, 6865, 6879, 7439
Ontario. Ministry of Labour. Women's Bureau. Research Branch. : 328
Ontario. Ministry of Labour. Women's Programs Division. : 2422, 3427
Ontario. Ministry of the Attorney General. : 2849
Ontario. Ministry of Treasury, Economics and Intergovernmental Affairs and Ontario Conference on Local Government. : 5380
Ontario. Office of the Provincial Secretary for Social Development. : 329
Ontario. Provincial Secretariat for Justice. : 5710, 5711
Ontario. Secretariat for Social Development. : 4134
Ontario. Task Force on Equal Opportunity in Athletics. : 618
Ontario Coalition for Better Daycare. : 1688
Ontario Educational Communications Authority. : 681, 686, 7553, 7554
Ontario Federation of Labour. : 3638
Ontario Human Rights Commission. : 1857, 3122
Ontario Institute for Studies in Education. Dept. of Adult Education. : 2102
Ontario Ladies' College. : 2065
Ontario Native Women's Association. : 1483, 4765, 4766
Ontario Progressive Conservative Association of Women. : 5488
Ontario Status of Women Council. : 320, 374, 617, 820, 2415, 2416, 2640, 3158, 3192,3536, 4045, 4131, 4929, 5017, 6123, 6926, 6974, 7241
Ontario Status of Women Council. Child Care Committee. : 1692

Payne, Julien D. : 6348, 6349
Payton, L. C. : 6626
Pazdro, Roberta J. : 515, 516
Peal, Emma. : 1131, 1863, 1864, 1982, 2297, 2707, 6709
Pearl, Brian. : 6036
Pearson, Mary. : 126, 1066, 1067, 2477
Pedersen, Diana L. : 4974
Pelletier, Gérard. : 5382
Pelletier, Jacqueline. : 7242
Pelletier, Jacqueline and others. : 6627
Pelletier, Pol. : 6516, 6517, 6518
Pelletier-Baillargeon, Hélène. : 1330, 7328, 7329
Pelrine, Eleanor. : 74, 75
Pelrine, Eleanor Wright. : 5101, 7100
Peltz, Barbara. : 7511
Pendergast, Barbara. : 1530
Penney, Jennifer. : 2298
Pennock, Mike and Mark Goldenberg. : 1694

Pepperdene, Barbara J. : 1202, 4866
Perkins, Craig. : 1746
Perly, C. : 2299
Perreault, Michel. : 76
Perreault, Yvette. : 5732
Perron, Marie et Jean Perron. : 5919
Perticaro, Barbara. : 6689
Pestieau, Caroline. : 7330
Peter, Karl and Ian Whitaker. : 7421
Peterkin, Audrey and Margaret Shaw. : 974, 7196
Peters, J. F. : 1937
Peters, John F. : 1935, 1936, 5739

Peterson, Rebecca, Gerda R. Wekerle and David Morley. : 2495
Pethick, Jane. : 848
Pettigrew, Eileen. : 2708
Pfeifer, Pat and Stanley J. Shapiro. : 1132, 5945, 6729
Pfeifer, Patricia. : 5606, 6730
Philip, Catherine. : 6999
Phillips, Frances. : 215, 216
Phillips, M. : 5713, 7101
Phillips, Paul. : 2388
Phillips, Rhys D. : 330
Picard-Pilon, Louise. : 4930
Piccolo, Ornella. : 5607
Piche, R. : 4848
Pié, Bette. : 331
Piéri, Monique. : 2892
Pierson, Ruth. : 2381, 2382, 7006, 7558
Pierson, Ruth and Beth Light. : 7136, 7557
Pierson, Ruth Roach. : 437, 438, 439, 440
Pike, Lois. : 5383
Pike, Robert. : 1938
Pilkington, Harry. : 2574
Pinard, Yolande. : 2966, 7389
Pineau, Jean. : 1939, 4178, 4179
Pineau-Ouellet, Ghislaine. : 5450, 7390
Pinet, Janine. : 5865, 6690, 6731

Prince Edward Island. University. President's Advisory Committee on the Status of Women in the University. : 6628
Prindiville, Joanne. : 5198
Pringle, Brenda. : 1649
Prodanou, Anna. : 5273
Progressive Conservative Party of Canada. : 5489
Prokop, Mary. : 4486, 4976
Propper, Alice. : 4565
Prost, Viviane. : 542
Prost, Vivian and Nell Tenhaaf. : 3108
Proulx, Marcienne. : 976, 4849, 6239
Proulx, Monique Cecile. : 676, 6039
Proulx, Serge. : 217
Provincial Council of Women of Manitoba. Arts and Letters Committee. : 518

Prus, Robert and Styllianos Irini. : 5519
Pulyk, Marcia. : 4325, 4326
Purcell, Myrtle. : 6458
Purdy, Harriet and David Gagan. : 5163
Purdy, Kris. : 334, 621, 4319
Purdy, Margaret. : 6781
Pyke, S. W. and C. Stark-Adamec. : 2968, 5613
Pyke, S. W. and J. C. Stewart. : 6486
Pyke, Sandra W. : 1770, 1865, 5608, 5612, 5947, 6040, 6086
Pyke, Sandra W. and Faye Weisenberg. : 6828
Pyros, J. : 3109
Québec. Bureau de la statistique. Service de la démographie et du recensement. : 3055
Quebec. Comité chargé d'étudier le problème du travail de nuit de la main-d'oeuvre féminine dans les établissements industriels. : 2453
Québec. Conseil des affaires sociales et de la famille. : 77, 78, 2789
Québec. Conseil du statut de la femme. : 79, 219, 335, 687, 826, 1426, 1429, 1709, 1866, 1942, 2040, 2642, 2643, 2853, 2854, 4951, 7331, 7332, 7333, 7347
Québec. Ministère de la Fonction publique. : 336
Québec. Ministère de la Fonction publique. Programmes égalité des chances. : 1430, 1431
Québec. Ministère de la justice. Comité d'orientation. : 827
Québec. Ministère de la justice. Service d'information. : 1943, 4181
Québec. Ministère de l'éducation. : 2041, 7334
Québec. Ministère de l'éducation. Direction générale de l'éducation des adultes. : 2042
Québec. Ministère des affairs sociales. Direction du personnel. : 337, 1432
Québec. Ministère des communications. Centre de documentation. : 7335
Québec. Office de revision du code civil. Comité du droit des personnes et de la famille. : 2855, 2856
Québec. Secrétariat d'état a la condition féminine. : 7336
Queen's University. Association of Women Teaching at Queen's. : 6629
Queen's University. Office of the Principal. : 6630
Queen's University. Principal's Advisory Review Committee on the Status of Women. : 6631
Queen's University. Principal's Committee on the Status of Women. : 6632
Quiggin, Betty. : 4566
Quigley, Jocelyne. : 6866
Rabkin, Brenda. : 5274, 6782
Racicot, Colette et Marie Tellier. : 4567, 7393
Radio, Vera. : 7484
Rae, Barbara J. : 1135, 2712
Rae, Jane. : 222, 7103
Rahn, M. Julie-Anne. : 3196
Ram, Bali. : 2303, 3056

Ramkhalawansingh, Ceta. : 2575, 3518, 3359, 3360
Ramu, G. N. : 2790, 2791, 3967, 3968
Randall, Nora Delahunt. : 657
Randall, S. J. : 2304
Rankin, Linda. : 2713
Rankin, Linda Marie. : 3873
Rao, N. Baskara. : 3057, 3058
Raphael, Dennis. : 5614, 5615, 5616, 7582, 7583, 7584
Rasky, Deena. : 2305
Rasminsky, Judy. : 828
Rasmussen, Linda and others. : 5164
Rasporich, Beverly J. : 3874
Ray, Janet. : 977, 2644, 3010, 4395, 7173
Ray, Marilyn Anne. : 4869
Ray, Ratna. : 3132, 4261
Rayfield, J. R. : 3361
Raymond, Valerie. : 3668
Read, Daphne, ed. : 7174
Read, Merilyn. : 6487
Réaume, Denise. : 2645, 3713
Recherches opérationnelles technique économiques. : 2306

Redmond, Sarah and Eileen Turcotte. :7243
Reed, Carol. : 549, 2714
Reeve, Phyllis. : 4977, 7021
Reeves, John. : 1206, 7104
Reeves-Morache, Marcelle. : 7394
Regina. University. President's Committee on the Status of Women. : 6633
Regina. University. President's Committee on the Status of Women. Sample Survey and Data
    Bank Unit. : 6634
Regina Plains Community College. : 6867
Reich, Carol. : 1410

Reich, Carol and Helen La Fountaine. : 1772, 1773, 6431, 6432,6433
Reich, Carol M. : 1771
Reid, Alison. : 3110
Reid, Diane and others. : 4978
Reid, Gayla. : 732
Reid, Laura. : 3440
Reid, Linda. : 1598
Repo, S. : 2646
Research, Action and Education Centre. : 2882
Réseau d'action et d'information pour les femmes. : 2647, 4301, 6488, 6489, 6928, 7338
Revolutionary Workers' League. : 2986
Reynolds, Louise. : 978, 5302
Reynolds, O. J. : 225
Rhodes, A. : 7105
Rhodes, Ann. : 733, 5070, 6380
Rhodes, Kathleen. : 1333
Ribeyron, Marie-Thérèse. : 3302, 4262, 4511, 5717, 6490
Rice, Richard M. : 4487, 4526
Rich, J. : 2949, 3969
Richard, Yvan. : 1070
Richardson, Ann. : 6041
Richardson, Karen. : 1484, 4717
Richardson, Kathy and others. : 4527
Richardt, Joan Marie. : 6829

Roch, Marcelle Hardy. : 2454
Rockett, Eve. : 622, 4302, 5480, 5649
Rodd, Catherine. : 6783
Roden, Lethem Sutcliffe. : 734
Roe, Kathleen Robson. : 442
Roger, Gertrude Minor. : 980
Rogers, Janet. : 543
Rogers, June. : 1296
Rogers, Sally and Catherine Carey. : 5481
Romaniuk, A. : 3061, 4643
Romaniuk, Anatole. : 3062
Romaniuk, Anatole and Victor Piché, : 3063
Romm, Tsilia. : 6830
Roney, Bronwen. : 1532
Ronish, Donna Ann. : 2136, 2137
Rooke, Constance. : 3876
Rooke, Patricia T. and R. L. Schnell. : 981, 5278, 6957, 6958
Rooney, Frances. : 4396, 4596, 6533
Roper, Julie Faye. : 6044
Rose, Marie-Georgette. : 831
Rose-Lizée and Ginette Dussault. : 1867

Rosenberg, Avis Lang. : 520, 521
Rosenberg, Harriet. : 1297
Rosenberg, Leah. : 982, 3362
Rosenbluth, Vera. : 5482
Rosenfeld, Rachael A. : 2309, 6931
Rosensweig, Donna. : 6207, 6959
Rosenthal, Star. : 3633
Ross, A. : 4419
Ross, A. D. : 1138
Ross, Aileen D. : 1137, 4263
Ross, Alexander. : 83
Ross, Anne. : 1072, 6784
Ross, Beatrice Spence. : 7237
Ross, Beverley. : 4597
Ross, David. : 5071
Ross, Eleanor C. : 1139

Ross, Hazel Miriam. : 3197, 5618
Ross, Henry. : 1140, 2310
Ross, Kathleen Gallagher, ed. : 1651
Ross, M. L. : 6491
Ross, Mary Lowrey. : 226
Ross, R. R. : 3490
Ross, R. R. and others. : 3491
Ross, Robert R., Claudia Currie and Barbara Krug-McKay. : 5483
Ross, Shirley Ann. : 84
Ross, Val. : 623, 735, 5279, 5280, 5387, 6173
Ross, Valerie. : 3303, 6045, 7106
Rosser, M. J. : 4264, 5019
Rossé, Glen Peter. : 6785
Rossiter, Sean. : 5304
Rosta, Helen : 85
Rosta, Helen J. : 86
Rothberg, Diane. : 1255
Rothman, Betsy. : 5796

Rouilland, Jacques. : 1441, 3657

Rouslin, Virginia Watson. : 5167

Rousseau, Yvette. : 1167, 2311

Routledge, Janet. : 832, 3606

Rovan, Rhonda. : 1256, 6150

Rowan, Renée. : 1747

Rowland, Robin. : 3464, 3465

Rowley, J. C. R. and D. W. Henderson. : 2792

Roy, Laurent. : 1946, 4720

Roy, Laurent and others. : 4719

Roy, Monique. : 522, 5439

Roy, Rosaire. : 3658

Royal Commission on the Status of Women in Canada. : 7137

Royce, M. V. : 2312, 7441, 7442

Royce, Marion. : 421, 2071

Royce, Marion V. : 2068, 2069, 2070, 2072, 2103, 2104, 2105

Roycroft, Marilyn M. : 5388

Rozovsky, Lorne E. : 87, 130, 3198, 4303, 4304

Rubenstein, Lorne. : 624

Rubin, Berte. : 6284

Rubinger, Catherine. : 3920, 3985

Ruff, Kathleen. : 1748, 3519, 6492

Rule, Jane. : 736

Rumball, Donald. : 1141

Russell, Bettina. : 155

Russell, Connie. : 5852

Russell, Mary. : 1599, 5720

Russell, Susan. : 6088, 6089, 6280, 6831

Russell, Susan Jessie. : 6046, 6047, 6279

Ryan, Edward. : 4054

Ryan, Edward F. : 3716, 3717, 6352

Ryan, H. R. S. : 131

Rymell, Heather. : 5103

Ryten, Eve. : 1207, 2313, 6710

Ryval, Michael. : 3669

S.O.S. grossesse. : 5440

Sabat, Christina. : 523

Sabia, Laura. : 2950, 5389

Sachdev, Paul. : 88

Sadoway, Geri. : 4935

Saint-Arnaud-Beauchamp, Jocelyne. : 2951

Saint-Martin, Fernande. : 1334

Saint-Pierre, Annette. : 7197

Sales, Judith. : 1652

Sallot, Lynne. : 1869

Salutin, Marilyn. : 1611

Salverson, Laura Goodman. : 983, 3386

Samler, Jolanta and Frankie Ford. : 625

Samson, Linda M. : 1073

Samson, Marcelle Germain. : 7138

Sanders, D. E. : 4722

Sanders, Doreen. : 2720

Sanders, Douglas. : 4721

Sanders, Karen E. : 3877

Sanders, Willie James. : 402

Sanderson, Kay. : 7001
Sandrock, Tom. : 5200
Sands, Gwen. : 524
Sangster, Dorothy. : 3796, 4488, 5281
Sangster, Joan. : 6267
Santi, Roberta. : 4470
Saskatchewan. Advisory Council on the Status of Women. : 339, 1711, 2858, 3142, 6151, 7403
Saskatchewan. Dept. of Labour. Research and Planning Division. : 6933
Saskatchewan. Dept. of Labour. Women's Bureau. : 2460
Saskatchewan. Dept. of Labour. Women's Division. : 1653, 1712, 2314, 2315, 2461, 2883,
    3770, 3931, 3991, 4305, 5020, 5072, 7404, 7411, 7412
Saskatchewan. Human Rights Commission. : 6125
Saskatchewan. Law Reform Commission. : 3771, 3772, 4191, 4192, 4193, 4194, 4195, 4306,
    6353, 6354
Saskatchewan. Office of the Co-ordinator, Status of Women. : 7405
Saskatchewan. Task Force on Women's Health. : 3199
Saskatchewan. University. University Studies Group. : 6635
Saskatchewan Federation of Labour, C.L.C. Women's Ad Hoc Committee. : 1713

Saskatoon Business and Professional Women's Club. : 7406
Saskatoon College of Law. : 3773
Saskatoon Women's Calendar Collective. : 7107
Saumart, Ingrid. : 737, 984
Saunders, Doris. : 7184
Sauvé, J. : 5797
Sauvé, Jeanne. : 3718
Sauvé, Jeanne and Lise Bacon. : 5390
Savage, Candace. : 3012, 7413
Savoie, Marie. : 4936
Sawada, Daiyo, Alton T. Olson and Sol E. Sigurdson. : 5949

Sawer, Barbara. : 2884, 2885
Sawer, Barbara J. : 2886
Sawyer, Alison. : 1074
Sawyer, Deborah C. : 6975
Sayer, Liz and Dormer Ellis. : 6868
Sayer, Lynda Anne. : 6832, 6869
Scanlan, Larry. : 443
Schafer, Juliet. : 1776
Schendlinger, Mary. : 833, 5282
Schlesinger, B. : 1983, 2316, 4265, 4266
Schlesinger, Benjamin. : 834, 1075, 1076, 1947, 2793, 2794, 3970, 5740, 5741, 5742, 5743, 5798,
    6208, 6209, 6210, 6211, 6212, 6213, 6214, 6223, 6786, 6976, 6977
Schlesinger, Benjamin and Alex Macrae. : 5744
Schmid, Carol. : 3719, 7108, 7175
Schmidt, Lanalee Carol. : 6048
Schmidt, Wolfgang and Jan de Lint. : 403
Schmidt, Wolfgang and Robert E. Popham. : 404
Schneider, Elizabeth M. and others. : 835, 5721
Schneider, Frank W. and Larry M. Coutts. : 6049
Schom-Moffatt, Patti and Cynthia Dale Telfer. : 1257
Schrank, William E. : 1777, 6694, 6934
Schreck, David Donald. : 1208, 1870
Schreiber, E. M. : 6050, 7109
Schreiner, J. : 2317, 2318
Schrieber, Dorothy. : 4723
Schrodt, Barbara. : 658, 659

Schroeder, Alana Shirley. : 6870
Schroeder, F. A. : 4093
Schroter, Candice. : 4267
Schull, Christiane. : 5430
Schulz, Linda Z. : 2887, 6986
Schwenger, Cope W. : 89
Science Council of Canada. : 5866
Science Council of Canada. Science and Education Committee. : 5867
Scott, Donna Lynn. : 3878
Scott, Howard. : 4421
Scott, Joan Pinner. : 5868
Scott-Brown, Joan M. : 4815
Scrivener, Leslie. : 2462
Scrutton, R. Edgar. : 3363, 4528
Scutt, J. A. : 5722
Sealy, Nanciellen. : 7206
Secord, R. C. : 836, 4307
Secord, Richard Calhoun. : 4055
Séguin, Claire. : 4724
Seifert, Carol. : 7139
Selman, G. R. : 2106
Semas, Phillip. : 6695
Semkow, Verna-Jean Amell. : 5619
Semotiuk, Craig. : 4778
Seneca College of Applied Arts and Technology. : 340

Seneca College of Applied Arts and Technology. President's Task Force on Affirmative Action. : 6636, 6637
Senior Citizens' Forum of Montreal. : 377
Sequin, Lucie. : 5185
Serre, Michèle. : 4644
Service, Dorothy Jane. : 3736
Service de la condition féminine CSN. : 341
Sex-Role Stereotyping and Women's Studies Conference, Sept. 28-30, 1978, Toronto. : 6051
Sexton, Christine S. : 3304, 6052
Shack, Sybil. : 1142, 1778, 4489, 6053, 6435, 6436, 6437, 6871

Shaheen, Ghazala and Cecilia A. Gonzales. : 1984, 4490
Shain, Merle. : 5186
Shapiro, Daniel M. and Morton Stelcner. : 2577, 6935, 6936, 6937, 6938, 6939
Shapka, Muriel. : 4322
Shaver, Fran. : 5021
Sheehan, Nancy M. : 6506
Sheinin, Rose. : 1209, 5870, 6055
Shepherd, Marian M. : 6638
Sheppard, Deborah L. : 3305
Sheppard, June. : 6987
Sheppard, Mary. : 3306, 4268
Sherbrooke. Université. Comité permanent de l'AUCC pour la situation de la femme à l'université. : 6639
Sherrard, Debbie and Camille Fouillard, comps. : 3200
Shershen, Eugene D. : 5620, 5950
Sherwin, Barbara Brender and others. : 5621
Shields, Barbara A. : 6872
Shipley, Nan. : 4814
Shirley, Marilyn R. : 1078
Shone, Margaret A. : 4082

Smart, Patricia. : 739, 3921, 3922
Smith, Bruna. : 3367, 7458
Smith, Donald J. : 1397
Smith, Dorothy. : 2796
Smith, Dorothy E. : 1779, 2795, 2987, 7487
Smith, Dorothy E. and others. : 1780, 6440
Smith, Dorothy E. and Sara J. David. : 4429
Smith, Elizabeth. : 986, 2321, 4397
Smith, Gerald P. : 5622
Smith, Janet. : 1398, 1399
Smith, M. Elizabeth. : 5886
Smith, Margot and Carol Pasternak. : 5168
Smith, Marilyn. : 7198
Smith, Patricia Keeney. : 6519
Smith, Sharon. : 3112
Smith-Cassill, Clarence. : 4726
Smookler, Kenneth. : 4136
Smye, Marti Diane and Jeri Dawn Wine. : 550, 5951
Smye, Marti Diane, Jeri Dawn Wine and Barbara Moses. : 551
Smyth, Donna E. : 740
Smyth, Frances E. : 6058, 6733
Snider, Nancy Jay. : 6833
Snider, Norman. : 4513
Snowden, Annette. : 232, 4455
Social Planning and Research Council of Hamilton and District. : 1695
Social Planning Council of Hamilton and District. : 1696
Social Planning Council of Metropolitan Toronto. : 1697, 1698, 1699
Social Planning Council of Ottawa and District. Committee on Day Care for Children : 1700
Social Planning Council of Peel. Interim Place Steering Committee. : 839
Sodoway, Geraldine. : 6268
Sonnemann, Sabine and Jean L'Espérance. : 2579, 3823

Soper, Mary. : 6216
Sorensen, J. : 1145, 4937
Sparling, Mary. : 526
Speare, Jean E. : 4816
Spears, George and Kasia Seydegart. : 6493
Spears, Kasia and Jan Barnsley. : 2424
Speirs, R. : 5799
Spencer, B. G. and D. C. Featherstone. : 4271
Spencer, Byron. : 4272
Spencer, Byron and Dennis Featherstone. : 4273, 4274
Spencer, Byron G. : 2322
Spink, Marilyn. : 1442
Spinks, Sarah. : 3608, 6251, 6269
Sport and Recreation As It Affects Women Conference. : 627, 3783
Spricer, Rosa. : 5623
Spring, S. : 3113
Squires, Nicole-marie. : 2724, 4398
Srivastava, Ram P. : 3368
Stacy, Stanley. : 164, 3308, 6059
Stamp, R. M. : 987, 2073
Stankiewicz-Bleszynski, Teresa I. : 3492
Stanko, Elizabeth A. : 6259
Stanleigh, Judy. : 6787
Stanley, F. : 4727

Stuart, Elizabeth. : 4984

Stuckey, Johanna. : 5521

Stuckey, Johanna H. : 1781

Stunell, Linda. : 1261

St. John, Clinton. : 6441

St. John's Local Council of Women. : 7185, 7225

St. John's Women's Bureau. : 3750

St.-Pierre, Nicole et Ginette Ruel. : 7348

Sullivan, Gail and Susan Watt. : 91

Sullivan, Nancy. : 6585

Sutherland, Sharon L. : 6734, 6834

Sutton, May. : 5074, 6978

Suzanne Veit and Associates Inc. : 4471

Suzuki, Barbara A. F. : 635, 6383

Swain, Sue. : 660

Swan, Carole. : 1875, 1876, 2324, 2325, 6549

Swan, H. F. : 1400, 4276

Swan, Susan. : 631, 741, 4598

Swanick, Lynne Struthers. : 7141

Swanick, M. Lynne. : 7207

Swanick, M. Lynne Struthers. : 5081, 5412

Swartz, Shirley. : 6697

Swartzen, Judy and others. : 6494

Swedlo, Mavis D. : 1298

Symons, Gladys. : 6735, 6736

Symons, Gladys L. : 1782, 6586

Synge, Jane. : 1783, 2044, 6063, 6091

Syrotuik, Janice Letitia. : 632, 6285

Szala, Karen Victoria. : 3972

Szlamp, Terry. : 1443

Tahon, Marie-Blanche. : 5207

Talbot, Jocelyne. : 4373

Tanaszi, Margaret J. : 3881

Tandan, Nand. : 2326

Tangri, Beverly. : 6550

Tannis, Wendy Bunt. : 6835

Tapp, John L. : 6218

Tardy, Evelyne et autres. : 5394

Tarrab, Gilbert, ed. : 92

Tasaka, Karen Joy. : 4939, 5823

Tausig, Christine. : 6587

Tausky, Thomas E. : 993, 3882

Taylor, Amy. : 147

Taylor, Connie. : 6443

Taylor, James A. : 5283

Taylor, K. Wayne, Neena L. Chappell, and Stephen Brickey. : 1600

Taylor, Linda. : 2726

Taylor, Norma. : 2888

Tcheng-Laroche, Françoise. : 6220

Tcheng-Laroche, Françoise and Raymond H. Prince. : 6219

Teasdale, Philip. : 4137

Teather, Lynne. : 7491

Tellier, Marie. : 1877

Temins, Irving D. : 1950

Temple, Anna. : 2074

Tennenhouse, Carol. : 4138, 4139, 6357

Tennyson, Brian D. : 6309

Tétreault, Jean Marie. : 4184

Texier, Catherine and Marie-Odile Vézina. : 5522

Texmo, Dell. : 3883

The Minus Ones, Winnipeg. : 6221

Theobald, William F. : 3784

Therien, C. : 2045, 2456

Thew, Carol Larson. : 5626

Thibaudeau, Huguette. : 3923

Thibault, André. : 2327

Thibault, Andrée. : 6495

Thibault, Gisele. : 3753, 6963

Thivierge, Nicole. : 2075, 7395

Thom, Pat. : 2108

Thom, Patricia, Anne Ironside and Eileen Hendry. : 1534, 7512

Thomas, Clara. : 742, 994, 3884, 3885, 5169

Thomas, David. : 3973

Thomas, E. M. : 3723

Thomas, Eleanor. : 1999, 5442

Thomas, Gregory Charles. : 633, 5627

Thomas, W. D. S. : 4817

Thompson, Arthur N. : 7422

Thompson, David. : 2581

Thompson, Edward. : 3200.1

Thompson, Jennifer. : 2115

Thompson, John H. : 6310

Thompson, Judy and Rhonda Gilby. : 840, 3309

Thompson, Martin. : 4779, 4780, 4781, 4782, 4783, 4784

Thompson, Nancy Ramsay. : 2140

Thompson, Patricia. : 1263

Thompson, Retta. : 4985

Thompson, Tony. : 236

Thomson, Aisla Margaret. : 5395

Thorpe, Wendy Lisbeth. : 4986

Thring, Beverley R. : 2109, 6241

Tierney, Ben. : 132

Timson, Judith. : 743, 1146, 5724

Timson, Judith and Bonnie Palef. : 3974

Tindal, Doug. : 2729

Tippett, Maria. : 529, 995

Tisseyre, Michelle. : 6520

Tisseyre, Michelle A. : 7115

Tivy, Louis. : 996, 7256

Todres, Rubin. : 5897

Toeplitz, Jerzy. : 4323

Toews, Lorette K. : 6064, 7377

Tolmie, Ellen. : 6270, 6271

Tomeh, Aida K. : 2798, 6065

Toronto. City Council. Special Committee, Places of Amusement. : 5523

Toronto. Dept. of Social Services. Day Care Planning Task Force. : 1701

Toronto. Mayor's Task Force On the Status Of Women in Toronto. : 7244

Toronto. Metropolitan Toronto Library Board. Audio-Visual Services. : 688

Toronto. Planning Council. Governing Committee. : 1702

Toronto. University. Committee on Employment Conditions of Full Time Women faculty :
6642, 6643

Toronto. University. Task Force to Study the Status of Non-Academic Women at the University of Toronto. : 6644
Toronto Abortion Committee. : 93, 94
Toronto Rape Crisis Centre. : 5725
Torrance Consulting Ltd. : 6534
Toscani, Ave. : 2481
Toumishey, Laura Hope. : 6788
Toupin, Louise. : 3660, 6444
Toupin, R. : 1336
Townesend, Michael. : 1602
Townson, Monica. : 1147, 1148, 1403, 1404, 1553, 1880, 1881, 1882, 1883, 2655, 2730, 3523, 3610, 5075, 5076, 5431, 6556, 6944
Towson, Shelagh M. J. and Mark P. Zanna. : 5628
Travers, Lincolne. : 1264
Travis, Gail Lesley. : 1603
Tremblay, Andrée. : 2141
Tremblay, Anne. : 3886
Tremblay, Henri. : 3524
Tremblett, Gwen. : 6445
Tremblett, Josephine. : 1784
Trent University. Presidential Advisory Committee on the Status of Women. : 6645, 6646
Trevelyan, Margot. : 4988, 6496
Trew, Marsha. : 1785
Trifiro, Luigi. : 6311, 6312
Trofimenkoff, S. M. : 7396
Trofimenkoff, Susan Mann. : 2385, 2976, 3887, 3924, 6313, 7397, 7398, 7569
Trofimenkoff, Susan Mann and Alison Prentice. : 7177
Trotter, Beth Sherran. : 6066
Trottier, Michel Jacques. : 3493, 3494
Trovato, Frank. : 3066, 4491
Trovato, Frank and Carl F. Grindstaff. : 3065
Trovato, Frank and T. K. Burch. : 3067
Trow, Susan. : 7257
Trudeau, Margaret. : 997, 998, 5305
Trudeau, Pierre E. : 3806, 6067, 7116
Tudiver, Judith G. : 6068
Tunis, Barbara Logan. : 4873
Tuohimaa, Anne. : 406, 6069
Turcotte, Bobbie and Mary Hemlow. : 999
Turcotte, E. : 2330
Turnbull, Andy. : 5760
Turner, Janice Shirlene. : 1714
Turner, Jean and Alan B. Simmons. : 3068, 6070
Turner, Lynda E. : 7117
Turner, Marion Diane. : 744
Turner, Wesley. : 7178
Turrittin, Anton H., Paul Anisef and Neil J. MacKinnon. : 2046, 5953
Turrittin, Jane S. : 3370
Turrittin, Jane Sawyer. : 3369, 3371
Twidale, Peter. : 1459
Tyndale, Eleanor. : 6260, 6698
Tyrchniewicz, Mabel Eleanor. : 1985
Tyrwhitt, Janice. : 634, 1337
United Community Services of the Greater Vancouver Area. : 1668
United Community Services of the Greater Vancouver Area. Social Policy and Research Dept. : 1080

United Electrical, Radio and Machine Workers of America. : 3612
Université du Québec à Montréal. Groupe interdisciplinaire pour l'enseignement et la recherche sur la condition des femmes. : 6647
Université du Québec à Montréal. Laboratoire sur la répartition et la securité du revenu / Québec. Conseil du statut de la femme. : 2457, 7340
Université Laval. Comité d'étude sur la condition féminine à l'Université Laval. : 6648
University of Alberta. Dept. of Extension. : 2110
University of Alberta. Institute of Law Research and Reform. : 6358, 6359
University of British Columbia. Committee of Mature Women Students. : 2047
University of British Columbia. Student Counselling and Resources Centre. : 1210
University of British Columbia. Women's Office. Women's Research Collective. : 6738, 6836
University of British Columbia. Women's Resources Centre. : 7142
University of New Brunswick. Faculty of Law. Women and the Law Project. : 1675
University of Saskatchewan. Saskatoon Women and Law Committee. : 2586, 4197, 4729
University of Saskatchewan. Women and the Law Committee. : 841
University of Western Ontario. President's Advisory Committee on the Status of Women. : 6649
University of Western Ontario. President's Advisory Committee on Women's Salaries (Academic). : 6650
University Women's Club of Edmonton. : 2111
University Women's Club of Regina. : 1715, 4570
University Women's Club of Toronto. : 4989
Urbas, Jeannette. : 3925, 3926
Ursel, Jane. : 3255
Usher, Sarah. : 2953, 4571, 5629, 6874
Usher, Susan. : 4277
Uwacgbutc, Adaoma C. : 3372, 4515
Vachon, Mary L. Suslak. : 6979
Vaillancourt, Germaine et Francine Paquin. : 5208
Vaillancourt, Louise B. : 2732
Vail, Susan E. : 635
Vallely-Fischer, Lois. : 1405
Valois, Jocelyne. : 5107
Valverde, Mariana. : 3613
Van Daele, Christa. : 7570
Van Der Gracht, Deb. : 5397, 6497
Van der Merwe, Marina Suzanne. : 3201
Van Der Merwe, Sandra. : 677, 1885, 2733, 2734, 2735
Van Herk, Aritha. : 745, 5398
Van Kirk, Sylvia : 4666, 4675, 5170, 7179, 7423, 7424, 7425
Van Luven, Lynne. : 7459
Van Norman, Catherine Bell. : 7258
Van Raalte, Sharon. : 530, 4818
Van Steen, Marcus. : 1001, 5187
Van Trigt, Maria. : 661
Vance, Catharine. : 1000
Vance, Joanie. : 5735
Vancouver People's Law School. : 1952, 4094
Vancouver Status of Women. : 239, 2859, 3527
Vancouver Status of Women Council. : 2656, 7012
Vancouver Transition House and the Women's Research Centre. : 842
Vancouver Welfare and Recreation Council. : 1669
Vancouver Women's Caucus. : 2048, 6446, 7493
Vancouver Women's Health Collective. : 4374
Vancouver Women's Network. : 4952
Vanderburgh, R. M. : 4769, 4770

Vanderburgh, Rosamond M. : 4768
Vandonselaar, Kodyn Herman. : 5630
Vargo, J. W. : 3162
Vastel, Michel. : 5284
Veevers, J. E. : 133, 2799, 3069, 3070, 3071, 3072, 3073, 3074, 3975, 3976
Venton, Anne, Ross Traub and Ellen Campbell. : 6126
Verduyn, Christl. : 3889, 3890
Verkruysse, Patricia Louise. : 3888
Verma, Ravi B. P. : 3075, 4492
Vernon, Philip E. : 5954
Verthuy, Mair. : 5129, 7571, 7572, 7573
Vertinsky, Patricia. : 636
Vézina, Marie-Odile. : 96
Vézina-Parent, Monique. : 7341
Vickers, Jill. : 6699
Vickers, Jill McCalla. : 5400, 5401, 5402
Vickers, Jill McCalla and June Adam. : 2142, 6588
Vickers, Jill McCalla and M. Janine Brodie. : 5399
Vickers, Jill McCalla and Patricia Finn. : 3614
Vickers, Joan. : 678, 5631
Vickers, Joan and others. : 637
Victor, Jean-Louis et Denise Roussel. : 7342
Victoria. University. : 6651
Victoria Day Care Services. : 1703
Vincens, Simone. : 1002, 5171
Vincent, Andrea L. and Patricia A. Cox. : 4278, 4572
Vincent, M. O. : 4401
Vineberg, Ethel. : 4990
Vinet, Alain, Francine Dufresne et Lucie Vézina. : 2458
Vingilis, Evelyn. : 5632, 5633
Vinohradova, Mary. : 5172
Vipond, Mary. : 5108, 5109
Vlassoff, Carol and J. W. Gartrell. : 3076, 5752
Vohanka, Sue. : 2587
Voice of Alberta Native Women's Society. : 4819
Voice of Women [Halifax]. : 2402
Voisey, Paul. : 6314
Wachowich, Elizabeth Louise. : 3310, 4279
Wachtel, Andy and Brian E. Burtch. : 6360
Wachtel, Eleanor. : 1750, 3615, 3671, 3724, 4060, 4061, 5422
Waddell, C. : 7445
Wade, Susan. : 3015
Waisberg, Barbara. : 5933
Waisman, Chaika. : 531
Wakil, S. Parvez. : 3977, 6739
Wakil, S. Parvez and E. A. Wakil. : 3978
Walen, Gregory G. : 4198
Walker-Leigh, Vanya. : 2332
Wallace, Catherine. : 1886, 5403
Wallace, Cecelia. : 1338
Wallace, Joan. : 1887, 5404
Walmsley, Ann. : 6361
Walmsley, P.Y. and M. Ohtsu. : 6946
Walsh, Richard T. and John R. Schallow. : 6071
Walsh, William D. : 2333, 4280

Walshaw, Anne. : 1604
Walters, Cyril Maurice. : 4797
Walton, Jo Anne. : 1211, 4941
Walton, Yvette M. : 638, 1003
Wanadi-Mboyo, Ea Booto. : 1953
Wand, Barbara. : 6837
Waniewicz, Ignacy. : 2112
Wanless, Janet L. : 5898
Ward, Eleanor. : 2736, 3441
Ward, W. Peter. : 6789
Ward-Harris, E. D. : 1004, 4851
Warskett, George. : 2334, 5872
Wasserman, David. : 6838
Wasylycia-Coe, Mary Ann. : 3824, 3825
Wasylynchuk, Mary Ann. : 662
Wasylyzia-Leis, Judy. : 2657
Waterloo. University. Library. Lady Aberdeen Collection. : 7143
Waterloo. University. President's Advisory Committee on Equal Rights for Women and Men. :
    6652
Waterman, Diane C. : 6072, 6281, 6839
Waters, Donovan. : 4062, 4185
Watson, Catherine Margaret. : 5484

Watson, Elizabeth. : 241, 242, 243, 244, 245, 246, 247, 248
Watson, Julie. : 2893
Watson, Louise. : 1005, 3616
Watson, Wendell W. . 37
Watterson, Georgia. : 532, 533
Waxman, Sydell Blossom. : 4402
Wayne, Jamie. : 639
Webb, Peter. : 2860
Webster, Daisy. : 2113
Webster, Jackie. : 746
Webster, Loyola Cathleen. : 379
Weeks, Margaret Wendy. : 5023
Weintraub, Laura S. : 3163, 3202
Weir, Lorna. : 3797
Weir, Lorna and Brenda Steiger. : 3798

Weir, Tamara and Ronald J. Burke. : 3311, 4281
Weiss, Star. : 7013
Weitz, Margaret Collins. : 7343, 7349
Wekerle, Gerda. : 6796
Wekerle, Gerda, Rebecca Peterson and David Morley. : 7574
Wekerle, Gerda R. and Novia Carter. : 6797
Welch, Frances. : 3785, 5761
Welch, Joan Sally Shewchuk. : 2049
Wendell, Susan. : 1876
Wener, D. and W. D. Cairns. : 6740
Wensel, Joan. : 7446
Weppler, Doreen. : 5405
Western Conference on Opportunities for Women. : 2114, 2336
Weyer, John. : 1081
Whalen-Way, Audrey. : 6447
Whissel-Tregonning, Marguerite. : 1006, 7245
White, Charles A. : 3257, 3433, 4063, 7496
White, Julie. : 3617, 6551

White, Nancy. : 4599
White, Terrence H. : 2337
White-Tanabe, Patricia Anne. : 6242
Whitehead, Ruth Holmes. : 534, 4652
Whitney, Beverley. : 5485
Whitson, David. : 640
Whittingham, Anthony. : 1554
Whittingham, Frank. : 4282
Whittingham, Ken. : 1786
Whittington, Hugh. : 1265
Whitton, Bob. : 2492
Whyte, John D. : 4730
Wiebe, Heather Rachael. : 344
Wieland, Joyce. : 535
Wigney, L. : 2050
Wilcox, V. and E. Dollery. : 2482
Wilensky, Marshall. : 6286
Wilkinson, Shelagh. : 6222
Wilks, Claire Weissman. : 5130, 5131
Williams, Jack. : 3618, 3619
Williams, Tannis M. : 6589
Williams, Tannis MacBeth and others. : 5634, 6741
Williams, Trevor. : 2051
Williamson, Lenny. : 2889
Willick, Liz and Sue Berlove. : 7460
Willis, Jane. : 1009, 4646

Willis, Janet. : 1787, 2052, 2115, 2116, 2117
Willis, Kathleen Diane. : 5635
Willman, Gwen. : 4943
Wilson, Edward. : 134
Wilson, Frances. : 7575
Wilson, I. : 2118, 6712
Wilson, L. J. : 4991, 4944, 7004
Wilson, Mary Carol. : 1010, 4403
Wilson, Patricia A. : 3891
Wilson, Rod. : 407
Wilson, S. J. : 2338, 4283
Wilson, Susannah J. : 5111, 5112
Wilson, Susannah Jane Foster. : 5110
Windsor. University. Faculty Association Sub-Committee on the Status of Women Academics. :
    6653
Windsor. University. Faculty Association Sub-Committee on the Status of Women Faculty. :
    6654
Windsor. University. President's Committee on Equal Rights. : 6655
Windsor Social Planning (A division of United Community Services). : 1704

Wine, Jeri Dawn. : 6092
Wine, Jeri Dawn and others. : 552
Winnipeg. University. : 6656
Winter, Maridee Allen. : 1151
Wintermute, Dianne. : 2143
Wires, David. : 1954
Wisniewski, Lawrence. : 1266
Wolfe, Jennifer. : 641, 1788
Wolfe, Margie. : 5113
Wolfe, Morris. : 6498

Wolfe, Sandra J. : 6875
Wollheim, Peter. : 3114
Wollison, Mary Anne. : 5921
Woloski, R. : 2861
Wolowyna, Jean E. : 3077
Women for Non-sexist Education. : 6127
Women for Political Action. : 5407
Women for Political Action and Ontario Committee on the Status of Women. : 5650, 6499
Women in Canadian History Project. (Ontario Institute for Studies in Education). : 2076
Women in Transition Research Project. : 843
Women's Counselling Collective. : 1535, 6243
Women's Employment Counselling. : 2395, 6876
Women's Hockey Workshop. : 644
Women's Liberation Movement of Sudbury. : 3726
Women's Movement Archives [Canadian Herstory Project]. : 425
Women's Research Centre. : 844, 1460, 7014, 7015, 7429
Wood, Beverly A. : 6128
Wood, H. Diane. : 5636
Wood, Jean. : 2743, 5080
Wood, Susan. : 3893
Wood, Ted. : 254, 255, 256, 257, 258
Woodcock, Lynda and Nancy Sullivan. : 6590

Woodcock, Penelope Jane Robinson. : 6877
Woodman, Marion. : 5637
Woods, David. : 4404
Woods, Sandra. : 3525
Woodsworth, K. C. : 1955, 4095, 6362
Woodsworth, Sheila. : 4363
Woodward, Joan. : 3634
Woolner, Susan. : 6790
Woolsey, Lorette. : 5638, 6073
Woolsey-Toews, L. : 6074
Working Women (formerly Women's Community Employment Centre). : 3375, 7461

Working Women's Association [Vancouver]. : 1273, 2371
Worthington, Bonnie. : 6521
Worton, Jean McBean. : 4084
Worzel, Richard. : 2744
Wouk, Judith. : 135, 2862
Woywitka, Anne B. : 5173, 7005, 7426
Wozney, Christine. : 7024
Wren, Derdri. : 6244, 6287, 6742
Wright, Bunny. : 4405
Wright, Helen K. : 1011, 3016
Wright, J. F. C. : 5288
Wright, James Frederick Church. : 1012
Wright, John de P. : 3672
Wright, Pat and Doris Wilson. : 1082
Wright, Susan, Andrew Griffith and others. : 1790
Wright, Vicki. : 6129
Wyckham, Robert. : 1892
Wyland, Francie. : 1279, 3799
Wylie, Betty Jane. : 6980
Wyman, Georgina. : 5114, 5409, 6591, 7120
Wynn, Sheila. : 3219
YWCA Women's Centre. : 3769

Yaffe, Phyllis. : 3894
Yaga, Baba. : 5524
Yam, J. : 5415
Yee, Paul H. N. : 5639
York University. Adviser to the President on the Status of Women. : 6657
York University. Presidential Advisory Committee on Sexual Harassment. : 6157, 6158, 6592, 6593
York University. Presidential Committee to Review Salaries of Full-Time Faculty Women. : 6658
York University. President's Committee on Staff Compensation and Personnel Policies. : 6659
York University. Senate Committee on Part-Time Faculty. : 6660
York University. Senate Task Force on the Status of Women. : 6661, 6662
Young Women's Christian Association of Canada. : 845, 846, 4992, 6536, 7121
Young Women's Christian Association (Montreal). Roles of Women Study Committee. : 7144
Young Women's Christian Association. Sexism in Advertising Committee. : 259
Young, Connie. : 5922, 6075
Young, Filson A. : 6076, 6878
Young, Leslie. : 347
Young, Mildred. : 747
Yukon Territorial Government. Dept. of Social Welfare. : 7430
Yuzwak, William J. : 4530
Zachon, Vivian. : 2596
Zaleski, Halina. : 5824

TO REMAIN AT THORNELOE

Title: Women in Canada:
        A bibliography

L.U. Women's Center
Centre des Femmes U.L.